The Papers of
George Catlett Marshall

The Papers of
George Catlett Marshall

Volume 1

"THE SOLDIERLY SPIRIT"
DECEMBER 1880–JUNE 1939

Larry I. Bland, Editor

Sharon R. Ritenour, Assistant Editor

THE JOHNS HOPKINS UNIVERSITY PRESS

Baltimore and London

1981

The Johns Hopkins University Press, Baltimore, Maryland 21218
The Johns Hopkins Press Ltd., London

Library of Congress Cataloging in Publication Data

Marshall, George C. (George Catlett), 1880-1959.
The papers of George Catlett Marshall.

Includes index.
Contents: v. 1. The soldierly spirit, December 1880-June 1939.
1. Marshall, George C. (George Catlett), 1880-1959.
2. United States—History, Military—20th century—Sources.
3. Generals—United States—Correspondence.
4. United States. Army—Biography.
I. Bland, Larry I.   II. Ritenour, Sharon R.   III. Title.
E745.M37 1981   973.918'092'4   81-47593
ISBN 0-8018-2552-0 (v. 1)   AACR2

Contents

Foreword

The contributions made by George Catlett Marshall to the United States, indeed to much of the world, during his more than fifty years of public service fully justify publishing his papers. A brilliant tactical planner and organizer in World War I and, as chief of staff of the United States Army, the organizer of United States contributions to the Allied victory in World War II, his military career alone makes him worthy of careful study.

But General Marshall's contributions did not cease with war's end. At President Harry S. Truman's behest, Marshall headed the special mission that sought to mediate the civil war in China, served two years as secretary of state, and held the post of secretary of defense during the Korean War. Between these latter two assignments, he served a short but important interlude as president of the American National Red Cross. It is therefore appropriate that the essential documents relating to his life be made available to the general reader, to students, and to scholars.

Beyond the immediate purpose of documenting Marshall's life and the development of his ideas and policies through his own papers is the broader expectation that this collection will help to illuminate the nature of the United States Army and certain aspects of the country's military and foreign policies during his career.

At the same time, no documentary collection can tell everything about the man, much less make comprehendible an entire era. Some of the limitations are inherent in the fragmentary nature of the available evidence, whether in Marshall's documents or in his recorded interviews. Others are found in the man himself: his desire for a private life, his reticence, and his disdain for self-glorification. Still others stem from the obvious fact that George C. Marshall was but one member—although a very important one—of a constellation of leaders who carried this country through its greatest war and who struggled with the stubborn problems of achieving a lasting peace.

In donating his personal papers to the George C. Marshall Research Foundation, General Marshall was keenly aware of the importance to succeeding generations of the documents he had produced and accumulated. He was, perhaps, less willing than many great men to put on paper his own explanation of his personal motivations, ideas, and policies. Except for a brief period after World War I, he kept no diary which might reveal his innermost thoughts, and he was reluctant to record his judgment of contemporaries. Even late in life, in the important collection of interviews undertaken by Forrest C. Pogue and used in his authorized biography, Marshall declined to comment on scores of questions and personalities. (Forrest C. Pogue, *George C. Marshall,* 4 vols. [New York: Viking, 1963–].)

As a result, despite the hundreds of thousands of documents available to and from Marshall and the scores of interviews undertaken by the biographer and others, the historian is still left with unanswered questions. Many important facets of George C. Marshall's character and milieu are illuminated by Dr. Pogue in his biography of General Marshall. The biographical narrative quite properly permits the use of both corroborative evidence—official documents and the personal papers and comments of contemporaries—and judgments by the author on the basis of his four decades of research in the period and on General Marshall. The documentary approach, however, must let the documents speak for themselves.

The George C. Marshall Research Foundation has played a key role in collecting information and documents pertaining to General Marshall. From its inception in 1953, this institution has encouraged and supported the accumulation of these papers, and thanks to the foresight and diligence of a large number of persons the documents now number in the millions. The assembling of relevant documents—those written either by Marshall himself or by contemporaries—was accelerated after the establishment in 1964 of the Marshall Foundation's Research Library, which faces the Virginia Military Institute's parade ground in Lexington, Virginia. Under successive scholars, archivists, and librarians, this collection has continued to grow in quality, quantity, and scope. Without this collection, the task of compiling this multivolume documentary edition would have been more difficult and time-consuming. Needless to say, the Marshall Foundation, both in its policies of collecting documents and secondary materials and in its support of the editing project, has in no way sought to circumscribe the editor's independence and judgment.

The ideal of objectivity, however, did not mean disinterest or inactivity. In assisting the project, the Marshall Foundation turned to three principal sources of outside support, and each has made a major contribution to the publication.

Chronologically, the first source was the National Historical Publications and Records Commission (NHPRC). The NHPRC recognized the potential of the foundation's own documentary resources and gave it the financial support necessary to launch the editing project. Although the commission has encouraged the foundation to adhere to the highest standards of scholarship, to develop its editorial talents, and to employ modern word-processing techniques to facilitate the effort, it has in no way sought to influence the specific content of the resulting volumes. The foundation cannot overemphasize the importance of the NHPRC in launching and sustaining this project.

The second major outside contribution to this publication came about as a result of the foundation's desire to seek the best historical and editorial skills available to it to guide the project. This took the form of an advisory committee, headed by the director of the foundation and composed of distinguished historians and editors in the field of military and diplomatic history. Their names and only the briefest indication of their activities are given below:

Richardson Dougall, former deputy director of the Historical Office, Department of State, and the editor of several major documentary collections of United States diplomacy.

William M. Franklin, former director of the Historical Office, Department of State, the supervisor of the series *Foreign Relations of the United States*, and the editor of special documentary volumes of American diplomatic history.

Maurice Matloff, chief historian of the Center of Military History, Department of the Army, writer of military history, and editor of numerous army historical volumes.

Forrest C. Pogue, the authorized biographer of General Marshall, author of books and essays on military history, one of the country's pioneers in oral history research, and the director of the Marshall Foundation from 1964 to 1973.

Edwin A. Thompson, director of the Records Declassification Division, National Archives and Records Service, a professional archivist, and a former member of the editorial staff of *The Papers of Dwight David Eisenhower*.

This group of distinguished historians has worked diligently at its duties. Not only was the advisory committee instrumental in drawing up the project's philosophical guidelines, but each member studied every proposed document and its annotation; the resulting specific suggestions as to form and content have been invaluable to the editor. With the wisdom of mature scholars, they have been perceptive and constructive but in no way restrictive in their advice. The Marshall Foundation extends to them its deepest gratitude and attributes to them much of the balance reflected in the selection, annotation, and arrangement of these papers.

The third influence external to the Marshall Foundation has been The Johns Hopkins University Press. The press not only recognized the quality of George C. Marshall's papers, but it was eager to support the foundation's use of modern technical methods for producing the volumes. Under the direction of Jack G. Goellner, the press has given the editor the benefit of excellent advice from its staff in areas of technical consistency, design, layout, and production. Moreover, the press's interest has been an inspiration to the editorial staff in achieving the difficult task of completing its work on schedule.

The editor of this volume, Dr. Larry I. Bland, and his assistant, Sharon R. Ritenour, are members of the Marshall Foundation staff. Their editorial skill and sound judgment in the selection of documents will be apparent to all readers of this volume.

August 20, 1981

Fred L. Hadsel
Director, George C. Marshall
Research Foundation
Project Director, *The Papers
of George Catlett Marshall*

Preface

THE MARSHALL PAPERS

George Catlett Marshall (December 31, 1880–October 16, 1959) was a public official throughout most of his adult life, from his commissioning as a second lieutenant of Infantry in the United States Army at the beginning of February, 1902, until his retirement as secretary of defense at the end of September, 1951. It is the nature of public officials, reinforced by statutory command, to collect and maintain records of their activities. Generally, the more exalted the position, the greater the quantity—sometimes even the quality—of an official's correspondence, and the more difficult it is for the person to draw a sharp line between official and personal records.

Marshall was little concerned with collecting self-justifying, reputation-enhancing historical documents. He consistently permitted papers that he might have retained for his private files to become part of official records. In part, this was a traditional attitude among professional soldiers. In addition to the often difficult conditions under which they served, they were naturally reluctant to burden themselves, during their frequent changes of station, with collections of documents in their household goods for which they might have to pay excess weight charges. Marshall once remarked: "My things of that nature have largely been lost or destroyed in the many moves I have made—to the Philippines several times, to China, in typhoons, and to other places in the United States— and a careless attitude on my part to all such manner of things." (Marshall, interviewed by Forrest C. Pogue, February 28, 1957, GCMRL.)

Marshall returned to the United States from France following World War I with but a single official document (not printed, but see p. 160). He began to maintain organized files of his correspondence only in the spring of 1932, shortly before leaving Fort Benning. After he began working in the War Department in mid-1938, he acquired a staff that saved and organized his correspondence. From that time until his death, most of his correspondence was handled by office staffs in Washington, D.C.

Marshall valued his own privacy and reputation as well as those of others. He did not encourage publicity about himself. In part this was because he felt that it was unseemly, since articles in the popular press appeared to him to be excessively critical or complimentary. Too much praise, he felt, could be as dangerous to an officer's career as too much criticism. "I am getting entirely too much publicity for my own good," he wrote just after he was named acting chief of staff of the army. "It will start up resentment in the Army, I think." (Marshall to Pershing, July 17, 1939, LC/J. J. Pershing Papers [General Correspondence].)

Collecting papers for future publication in memoirs did not appeal to Marshall. Although he prepared a draft memoir of his experiences in World War I (see p. 259), he decided not to publish it. His attitudes toward memoirs were influenced by some of the bitter word-battles carried out in memoirs of World War I by participants he knew personally. "Practically every one of position who has written about the war has lost somewhat by doing so," he warned General Pershing (p. 369). In 1950, a magazine published the following Marshall quotation: "I long ago made up my mind that I was not going to write any memoirs. To be of any historical importance, they have got to be very accurate. That is, you mustn't omit and make it pleasant reading. Now, if you do put it all in, you may do irreparable harm. Inevitably the press reaction, the public reaction, devotes itself to the critical item, although it may be only one paragraph in the entire book. You almost ruin a man. But if you don't mention that, it is not history, because it had a very important bearing on the procedure." (*Infantry Journal* 66 [May 1950]: 7.)

Marshall's attitude toward saving documents and writing memoirs did not settle the issues of later scholarly or public access to his papers or of how and where the valuable collection should be preserved. In 1956, General Marshall deeded his papers to the George C. Marshall Research Foundation. Even before the foundation opened its library building in Lexington, Virginia, the process of moving and cataloging Marshall's papers and memorabilia had begun. By 1980, the progress of declassification and the publishing of Forrest C. Pogue's biography of Marshall permitted the transfer of nearly all of the remaining papers to the library.

In the Marshall Library's archives, the documents Marshall himself or his office staff collected are divided into twelve subgroups corresponding to the various positions he held and to his retirement. Although there is some overlapping, the subgroups are arranged chronologically: Fort Benning (1932); Fort Screven (1932–33); Fort Moultrie (1933); Illinois National Guard (1933–36); Vancouver Barracks (1936–38); Pentagon Office (1938–51); China Mission (1945–47); Secretary of State (1947–49); American Battle Monuments Commission (1949–59); American National Red Cross (1949–50); Secretary of Defense (1950–51); and Retirement (1951–59).

All twelve groups of General Marshall's correspondence total approximately eighty linear feet of documents. The first five subgroups—congruent with his last five assignments prior to his War Department assignment in July, 1938—amount to approximately sixteen linear inches. The Pentagon Office subgroup constitutes Marshall's papers as army chief of staff, 1939–45, but it includes a significant amount of correspondence prior to and subsequent to that period. Arranged alphabetically rather than chronologically, as the previous five subgroups are, Pentagon Office is the largest single subgroup of documents, amounting to slightly more than forty percent of the total available in the Marshall Library. Of the eight series in this subgroup, the three most important for this volume are the General Correspondence, Selected Correspondence, and Speeches and Testimonies. The Selected Correspondence was chosen by Marshall's office staff; it was filed in locked cabinets in Marshall's office.

Even before the establishment of its library in Lexington, Virginia, the Marshall Foundation inaugurated a policy of collecting original Marshall papers to supplement those that the general had donated. In addition, programs were initiated to microfilm and photocopy Marshall documents and related items in other repositories; to collect research notes and secondary sources bearing on Marshall's life and times; and to collect photographs of Marshall, his family, and his associates.

In order to support his biographical research, Forrest C. Pogue started, and the library has maintained, an extensive research file. For this volume, the two kinds of documents cited to this file are a few photocopies of original documents given to the library by owners who wished to retain the originals, and numerous letters to Dr. Pogue from persons who had been asked by him to discuss their relationship with Marshall.

Also on deposit in the library and available for this project were Dr. Pogue's notes and transcripts on forty hours of interviews, conducted in late 1956 and 1957, which show the general's remarkably accurate memory. In addition to these, Dr. Pogue conducted scores of interviews with Marshall's associates and acquaintances.

DOCUMENT SELECTION

The volumes in this series constitute a selected edition of documents by, to, and about George C. Marshall. Of the 506 documents reproduced in this book, 83 were Marshall holographs, 39 were typed by him, 337 dictated by him, 26 were directed to him, and 21 were between second and third parties about him. Approximately three to fifteen percent of the Marshall documents for a given year have been reproduced, the percentage being highest in the early years of Marshall's career.

Documents issued "by order of" Marshall were usually written by others and are not considered Marshall papers, unless otherwise noted. Similarly, the thousands of routine messages and directives sent over his signature were usually written by other persons. Documents in these two categories were frequently not filed with Marshall's correspondence, although they appear in numerous official records in the National Archives and sometimes in the personal files maintained by the recipients. Most brief notes of congratulations, condolences, and thanks have been excluded from this volume.

Documents selected for inclusion are those discussing or having some influence on important events or persons; those bearing on civil-military relations; those showing the influence of experience (particularly of World War I) on Marshall's thinking; those pertaining to the organization, operation, and morale of the military establishment; and those demonstrating Marshall's military judgment. Also selected were documents showing the development of Marshall's character, interests, and career.

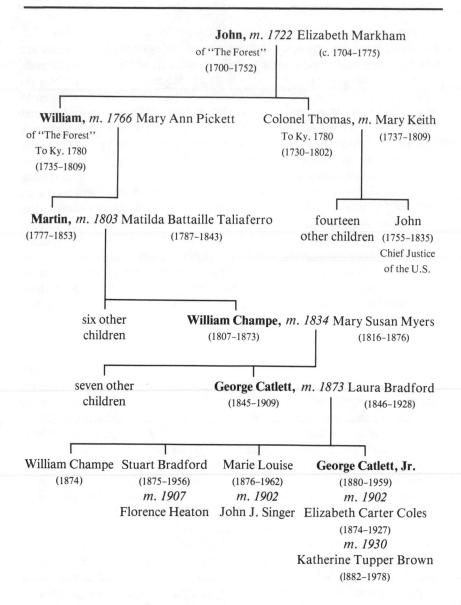

MARSHALL GENEALOGY

General George Catlett Marshall and Chief Justice of the Supreme Court John Marshall were distantly related, a fact which intrigued the general's father (see pp. 3, 11) and numerous persons since. The chart given here is meant only to show the relationship between the two famous Marshalls; it is by no means complete.

ANNOTATION

The editors have attempted, insofar as possible, to identify all events and persons mentioned in the documents. The graduates of Marshall's alma mater, the Virginia Military Institute, and of the United States Military Academy are identified by their year of graduation (e.g., "V.M.I., 1901"). Certain men attended both schools, usually leaving V.M.I. for the greater certainty of an army commission upon completion of the Military Academy course (e.g., George S. Patton, Jr., V.M.I., 1903–4; U.S.M.A., 1909). The graduates of other institutions may also be identified on occasion, but no systematic effort has been made to do this for every college graduate. The annual *Army Register* usually gives such information for Regular Army commissioned officers. Persons are identified initially only as to their status, rank, or role at the time of the citation. Subsequent citations usually give only the changes since the previous identification. The index should enable the reader to follow a particular individual's development or relationship with Marshall.

Standard sources of biographical and career information have been used but not cited. These include: War Department, Adjutant General's Office, *Army Directory: Reserve and National Guard Officers on Active Duty* (1941); War Department, Adjutant General's Office, *Army List and Directory*; War Department, Adjutant General's Office, *Army Register*; War Department, Army War College, *Order of Battle of the United States Land Forces in the World War*; United States Military Academy, Association of Graduates, *Biographical Register of the Officers and Graduates of the U.S. Military Academy*; United States Military Academy, Association of Graduates, *Register of Graduates and Former Cadets of the United States Military Academy* (1975); Virginia Military Institute, *Register of Former Cadets* (1957); *Who Was Who in America*; and *Who's Who in America*.

Whenever appropriate and feasible, quotations from Marshall and his correspondents have been used to annotate the documents. Citations to secondary sources have been avoided except for Robert E. Sherwood's *Roosevelt and Hopkins: An Intimate History* (New York: Harper and Brothers, 1948); the United States Army's official history series *United States Army in World War II* (Washington, D.C.: Government Printing Office, 1947–); and the Air Force's *Army Air Forces in World War II* (Chicago: University of Chicago Press, 1948).

One of the most important primary sources used in annotating this volume was the nineteen oral history tapes by Marshall. Some of these were created when General Marshall spoke in response to questions sent to him by Forrest C. Pogue; others were interviews with Dr. Pogue. The transcripts are stored in the Marshall Library and were cited in this volume as Interview, with a date (e.g., "Interview, February 21, 1957"). Interviews with other persons were cited by interviewee, interviewer, date, and repository (e.g., "Major General Morrison C. Stayer, interviewed by Forrest C. Pogue, January 20, 1960, GCMRL").

Marshall's *Memoirs of My Services in the World War, 1917–1918* (Boston: Houghton Mifflin, 1976), and Katherine Tupper Marshall's *Together: Annals of an Army Wife* (New York and Atlanta: Tupper and Love, 1946) were valuable sources for annotating this volume. The manuscript of the former and a photocopy of the manuscript of the latter are on deposit in the Marshall Library. General Marshall made extensive changes in and additions to the *Together* manuscript. His memoirs of World War I are hereinafter cited as *Memoirs*.

ACKNOWLEDGMENTS

The editor is indebted to far more persons than can possibly be mentioned in this short notice. They include not only those whose immediate help has been invaluable, but also many individuals unknown to the editor who worked on the document collection during the early years of the Marshall Foundation.

Among these early supporters of comprehensive documentation of the life and times of George Catlett Marshall were loyal members of his staff and colleagues, his many admirers, and the trustees and supporters of the Marshall Library when, as an institution, it was no more than an aspiration. General of the Army Omar N. Bradley, head of this group of supporters, and later chairman emeritus of the foundation, was instrumental in assuring the deposit of General Marshall's personal papers in the library's archives. Equally important has been the leadership of the chairman of the foundation's Board of Trustees, The Honorable Robert A. Lovett, and its president, Lieutenant General (Ret.) Marshall S. Carter, as well as the foundation's trustees, in assuring the growth of the archives to the point that it could become the principal source of this and succeeding volumes of the Marshall papers.

Two other persons were of critical importance during the first three decades of this development. The authorized biographer, Dr. Forrest C. Pogue, has spent over three decades of his career in collecting documentary and oral material concerning General Marshall which has been invaluable to the editor. The first librarian, the late Eugenia Lejeune, worked indefatigably in helping to assemble additional documentation for the foundation. Without the help of these and many other persons, this collection of *The Papers of George Catlett Marshall* would have had to be postponed for many years.

Other Marshall Foundation staff members, past or present, also contributed in many different ways to this volume. Royster Lyle, now curator of collections, assisted the editor by knowledge gained through his long association with the library. Barbara P. Vandegrift was likewise helpful during her period as librarian with the foundation. The current archivist, John N. Jacob, and his predecessor Anthony R. Crawford, were of critical importance in the organization of the papers and in their knowledge of their contents. Thomas E. Camden and Michael I. Shoop helped in research, photographic coverage, and bibliography. Ted M. Camper expertly handled the project's accounting. Two recently retired members of the staff, Wilbur J. Nigh and Juanita D. Pitts, worked for many years in the National Archives, where their assistance in obtaining, declassifying, and indexing documents pertaining to General Marshall was invaluable to this and will be invaluable to succeeding volumes of the Marshall papers.

In addition, the archivists at the National Archives, and specialists such as Timothy K. Nenninger, formerly of the Navy and Old Army Branch, contributed general advice and specific assistance in the photographic and cartographic collections. Similarly, the archivists at the Library of Congress provided numerous services which supplemented at key points the documents available to the editor.

Local assistance in the preparation of this volume was also extremely helpful. The staffs of the library, archives, and file room of the Virginia Military Institute gladly provided the editor with information available nowhere else, while the reference librarians of the Washington and Lee University Library were also helpful in the same generous spirit. The staffs of two area newspapers provided the editor with the benefits of their expertise. The *Buena Vista News*, and publisher Thomas A. Garlow, helped with the typesetting. The publisher of the Lexington *News-Gazette*, and particularly James E. Dedrick of the production staff, assisted the editor in learning typesetting; the latter also reproduced numerous illustrations for this volume. The Andre Studio of Lexington likewise assisted in preparing the illustrations.

The editor gratefully acknowledges the permission of the following individuals, publishers, and institutions to reprint selected materials as noted: the American Battle Monuments Commission, Washington, D.C., for three maps of World War I from its *American Armies and Battlefields in Europe* (Washington, D.C.: Government Printing Office, 1938); the *Deseret News*, Salt Lake City, Utah, William B. Smart, editor and general manager, for Marshall's August 25, 1916, lecture on marching; the Houghton Mifflin Company for excerpts from Marshall's *Memoirs of My Services in the World War, 1917-1918* (Boston: Houghton Mifflin, 1976); the Northwestern University Library, Special Collections Department, Evanston, Illinois, R. Russell Maylone, curator, for documents from the Papers of Charles G. Dawes; the Oregonian Publishing Company, Portland, Oregon, Fred A. Stickel, president and publisher, for two photographs and a map of the Vancouver Barracks C.C.C. District; Lewis Perry, Jr., Paul Sadler, Jr., and *The Phillips Exeter Bulletin*, 77 (May 1978), for Marshall's December 20, 1920, Field Orders, No. 1; the Smithsonian Institution, Military History Division, for four World War I watercolor portraits by Joseph Cummings Chase; and the Yale University Library, Manuscripts and Archives Department, New Haven, Connecticut, Judith A. Schiff, chief research archivist, for Marshall's December 22, 1927, letter in the Henry L. Stimson Papers.

Information or documents of value to this project were also provided by the archives and the Information Center of the *Chicago Tribune*, the Illinois State Library, the Franklin D. Roosevelt Library, and the United States Army Military History Institute.

Anne Katherine Pond, former chief, Documentary Editing Section, Department of State, proofread the final version of this volume with great promptness and accuracy. The editor benefited greatly from her knowledge and suggestions.

Numerous members of The Johns Hopkins University Press have worked with the editor to improve the quality and appearance of this volume. The editor wishes to express his particular appreciation to Henry Y.K. Tom, social sciences editor; Barbara Lamb Kraft, managing editor; Alan C. Carter, designer; and Susan Bishop, formerly the designer for the press.

The editor would also like to express his appreciation and thanks to the National Historical Publications and Records Commission and to its staff, particularly Executive Director Frank G. Burke, Publications Director Roger A. Bruns, and Research Supervisor Mary A. Giunta. The NHPRC's Institutes for the Editing of Historical Documents, which both the editor and the assistant editor attended, were uniquely valuable training programs. The influence of the NHPRC's staff far exceeds the modest limits of its budget.

Three present members of the George C. Marshall Research Foundation staff were of such critical importance in the editing of this volume that they deserve special mention. The assistant editor, Sharon R. Ritenour, provided essential research, important portions of the editing and make-up, and critical and helpful advice, as well as long hours of overtime work. Joellen K. Bland has been especially helpful in operating the editing terminal and in proofreading the text. Kathi Mullenax-Howard contributed to this volume through her painstaking preparation of the camera-ready copy. Without these efforts, this volume could not have been completed.

Larry I. Bland
Editor

Guide to Editorial Policies

STYLE

In the annotation, matters of style are intended to conform to *A Manual of Style,* twelfth edition, revised (Chicago and London: University of Chicago Press, 1969). In the documents, the document writer's style is followed, except as explained immediately below.

TEXTUAL CHANGES AND INSERTIONS

Document Heading.   The documents reproduced in this volume frequently do not contain an inside address. The organization, sequence, and sometimes the content of the heading (i.e., writer or recipient, security classification, date, place of origin, and document title or subject) are supplied by the editor.

1. Writer or recipient.   Letters are always addressed to or from some person or office (e.g., TO THE ADJUTANT GENERAL; FROM GENERAL JOHN J. PERSHING). As it is often impossible to determine what title, if any, Marshall prefixed to civilian addressees, titles are used only with military officers. Frequently, Marshall addressed as "General" all ranks of general officer (similarly with the two ranks of colonel and lieutenant, and with certain enlisted grades). The editor has supplied the writer's or recipient's correct rank at the time the document was written.

Telegrams, speeches, lectures, reports, and memorandums will be designated as such.   Memorandum address lines are printed as Marshall wrote them (e.g., MEMORANDUM FOR GENERAL WESSON).

In some instances the editor has established that Marshall wrote a document signed by another person. This is indicated by "[s. King]," with the signer's last name in the brackets. For example,   "TELEGRAM TO BENJAMIN IDA WHEELER [s. Bell]," was written by Captain Marshall but signed by Major General J. Franklin Bell (p. 99). Documents signed by Marshall but written by another person are not considered Marshall papers, and, therefore, not selected unless otherwise noted.

2. Security Classification.   The security classification is given in italic type beneath the sender-recipient line. Before 1917 and during the interwar period, until he began working in the War Department's War Plans Division in mid-1938, Marshall handled relatively few classified documents. The file copies of such documents were sometimes not marked as to classification; the classification is printed in this volume *only* if it was written, typed, or stamped on the source text reproduced in this volume. Occasionally, an unofficial classification such as "personal" or "confidential" is printed if it was put on the document by the writer (e.g., Pershing to Marshall, December 16, 1935, on p. 479).

3. Date.   Marshall usually wrote his dates in the month-day-year form used in this volume. Brackets indicate that all or part of the date has been supplied; they may also mean that a spelled-out date has been converted to the standard form: "Sunday the tenth" = [July 10, 1927].

4. Place of Origin.   This is frequently supplied by the editor. During World War I, most documents simply indicated that the issuing headquarters or office was in France. As organizations kept detailed records regarding their various locations, it was usually easy to establish a document's place of origin. Bracketed additions were also necessary because many documents in this volume were reproduced from the carbon copies of typed letters which were usually typed on plain rather than letterhead stationery.

5. Title or Subject.   Many memorandums and reports and a few speeches have a formal title or subject designated on the manuscript. This is printed as written in the original but is centered over the document text.

Salutation and Complimentary Close.   These elements are important in any assessment of Marshall's relationship with his correspondents. Not given to easy familiarity, he used first names in salutations and such phrases as "affectionately yours" in the complimentary close only with special friends. For example, see his reaction to President Roosevelt's calling him "George" (p. 651). In order to save space, the salutation and the complimentary close have been printed with the first and last lines respectively of the document text, rather than on separate lines as they appear on the original manuscript. The punctuation and capitalization of these elements remain as in the original.

Signature.   A name or initials at the end of a document indicates that the editor has used the signed copy as a source. No indication of a signature or initials means: the original document was not signed (rare); a typed or stamped signature-block appeared at the end of the original document; or a carbon or other copy with no indication of signature style was used. Even on letters to friends, Marshall usually signed "G. C. Marshall," using the salutation and complimentary close to indicate familiarity and regard. Signed originals are always used in preference to copies as sources in this volume, where both have been found.

Marshall-edited Materials.   Marshall sometimes made changes in his letters and other documents before sending them, but he generally did so only to correct minor errors of spelling or punctuation. Numerous documents in this volume were initially dictated to a secretary, and Marshall would correct letters, words, or punctuation in the final version. In most instances, these corrections appear only on the signed copy and not on the carbon or file copy. He rarely inserted new words or phrases by hand, made changes significantly affecting the meaning, or added handwritten postscripts that do not appear on the typed file copy. One significant exception was his letter concerning his health to Morrison C. Stayer on pp. 638–39.

When Marshall wished to write something that he did not want his secretary or his office staff to see, he would write by hand or type the letter himself. He was a reasonably proficient typist. For example, see his two letters to Stayer on pp. 682–83 and 696–97.

This volume contains very few documents on which Marshall made significant changes. For example, see his draft for General Pershing's "Address at Army War College Graduation Exercises," June 22, 1923, on pp. 231–33. Even in this instance, Marshall's changes were mainly to improve the grammar and style. In this volume, the final, author-edited version is the text chosen for reproduction.

Brackets.   Bracketed additions or "[*sic*]" within the text of documents have been avoided unless there appears to be a danger of confusion or misinterpretation by the reader. In bibliographic and manuscript-source citations, brackets are used to separate material within parentheses. Although there are several instances of Marshall's using parentheses in his own documents (e.g., "American (?) Historical Association" on p. 222), there is no instance of his using brackets. Thus all bracketed material is editorial. If the word or letter in brackets is in italic type, it indicates that this is to be read in place of the preceding word or letter (e.g., "fixed up for these four [*three*] divisions," p. 116). If the bracketed material is in roman type, it indicates additional, rather than substitute, material (e.g., "Wednesday afternoon [August 1] General Pershing and I," p. 233).

Ellipses.   To save space, particularly in a few long reports or speeches, certain insignificant passages have been omitted. These are usually reminiscences, social amenities, or historical background, and their omission is marked by ellipsis points. Significant omissions, in terms of content or length (i.e., over twenty to thirty words), are explained by footnotes.

Romanization of Chinese.   The State Council of China decided that as of January 1, 1979, the Chinese phonetic alphabet, Pinyin, would be used exclusively to standardize the romanization of Chinese names and places. The United States government also adopted the system on that date. The previous system—the Wade-Giles (named for two nineteenth-century linguists)—was the one used by Marshall and his contemporaries. The editor has not attempted to include the new forms (e.g., Tientsin = Tianjin) in this volume.

Inclosure and Indorsement.   The official United States Army spelling for both of these words is with an *i*, although Marshall sometimes used *e*. The official spelling has been followed in the annotation in this volume. An "indorsement" is an official notation placed upon a military communication. In the army, original official letters are not retained by the recipient to be answered separately. They are returned to the sender with whatever remarks are required embodied in a formal "indorsement" which is invariably numbered. A document proceeding through "military channels" gets an "indorsement" from each succeeding headquarters through which it passes. (For example, see pp. 32–34.)

DOCUMENT SOURCE CITATIONS

Source Line. At the end of each document reproduced in this edition—and prior to any footnotes— is the line giving the source of that document. There was rarely more than a single copy made of Marshall's correspondence. But it was common to make multiple copies of official documents, and these were distributed in various files. It was difficult—frequently impossible—to find the original, signed document. Only the location of the version used in this volume is given. The source line does not attempt to locate the document precisely within a collection. Its purpose is to give the approximate location at the time of this publication.

In a few instances, a document apparently exists only in printed form. These are cited to the publication from which they were taken (e.g., *"Phillips Exeter Bulletin,* May 1978," on p. 205). Except for this kind of citation, the elements of the source line are: "Repository/Collection (subgroup, sub-subgroup); manuscript type."

Most Marshall manuscripts used in this volume came from but four repositories and a few from four others. Collections within a repository are cited by name (e.g., G. C. Marshall Papers, J. J. Pershing Papers). Record group (RG) numbers rather than collection names are used if this is the practice of the repository (e.g., VMI/RG 2; NA/RG 407). Marshall's personal file, which was maintained by the Adjutant General's Office, is cited as "NA/201 File."

Abbreviations. The following abbreviations are used for the repositories cited in this volume.

FDRL = Franklin D. Roosevelt Library, Hyde Park, New York

GCMRL = George C. Marshall Research Library, Lexington, Virginia

LC = Library of Congress, Washington, D.C.

NA = National Archives and Records Service, Washington, D.C.

NU = Northwestern University Library, Evanston, Illinois

USAMHI = United States Army Military History Institute, Carlisle Barracks, Pennsylvania

VMI = Virginia Military Institute Library, Lexington, Virginia

YU = Yale University, Sterling Library, New Haven Connecticut

Manuscript-type Notation. Approximately eighteen percent of the documents written by Marshall in this volume are holographs. The editor has strong evidence to suppose that another eight percent were typed by Marshall. Holographs are designated by an "H" at the end of the document source line, and Marshall-typed documents are designated by a "T." In both kinds of documents, silent corrections have been made very rarely (e.g., the addition of an omitted period at the end of a sentence which itself ends at the edge or the bottom of a page on the original manuscript). The reproductions of these documents were given especially careful proofreading.

Marshall documents not designated by "H" or "T" are presumed to have been produced by a clerk or secretary from dictation, notes, or a draft. With one exception (Marshall's report to the military governor of Mindoro, September 14, 1902, p. 26), these documents are typed. In such documents, obvious errors in spelling—and occasionally in capitalization and punctuation—have been corrected. Marshall may have made some or all of these corrections on the signed original before it was sent.

DOCUMENT SEQUENCE

A chronological arrangement of documents is generally maintained throughout the volume. Occasionally, a particularly interesting or relevant document— such as one in which Marshall reminisces about earlier events—is inserted thematically rather than chronologically. Examples of these are the second and the last documents in the volume.

ABBREVIATIONS

Technical endeavors and complex bureaucracies seem to lend themselves to abbreviations and acronyms. Although it may be argued that even in the military profession the golden age of such shortened forms began only with World War II, there were a significant number prior to that time. In general, the editors have tried to exercise restraint in the use of abbreviations in the annotation. If a particular abbreviation appears but once in the volume, it is identified immediately in brackets or in a footnote. Recurring abbreviations are listed below. Some of these forms may appear in the documents with or without periods (e.g., VMI, V.M.I.). In editorial matter, with the exception of the document source lines, periods are used in abbreviated words.

A.D.C.	=	aide-de-camp
A.E.F.	=	American Expeditionary Forces
A.F.C.	=	United States Army Forces in China (also U.S.A.F. in C.)
A.G.	=	adjutant general (but not TAG)
A.R.	=	army regulation
B.G.	=	brigadier general
Bn.	=	battalion
Cav.	=	Cavalry
C.C.C.	=	Civilian Conservation Corps
C.M.T.C.	=	Citizens' Military Training Camp
C.O.	=	commanding officer
Col.	=	colonel
C.P.	=	command post
C.P.X.	=	command post exercise
C.S.	=	Chief of Staff of the Army (sometimes C. of S.)

C.W.A. = Civil Works Administration
Dist. = district
Div. = division
D.S.C. = Distinguished Service Cross
D.S.M. = Distinguished Service Medal
F.A. = Field Artillery
G-1 = Personnel Division, General Staff
G-2 = Intelligence Division, General Staff
G-3 = Operations Division, General Staff
G-4 = Logistics Division, General Staff
G-5 = Training Division, General Staff (A.E.F. G.H.Q. only)
Gen. = general
G.H.Q. = general headquarters
G.O. = general order
Inf. = Infantry
Lt. = lieutenant (also lieut.)
N.C.O. = non-commissioned officer
N.G. = National Guard
O.C.S. = Office of the Chief of Staff of the Army
P.M.S.&T. = professor of military science and tactics
P.W.A. = Public Works Administration
Q.M. = quartermaster
Q.M.C. = Quartermaster Corps
R.F.C. = Reconstruction Finance Corporation
R.O.T.C. = Reserve Officers' Training Corps
S.O. = special order
S.O.S. = Service of Supply (A.E.F.)
T.A.G. = The Adjutant General of the Army
T. of O. = tables of organization (also T/O and TO)
T.R. = training regulation
U.S.A.T. = United States Army Transport
U.S.M.A. = United States Military Academy
U.S.N.A. = United States Naval Academy
U.S.S. = United States Ship (or United States Naval Vessel)
V.M.I. = Virginia Military Institute
W.D. = War Department
W.D.G.S. = War Department General Staff
W.P.A. = Works Progress Administration
W.P.D. = War Plans Division (War Department)
Y.M.C.A. = Young Men's Christian Association

Sources of Illustrations

The following are the sources for the illustrations used in this volume. The abbreviations and the format of the source line are described in the "Guide to Editorial Policies."

Marshall Chronology

The following is a brief outline of the major events in George C. Marshall's life during the period covered by this volume:

December 31, 1880	Born in Uniontown, Pennsylvania
September 1897– June 1901	Cadet, Virginia Military Institute (Lexington, Virginia)
September 1901– December 1901	Commandant, Danville Military Institute (Danville, Virginia)
February 2, 1902	Commissioned a second lieutenant of Infantry
February 11, 1902	Married to Elizabeth C. Coles
May 1902– November 1903	Duty in the Philippine Islands (Manila; Mangarin, Mindoro)
December 1903– August 1906	Duty at Fort Reno, Oklahoma (detached service for mapping, Texas, summer 1905)
August 1906– June 1910	Student (1906–8) and instructor (1908–10), Army Service Schools (Fort Leavenworth, Kansas)
March 1907	Promoted to first lieutenant
June 1911– September 1912	Inspector-Instructor, Massachusetts Volunteer Militia (Boston, Massachusetts)
September 1912– June 1913	Duty with the Fourth Infantry (Fort Logan Roots, Arkansas; Fort Snelling, Minnesota; Texas City, Texas)
August 1913– May 1916	Duty in the Philippine Islands; aide-de-camp to Major General Hunter Liggett
July 1916– July 1917	Aide-de-camp to Major General J. Franklin Bell (San Francisco, California; Governors Island, New York)
October 1916	Promoted to captain
July 1917– April 1919	Duty with the A.E.F., France: assistant chief of staff, G-3, First Division (June 26, 1917–July 12, 1918); G-3 section, G.H.Q. (June 13–July 12, 1918); assistant chief of staff, G-3, First Army (October 17–November 19, 1918); chief of staff, Eighth Corps (November 20, 1918– January 15, 1919); G-3 section, G.H.Q. (January 15–April 30, 1919) Temporary promotions: major, August 1917; lieu- tenant colonel, January 1918; colonel, August 1918

May 1919– June 1924	Aide-de-camp to General John J. Pershing (France and Washington, D.C.)
July 1920	Promoted to major
August 1923	Promoted to lieutenant colonel
September 1924– May 1927	Duty with the Fifteenth Infantry (Tientsin, China)
July 1927– October 1927	Instructor, Army War College (Washington, D.C.)
September 15, 1927	Death of Elizabeth C. Marshall
October 1927– June 1932	Assistant commandant, Infantry School (Fort Benning, Georgia)
October 15, 1930	Married to Katherine Tupper Brown
June 1932– June 1933	Commanding Fort Screven, Georgia, and Civilian Consevation Corps (C.C.C.) District "F"
June 1933– October 1933	Commanding Fort Moultrie, South Carolina, and C.C.C. District "I"
September 1933	Promotion to colonel
October 1933– October 1936	Senior instructor, Illinois National Guard (Chicago, Illinois)
October 1936	Promoted to brigadier general
October 1936– June 1938	Commanding Fifth Brigade of the Third Division, Vancouver Barracks, Washington, and C.C.C. District
July 1938– October 1938	Assistant chief of staff, War Plans Division, War Department (Washington, D.C.)
October 1938– June 1939	Deputy chief of staff, War Department (Washington, D.C.)
July 1, 1939	Began duties as acting chief of staff

Introduction

December 1880–February 1902

T HE MARSHALLS of Uniontown, Pennsylvania, at the time George Catlett, Jr., was born on the last day of 1880, were a solidly middle-class family, respectable and churchgoing. George C. Marshall, Sr., had developed a prosperous business which manufactured coking coal in competition with Henry Clay Frick, the region's dominant figure.

Although after their marriage in 1873 Laura Bradford and George Marshall established themselves in southwestern Pennsylvania, both were descendants of a long line of Kentucky and Virginia ancestors, some of prominence. George C. Marshall, Sr., was particularly interested in his connection with Chief Justice John Marshall, his grandfather's first cousin. George C. Marshall, Jr., was somewhat embarrassed by his father's keenness regarding the relationship. In later years he remarked that "the continued harping on the name of John Marshall was kind of poor business. It was about time for somebody to swim for the family again." (George C. Marshall, interviewed by Forrest C. Pogue, February 28, 1957, George C. Marshall Research Library, Lexington, Virginia, hereafter cited as Interview.)

Uniontown was the quintessential small town during Marshall's childhood. The family lived in the last house on West Main Street beside a small stream. Hilly fields and woods stretched beyond the creek. Marshall's world normally had a radius of perhaps five miles, but it encompassed fishing holes and hunting grounds; a few miles beyond lay historic sites like General Braddock's grave and George Washington's Fort Necessity. This small world was bisected by Main Street—the famous and busy National Road that ran westward from Cumberland, Maryland—and into it came circuses, fairs, and an occasional trial at the town courthouse. ★

TO ELIZA STUART[1]   [September, 1890?]
                                                     [Uniontown, Pennsylvania]

Dear Aunt   The Church gave fifty dollars and we gave eighty dollars and eighty cents. Papa gave me a new prayer book and hymnal for doing without molases. Papa went to Lexington in Virginia.[2] Love to Ted and Jack.

                                                            George Marshall

GCMRL/Museum; H

1. Marshall's mother's aunt lived with the family for a time. Marshall remembered her as an elderly, well-educated woman who was determined that he also be well educated. "She began teaching me at about five years old and she so soured me on study and teaching that I liked to never have recovered from it. Because I would be held by her chair while she taught me and I could see out in the streets my friends playing. That was particularly horrible to me on Saturday mornings." (Interview, February 28, 1957.)

2. Marshall's brother Stuart (b. 1875) entered the Virginia Military Institute in Lexington, Virginia, in September, 1890.

*To Eliza Stuart from George C. Marshall, Jr.,
September, 1890(?).*

MARSHALL said in 1957: "My first very clear recollection is going out to our barn in which we kept a horse and a cow . . . climbing up the ladder, which was fastened to the side of the barn, in an effort to get to the haymow—the first time I had ever tried this. . . . And as I climbed up the ladder, being very cautious and a little frightened, I came to a windowless opening which I could look out of between the rungs of the ladder. In a sense . . . this was my first look at the world." (Interview, February 21, 1957.)

The family's prosperity ended suddenly in 1890. Earlier that year Marshall's father had sold a large part of his coking business to the expanding Frick enterprises and had used the income to invest heavily in the Shenandoah Valley land boom. The investment was wiped out a few months later when the speculative bubble burst, plunging the family into unaccustomed financial straits. "We had to economize very bitterly," Marshall recalled, and only his mother's modest income from some Pittsburgh property saved the situation. (Interview, February 28, 1957.) ★

To Mrs. Chester M. Davis   November 19, 1952
                                            [Pinehurst, North Carolina?]

My dear Mrs. Davis: I receive so many requests somewhat similar to yours that it is not practicable for me to meet them. However, I will try, in a few words, to give you a partial answer to yours.[1]

My mother exercised a constant and lasting influence on my life. I was always very close to her, as her youngest child and because for some years my brother and my sister were away at school while I was at home with her. She was both gentle and firm, very understanding, and had a keen, but quiet, sense of humor, which made her my confidante in practically all my boyish escapades and difficulties.

She was a conscientious churchwoman and saw that I was always regular in my attendance. What I came to admire most about her while I was still young, and much more later on, was the way she bore a very heavy burden during the great financial depression of the nineties. She was in poor health, yet did all the work of our home and made it a cheerful place, where most of the young people of our various groups would assemble in the evenings when we were free, for music, good times, and interesting discussions. This was most uncommon in our community at that time. The custom was brought north by my parents from Kentucky.

All my mother's life, she sent me a check for $10.00 on my birthday. The point was, she gave me. Our only quarrel that I can think of was her insistence on my mailing her letters immediately they were written, and they generally seemed to be written very shortly after the carrier had collected the mail. I recall that when I returned home in 1927 from China to find her confined to her bed shortly before her death, she immediately directed me to mail a letter in the mailbox across the street, though it was then 6:30 in the morning and I had but greeted her a few moments previously after a three years' absence. I thought she was joking, but she was merely being her same self—always thoughtful of others, but determined in a few small things for herself.

She was a very wonderful mother, and I was very lucky to be her son.   Faithfully yours,

GCMRL/G. C. Marshall Papers (Retirement)

1. Mrs. Davis (Elisabeth Logan Davis) had written General Marshall on November 4, requesting information about his mother for a biographical sketch. Mrs. Davis was writing *Mothers of America* (Westwood, N.J.: F. H. Revell, 1954), a book about mothers of famous American men. Laura Bradford Marshall is not mentioned in the book.

To Reverend Bernard C. Newman[1]   August 6, 1943
                                                   [Washington, D.C.]

My dear Mr. Newman: I have received your note of August fourth and I am sending you a photograph for the Parish House as requested.

Your letter recalled to me the days of my youth when Saint Peter's and Mr. Wightman exercised a profound influence on my character and life. I mentioned Mr. Wightman because while I was a mere boy in my early teens he honored me with his friendship. We often took walks in the country together and I spent many hours with him at the Parish House which had just been constructed.[2]

You are wrong about my singing in the choir. Up to the present day it would be quite impossible for me to qualify for such service. I did engage in church work, soliciting funds, doing odd jobs, but more particularly in pumping the organ until, to be perfectly honest about this business, I was discharged for failing to provide air at a critical moment, having become deeply engaged in a Nick Carter novel. Miss Fannie Howell was my boss upon whom this unpleasant duty fell but I suffered more at home after the event than from Miss Fannie.[3]

Thank you for your letter and for your prayers. I need them. Faithfully yours,

G. C. Marshall

GCMRL/B. C. Newman Papers

1. Newman was rector at Saint Peter's Episcopal Church in Uniontown, Pennsylvania.

2. Reverend John R. Wightman, a young minister new to Saint Peter's Church, became an intimate friend of Marshall. The men of Uniontown worked during the day, and Wightman had few male associates and welcomed Marshall's company. (Interview, February 28, 1957.)

3. United Press released Marshall's account of the organ-pumping incident on September 23, 1943; and the story was published in several newspapers, including the New York *Herald Tribune*.

U NTIL HE was eight years old Marshall was rather casually educated in a succession of private schools in Uniontown. In September, 1889, he enrolled in the local public school. There he was embarrassed and his father dismayed by his lack of knowledge in comparison to his peers, particularly in arithmetic, grammar, and spelling. Although his interest in and knowledge of history was more acceptable, Marshall remembered his four years in public school as "humiliating" and "a very painful time." When the pain had been eased by the passage of more than sixty years, Marshall agreed that his public-school years had been a valuable and necessary democratizing experience, "very important, I think, in the life of every young American." Nevertheless, as soon as the family's financial position improved sufficiently in 1893, he enrolled in Uniontown Academy, a private school.

GEO. C. MARSHALL, PRES'T.   A. W. BLISS, SEC'Y.   L. DE SAULLES, SUP'T.

PERCY MINING CO.

CONNELLSVILLE COKE.

72-HOUR FOUNDRY COKE A SPECIALTY.

FREIGHT RATES AND PRICES FURNISHED ON APPLICATION.

Percy, Fayette Co., Pa., *11 Sep* 189

Genl. Scott Shipp,

    Lexington Va.

      My Dear Genl.

             I Send You My Youngest ,And Last. He Is Bright, Full

Of Life,And I Believe Will Get Along Very Well .

A Cousin Of His Will Also Go,Depending On His Eyes. Enclosed Find

Ck. For $200. Any Extras George May Need,Please Advise Me,And I

WillSend You Ck.

          Kind Regards

To Brigadier General Scott Shipp (superintendent of the Virginia Military Institute) from George C. Marshall, Sr., September 11, 1897.

By his mid-teens, Marshall had begun to look toward a military career. His parents were not pleased by his interest in the tiny, low-status army. Marshall would have liked to attend the United States Military Academy. Education there was free—a consideration of great importance to the family—and a commission was guaranteed to successful graduates. But in his congressional district Academy appointments were based on competitive examination, and Marshall's scholarly credentials were weak. Moreover, his father was a staunch Democrat in a Republican district. Finally, a painfully injured right elbow probably would have prevented his meeting the physical requirements for entrance.

Stuart Marshall had graduated with a creditable academic record in chemistry in 1894 from the Virginia Military Institute. When George was begging to be allowed to attend, he overheard his brother trying to persuade his mother against it, because he thought the family name might be disgraced by George's apparent lack of scholastic ability. That, Marshall later recalled, "made more impression on me than all the instructors, parental pressures or anything else, and I decided right then that I was going to 'wipe his face' or 'wipe his eye,' and I ended up at the V.M.I." His mother sold some property to raise the tuition. (Interview, February 21, 1957.)

The cadet routine at the Virginia Military Institute was, Marshall remembered, "very austere." School ran from early September through June with few holidays, little respite from discipline, and practically no provisions for entertaining the cadets. For a boy in the fourth class—a "rat"—hazing by upperclassmen made life "quite an ordeal." Marshall's natural stoicism helped him survive. "The routine of cadet life I became accustomed to and accepted. I think I was a little bit more philosophical about this thing than a good many boys. They would get very exercised over something of that kind. It was part of the business and the only thing to do was to accept it as best you could and as easily as you could." Having agreeable roommates made surviving easier. (Interviews, March 6 and 13, 1957.)

The most exciting event of Marshall's "rat" year was the war with Spain. On April 23, 1898—the day after Congress authorized the president to organize volunteer units "possessing special qualifications"—the cadets unanimously voted to offer their services. (*Lexington Gazette,* April 27, 1898.) By the time Marshall returned to Uniontown for summer vacation, the local National Guard company had left for the Philippine Islands with the rest of the Tenth Pennsylvania Infantry Regiment. Company C's heroic return the following summer had a profound impact on Marshall, who by then was half-way through V.M.I. and was already winning military—although not scholastic—honors. ★

SPEECH[1]   September 9, 1939
                                                                        Uniontown, Pennsylvania

. . . The life of a man reflects the impressions of youthful surroundings, and this has been my personal experience. My first great emotional reaction came, I believe, with the parade of old Company C of the 10th Pennsylvania regiment of infantry, on its return with the honors of war from a campaign in the far-off Philippine Islands.[2] Few of us had ever heard of the Philippines until that year. We had heard of manila rope, but we did not know where Manila was; and when this fine old regiment left Western Pennsylvania for San Francisco, to sail across the broad Pacific and carry the flag ashore in distant Manila, it had a broadening effect, geographically, on the inhabitants of Fayette County. Later on, in the spring of 1899, when the cables arrived describing the fighting in which some young men well-known to us were mentioned for conspicuous courage and others were reported as casualties, local interest grew intense. I have sometimes thought that the impressions of that period, and particularly of that parade, had a determining effect on my choice of a profession.

It was a wonderful scene, that parade. The bricks of Main Street were painted red, white, and blue, and triumphal arches erected in every block—there was even an arch of coke constructed by the Frick Company. And when the head of the procession finally appeared, the individual excitement surpassed, as I recall, even that of the splendid so-called Victory parades of 1919 in Paris and London, in which I participated as an Aide to General Pershing.

No man of Company C could make a purchase in this community. The town was his. He had but to command and his desires were gratified—a medal for every soldier and a sword for each officer. And there was a final jubilation at the Fair Grounds. It was a grand American small town demonstration of pride in its young men and of wholesome enthusiasm over their achievements. Years later most of us realized that it was much more than that. It reflected the introduction of America into the affairs of the world beyond the seas. . . .

GCMRL/G. C. Marshall Papers (Pentagon Office, Speeches)

1. This speech was delivered when Marshall visited Uniontown shortly after his promotion to army chief of staff on September 1, 1939. Marshall wrote on the file copy of this speech: "Only a portion of this—approximately was used." About twenty percent of this speech is printed here. The omitted parts include a brief introduction as well as recollections of his early career, his poor scholastic record, the historical importance of the Uniontown area in early American history, and the problems of the current (1939) world situation.

2. The Uniontown parade was on August 29, 1899.

M ARSHALL began his "rat" year while recovering from typhoid fever; later he was injured in a hazing incident. Despite these initial trials, he quickly demonstrated his military interests and abilities by successively holding the highest cadet positions available in each class: first corporal, first sergeant, first captain. When asked what he had done to make himself first captain, he replied: "The first thing was I tried very hard. . . . I was very exacting and exact in all my military duties and I was gradually developing in authority from the very mild authority, almost none, shown by a corporal to the very pronounced authority as first sergeant." (Interview, March 13, 1957.)

His responsibilities were large for one his age; he had to learn to exercise authority in such a way as not to create resentment. "The impact of the V.M.I. on my later leadership was probably much greater than I realized at the time. Having been a first sergeant and later a first captain meant a great deal in control. I had specific things to do. I was responsible for the men, and you couldn't go to sleep on that. That required your attention every minute. You had to know just what you were doing, and you had to have some talent at putting it over. This was particularly true of the first captain, because he took the lead on such matters." (Ibid.)

In later years Marshall recalled that his academic performance at V.M.I. steadily improved after a poor start. In fact, he began and remained a mediocre scholar. His grades in English improved, but he tended to do poorly in mathematics and science. Marshall finished fifteenth of the thirty-three graduates, but managed to stand fifth in civil engineering, his major. Not surprisingly, he did well in military subjects. (Interviews, February 21 and 28, 1957; V.M.I., *Official Register,* 1898–99 to 1901-2.)

The most serious challenge Marshall faced in his final year at V.M.I. was not scholastic or even romantic—he had fallen in love with the belle of Lexington, Elizabeth ("Lily") Carter Coles—but getting an army commission. Fortunately for him, the United States Army, consonant with the nation's new world position and at Secretary of War Elihu Root's insistence, was more than three times as large in 1901 as it had been when Marshall entered V.M.I.

A law taking effect on February 2, 1901, required the appointment of 837 new first and second lieutenants. First priority was given to West Point graduates, next to successful applicants from the ranks, then to former officers of the volunteers, and finally to civilians. Although he had graduated from a military school, Marshall had to compete with others from civil life. Excepting West Point graduates, all applicants had to take an admission test. In order to take the examination Marshall needed a letter of authorization from the War Department. (*Report of the Secretary of War, 1901* [Washington, D.C.: Government Printing Office, 1901], pp. 7–10; Major William Murray Black, "The Education and Training of Army Officers," *Journal of the Military Service Institution* 32 [January–February 1903]: 17, 20, 30–31.) ★

To Brigadier General Scott Shipp   January 21, 1901
From George C. Marshall, Sr.   Uniontown, Pennsylvania

My Dr Sir:–   It has been George Jr.s ambition to go in the regular service, and he has been bending his energies to that end. While his Mother and I both were against it I believe in taking him on his own judgment etc. I have many warm and influential friends of the administration and quite close ones at that. They will do for me all that it is possible to do. Even so far as making it a personal demand. On that score I am fully satisfied and assured—[1]

Now my object in writing is to ask of you a letter simply giving me your opinion as to George's fitness. Whether he possesses those qualifications, so essential to the making of an officer that would be a credit to the Institute or not particularly as it comes from the V.M.I. the West Point of the South.[2] At any rate I will present them in person, and do the talking for the V.M.I—

By doing this, you will greatly oblige   Yrs very truly

G. C. Marshall

P.S.—All I can say is that if he only makes as great a success in his line as Stuart has in his I will be both satisfied and proud of him—[3]

G. C. M.

VMI/Alumni File; H

1. At the request of George C. Marshall, Sr., John S. Wise wrote a letter of recommendation to President McKinley on January 30, 1901. Wise cited George's relative, "the illustrious John Marshall . . . and the records fail to disclose since then one of the name who was either fool or coward. They are filled with instances of intelligent brave gentlemen of this name and this boy bears it most worthily. I heartily commend him." (NA/RG 94 [Document File].) Wise, a V.M.I. graduate (1866) and the son of a former governor of Virginia, had switched to the Republican party, moved to New York, and helped William McKinley win the 1896 presidential nomination.

2. In response to Mr. Marshall's request, General Scott Shipp wrote a letter of recommendation on January 23, 1901: "I was a Confederate officer, and for nearly forty years have been Comm^r or Suptd^t of this school. I have served on B^d of Visitors to both West Point and Annapolis. With this experience I assert with absolute confidence that if commissioned in the army, young Marshall will in all respects, soon take his stand much above the average West Point graduate." (Ibid.)

On February 12, 1901, George C. Marshall, Sr., requested General Shipp to write a personal letter to President McKinley, much like the one that Wise had written. Superintendent Shipp responded with a letter to the president on February 14, recommending Marshall for a second lieutenancy and commenting that "Marshall is fully the equal of the best." (Ibid.)

3. Upon graduation from V.M.I. in 1894, Stuart B. Marshall joined the Dunbar Furnace Company in Dunbar, Pennsylvania, where he soon became chief chemist.

YOUNG MARSHALL had reason to press vigorously for action: the positions in the expanded army were being filled rapidly. By September, 1901, when he was finally able to take the qualifying examination, there were only 142 vacancies for the new lieutenancies and over 10,000 applications on file. (*Report of the Secretary of War, 1901,* p. 11.)

In April, armed with one of his father's business cards and some letters of introduction, Marshall journeyed to Washington, D.C. There he visited the newly appointed attorney general, Philander C. Knox, a friend of his father; the chairman of the House Military Affairs Committee, John A. Hull, distantly connected with his mother's family by marriage; and finally President McKinley himself. (Interview, February 28, 1957.) But these meetings were perhaps less important than the letters of recommendation his father had persuaded the Republican senators from Pennsylvania, Boies Penrose and Matthew S. Quay, to write to the War Department. (Copies of the documents concerning Marshall's efforts to obtain permission to take the test are in NA/RG 94 [Document File].)

One of the few extant documents produced by cadet Marshall, the report written at the end of his final year at V.M.I., appears on page 16. ★

George C. Marshall, Sr. (1845–1909).   *Laura Bradford Marshall (1846–1928).*

George C. Marshall, Jr., about 1885.

First Classman Marshall wearing his furlough coat. General Shipp said of him: "He is of fine physique and soldierlike appearance; a young man of marked character and ability, with natural powers of command and control." (Shipp to Whom It May Concern, January 23, 1901, NA/RG 94 [Document File].)

13

George C. Marshall, third from the left in the front row, with the V.M.I. cadet staff, 1901.

The Marshall-Coles wedding party poses on the front porch of the bride's Lexington home, where the Episcopal ceremony took place. Left to right are Marie (George's sister), Elizabeth Carter ("Lily") Coles, George C. Marshall, Jr., Stuart (George's brother), Mr. and Mrs. George C. Marshall, Sr., and Mrs. Walter Coles.

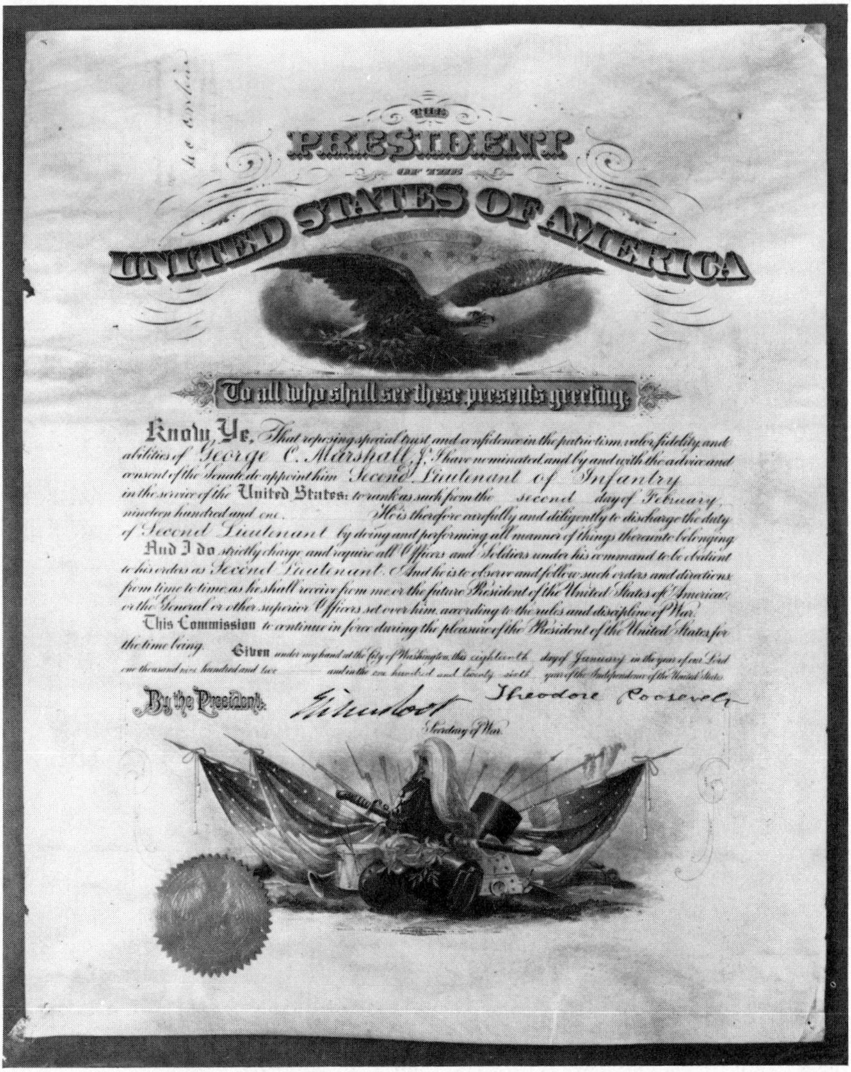

THE PRESIDENT OF THE UNITED STATES OF AMERICA

To all who shall see these presents greeting:

Know Ye, That reposing special trust and confidence in the patriotism, valor, fidelity and abilities of George C. Marshall Jr. I have nominated and by and with the advice and consent of the Senate do appoint him Second Lieutenant of Infantry in the service of the United States: to rank as such from the second day of February nineteen hundred and one. He is therefore carefully and diligently to discharge the duty of Second Lieutenant by doing and performing all manner of things thereunto belonging.

And I do strictly charge and require all Officers and Soldiers under his command to be obedient to his orders as Second Lieutenant. And he is to observe and follow such orders and directions from time to time, as he shall receive from me, or the future President of the United States of America, or the General or other superior Officers set over him, according to the rules and discipline of War.

This Commission to continue in force during the pleasure of the President of the United States for the time being.

Given under my hand at the City of Washington this eighteenth day of January in the year of our Lord one thousand nine hundred and two and in the one hundred and twenty sixth year of the Independence of the United States.

By the President: Theodore Roosevelt

Elihu Root
Secretary of War.

Marshall's commission as second lieutenant of Infantry.

REPORT TO MAJOR RICHARD C. MARSHALL, JR.[1]   June 11, 1901
Lexington, Virginia

Report of the Superintendent of the Mess Hall.

Sir:–   I have the honor to submit the following report on the Mess Hall:

During the time I have had charge of the Mess Hall I have not found it necessary to make any definite complaint to the Quartermaster. On a few occasions I have found reason to call the attention of the head waiter to untidiness in the setting of the tables and any lack of neatness in the dress of the waiters.

The fare is an improvement on that of the last three years, and in my judgment is all that could be expected, except in the manner of cooking the meats. The meat itself appears to be of a good quality, but it seems to have been dried up in the cooking.

To the best of my knowledge, no serious breaches of discipline have so far occurred, and the few minor ones have been reported as far as possible.

The practice of carrying coffee, bread, etc., from the Mess Hall has been entirely broken up. I have no knowledge of any cases of this sort, either officially or unofficially, since it was especially forbidden.   Very respectfully,

VMI, *Annual Report of the Superintendent, 1900–1901*

1. Major Marshall (no relation to George) was a V.M.I. graduate (1898) and the acting commandant of cadets.

TO MAJOR GENERAL JOHN R. BROOKE   September 23, 1901
FROM JOHN S. WISE   New York, New York

My dear General   This will be presented to you by my young friend Geo: C. Marshall jr, who goes before your Board for examination.[1] I sincerely hope he may succeed. This boy has the very highest testimonials. He was first Captain at the V^a Mil: Ins: & had a good class standing. Gen: Shipp, the Sup^t regards him as one of the fittest pieces of food for gunpowder turned out by his mill for many years—

Commending him to your tender mercies I am   Yrs: trl

Jno: S. Wise

NA/RG 94 (Document File); H

1. The three-day examination for commission had originally been scheduled at Governors Island in New York Harbor in early September, but President McKinley's assassination and funeral caused a postponement until September 23.

F OLLOWING his examination, Marshall returned to his new job in Danville, Virginia. Since September 16 he had held the rank of major and the position of commandant of cadets at the Danville Military Institute, a hedge against the uncertainty of gaining a commission. At the Institute he taught the approximately ninety boys in the elementary and secondary levels arithmetic, algebra, history, and English, in addition to drill and discipline. (Marshall, "Form for Individual Record of Applicant," NA/RG 94 [Document File].) ★

To Brigadier General Scott Shipp   October 2, 1901
                                                   Danville, Virginia

My dear General Shipp   I have been very busy since my return from Governor's Island Sunday night and this is the first opportunity to write to you I have had since my return. I was put on my honor, to a certain extent, in regard to giving people information about the questions asked me in the examinations, but I think I am free to give you some general information as to the method and character of the examinations. I reported at G's. I. on Monday morning, September 23rd, and was told to be at the War building on Tuesday morning. On Tuesday I stood arithmetic, algebra and geometry.

The first two were extremely simple, all the fundamental operations such as addition, subtraction and multiplication and one simple problem. The Geometry was hard, much harder than I had understood it would be. There were five questions, four of them demonstrations and one problem. I was fortunate in having glanced at each demonstration we were given before I went in or I think I would have failed, as it was I practically maxed it, I think. On Wednesday I stood Logarithms, Trigonometry, Surveying and Geography. All the questions on the first of these were simply for definitions and all very easy. The Trigonometry was fairly hard, solutions of right triangles and relation of different functions of angles. The Surveying was easy and only required common sense, such questions as solution of angles given sides in chains &c., percent of grade and similar questions. The Geography was catchy as it usually is according to accounts I have heard, but I had prepared for such questions. They asked what states crossed by lines through different points, the location of the newly acquired possessions of the U.S., and capes and bays, especially those in the vicinity of some country over which there has been discussion at any time. On Thursday I finished up the mental taking exams in Grammar, History, Constitutional Law and International Law. In the Grammar they asked definitions and how to form plurals and feminines of words and also gave a sentence to analyze.

The History was extremely general the questions covering all countrys, particularly Italy and the U.S. One question was "Locate, describe and give seating capacity of the Coliseum". Luckily I have read a great deal and found ready answers to most of the questions in the History. The Constitutional Law was long but I am positive I maxed it. All the questions were on the Constitution itself. I had only looked at the International Law given in the back of our Government Law book and not a question on the examination was answered in it. I had to use my head and guess and I found out afterwards that I got all but one question practically right. The questions were such ones as "Discuss the International Law in connection with the St. Lawrence River as a boundary line", "What is the marine Leaugue and give reasons for having such an agreement?", "Discuss the general principles of allegiance", &c. On Friday we were each given a company to drill. It was optional with the civilians but I took it, thought I was the only one who did so. I had to put the company through the ordinary movements. The physical examination was strict but I was not given any reason to claim any failure, if I am so unfortunate, on that part of the examination. I am not yet informed as to the question about my age but from what little General Brooke would tell me it will be all right. I expect to hear the result in about three weeks or a month.

I hope I have not written you too long a letter but as I feel entirely indebted to you for my appointment I want to give you all the information in my power about the examination since it may be of use to you in advising some of your men.   Faithfully yours

G. C. Marshall, Jr.

GCMRL/VMI Collection; H

MEMORANDUM BY THE EXAMINING BOARD   [October 8, 1901]
Governors Island, New York

The board met at the call of the president, and proceeded with the examination of George Catlett Marshall, Jr., Danville Military Institute, Danville, Virginia, who appeared before the board in accordance with instructions from the War Department and from the board.

The standing of the candidate in the various subjects upon which he was examined, as per instructions from the War Department, and under General Orders, as shown by appended papers, is as follows:

No.	Subject	Aver-age	Relative weights	Products of multi-plication by rela-tive weights
1	English grammar, etc.	75	3	225
2	Mathematics	86	4	344
3	Geography........................	65	2	130
4	History	89	3	267
5	Constitutional and international law	65	2	130
6	Army and drill regulations, etc.			
7	Military record.....................			
8	Physique	100	3	300
9	Moral character and antecedents	100	3	300
			20	1696
				84.80

The applicant, George Catlett Marshall, Jr., Danville Military Institute, Danville, Virginia, having attained an average in each subject of 65 per cent, and having attained a general average of 70 per cent, the board considers him as having passed, and as well qualified for the position of a commissioned officer in the United States Army.

The board, however, finds that Mr. Marshall will not be twenty-one years of age until December 31, 1901. It therefore recommends that he be commissioned after that date. He is recommended for artillery on account of high standing.[1]

NA/RG 94 (Document File)

1. On his application form Marshall listed his preference of service branches as "1st Artillery 2nd Infantry 3rd Cavalry." West Point graduates, primarily because of the mathematical emphasis of their training, were recommended for commissions in the Engineers, Ordnance, Artillery, Cavalry, and Infantry in the order of their graduation standing, thereby establishing a rough order of status for the branches. (Black, "The Education and Training of Army Officers," p. 30.)

Not only was the wait for the results of the examination nerve-wracking, but the commissioning process was delaying Marshall's marriage to Lily Coles of Lexington. In addition to being twenty-one years old, civilian appointees had to be single at the time of commissioning. ★

To Brigadier General Scott Shipp   December 12, 1901
                                     Danville, Virginia

My dear General   I am glad to be able to tell you that I have received a letter
from the War Department telling me that I passed my examinations successfully,
and was recommended for a commission as lieutenant in the Army after
becoming of age. The commission is to be sent after December 31st. A little late,
but very acceptable Xmas gift.

As I will be in Lexington during the holidays I can explain all the details of the
affair to better advantage then. Please pardon this paper[1] and believe me—
Faithfully yours

G. C. Marshall, Jr.

VMI/Alumni File; H

1. Marshall wrote on lined notebook paper.

M ARSHALL resigned his position in Danville and returned to his home in
Uniontown. On January 6, 1902, his nomination for a commission in the
Thirtieth Infantry Regiment, a unit stationed in the Philippines, was sent to the
adjutant general of the army. Having assumed that he would receive an Artillery
Corps commission, Marshall was nonplussed when he received the news. His
father prevailed upon two Uniontown friends to write to Senator Matthew Quay,
who queried the War Department. The adjutant general replied that there were
"no vacancies as second lieutenants of artillery to be filled by candidates from
civil life. The only remedy for Mr. Marshall is to arrange a mutual transfer with
someone in the artillery who desires infantry." (TAG to Quay, January 30, 1902,
NA/RG 94 [Document File].) Marshall returned his signed oath of office as an
infantryman on February 3.

Elizabeth Carter Coles and George C. Marshall, Jr., were married in an
Episcopal ceremony in the bride's home in Lexington, Virginia, on February 11.
The next morning the new couple took the train for Washington, D.C. As
Marshall had orders to report on the thirteenth, they expected but a single day's
honeymoon. Fortunately, when Lieutenant Marshall reported to the War
Department building, he met Major William H. Carter, the assistant adjutant
general and a man who became a good friend in later years. (Interview, March
13, 1957.) Carter was sympathetic to the plight of newlyweds facing a long
separation and directed that revised orders be issued delaying for ten days
Marshall's departure for foreign duty. ★

Young Officer

February 1902–June 1917

FORT MYER, VIRGINIA, was Second Lieutenant Marshall's first duty assignment. But in less than a week he was off to Fort Slocum, New York, and from there, on March 17, 1902, he boarded a westbound train for the first leg of the trip to his new post in the Philippine Islands. The month-long second leg, aboard the army transport *Kilpatrick*, which sailed from San Francisco, stuck in Marshall's memory as being long, dull, and somewhat dangerous. But he remarked: "It was rather interesting on the boat. . . . There were quite a few officers who had been volunteers in the Spanish-American War and the Philippine Insurrection and now had received Regular commissions; and some of them were very industrious in telling me—particularly who had come from civil life—how I should function. They understood it all. Later on I discovered they knew damn little." (Interview, March 13, 1957.)

The Philippine Insurrection was sputtering out by the time Marshall arrived in Manila in May. President Theodore Roosevelt declared peace officially on July 4, 1902. Marshall landed in the capital of America's new Pacific outpost in the midst of a severe cholera epidemic. He also needed to reach his new station quickly. Manila was an expensive city and he had little money. Taking hurried leave of the city, Marshall experienced a harrowing boat trip through a typhoon. Finally, he arrived at Calapan, the capital of the island of Mindoro, where his detachment of Company G, Thirtieth Infantry, was stationed.

Marshall had hardly had time to get acquainted when the cholera epidemic struck the region, necessitating the most rigorous enforcement of discipline on the soldiers in order to prevent their infection. When the quarantine was finally eased, Marshall, the most junior officer, was given the job of staging a Fourth of July field day and talent show. His memory of the situation was vivid. "Some of the older officers were laughing at me because the morale of the garrison had just been knocked galley-west by the arbitrary and tyrannical handling of the place by a predecessor of the then commanding officer. And [the men] were all sore and all outraged and just in a sort of a sullen silence." (Ibid.) His success in raising the command's morale demonstrated his ability to take charge in a difficult situation. Further, it was the first evidence of his career-long concern with maintaining high troop morale. ★

To CLYDE A. BENTON[1]   January 11, 1950
                                          [Pinehurst, North Carolina]

My dear Benton: I have your letter of December twenty-ninth regarding the incident of the Fourth of July Field Day sports at Calapan, Mindoro, in the Philippine Islands some forty-eight years ago.

I recall your winning the first event, the 100-yard dash, but there was more to the affair than you realized. I was the youngest officer of the garrison and newly arrived in the Islands, so I was given the chore of organizing the celebrations of the day in a rather gloomy, depressed command.

Entries for the sports were supposed to be submitted in advance. But few came forward and you were one of the only two entries for the first event. I had collected money for prizes to the first four places, so I gave it all to you two competitors in that first race, over the objections of some of the older officers. As an immediate result I had a wealth of competitors for the following events and I recall that we inserted a bare-back pony race—and they were wild little captured ponies. One bolted into a native thatch house, wrecking it and dropping the girls hanging out the windows of the second story to the ground amidst much excitement and the first laughter I had heard in Calapan.

Later on that evening we had an amateur show with hardtack boxes for a stage and tent flies for a curtain. I persuaded the commanding officer to parole a prisoner to me and permit me to take off his shackles. He was the dancing hit of the show.[2]

In those far-off days the soldiers of the regular Army got little attention or consideration from the Government or the public. As I recall, the ration was sixteen cents and privates (there was only one class) got $13.00 a month plus ten percent on foreign service. There was no turkey, chicken or fresh vegetables. Dried peaches and apples and desiccated potatoes were a daily portion. No ice in a tropical hot season. Doughnuts and hot chocolate, Salvation Army and Red Cross girls were unheard of. Cholera was raging throughout the Islands, and in our little village of Calapan of about 1200 natives, I think we lost almost 500— and only one doctor in attendance.

The only contribution I recall during my first year was a box of forty books from Helen Gould.[3] In contrast today I am busy with the efforts of the Red Cross, among other notable things, to bring a touch of home to our many soldiers abroad, to keep them in touch with their families. . . . Faithfully yours,

GCMRL/G. C. Marshall Papers (Pentagon Office, General)

1. At the time Marshall wrote this he was head of the American National Red Cross and was attending Red Cross meetings throughout the country. Benton requested that he be allowed to shake the general's hand when the latter visited Oklahoma City. Marshall asked the local committee to invite the former member of Company M, Thirtieth Infantry, to the January 26, 1950, meeting.

2. In his recorded interview of March 13, 1957, Marshall described the events of that Fourth of July in considerable detail, "because it had quite a bit to do with my standing in the regiment afterwards, particularly with the men." His insistence on paroling the man, one of the most popular soldiers on the post, in the face of the colonel's and the adjutant's doubts, proved to be a great boost to morale. Marshall thought that the soldier "had suffered a little bit for what I call this tyrannical handling of the place beforehand."

3. Helen Miller Gould (1868–1938), eldest daughter of financier Jay Gould, was widely known for her philanthropy and her interests in education. During the Spanish-American War she had made gifts to United States Army hospitals.

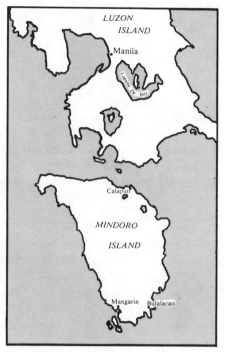

*Sites of Marshall's 1902–3 Philippine
assignment.*

REPORT TO THE ADJUTANT, SECOND BATTALION   August 1, 1902
                                                        Mangarin, Mindoro[1]

Sir:–   I have the honor to report that no insurgents surrendered or were captured at this post since last report.[2]   Very respectfully

                                                        G. C. Marshall, Jr.

NA/RG 395 (Mangarin, Letterbook)

1. Marshall arrived in Mangarin from Calapan on July 12, 1902. Owing to the temporary
absence of Captain Henry E. Eames, Marshall assumed command of Company G until
September 19. At various times, he was also acting quartermaster, commissary, and summary
court trial officer.

2. Some insurgent bands, having been driven out of Luzon, continued to resist on Mindoro
during 1902. Marshall recalled that when he arrived at Calapan, "the hills were full of in-
surrectos who would shoot into the town from time to time." (Interview, March 13, 1957.)
Mangarin, a village at the other end of the island, was less troubled. As acting company
commander, Marshall was required to file bimonthly the above report and monthly a report on
the number of persons taking oaths of allegiance to the United States.

REPORT TO THE MILITARY GOVERNOR   September 14, 1902
                                                    Mangarin, Mindoro

Sir:- I have the honor to make the following report in regard to the civil prisoners in confinement at this post. On the night of Sept. 6th, one native prisoner Alamacio Nagalay escaped during a heavy storm taking advantage of the noise by climbing through a hole in the floor.[1] I am of the opinion that no one was responsible due to any neglect. A combination of circumstances rendered this man's escape possible. I am trying to locate his hiding place in the mountains now, and am going on a search for him in a few days; as soon as the U.S.A.T. Isla de Negros comes in.[2] On the morning of Sept. 10th I left this post in a sailing banco accompanied by seven soldiers and one native prisoner Placido Carpio who acted as guide. I arrived about ten miles north of Bulalacao that evening and camped for the night. The next morning before daylight I took five men and the guide and struck back in the mountains. I was acting on information given me by the guide of some ladrons[3] who he said lived in the vicinity. One of these men, he said, was the head or chief ladron of this Island. At noon we reached this rendevous and found it had been deserted some time. From there we marched in a northeasterly direction and near the coast found a house where our guide claimed a ladron lived named Judas Bartos. We succeeded in capturing this man; the only evidence against him is that of our guide. The Presidente of Bulalacao says that Judas Bartos is a good man, but I am not so certain that the Presidente always means what he says. I request that I be instructed whether to liberate this man or not. On the day of Sept. 8th the Presidente of Mangarin turned over to me a manyan, one Paulinos Calaguip accused of the murder of one man and his two children. One native Nicholas Tiris, accused of theft in Calapan, is also in confinement here.

                                                    G. C. Marshall, Jr.

NA/RG 395 (Mangarin, Letterbook)

  1. The Guard House at Mangarin, like nearly all the buildings on the post, was a "nipa shack," a wood and bamboo framework covered with nipa palm thatch and having a springy, split-bamboo floor. The whole hut was built atop heavy log pilings to keep it off the ground.

  2. The U.S. Army Transport *Isla de Negros* provided the inter-island passenger and supply service to the scattered garrisons. Marshall retained vivid memories of his first trip on the ship going to Calapan in May, 1902. It had a Spanish captain, a Spanish first mate, and a Filipino crew. "The boat was very greasy and dirty. The food was particularly greasy, it seemed to be bathed in it, and the major domo was a one-eyed performer who won my antagonism immediately." Marshall and another new lieutenant were forced to take the wheel during a typhoon to prevent the ship's wrecking. (Interview, March 13, 1957.)

  3. *Ladron* meant "outlaw" or "thief" in Spanish.

TO BRIGADIER GENERAL SCOTT SHIPP   January 4, 1903
                                                    Manila, Philippine Islands

Dear General   In view of the fact that I practically owe my present position to you I always feel a desire to let you know how I am getting along in the Army.

My company took station here in the City the day before Xmas, though I did not report until January 1st as I was left behind at our former post, Mangarin, Island of Mindoro, with a detachment of the company, awaiting the arrival of some Native Scouts to relieve me. With the exception of the last few days all my service out here has been on Mindoro. While I have seen no actual fighting yet I had some hard hiking after ladrones in the mountains, but they offered little or no resistance when cornered. Mangarin was a very isolated post, a month between boats when I first reached there. Afterwards we had a boat every three weeks. This was very disagreeable as regards mail from home, but I found it more agreeable from an official standpoint, as I was left to my own judgement since it took two months to receive a reply to any communication from Manila, and as the times were not serious the freedom it gave me was not offset by the responsibility. So far I have found this life even pleasanter than I had imagined it would be and I think it will improve with time. Last night as I came out of the theatre I was very much surprised by meeting Epes, class of 1900, but I was only able to talk to him a very few moments and did not learn much of what he is doing out here.

I believe he said he was in the Educational Department. I am expecting him out here at the barracks next week to talk over old times. I was with Lansing, "95", a few days in May. Since then he has gotten his 1st Lieutenantcy.[1] Though my first year of foreign service has not expired I am looking forward to the time of our departure for the States.

During the days of the fighting the time passed more quickly than now, with the routine of garrison duty, especially in Manila.

At Mangarin there was fine hunting, deer, wild bore and ducks to while the hours away, and we also did a great deal of sailing.

I asked my wife to have a catalogue of the Institute sent me, but she evidently overlooked it. I would like to get the one that came out last spring and the next one, when it comes out, as I want to keep in touch with the progress of the Institute. I see by the Army and Navy Journal that we were well represented in the last batch of appointees. All the officers I meet are very complimentary in their opinion of the Institute. General Carter, the former Assistant Adjutant General, was exceptional generous in his praise of the V.M.I. when I was talking to him in Washington last February.

Certainly as far as numbers go the graduates present a very creditable appearance in the Register.[2] I understand that a great many improvements are being made, and I hardly expect to recognize the place if I am fortunate enough to see it again. I am afraid this letter will be an imposition on your good nature, so this must be the last page. Believe me, General, with best wishes, and the hope that this new year will find you in better health than ever, I am— Faithfully yours

G. C. Marshall, Jr.

GCMRL/VMI Collection; H

1. Branch J. Epes (V.M.I., 1900) was a teacher working for the United States Department of

Agriculture. Cleveland C. Lansing (V.M.I., 1895) had served with the volunteers in the Philippines during the Spanish-American War. He accepted a commission in the army in June, 1901, and became a first lieutenant of Field Artillery in June, 1902.

2. The *Official Army Register for 1903* lists twenty-seven V.M.I. graduates in the following departments: Medical, two; Chaplain, one; Cavalry, four; Artillery, seven; Infantry, thirteen. Most of these were lieutenants.

O N JANUARY 24, 1903, Marshall's company moved from Infantry Garrison Hospital No. 3 in Manila to Santa Mesa Garrison, three miles east of the center of town. There it remained until September 21, when it was sent for six weeks of garrison duty at the Malahi Island Military Prison, a post Marshall disliked intensely. This ordeal completed, Company G joined the regiment in boarding the U.S.A.T. *Sheridan* for the United States. Following brief stopovers at Nagasaki, Japan, and Honolulu, Hawaii, the ship reached San Francisco on December 15, 1903. There the regiment divided; Marshall and his company entrained for Fort Reno in Oklahoma Territory.

At Fort Reno the new enemies were neither ladrons nor cholera, but routine and boredom. The army was still dominated by its frontier Indian-fighting heritage. The regiment was dispersed to three widely separated posts. Garrison duties—drill, inspection, administration—required perhaps half an officer's day. There was an intense concern with "spit and polish," appearance and orderliness. Marshall had plenty of time for riding, an activity he took up seriously only after joining the army, and for hunting. The hunting was superb, he recalled. "We went shooting almost every day of the year for something or other." (Interview, March 13, 1957.)

There was some attempt at education during the winter months. Secretary of War Elihu Root believed that "other things being equal, the officer who keeps his mind alert by intellectual exercise, and who systematically studies the reasons of action and the materials and conditions and difficulties with which he may have to deal, will be the stronger practical man and the better soldier." (*Report of the Secretary of War, 1901,* p. 21.) Marshall remembered the new garrison schools as the beginning of his formal military education, although "the schools didn't amount to very much." (Interview, March 13, 1957.)

Marshall's routine assignment at Fort Reno was interrupted in the summer of 1905 by detached service. The army had taken up again the enormous task of making a detailed, confidential map of the country's strategic border regions: the Progressive Military Map. Teams composed of one officer and a few selected enlisted men were sent into the field with instructions to fill in, on a scale of one inch equals two miles, details on the skeleton maps they had been issued. In early

June, Marshall journeyed to Fort Clark, Texas, to make preparations to map nearly two thousand square miles of dry, largely uninhabited land. ★

TO CAPTAIN JOHN C. OAKES[1]   June 13, 1905
                                                           Fort Clark, Texas

Sir:- I have the honor to inform you of my arrival at this post. I spent yesterday getting all the information possible regarding my sheet (403 N. Langtry)[2] from the old packers, teamsters and guides in the post and from several civilians in the adjacent town of Brackettville who were familiar with that locality.

They all agree on one point—that it will be almost impossible to get a wagon along the main trail and absolutely impossible to take a wagon off that trail. They tell me a pack train is the only method of getting around west of Devils River and the commanding officer here, Colonel Hughes, instructed me to say that he recommended that no attempt be made to use wheel transportation west of Devils River. There is a pack train here of twenty one mules and two packers which I would like to have authority to use.

My principal trouble will be in securing water, there being practically no water off the one trail which can be used, except in the small portion near Devils River. I am told the Pecos has always been brackish and has grown even more so and to such an extent that even the mules sicken after drinking it. At most of the stations shown along the railroad the section hands use barreled water hauled by the Southern Pacific. If the use of a pack train is authorized a number of mules will be fitted with two ten gallon kegs each.

In regard to buying rations & forage in the field I am told by reliable persons that except at Langtry, nothing can be bought and very little of anything there. Some sheep may be found and possibly a few goats.

As it is two days march from here to Del Rio which is a few miles east of that edge of my sheet, I think the only practicable arrangement would be for the Quartermaster here to ship me rations & forage to such station as I may be near. Otherwise I will consume most of my time coming & going. I request that such authority be secured for the Quartermaster at this post.

Would it be possible for me to secure authority to make at least one trip a month from such station as I may be near to Spofford Junction, the Fort Clark R.R. Sta., and return?

If this could be arranged I could come in and settle up with the Quartermaster and Commissary attend to such other business as will be apt to come up, and only consume from two to three days. Whereas if I attempt to ride in from any but the extreme eastern part of my sheet I will be eight or ten days at the least. I have secured such instruments as I will need, except a stopwatch for timing my horse.[3] I will report later where I have gotten the instruments.

I will go ahead and make such preparations as possible pending the receipt of a reply to this or the necessary authorities.   Very respectfully

G. C. Marshall, Jr.

NA/RG 393 (Southwestern Division); H

1. Oakes (U.S.M.A., 1897), Corps of Engineers, engineer officer for the Southwestern Division, was responsible for the construction of the Progressive Military Map in Texas.

2. The officer in charge of each expedition was given a skeleton map of an area one degree of longitude by one-half degree of latitude (approximately sixty by thirty-five miles) and was expected to sketch in details. The officers selected for this duty were supposed to have special aptitude for reconnaissance duty. Marshall later told an acquaintance that he did part of his "fill-in" sketching in Judge Roy Bean's famous old cabin at Langtry. (Marshall to Bennett Foster, April 9, 1956, GCMRL/G. C. Marshall Papers [Retirement].)

3. "I had to walk the track and count the rails. That gave me an exact measurement which I needed as a base-line. I got my distances otherwise from the odometer on the wheel of the wagon and from the time scale on the walking of my horse." (Interview, March 13, 1957.)

To the Military Secretary,   August 31, 1905
Southwestern Division   Thirty miles due north of the
                                         railway on Devils River, Texas

Sir:-   . . . In regard to the purchase of the necessary forage in the field as I was instructed to do by the Engineer Officer,[1] I have the honor to make the following statement: The instructions directed me to make arrangements with the Post Quartermaster at Fort Clark to purchase forage in the field when returning to Clark would involve too much delay. Your office furnished me with a copy of a letter to the Dept. Commander, dated May 22nd 05, in which he was instructed to make arrangements for me to purchase rations and forage in the field. The Post Quartermaster gave me a number of blank Q.M. Form 10 to Abst. "A" with which to make the purchases. From what I could learn of the country I was to map I believed I would not always be able to purchase forage (which I found later to be correct) as there were but two small stores in my sheet, so I requested additional authority to have forage and rations shipped me when such was the case. During the nine weeks I have been out I have made but four purchases of forage for my fourteen animals, having my forage shipped me whenever possible on account of the high price and inferior grade of all that could be bought out here.

It has never been practical to go into Clark for forage as the nearest point to Clark in my sheet is fifty miles and the furthest two hundred miles by road.

In yesterdays mail I received back the vouchers for the first two purchases of forage, one June 26th 05 in Del Rio, Tex., and one July 3rd 1905, in Comstock,

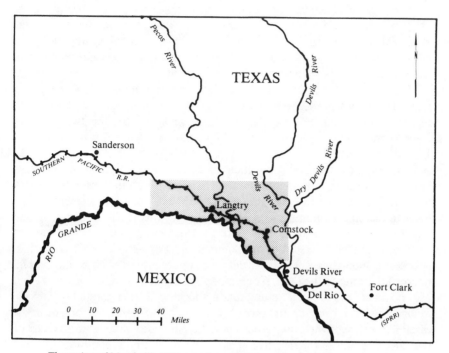

*The region of Marshall's 1905 mapping expedition. The shaded portion was the
area he was assigned.*

Tex. These have never yet been settled and I am directed to furnish certificates in
duplicate for each set of vouchers showing the extreme emergency for such
purchases and stating my authority for making them. I do not suppose the last
two purchases made have been settled for either. In an endorsement on the letter
of transmittal the Dept. Quartermaster states that the records of his office do not
show that I have ever been granted authority for such purchases or requested
any, and juding from the tone of the endorsement there seems to be a possibility
of the purchases being disallowed. He also states that I should make such
purchases only in cases of extreme emergency and then only on the order of the
Post Commander at Fort Clark.

While in every case there was ample emergency to justify my purchasing the
forage I do not see that any emergency, other than the excessive distance from
Fort Clark (if that could be called one) was necessary. Under my instructions
from your office it appears to me I could have made weekly purchases and the
fact that I didn't was due to my own arrangement to have grain shipped me. I do
not see that there was any reason for me to apply to the Dept. Quartermaster for
authority to make such purchases as I already held a copy of the Division
Commander's instructions to the Dept. of Texas, furnished me for my guidance,

directing that arrangements be made for me to make such purchases, as well as direct instructions to the same effect sent to me, only requiring me to make the arrangements with the Post Quartermaster. I have already had inquiries as to when these long delayed forage bills will be settled and I respectfully request that some arrangement be made to secure the settlement of all.

There will be no further necessity of my purchasing forage while engaged in mapping this present sheet but I request that I be informed as to whether I am to furnish certificates showing the extreme emergency for the last two purchase made by me. I will make out and mail the certificates for the first two purchases at once.

In regard to the purchasing of rations in the field as was contemplated in your instructions I endeavored to make some arrangement with the Post Commissary to do so but he stated he had no means of making such arrangement. I then wrote to the Chief Commissary of the Dept. direct to avoid delay, requesting that arrangements be made for me to make such purchases as directed in your instructions, and he referred it to the Commanding Officer at Fort Clark for him to order such purchases. The latter did not consider me under his command and returned the letter to the Dept. Commissary from whom it came back to me but with no arrangement made stating that authority had been granted to ship me rations, the latter being on my own application, as referred to before, as in the case of the forage when no rations could be purchased. I gave up the idea of purchasing rations in the field as I could manage to carry a months rations and touch the railroad frequently enough to get fresh ones.

There seems to have been some misunderstanding about the supplying of my detachment and I respectfully request that I be informed as to whether I have been at fault or not though my instructions be so clear as to hardly permit of being misconstrued.   Very respectfully

G. C. Marshall, Jr.

NA/RG 393 (Southwestern Division); H

1. In the first indorsement of Marshall's letter of June 13, John C. Oakes had recommended that "the Post Quartermaster be directed to ship rations and forage to such stations as Lieut. Marshall may designate when it is impossible for him to buy supplies." Lieutenant Colonel James S. Pettit (U.S.M.A., 1878), the military secretary of the Southwestern Division, granted this authority on June 30.

WHILE HIS letter of August 31 bounced back and forth between Southwestern Division headquarters in Oklahoma City and Texas Department headquarters in San Antonio, Marshall became incensed at the "dyed-in-the-wool spirit of the commissary staff." (Marshall to Major General G. V. H. Moseley, September 9, 1938, GCMRL/G. C. Marshall Papers [Pentagon Office, Selected].) Hardly had he completed "the hardest service I ever had in the army" (Interview, March 13, 1957), when his honor seemed to have been impugned. The following is Marshall's handwritten tenth indorsement to his own letter. ★

To the Military Secretary,   September 26, 1905
Southwestern Division   Fort Clark, Texas

Respectfully returned to the Military Secretary, S. W. Division, through the Adjutant, Fort Clark, Texas. While this letter has already caused considerable clerical work I do not care to drop the matter with the following statement of the Chief Comsy. of the Dept. in the 5th End. hereon remaining as an apparently accepted fact: "By comparing these papers with that part of Lieut. Marshall's letter of August 31, 1905, to the Military Secretary of the Southwestern Division which refers to the purchase of rations, it is thought the letter will show a *varying from the facts."* [1]

To me the conclusion of the foregoing is a most serious charge questioning my veracity and my status as an officer and a gentleman.

I have most carefully gone over the copy of my letter to the Dept. Com'sy., its appended endorsements and my remarks in the within communication and I fail to see wherein I have varied from the facts in the smallest particular. Following the above extract from the 5th Endorsement is the following: "His letter to this office did not ask for rations to be shipped, nor would I have any authority to have authorized such shipments, but he infered the shipments would be made from Fort Clark." There is absolutely nothing in the within letter referring to any request by me to the Dept. Comsy. for authority to have rations shipped me and therefore I fail to see the reason for the foregoing statement.

I fully understand he had no authority to authorize such shipments and had applied direct to the Engineer Officer of the S W Division to secure it for me which he did. I think that if the copies of the endorsements on my letter to the Chief Comsy. of the Dept., on June 23 –05, are read it will be seen that at the conclusion of that correspondence no arrangements had been accomplished whereby I could purchase rations in the field as it was intended for me to do.

I saw the Post Commissary at this post yesterday and he stated that he now has no way of or authority for making arrangements for me to purchase rations in the field nor had he had any since I started on this work.

After seeing the course to be followed in purchasing forage outlined by the Chief Quartermaster of the Dept., after the receipt of this letter I suppose that would be the method to be followed in purchasing rations, but that information was never furnished me or the Post Commissary here.

I do not care to appear in the light of a complainer no as attempting to deceive by incorrect or false statements and I feel confident that if these papers are carefully reread I will be be found guilty of neither. I have completed my work on the military map and there is no further necessity of purchasing rations &c. by me, but I respectfully request that careful consideration be given this matter as it now stands. [2]

G. C. Marshall, Jr.

NA/RG 393 (Southwestern Division); H

1. Captain Samuel B. Bootes was chief commissary of the Department of Texas. His concern was that regulations stipulated that purchases in the field be made only in emergencies. He

did not consider Marshall's situation to have been an emergency.

2. Marshall went to see Brigadier General Jesse M. Lee, a Civil War veteran who commanded the Department of Texas. The matter was settled, but it had required fourteen indorsements of Marshall's original August 31 letter and nine weeks of paperwork. Special Orders, No. 134, was issued declaring that Marshall's purchases had been made under emergency conditions, and the $52.12 was paid.

To Brigadier General Scott Shipp   March 3, 1906
Fort Reno, Oklahoma

My dear General,   I see by the Army and Navy Journal that Major Strother has been ordered away from the Institute.[1]

Now, while I feel that you will consider that I have not enough years on my shoulders yet, I wish to tell you that I would like myself to be considered as an applicant for the detail as Professor of Military Science and Tactics at the Institute now, or at any other time the position may become vacant. I am putting this in the form of a personal letter to you as I do not care to have my name submitted to the Board of Visitors as an applicant for the detail unless accompanied by your recommendation. If you do not see fit to recommend me then the subject can be dropped with the receipt of this letter by you.

Circular No. 101, War Department, series 1905, states that no officer having less than five years service is eligible for the detail. On September 2nd next I will lack five months of having five years service. If this application should be favorably considered I feel sure the War Department would waive the point as I would lack by such a short period of having completed the necessary five years. Please be perfectly frank with me, General, and do not try to avoid hurting my feelings as I really am not at all optimistic about the probable result of this application.

I was much pleased to see of Arthur's detail as A.D.C., to General Buchanan.[2] It is a sure and very flattering sign of his efficiency and popularity.

I spent the past summer in southwestern Texas along the Pecos River and the Rio Grande making a topographical map. The heat was terrific and the country a rocky desert covered with a network of deep canons. I never expect to suffer again such hardships as I did there, but I feel partly repaid since I received a letter from the Chief Engineer Officer of the Division complimenting me on my map and saying it was the best one received and the only complete one. I had a full four months leave after finishing in Texas and went up to New York by boat from New Orleans.[3]

Nicholson,[4] of my class at the Institute, was to have been married at the time I went through New Orleans and had asked me to be best man, but the yellow fever caused the wedding to be postponed.

After my long rest I returned here to find little time for anything but work as I am adjutant, in command of my company and judge-advocate of a general court. Mrs. Coles mentions seeing you, in her letters very frequently. I expect her to arrive here with Mrs. Marshall in about two weeks.[5]

Hoping this will find you enjoying the best of health, believe me,   Faithfully yours,

G. C. Marshall, Jr.

VMI/Alumni File; T

1. Lewis H. Strother (V.M.I., 1877), Twenty-eighth Infantry, was professor of military science and commandant of cadets, 1903–5.

2. Arthur M. Shipp (V.M.I., 1897), Superintendent Scott Shipp's younger son, was a first lieutenant in the Twentieth Infantry in the Philippines. On October 16, 1905, he had been appointed aide-de-camp to Brigadier General James A. Buchanan, temporary commander of the Department of Mindanao. By the time Marshall wrote, Shipp had left the Philippines for the United States.

3. Marshall was on leave from September 27, 1905, to January 26, 1906.

4. Leonard K. Nicholson (V.M.I., 1901), Marshall's roommate all four years at V.M.I., was heir to the New Orleans Times-Picayune Publishing Company. Marshall thought his roommate remarkable because he never lost his temper. (Interview, March 13, 1957.)

5. Lily Marshall did not immediately join her husband at Fort Reno when he arrived in 1904. She had a heart condition that mitigated against a strenuous life. Possibly she was delayed as long as the March, 1906, trip mentioned in this letter.

FROM BRIGADIER GENERAL SCOTT SHIPP   March 7, 1906
                                                  [Lexington, Virginia]

Dear Marshall   We had entered into correspondence with officers, who are graduates of the Institute, before your letter was received. I have always thought of you as one for that detail; but just now I think it better to have an officer of higher rank, an older man.[1] There is nothing but time, the amount of which varies in different cases, which will give the experienced, basic, matured judgment required for the very difficult position of Cmdt in this place. You think you know what is required, but you would find the difficulties vastly greater than anything you apprehend. Saunders told me what an effective Cmdt you made,[2] but the problem here is a very different one. . . .   Sincerely yrs

Scott Shipp

VMI/RG 2; H

1. Captain Morrell M. Mills (V.M.I., 1897), First Field Artillery, was chosen. He had been assistant professor of mathematics and tactics during Marshall's first year at V.M.I.

2. Colonel Isaac H. Saunders (V.M.I., 1884), president of Danville Military Institute, had written to Shipp on December 12, 1901, following Marshall's resignation as commandant, praising the former first captain as "a splendid officer. He possesses rare judgment, discretion and tact for one so young." (VMI/RG 2.)

M ARSHALL returned to Fort Reno at the end of January, 1906, but his stay was destined to be a short one.

Brigadier General J. Franklin Bell—commandant of the Infantry and Cavalry School, the Signal School, and the Staff College at Fort Leavenworth, Kansas—had been striving to improve the quality of student sent to his schools as well as the quality of instruction. After leaving Leavenworth to become the army chief of staff on April 14, 1906, Bell continued to struggle to overcome the anti-intellectual bias among many army officers. Some regimental commanders, a friend observed, seemed to "give the detail at Leavenworth to their regimental idiot." (Colonel A. L. Wagner to Bell, February 21, 1905, NA/RG 393 [Leavenworth].)

At Fort Reno, Marshall recalled, "we had a competition in the Post School for the Leavenworth detail and I had always come out [number] one [for] two years, but I was never given it. It always went to some higher ranking officer, none of whom did at all well, and all of whom came back with many criticisms and attacks on the Leavenworth procedure. The third year nobody put in for it; and they sent a list around later, on account of an inquiry from regimental headquarters, and it developed afterwards that I was the only one that put down 'yes' that I wanted to go, and therefore I got the detail." Probably equally important was the Fort Reno commander's opinion that Marshall was "an excellent officer." (Interview, April 4, 1957; Efficiency Report, June 30, 1906, NA/RG 94 [Document File].)

Upon arriving at the school, Marshall was dismayed to find that some of the other fifty-three students, particularly those from the Cavalry, had been coached on what to expect and even had copies of the previous year's examinations. "I wondered what was going to become of me without any preparation of any kind." Marshall had never seen academic tactical problems of this sort. "So I knew I would have to study harder than I ever dreamed of studying before in my life." (Interview, April 4, 1957.)

Approximately the top half of the graduates of the Infantry and Cavalry School (the name was changed to the Army School of the Line in 1907) were selected for the second year's prestigious General Staff course. Completion of the second year was usually a prerequisite for attending the Army War College in Washington, D.C.

During the first few weeks of school in August and September, 1906, Marshall heard many of his classmates speculate on who would be the top students; his own name was not mentioned. He perceived that the "game" at Fort Leavenworth was hard work, concentration, and competition. (Interview, April 4, 1957.) In recalling his experiences on the mapping expedition and with the commissary staff afterwards, he noted that hardships and lack of sympathy were "part of the game and it was a great lesson to me and a very valuable one." (Interview, March 13, 1957.) After a few weeks at Fort Leavenworth, Marshall

---

INFANTRY AND CAVALRY SCHOOL

Fort Leavenworth, Kansas, July 1, 1907.

Class Standing of Marshall, George C. Jr., 2d Lieutenant, 30th Infantry.
Graduated June 29, 1907.

CLASS STANDING:		ORDER	WEIGHT	PERCENTAGE	
DEPT. MILITARY ART	Theoretical	1	141.691	97.72	Number of Officers in class, 38. Total Weight of course, 1000
	Practical	3	224.000	95.32	
DEPT. ENGINEERING	Theoretical	3	116.46	97.05	
	Practical	3	173.93	16.63	
DEPT. LAW		2	126.090	96.98	
DEPT. SPANISH		11	146.85	97.90	
DEPT. CARE OF TROOPS		10	39.740	96.85	
General Merit – – – –		1	967.751	96.78	

Report of Academic Board under paragraph 78, G. O. 145, W. D., 1906.

In comparison with his classmates during their course of instruction, in the opinion of the ACADEMIC BOARD, this officer:

Has shown marked proficiency in:

Has exhibited qualities which would appear to fit him *especially well* for the following professional employments:

Post engineer officer.
Aide-de-Camp.
Adjutant General.
Recruiting officer.
Line officer with volunteer troops.
Duty with organized militia (Governor's Staff).
Duty with organized militia (special detail conducting field exercises in summer camps).

Topographical officer on marches, expeditions & explorations.
Military Attache.
College detail.
Staff officer with volunteer troops, with advanced rank (two grades).

Appears *well* fitted for the following professional employments:

Inspector General.
Subsistence Department.
Ordnance Department.
Acting Judge-Advocate of Department.
Organizing and commanding native troops.
Assistant instructor I. & C. School, Military Art & Law.

Quartermaster's Department.
Pay Department.

Recommended

Remarks of Commandant:
Opinions and recommendation of Academic Board concurred in.
Above action taken after careful discrimination and consideration.
in conference with the Board.

Brigadier General, U. S. A.,
Commandant.

[Duplicate attached to efficiency report.]

Marshall's 1906–7 class standing report.

recalled proudly, "I developed a position which put me in another light to my classmates who had left me out entirely of the estimate of who was going to be in the next year's staff class." (Interview, April 4, 1957.) ★

To the Adjutant General   July 7, 1907
                                                    Mt. Gretna, Pennsylvania

Sir:– I have the honor to respectfully request that the order directing me to attend the encampment of the 2d Brigade, National Guard of this state at Tipton, Penna., be revoked for the following reasons:

On finishing the term at the Infantry & Cavalry School at Leavenworth this year I took my wife to a summer resort in Minnesota. We arrived late at night July 3d, and at 8.00 A.M. the next morning I received a telegram from the Secretary of the I. & C. School informing me that I was directed to proceed to Mt. Gretna at once. This I did, leaving for here a half hour later. On arriving here I learnt for the first time of the order directing me to report for duty at the Tipton encampment July 20th to 28th. This will not permit me to return to my wife until July 31st. Meantime she will be alone, among total strangers, at a place I personally know nothing of except through hearsay. Her health does not permit of her traveling from Minnesota to Pennsylvania alone, nor does the pay of my position permit of my going back for her, and bringing her east to be near me or with relatives, during the week intervening between this and the Tipton encampment. I expected Mrs. Marshall to be alone for some ten days, but I can not leave her alone for a month under the present circumstances. Had I known when I received the telegram in Minnesota that I was due at another encampment, I could have satisfactorily arranged for it at once and entirely avoided my present dilemma.

I have hesitated in making this request because I dislike such action and also because two other officers here with me have already made it for various reasons. Also, aside from the matter of duty, it would be greatly to my advantage to attend the Tipton encampment as the troops of the 2d Brigade are from the immediate vicinity of my home, but as my request is not based on a question of my pleasure or comfort or of ordinary inconvenience, but on absolute necessity, no other solution to which I can arrive at, I am compelled to make it.

This is the first favor of any sort I have asked since entering the service and I earnestly request that it be favorably considered and that I be informed of the decision by telegraph.[1]   Respectfully

                                                    G. C. Marshall, Jr.

NA/RG 94 (Militia); H

1. Special Orders, No. 161, July 11, 1907, revoked the order sending Marshall to Tipton; he returned to duty at Fort Leavenworth on July 20.

Report to Captain Charles D. Rhodes[1]   July 28, 1907
                                                    Fort Leavenworth, Kansas

Sir:– In compliance with your verbal instructions, I have the honor to submit the following report of my observations of the 13th Regiment Pennsylvania National Guard while encamped at Mt Gretna, Penna., July 6th to 13th last:

Sewage System . . .

Clothing and Equipment . . .

How Subsisted

. . . Practically the regular army ration was issued by the Brigade Commissary—one three day and one five day issue—but this hardly indicates the character of the food provided as each man contributed on an average of $1^{50} towards the mess for the eight days.

The company officers stated that they could handle the regular ration and make it do, but as the encampment was in the nature of the only outing the majority of the men had during the year, it was necessary to set a bountiful table. . . .

Drills and Ceremonies . . .

Personnel and Discipline

The personnel of the commissioned officers of the regiment was high, all appearing to be educated, ambitious and energetic men and very enthusiastic regarding the efficiency of the regiment.

Every officer, from the colonel down, seemed anxious to acquire all the practical knowledge possible of Military Art and were apparently ready and anxious at all times to listen to suggestions and follow them at once. They appeared to realize the futility of spending all the valuable hours of the encampment in normal "parade ground" drills and ceremonies, and endeavored to utilize all the time practicable in advance and rear guard, outpost and attack formations adapted to a varied terrain and approximating actual conditions as closely as possible. The drills were seldom held on the parade ground. My criticisms and suggestions were solicited and followed out to a flattering degree.

The enlisted personnel of the regiment was good. Men of all vocations were to be found in ranks, from the superintendent of a county school system, down through the various grades of labor. The men were generally of good physique, some few were undersized in those companies from the coal region where the labor element are strongly opposed to the National Guard organization, and recruits therefore difficult to secure.

The conduct of the enlisted men in camp was very good.

Apparently not much importance was attached to the practice of saluting but an improvement in this was noted during the week.

The average age appeared to be about 22 years.

There was a wide difference in the opinion of the different company commanders as to the number of men who would reenlist, ranging from 15 to 90 percent. Judging from the company records of past reenlistments, 15 percent seemed more nearly the correct number.

All stated that 90 to 100 percent would volunteer in case of a foreign war.

Guard Duty . . .

Target Practice . . .
Record Keeping . . .
Instruction Given . . .
General Remarks.
Inspection and Rating System

There are two general inspections of the State troops, one held in the armory in the Spring—the "minute inspection"—and one held while the troops are encamped each summer. As I understand it, the rating of each company or similar unit, is based on the result of these two inspections and the total percentage of each company published showing the relative efficiency of all the companies in the Guard, therefore the goal for which all strive is the obtainment of the highest possible percentage, and the success of the companies in obtaining good recruits, &c., depends in a large way on its rating.

Naturally the methods of work pursued, character of drills conducted most energetically &c., is that which brings results calculated to secure the highest percentage at the semi-annual inspections. I had the opportunity at this encampment of closely observing the summer inspection, and, based on my observations, I came to the conclusion that the method adopted is one that discourages progressive, practical work on the part of the regimental officers and fosters a system of "cadet training" which spends itself in encouraging a natty appearance, ceremonies, parade ground drills and the execution of few practical field formations, and then in a cut and dried fashion following the diagrams of the text books regardless of terrain, circumstances or similarity to actual war conditions. . . .

In a general way, it appeared to me that too much of the short time available, (one day,) was consumed in inspecting details that could be thoroughly covered at the home stations of the companies and not enough advantage taken of the opportunity to observe the condition of preparedness for war by field maneuvers. Certainly a much better idea of the field efficiency of the Brigade could have been obtained by observing the work of the officers and men in the maneuver of July 9th, than on the open parade ground.

What is more important, in fact all important and my reason for commenting so particularly on the method of inspection and consequent rating, an inspection made under such circumstances would have been a great incentive to all the officers to thoroughly drill themselves in and study the most important essential to war preparedness—field evolutions and maneuvers. As I have mentioned before, officers informed me that it was only practicable to drill at night at the home stations therefore it would seem all important to encourage or require all to derive as much advantage as possible from the opportunity presented in camp of operating in practical exercises over a varied terrain.

Men can be taught to salute, squads right and left, &c., in the armories, but a correct idea of advance guard and outpost duty and a correct handling of troops in the advance to the attack and on the defensive, can only be secured by movements on varied ground with as close an approximation to war conditions as possible.

When a choice must be made as to what to devote most of the short time available in one weeks encampment, it would seem that the majority of the work should be devoted to that which cannot be learnt from the books or managed on the armory floors—field maneuvers—and the smaller portion of the time in camp to that which can, to a large extent, be so derived—battalion and regimental drills. A well planned, umpired and criticized maneuver, however small—in fact, preferably so, furnishes food for thought and study for many days afterward, while an objectless and perfunctory advance guard or attack formation, is generally forgotten with the sounding of recall.

The 13th Regiment spent little time in close order drilling but if instead of the numerous advance guard and outpost and attack formations, a number of small, carefully prepared maneuvers for companies or battalions operating against each other and necessitating but two or three hour's time, had been held either in the mornings or afternoons, after the first two days in camp, much better results would have been achieved.

In this connection, I wish to make special mention in this report of the spirit in which all of the officers of the 13th Regiment entered into the maneuvers of July 9th, and especially of the manner in which the criticisms following it were received and the enterprising and enthusiastic fashion in which all strove to make use of the few remaining days in camp in correcting the errors in the training of the men, shown up by the maneuvers. All seemed convinced immediately of the fact that the regiment was in fair shape for ceremonies and parade ground drills, but was greatly lacking in the practical knowledge necessary to qualify it for the purpose for which it is intended—field service.

I think it was demonstrated to all that a small maneuver is less tiresome to the troops than a parade or review and that it stimulates and holds the interest of the enlisted man as no other work does.

———

In conclusion I wish to report that I was treated with every possible consideration and kindness by the Brigade Commander and Colonel Stillwell and his officers.

My tour of duty with the 3d Brigade, Pennsylvania National Guard was made as pleasant and enjoyable as work can be.

Note   A portion of my notes, including a diagram of the camp giving distances &c., was removed from my suitcase accidentally, I suppose, by the negro cleaning my tent. In this respect my report is incomplete.   Respectfully submitted

G. C. Marshall, Jr.

NA/RG 94 (Militia); H

1. Rhodes (U.S.M.A., 1889), Sixth Cavalry, was the senior instructor at the Pennsylvania National Guard's summer camp. He had finished second to Marshall in the Fort Leavenworth

class standings. Marshall's thirty-one-page handwritten report was filed as inclosure "D" to Rhodes's report. The first section comments in detail on the poor sanitation practices of the troops in camp. The second section describes the varied uniforms of the officers and enlisted men. Concerning "Guard Duty," Marshall was critical of the lack of practical maneuvers, as demonstrated by "the rigidity of the formations and the closeness with which the models given in the text books were adhered to, regardless of the terrain." He did note considerable improvement as the camp progressed, however. Marshall details his own participation in "Instruction Given." He lectured several times, conducted formations and drills, and offered critiques of the various maneuvers and formations.

TO THE SECRETARY OF WAR   July 27, 1907
FROM COLONEL FREDERICK W. STILLWELL   Scranton, Pennsylvania

Sir;   The officers of the 13th Regiment Infantry, N.G.P. recently encamped at Camp Theodore J. Wint, Mt. Gretna, Pa., have requested me to formally express to you our thanks for the invaluable assistance received, and the lasting benefit derived by this regiment on its last annual tour of duty, by reason of the presence of the officers of the U.S. Army, who were present in pursuance of orders of your Department.

We wish also to particularly express our appreciation of the zeal, the energy, the intelligence, and the many helpful suggestions of Lieutenant George C. Marshall, 30th U.S. Infantry, who was detailed to this regiment, and whose presence and faithful work with and among us was very beneficial to every officer and enlisted man of this command; so much so that if it be possible and in accord with your and his circumstances at the time, we would respectfully request that he be detailed to this regiment again at our next annual encampment.   Very respectfully,

F. W. Stillwell

NA/RG 94 (Document File)

SPEECH[1]   October 13, 1939
                                                Washington, Pennsylvania

. . . I completed the first year of the course at the Infantry-Cavalry School at Fort Leavenworth and immediately hurried off to a summer of relaxation on a lake in Minnesota.[2] I had just enough money to get me there and knew I would have to wait for the next month's pay to be able to pay my bill while there. My wife and I arrived at ten o'clock at night and she was in grave doubt as to the character of the place. At six o'clock in the morning—it was the 4th of July—I was awakened by a messenger with a telegram which directed me to leave by the next train for Mt. Gretna, and that was my introduction to the Pennsylvania National Guard.[3] I started that day toward St. Paul, while presumably my baggage, which included my bedding roll, was still on the way to the camp I had just left. I wondered what I would do without field equipment.

I have always taken a great deal of pride in my solution. I found out what train my baggage was arriving on and also on what siding the train would be. I had only a minute or two and ran down along my train to the baggage car of the other train. It started to move but there were windows in the baggage car and I managed to climb through one. I saw my bedding roll, and the baggage master saw me. He grabbed me, but I grabbed my roll and kicked it out of the door. He grabbed me again but I managed to jump out of the car. There were five officers of the Regular Army at Mt. Gretna and I was the only one who had his field equipment.

. . . Everybody received us with the greatest cordiality and enthusiasm and were very remarkable in their acceptance of our multitude of criticisms. In our youthful enthusiasm, fresh from a theoretical course at Leavenworth, we were inclined to be hypercritical. I have never gotten over that early impression of the willingness of the National Guard to accept the criticisms of Regular officer instructors. I have always counted on the fact that as long as our own purpose is serious, and we are doing our best to help, our criticism will be acceptable and will be received in fine spirit by all members of the National Guard. That has been my personal experience.

The next summer [1908], following some correspondence with General Dougherty during the winter,[4] maneuvers were arranged in connection with the horseback tour of the second year graduates of the Staff College, of whom I was one.[5] We started at Manassas and rode about six hundred miles, completing the ride at Gettysburg, and twelve of us remained there for the concentration of the entire Pennsylvania Division. I believe it was called a Division in those days, although I think there were fourteen regiments of Infantry and Cavalry. There were electric storms, balls of fire, and all sorts of accidents, but we put on maneuvers there again, this time for the other brigades. General Dougherty arranged that. I learned a tremendous amount while there about how to do a great deal in a short time, as we had very little time available. Troops were arriving one day and going into maneuvers the next. We were running eight to ten maneuvers on the road. I shall never forget the lesson I learned from the human reactions and from what goes to make attacks, apart from the maps. . . .

I came back to Pennsylvania a number of times. I remember one of my last experiences was an Officers' Camp which we had in those days in early June. . . .[6] That also was at Mt. Gretna and it was very instructive to me. It gave me a chance on the job, as you might say, which was an infinite help to me later on, particularly as we moved into the World War. There was one thing that made a great impression on me in my first year [1907]. The report I submitted was printed. That was the first written word of mine that ever found print. I knew I had gotten into trouble, particularly when the Inspector General of the State, Colonel Sweeney, took decided issue with me because my comments reflected on the Inspector General's Department as to the effect of their duty in relation to preparation of troops and maneuvers. I was idealistic in the extreme, and I presume very impractical, but my intentions were of the best. The point with me was, that next summer [1908] when I was taking the officers on the tactical walks, Colonel Sweeney went everywhere with us, and sat and listened to everything I had to say, and talked to me at great length afterward and in every way treated me with the greatest possible respect. I was a second [*first*] lieutenant, he was thirty years older than I. I never forgot that lesson and the satisfaction and assurance he gave me.

Coming back from the Philippines in 1916, or rather on my arrival at San Francisco in the summer of 1916 following our sudden concentration that spring, I found waiting me in the mail a copy of a General Order—which I came across not so long ago among my papers—for a brigade of the Pennsylvania National Guard at Mt. Gretna going into camp preliminary to that concentration, and they had their training program marked in red. They sent it to me because they knew I was interested in training, but they also sent it to me for a different reason. I never discovered the reason until after the World War, and never thanked anybody for what really was the great thrill of my life up to that moment. I found in the last paragraph, in an inconspicuous place, that they had paid me a high compliment. They had named the camp, Lieutenant George Marshall. Up to that moment, I had never had anything named after me except a dog. The point to that story is this: When I wrote after the War and apologized for not thanking them, they told me in a jocular way that one of the reasons they did this was that it was in the way of thanks and appreciation for the fact that I had made an effort to put over a maneuver by myself for a regiment of infantry, cavalry and artillery. . . .

GCMRL/G. C. Marshall Papers (Pentagon Office, Speeches)

1. This version of Marshall's speech at the annual banquet of the National Guard Association of Pennsylvania was taken from a reporter's notes and edited, probably by someone on Marshall's staff. About four-fifths of the speech—introductory remarks, an anecdote, and comments concerning contemporary War Department and National Guard issues—have been omitted here.

2. Marshall and his wife had planned to vacation at the Lake Pulaski House in Buffalo, Minnesota.

3. Pennsylvania's ten-thousand-man National Guard was the second largest (after New York) such organization in the country. Previously, the Pennsylvania state government had held its troops aloof from combined encampments with the Regular Army on the grounds that they had nothing to learn from the army. The chief of staff, General Bell, thought he detected a change in this attitude and wished "to take advantage of every opportunity to cultivate more cordial and friendly relations with the National Guard of Pennsylvania." But only one officer, Captain Charles D. Rhodes, was assigned to that state's summer encampments. Bell directed that several "especially qualified" officers be sent from Fort Leavenworth to assist Rhodes. Marshall was one of the six Bell named. (Bell to Major General Fred C. Ainsworth [the military secretary], June 30, 1907, NA/RG 94 [Militia].)

4. Brigadier General Charles B. Dougherty was the commander of the Third Brigade,

Pennsylvania National Guard. In civil life he was superintendent of the Pennsylvania Coal Company. Some army officers considered Dougherty to be "very progressive in his military ideas, and in sympathy with the wishes of the War Department in regard to desiring the militia to conform to regular army standards, so far as is practicable." (Captain Charles D. Rhodes, Report to TAG, August 12, 1907, NA/RG 94 [Militia].)

5. Following the completion of the Staff College year on June 30, 1908, the entire class and some of the instructors left Fort Leavenworth for a two-week horseback ride from Manassas, Virginia, to Gettysburg, Pennsylvania. At various times during the ride the students read research papers each had prepared on some aspect of the Civil War campaigns in the area. Marshall delivered the final paper (not printed) summarizing the lessons to be learned from the Battle of Gettysburg (July 1–3, 1863). Following this, Marshall reported for duty with the Third Brigade of the Pennsylvania National Guard encamped near Gettysburg. He was at the camp from July 15 to July 24.

6. Marshall was an instructor for the Pennsylvania National Guard between July 10 and 30, 1909. The Officers' Camp he describes took place between May 13 and 20, 1911.

7. This demonstrable change in Sweeney's attitude was considered a major victory for the Regular Army and for General Dougherty. (See Rhodes's Report to TAG, August 12, 1907, ibid.)

To Colonel Bernard Lentz[1]   October 2, 1935
                                                               [Chicago, Illinois]

Dear Lentz: I found your letter about General Morrison on my return from leave ten days ago. To date I have been too busy catching up to reply.

General Morrison and I reached Leavenworth the same year, but in slightly different capacities.[2] He was practically unknown to the students. His work that year was exclusively (at least for most of the year) with the Junior Class and not with the staff class.

Reports soon circulated that here was an instructor in tactics that talked a totally different language from all the others. After listening to him it began to appear that the others were talking about technique and calling it tactics; that he talked the simplicities of tactics and cared (or maybe knew) nothing of technique. In the marking of problems we were given minute cuts on dozens of little errors in technique, until we came to him, and then we lost shirt, pants and shoes in one swat, for violating a fundamental tactical principle which none of us had recognized as such. Theretofore we could recite the principle, but rarely recognized it in action. His problems were short and always contained a knockout if you failed to recognize the principle involved in meeting the situation. Simplicity and dispersion became fixed quantities in my mind, never to be forgotten, and their application realized to almost any situation, from garrison police to an army battle.

He spoke a tactical language I have never heard from any other officer. He was self-educated, reading constantly and creating and solving problems for himself. He taught me all I will ever know of tactics.

Here, in my opinion, were his defects; ones that prevented him—aside from ill health—from rising to the top as a leader:

He was a miserable judge of men. Not that a bum could fool him, but he couldn't distinguish between the doer and the pedantic or mediocre type.

He couldn't hear—or rather concentrate sufficiently to understand—views other than his own. There was no difficulty in tactical matters, but that was because he was so much wiser than all the others that there could be no possible grounds for argument—merely the necessity for further exposition by him. But on other subjects I found he really did not even hear what you were saying, though he was easily approachable and listened—apparently—patiently.

He understood nothing of the necessity of compromise. This is a magnificent, but rather unpractical trait. In almost every public position in life compromises must be made. The great man is he who makes the minor adjustments—without dishonor—that permit the great issues or important matters to be carried to proper completion. In General Morrison's case, this came about through his lack of contacts—too many hours in the library and too few with men.

One afternoon at Leavenworth will illustrate something of this. He and I were leaving to play golf. Both of us were terrible. My balls flew off at a tangent and never went down the course (they still do); his topped balls bounced pathetically along the fairway. He invariably remarked "Well, I have good direction." Never, in my memory, did he lift but one ball off the ground, and that struck the saddle horn of a civilian driving cattle near the cemetery. I calmed the cussing man, and General Morrison very sonorously remarked, "My direction wasn't so good that time." Not a hint of a joke.

As we walked home in the dusk, across the West Parade, I suggested that we stop at the Club. He begged off, but I insisted. We really created a sensation as we entered—Joe Louis as my companion could not have been more surprising. I steered Colonel Morrison to a table where E. T. Collins, J. M. A. Palmer, Bjornstad and E. J. Williams were sitting. They welcomed him with honor and delight. Having had a few drinks they continued their badinage. We had a couple of cocktails and General Morrison joined in the laughter about this and that. Finally, he and I started home. It was late, after his dinner hour and he commented on that. Then, after a little silence, he made a remark that stuck in my mind throughout the remainder of his career. "Marshall," he said, "I don't mix enough with other officers."[3]

The foregoing is probably not what you wanted, but it represents my impressions. However, do not quote me.   Faithfully yours

GCMRL/G. C. Marshall Papers (Illinois National Guard)

1. Lentz, whom Marshall had known since 1908, was interested in writing a story for the *Infantry Journal* on John F. Morrison (U.S.M.A., 1881). He had written to Marshall requesting "some anecdotes, wise sayings, etc., that would be helpful in giving our many younger officers something of the spirit of this truly great officer and teacher." (Lentz to Marshall, September 14, 1935, GCMRL/G. C. Marshall Papers [Illinois National Guard].)

2. Morrison, then a major in the Twentieth Infantry, arrived at Fort Leavenworth in September, 1906, to take the position of assistant instructor in the Department of Military Art at

the Infantry and Cavalry School and the Staff College. The next year he became the senior instructor and in 1908 the assistant commandant.

3. This incident must have happened during the 1909–10 school year when Marshall was an instructor in the Engineering Department. At that time Captain Edgar T. Collins (U.S.M.A., 1897), Sixth Infantry, was a student in the School of the Line, and Captains John McA. Palmer (U.S.M.A., 1892), Fifteenth Infantry; Alfred W. Bjornstad, Twenty-eighth Infantry; and Ezekiel J. Williams, Fifth Infantry, were students in the Staff College.

A T THE END of the Staff College year in June, 1908, Marshall was one of five graduates selected unanimously by the senior instructors to remain with the school as teachers for the coming year. The other four were captains, the most junior of whom was nearly five hundred files ahead of Marshall in rank. Major Morrison told the army adjutant general: "Lieutenant Marshall will be used as an assistant instructor in the Engineering Department and Military Art Department. He is an exceptionally capable man and will be very valuable to both the departments, and his services are greatly needed." (Morrison to TAG, July 1, 1908, NA/RG 94 [Leavenworth].) ★

From Major General Edward W. Nichols[1]   May 27, 1909
                                                  [Lexington, Virginia]

My dear Marshall: I write to ask whether you would like to have your name considered in connection with the detail as commandant here for the three years beginning August 15th., next. Capt. Mills' term expires on the 17th. of August, and the matter is to be determined by the Board of Visitors at their meeting to be held here on June 19th.

We have noted with increasing interest your success, and wish for you all good things that the Army may afford. With kindest regards to Mrs. Marshall, believe me to remain,   Yours very cordially,

P.S.—I think it is probable that we could overcome any difficulties that may be presented at Fort Leavenworth arising from your present position through Gen. Bell, Chief of Staff, who is a great friend of the institution. In the event of your desiring your name considered in this connection, please send me an outline of your record since you left us.

VMI/RG 2

1. Nichols (V.M.I., 1878) had been the professor of mathematics when Marshall was at V.M.I. On July 1, 1907, he succeeded Scott Shipp, who had retired, as superintendent.

To Major General Edward W. Nichols   June 1, 1909
                                                  Fort Leavenworth, Kansas

My dear General:- Your letter of May 27th., received and I desire to thank you for considering me in connection with the detail of commandant at the Institute. I will be very glad to have you place my name before the Board of Visitors on June 19th. As I will have completed three years of detached service August 15th., next, and four years is the supposed limit, there may be some difficulty for this reason in securing favorable action from the War Department in regard to my detail, though of late this regulation has frequently been departed from.

I am now an instructor in the Department of Engineering of the Army School of the Line and of the Army Staff College, and as my relief from this duty at this particular time of the year would tend to disarrange the plans of the Department for the coming term, I will appreciate your telegraphing me, collect, the action of the Board. This will also be of considerable convenience to me as I had intended moving into new quarters the last week in June, before leaving for some maneuvers in Pennsylvania, where I will be on duty during July.

In compliance with your request I enclose an outline of my record since leaving the Institute. I trust this is in the form you desire.

Mrs. Marshall left Saturday night for Virginia to spend the summer with her mother near Charlottesville. I hope to spend a week or ten days there in August.

I appreciate very much your expressions of interest in my Army career, and I wish to assure you that your congratulatory letter of two years ago has served me as a constant incentive.

With kindest regards, believe me,   Very respectfully yours,

                                                  G. C. Marshall, Jr.
VMI/Alumni File; T

To Major General Edward W. Nichols   June 24, 1909
                                                  Fort Leavenworth, Kansas

My dear General:- I owe you an immediate explanation of my telegram of this morning requesting you to withdraw my name as a candidate for the detail of commandant at the Institute.

From your letter of May 27th I gathered the idea that the Board of Visitors would meet and decide the matter on the 19th. In case I was selected this would give the Department of Engineering here an opportunity to select my successor from among the members of the present Staff Class, who graduate and leave here on June 30th. No telegram having been received up to yesterday morning, the head of the Department, Captain Cole,[1] became worried and rather reconsidered his original approval of my trying for the detail at Lexington. For that reason I telegraphed you to find out if the Board of Visitors had already acted on the matter. In case it had I was prepared to leave, but otherwise I would be under obligations to act as I finally did.

I enclose a letter the head of the Department addressed me yesterday which is self explanitory,[2] and I trust you will understand my position and approve of my action.

I regret to lose this chance of possibly being detailed at the Institute and trust I may have another opportunity at some future date.   Very respectfully yours,

G. C. Marshall, Jr.

P.S. Please return the enclosed letter.

VMI/Alumni File; T

1. Captain Edwin T. Cole (U.S.M.A., 1889), Sixth Infantry, was the senior instructor in the Department of Engineering. When Cole died in 1940, Marshall wrote: "He was instrumental in having me selected as Instructor though I was but a young lieutenant at the time and the students were all my seniors, some by many years." (Marshall to Captain Charles M. Delp, February 27, 1940, GCMRL/G. C. Marshall Papers [Pentagon Office, General].)

2. This letter was not found in the Marshall papers or in the Alumni File.

TELEGRAM TO BRIGADIER GENERAL   July 1, 1909
WILLIAM W. WOTHERSPOON   Fort Leavenworth,
FROM MAJOR GENERAL J. FRANKLIN BELL   Kansas

Referring to your telegram of yesterday Lieut. Marshall already absent from regiment three years.[1] Full college detail would keep him absent seven years in succession. On account of low rank such absence would certainly result in his ruination as a line officer besides being an utter disregard of regulations and orders of the President. In addition he is a valuable instructor here with one more year to serve. His detail can not be so important at any college as to justify a disregard of all the above considerations.

NA/RG 165 (OCS, General)

1. Wotherspoon was acting army chief of staff in Washington in Bell's absence. Superintendent Nichols was in Washington on July 1 and had visited the chief of staff's office. In a telegram later the same day, Bell said: "[Brigadier General George B.] Davis [the judge advocate general] has message from Nichols requesting he persuade me to let him have Marshall. V.M.I. is important institution but no more so than this one. Cannot consent to establishment precedent taking instructors away from here for any college whatever. Won't recommend Marshall under any consideration whatever. There are other men equally as good and more available."(Bell to Wotherspoon, July 1, 1909, NA/RG 165 [OCS, General].)

W ITH THE END of the 1908-9 school year, Marshall was again detailed as
instructor with the Pennsylvania National Guard, July 10-30. As soon as
the camp ended on July 30, Marshall hurried southward to join his wife for a
brief vacation in Virginia. He arranged to stay the night at the Fort Myer,
Virginia, apartment of a friend from Fort Leavenworth, First Lieutenant
Benjamin D. Foulois.

At Fort Leavenworth some of Foulois's classmates and instructors had considered him somewhat odd because of his belief that "the dynamical flying
machine" would have a profound impact on military tactics within a few years.
(Benjamin D. Foulois, *From the Wright Brothers to the Astronauts: The
Memoirs of Major General Benjamin D. Foulois* [New York: McGraw-Hill,
1968], pp. 43-44.) But as a student in the General Staff School the previous year,
when Foulois was in the Signal Corps School, Marshall had been present at a
lecture delivered by the head of the Signal School, Major George O. Squier
(U.S.M.A., 1887). Marshall later recalled Squier's "startling statement that two
brothers, named Wright, were actually reaching the solution of flight by heavier-
than-air machines. I knew nothing of this at the time, having seen no reference
to it in the press, and I have never forgotten the profound impression it made on
my mind." (Speech, September 19, 1938, Air Corps Tactical School, Maxwell
Field, Alabama, GCMRL/G. C. Marshall Papers [Pentagon Office, Speeches].)

Marshall arrived at Fort Myer on July 30 to find some seven thousand persons, including cabinet officers, ambassadors, and diplomats, "present to see the
miracle—an effort to fly twenty miles, with two passengers, at a speed of at least
forty miles an hour." His friend Foulois had been the navigator-passenger on the
historic flight piloted by Orville Wright, and that evening his apartment was full
of reporters searching for newsworthy comments. (Ibid.)

Following their Virginia vacation, the Marshalls returned to Fort Leavenworth
for the 1909-10 school year. During his two-year duty as instructor, Marshall
produced most of the small amount of technical writing he did during his career.
In 1909 he collaborated with Captain Clarence O. Sherrill (U.S.M.A., 1901) in
issuing a manual on *Cordage and Tackle.* During this period Marshall was also
an associate editor of the *Infantry Journal,* although he wrote but one essay
himself: "A Record in Military Mapping," 6(January 1910): 546-50.

After classes ended on June 30, 1910, Marshall reported for a month's duty as
inspector-instructor at several state militia officers' camps of instruction. The
War Department, pleased with the success it had had with militia camps since
1908, and determined to "undertake a general movement along these lines in
1910," specified that "such instructors as will be needed should be selected from
the best qualified officers of the Regular Army." (General Orders, No. 4,
January 12, 1910.) Marshall attended four such camps: July 2-6 with the New
York National Guard; and July 9-30 with three different units of the
Massachusetts Volunteer Militia. ★

REPORT TO THE COMMANDING GENERAL,   [August, 1910]
DEPARTMENT OF THE EAST   [Camp Perry, Ohio]

"Report on Field Inspection of the
Organized Militia of Massachusetts. 1st Corps of Cadets"[1]

. . . CONDITION OF UNIFORMS, ARMS, AND EQUIPMENTS
OF OFFICERS AND ENLISTED MEN.

. . . In connection with the equipment I wish to repeat my recommendation of last year—that each state be issued sufficient equipment to completely equip each organization to its war strength on short notice. The excess not in use should be kept at the state arsenal. This would vastly simplify the work of the War Department or territorial departments in case it should become necessary to suddenly order out all the state troops for actual service. It affords an easy and effective means of decentralizing such work.

SANITATION.

. . . The police of the camp was excellent. If any comment is made it might be said that too much time was set aside and devoted to the police of the camp.

DRILL AND INSTRUCTION.

. . . In order to give the men the maximum amount of instruction in their drill, etc., only five enlisted cooks did any cooking. These were assisted by 51 colored servants who waited on the tables, cooked, washed, etc. As it has been the custom in this organization when in camp on its home grounds to receive all the veterans of the corps, supporters, etc., a great many extra meals had to be served which necessitated a large staff in the mess department. The straight government rationed was not used and the cooking and meals were excellent. The corps had camped under service conditions during the past two summers, so were familiar with the handling of the regular ration. . . .

MISCELLANEOUS REMARKS OF INSPECTOR.

. . . *Selection of Officers:–* While according to the law the officers are supposed to be elected by the enlisted men, as a matter of fact in this organization they are practically appointed according to seniority, when efficient. As a result they are far above the average in efficiency. The election of officers should be discontinued and promotion by seniority required, the promotion being company, battalion or regimental according to the location of the units mentioned.

Where only one company comes from a town promotion from junior corporal to captain should be by seniority, provided the man passes suitable examinations. All seem to believe that this would do much to improve the National Guard, and their belief appears to be justifiable in every respect.

Drill Regulations and Guard Manual:– The experience of the instructor at nine camps with National Guard troops during the last four years leads to the belief that the infantry drill regulations and the manual of guard duty were not written with a view to the instruction of our National Guard troops and the large bodies of volunteers we will be compelled to hastily raise and train in case of war—these two forces presenting our greatest military problem. There appear to be many unnecessary details in both these volumes, which vastly increase the difficulty of quickly instructing new men in the first principals of soldiering. It would appear that at least fifteen movements in the manual of arms could be eliminated to advantage. For instance such movements as from right shoulder arms to present and the reverse, the various movements to and from left shoulder arms, serve no purpose, but as they appear in that part of the regulations detailing the elementary instruction for the recruit they should be thoroughly learned and not slighted. There are possibly close order formations that have no good purpose, too many rigid rules and too few general principles. The guard manual is complex and exceedingly difficult to the average private, even in the regular service. It is unfortunate considering the amount of instruction the individual soldier is given in guard duty that there is not more general similarity between the duties of a sentinel on an ordinary post and on outpost.

The 1st Corps of Cadets was organized in 1741; it has many interesting customs and traditions which are observed today; it has a great many veterans and a large following who support it. As a result the personnel is unusually high, the officers and enlisted men, practically all being from the better walks of life, men of college education and consequently of a high order of intelligence. The discipline is as near perfect as could ever be expected in a National Guard organization. The "esprit" of the organization has been developed to the highest point and is deserving of great commendation.[2]   Respectfully submitted,

G. C. Marshall, Jr.

NA/RG 393 (Department of the East); T

1. Marshall inspected the cadets at their camp at Hingham, Massachusetts, July 9–16. This report was written in August while Marshall was at Camp Perry, Ohio, where he was a statistical officer at the annual National Rifle and Pistol Matches. He had requested this duty and delayed his vacation trip in order to get it.

2. Captain Monroe C. Kerth (U.S.M.A., 1898), a General Staff officer who had been in Marshall's class in the School of the Line and the Staff College, sent a memo to the chief of the Division of Militia Affairs quoting Marshall's recommendations under *Drill Regulations and Guard Manual* at length (February 6, 1911, NA/RG 168). Kerth added: "Lieutenant Marshall's experience with the Organized Militia, and his splendid record as an officer in the Regular Service, entitle his comments and recommendations to serious consideration. My own experience has been such that I not only agree with Lieutenant Marshall in his statements, but desire to emphasize the same, if possible."

EARLY IN September Marshall and his wife went abroad for six months of leave. It was "quite a feat on a lieutenant's pay," he recalled; "we had to do it on a shoestring, but we managed to cover six countries—two of them while I was on half pay. We had a very interesting time, particularly because we didn't try to hurry. We would stay at a place for weeks."

The couple's first stop was England, where they remained for over a month. In mid-September, Marshall took a busman's holiday and attended the British Army maneuvers at Aldershot in Surrey. First he applied to the United States Embassy for permission. "But, of course, they could do nothing for me. So I just rented a bicycle up near Aldershot and went there and went through all the maneuvers and saw about three times as much as our attache saw because I wasn't restricted. I just rode all over the place as I wanted to and had an interesting time of it." (Interview, April 4, 1957.) ★

To the Adjutant General   September 19, 1910
                                                                  London, England

Sir:–   I have the honor to request that the leave granted me by par. 15, S.O. # 94 War Department, C.S. be extended one month on half pay. The ocean voyage to Europe and back is so expensive that in all probability I will not be able to take it again, and for this reason I desire very much to continue my stay abroad an additional month in order that I may not have to slight some things which I have a particular desire to see.[1]   Very respectfully,

                                                                  G. C. Marshall, Jr.
NA/RG 94 (Document File); H

1. Colonel William Paulding, commanding officer of the Twenty-fourth United States Infantry, Madison Barracks, New York, advised rejection of Marshall's request, because Marshall had been on detached service at Fort Leavenworth and had "never served with this regiment." However, Major General Frederick D. Grant (U.S.M.A., 1871), at Department of the East headquarters, Governors Island, New York, approved the request "in order to enable Lieutenant Marshall to take full advantage of his trip to Europe." (NA/RG 94 [Document File].)

FOLLOWING their visit in Britain, the Marshalls journeyed to France, Italy, and Austria before beginning their return. "We had a very stormy trip home," he remembered. "We didn't see anything of interest in Africa [Algiers] except to argue with the carriage men and others about the prices they were charging—Mrs. Marshall being very embarrassed about my refusal to pay the price they put up." (Interview, April 4, 1957.)

Marshall reported for duty—"in a blizzard"—on January 30, 1911, at Madison Barracks, on Lake Ontario near Sackets Harbor, New York. He was assigned to command Company D of the Twenty-fourth Infantry, the regiment to which he had been assigned upon his promotion to first lieutenant on March 7, 1907. This was the first time Marshall had served with his regiment, and his stay proved to be a brief one.

Early in March, 1911, Marshall was ordered to Washington. There he found War Department planning in its final stages for the concentration of a "Maneuver Division" on the Mexican border, the first division-sized gathering since the Spanish-American War. Marshall was immediately assigned as an assistant to the division's chief signal officer, Major George O. Squier. Marshall arrived at the headquarters at Fort Sam Houston in San Antonio, Texas, on March 11, and was assigned to special duty with Company D of the Signal Corps. "I found when I got down there," he recalled, "that they had taken me into the Signal Corps affair just to get me present." (Ibid.) Unfortunately, "the weather conditions could hardly have been more unfavorable" for maneuvers. (Major General William H. Carter to TAG, June 13, 1911, NA/RG 94 [Maneuver Division].) Nevertheless, with innovations such as field telephones, wireless transmitters, and airplanes to assimilate, the experience was highly educational for the nearly sixteen thousand officers and men present.

Marshall arrived without equipment of any kind. "I just came by myself. Now they kept sending men in to me which formed a sort of echelon of men in connection with communications detail. So I had command of this outfit." He also had to act as his own depot quartermaster, drawing supplies for which he was personally responsible. It was a complex situation involving "a lot of paperwork." (Interview, April 4, 1957.)

The division's chief signal officer had been assigned three army pilots and their two planes. The latter Marshall recalled vividly. "I turned out every morning at 5:30 in the cold of a Texas winter to avoid a possible calamity, as the planes in taking off barely cleared my tent. I saw the Curtiss crash, and I saw the Wright run through a horse and buggy, or rather I saw the horse run over the machine." (Marshall, Speech at the Air Corps Tactical School, September 19, 1938, p. 632, below.)

When the aircraft were undergoing repairs—which was often—or the weather was bad—also often—the pilots acted as communications officers. Marshall, having organized the headquarters communications center, "worked out a brief plan of having maneuvers with all the staff, headquarters, communications details, and things of that sort instead of the troops at first. And that took the chief signal officer very strongly; and he advertised it very thoroughly and put it on and had me to draw up the problem and all for the procedure. It involved the whole division and a Cavalry brigade." (Interview, April 4, 1957.) ★

TACTICAL PROBLEM   April 3, 1911
                                                      San Antonio, Texas

Tactical Problem No. 1
for Company D., Signal Corps, and attached officers.

The orders of the Division Commander and a brief outline of the essential details of the orders of his principal subordinates, are given.[1] With these as a basis the company will be disposed so as to furnish the communication desired.

Attached officers will be designated to act as commanders of the several fractions of the command.[2]

They will be required to make decisions and give such commands from time to time as the situation may require, and they are particularly charged with keeping track of the length of the columns, where the heads of the various elements are, etc., for the information of the Signal Troops.

The rate of march per hour of the imaginary troops of the Division will be taken as 2½ miles for infantry and 3½ to 8 miles for cavalry.

The tent of The Chief Signal Officer will be considered as that of the Chief of Staff for the purpose of the problem.

G. C. Marshall, Jr.

NA/RG 111 (Maneuver Division)

1. Attached Field Order No. 1, written by Marshall, is not printed.

2. Marshall, acting as "Colonel D., Chief of Staff," designated the three army pilots as umpires to keep the maneuver running properly. Lieutenant Benjamin D. Foulois was "Brigadier General E" assigned to the Independent Cavalry Brigade and commanding the wireless platoon. Lieutenant John C. Walker, Jr., was "Brigadier General A" with the Right Column, and Lieutenant G.E.M. Kelly (killed on May 10 in a plane crash) acted as "Brigadier General B" with the Left Column.

T HE MOST memorable aspect of this Signal Corps headquarters exercise for Marshall was his use of the Maneuver Division's wireless transmitter. The three army pilots acted as commanders of the three groups of imaginary troops sent to repel the imaginary enemy advancing on San Antonio from the northeast. Two of the "generals" were to report to Marshall by telephone. The third (Benjamin Foulois) was given a platoon of men and the hand-cranked wireless set. Marshall was amused by the first American military radio message he ever knew to be received; Foulois reported that he and the Cavalry were "just west of the manure pile." Unfortunately, no one at headquarters knew where the manure pile was. (Interview, April 4, 1957.)

The point had been made, however. In his report, Major Squier predicted that the days when generals operated their forces largely by commands given personally in the field were over. Henceforth, the commanding general would sit well behind the lines, surrounded by specialized staff experts and communications equipment. In addition, he noted, "if there was any doubt in the minds of individuals of this command as to the utility of the aeroplane, for military purposes, that doubt has been removed by the aeronautical work done in this division." (Squier to Chief Signal Officer, War Department, July 13, 1911, NA/RG 111 [Maneuver Division].)

On May 4, Marshall received orders to report to the headquarters of the

Department of the East at Governors Island, New York, for reassignment as inspector-instructor to the Massachusetts Volunteer Militia. A law passed on March 3, 1911, permitted the assignment of Regular Army officers for long-term duty with state militias, rather than for brief tours at summer camps only.

In mid-October, 1910, as the bill to permit such assignments was being contemplated, the governor of Massachusetts wrote to request Marshall's assignment. (Eben S. Draper to Major General Frederick D. Grant, October 11, 1910, NA/RG 98 [Department of the East].) On May 13, Marshall arrived at Mt. Gretna, Pennsylvania, for the first of two week-long officers' camps (the second being at Luray, Virginia, May 22–30) to which he had been detailed prior to reporting to Boston. General Dougherty, head of the Pennsylvania National Guard, attempted to get the War Department to change Marshall's Massachusetts assignment. ★

To CAPTAIN CHARLES D. RHODES   May 15, 1911
FROM MAJOR GENERAL CHARLES B. DOUGHERTY[1]   Mt. Gretna,
                                                              Pennsylvania

My dear Captain Rhodes:- . . . You know with what esteem and regard Lieutenant Marshall is held by the officers and men of the National Guard of Pennsylvania. He has served with us so often; he is so capable in every way, and has kept in such constant touch, by correspondence, with some of the Colonels and helped them in their efforts to increase the efficiency of their commands that I feel he can accomplish a great deal of good in Pennsylvania if we can only have him detailed to this State.

He is, I understand, under detail to go to Massachusetts. As you probably know, Lieutenant Marshall is a native of Pennsylvania, and on that account, is deeply interested in the progress of the National Guard of this State. He is so fit for the work we have in mind and can be so helpful to us that I feel, with your sure knowledge of the situation, that I may call upon you to help to do something to get the detail to Massachusetts revoked, and have him sent to us here in Pennsylvania.[2] . . . Sincerely yours,

                                                            C. B. Dougherty

NA/RG 165 (OCS)

1. Dougherty had become commander of the entire Pennsylvania National Guard division. Rhodes was a member of the General Staff Corps and assigned to the Office of the Chief of Staff.

2. Inclosed with this letter was one that Dougherty wrote to Brigadier General Thomas J. Stewart, the adjutant general of Pennsylvania, concerning Marshall's assignment: "If there is anything in the world that you can do to bring this about, it will be rendering valued service, not only to the State, but to the Division Commander as well." Stewart wrote a "personal and unofficial" letter to Major General Leonard Wood, the army chief of staff, urging Marshall's assignment to Pennsylvania. Rhodes replied on May 19 that the chief of staff did not feel that he could "revoke Marshall's order without being accused of injustice toward Massachusetts." (NA/RG 165 [OCS].)

M ARSHALL reported to Massachusetts Adjutant General Gardner W. Pearson on June 3, 1911, for duty as one of the inspector-instructors assigned to the state. His first job was to assist Captain George E. Thorne, who was in charge of the officers' camps of instruction for 1911 in the Department of the East, with the program for the Massachusetts militia officers' school to be held June 23–27.

Following this, Marshall assisted Captain Matthew E. Hanna (U.S.M.A., 1897), whom he had known at Fort Leavenworth, in drawing up plans for a major state maneuver to be held July 23–30. Marshall, the only lieutenant along with fourteen captains of the Regular Army present, and Hanna acted as umpires and assistants to the commander in chief.

"War is now on in this state," the *Boston Globe* reported on July 23, "and some 6,000 troops . . . are in the field." Another ten thousand persons visited the camps and watched the opening of the spectacle. On July 27, Major General Frederick D. Grant, commander of the Department of the East, came up from Governors Island to observe. Hanna praised the maneuvers as "unqualifiedly the most successful" militia exercise ever held in the United States. (*Boston Globe,* July 30, 1911.)

At the beginning of September, Marshall leased an apartment in Boston, and he and Lily again attempted to set up housekeeping. But the job of teaching and inspecting scattered units was demanding and required considerable travel. He later recalled that "the work with the Massachusetts Organized Militia was very interesting, very instructive, and a very hard job. I rarely ever was home in the evening—had to travel a great deal. All the men responded, though they thought they were getting too much work. I developed a number of what I thought were interesting courses of instruction. . . . This was quite an educational treat to me. The teacher was being educated at the same time he was instructing. But they accepted everything that I put up. And I was able to experiment and enlarge and subtract and so on." (Interview, April 4, 1957.) ★

REPORT TO THE CHIEF,   October 2, 1911
DIVISION OF MILITIA AFFAIRS   Boston, Massachusetts

Sir: In compliance with instructions from your office in a letter dated July 13, 1911, I have the honor to submit the following report of the duties I have performed, etc., for the period June 1 to September 30, 1911.

I reported for duty to the Adjutant General of Massachusetts on June 3 and found everyone busy with preparation for the extended maneuvers to be held the last week in July. During June and the first three weeks of July, my time was entirely devoted to work in preparation for these maneuvers. I had charge of a number of the arrangements made in the office of the Adjutant General for the organization of a provisional division and the two combatant brigades, the preparation of maps, the leasing of camp sights, etc.

I also conducted a number of tactical walks on Saturdays and Sundays for officers and non-commissioned officers of battalions; gave several lectures; conducted a school of instruction for staff officers of the brigade, method of keeping records of orders issued, messages sent and received, etc. For one week I conducted a series of progressive map problems, or "one sided" war games, for the instruction of one of the brigade commanders. These sessions were about five hours long and a stenographer was used.

During the last week in July, I was assistant to the chief umpire, his Excellency, the Governor, the Commander in Chief, during the maneuvers. I also had charge of a number of details at the Headquarters of the Provisional Division.

During August no schools were held, no instruction given. I was engaged in the preparation of a comprehensive report on the maneuvers, and schedules for the winter training of the troops.

During September I was still engaged in the work on the report, and perfecting schedules for drill instruction, schools, etc. In this month the first meeting of the school for instruction of brigade staff officers was held, the primary object being to instruct these officers in their duties when handling their assembled brigades in the field.

I found during the maneuvers that it was very dangerous to attempt maneuvers involving the handling of brigades, where the troops move constantly from camp to camp, without having given most careful instruction to the brigade staff officers. Heretofore these officers have received little or no instruction in such duties, and are only actively engaged with military matters during the one week of the summer camp. The brigade staffs, therefore, have not a clear conception of their duties, their relations with each other, their commander, and the troops, and consequently there is an utter absence of team work. As I was able, previous to the maneuvers, to give the staff officers of one brigade several evening's work in practical problems on the map, involving their duties, I had an opportunity of comparing the work of this staff with that of the other brigade, and its effect on the troops was most marked, having a decided influence on the course of the maneuvers.

During the period covered by this report the undersigned had not taken up the routine duties of his position. The early part of the period was entirely devoted to strenuous efforts, exerted to make the summer maneuvers a success. During August and September the time was mostly utilized in preparation for the winter work, investigating and reporting on the methods of conducting business, etc., in the Adjutant General's office and preparation of reports.   Very respectfully,

G. C. Marshall, Jr.

NA/RG 168 (Camps)

Lieutenants Bruce Palmer and George Marshall take a break during engineering class at Fort Leavenworth in the spring of 1907.

Lieutenant Marshall (first row, fifth from the left), Captain Henry E. Eames, and the men of Company G, Thirtieth Infantry, probably at Santa Mesa Garrison near Manila, 1903.

George and Lily Marshall, Fort Leavenworth, about 1908.

Army Service Schools leaders, 1908–9: Brigadier General Frederick Funston, commandant (left); Major John F. Morrison, assistant commandant; Captain Edwin T. Cole, senior instructor, Department of Engineering.

Regular Army officers (left to right: Captain George E. Thorne, Captain Matthew E. Hanna, Major General Frederick D. Grant, and First Lieutenant George C. Marshall) confer on the progress of the Massachusetts militia maneuvers, late July, 1911.

First Lieutenant Marshall of the Fourth Infantry (September 4, 1912, to June 22, 1913).

*Captain Marshall and Major General J. Franklin Bell, Governors Island,
New York, spring, 1917.*

REPORT TO THE CHIEF,
DIVISION OF MILITIA AFFAIRS

January 1, 1912
Boston, Massachusetts

Sir: I have the honor to submit the following report as Inspector-Instructor on duty with the Organized Militia of Massachusetts, for the quarter ending December 31, 1911:

During October my office hours were occupied in preparing a report on the maneuvers of the past summer, in preparing data for the correspondence schools, and in assisting in business connected with the Adjutant General's Office. My evenings were occasionally devoted to conducting schools.

From October 26th to November 30th I was engaged in visiting the majority of the infantry companies in the state. Where it was not possible for me to visit a company, its officers were present at some other company's armory. The principal purpose of these visits was to observe the manner in which company officers conducted their armory instruction; to start them off properly with the new drill regulations; and to give the noncommissioned officers a proper idea of their duties, how to give commands, lead their squads, platoons, &c. An effort was made to explain to all the officers and noncommissioned officers the possibilities of their position at the present time in connection with the National defense, emphasizing the suddenness with which they might be called out for active service; the consequent necessity for developing the discipline of their organizations during the armory season by properly conducted close order drills, &c; the meaning of discipline and its test in actual campaign, etc. I also conducted several schools on evenings during this month. During my office hours I was engaged in routine business and preparation of problems, &c., for schools.

In December I was occupied in preparing problems, solutions, and other data for six school courses, four purely correspondence and two correspondence supplemented by personal instruction. It was necessary for me to prepare this work in advance for January, February and March, as my time will be occupied from January 22^d to the first week in March with the annual Federal inspections. . . .

I was also engaged during December in delivering lectures to officers and noncommissioned officers on the recent maneuvers, pointing out in detail the mistakes made, their effect, and methods for avoiding them in future.

I also visited the drills of three battalions of the high school boys. I deem this matter of sufficient importance to merit a separate report, which will soon be submitted.[1]

ARMORY INSTRUCTION.

Observation of the state of efficiency of the National Guard organizations when they first arrive in camp in the summer, and of their methods of work in their armories, convinces me that the most serious defect in their system of training is a failure to properly understand the purposes of the close order drills.

The latter are rarely ever conducted in such a manner as to develop discipline, and, as a matter of fact, they are usually so conducted as to hurt discipline and waste time. If the time now devoted to armory instruction is properly utilized, I am convinced that organizations can report for their summer tours of camp duty in such a state of discipline and so instructed in squad, platoon and company leadership, map reading, sanitation, supply, and minor tactics that their field instruction can be conducted along lines much further advanced than in the past.

To sum up: The present position of the National Guard in the first line of our military force demands that their field efficiency be greatly increased. They cannot undertake more complicated field exercises while reporting for summer camps at the state of efficiency they have in the past. The change must first be effected during the armory season; and to me it is apparent that during this period almost fifty per cent. of the working time has been wasted. Therefore the principal problem before us is to devise ways and means of obtaining more efficient armory instruction.

RECRUITING.

Obtaining recruits is one of the greatest difficulties with which a company commander has to contend. Of the methods employed in this state I think the scheme whereby corporals are charged with keeping their squads properly recruited is the best. This is made one of the most important of the corporal's duties and if he cannot obtain suitable recruits, it is understood that he is not capable of being a corporal.

I think some clever mind must devise a scheme whereby a member of the National Guard is by law given some status, privilege, or position which gives him an advantage over other civilians *eligible* for enlistment in the National Guard. Exemption from jury duty is an unsatisfactory example of such a privilege. The other extreme would be the right to vote, others being ineligible. This last is, of course, wholly impracticable, but between the two something might be determined upon which would operate without cost to the state, would not make service compulsory, and yet would make it distinctly desirable for a man to have honorably served one enlistment in the Regular Army or National Guard. An addition of ten per cent. to the percentage obtained in a civil service examination has been suggested as an advantage to be given every man who is serving or has served an enlistment in the Regular Army or National Guard, but this would only be an advantage to the few who were desirous of obtaining a civil service appointment and therefore would not be sufficiently general in its application.

RESERVE LIST.

I have been contemplating the preparation of a memorandum for The Adjutant General of this state recommending that a special enlistment contract be prepared to present to a man on his discharge from the present state force. This contract to obligate the man for a period of three years to report to a designated rendezvous in case the state troops were called out by the Federal Government for active service. The average man always feels that he would enlist in case of war and also feels that there is little chance of a war occurring. For this reason I do not think a man would ordinarily hesitate to enter into a contract which required no service of him, other than his advising the proper office of any change of address, except in case of war, for which he would probably desire to enlist in any event.

PRIVATES MANUAL. . . .

SCHOOLS.

I have already referred to the schools being conducted in this state. The present system of courses is probably more elaborate and comprehensive than in other states and it is still too early to report on its success. The school for enlisted candidates for commissions is apparently a splendid idea and is intended to offset the evils of promotion by election. This course is to be carefully prepared for next year in the form of pamphlets similar to those used in the commercial correspondence schools.

In all tactical problems an especial effort is being made to teach the officers the details of troop leading—how to execute orders in all the various details involved, from fighting to cooking. A weakness in this respect was apparent throughout the recent maneuvers.

The majority of the problems are being solved on the map used during the maneuvers and the problems themselves are frequently reproductions of situations that arose during the maneuvers. A war game map of a portion of this area is being prepared.

I think it exceedingly important that every state should have a map of ground with which the officers are personally familiar. This makes war games far more feasible and instructive, and the officers unconsciously learn how to read a map.

PROGRESS IN MASSACHUSETTS.

I think all the infantry organizations, and particularly some of the staff officers, have made good progress in their practical and theoretical work this fall. They take their work seriously and are laboring to correct all the weaknesses developed by the maneuvers.

Last summer after observing the many and surprising difficulties of company, battalion and regimental commanders, and of all the staff officers, in handling their organizations, when part of a large force moving as a unit from bivouac to bivouac, I am convinced that ordinary prudence demands that all state troops which have reached a fair state of efficiency should be maneuvered for about two days every summer as part of a reinforced brigade, bivouacing two nights, carrying *everything* with them, and not having a standing camp to return to. Very respectfully,

G. C. Marshall, Jr.

NA/RG 168 (Camps); T

1. This report was not found in the records of the National Guard Bureau (NA/RG 168).

To Major General Edward W. Nichols January 20, 1912
Boston, Massachusetts

My dear General:– I have your letter of January 16th and I sincerely appreciate the honor you do me in expressing a desire to have me as Commandant.[1]

While my present detail does not expire until June 1913 I have almost decided to ask to be relieved at the close of the field work next July or August, as I have had an overdose of National Guard instruction work during the past five years and hardly feel equal to the exacting strain of another year of it.

Because of the details that have been given me since 1906 I am not in a position to ask for anything but service with troops, and I therefore could not make application for the detail as Commandant at the Institute. However, if you care to ask for my detail and the War Department sees fit to grant your request, the resulting order would be very pleasing to me.

I regret that on both occasions you have written me in regard to this matter I have had to make such circuitous replies.

Mrs. Coles and Mrs. Marshall join me in warmest regards. Very respectfully yours,

G. C. Marshall, Jr.

VMI/Alumni File; T

1. Nichols said: "I write to ask if you would like to have the position. We wanted you, you recall, three years ago." (VMI/RG 2.) Originally Nichols wanted Morris E. Locke (V.M.I., 1899), one of Marshall's classmates at Fort Leavenworth, 1906–8, and a captain in the Third Field Artillery, as commandant of cadets at the Virginia Military Institute, but Chief of Staff Leonard Wood rejected this request. College details were limited to lieutenants of over five years' service because of "the great number of captains detached from their regiments, resulting in a loss of efficiency which was so marked as to require remedy." (Nichols to Wood, January 6, 1912; Wood to Nichols, January 10, 1912, NA/RG 165 [OCS].)

Report to the Chief, Division of January 30, 1912
Militia Affairs[1] Boston, Massachusetts

At the present time there are five battalions of infantry and two troops of cavalry of the organized militia of Massachusetts on duty preserving order in the city of Lawrence.[2] In calling out for military duty all the men concerned, there has been but one case where a man's employers have endeavored to have him excused from performing this duty. Unfortunately this one instance is the case of Lieutenant Brown, Company A, 8th Infantry, M.V.M., who is employed at the government arsenal at Watertown. In view of the well known difficulties with which the National Guard authorities all over the country have had to contend in educating the labor employers up to the point of considering it a patriotic duty to permit their men to perform their duties in the National Guard without hindrance or disadvantage, it would appear that the federal government should be exceedingly careful to set a proper example in this matter. The instance referred to above has resulted in the most unfortunate comment.[3]

NA/RG 168 (Document File)

1. The original letter is not in the file. This version is from a descriptive card which apparently quotes the original and subsequent indorsements fully.

2. As the militia's Regular Army instructor, Marshall was in Lawrence in civilian clothes frequently during the mid-January to mid-March textile strike. (See Charles A. Ranlett to Marshall, May 4, 1939, GCMRL/G. C. Marshall Papers [Pentagon Office, Congratulations].) Marshall returned to Lawrence on the afternoon of January 29, following incidents of violence that morning. On January 31, in response to a letter from Captain George Van Horn Moseley regarding new militia regulations, Marshall wrote: "I have been so busy with the militia during this strike at Lawrence (purely instruction work) that I have not had time before to look over the enclosed tentative regulations carefully. As I go back to Lawrence tomorrow I will give you my views on the subject today, without further delay." (Marshall to Moseley, January 31, 1912, NA/RG 168 [Document File].)

3. The commanding officer at Watertown Arsenal replied by indorsement that Lieutenant Brown's particular skill was of such importance that the facility would be forced to close if he joined his militia unit. Marshall was directed to give this information to those making unfavorable comments. On July 1, 1912, Marshall again raised the issue of critical-skills deferments, this time asking for a definite War Department ruling. The department preferred to handle each case on an ad hoc basis.

TO THE CHIEF, DIVISION OF MILITIA AFFAIRS   February 1, 1912
Boston, Massachusetts

Sir:– I have just received official notification that I am to be relieved from my present duties May 1st and returned to duty with my proper organization. I therefore have the honor to respectfully request that in relieving me from duty here on May 1st the order be so worded as to permit me to draw commutation of quarters, fuel and light until August 31, 1912, for the following reasons:–

On reporting here for duty last summer I found that the lease year commenced either September or October 1st and that they would make no exception in my case. I also found it impossible to lease any quarters (except in expensive apartment hotels) with a provision in the lease which would permit me to cancel the lease on two months notice—similar to the usual provision in all Washington leases. I even offered to pay ten percent more rent in consideration for some such provision. I had reason to feel that my present detail was for two years under ordinary circumstances, and I now find myself confronted with the proposition of paying $200 out of my pay, for the four months beginning May 1st. The reliable realestate dealers here, and others, inform me that it is practicably impossible to sublease the ordinary apartments in Boston for the summer months, as every one here leaves town for nearby shore resorts.

Without request or application on my part I have been moved about so frequently during the past eighteen months that I have been subjected to very heavy extra expenses. I left Fort Leavenworth in August 1910, sttled at Madison

Barracks February 1, 1911, was ordered away from there March 8, 1911; settled here in Boston last summer; and am now to pack up again and leave here May 1st. Furthermore, despite strict economy, I have found it almost impossible to maintain myself on my present detail in a manner suitable to the position I hold, and live within my pay. This last condition I fully expected when I came here and was prepared to make the best of it, but I think this prospective extraordinary expense, considered in connection with the frequent moves I have been ordered to make recently, justifies me in hoping for some special consideration. Such unusual expenses are wholly out of keeping with the pay of a first lieutenant of Infantry.[1] Very respectfully,

G. C. Marshall, Jr.

NA/RG 168 (Camps); T

1. The pay of a first lieutenant with five years in grade, which Marshall would have after March 7, 1912, was $183.33 per month. Marshall's letter prompted the War Department to change its plans. The army chief of staff decided to reassign him, and seven other similarly affected inspector-instructors, only after the National Guard's summer encampments in their respective states. (Major William J. Snow [acting chief, Division of Militia Affairs] to the Chief of Staff, February 9, 1912, NA/RG 168 [Camps].)

TO MAJOR GENERAL EDWARD W. NICHOLS   February 3, 1912
                                            Boston, Massachusetts

My dear General:–   I received your letter of January 31st this morning and was naturally very much interested in what you had to tell me about your interviews with Generals Wood and Carter. I appreciate very much the effort you have made to have me detailed as Commandant—in any event your display of interest in me will go far towards bettering my status with the War Department.[1]

When I answered your first letter I felt that there was not much chance that the authorities in Washington would agree to starting me on a fresh term of detached service. Because of the fact that the congressional resolutions refer to "regimental" duty I, personally, am done some injustice.[2] I was on detached service on two occasions when the duty was more trying than that in actual campaign. In 1905 I was ordered down to the Texas border to map 2000 square miles from a horse's back, with water about once every thirty miles. I labored out there for a number of months with the thermometer varying from 100 to 130 degrees, and at least a month of the time without even a tent; but that is not considered as regimental service. However, I realize that I am but a very small cog in the wheel and have no right to feel that I am not receiving everything that is due me.[3]

Mrs. Marshall will feel much outraged when I tell her that we must pack up again before May 1st. We just unpacked last September; and the previous February I reported for duty at Madison Barracks, unpacked, and four weeks later was ordered to Texas, leaving her to crate things up again. I think a few peaceful, housekeeping years in Lexington would appeal to her more than all the glories of war.

With kindest regards from Mrs. Coles and Mrs. Marshall, believe me,   Very respectfully yours,

G. C. Marshall, Jr.

VMI/Alumni File; T

1. Major General Leonard Wood was army chief of staff; Major General William H. Carter was commander of the "Mobile Army Division" (formerly called the "Maneuver Division"). Nichols told Marshall that his name was on a list that the War Department had prepared, at the Senate's insistence, of officers with considerable detached service and little troop duty. Although "the intimation was very strong that it would be very doubtful," Nichols thought both Wood and Carter "disposed . . . to do anything that they can for us. . . . I want you to know that the board [of Visitors, V.M.I.] has applied for your services here, and if we can't secure you it is not our fault. I shall send in a list of officers in the order of our preference, and your name will head the list. Both Gens. Carter and Wood know of you, and spoke of you in the highest terms." (Nichols to Marshall, January 31, 1912, VMI/RG 2.)

2. The congressional resolutions were written into law in the army appropriation bill for 1913, approved August 24, 1912, and published by the War Department as General Orders, No. 32, September 18, 1912. The law provided that, in peacetime, any army officer below the rank of major who had not been "actually present for duty for at least two of the last preceding six years" with troops of his branch, would not be permitted to remain detached for any duty. Moreover, any superior officer who permitted such detached duty forfeited from his own pay the pay and allowances due the detached officer. This law quickly became known as the "Manchu law." Many officers were pleased with this "revolution." One cavalryman wrote: "What is a Manchu in our service? He may be described as an officer with a penchant for revolving chair work and an aversion for troop duty, and who in pursuance of that policy rarely does any actual troop duty. The first orders for the eviction of the Manchus from Washington was synchronous with the revolution expelling the then reigning family from the throne of what is now the newest republic [China]. Hence, the designation 'Manchu.' " (H.R.H. [Captain Howard R. Hickok, Fifteenth Cavalry, one of Marshall's classmates at the Staff College in 1907–8], "The Manchus," *Journal of the United States Cavalry Association* 23[January 1913]: 697.)

3. The War Department rejected the Institute's request because of Marshall's "excessive detached service of which he has had 5½ years out of the past six and for which he is now under orders to return to duty with his arm." (TAG to Nichols, March 21, 1912, VMI/Alumni File.)

REPORT TO THE CHIEF, DIVISION   [April (?), 1912]
OF MILITIA AFFAIRS[1]   [Boston, Massachusetts]

. . . *Camp and Field Duty:* During this period, most of the infantry organizations had a two weeks tour of duty in connection with the strike at Lawrence, Massachusetts. The inspector-instructor was frequently present for one to three days at a time, during which period he inspected most of the organizations for the Federal inspection (not counting property). Owing to the strenuous nature of the duty performed, it was not possible to give much personal instruction to companies, and it was not even found practicable to utilize the sergeant-instructors for this purpose. . . .

Strike Duty: During a period of eleven weeks, from three to twenty-one companies of infantry were on duty at Lawrence, Massachusetts, in connection with the strike.[2] During the early part of this period, when the strikers were allowed to parade by the thousands, the troops were confronted by many serious situations, and the discipline, control of the men, etc., at such times was excellent. Throughout the period the troops performed their duties in an exceedingly businesslike and methodical fashion, and as a result their prestige in the state is greatly improved.

The non-commissioned officers and privates received a good deal of instruction in guard duty, patrolling, care of the rifle, and company drills during this period. . . .

NA/RG 168 (Document File)

1. The original of Marshall's first quarter report is not in the NA/RG 168 files. This version is taken from an undated memo ("Extracts from Reports of Inspector-Instructors," probably spring, 1912) by Brigadier General R. K. Evans, Chief, Division of Militia Affairs. Approximately one-third of the portion Evans quoted is printed here.

2. The militia was first called to Lawrence on January 15. The strike was essentially over on March 12, when the strikers voted to accept new contracts. The last militia troops left on March 25.

I N LATE April Marshall received a list of six officers' camps to which he was assigned in June and July. On May 3 he left Boston for the first, at St. Augustine, Florida, May 6–10. After Florida, he expected to attend camps at Raleigh, North Carolina; Winchester, Virginia; Mt. Gretna, Pennsylvania; New Haven, Connecticut; and West Newbury, Massachusetts, before returning to his station in Boston. (TAG to Marshall, April 22, 1912, NA/RG 393 [Eastern Division, AG].)

On May 9 Marshall was surprised to receive a telegram ordering him to report to Governors Island instead of Raleigh. (Marshall to the Adjutant General, Eastern Division, May 9, 1912, ibid.) He was assigned to temporary duty assisting Brigadier General Tasker H. Bliss, commander of the Eastern Division, in planning and running the Connecticut Maneuver Campaign scheduled for August 10–20.

The scenario Marshall had to develop was that of a surprise invasion by 100,000 troops of a European power landing in Connecticut and marching on New York City. A total of 17,331 officers and men were to participate, including 2,324 Regular and 15,007 National Guard troops. New England (i.e., Massachusetts, Connecticut, Maine, and Vermont) would attack troops from New York and New Jersey; Regular Army troops would fight on both sides. (*Report of Brigadier General Tasker H. Bliss,* NA/RG 94 [Militia].)

Marshall recalled that he had to "develop the maneuver and everything connected with it and still was tied down to the necessity of having very short marches—. . . four miles a day I think was the first march. Even that took the blisters on all the feet. But it made it very hard to get a tactical problem that was logical with these restrictions in distances. But that was the way it had to be done. . . . Because you can't take a man from behind the counter in a store and put him in heavy marching shoes the next day and expect him to be able to trudge about the country without just taking all the hide off his feet.'' (Interview, April 4, 1957.)

As the final battle approached, a journalist commented: "That weary looking young gentleman with a single bar on his shoulder strap over there by the umpire's car is Lieut. G. C. Marshall, the busiest man on the field. May 10 last he was especially detailed to work out this entire campaign; the most effective and satisfactory military movement ever held in this country in time of peace is the child of his brain. Next Monday he will get his first real night's sleep in weeks." (New York *World,* August 17, 1912.) ★

FROM BRIGADIER GENERAL TASKER H. BLISS   August 22, 1912
                                                          Governors Island, New York

Sir:– With reference to the Connecticut Maneuver Campaign of 1912, just ended, it is recognized that a very great measure of the success of the maneuvers is due to the skillful manner in which you planned the various situations of the campaign.

I wish to thank you personally and officially for your efficient services and to express the belief that such ability as you have shown in this task will surely result in high honor to yourself and to the military profession.   Very respectfully.

NA/RG 94 (Document File)

D ESPITE General Bliss's efforts to retain Marshall on his staff for the several months it would take to complete the maneuver report, Marshall was ordered to proceed to his new regiment. Assigned to the Third Battalion, Fourth Infantry, then stationed at Fort Logan H. Roots, near Little Rock, Arkansas, Marshall reported to the post commander, Lieutenant Colonel Elmore F. Taggart (U.S.M.A., 1883), on September 4, and was sent to Company M, Captain Fine W. Smith (U.S.M.A., 1895) commanding.

In December, Captain Smith was ordered to New York City for recruiting duty. Command of the company fell to Marshall, who held this position from December 23, 1912, until June 7, 1913, except for a week in March when he was sick in the hospital. During this time, the company made two major changes of station. In February, 1913, the battalion was ordered to Fort Snelling, just south of St. Paul, Minnesota. Only ten days after arriving on February 14, the battalion was suddenly ordered to Fort Crockett, near Galveston, Texas, to join the newly formed Second Division under Major General William H. Carter. This concentration of 11,450 men was prompted by the growing tension along the southern border resulting from fighting in Mexico following General Victoriano Huerta's coup.

On February 28, Marshall and Company M arrived at Fort Crockett after a four-day train trip. There they remained, except for two brief marches, until Marshall left for the Philippine Islands on June 22. (NA/RG 94 [Regimental Returns, Fourth Infantry].) ★

TO THE ADJUTANT GENERAL   April 10, 1913
                                                         Fort Crockett, Texas

Request for assignment to foreign service.

1. In view of the fact that I am now within a very few numbers of the top of the foreign service roster, I request foreign service as soon as possible, in the following order of preference:

    1. Hawaii.
    2. Alaska.
    3. China.
    4. Panama.
    5. Philippines.

2. While I understand, unofficially, that there is a ruling that officers who are near the top of the foreign service roster, will only be assigned to Philippine regiments, I request consideration of the following statement of the unusual conditions in my case which makes it of the greatest importance to me to avoid service in the Philippines during the next five years— My wife is suffering from a very serious organic lesion of the heart. She has been forbidden by all the specialists she has consulted, to attempt to live in the climate of the Philippines. She could go to Alaska, Hawaii, China or Panama (the last named place because it is but a short trip from the U.S.)

I have been separated from my wife during one Philippine tour, and I am naturally very anxious to avoid another, for three years, in the immediate future.

3. In case the foregoing application is granted, I request that I be ordered to my new station via Fort Snelling in order to pack up my household goods for shipment or storage.

4. This letter has been read and approved by my regimental commander, and, in view of its personal nature, I received his permission to forward it direct.

                                                                G. C. Marshall, Jr.

[1st Indorsement: Major Francis J. Koester, Adjutant General,
April 15, 1913.]

1. Under the rules established by the Secretary of War governing details to foreign service, requests for such service, except in the Philippine Islands, cannot be considered.

2. When Lieutenant Marshall reaches the head of the roster, he must be sent to duty wherever the first vacancy occurs,—whether the Philippines, Hawaii or Panama.

[2nd Indorsement: Marshall to TAG, May 5, 1913; H.]

1. Returned, requesting that the within letter be considered as an application for immediate service in the Philippine Islands, which was the intent of the letter in case other foreign service could not be considered.

2. Assignment to the 15th Infantry is preferred. . . .

G. C. Marshall, Jr.

NA/RG 94 (Document File); T

To Major General Edward W. Nichols   July 4, 1913
San Francisco, California

My dear General Nichols– I sent you a very hurried telegram from Galveston acknowledging your letter regarding my detail to the Institute and explaining the impossibility of my being given such a detail before the fall of 1914.[1]

I should have written to you in reply to your letter before this, but I have been very busy in making all the preparations for a long journey and covering the first lap.

Mrs. Marshall and myself sail for Manila at noon tomorrow on the Army Transport "Logan". We should arrive at Honolulu in about a week, at Guam two weeks later and at Manila August 5th.

I have been assigned to the 13th Infantry, which is stationed in Manila. I am now paying the penalty for having had too many good things during the past seven years—six years of various detached service away from troops and no foreign service in nine and one half years.

However I should soon come back from the Islands with a clean slate on all counts. I made personal application for this foreign service I am now starting on—but I knew it was soon to come in any event.

I seem fated as regards a detail to the Institute, but the fact that you consider me a desirable person for the detail is the source of great satisfaction to me.

Mrs. Marshall joins me in warmest regards to Mrs. Nichols and yourself. Very respectfully yours,

G. C. Marshall, Jr.

VMI/Alumni File; H

1. Nichols's letter of June 5 offered Marshall the position of professor of military science. "It is my idea to have the professor of military science connected directly with me as post adjutant and as military adviser. He will, of course, teach the military branches. The position will be somewhat in the nature of an inspector-instructor, the duties of which office you are familiar with from your experience in Massachusetts." The position paid $800 per year, which would be added to his army salary. (Nichols to Marshall, June 5, 1913, VMI/RG 2.) In his telegram of June 16, Marshall stated that he would not be eligible for detached service until October, 1914.

MARSHALL was struck by the changes that had taken place in the Philippines since his previous tour in 1902-3. "The greatest difference of all was the fact that under a very fine road policy, when they built these macadam roads and had men to tend them and sweep the macadam and rocks and powder dust back into all the places where the water would accumulate, the Philippines had a better road system at that time, so far as extensiveness and being connected up, than in most places I knew in the United States. Living conditions were, of course, very much better because you had good houses and very good servants. And you had a very good general commissary to bring things out so that you got good things to eat and sufficient fresh things to eat. So it was a tremendous improvement over the Philippines of the old days when maybe you got it and maybe you didn't." (Interview, April 4, 1957.)

Sometime during 1914, Marshall purchased a new Model-T Ford from his Fort Leavenworth colleague Major Clarence O. Sherrill of the Corps of Engineers. This facilitated Marshall's study of the military campaigns during the Philippine Insurrection. "I got very much interested in visiting the battlefields," he said later. (Ibid.)

Marshall had been somewhat "ashamed" of his lack of knowledge concerning the Philippine Insurrection. When the War Department offered free copies of its voluminous reports on the Insurrection, Marshall took all he could get. When he returned to the Islands in 1913, he began to study the books seriously. "I went through them all in great detail," he recalled. He was particularly struck by the reactions of the troops and their officers to the problems they faced in a guerrilla war in the jungle, noting the possibilities for their actions getting "out of hand when they are on their own in critical situations." Furthermore, he was interested in the conflicts between the civilian government then being established and the soldiers who had suffered during the Insurrection. It was, he later observed, "all together a regrettable situation" in which both sides were wrong. (Interview, March 13, 1957.)

A few weeks after he arrived in Manila, planning began for a major training exercise to be held early in 1914. Marshall was appointed adjutant for the "White Force" (also called "Detachment No. 1") that was to act as the invader who, having landed at Batangas (about 115 kilometers south of Manila), would attempt to capture the Philippine capital. This provided Marshall some relief from the routine of garrison duty with Company F, Thirteenth Infantry, at Fort McKinley.

Planning for the exercise continued into early January, 1914. The White Force of 4,842 officers and men was to face the defending "Brown Force" (or "Detachment No. 2") of 3,245. It had been customary in arranging such maneuvers to furnish detailed information concerning the starting date, concentration points, and so on, to the troops and supply departments thirty to ninety days beforehand. But General Bell, the Philippine Department commander, kept the exact date secret. Rumors put the starting date about February 15. (Colonel James B. Erwin [chief umpire] to Bell, March 20, 1914, NA/RG 165 [War College Division].)

Shortly after eight o'clock on the morning of January 22, a surprised Marshall was called away from a company skirmish-run to report to headquarters in his "soaking-wet flannel shirt." (Interview, April 4, 1957.) Having received their maneuver instructions, Colonel William C. Buttler (U.S.M.A., 1876), Twenty-fourth Infantry, White Force commander, and his staff went to Marshall's quarters to eat lunch and begin their preparations.

Marshall, whose duty was to issue all the detailed orders to the various units, recalled that he spent most of the luncheon "on the telephone mobilizing this outfit and arranging for it to move to Batangas. And it came from all sorts of places in northern Luzon and they had to move by various ships and all, and I had to get the whole thing together."

"I was having a great deal of trouble. I didn't realize the full reason for the trouble, because I was mobilizing the larger detachment of the two. I was just a lieutenant, and on the other side two full colonels were at the top, and they were mobilizing their detachments and getting all the preference on account of their rank. So I was having a very hard time. I finally had to go in and see the quartermaster and tell him I had to get this, and finally he said I didn't have approval to see him. I said I came in because it was the only way I could get in. I had to get this outfit underway, and I had to have stalls on the boats for some eighteen hundred horses before we could get that part of the command out. Well, he said he couldn't talk to me then. I said I am sorry, but we've got to have an understanding. If you are not going to deal with me except as a lieutenant, I will communicate with General Bell, who is in the southern provinces, and find out what he wants me to do. Well, of course, then he wilted and right away gave me a reasonable break as to what I should get. But I was always up against the fact that I was dealing with a colonel, and my opponents were colonels, and I was just a lieutenant." (Interview, April 4, 1957.)

Captain Jens Bugge (U.S.M.A., 1895), a close friend of Marshall, despite being over six hundred files senior, and one of Marshall's former students at Fort Leavenworth, had been detailed to act as the detachment's chief of staff. But on the trip to Batangas, Bugge suddenly became ill and had to be sent back to Fort McKinley. Marshall was designated to replace Bugge, making him de facto commander of the White Force.

As Marshall recalled, "the commanding officer was found ineffective by the Inspector General who was cruising around. He was about to retire very shortly, I think, anyway, and General Bell wrote him a letter and notified him that he could either be retired immediately or he could continue through the maneuver, but he would have to leave all the commanding to be done by me. The reason they did it just that way was because the next man in rank was about as bad as he was. They told me they were going to relieve this first fellow, who was a very courtly gentleman, very nice fellow. He carried a zinc-lined suitcase with him which he worked on most of the time. He would ride in the spring wagon, and I would ride the horse. But every time we would stop, the suitcase would be opened and he would refresh himself against the Philippine heat. But when they told me they were going to . . . retire him, I objected because I knew I was going to have a much more difficult time with the other man. So the arrangement was made whereby he continued through maneuvers, but he must agree not to give me any instructions of any kind, but leave me free to act. So I had the advantage of being a first lieutenant with the largest force of troops in the Philippines, which I could command in a very extensive maneuver campaign." (Interview, April 4, 1957.)

The following are two of the documents—typical of the dozens Marshall issued from White Force headquarters during the January 25–February 4 maneuver—included in the chief umpire's report to General Bell. ★

FIELD ORDERS, NO. 1

January 25, 1914
Camp McGrath, Batangas

1. Mounted patrols of the enemy (BROWN) have been seen in the vicinity of SAN JOSE. Nothing further has been learnt of the enemy.

The greater portion of this Detachment should be concentrated at this place tonight.

2. This Detachment will remain in its present camps tonight strengthening the outpost line.

3. The Commanding Officer, 24th Infantry, will relieve the present outpost with 6 companies, 24th Infantry, by 7 P.M. tonight, establishing the outpost for the Detachment along the general line—LONGOS RIVER—PATAY—SAN PEDRO—SAN PAGA.

A detached post of one squad will be posted on IBAAN HILL, particularly charged with preventing hostile reconnaissance from that point.

The outpost positions will be intrenched.

Cavalry patrols have been posted at BALIBAC, SAN JOSE and IBAAN by the Commanding Officer, Detachment, 7th Cavalry. These patrols are under control of the Cavalry Commander, who will be consulted by the Outpost Commander as to the orders given the Cavalry patrols.

The Cavalry Commander will make no changes in the disposition of his outpost patrols without first informing the Outpost Commander.

4. Messages will reach the Detachment Commander at the Recreation Room, Camp McGRATH.

NA/RG 165 (War College Division)

To Major Henry W. Parker[1]   January 27, 1914
                                    Crossing of LIPA-BATANGAS road
                                                  and IBAAN trail

The hostile Cavalry has fallen back to SAN JOSE. Has an officers' patrol on SAN JOSE-IBAAN road. Your message to attack the BROWN Cavalry at the two bridges is therefore revoked. Instead you will select a concealed bivouac and bivouac (in advance) of our outpost line and strike the rear of any Cavalry. Rushing forward from SAN JOSE early tomorrow. Your orders for establishing the outposts of the Detachment tomorrow morning will be awaiting you at the two bridges.

NA/RG 165 (War College Division)
1. Major Parker commanded the Philippine Scouts detachment with the White Force.

O N FEBRUARY 4, the maneuver was declared ended, and Marshall was relieved as chief of staff. The maneuver's chief umpire called the exercise "by far the best that I have ever attended." The chief umpire with the White Force reported that "the orders issued from Headquarters Detachment No. 1 were excellent. In several cases they are models that show a clear grasp of the situation, and attention to every necessary point of tactics, and are so clear and definite as to be impossible to misconstrue." Moreover, despite the great handicap under which Marshall worked, the exercise had been "a severe task which he carried out successfully and for which he deserves great credit." (Colonel James B. Erwin [chief umpire] to Bell, March 20, 1914, NA/RG 165 [War College Division]; Lieutenant Colonel Clarence E. Dentler [chief White Force umpire], report included in Erwin to Bell.) ★

To Major General Edward W. Nichols   March 5, 1914
                                                    Yokohama [Japan]

My dear General Nichols— As I have heard nothing from you since your letter of last June, addressed to me at Galveston, regarding the detail as Military Instructor at the Institute, I am wondering if you could have been offended at my delay in answering. I was absent on leave from Galveston at the time your letter arrived there, and on my return I only had time to telegraph you in reply, as I left immediately for San Francisco. I believe I wrote to you from San Francisco.

Upon my arrival in Manila I was put to work on the problem of the mobile defense of the elaborate fortifications at the entrance to Manila Bay, and was made Adjutant General of the force organized for this purpose—all this in addition to the performance of my regular regimental duties. As this force consists of the bulk of the mobile organizations in the Islands—infantry, artillery (mountain), Scouts, Engineers, &c., all at war strength, it involved considerable extra work on my part. When the annual maneuvers occurred in January, I went out as Chief of Staff of the force which put to sea, landed on the beach at Batangas and Lucena and advanced on Manila (60 miles) representing an invading force hostile to the U.S.

You can gather some idea of the difficulties involved in landing, thru the surf, 1100 animals, 125 vehicles, 130,000 rations, 20 days forage, &c. However, I think we pretty convincingly licked the other side (7th Cav., 8th Cav., 8th Inf., Bn. F.A., Scouts Engrs., &c.) When the campaign was completed Gen. Bell gave me two months sick [leave] in which to regain a few lost pounds, and Mrs. Marshall and myself came up here for the cold weather.[1] I have applied for two months regular leave and we expect to go thru Korea, Manchuria (to see all the battle fields) and on down the China Coast to Hong Kong, reaching Manila about June 15th.

Both of us are feeling splendidly and enjoying every moment of the trip.

My tour out here will be completed June 15th, 1916, by which time I hope to have been promoted. We plan to return by the trans-Siberian Ry., and to spend a long time in France, as I hope to be attached to a French regiment for a year.

Mrs. Marshall joins me in warmest regards to Mrs. Nichols and yourself.   Very respectfully yours,

                                                    G. C. Marshall, Jr.

VMI/Alumni File; H

1. On February 5 Marshall entered the military hospital in Manila with an illness diagnosed as "neurasthenia, subacute." He remained hospitalized until February 15. ("Statement of medical history . . . ," May 6, 1916, NA/RG 94 [Document File].) Because of his wife's heart condition, during his tour of duty in the Philippines, Marshall had her go to Japan for about three months each year during Manila's tropical summer. (Interview, April 4, 1957.)

To Stuart B. Marshall   March 21, 1914
                                                    Yokohama [Japan]

My dear Stuart– I wrote you a short train letter on my way up here from Nagasaki, which I hope reached you all right. Tomorrow we leave for the Fujiya Hotel at Miyanoshita—a celebrated hotel in a wonderfully beautiful mountain region, with Fujiyama standing off in bold relief. We will probably stay there several weeks or a month.

On the assumption that you may be interested in the plan of the maneuvers which led up to my sick leave, I am going to give you a very brief description of them. To assist you in understanding I am enclosing a little skeleton map of the district concerned, which I tore out of one of "Cook's" guide books.

The troops in the Islands are divided into two detachments. No. 1, and the most important, is for the land defense of the coast batteries at the entrance to Manila Bay—notably Corregidor which has been made stronger than Gibraltar. I am adjutant of this Detachment or Adjutant General as they formerly termed it. Det. No. 2 is principally composed of cavalry and is to operate against the rear or line of communication of any invading force landing north or south of the entrance to the Bay—at Batangas for example.

These detachments were first organized last September and I had been working on the mobilization, concentrations, supply plans, &c., of No. 1 all Fall. The Chief of Staff of No. 1 was absent during this period big game hunting in Indo-China, so I had all his work to do—particularly as the senior officer of the Det. (its commander) was not stationed near Manila and unfortunately was incapable of assisting and they were trying to force his retirement for mental and physical disability. All my work in this matter had to be done in addition to my full regimental duties—which used up all my evenings, Sundays and holidays.

Early on the morning of Jan. 22^d I was called down to Gen. Bell's head-quarters and notified that the annual maneuvers would start that morning (no previous notice) as I was the only representative of the headquarters of Det. No 1 I was given the maneuver situation. In brief—Det. No. 1 was directed to embark immediately, put to sea and (representing an invading force hostile to the U.S.) land on the beach at Batangas and Lucena—and from there move on Manila (60 miles from Batangas). The maneuver was therefore to test out Det. No. 2 in its work in case of an actual invasion. My Det. No. 1 was to be theoretically considered concentrated on Corregidor.

Within fifteen minutes I had sent off the mobilization telegrams to most of the units. I then rushed out to McKinley, converted our house into an office and started to bring about the concentration and embarkation of the Det. at Manila, and its dispatch to Batangas. Some troops were 150 miles up country, others on the Islands at the entrance to the Bay.

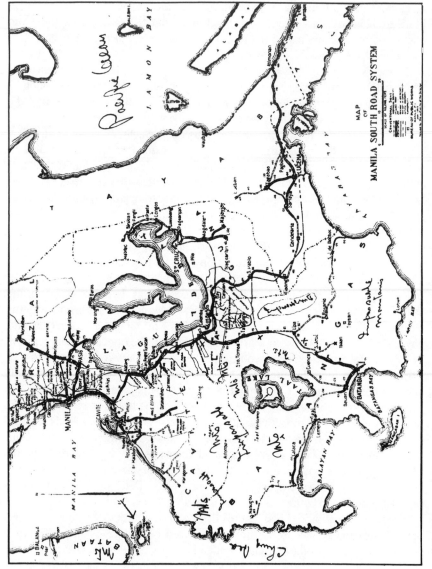

Map of the maneuver area, with Marshall's handwritten notations, included in the March 21, 1914, letter to his brother.

Stalls had to be built in the transports that were in the harbor, &c. The transport "Merritt" left that same evening with ½ a regiment, 30,000 rations, the advance ordnance depot and the Field Bakery.

The "Warren" had 300 stalls finished by mid night and sailed with that number of animals, and troops and vehicles at 10 A.M. the 23^d. I left on Gen. Bell's yacht on the night of the 24th. By the 27th the following had concentrated at Batangas:

24th Inf. (regiments out here are at war strength. This one for instance, had 1700 men, 30 vehicles, 170 animals, 2 machine guns, &c.)

13th Inf.

2^d Battalion 15th Inf.

4 battalions of Philippine Scouts.

1st Bn. 2^d Field Artillery (12 guns, 400 mules, &c.)

Troops G and H, 7th Cavalry

Co. K, Engineers (50 mtd. men, 100 dismounted men, pack train, &c.)

½ Co. F. Sig. Corps. (40 mtd men, 2 reel carts with 5 miles of ground wire each, &c.)

Field Bakery (capacity 6500 loaves of bread per day.)

Field Hospital

125,000 rations, 20 days forage for 1050 animals. There were about 100 army wagons.

You can imagine the difficulty of landing on the beach all the animals and impediments concerned, particularly when the boats could not stand in closer than ¾ miles from shore and no dock. The hostile cavalry was into our outpost line by the 25th.

As Chief of Staff (with a mere figure head as a commander) I had practically the entire burden of the thing, coupled with the difficulties connected with a first lieutenant's ordering colonels, &c., in the regular army. But it had to be done and Gen. Bell told me to hesitate at nothing in the way of precedents.

There were no restrictions on the campaign, except as to real bullets. The maneuver was continuous day and night from Jan. 22^d. There were countless small skirmishes, cavalry forays against wagon trains, outposts, &c., and three big fights—one just south of Lipa, one 6 miles north of Lipa and one near Calamba.

Det. No 1 chewed the other side up, captured two of their six cavalry squadrons, and smashed up their infantry. We reached Manila Feb. 4th.

Det. No. 2 consisted of:

22 troops in all $\Big\{$	7th Cavalry (less 2 of the 12 troops)	1st Bn. 2^d Field Artillery
	8th Cavalry	Co. Engrs.
	8th Infantry	some scouts, and the
		remainder of the trimmings.

In some of the brushes, particularly at night, the men became so intense on the thing that arms, ribs, heads, &c., were broken in cavalry charges, &c.

When the troops reached Manila I was exhausted from my months of overwork, coupled with this final strain, so I let down when the thing was over and was put on sick report and Gen. Bell had them give me two months sick leave in Japan.

He leaves in April to command the troops in Texas, and he told me the instant the orders came to go into Mexico he would cable or telegraph the War Department to have me on his staff. So I hope this will obviate the necessity of trying to use "pull" for this purpose.[1]

Most of what I have told you, you must treat as really confidential for two reasons—first because all plans for the defense of the Islands are most secret, and second because a criticism by me of my superior would ruin me if made public.

Between you and myself, I had an opportunity that rarely ever comes to a Colonel, and has never been heard of before being given to anyone below that rank, except Gen. Pershing—but he was then 42 years old and a senior Captain. I had absolute command and control of the Detachment, appointed even the adjutant and aides. The Colonel was ignored by Gen. Bell and his Chief Umpire and not even consulted. His retirement has been ordered. But they wouldn't relieve him from supposed command during the maneuvers as they did not want a more assertive Colonel to fall into command and relieve me of actual control. I trust that you will read this to yourself, tear it up and disabuse your mind of the idea that I am rather a remarkable braggart. I don't tell you things about myself—successes—but this one was rather unique and unheard of during peace times in our conservative army and I thought should prove an exception to my usual rule.

I weigh 170 now and feel splendidly. Lily has also gained a number of lbs. up here and looks very well. We are having such an enjoyable time. I wish you could have a share in it with Florence and Stuart, Jr.

I am still waiting to hear from my application for two months regular leave, before completing my arrangements for seeing Korea and the Ruso-Jap battle fields.

I hope Mother is feeling better now.

Lily joins me in much love to you all,   Your affectionate brother,

George

GCMRL/S. B. Marshall Papers; H

1. The Second Division had been concentrated along the Texas-Mexico border to guard against border violence as the revolutionary groups in Mexico struggled for power. Mexican-American relations had seriously deteriorated during 1913 and 1914. United States President Woodrow Wilson refused to extend diplomatic recognition to Mexican President Victoriano Huerta's government, which Wilson considered illegal.

REPORT TO THE ADJUTANT GENERAL   June 15, 1914
                                                    Fort McKinley, Philippine Islands

Report of visit to Manchurian battlefields,
with recommendations.

1. I am making the following report in compliance with Par. 62, A. R., 1913,[1] and with the special object of pointing out the material professional advantages to be derived from a visit to the Manchurian battlefields, the relatively small expense of such a trip, the great desirability of formally ordering large parties of our officers to make this tour as illustrated by the practice of the English Army in this respect, and the most desirable route to be travelled.

2. On April 1, 1914 I mailed to our Military Attache in Tokio, an itinerary of the trip I desired to make, giving hour of arrival and departure at each place, portions of each battlefield I desired to see, etc., I requested that such assistance be secured for me from the Japanese War Office as practicable. On April 14, 1914, the War Office notified Colonel Irons that they had arranged for assistance to be given me in securing guides, hiring horses, etc., but that it was impracticable to furnish me a non-commissioned officer at each place and there were too few army horses in the district to provide me with a mount.[2] However, as will be seen later, I was furnished an army mount at each place, except Port Arthur where they provided a two horse carriage for me, and a commissioned officer accompanied me on my daily trips.

3. My original itinerary contemplated the following trip: . . .

4. Captain M. C. Kerth, 15th Infantry, Tientsin, China had cabled me to arrange for this same trip for him, he to meet me at Dairen. However, when I arrived at Dairen I found a telegram from him stating that his Colonel had cancelled his leave owing to the Mexican crisis.

5. I purchased a first class circular tour ticket from Kobe, Japan, to Moji by rail, thence by boat to Dairen; thence by rail through Telissu, Liao-yang, Mukden and Antung to Fusan, Korea; thence by express boat to Moji or Shimonoseki; and thence by rail to starting point—Kobe. The ticket cost $41.50 gold, not including about $12.50 for berths and de luxe express fares. It did include meals and berth on each boat on which the service was very good. The trains throughout, especially in Manchuria and Korea are splendidly equipped and served. This same ticket can be purchased so as to start and finish the trip at Tokio, Yokohama, Nagoya, Kyoto, Osaka and Shimonoseki—the difference in fare for the varying distances being very slight. Ticket is good for 60 days. You can also arrange to go from Kobe to Moji or the reverse by boat.

6. I landed at Dairen at 5:30 a. m., April 28, 1914, and was met at the dock by

a porter from the Yemato (Government) Hotel, who informed me that the unexpected hour of the arrival of my boat had prevented the proper official from meeting me, but that a room was engaged for me at the Hotel. At 7:00 a. m. Dr. Uyeda, Secretary to the President of the South Manchurian Railroad, (Government affair,) called upon me and submitted a schedule of trains, including passenger and goods trains, for my trip. The news of the Mexican crisis was so disturbing that I felt called upon to shorten my trip, and Dr. Ueyda assured me that he could arrange for any changes that I cared to make by telegraphing to the army and railroad officials at each point. I therefor decided to shorten my stays at Port Arthur, Liao-yang and Mukden by one day each, and to omit the stops at Telissu as no express would be going through there on the day I would pass and there was no place for me to spend the night.

7. Having rearranged my schedule I made the following trip:-

April 28, 1914: Left Darien at 9:45 a. m., arriving at Chin Chou, (Nanshan station) about 11:00 a. m. Visited battlefield accompanied by an officer of the civil administration, returning to Darien via goods train at 4:00 p. m. Station master at Chin Chou entertained me with tea and many attentions. He had been notified to expect me and see that my visit was a success. The same was the case with each train master. The Yamato Hotel provided me with a lunch or tiffin for this trip.

April 29, 1914: Left Darien at 7:55 a. m., arriving at Port Arthur at 9:20 a. m., I was met at the train by Lieutenant Fujita, 30th Infantry, and conducted to the Staff Headquarters where I called upon the Governor General, General Baron Fukushima and had tea. General Fykushima was most cordial, talking to me for more than a half hour, and incidentally reading me his special bulletin of Mexican despatches.

Lieut. Fujita then took me to 203 Metre Hill, Akasayama, 174 Metre Hill and Fort Itzushan. We used a carriage hired by the Staff Office. After tiffin we visited the War Museum, Charnel Shrine and top of Battle Monument on Quail Hill, looked over the harbor and returned to the Hotel, (Government) at 5:30 p. m.

That evening a representative of Baron Fukushima called upon me expressing regrets that the Imperial mourning forbade my being entertained at dinner.

April 30, 1914: Lieut. Fujita called for me at 7:15 a. m., and we drove to Fort Sungshushan and visited each fort and battery in turn around to the east coast. We had carried our tiffin out and ate it in the ditch of North Fort. We returned to the Yamato Hotel at 5:45 p. m.

Lieut. Fujita spoke English and had made a special study of the fighting around the most important forts. He was very companionable, instructive and made my stay at Port Arthur unusually interesting and pleasant. Owing to his night language classes he could not accept an invitation to dine with me.

May 1, 1914: Left Port Arthur at 6:55 a. m. Lieut. Fujita was at the train to see me off. Arrived at Darien at 8:30 a. m., breakfasting at the hotel and left one hour later for Telissu and Liao-yang, taking a tiffin box from the hotel.

Mr Mullet-Merrick, English adviser to the President of the South Manchurian Railroad did much to make my stay in Darien pleasant, and accompanied me to the train on this morning. The American consul was also very considerate.

The train master took special pains to make my trip north comfortable and interesting. He had tea served to me at amusingly frequent intervals and pointed out many important lines of the Telissu battlefield.

I arrived at Liao-Yang at 6:30 p. m., and was met at the station by Lieutenant General Akiyama's Chinese and English Interpreter—an officer. we immediately decided upon the next days trip and I proceeded to the Ryoto Hotel, a Japaneese Inn, where I had to furnish my own blankets and pillow and was served plain foreign food. The proprietor had been notified to expect me and see that I was made comfortable.

May 2, 1914: Left at 6:15 a. m., on Yentai coal train with Interpreter Shimidzi, dropping off train at a siding about 18 miles from Liao-yang (On this same caboose were all the officers and non-commissioned officers of a company on their way out in the country for a day of field firing. They put their paraphenalia in an empty gondola car.) We walked across fields and through villages nearly six miles to Manjuyama and Hill 131, eating our tiffin lunch on Manjuyama. In the afternoon we walked 12 miles to the Yentai mines and had a Japanese bath there and took a coal train for Liao-yang.

Upon my return to the inn I found that General Akiyama had sent me a present of several bottles of wine. I called upon him in General Kuropatkin's old quarters, and was served tea, cakes and champagne and had a most interesting talk with the General about the cavalry operations during the Mukden campaign.

That night I dined with Dr. Alex MacDonald Westwater, an English missionary, who has lived in Liao-yang for 33 years. He was most entertaining regarding his experiences during the war and those of the various military observers and war corespondents who had stayed with him.

May 3, 1914. General Akiyama provided me with the horse of Lieut. General Morikawa and with the interpreter on a machine gun horse. We started off at 7:30 a. m. for Shoushan pu and the Tassu Brook positions, carrying our tiffin with us. We returned to the hotel at 5:40 p. m., having visited three redoubts or forts of the inner line on our way out and in.

I left at 6;30 p. m., arriving at Mukden at 7:50 p. m. There I found Major Shirai, Captain Hirano and Lieutenant Takahaski, of the 56th Inf., at the train to meet me and accompany me to the Yamato Hotel, (Government) We immediately arranged for the next day's trip and they then left.

May 4, 1914: At 7:15 a. m. Capt. Hirano and Lieut. Takahashi called for me at the hotel with an officer's mount and a mounted orderly. We rode 6 miles west of the railroad to the scene of the desperate night attack at Yukuantun, and from there followed the battle line north and north east for 17 miles. We inspected the scene of the celebrated night attack by Hirano's former regiment, 28th, at the north west corner of the Pei-lie Forest or Royal Hunting Park, rode through the forrest to the North Tomb, followed along the scene of the confused fighting across the Simintun high road, and finally rode through the walled city of Mukden, and reached the hotel at 6:00 p. m. (A 32 mile ride.)

That night Major Shirai, Capt. Hirano and Lieut. Takahashi dined with me and accompanied me to my train when I left for Korea after midnight.

May 5, 1914. I arrived at Antung on the Yalu River at 8:30 a. m., having had a hurried view of Hamatan. I had a half hour in which to gather an idea of the terrain involved in the Battle of the Yalu. I then continued on to Seoul, Korea.

8. Throughout the trip I was continuously the recipient of many courtesies. All train masters, station masters and hotel proprietors with whom I came in contact seemed to have been advised to expect me and make an effort to smooth the way. The officers were invariably pleasant and interesting and made an excellent pretense of enjoying their day's excursions with me. They talked freely, had large scale special maps of local incidents in the fighting and gave me many thrilling descriptions of the troop leading of regiments, battalions and companies.

I was told that as far as they knew I had seen more of the Mukden Battlefield than any foreign officer who had visited it during their stay in Manchuria. Interpreter Shidmidzi had been in the Liao-yang fight and Capt. Hirano had been badly wounded on the top of 293 Metre Hill in the November 30th assaults. I met many officers on the trains and had interesting conversations with them. At Liao-yang at the scene of Major Tashibano's (?) death, just west of Shoushan pu, I met 11 officers of the 58th Infantry lecturing to their non-commissioned officers on the details of the heroic death of Tashibano.—who has been deified as one of their few war gods. In this connection I learned the interesting fact that an heroic death does not make a great hero for the Japaneese unless the previous life of the man has been one of complete and austere dedication to duty. In speaking of this Major's life they remarked, among many other things, that he always had gone to his daily duties at 4:00 a. m. and daily engaged in bayonet combat with his men.

9. Some years ago I made a staff ride over a number of the battlefields of the Civil War, but in spite of that experience I was astonished at the amount of valuable professional knowledge I apparently acquired on this recent trip.

While a student of the Army School of the Line and the Staff College and later when I was instructor there I had made a serious study of the events of the Russian-Japaneese War. Since then I have continued my studies of the War with considerable energy. In preparation for this trip I made special studies of the battlefields I was to visit, and during the trip I devoted every free hour on the trains, boats and at the hotels to study. Yet I found that a few hours on the actual field apparently did more to instruct me in the details of troop leading and the larger phases of tactics than years of theoretical study. I came away with a new idea of those fights and entirely different ideas as to the proper methods to follow in peace training. In this connection I had dozens of opportunities to watch the Japanese troops at work, and the officers I went about with told me of changes they had made in their system of training since the war—and why they had made them.

I was particularly impressed with the following things.

(a) *Bayonet Combat:* The battlefields in Manchuria demonstrate the certainty of the bayonet being called upon to decide the issue at the crucial points in every large battle. As a result I saw the Japaneese Infantry working at bayonet combat at all hours of the day from 7:30 a. m. until 5:00 p. m., We have bayonet *fencing.* They have *bayonet* combat. Where our men, as a natural result of the spirit of the new manual, spar and dance about with efforts to make clever feints and thrusts, the Japaneese rush at each other and one opponent is more than likely to land violently on his back. They do not rush in a blind bull like manner—it is done with great skill and involves parries, etc.—but the entire spirit of their instruction involves first of all the utmost use of the momentum of the man. I do not think that THE FEATURES of our complicated attack and defense, without great stress being laid on the momentum of the man as the most important feature of the system, will succeed for one instant on the parapet in battle.

(b) *Night Attacks:* It was plain at Liao-yang and doubly so at Mukden that almost every important point in a great battle must be assaulted at night if success is to be hoped for. I had studied over the night attacks many times, but not until I actually visited the ground and had the details of the local troop leading of companies, battalions and regiments explained did I really absorb or comprehend the true necessities in this sort of work. We have orders requiring night exercises, but with the sole exception of two night exercises I heard of being conducted by a brigade at Texas City, I have never participated in or learned of a night exercise being conducted in our army along the lines that would of necessity have to be followed in delivering a night attack in a large battle. We have night marches, outposts, partial deployments, etc., but we do not practice the formations that seem to be necessary in order to initiate and carry home a night assault, nor do we familiarize our officers and men with the devices utilized at such times—such as phosphorescent compasses, magnesium fire balls, star rocketts, etc. To attempt to utilize formations and devices for the first time on the battlefield and in darkness will lead to but one result according to all studies in psychology of warfare—that is total failure, if not route and panic.

(c) *Hand grenades:* Because of the decisive results obtained by the constant use of hand grenades in the Russian-Japaneese War, the soldiers of the Japaneese infantry are very carefully trained in the different methods of throwing hand grenades. The defense of Corregidor against landing parties or of any fortifications that may be built on Mariveles Mountain, would inevitably involve the promiscuous use of hand grenades by both attackers and defenders. I doubt if there is a private in the ranks of the infantry forming the mobile defensive force for Corregidor who has ever heard of a hand grenade. A little training along this line would probably prove much more valuable than the constant training received in individual signalling.

10. English Army Officers from Hongkong, Indian and other Far East garrisons frequently visit the battlefields in Manchuria. At intervals they have sent large parties of officers on such trips, just as our War College and Staff College classes go over Civil War Battlefields. As some high ranking officer is in charge, usually a brigade general, the Japaneese officials do much to assist in making an instructive success of these trips, that they could not afford to do for the unofficial visits of one or two officers, as in my case.

I inquired particularly about the visit of one party of thirty English officers sent out from India by General Lord Kitchener. A Brigade General was in charge and one officer who had been an observer during the war and spoke Japaneese—the Captain Vincent so frequently mentioned by General Sir Ian Hamilton in his book—accompanied the party to assist in the instruction and promote harmonious relations with the Japaneese. Cooks, tents and a mess outfit were brought to Manchuria, one officer acting as Quartermaster of the expedition. They stayed at the Yamato (Government) Hotels at Darien and Port Arthur and camped at other points. They were entertained everywhere by the Japaneese Generals in command. Japaneese General Staff Officers were specially detailed to accompany the party and lecture on the various fights at each point visited in the field, and usually an officer who had actually participated in the local combat being studied was sent along to give more color to the descriptions.

The party visited Nanshan, Port Arthur, Telissu, several of the smaller battlefields which occured between Telissu or Takushan and Liao-yang. From the latter place they rode east and south east over the route of General Kuroki's advance from the Yalu, touching especially on the forcing of the Motieling Pass.

The Japaneese could not furnish horses for so large a party, but they gave the necessary assistance in arranging for the hire of ponies, mules and carts. Incidentally the party failed to advise the local Chineese officials east of Mukden and Liao-yang of their proposed movements, and they were fired on by Chineese huntz hutzies (?) east of Motieling.

11. The location of so many of our officers in the Philippines and China, within easy access of Manchuria, the monthly trips of the transports to Nagasaki, and the frequent trips of the "Warren" to China, make it possible to give a great many *selected* officers the great professional advantage of studying the battlefields of the war upon which the tactics of the immediate future are bound to be based. Even if the government will not permit the expenses of such an expedition to be paid out of federal funds, the officers need not be placed upon a leave status; they can be sent on transports with the proper tentage, and the arrangements with the Japaneese War Office can be made by the proper authorities.

12. As every foreigner's movements in Manchuria are closely watched by Japaneese officials and as all preliminary arrangements are made and carried out

with rigid exactness, it is essential in planning such a trip to notify the War Office several months in advance, giving a most detailed itinerary of the trip it is desired to make, and then to comply rigidly with the approved itinerary. Colonel Irons informed me that some of our officers had made request to the Japaneese War Office for certain courtesies and then failed to appear at the appointed place. Such actions react in a most unfortunate manner on individuals or parties who follow later, and constitute to the Japaneese an unexplainable and unpardonable breach of etiquette.

13. The last week of April and the first part of May afford about the best season for visiting Manchuria. At that time the temperature is pleasant there is little or no rain and a minimum of the frequent and trying dust and wind storms. The English Officers took entirely too much baggage, according to the accounts I heard.

An officer should not be favored with a specially arranged visit to Manchuria unless he can give assurance that he has studied the campaign seriously—which means eight or ten months study at the least. In organizing a large party I consider that officers should be allowed to compete in an examination of their knowledge of those portions of the campaign which are to be visited. It is a great waste of time to visit those battlefields if one has merely read over the accounts several times.

The British General staff account of the war is the best authority to study—more recent and complete than the German General Staff account. Other good books to study in preparation: General Sir Ian Hamilton's Staff Officers' Scrap Book; Colonel Tetrahof, (?) 5th Siberian Regiment, account of Nanshan and Port Arthur, (he had charge on 203 Metre Hill.) Human Bullets by Lieutenant Sakurai (gives the best idea of the spirit of the troops at Port Arthur;) the reports of our military observers, particularly Major Kuhn's on Port Arthur and Captain March's description of Manjuyama at Liao-yang; our translation of the Russian study of the effects of the siege of Port Arthur on fortifications.[3]

14. In closing I wish to report again on the extreme courtesy and kindness of the Japanese army and railroad officials who assisted me during my visit in South Manchuria.

[1st Indorsement: Captain Ezekiel J. Williams, Company F,
June 15, 1914.]

. . .3. In the case of this officer attention is invited to the special excellence of the above report, and to the further fact that he bore the expense of the trip out of his own private funds and devoted time out of his ordinary leave to the making of the study and securing of the information on which it is based.

[2nd Indorsement: Colonel George W. McIver, Thirteenth Infantry,
June 19, 1914.]

1. Forwarded concurring in remarks contained in 1st indorsement.

2. Referring to paragraph 9(c) of the report the importance of grenades as one

of the elements of the defense of Corregidor has not been entirely overlooked as may be seen from the fact that an expenditure of rifle and hand grenades is allowed for the two (2) infantry regiments assigned to duty on Corregidor and in case of the 13th Infantry at least some instruction in the use of these missiles was given in both the 1913 and 1914 maneuvers on Corregidor. The allowance at present inadequate, should be made sufficient for the instruction of a complete squad in each infantry company of the Corregidor garrison.

3. The professional interest of this report is so great that Lieutenant Marshall has been directed to prepare a lecture on the subject of his visit to the Manchurian battle fields for delivery to the assembled officers of the 13th Infantry, the report to be expanded into lecture length through the addition of details and observations of possible interest not included in the report, and through the amplification of paragraph 9 of the report with the idea of showing more in detail how our own methods of infantry training may be improved upon.

[3rd Indorsement: Brigadier General Eli D. Hoyle, Fort McKinley, June 20, 1914.]

1. This interesting report is such as might have been expected from Lieutenant Marshall, who has made, and is making, a serious study of tactics and strategy. Specially endowed by nature he avails himself of every opportunity for professional improvement, and with marked success. The points he emphasizes, under (a), (b), and (c) . . . are worthy of serious consideration.

2. I will arrange for the attendance of all the officers of the post at the lecture to be delivered by Lieutenant Marshall, referred to in paragraph 3, 2^d indorsement.

GCMRL/M. M. Singer Papers; T

1. This regulation states: "An officer of the Army visiting foreign countries, whether on duty or leave, will avail himself of all proper opportunities to obtain military information, especially such as pertains to his branch of the service. He will report the results of his observations to The Adjutant General of the Army on his return to duty, or sooner if practicable."

2. Colonel James A. Irons (U.S.M.A., 1879) was military attache in Tokyo.

3. The books cited are: Ian Hamilton, *A Staff-Officer's Scrap Book during the Russo-Japanese War*, 2 vols. (London, 1905–7); Nikolai A. Tretiokov, *My Experiences at Nan Shan and Port Arthur with the Fifth East Siberian Rifles* (London, 1911); Tadayoshi Sakurai, *Human Bullets, A Soldier's Story of Port Arthur* (Boston, 1907); U.S., War Department, General Staff, *Reports of Military Observers Attached to the Armies in Manchuria during the Russo-Japanese War*, 5 vols. (Washington, 1906–7); A. von Schwartz, *Influence of the Experience of the Siege of Port Arthur upon the Construction of Modern Fortresses*, Military Information Division Study No. 12 (Washington, 1908).

O N JUNE 5, 1914, Marshall returned to garrison duty at Fort McKinley with Company F. On his year-end efficiency report, his company commander, Captain Williams, wrote of Marshall: "This officer, for his years of service, age and rank, is one of the most completely equipped for military service it has been my lot to observe. He has excellent tactical sense, is keen of perception, prompt to decide and act, attentive to duty, intelligent, a thorough gentleman, devoted to his profession, and quick to take advantage of opportunities for improvement. His bearing is that of a military man and he is temperate. Should the exigencies of active service place him in exalted command I would be glad to serve under him." (December 31, 1914, NA/RG 94 [Document File].)

On February 25, 1915, Marshall was transferred to Company M, Thirteenth Infantry, and appointed an aide-de-camp by the new commander of Fort McKinley, Brigadier General Hunter Liggett. "General Liggett made me his aide in order to prevent my being transferred from Fort McKinley down to the southern end of Batangas Province at Fort Batangas," Marshall recalled. They had met several years before when Liggett had informally taken the Fort Leavenworth staff officer's course under Marshall. "I would give him the problem after the class got it and then I would go over his work, correct his work, after I had the approved solution. He went through the whole course like that and then went to the War College." (Interview, April 4, 1957.) ★

To Major General Edward W. Nichols

October 4, 1915
Fort McKinley,
Philippine Islands

My dear General: Captain E. J. Williams, 13th Infantry, now detailed as a Major of Philippine Scouts, has asked me to write to you regarding the admission of his son James into the 4th Class at the Institute next September. James will then be seventeen years old, and is a boy of excellent habits, fine physique and pleasant personality. His schooling has been carefully supervised by his father with a view to preparing him for the V.M.I. I gave Captain Williams the Institute catalogue about eighteen months ago so that he could look up the entrance requirements. Since then he has had James under a private tutor until last April, when he sent him to Bishop Brent's fine boys school at Baguio—the summer capitol in the high mountains of Benguet.

James is to be educated as an electrical engineer, for which profession he has a marked talent and fondness. His father hopes to have him go through the V.M.I., and then finish at the Boston "Tech."

Captain Williams plans to send James back to the States next May, but he hesitates to start him on this long journey without some assurance that there will be no difficulty regarding his being accepted at the Institute. For this reason he has asked me to write to you and explain the circumstances. I am positive that James will be fully prepared to start with the 4th Class at least, and I think he will make a most desirable cadet.

Captain Williams is now stationed about 300 miles south of Manila in Mindinao. He will write to you direct about the matter.

Mrs. Marshall and myself continue to enjoy our tour of foreign service. McKinley is a very gay and attractive post—far more desirable than the Texas border. My duties for some time past have been very agreeable, as aide-de-camp to General Hunter Liggett, the former Director of the War College in Washington. I expect to start for home next April, though the War Department may hold me out here until June or July, when my three years will be up. I applied for an extension of my tour beyond the two year point, but I do not expect to stay until General Liggett goes home in January 1917.

I have been much worried at times for fear I would miss an advance on the City of Mexico, but I may go home at the expiration of my tour and still be in time. General Bell sent me a letter of the Chief of Staff's last November, agreeing to order me home for duty on General Bell's staff in case he went into Mexico. This has served to make me feel more at ease over the situation. I see now that Locke has been redetailed on General Bell's staff. The latter and Mrs. Bell think the world of Locke.[1]

I did not leave the Islands this year, but Mrs. Marshall went up to Japan for two and a half months, ostensibly for her health and to miss the hot season, but I think she went for clothes. We have a little Ford and ride from twenty to sixty miles almost every evening. The roads out here are wonderfully fine—so much better than the roads in the States—and the scenery is magnificient. The main automobile highways are the "Manila North Road"—165 miles long and ending at Baguio 5000 feet above the sea, and the "Manila South Road"—running south 133 miles to Antimonan on the Pacific side of southern Luzon.

Mrs. Marshall looks very well and I am enjoying good health. I ride horseback an hour or more every morning before breakfast, and usually play several sets of tennis in the afternoon. The golf links run almost under our door steps, but I only play the game at infrequent intervals and then very badly.

The absolute stagnation in promotion in the infantry has caused me to make tentative plans for resigning as soon as business conditions improve somewhat. Even in the event of an increase as a result of legislation next winter, the prospects for advancement in the army are so restricted by law and by the accumulation of large numbers of men of nearly the same age all in a single grade, that I do not feel it right to waste all my best years in the vain struggle against insurmountable obstacles. The temptation to accept an absolutely assured and fairly fat living, with little or no prospect of reasonable advancement, is very great when you consider the difficulties and positive dangers of starting anew in civil life at my age. However, with only one life to live I feel that the acceptance of my presnt secured position would mean that I lacked the back bone and necessary moral courage to do the right thing. All this is, of course, confidential, and I am afraid I am boring you with my personal affairs; but I place such a value on your judgment or opinion that I have written so much of my personal affairs.[2]

There are two or three V.M.I., men out here now. Captain Peek in the C.A.C., Lieut. Gill, 8th Infantry, Lieut. Falligant, 8th Cavalry and Magruder in the Field Artillery. The last named is a splendid officer, though they are all good men. A young fellow named Speer came out last year as a lieutenant in the 13th Infantry. He was a bad egg, worthless, untrustworthy and undesirable. His resignation was soon forced and I now understand that he has entered the Canadian Army. I was sorry to see him put a blemish on the fine record of all our men—but despite his unfortunate personal misconducts he made an excellent impression as an officer.[3]

I see that you have Derbyshire and Hodges with you now.[4] Hodges and I were in the same class at Leavenworth. He is a very hardworking and bright officer. Please give my regards to both of them and to the members of the faculty who may still remember me.

I remember writing to you from Japan last year, but I believe that was before I crossed over to China and Korea. I made a very interesting trip over the battlefields of the Russian-Japanese war. The Japanese officers in Manchuria treated me royally. I was entertained by General, Baron Fukushima, the Governor of Manchuria, at Port Arthur and by Lieutenant General Akiyama, their greatest cavalry leader, at Liaoyang. Officers were detailed to accompany me every where and they furnished riding horses, carriages, etc. I rode horseback from twenty five to forty miles every day for ten days, and sometimes walked long distances in addition. Starting at Dalney I visited Nanshan, Port Arthur, Tellisu, Liaoyang, the Sha ho, Mukden and the Yalu River. The weather was perfect, the scenery in some places was magnificient, and the Chinese villages far off the railroad were most interesting.

This letter has become entirely too long and contains too many "I's", but I trust to your patience. Mrs. Marshall joins me in kindest regards to Mrs. Nichols and yourself.　Sincerely yours,

G. C. Marshall, Jr.

VMI/Alumni File; T

1. Captain Morris E. Locke.

2. On May 2, 1939, Colonel Harry H. Pritchett wrote to Marshall congratulating him on his appointment as army chief of staff, and reminding him of "a conversation I had with you back in 1913. We were sitting on a bench beside that old cement tennis court at Fort Wm. McKinley, P.I., waiting for a chance to play, and I had remarked that, judging from the slow rate of promotion, it would take me twenty years to reach the grade of captain. You replied that the prospects were certainly discouraging, and that retirement in the grade of major was about all you could see ahead; also if matters did not improve you might seriously consider resigning upon returning to the United States, as you felt if you worked as hard in civil life as you had tried to do in the Army that better success might lie in that direction." (GCMRL/G. C. Marshall Papers [Pentagon Office, Categorical].)

3. First Lieutenant (Captain, effective July 1, 1916) George M. Peek, of the Coast Artillery Corps, and Second Lieutenant William H. Gill, of the Eighth Infantry, were members of the V.M.I. class of 1907. Second Lieutenant Louis A. Falligant, who was in the Fifteenth Cavalry

by the time Marshall wrote, was a member of the V.M.I. class of 1909, but did not graduate. First Lieutenant John Magruder, of the Third Field Artillery, was a graduate of V.M.I. in 1909. Second Lieutenant George A. Speer, Jr., formerly of the Thirteenth Infantry, was a graduate of the V.M.I. class of 1912.

4. Captain George A. Derbyshire (V.M.I., 1899) was assistant professor of German, English and tactics. Colonel Harry L. Hodges (U.S.M.A., 1902), commandant of cadets and professor of military science and tactics, was on detached service from his duties as first lieutenant in the First Cavalry.

FROM MAJOR GENERAL EDWARD W. NICHOLS   November 22, 1915
[Lexington, Virginia]

My dear Marshall:–   . . . With reference to young Williams, we should, of course, be delighted to have him with us at the beginning of another year. . . .[1]

Now as to the personal reference to yourself. I know of no one in the army of your grade who stands higher. You will perhaps recall the conversation I had with Gen. Weaver about you when, a few years ago, I was trying to secure your services here.[2] Now my dear fellow, I would think twice and think long before I gave up my commission were I in your place. You are an eminent success in your present line of endeavor, highly esteemed by every one who knows you and with a standing in the service of the very highest bar none.

Beside, every indication points here to a material increase in the regular establishment. The plan of the administration recently made public contemplates among other things an increase of fifteen regiments in the infantry. This will give you a captain's commission and obviate the stagnation arising from so large a number of your age and grade.

I would advise you to stick to it. If you do I am very sure in time you will be among the high ranking officers in the service. . . .

Yours very cordially,

VMI/RG 2

1. Edwin J. Williams graduated with the V.M.I. class of 1920.
2. Brigadier General Erasmus M. Weaver was chief of the Coast Artillery Corps. Nichols may have meant Major General William H. Carter rather than Weaver. (See above, Marshall to Nichols, February 3, 1912.)

WHILE MARSHALL was contemplating his army career, he was also engaged in planning for, and then participating in, a ride by General Liggett's staff up the central valley of Luzon to the Lingayan Gulf and back—January 14–29, 1916—to study the potential for defense in the event of a Japanese attack from that direction. That, and the possibility of military involvement with Mexico, seemed more likely at the time than American participation in the European war. (Marshall to Captain William T. Sexton, January 23, 1940, GCMRL/G. C. Marshall Papers [Pentagon Office, General]; Interviews, March 13 and April 4, 1957.)

In mid-May, 1916, a few weeks after General Liggett had been appointed Philippine Department commander, Marshall's foreign tour was completed, and he was ordered back to the United States. After spending a month's leave in Japan, the Marshalls sailed on the U.S.A.T. *Thomas* for San Francisco, arriving there on July 13. Marshall had orders to report to the Sixteenth Infantry, then part of Brigadier General John J. Pershing's punitive expedition, at Colonia Dublan, Mexico.

General Bell—since August, 1915, commander of the Western Department, with headquarters at the Presidio, San Francisco—"had lost almost all of his officers to this duty on the Mexican border," Marshall remembered, "and he only had retired officers helping him out and he was organizing three training camps. So he held me by the means of getting me detailed as an aide." (Interview, April 4, 1957.)

Marshall's first assignment was to assist Brigadier General William L. Sibert (U.S.M.A., 1884) with his civilian training camp for business and professional men at Monterey, California. Successful there, he was sent to another camp— August 21 to September 16—at Fort Douglas, near Salt Lake City, Utah. In addition to drilling and inspecting the volunteers, Marshall gave illustrated lectures. A local newspaper reported part of one such presentation. ★

LECTURE ON MARCHING   August 25, 1916
                                                              Fort Douglas, Utah

The infantry drill regulations state that marching constitutes the principle occupation of troops in a campaign, and is one of the heaviest causes of loss. This loss may be reduced materially by training and by proper conduct of the march. This does not sufficiently emphasize the subject. Our military history is crowded with incidents of battles, and even campaigns, lost through the inability of our hastily-raised troops to march. Present experiences prove to the regular army officer that marches mildly imitating the conditions of campaigns generally result in the complete demoralization of national guard and other hastily-trained troops.

Your training thus far has involved only the marching requirements of the drill ground, at the drill cadence, and without packs to burden your shoulders. Next week your company commanders will take you on short road marches for the double purpose of hardening you and of reaching the terrain assigned for your instruction. Your real training in marching and in march discipline will then commence. The effort required for an ordinary walk of 25 miles will be equalled in 15 miles in the ranks of a company, in marching 12 miles in a regiment and 10 miles in larger forces.

When you march in a column all but the first four men of the thousands who follow breathe in a cloud of dust from the time the march is started until it stops. The eyes become full of dust and it sifts through the clothing, producing thirst. The most fatal thing is to drink from the canteen. Even to wash your mouth will create thirst which must be satisfied. One drink will require another, and before the march is half concluded you will not even have the luxury of "spitting cotton." Probably you will have to fall out. An old campaigner never drinks from the time he leaves camp until the new camp is reached, except in the case of sickness after he has fallen out.

Squad discipline requires that no man be allowed to fall out, and the squad leader must insist on his men remaining in the ranks unless actually sick. The men falling out report to the rear, where an officer will generally put them back in the ranks. If the man is really sick, he will receive a note to report to the ambulance when it passes.

When the signal to halt comes, the men fall out instantly to the side of the road, leaving the roadway clear, and sit down to rest. The men should be required to reserve their strength and not indulge in horseplay during the first halts. The first halt is usually made at the end of the first half hour and continues for 15 minutes. The following halts will be made each hour, extending for 10 minutes. When the march is long, a noonday halt of an hour should be made.

Deseret Evening News (Salt Lake City, Utah), August 26, 1916

A FTER THE UTAH CAMP, Marshall returned to San Francisco where he got his first close look at Major General J. Franklin Bell. They had met before, at Fort Leavenworth and during the 1914 maneuvers in the Philippines, but Marshall did not know him personally. "General Bell was a very remarkable character," Marshall said forty years later. "As a fighter, I don't think he had many equals. He held the Medal of Honor and should have been awarded it on several occasions. He was attacked by many older officers, particularly when he won preferment and promotion over their heads, but actually he was so far ahead of them in ability that there was no question about it." (Interview, April 5, 1957.)

Marshall did not believe that Bell had been particularly successful as chief of staff of the army. "He tried to handle things too much by personal associations, by letters. . . . All of General Bell's efforts to modernize the army were being ruthlessly attacked by those who were opposed to anything of that sort largely because they didn't want to do it themselves personally." If Bell had a failing, it was in making too many speeches; "he overdid it very badly, but nobody could tell him so. When I became his aide—I was getting pretty well along in years for that sort of duty—with some hesitation, but nevertheless with a firm intention, I made it plain that I thought he was making a great mistake in making these speeches. Mrs. Bell was shocked that I, a comparative unknown, should dare to make such a criticism of General Bell. But I was convinced that that was the trouble and thought that it was my duty to tell him, and if he didn't like that he could relieve me as an aide because I wasn't after that kind of a job. But we got along. Mrs. Bell didn't like me at all at first, and afterwards we became devoted friends." (Ibid.)

On October 13, Marshall was officially promoted to captain—with rank to date from July 1—and transferred to detached service in the Eighteenth Infantry, a regiment he never joined. Instead, he spent much of his time as aide handling requests from an increasingly worried public for Bell's advice and influence in furthering various preparedness schemes or in obtaining military appointments.

During the early months of 1917, the German-American diplomatic crisis that was the chief cause of these preparedness efforts escalated. Germany began unrestricted submarine warfare on February 1, and two days later President Wilson broke diplomatic relations. On March 1, American newspapers published the Zimmermann Telegram which instructed the German minister in Mexico City to propose a Mexican-German alliance against the United States. By mid-March word of American ships sunk began to reach the public. War was clearly very near. By the end of the month, Marshall was busy helping to coordinate the Western Department's efforts to mobilize the scattered National Guard units and to assign them to guard hundreds of bridges, tunnels, docks, and other potential targets of sabotage.

On April 2, President Wilson delivered his war message to Congress. Four days later the United States was officially at war, and the army was deluged with volunteers. Marshall sent versions of the following telegram to several university presidents. ★

TELEGRAM TO BENJAMIN IDA WHEELER [s. Bell][1]   April 7, 1917
San Francisco, California

I am informed that a number of students at the University of California have enlisted. Of course, everyone appreciates highly the motives leading these young men to this action, but it is very desirable that this impulse on the part of the student body should be restrained at this time for a few days at least. I think it highly important that your portion of your student body available for military duty should be held as nearly intact as possible until the plans of the War Department now in process of formulation are completed and published. Tentative plans known at these headquarters will permit of all of the senior class in your military department entering three months training course preparatory to commission as officers. I believe it is highly probable that such modification of the tentative regulations will be made as will permit juniors also to enter this training course. The use to which other classes can be put is yet to be determined, but I think for the present they can render the government the best service by continuing in their regular course of instruction at the university. With your permission I shall give this telegram to the press for the benefit of other institutions in this department to which similar advice may apply.

NA/RG 394 (Western Department, Ninth Corps Area)

1. Wheeler was president of the University of California at Berkeley.

ALMOST AS SOON AS war was declared, General Bell was ordered to take command of the reorganized Department of the East, formerly under Major General Leonard Wood. Marshall left for Governors Island about April 26. Bell, who stopped by his hometown in Kentucky, contracted influenza on the train. Upon arriving at headquarters on May 1, about one-half day after Marshall, Bell went immediately into seclusion for treatment at the Rockefeller Institute in New York City. (George C. Marshall, *Memoirs of My Services in the World War, 1917–1918* [Boston: Houghton Mifflin, 1976], p. 1.)

It was a very strenuous time for Marshall. Bell had told his headquarters staff that he had to go on a trip and that Marshall would represent him, issue orders in his name, and transmit instructions to the staff. "So he went off and left me with a staff of about fifteen old colonels at the head of all the various departments, and I was the [captain] and all the pressure of the war was coming on." (Interview, April 4, 1957.)

One of the chief sources of pressure on Marshall was from people wanting to get themselves or someone else promoted or into the officers' training camps—modeled on the Plattsburg, New York, camp started by General Wood before the war—then in the process of formation. "The Governors Island ferryboat would be jammed with fellows coming over" seeking admittance. (Ibid.) "Everybody who was anybody, in a sense, was trying to get in and each of them seemed to feel that political pressure was necessary, and I was trying to demonstrate that it wasn't necessary. We would go at these things just on their face value and without any reaction to pressures. . . . All seemed to think they could get what they wanted right away just by the stating of their desire. I guess I probably stood this off better than General Bell could, because I didn't know them and they didn't know me. . . . I was using three phones at the time, and I was being seen by everybody that came to the Island; so it was exceedingly hectic, and I had to learn how to do business very quickly." (Interview, April 5, 1957.)

Rebuffed by Marshall, favor-seekers sought to discover General Bell's whereabouts. But Marshall kept it a careful secret, although he himself had to go to the hospital every other day during the two weeks Bell was there. "It was quite a long drive and took quite a lot of time. The visit there always took time, because he was intensely interested in everything that was going on; and I tried to tell him exactly what it was and particularly to tell him of the displeasure of his senior staff officers with the fact that I was doing several things." (Ibid.)

Supplying the score or so of training camps in the department was another of Marshall's chief worries, and his solution rankled some of the older officers. Daily complaints from the camps regarding lack of various supplies was evidence that something was wrong. But when Marshall and Bell's other aide, Captain John B. Murphy, "went to ask the staff about it, these older staff officers, these senior colonels, they just turned us down as not knowing anything about the thing." Murphy had made a list of all the supplies needed per hundred men, and Marshall had him visit the camps and telegraph back what was lacking. The Plattsburg camp, scheduled to open May 15 with twenty-five hundred men, was grievously short of bedding. "Then we began to experience the first knowledge of what the war shortages were really going to be, which started in this very small way. We found we couldn't get the blankets. First the quartermaster didn't have them and, next, the shops in New York didn't have them. We were getting mattresses and blankets and pillows from as far west as Chicago in order to provide for this camp." (Ibid.)

"I found that [in] trying to get these things I wasn't making much headway with the staff. I directed that everything be sent by express, and that raised a racket right away because that would be very expensive. Well, I didn't think the expense was going to mean so much with these men freezing up there. The reaction—the public reaction—was going to be very severe. And the men would probably all get colds . . . and pneumonia." Marshall's unorthodox actions finally stirred the department quartermaster to protest. Marshall was able to calm his fears and showed him Murphy's complex supply formula. "Well that made quite a change in him right away, because he saw that we really had something he didn't have. And he was very much reassured and went ahead from that time on filling the orders that came in over my desk." (Ibid.) Bell was out of the hospital in time to inspect the Plattsburg camp on May 13, just before it opened. ★

To E. G. KERTH   May 17, 1917
                                                        [Governors Island, New York]

My dear Mr. Kerth: General Bell has received your letter of May 9th regarding your application to the Secretary of War concerning the promotion of your brother, Major Monroe C. Kerth. He is so occupied at the present time he is unable to write to you himself and has directed me to tell you that there are many officers to whom he feels under special obligations for valuable personal service rendered him in the past; that he is endeavoring to help them and does not feel at liberty to help others in competition with them until they are first provided for.

General Bell regrets that he cannot see his way clear just at this time to assist Major Kerth and wishes you to feel that his decision in your brother's case is based solely upon a desire to help those to whom he owes a very definite service.

I personally know your brother very, very well. I was a classmate of his at the Army School of the Line and the Army Staff College at Fort Leavenworth. I regard him as one of my most valued friends in the service. I think I can assure you that his record on file in the War Department will be sufficient to secure for him all the recognition he could possibly hope for. He has few equals in the Infantry service.   Sincerely yours,

NA/RG 120 (Seventy-seventh Division, Bell's Correspondence)

To Eugene V. Daly   May 22, 1917
[Governors Island, New York]

Dear Sir:–   General Bell has received your letter of May 16th, and given it very careful consideration. Having received many other communications of a similar nature he turned the matter over to a committee of officers on his staff for report.[1]

He directs me to inform you that he agrees with you in believing it highly desirable to provide some means for utilizing the services of the large number of citizens who are disqualified in one way or another for the present military duties. Much as he would like to adopt some such scheme as you propose, he finds it utterly impossible for the military authorities at this time to plan or conduct anything of that nature.

We are suffering from a serious lack of sufficient officers and non-commissioned officers of the regular army, particularly at the larger headquarters and training camps. The commissioned officers now available are simply overwhelmed with work. Difficulty is being experienced in obtaining the necessary supplies for the present camps. Tentage is not available. Cantonments for some 200,000 men must be built in this department within two months.

After consideration of the above, I think you will understand why it is impractical and impossible at this stage of the war for the army authorities to undertake the instruction or employment of any groups of men outside of those regularly enlisted for service. It is hoped that after two or three months conditions may change, and the army authorities be enabled to take some action along the lines you suggest.   Very truly yours,

NA/RG 120 (Seventy-seventh Division, Bell's Correspondence)

1. Daly's letter was prompted by his desire to serve the country in a military capacity while maintaining his business. He suggested that the army conduct half-day camps near the city for business and professional men between the ages of thirty-five and fifty.

To MAJOR GENERAL EDWARD W. NICHOLS   May 27, 1917
Governors Island, New York

My dear General: In compliance with your request at the Alumni Dinner the other evening in New York, I am sending you herewith a statement of my military service to date. I am also sending you a copy of my efficiency report for the year 1916, now on file in the War Department. I feel rather embarrassed in sending you the efficiency report, as it is much better than I deserve and much better than I will ever receive in the future. Colonel Hagood likes me and was extravagant, to put it mildly, in his estimate of my ability. However, as the report includes a rating of me by two of the present Major Generals of the Army, I value it very highly. Officers are not supposed to see their own efficiency reports unless they call personally at the office of the Adjutant General in the War Department. General Bell handed me mine so that I could see what Colonel Hagood had written, and I then made a rough copy. They are supposed to be confidential, but I merely wanted you to know just what was on file regarding my record for the past year in the War Department.[1]

I wrote to you yesterday for General Bell. Today I received a notice of the commencment exercises. I see that General Black will be present. If I can possibly arrange it I want to be there at least one day that week.

With renewed thanks for your kind offers of the other night, Very respectfully yours,

G. C. Marshall, Jr.

VMI/Alumni File; T

1. Generals Liggett and Bell rated Marshall "excellent" on all points, highly praising his military knowledge, judgment, and discretion. Both thought him qualified to be chief of staff of a division or a corps. Bell remarked that Marshall was "an exceptionally rapid, systematic worker. Never forgets and is capable of accomplishing much in time available. Always cheerfully willing, never excited or rushed, cool and level-headed. A good countervail for me."

Lieutenant Colonel Johnson Hagood, under whom Marshall served at Fort Douglas, Utah, in response to a question as to whether he would like the officer being evaluated to be under his command stated: "Yes. But I would prefer to serve *under his command.*" Hagood also thought Marshall should be a major general of volunteers. "In my judgment there are not five officers in the Army as well qualified as he is to command a division in the field." Was Marshall fitted for promotion to the next highest grade? "Yes. He should be made a Brigadier General in the Regular Army and every day this is postponed is a loss to the Army and to the Nation." Finally, under "Remarks," Hagood wrote: "I have known this officer many years by reputation and served with him in the P. I. during the Batangas Maneuvers [1914]. He is a military genius and one of those rare cases of wonderful military development during peace. He is of the proper age, has had the training and experience, and possesses the ability to command large bodies of troops in the field. The army and the nation sorely needs such men in the grade of General Officer at this time, and if I had the power I would nominate him to fill the next vacancy in grade of Brigadier General in the line of the army notwithstanding the law limiting the selection to Colonels. He is my junior by over 1800 files." (Marshall's typed copy of the efficiency report is cited here. The original is in NA/201 File.)

ON MAY 28, Major General John J. Pershing and his staff came to Governors Island, rendezvousing in Marshall's office before sailing to Europe. It was Marshall's first meeting with the commander of the American Expeditionary Forces (A.E.F.). "General Pershing arrived in civilian clothes and straw hat," Marshall recalled. "We put him on a ferryboat at Governors Island at a secluded dock and sent him over to the *Baltic* which he boarded for his trip to Europe." What Marshall did not then know was that Pershing's chief of staff, Lieutenant Colonel James G. Harbord, had requested Marshall's services. But when Pershing discovered that Marshall was Bell's aide, he ordered the request dropped. (Interview, April 5, 1957.) Watching the officers depart, Marshall was "in a most depressed frame of mind over being left behind." (*Memoirs,* p. 3.)

On June 3, troops of the hurriedly collected First Division began to leave their camps in Texas and Arizona for Hoboken, New Jersey, where they were to embark for France. The same day, Marshall was handed the following telegram from the new division's commander. Bell allowed him to write the reply. (Ibid., p. 5.) ★

TELEGRAM TO MAJOR GENERAL J. FRANKLIN BELL   June 3, 1917
FROM BRIGADIER GENERAL WILLIAM L. SIBERT   [Washington, D.C.]

Would you consent to Captain George C. Marshall's detail as a General Staff officer on my divisional staff for immediate service abroad. Answer care of Chief of Staff's Office, Washington.

NA/201 File

TELEGRAM TO BRIGADIER GENERAL   June 4, 1917
WILLIAM L. SIBERT[s. Bell]   Governors Island, New York

Just received your wire regarding Captain George C. Marshall. Detail suggested agreeable to me.

NA/201 File

To Major General Edward W. Nichols   June 9, 1917
Governors Island, New York

My dear General: I have been detailed on the General Staff, and appointed as assistant Chief of Staff of the First Expeditionary Force. By the time you receive this letter I will be out of the country.

As you were good enough to offer to assist me, I wish you to know how matters have turned out. The information contained in the first paragraph of this letter is confidential for the present, that is, until the safe landing has been announced. I suppose I am rendering myself liable to a severe penalty in writing this freely to you.

The "First Captain" of the 1915 class,[1] who is a First Lieutenant in the Reserve Corps, was selected to go attached to one of the regular companies to which additional officers had been added. He was one of the three men picked out of the Fort Myer camp. I thought this would interest you.

Mrs. Marshall has left New York to join her mother in Charlotte, N.C. She will probably come with her mother to Lexington immediately after the "finals" to settle there semi-permanently; that is, for the duration of the war.

With assurances of my respect and warmest regards.   Sincerely yours,

G. C. Marshall, Jr.

VMI/Alumni File

1. Claude R. Cammer.

World War I

June 1917–April 1919

OPERATIONS OFFICER with the first division sent to France was the job Marshall "particularly desired." General Sibert's telegram meant duty in France, but Marshall did not know that the general was to command the First Division, and he did not know in what general staff capacity he was to serve. On June 8, when Sibert formally took command of the division, Marshall learned that he was to be the assistant chief of staff for Operations. (*Memoirs,* p. 5.)

The troops began boarding their hastily and inadequately prepared ships on the night of June 10. The next day, the division's staff assembled for the first time aboard the United States Army Transport *Tenadores,* formerly a United Fruit Company banana boat. Marshall shared a stateroom with the division's other assistant chief of staff, Major Lesley J. McNair (U.S.M.A., 1904), who was in charge of training. Marshall also became friendly with a casual passenger on the ship, Major Frank R. McCoy (U.S.M.A., 1897), who was on his way to become assistant chief of staff at Pershing's headquarters in Paris. (Ibid., p. 7.)

The troops, Marshall discovered, "had been given their arms on going to the train. They were about twenty percent of the original regiment—the rest of the regiment had been taken to form new regiments. . . . It was quite a messed-up affair when they arrived in Hoboken [New Jersey]. They had no knowledge of how to drill, no knowledge of how to handle their rifles, and they were eighty percent of the strength of the companies. Together with the fact that all the men loading the ships seemed to be bull-necked Germans, it wasn't a very encouraging outlook." (Interview, April 5, 1957.) ★

FIRST DIVISION WAR DIARY[1]   June 12, 1917
                                               Aboard the U.S.A.T. *Tenadores*

Weather Fair, Health good.

1. As the loading of several of the transports was completed they cleared the Hoboken Docks and moved out into the stream, at least five anchoring in North River, the "Tenadores" opposite 96th Street and others lower down.[2]

2. Owing to the lack of facilities for communication and the necessary secrecy maintained by the Naval authorities in control, exact details as to time of movements of the several transports and their present location cannot now be given.

G. C. M.

NA/RG 120 (GHQ, War Diaries)

1. Army regulations required divisions to keep journals of march in peacetime and war diaries on campaign. The journal was to contain a historical record of the march, facts as to equipment, clothing, supply, shelter, roads, weather, health of troops, and incidents of any kind that might have value. Marshall made most of the entries in the First Division War Diary between June 12 and December 8, 1917.

2. The convoy included ten army troop transports, four cargo transports, three navy troop transports (for the Fifth Marine Corps Regiment), plus navy escort vessels. The convoy sailed in four sections with the *Tenadores* in the first.

FIRST DIVISION WAR DIARY   June 14, 1917
                                            Aboard the U.S.A.T. *Tenadores*

Weather overcast. Health good.

1. The Tenadores in company with other transports left anchorage at 4 A.M. and moved down North River. Owing to a heavy fog all anchored for several hours off Governor's Island, later moving down the harbor and out to sea.

                                                            G. C. M.

NA/RG 120 (GHQ, War Diaries)

FIRST DIVISION WAR DIARY   June 21, 1917
                                            Aboard the U.S.A.T. *Tenadores*

Weather overcast. Health good.

1. About 10:30 P.M. members of the watch observed the wake of a torpedo, (clearly disclosed by the highly phosphorescent state of the water) crossing fifty feet in front of the bow of the Tenadores from Starboard to Port. Two alarm shots were fired by the DeKalb.[1] About the same time army officers aboard the Saratoga observed the wake of two torpedoes passing in front of the bow of that boat and naval lookouts on a destroyer observed the wake of a torpedo passing under their boat and continuing on in front of the naval cruiser Seattle. The wake of this torpedo was also observed from the Seattle. The Tenadores increased speed and changed course ninety degrees.[2]

                                                            G. C. M.

NA/RG 120 (GHQ, War Diaries)

1. The Navy Transport *DeKalb,* formerly a German passenger ship and then the auxiliary cruiser *Printz Eitel Friedrich,* was transporting part of the Fifth Marine Regiment. The *Saratoga* was an army transport carrying part of the Sixteenth Infantry Regiment.

2. Marshall originally recorded this day as "uneventful." He and several other officers who witnessed the incident thought that "some amateur lookout had received a too vivid impression from the train of a porpoise or shark." But after hearing Rear Admiral Albert Gleaves, the commander of convoy operations whose flagship was the *Seattle,* declare that a naval engagement with a submarine had taken place, General Sibert ordered Marshall to change the war diary account to agree with the navy version. On July 4, George Creel, chairman of the Committee on Public Information, released an account of the alleged encounter to the American press. Marshall states that he and the other division officers involved "were entertained in reading the thrilling account of this affair." (*Memoirs,* pp. 9, 14–15.)

FIRST DIVISION WAR DIARY   June 25, 1917
                                            Aboard the U.S.A.T. *Tenadores*

Weather Overcast to Fair. Health good.

1. Two French Naval boats joined the convoy.

2. Belle Isle was sighted about 5 P.M. and the coast of France about 7 P.M.

3. A French aeroplane scouted over the convoy about 7.30 P.M.

4. A pilot boarded the Tenadores about 10 P.M., and a little later the ships anchored in La Crosique Bay.

G. C. M.

NA/RG 120 (GHQ, War Diaries)

FIRST DIVISION WAR DIARY   June 26, 1917
                                        Aboard the U.S.A.T. *Tenadores*

Weather fair. Health good.

1. Anchors were hoisted after daylight and the ships steamed up the Loire to St. Nazaire, the Tenadores docking at 9 A.M. U.S. Army and Navy officers, from the Port of Debarkation established at St. Nazaire, and French Army officers boarded the Tenadores before she docked.

2. Unloading of freight was started immediately, the Division Commander and Staff Officers inspected the camp sites and the troops were taken ashore for exercise marches.

3. All troops remained on the transports on this night. Orders were issued providing for censorship of the mail, . . . and for the disembarkation of the command at 8.15 A.M. on June 27th. . . . The camps were not ready on this date.

4. The first convoy consisted of the transports Tenadores, Pastores, Havana and Saratoga.

5. The naval converted cruiser DeKalb carried one battalion of Marines. It appears that the Officer in charge of the Port of Debarkation had no information regarding the regiment of Marines attached to this Division until our arrival June 26th.

G. C. M.

NA/RG 120 (GHQ, War Diaries)

F ORTY YEARS afterward, Marshall still vividly remembered his first days on French soil. By a "fortunate coincidence I was the second man ashore. I was just behind General Sibert on our first expedition when we landed at St. Nazaire. And when we finally got permission to go ashore that evening—some of the officers—and walk about the town, it was very depressing. They had just gotten the news of the terrible losses on the Somme when the Germans had thrown back this offensive. . . . Every woman seemed to be in mourning, and everyone seemed to be on the verge of tears. The one thing we noticed most of all was there was no enthusiasm at all over our arrival. The Canadians had come and were going to settle the war in a month or two and nothing happened. Now the Americans had come and were going to settle the war right off—and nothing happened. The whole thing was a very depressing affair. The surroundings—everything about it, our first taste of the effect of the war, particularly on the rear areas—left a lasting impression on my mind and a deep sympathy for the French and, I think, an understanding such as other officers in high staff positions—[who] had not gone through this affair—did not comprehend, and [who] were rather intolerant of the French in some of their peculiarities. . . . I might say that everything in the way of large war measures was a peculiarity to us." (Interview, April 5, 1957.) ★

FIRST DIVISION WAR DIARY   June 27, 1917
                                                 St. Nazaire, France

Weather fair. Health good.

1. The troops of the First Division of the Convoy disembarked as ordered and proceeded to their respective camps. The battalion of Marines was temporarily accommodated in the cantonments assigned to organizations on the Third Division of the Convoy. While the men are crowded in quarters and there is practically no ground available for drills or formations in or out of camp, the portable cantonments set up by the French are most comfortable and the camp sites located on healthful ground.

2. The Second Division of the Convoy arrived and docked during the morning. The following transports formed this division: Momus, Antilles, Lenape and the Naval Transport Henderson. The commanders of the troops reported an uneventful trip, but the naval authorities reported the sinking of a submarine by one of our destroyers about 200 miles off the coast.

3. The same procedure was followed by the troops in this division of the convoy as prescribed for the first division.

G. C. M.

NA/RG 120 (GHQ, War Diaries)

FIRST DIVISION WAR DIARY   June 28, 1917
                                               [St. Nazaire], France

Weather rainy. Health good. Supplies good, but hard to obtain owing to muddy roads and few trucks.

1. The Third Division of the Convoy, consisting of the transports Mallory, Finland and San Jacinto, arrived in the harbor during the morning after an

uneventful voyage. The troops aboard were directed to follow the same procedure as those in the First Division of the Convoy.

2. A portion of the troops in the second division of the convoy disembarked during the morning and proceeded to their camps. Two companies of the 28th Infantry, and two battalions of the 26th Infantry remained aboard owing to difficulties encountered in moving their wood and rations to camp. The mud caused the few trucks available to stall. The two battalions of Marines remained aboard the Henderson as there were no cantonments or tents available.

3. The Commanding General, U. S. Expeditionary Forces arrived in St. Nazaire in the morning and made a close personal examination of the camps.

4. Orders were issued for the instruction and training of the troops . . . and concerning relations with the French people. . . .

G. C. M.

NA/RG 120 (GHQ, War Diaries)

First Division War Diary   July 5, 1917
                                                          [St. Nazaire], France

Weather fair. Health good. Supply good.

1. Three automobile trucks have been fitted with improvised bodies and were made available for use this date. The bodies of the trucks have only partially been located and many of these are broken. Division Headquarters automobiles and motor-cycles not yet located. Horses not yet available; undergoing mallein test.[1] Absolute lack of any transportation, except one small French automobile and a limited number of French trucks, makes the efficient organization and administration of the Division unsatisfactory and difficult.

G. C. M.

NA/RG 120 (GHQ, War Diaries)

1. A test for the presence of the bacterium that causes the highly contagious and destructive horse disease called glanders.

First Division War Diary   July 11, 1917
                                                            St. Nazaire, France

Weather fair. Health good. Supply good.

1. The 28th Infantry entrained in five sections and left for its billets in the training area. The first section left thirty eight minutes late, owing to the late arrival of the horses, the fact that the train was not made up as expected and freight had to be carried by hand for considerable distances, and the instructions from Base Section, Number One, directing that the organizations should not

arrive at the entraining point until thirty minutes before scheduled time for departure. Some delay was also due to the fact that most of the officers and non-commissioned officers were entirely inexperienced and most of the men recruits. The remaining four trains left on time or approximately on time.

2. The French trains are made up of fifty cars adapted to their organization, which naturally does not entirely suit ours; particularly as regards wagons, which must be loaded from the side, and the extra impedimenta which is being carried oversea by our troops.

3. All organizations are without rolling kitchens, which did not arrive on this convoy. It now appears that no automobiles for Division Headquarters were shipped on this convoy, though the cars were on the docks at Hoboken when the transports were being loaded.

G. C. M.

NA/RG 120 (GHQ, War Diaries)

First Division War Diary   July 12, 13, 14 & 15, 1917
                                                  Gondrecourt, France

July 12.
1. The Division Commander with several members of his Staff left at 7 A.M. for Gondrecourt, via Paris, by automobile. Colonel Coe, Chief of Staff, and Captain Marshall, Assistant Chief of Staff, proceeded to Paris by rail.[1] The 26th Infantry, Outpost Company, Signal Corps, Division Headquarters Troop and the Division Headquarters clerical force entrained during this date for Gondrecourt. The Division Inspector and one Quartermaster officer from the Division Staff remained at St. Nazaire to observe and assist in the entrainment of the remainder of the Division.

June [*July*] 13.
2. The Division Commander, with most of the officers of his Staff arrived in Paris on this date and reported at General Headquarters.

June [*July*] 14.
3. The Division Commander and his Staff remained in Paris.[2]

June [*July*] 15.
4. The Division Commander and Staff proceeded by automobile and rail to Gondrecourt, arriving between 6 and 7 P.M.[3] All troops, excepting the organizations of the 5th Regiment of Marines, had arrived at their designated billeting areas after uneventful trips.

G. C. M.

NA/RG 120 (GHQ, War Diaries)

1. Frank W. Coe (U.S.M.A., 1892) was a colonel in the Coast Artillery Corps; in August he was promoted to brigadier general and left the division. Marshall and Coe were met at the Quai d'Orsay train station by Captain George S. Patton, Jr., (V.M.I., 1903–4; U.S.M.A., 1909) who had been with Pershing at Governors Island in May and who was now commanding Pershing's Headquarters Troop. (*Memoirs,* p. 16.)

2. Marshall and the rest of Sibert's staff watched the Bastille Day parade. Marshall later wrote that this "was our initial glimpse of first-class fighting troops of the French." (Ibid., p. 17.)

3. Accompanying General Sibert in his automobile, Marshall recalled that en route they passed "along a portion of the battlefield of the Marne, and near Bar-le-Duc we saw the first evidences of devastation." (Ibid.)

FIRST DIVISION WAR DIARY

July 17, 1917
Gondrecourt, France

. . . 2. The Chief of Staff and his assistants inspected the offices and working arrangements of the General Staff Officers of the 47th French Division.[1] It was decided to adopt virtually the same arrangement for this Division, excepting the 1st Bureau of the French organization which corresponds to our Division Adjutant's Office.[2]

G. C. M.

NA/RG 120 (GHQ, War Diaries)

1. The Forty-seventh Chasseur Division, commanded by General de Poudrygain, had been sent to Gondrecourt to assist in training the First Division. The French soldiers "made a wonderful impression on our men," Marshall wrote afterwards. (*Memoirs,* p. 18.)

2. The French General Staff was divided into four bureaus; to each of these the United States Army gave a "G" (General Staff) designation.

1st Bureau (Personnel)	=	G-1 (Personnel and Training)
2nd Bureau (Intelligence)	=	G-2 (Intelligence)
3rd Bureau (Operations)	=	G-3 (Operations)
4th Bureau (Supply)	=	G-4 (Logistics)

At A.E.F. General Headquarters, Training was made G-5.

MARSHALL was not only involved with training the division for duty, but in late July and early August he was also given the job of locating billeting and training facilities for the next three American divisions—the Twenty-sixth, Forty-second, and Second—scheduled to arrive before the end of 1917. "I had to figure out what was required in the way of mess halls and bunkhouses and headquarters and hospital buildings and everything of that sort. Nobody advised me—they didn't have time—they just told me to do it. One of my old friends, a student officer from Leavenworth, [Colonel] John [McAuley] Palmer, who was one of the fine intellectuals of the army, was G-3 [at General Headquarters] at that time. He just sent me a telegram that they could give me no advice; so just go ahead and do what I thought was wise. I had a pretty large order for a young officer there, and I proceeded to undertake it in as large a way as I could. The only trouble was I got everything fixed up for these four [*three*] divisions and I didn't realize that nobody had fixed up anything for the First Division. So my own division was behind all the others in getting the necessary things." (Interview, April 5, 1957. For Marshall's detailed description of his activities and his problems with French officials, see *Memoirs*, pp. 23–25.) ★

REPORT TO THE COMMANDING GENERAL, A.E.F.   August 1, 1917
[Gondrecourt], France

Billeting and training facilities in vicinity of Neufchateau.

1. In compliance with the instructions contained in the letter from your headquarters to the Commanding General, 1st Division, A.E.F., dated July 17, 1917, the *attached* report on the billeting accommodations, water and training facilities for one division *around Neufchateau,* is submitted.[1]

This area will be ready for all the troops of the division by August 15th. Some of the mess, recreation, kitchen and stable buildings will not be completed by this date for the artillery and certain of the special units, but these are not essential to immediate occupancy.

2. On July 21st I proceeded to Mirecourt, the headquarters of the Eastern Armies, and met the Commandant d'Etapes in charge at Neufchateau. Since that date I have made as frequent trips to Neufchateau and the surrounding country as the opportunity of working with the above official occurred. On July 21st I found that work had been under way for about two weeks on the preparation of the area around Neufchateau.

3. *Reports on other areas.*—

Reports on the cantonment and training ground areas for the other two divisions will be submitted as soon as the French officials have prepared their data for billeting the troops. A commandant d'etapes for each of these cantonments has just been appointed and I will not be able to go over the ground thoroughly until they have had an opportunity to complete their preliminary plans.

It appears that the cantonment for the "second" division, located immediately south of the Neufchateau Area, with headquarters at Bourmont, should be ready for the troops by September 1st and possibly earlier. The area for the remaining division is located southeast of the Bourmont Area, and includes Vittel and Martigny.

4. *General character of the country.*—

The country covered by the areas above referred to consists of broad, fertile valleys bordered by high hills. It is well watered, not too heavily timbered for military training, devoted largely to hay and grain crops and dotted with villages above the average in general appearance. When the harvest is completed about August 20th, there will be excellent facilities for training troops—drill, target practice (infantry and artillery), special trench warfare and divisional maneuvers. In short, it appears to be healthful, is beautiful and seems to be admirably adapted to the training of troops as compared to other sections of France with which I am familiar.

5. *Inhabitants.*—

I have found the inhabitants of the region enthusiastic over the expected arrival of United States troops. While some of this enthusiasm may be due to expected financial profit, yet their attitude seems genuinely friendly to a greater degree than would ordinarily be expected. This should make the actual billeting of the troops more easily adjusted than it otherwise would be.

6. *Neufchateau Area.*—

I have found the Commandant d'Etapes at Neufchateau, Major Bluem, who is in charge of that area, a very obliging, effective and direct officer to deal with. His original plans, prepared before seeing me, contemplated much more in the way of special accommodations than has been provided for the 1st Division at Gondrecourt. Generous billeting assignments have been made, supplemented wherever necessary by a total of about sixty portable barracks, generally of the straight side type, twenty meters long.

After the crops are harvested practically the entire area can be utilized for maneuvering troops. The "camp" (training area within which trenches may be dug, etc.) is indicated on a map attached to the report of the Neufchateau Area. This "camp" is also to be used by the troops of the Bourmont Area. However, ordinary drills and maneuvers are not limited to the area of this "camp"—all the terrain, excepting scattered truck gardens and potato fields, being available.

7. *Portable barracks.*—

At a conference yesterday with the Commandant d'Etapes from General de Castelnau's headquarters, General l'Etoile (?), I arranged for the erection of one barrack for each battalion to be used as an infirmary.

The following special buildings have been or will be erected in each area—these in addition to the sixty for quarters above referred to:

1 barrack per company for a mess hall.
1 barrack per battalion for a recreation room.
1 barrack per battalion for an infirmary.
1 kitchen building for each two to four companies.
(Kitchen buildings are generally not required for artillery units as their billeting accommodations are usually considerably in excess of their requirements owing to the necessity of spreading out the units sufficiently to secure billeting accommodations for animals.)
Such stables for animals as are required in addition to the available billets.
1 shower bath house for each village.

The barracks are ceiled and floored. Stoves were reported to be available for issue when the cold weather arrives. I saw a number in one village.

8. *Liaison Officer.—*

In order to facilitate materially and expedite the transaction of all business which involves any relations with the French officials, military or civil, I recommend the immediate detail of a liaison officer (one who can speak some French) for duty in the office of the Commandant d'Etapes at Neufchateau, Major Bluem, and the detail of similar officers for duty in the other two areas at least two weeks before the arrival of troops.

9. *Town Majors.—*

These officers, each accompanied by a non-commissioned officer, an interpreter and a motorcycle with a driver, should precede the troops to their billets by at least one week. Much confusion and many misunderstandings between the troops and the inhabitants will thus be avoided, and the existing good will of the inhabitants will be maintained. A brigade commander, the division quartermaster, some clerks, at least two automobiles and as many auto trucks as possible, should arrive at the headquarters of the area with the Town Majors. Transportation for all these officers is essential, for without it their efficiency is reduced at least fifty percent and the troops will ultimately suffer in consequence.

10. *Individual instructions to soldiers.—*

The conditions under which a soldier lives in billets are so different from what our men are accustomed to, wine is so cheap and much in evidence, amusements are so few and the rate of pay of our men is so high, that a brief pamphlet of information and advice might well be issued to each soldier before he reaches his first billet. It could describe the general character of a billet and the necessity for immediate hard work and ingenuity in cleaning and fixing it up; the necessity for considering the interest and feelings of the owner of the billet might be explained; cautions could be given against too free indulgence in wines and association with women who are generally diseased; advice to deposit or send home most of each month's pay—explaining the low rate of pay received by the French soldier—would be appropriate; and the soldier could be counseled against needlessly incurring the enmity of the poorer classes of the French people by overpaying for services and supplies and thus raising the prices beyond what the inhabitants can afford to pay. . . .

NA/RG 120 (First Division, Historical File)

1. Marshall's "Report on Cantonment for One Division in Neufchateau Area" is not printed, as it repeats much of the document printed here.

MEMORANDUM[1]

August 27, 1917
[Gondrecourt], France

Notes for Inspector General.

QUARTERMASTER SUPPLIES.

Lumber.

Requisition for 20,000 board feet of lumber, made by the Division Quartermaster on Quartermaster of the Base Section at St. Nazaire, before troops left St. Nazaire, to be delivered to Gondrecourt. Requisition not filled.

Personal appeal made by Division Quartermaster to Chief Quartermaster Army Headquarters, Paris, on July 13, for lumber. Instructed to purchase lumber in open market in vicinity of training camp. French authorities at Gondrecourt stated that they did not desire any effort to be made to purchase lumber other than through military authorities.

Request was made on French authorities for 100,000 board feet. To date 13,000 feet have been delivered and all used for mangers and feed stalls required for animals without nose bags. No lumber has been available for issue to organizations to be used for needed repairs in billets, steps, tables, shelves, etc.

Barracks.

To prepare quarters for men who can not be accommodated after harvest, mess halls, battalion recreation rooms, kitchens, etc., formal request was made on July 28th to the French authorities for 114 barracks and 14 kitchen buildings. To date 34 sectional barracks have been delivered to the Division.

Rations.

Since the daily issue of rations, shipped from the base at Nevers, commenced on August 17th, there has never yet arrived in any one day shipment of all the articles of the ration. At first the matches and soap, etc., failed to arrive; then the fruit failed to arrive; then vinegar failed to arrive. No pickles have been received at any time. From time to time errors were made in loading rations. On August 24th, shipment was short 4 crates of baking powder. Twice sacks of beans weighing 85 pounds net, were sent as weighing 100 pounds. Two cases of pumpkins were sent in place of tomatoes. Today three kegs of syrup were sent in lieu of four kegs.

In the issue made today, August 27th, for August 30th, the following items were short: Jam; Apples, evaporated; vinegar; pickles; butter. 225 pounds out of 1590 pounds of beans, and one keg out of four kegs of syrup.

In a telegram sent from the base at Nevers today the following shortages are indicated in the car of rations just leaving that place: Jam; vinegar; pickles; and butter. The telegram states that the articles are not on hand.

Automobile supplies.

There is a shortage of tire tubes of all sizes and of lubricating oils, (American.) A small supply of tire tubes has been secured from the French, and the necessary lubricating oil. It is understood that a large shipment of lubricating oil reached St. Nazaire on the first Convoy. Repair parts for cars, trucks and motorcycles are urgently needed.

Tobacco.

To date the following tobacco has been received.

25,920	packages, (one ounce,) Bull Durham.
1,744	lbs. tobacco, chewing.
411,160	cigarettes.
4,320	two ounce packages tobacco, P. A.
864	packages tobacco, Tuxedo.
	A limited supply of cigars.

Miscellaneous.

Many articles of clothing for sales stores and small issues are lacking. There has been a lack of horse-shoes and farrier tools, as well as of many property articles.

ORDNANCE STORES.

Request was made on the Chief Ordnance Officer, A.E.F. for target material, etc., necessary for use in target practice. Following instructions from him a formal requisition for ordnance supplies was submitted to the French authorities through the Commanding General 47th French Division, on July 6th. To date only negligible quantities of these supplies have been received.

SHORTAGE OF OFFICERS.

Owing to the number of officers who have been detached from the Division for various Staff duties in France, or have been promoted and relieved from duty with the Division, and to the number of officers required for duty as Town Majors, etc., there exists a serious shortage of field and company officers in the command. There are companies with only two officers present for duty and the latter have rarely had more than five months' service, and frequently less. It has been considered highly desirable to send officers to the front as frequently as practicable to observe conditions. This results in a further shortage. The Divisional Schools are about to be inaugurated. Under instructions from A.E.F. fifteen officers per regiment should be detached from each regiment to take the proposed courses.

G. C. Marshall, Jr.

NA/RG 120 (First Division, Historical File)

1. This memorandum was not directed to any office or officer and was perhaps a personal aide-memoire. Usually such unaddressed memorandums had a long attached distribution list.

TO THE COMMANDER IN CHIEF, A.E.F.   September 11, 1917
FROM THE COMMANDING GENERAL,   [Gondrecourt], France
FIRST DIVISION

. . . 2. I have been deeply impressed with Captain Marshall's marked ability in General Staff and all other duty entrusted to him, and strongly recommend that he be given a temporary commission as Lieutenant Colonel in the National Army and kept on General Staff work—he is fully qualified to perform the duties of Chief of Staff of a Division.[1]

Wm. L. Sibert

NA/RG 120 (GHQ, AG File)

1. Marshall had served as acting chief of staff from August 23, when Brigadier General Frank W. Coe left, until September 3, when Colonel Hanson E. Ely (U.S.M.A., 1891) took over. No reply to General Sibert's recommendation was forthcoming because the question of promotion by selection was being studied at General Headquarters, and General Pershing did not then have the authority to make such promotions. On January 7, 1918, a telegram arrived at division headquarters announcing Marshall's promotion. Meanwhile, Marshall was made a temporary major with rank dating from August 5.

MARSHALL termed the six months he spent with the First Division at Gondrecourt—July 14, 1917, to January 18, 1918—"the most depressing, gloomy period of the war. We often referred to it as the Winter of Valley Forge." His fortunate and pleasant housing and dining arrangements with a small group of companionable officers at the home of M. and Mme Jouatte "was in no small measure responsible for my being able to keep a stiff upper lip and wear an optimistic smile those days." (*Memoirs*, p. 18.)

Along with the difficulties of outfitting and training the raw division went the problem of dealing with the French command and with Pershing's headquarters at Chaumont. The division's officers and men were constantly being ordered away to new assignments, and its leaders were constantly being scrutinized, paraded, and criticized from every side. (Ibid., pp. 21–22.)

On October 3, Pershing and some of his staff arrived at Gondrecourt to witness a demonstration which Marshall had had to arrange on short notice. In his memoirs, Pershing noted that he was "much pleased with the evidences of efficiency in this organization." (John J. Pershing, *My Experiences in the World War* [New York: Frederick A. Stokes, 1931], p. 192.) But Marshall recalled a different reaction. When General Sibert and Chief of Staff Hanson Ely failed to give a sufficiently cogent critique of the exercise, Pershing was furious. "He just gave everybody hell, and he was very severe with General Sibert . . . in front of all the officers. Among other things, he said that we didn't show any signs of much training; we had not justified the time we had had here; . . . and generally he just scarified us. He didn't give General Sibert a chance to talk at all. . . . So I decided it was about time for me to make my sacrifice play. . . . I went up and started to talk to General Pershing, who dismissed the chief of staff rather contemptuously and was going off. . . . He shrugged his shoulders and turned away from me, and I put my hand on his arm and practically forced him to talk." (Interview, April 5, 1957.)

According to Benjamin F. Caffey—Marshall's assistant in the Operations Section during 1918 and later a brigadier general—when Marshall was angry "his eyes flashed and he talked so rapidly and vehemently no one else could get in a word. He overwhelmed his opponent by a torrent of facts." (Caffey to Forrest C. Pogue, January 14, 1961, GCMRL/Research File [World War I].) Marshall himself recalled that he was "just mad all over. I thought I had gotten in it up to my neck; I might as well not try to float but to splash a little bit. I've forgotten all that I said, but I had a rather inspired moment. The others were horrified, and General Pershing walked away from me by saying, 'Well, you must appreciate the troubles we have.' I said, 'Yes, general, but we have them every day and many a day, and we have to solve every one of them by night.' Then I left. . . . General Sibert was very regretful that I had done this, and some of my bosom friends came up to me and said . . . I was finished and I'd be fired right off." Marshall himself thought that the worst that would happen was that he would be removed from the staff and sent to duty with troops, "and certainly that would be a great success." But instead of ruining him, it helped. Afterwards, when Pershing would come to the division, "he would get me off away from the others and talk to me about the condition of affairs." (Interview, April 5, 1957.) ★

FIRST DIVISION WAR DIARY   October 17, 1917
                                                      [Gondrecourt], France

Weather fair. Health good. Supplies good.

1. The Chief of Staff, Col. Ely, accompanied by the Assistant Chief of Staff, Major Marshall, and two officers from general headquarters, (Col. Malone and Col. Drum)[1] left to make a reconnaissance of the sectors to be occupied by the battalions of the Division in the front line.

2. The battalion adjutant and one officer per company of the first battalions of each infantry regiment left for the front to make preparations for the reception of their battalions.

                                                                    G. C. M.

NA/RG 120 (GHQ, War Diaries)
1. Colonel Paul B. Malone (U.S.M.A., 1894), a Fort Leavenworth student for two years when Marshall was an instructor, was assistant chief of staff G-5 (Training). Colonel Hugh Drum was in the Operations Section.

THE FIRST DIVISION was assigned to replace French troops in the Einville sector on the Lorraine front east of Nancy, an area relatively quiet since the first months of the war. The first deployment of American troops to the front was accomplished in three successive shifts. The first battalion of each of the division's four Infantry regiments entered the front lines on October 23; the second battalions replaced them on November 2; and the third battalions replaced the second on November 11. The division was relieved on November 20, having suffered thirty-six killed, thirty-six wounded, and eleven taken prisoner.

Marshall went to the Einville sector with the second battalions and was billeted in Sommervillers. From there he made daily inspection trips. He wrote in his *Memoirs* (p. 43) that "the wide front over which the troops were distributed and the distance one was compelled to travel on foot to reach the front made my task of keeping in touch with the battalions a very onerous one. Starting at daylight I would generally be occupied until late in the afternoon tramping from one center of resistance to another." ★

FIRST DIVISION WAR DIARY   October 29, 1917
                                                              [Gondrecourt], France

Weather: fair. Health: good. Supplies: good.
. . . 2. The heavy rains have so washed and flooded the roads that difficulty is being encountered in hauling supplies for the troops and lumber for barracks and for the Corps Schools.
3. The 3rd Battalion of each Infantry Regiment started on a special schedule of training in preparation for a tour of duty at the front. Owing to the fact that the 2nd Battalion of each Regiment is preparing to leave for the front October 30th, and the 1st Battalions are at the front, heavy fatigue details are required from the 3rd Battalions for the Corps Schools, the Ordnance and Engineer Depots at Demange-aux-Eaux, the improvement of all picket lines which are badly flooded and the guarding of villages temporarily vacated by the 1st and 2nd Battalions. This special training is therefore being conducted under many difficulties. . . .

                                                                    G. C. M.
NA/RG 120 (GHQ, War Diaries)

REPORT FOR THE CHIEF OF STAFF,   November 3, 1917
FIRST DIVISION   Einville, [France]

German raid on sector held by 2d Bn. 16th Infantry.

1. At 7:30 A.M. today I learnt at Division Headquarters[1] that there had been a

very heavy hostile bombardment of the front line trenches from Aero to the south and that two soldiers of the 16th Infantry had been killed and two more of the same regiment wounded. This information was telephoned by Lieut. Hugo and myself to Colonel King at Gondrecourt.[2] I started out with General Bordeaux about 8:00 A.M., and went to Infantry Headquarters at Einville. There we heard that one French soldier had been killed, in addition to the two Americans. We went on to Regimental Headquarters but learnt nothing new there. On our way up to the Artois Post of Command at Gypse we met an Artillery Major who had heard that some Americans were missing, but as there were no traces of a raid, it was thought that these men had been lost in the taking over of the sector that night. At the Battalion P.C. we met the French Battalion Commander and Major Burnett, 16th Infantry. There we were told that three Americans had been killed and five wounded by the bombardment, etc., and that they were still investigating the absence of fifteen men, but had not yet located them. We went forward and located the Commanding Officer, Co. F, 16th Infantry, Lieut. Comfort, whose company occupied the Artois Strong Point. He was still somewhat dazed by the shell shock of the bombardment. He conducted us forward. After reaching the doubling trench we met a French lieutenant who said that there had been a raid as they had found a German helmet and a German rifle. We continued on up to Lieut. McLoughlin's (?) platoon and found him slightly wounded in the face, his helmet bent by a shell fragment and he himself very much shaken by the bombardment he had experienced. The trenches had been badly knocked about, the communication trenches almost destroyed in several places. The general facts of the affair were still in much doubt, but a short investigation quickly cleared things up. The following is about what happened.

2. About 2:50 A.M., Nov. 3d, a heavy bombardment was delivered by the enemy on our line from Aero to the south, including Bures. In the vicinity of the Artois salient it was extremely violent. It lasted about fifty minutes. Apparently the tip of the salient was only lightly bombarded with 77 mms., as it was only slightly damaged. The men generally sought shelter in their dugouts. Lieut. McLoughlin, commanding the platoon holding the salient, sought to get his men back to the doubling trench, but the the latter was under the heaviest bombardment and he was knocked down several times by shell blasts. During this bombardment the enemy exploded long, gas pipe dynamite charges under the wire in front of each face of the tip of the salient. When the bombardment lifted on the front trench about forty of fifty Germans rushed in from the two sides, killed or drove off the one or two soldiers who had come out of their dug outs, and carried off twelve of our men. Three soldiers of Co. F, 16th Infantry were killed. One had had his throat cut; one had been shot by a revolver as he stepped to the door of his dug out; and the third had had his head crushed in—whether by a club or a piece of shell fragment I do not know. One man was wounded by a bullet from a rifle or revolver. The man with the cut throat was found, I un-

derstand, on top of the parapet. I have not yet had an opportunity to question the wounded and I now understand that a German was wounded by the German barage and has come in to our lines, stating that the raid was planned in August and 250 volunteers called for, and that fifty participated in the raid. Every thing regarding the Germand-prisoner is new to me and as yet unchecked. Practically all the other details I found out for myself.

3. In order to get this off by the courier have written it the moment I reached Einville and it is therefore disconnected and hurried. I will make a rough sketch to enclose. I am sending with this the list of names of killed, wounded and missing. Also the orders for that center of resistance, etc. The company had just taken over the sector about ten o'clock last night and only a few of the non-commissioned officers had ever seen the trenches in day light.[3]

G. C. Marshall, Jr.

NA/RG 120 (GHQ, AG File); T

1. The headquarters indicated is that of the French Eighteenth Division at Sommervillers. The division was commanded by General Paul E. J. Bordeaux.

2. Jean Hugo (great-grandson of Victor Hugo) was Marshall's billet-mate at Mme Jouatte's, the interpreter and liaison officer at division headquarters, "and a very fine fellow." (Interview, April 5, 1957.) Colonel Campbell King was First Division adjutant.

3. Following Marshall's signature, the division chief of staff, Colonel Ely, wrote: "P.S. Later telephone report states that the captured German prisoner stated this attack had been planned over a month ago and 350 men were engaged in it. They did not know the Americans were there."

POLITICAL considerations magnified the importance of this small action. General Bordeaux questioned the wounded closely. Marshall recalled that Jean Hugo whispered to him that the general was trying to discover whether the Americans had resisted with sufficient vigor. "So I interrupted him and said, 'General, I understand you are trying to find whether the Americans showed fight or not. I don't think that is the thing to investigate. I think it would be very much more to the point if you look into the fact that you forbade the Americans to go beyond the wire in any reconnaissance and now they are surprised by the assault right through the wire. I think General Pershing is going to be very much interested in that reaction of a French commander to American troops.' " (Interview, April 5, 1957.)

Marshall further shocked General Bordeaux and the corps chief of staff by threatening, despite his low rank, to see the French corps commander personally about the restrictions. "I was representing the division commander who was one hundred or more kilometers away, so my rank didn't cut any figure with me as far as I could see. My job was to represent him and his interests; and his interests were very heavily involved here. This was the first American action and we had been surprised; prisoners had been taken, and the Germans were advertising it." (Ibid.) ★

REPORT FOR THE CHIEF OF STAFF,   November 3, 1917
FIRST DIVISION   Sommervillers, France

German raid on sector held by 2nd Battalion, 16th Infantry.

1. In addition to what was related in my report on this subject at 2:30 P.M., the following has been ascertained from a German prisoner, left in our lines from the raiding party, and from one of our wounded men I questioned.

(a) The raid was prepared in August and was not to have been held this A.M., but as American or strange helmets has been observed on the front it was decided to stage it immediately.

(b) 250 Germans participated in the actual raid and 16 batteries fired on the Aero and Artois positions. The prisoner had been in patrols up to the raiding point five different times during the past two months.

(c) The American soldier wounded by a rifle bullet told me that he was in the "doubling trench" during the bombardment with one other man; that he suddenly heard cries or yells in the front trench; that at about the same moment 3 Germans jumped down into his trench 10 feet away, the first man dropping on the floor of the trench and firing the shot that wounded him (the American soldier); that he fired back and the 3 Germans ran off in the trench; that 5 or 10 more Germans appeared on top and some threw bombs at him; that he thought the Germans were in the trenches about 20 minutes (probably five minutes, I expect); that he is confused as to what happened next. He was just recovering from an anesthetic when I questioned him and will probably be able to talk more later.

(d) As our men took over the sector about 10 P.M. in the rain and dark they had no opportunity to familiarize themselves sufficiently well with the trenches, location of dugouts, dumps of grenades, etc. The last was the most serious difficulty.

(e) The bombardment was so sudden, violent and accurate that all were dazed by the shock of the explosions and had much difficult in reaching their dugouts.

2. The men of the company not in the platoon raided seemed in very fair spirits considering their experiences. The men of the company in the rear trenches seemed unconcerned.

NA/RG 120 (GHQ, AG File); T

I N RESPONSE to the raid, not only did the French reduce the restrictions on the American troops under their command, but they staged an elaborate funeral for the three dead men. Both Marshall's memorandum on the ceremony and General Bordeaux's speech are printed in Marshall's *Memoirs,* pp. 48–50. General Pershing's headquarters—"still in the business of trying to command minor units,'' Marshall later recalled (Interview, April 5, 1957)—demanded an immediate report from Marshall and convened a board of officers to investigate and to draw lessons from the raid. ☆

TO WILLIAM D. SCHOLLE   November 25, 1917
                                                          [Gondrecourt, France]

My dear Scholle: Your letter to me of Aug. 20th reached me here in France two weeks ago and I was very glad to receive it.[1] I left Governor's Island June 10th and came over as assistant Chief of Staff of the 1st Division. I have been acting Chief of Staff for a time and very, very busy all day, every day since I landed nearly six months ago.

It happened to be my portion to write the order for the going into the line of the first American troops—infantry, field artillery and engineers and it was also my good fortune to be practically on the spot at the time of the first German raid. We were not particularly pleased over having eleven men captured; but, considering that the new command had gone with the front line for their first time at 10 P.M. that night in rain and fog and that the one company command had a number of guns turned on it equal to 45 percent of the total field artillery in the U.S. Army on July 1, 1916 and that the raid was pulled on part of one platoon at 3:30 A.M. that same night by 210 Germans—why, I think the men did splendidly. They were not disorganized; their trenches were practically destroyed; the platoon commander was a Plattsburgh Training Camp man who had joined 10 days before and the company commander had served with troops since last April. Divided authority with the French accounted for most of our troubles. This, of course, is all entre nous.

I was very sorry that Mrs. Marshall and I left so soon and so hurriedly that we had no opportunity to have Mrs. Scholle with us on the Island. I did not even have the pleasure of meeting her. However, I trust that all those pleasant things are merely being held in abeyance until 1918 or 19.

Mrs. Marshall is in Lexington, Virginia, where she expects to remain until I return.

War and training here is *mud* and *rain* and *cold*. The officer, platoon chief, who can keep his men's socks and shoes greased and dry and his horses groomed and picket lines above the flood of water and mud—he is the greatest contributor to our success in this war.

With kindest regards,   Sincerely,

                                                          G. C. Marshall, Jr.

GCMRL/G. C. Marshall Papers (Pentagon Office, Selected); H

1. Scholle had been first sergeant at the Monterey, California, training camp in the summer of 1916; and in February, 1917, Marshall had recommended him for a commission. On May 5

he was appointed first lieutenant of Infantry in the Officers' Reserve Corps and ordered to report to the Plattsburg, New York, training camp within ten days. Scholle's letter of August 20 is not in the file. He sent Marshall a copy of the letter printed here on April 14, 1943.

FIRST DIVISION WAR DIARY   November 26, 1917
                                                          [Gondrecourt], France

Weather: snow. Health: good. Supplies: good.

1. Troops resumed their training after a week of fatigue work. The departure for the Staff College or Corps Schools of nine out of twelve infantry battalion commanders has seriously handicapped regimental commanders in starting the first week of the regimental training. These battalion commanders have had to be replaced by officers who just arrived from the United States with the replacement battalions or by very young and inexperienced Captains. The former are not prepared to give any instruction or to carry out regimental orders in the tactics of trench warfare, and the latter have not yet mastered the details of commanding a company. The frequent changing of commanders for battalions and companies and of regimental adjutants has had a demoralizing effect.

2. The Inspector General, A.E.F., accompanied by three members of the Training Section, A.E.F., arrived to inspect training work.

G. C. M.

NA/RG 120 (GHQ, War Diaries)

FIRST DIVISION WAR DIARY   December 8, 1917
                                                          [Gondrecourt], France

. . . 2. Shortage in forage still continues. Shortage in leggins, winter gloves or mittens, and shoes exists. Owing to hard work, continuous muddy roads and necessity for wearing very heavy socks (generally 2 pairs, one light and one heavy) the men require larger sizes in shoes than was found necessary in the warmer and drier climate where our troops usually operated before the war. Apparently, as a result of this change, it has been found impossible to secure a sufficient number of shoes of the sizes between 8½ and 12. The wearing of tight shoes has resulted in a number of men developing sore feet during the recent open warfare maneuvers. Many men only have one pair of shoes at the present time.

G. C. M.

NA/RG 120 (GHQ, War Diaries)

GENERAL SIBERT was relieved of command on December 14 and replaced by the former commander of the division's Second Infantry Brigade, Brigadier General Robert L. Bullard (U.S.M.A., 1885). Pershing's headquarters staff thought Sibert, who was basically an engineer with little troop service, overly conservative in his approach to training, and pessimistic, by which they meant that he accepted too fully French tendencies to train primarily for trench warfare rather than for a war of maneuver. (Robert L. Bullard, *Personalities and Reminiscences of the War* [Garden City, N.Y.: Doubleday, Page, 1925], pp. 98–99; James G. Harbord, *Leaves from a War Diary* [New York: Dodd, Mead, 1926], pp. 201–2.)

During the autumn of 1917, while Marshall was acting chief of staff, Bullard had complimented him on his handling of the job. When Bullard arrived at First Division headquarters in mid-December, it was with the intention of making Marshall permanent chief of staff, although Marshall did not know this until much later. But at the time, Marshall and some other of the staff officers were infuriated with General Headquarters' "misunderstanding of our situation. . . . These fellows at G.H.Q. were almost all my close friends and associates at Leavenworth, and most of them had been student officers under me . . . , but we were wholly out of sympathy with each other, and I felt that they didn't understand what they were doing at all. They had become very severe and they didn't know what they were being severe about. . . . General Pershing was severe, so they modeled their attitude on him. I was so outraged by this that I talked a great deal and I made a great mistake . . . I learned the lesson then I never forgot afterwards. . . . What I did was I demonstrated to General Bullard that I had no business being the chief of staff in that state of mind. . . . He made Campbell King chief of staff, who was a much more moderate person and didn't get 'het-up' to the extent I did. . . . I never made the mistake—I don't think—again. . . . I think it delayed [me] a great deal. I think I would have been chief of staff of the division, and I would very quickly have been made brigadier general." (Interview, April 5, 1957.)

Repeated warnings of an impending major German offensive in the spring of 1918, and Pershing's determination that the American troops give a good account of themselves, resulted in a period of intensive training during December and January. Marshall wrote that "the suffering of the men at this time exceeded any previous or subsequent experience." On January 14, the division began moving to the Ansauville subsector, north of Toul, on the south side of the St. Mihiel salient. Division headquarters was established at Menil-la-Tour, which Marshall described as "a small, cheerless village." (*Memoirs,* pp. 53, 59, 61.)

Although the sector was a relatively quiet one, it was the first time the American staff had administered so large and elaborate an area, and Marshall found the job demanding. "The work had generally to be carried on with four or five observers from G.H.Q. standing at one's elbow to watch how it was being done. This did not tend to quiet the nerves and promote the assurance of the division staff during their novitiate," Marshall recalled. His job during this period "was divided between working on the new plans for the dispositions of the troops, and familiarizing myself with the sector by frequent tours of the front." (Ibid., pp. 61, 66.)

Near the end of February, Marshall became convinced that the Germans were preparing to raid the First Division's lines. He wrote the following instructions for Chief of Staff Campbell King's signature. (Ibid., p. 68.) ★

INSTRUCTIONS NO. 15 [s. King]   February 27, 1918
Secret[1]   [Menil-la-Tour], France

DEFENSE OF ANSAUVILLE SECTOR
Provisions for all alerts.

1. The reason for all alerts is to prevent surprise by the enemy.

2. To insure intelligent action throughout the command during alerts and in case of possible developments following an enemy attack, the following information will be disseminated by Brigade, Regimental and Battalion Commanders throughout the Commissioned personnel of the Division:

The enemy is conducting behind his lines maneuvers of rupture, which he intends to put into effect in a great offensive to be launched suddenly and without warning. These maneuvers follow in a general way the British offensive at CAMBRAI, and the enemy's offensive at RIGA and on the ISONZO.[2] That is, they include a sudden, violent, unexpected assault and the development of an assumed success by deep penetration through trench lines and a renewal of open warfare.

The notable feature of these maneuvers is the concealment of preliminary preparations, the power and above all the brevity of the preparations for rupture of the line, and the depth of the penetration. In one maneuver the actual open preparation lasted a bare fifteen minutes, as opposed to previous preparations of at least several hours. Following the preparation the attacking troops went forward at dawn and at nightfall had penetrated twelve kilometers.

Harassing fire on trenches, communications, P.C.'s, O.P.'s and artillery emplacements, especially with gas shells, can be expected for days preceding as well as immediately before the assault.[3] But the necessary preparation for rupture of an organized position can be secured in fifteen minutes only by an overwhelming use of minenwerfers or of tanks.[4]

3. Defense in the case of the enormous use of minenwerfers must consist in a proper distribution of troops in depth. Defense of Position 1 must consist of determined resistance of such elements as have not been put out of action by the

bombardment. Defense in case of an extensive use of tanks must consist in the determined defense of strong points containing anti-tank guns, the use of all available artillery as mobile anti-tank guns, and the destruction of tanks by explosive charges or Stokes bombs, dropped on them or placed in their path.[5]

In this connection it must be noted that tanks might conceivably penetrate as far as ANSAUVILLE-RAULECOURT. In such a contingency all troops are charged with holding their advance by any means at hand.

NA/RG 120 (First Division, Historical File)

1. Most documents intended for internal use by the A.E.F. were restricted by some level of security classification. That classification is printed here only if it was indicated on the copy used by this project. An additional method of maintaining secrecy was by issuing a document only to a limited distribution list. These lists are not printed here.

2. At Cambrai, France, the British attacked the Germans without artillery preparation, but with 381 tanks, on November 20, 1917; the initial success turned to near disaster nine days later. On September 1, 1917, the German Eighth Army attacked the Russian Twelfth Army, capturing the city of Riga, Latvia, in three days. The Twelfth Battle of the Isonzo (Caporetto) began on October 24, 1917, when twelve German and Austrian assault divisions suddenly attacked the Italian Army across the Isonzo River, forcing a disastrous Italian retreat.

3. P.C. = Post of Command.   O.P. = Observation Post.

4. A Minenwerfer ("mine-thrower") was a German muzzle-loading trench gun used to destroy machine-gun nests.

5. The Stokes trench mortar, named after its inventor, Sir Wilfrid S. Stokes, was a British-made, light, three-inch, muzzle-loading mortar that fired a projectile (Stokes bomb) weighing eleven pounds.

AT DAWN on March 1, the expected blow fell on the Americans' empty forward trenches. The attackers were "badly cut up" by the First Division's counterattack. Marshall later wrote that the men "fought beautifully and viciously, and covered themselves with glory. The result was apparently tremendously reassuring to the higher French officials." Premier and Minister for War Georges Clemenceau himself journeyed from Paris to decorate certain of the American defenders. (*Memoirs,* pp. 68–70.)

The First Division's attempt to raid German lines in retaliation met with several delays, but finally it occurred on March 11. Marshall wrote the complex "Special Operations Order" for this first American raid. The order itself is four typed pages long and quite technical. The following two are typical of the ancillary documents necessary for such an operation. ★

MEMORANDUM FOR CAPTAIN GRAVES,[1]   March 8, 1918
SIXTEENTH INFANTRY   [Menil-la-Tour], France
Confidential

Preliminary arrangements and movements RICHECOURT raid.

1. *Patrolling:*

Special patrols will be sent out before J Day to note changes in aspect of enemy's wire and lines.

2. *Route forward from Position 1 bis.*

The movement of your party forward by daylight from RAMBUCOURT to subcenter H/1 is a very delicate operation. You will have the leader of each small group which is to go forward from RAMBUCOURT to Center H, reconnoiter the route before J Day. You will arrange for guides to be posted in the communicating trenches to be used between RAMBUCOURT and subcenter H/1.

3. *Checking Officer.*

You will prepare a plain, accurate list of your entire party, including every man who goes forward to jumping off point. Your Quartermaster, stationed at a selected point in subcenter H/1, will be charged with checking off each man and officer as he returns. All will be instructed as to the importance of this and the guides will be posted and instructed so that men will be passed back to checking officer.

A copy of the list will be given the Adjutant, 26th Infantry at RAMBUCOURT and arrangements made for rechecking the party at that point.

A copy of the list will be furnished these headquarters.

4. *Movements from JOUY sous les COTES.*

3:30 A.M. J Day – Leave JOUY in 4 trucks for RAMBUCOURT.

3:00 P.M. J Day – Pioneer groups leave RAMBUCOURT for P.C. of subcenter H/1, followed at intervals by remainder of party in small groups.

5. *Movements returning from raid.*

Leave RAMBUCOURT by four trucks as soon as party has been checked up, returning to JOUY. Capt. Graves to report direct to Division Headquarters.

NA/RG 120 (First Division, Historical File)

1. Captain Sidney C. Graves (U.S.M.A., 1915). A similar memorandum was given to the leader of the other raiding party, Captain Joseph Quesenberry, Eighteenth Infantry.

MEMORANDUM FOR BRIGADE   March 10, 1918
COMMANDERS [s. King]   [Menil-la-Tour], France
Very Secret

Day and hour for special operations and pass word.

1. *REMIERES RAID:*

J day will be March 11th.

H hour will be 5:50 A.M.

Troops on the front lines of Center F will be notified by their officers at 5:20 A.M., March 11th, of the hour of the raid. The pass word "BOSTON" will be used

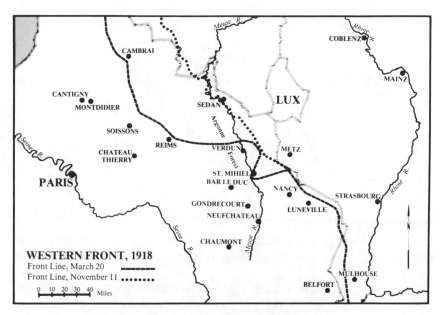

Some of the sites of Marshall's activities in the war.

to identify returning members of the raiding party who may return at any point of the line.

2. *RICHECOURT RAID:*

J day will be March 11th.

H hour will be 7:40 P.M.

Troops on the front lines of Center H and left of Center F will be notified by their officers at 7:10 P.M., March 11th, of the hour of the raid. The pass word "MEXICO" will be used to identify returning members of the raiding party who may return at any point of the line.

3. *CAUTION:*

Every possible precaution will be taken to prevent men in Center F from knowing that another raid is scheduled to be carried out following the one at the REMIERES salient.

The telephone will not be used to convey information regarding preparations for the raids. This prohibition does not apply to necessary technical artillery messages.

Information regarding the plans and time for these raids will only be given to those officers or non-commissioned officers who require the information in order to perform their duties effectively.

NA/RG 120 (First Division, Historical File)

To Commanding General, First Army Corps   March 9, 1918
From Chief of Staff, A.E.F.[1]   [Chaumont], France

Major Erickson and Colonel Marshall.

1. Special orders are being issued directing Major Erickson to report to you for duty with the 1st Division.[2]

2. The object of this order is the eventual transfer of Lieut. Colonel Marshall (Operations Section, 1st Division) to duty at these Headquarters.

3. The necessity for increasing the number of Infantry officers in G-3 (Operations) at these Headquarters is urgent.

It is believed that we have now arrived at the time when the General Staff here should be replenished from the troops. Under these conditions the reasons for the transfer of Colonel Marshall are obvious.

4. Nevertheless, the Commander-in-Chief is determined not to handicap the 1st Division in any way. It is therefore his desire that you and the Commanding General, 1st Division, should agree upon the feasibility of relieving Colonel Marshall.

To this end it appears that the only practicable solution is to send Major Erickson, who at present appears to be the only suitable officer available, for duty with the Operations Section of the 1st Division, General Staff, and to defer issuing orders in the case of Colonel Marshall until you and General Bullard have decided that the change may be effected. It is anticipated that a month or six weeks must elapse before this can be done.

5. In the unexpected event that Major Erickson should not prove satisfactory, effort will be made to find another officer to replace Colonel Marshall.

NA/RG 120 (GHQ, G-3 Reports)

1. The First Army Corps was created on January 15, 1918. Major General Hunter Liggett took command five days later. In addition to the First Division, the Second, Twenty-sixth, Thirty-second, Forty-first, and Forty-second Divisions were assigned to Liggett's command at this time. The A.E.F. chief of staff was Brigadier General James G. Harbord.

2. Hjalmer Erickson, who had been born in Norway and had begun his career as a private in the Eighth Cavalry, was a major in the permanent establishment. At the time of this memorandum, however, Erickson was a lieutenant colonel in the "National Army," i.e., the draft-based army as distinct from either the National Guard or the Regular Army.

To Commanding General, Thirty-Second   March 12, 1918
Army Corps [s. Bullard][1]   [Menil-la-Tour], France
Confidential

Special Operations Report.

1. *Raid on Remieres Salient.*

(a) At 5:50 A.M., March 11th, a detachment of 5 officers and 87 men of the 18th Infantry and 1st Regiment of Engineers, commanded by Captain Quesenberry, 18th Infantry, carried out a raid on the salient north of the western edge of the BOIS REMIERES. Twelve Engineer soldiers of the party formed a reserve with long torpedo charges to be used in case the breach in the wire made by the artillery on March 10th was not found to be satisfactory. As the breach was satisfactory, they were not required to go forward from our lines.

(b) The raiding party carried out their operation as planned. Not more than 11 Germans were found in the position raided. 1 was found killed by shell fire and 3 were killed by revolver or rifle fire. 7 retreated into our box fire, pursued by members of the raiding party. They were probably casualties. The condition of the trenches and dugouts was such that no estimate could be formed of other losses suffered by the enemy as a result of the artillery fire. All dugouts were caved in and the trenches were practically demolished and holding a great deal of water.

The raiding party remained in the enemy's position 20 minutes without suffering any casualties. 2 men were wounded by machine gun fire during the return across No Man's Land and 1 man was wounded by shell fire within our lines. He died later.

(c) It was apparent that the enemy had withdrawn the usual garrison of the salient as soon as the breaches were cut in the wire.

2. Raid on Eastern Flank of RICHECOURT salient.

(a) At 7:40 P.M. on March 11th, a detachment of 4 officers and 70 men of the 16th Infantry and 1 Engineer officer, commanded by Captain Graves, 16th Infantry, carried out a raid on the eastern flank of the RICHECOURT salient, a gap in the wire having been cut by artillery fire on March 10th.

(b) The raiding party carried out the operations as planned. About ten Germans were seen, of whom four were killed by a Stokes Mortar bomb thrown into the shell hole they had established themselves in and one or possibly two more were killed by grenades. No deep dugouts were found, only light shelters and these had been badly damaged. The trenches were found to be in a miserable state of repair, filled with water in many places and generally caved in.

2 officers and 3 men of the raiding party were lightly wounded by grenade fragments. No other casualties.

3. General remarks.

(a) The work of the French and American artillery was excellent, the enemy's reaction in each raid being practically negligible. The fact that our infantry was able to penetrate from 150 to 250 yards within the enemy's lines twice in one day without the loss of a man has served to inspire them with great confidence in our artillery. Their observation of the German trenches has also served to give them greater confidence in the strength of their own positions, as well as a poorer opinion of the strength of the enemy's.

Both raiding parties went into action in high spirits and came out with increased morale, though much disappointed in not taking any prisoners.

(b) This Division is greatly indebted to the 69th D.I. on our right and the 10th Colonial Division on our left for the strong support given during these two operations.

NA/RG 120 (First Division, Historical File)

1. At this time the First Division was part of the French Thirty-second Corps, which was commanded by General Passaga, whom General Bullard later praised for his aggressiveness and for his abilities to inspire confidence and to "win the American heart." (Bullard, *Personalities and Reminiscences of the War,* p. 289.)

MARSHALL'S transfer to General Headquarters at Chaumont was delayed longer than anticipated by the German spring offensive of 1918. On March 20, Marshall left Menil-la-Tour under orders to report to the American General Staff College at Langres, where he was to deliver a series of lectures on the practical administration of the First Division. The next day, March 21, the first of the five great German attacks of 1918 was launched against the British. Marshall had to pick up the classroom slack left by hurriedly departing British instructors. He wrote in his *Memoirs* (p. 76) that there "was not much time for personal thoughts with this variety of new duties to be assimilated, but I did have a feeling of great depression over being separated from the First Division just as the active fighting began."

On March 29, Marshall was ordered back to the division to help prepare for the move to the front, somewhere in Picardy. By April 5 the division was on the move. Two days later its headquarters was established at Chaumont-en-Vixen. Training began at once to assimilate the lessons taught by the German offensive. Eleven days later the division was moving again, replacing two French divisions in the Cantigny Sector by April 26. The First Division's command post was located in the wine cellar of a small chateau at Mesnil–St. Firmin, near the apex of the salient the first German drive had put into the French lines.

The division worked furiously on preparations against the expected renewal of the German attack around mid-May. The operations section planned a counterattack. Meanwhile, both sides deluged their enemies with continuous shellfire. When the expected attack did not materialize—the Germans were then preparing to strike fifty miles to the east—the First Division began to plan its own attack against the village of Cantigny. ★

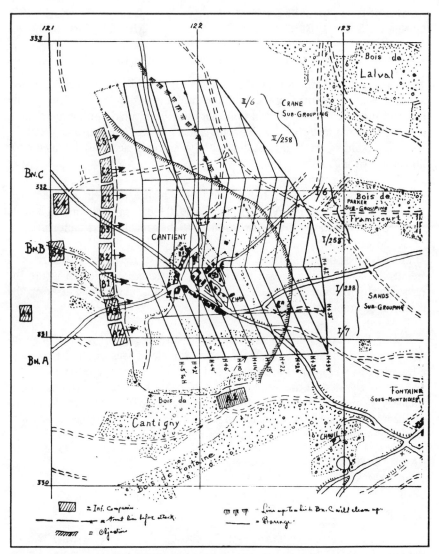

Map of the proposed Cantigny advance drawn by Marshall's Operations Section (G-3).

MEMORANDUM FOR THE COMMANDING   May 17, 1918
GENERAL, SECOND BRIGADE[1]   [Mesnil-St. Firmin], France

Alert arrangements, advance posts, alarms.

1. During the present period of moonlight nights while large working parties are employed well to the front and a heavy offensive action by the enemy at any moment must be considered as a possibility, it is particularly important that all commanders, particularly subsector commanders, make careful arrangements:
—for obtaining early information of the enemy's activities by means of numerous, strong patrols
—for obtaining prisoners
—for disposing of the troops at work in advance of their assigned alert positions in case of alarm. (*Note:* If practicable, these troops will immediately be returned, by *previously* reconnoitered routes, to their regular alert stations.)
2. *Advance Posts.*
The advance posts established in front of the line of resistance will be relieved frequently. Their positions will be changed, if necessary, so as to insure the protection of the line of resistance against a surprise attack and to keep the enemy in ignorance of their location.
3. *Alarms.*
During the recent German offensive there were instances where German infantry reached the line of resistance before the alarm was given. Patrols and advance posts will be instructed in several methods of giving the alarm quickly and effectively, despite the noise of bombardment. All front line troops will be similarly instructed. Whistle signals, rifle and revolver fire, "to arms" sounded on the bugle and any other available means will be employed to give the alarm to rear echelons in time to permit them to man their trenches.

G. C. Marshall, Jr.

NA/RG 120 (First Division, Historical File)
1. Brigadier General Beaumont B. Buck (U.S.M.A., 1885).

MEMORANDUM FOR COMMANDING GENERAL,   May 22, 1918
SECOND BRIGADE [s. King]   [Mesnil-St. Firmin], France

Prisoners.

1. The present critical situation makes it vital that prisoners be obtained on our front, particularly from the unidentified division facing the northern portion of our sector.
2. No prisoners have been obtained since May 2nd. Our ambuscade patrols have so far been unsuccessful. It is quite evident that the enemy is carefully avoiding the possibility of losing prisoners.

3. The Division Commander therefore directs that a determined effort be made to obtain prisoners in the shortest practicable time by means of patrols, larger combat groups, silent raids or raid with artillery support. For the last mentioned there is no time for training and long preparation. Heavy fire on a designated area, possibly followed by a box barrage of such dimensions as not to require careful advance registration, can be furnished by the artillery on request. A concise statement with sketch showing:

  area of preparation fire by artillery, amount and time

  limits of box fire and time,

should accompany requests for artillery preparation.

Campbell King

NA/RG 120 (First Division, Historical File)

OPERATIONS REPORT   May 28, 1918

[Mesnil-St. Firmin], France

From 10 A.M. May 27 to 10 A.M. May 28.

I. *General Characteristics of the Day:*

  We successfully attacked and took CANTIGNY.

II. *American Activity:*

  (a) *Infantry.–*

After a heavy destructive fire by our artillery the 28th Infantry advanced and took CANTIGNY in accordance with Field Orders #18. All objectives were taken and the ground is now being consolidated. 175 prisoners, of whom 3 are officers, have been counted. It is impossible to estimate the enemy's losses in killed and wounded, but they were very heavy. Our casualties are estimated to be about 300. Details will be furnished later. . . .

NA/RG 120 (First Division, Historical File)

CANTIGNY was the first American offensive. It had been ordered primarily to improve British and French morale. For the First Division to have withdrawn in the face of German counterattacks would have been a serious blow to American prestige and morale. For that reason, the Germans launched repeated and intense assaults on the new line. Pershing reported to the army chief of staff and the secretary of war that the division's attack had been "well planned and splendidly executed. . . . It is my firm conviction that our troops are the best in Europe and our staffs are the equals of any." (Pershing to March and Baker, June 1, 1918, NA/RG 120 [GHQ, Command File].)

But the small victory was overshadowed by the Third Battle of the Aisne which began on May 27. To replace French troops sent to meet the new threat, the First Division stretched its front. On June 4, division headquarters moved to the Chateau de Tartigny. Here, Marshall noted, the staff was "established in comparative luxury." They could even sleep above ground. Meanwhile, they planned to meet a German assault expected in about one week. (*Memoirs,* pp. 101–3.) ★

MEMORANDUM

June 4, 1918
[Tartigny], France

Liaison.

The present situation demands perfect liaison on the part of all unit commanders and their subordinate commanders. Therefore the Division Commander directs that:

(a) In every movement (relief, change of station in sector or rear area, alteration of combat position, etc.) a report will be made to the next higher commander *immediately upon the completion of the movement,* and when unexpectedly made, before it is initiated. Brigade and separate organization commanders will keep the G-3 section, Division Headquarters, constantly informed as to every movement so that there can be no doubt at any moment as to the location of the various units in the command.

(b) Battalion, company and platoon commanders in rear of the Intermediate Position will keep their units well in hand and will keep in close touch with their higher commanders.

G. C. Marshall, Jr.

NA/RG 120 (First Division, Historical File)

TO CHIEF OF STAFF, A.E.F.
FROM COMMANDING GENERAL, FIRST DIVISION

June 6, 1918
[Tartigny], France

Promotion of Lieut. Col. G. C. Marshall, Jr., G.S.

1. I believe that this officer's superior merit is recognized. He has had, of all officers of the General Staff up to the present time, the widest experience in actual staff work as G-3. That work, it seems to me, has been well up to the standard of the best armies with which the American Expeditionary Forces is serving. I believe it would be a mistake to keep Lieut. Col. Marshall, with his experience and ability, in as low a grade or as low a plane as he now occupies,

and I recommend his promotion to the next grade as fitting to the higher place to which he is sure to soon be called. . . .

NA/RG 120 (First Division, Record Card 8490)

To Colonel Hamilton A. Smith[1]   June 12, 1918
[Tartigny], France

My dear Colonel Smith: I have just received your note regarding memorandum on raids.[2]

The memorandum had a two-fold purpose, first: to have each regiment prepared so that if the Corps or Army made one of its sudden calls upon us as has been done in the past the regimental commander would have some chance to carry out a raid which had been carefully thought out; and second: to get the raid business started all along the front—that is, to have them doing in each regiment what you did in your regiment when you carried out your raid the other day.

What you say about the time required to arrange for a raid after it is planned is well understood. Our trouble has been that the demand has been made upon us in the afternoon to get prisoners the same night. Similar demands will probably be made in the future; but if all the plans have been prepared it will not be quite so unfair for the men. However, we have already established a great reputation with the Corps and Army for the daring patrolling that is continually carried out on our front and if we add to that, without any orders from the Army, frequent raids made at times chosen by the regimental commanders, I doubt if we receive many eleventh hour requests.

I do not think that there can be any question but what these raids are a military necessity at the present time. Every prisoner taken has contributed to the killing effect of our artillery fire, and has either reassured us as to the conditions in our front or given us some form of warning of what might be expected.

I think everyone here agrees with you about going to the Avre. Certainly the men would prefer to do something active rather than sit and take what is handed to them. However, no replacements are in sight. All our divisions are fast being employed and it is going to be pretty strenuous business pulling thru the next two months and if the division gets badly knocked about just at this time there is nothing to relieve it.

Here are some points that were reported by one of the Staff officers inspecting in the BELLE ASSISE region early yesterday morning:

— the wire in front of the line of resistance needs strengthening as there are only a few strands in most places;

— a great deal of paper (probably hard tack boxes, etc.) is strewn along in the vicinity of occupied trenches. This would photograph distinctly and give quite a clew as to our disposition;

— there were no alternate emplacements, or selected positions without emplacements, for the machine guns in LA LONGUE HAIE. As these woods would probably be heavily gassed the M.G.s to defend the draw would probably be put out of action;

— telephone wires were lying on the bottom of the boyaux where they are much more easily cut by shell fire or broken by passing men than if fastened to little stakes against the side of the trench.[3]

In connection with the above please do not think that we feel back here that no one is working up front, for we believe we have a pretty fair appreciation of how much everyone has done and how tired the men are.   Sincerely,

Marshall

NA/RG 120 (First Division, Historical File)

1. Smith (U.S.M.A., 1893) had been with Marshall on the *Tenadores* and at Mme Jouatte's in Gondrecourt. At this time he commanded the Twenty-sixth Infantry. He was killed at Soissons in mid-July.
2. The memorandum could not be found.
3. *Boyaux* were zigzag connecting or approach trenches.

To Major General Edward W. Nichols   June 14, 1918
                                                        [Tartigny], France

My dear General Nichols: I just learnt something a few minutes ago which I think will be of great interest to you. On May 28th troops of our Army made their first offensive operation, advancing on a front of over 2 kilometers and penetrating the enemies line for over a kilometer—they captured Cantigny, near Montdidier. I had been dealing with some men's names who were involved in the fighting, but not until a moment ago did I discover how creditable a part the V.M.I. played in the performance.

One company of Engineers participated in the attack. It lost 2 officers killed and 2 wounded and suffered heavy casualties among the men—but it stuck to its difficult job beautifully. It was commanded by Smith,[1] Class of 1915.

One battalion of infantry had to reinforce the line with some companies in broad daylight, under a terrific bombardment of very heavy artillery and a deadly machine gun fire. It also had to send companies forward under similar conditions and during a counter attack to carry up ammunition. Its battalion commander, fearing some difficulty about direction or delay due to the violent hostile fire, personally *led* some companies forward and saw them properly located in place. This was Creswell[2] of 1914, I think. He was recently promoted major for previous good work and also was commended for personally directing the work of digging jumping off trenches during the two nights before the attack when the hostile artillery was raising hell over the place. The machine gun company in Creswell's battalion is commanded by Cammer of 1915,[3] who is making a fine record.

As a last interest of the V.M.I. in the first attack, it happened to be my good fortune to have the opportunity of drafting the plans and writing the orders for the operation. This last statement is out of place among the descriptions I have given you of how some of our men fought, and it is for *your private ear alone.* It would ruin me to be making such a claim.

Al Tucker went in with his company to relieve the troops after the cessation of the counterattacks, and was wounded by a bursting shell. I think he will be all right very soon. He has been making a fine record.[4]

I feel sure you will be glad to know of the honorable part some of your men played in the hard fighting around Cantigny.

This is a very crude letter, but I only have a few moments and I feel sure you will understand the pencil and the disjointed English.

Always Sincerely respectfully yours,

G. C. Marshall, Jr.

GCMRL/VMI Collection; H

1. Captain Horace L. Smith, Jr.
2. Major Harry I.T. Creswell, class of 1913.
3. Lieutenant Claude R. Cammer.
4. Albert S.J. Tucker, a Lexington, Virginia, native, was temporarily with the First Division's Sixteenth Infantry as captain of Company G.

MEMORANDUM

June 18, 1918
[Tartigny], France

Utilization of information of the enemy.

1. Commanders of companies, infantry and machine gun, have stated, in several instances, that they have never seen photographs of the enemy's organization in their front and that frequently they have been compelled to arrange for their patrolling by means of small scale maps. If this is the case, it means that many opportunities for capturing prisoners have been lost and it also means that the lives of our men and officers have been needlessly risked or sacrificed.

2. Photographs have been furnished regiments of their entire front. The attention of company commanders in the front line should be called to the interesting points on the photographs, (organized shell holes, advance posts, etc.). It is not fair to the officers and soldiers to require them to work in No Man's Land without giving them the benefit of every assistance possible. The enemy takes advantage of every item of information he secures regarding our troops.

We must do likewise in order to successfully compete with him, no matter how courageous our men may be.

NA/RG 120 (First Division, Historical File)

TO THE ADJUTANT GENERAL, A.E.F.   June 18, 1918
[Tartigny], France

Duty with troops.

1. Request that I be relieved from duty on the General Staff and assigned to duty with troops.

2. I have been on staff duty since February, 1915, and I am tired from the incessant strain of office work.

G. C. Marshall, Jr.

[1st Indorsement: Major General Robert L. Bullard, June 19, 1918.]

1. Forwarded.

2. I cannot approve because I know that Lieut. Col. Marshall's special fitness is for staff work and because I doubt that in this, whether it be teaching or practice, he has an equal in the Army to-day. But his experience and merit should find a wider field than the detailed labors of a Division Staff.

R. L. Bullard

[2nd Indorsement: Colonel Malin Craig, Chief of Staff,
First Army Corps, June 26, 1918.]

1. Forwarded, preceding indorsement concurred in. If available, the services of Lieut. Col. Marshall will be very acceptable at these headquarters.

Malin Craig

NA/RG 120 (GHQ, AG File)

Marshall; Colonel Alvin C. Voris, the First Division's chief signal officer; Lieutenant Jean Hugo, French interpreter and liaison officer; Captain Jesse C. Drain, the First Division's ordnance officer; Madame Jouatte, in whose home the others were billeted at Gondrecourt; a French refugee and her daughter, 1917.

145

Colonel Campbell King, chief of staff; Brigadier General John L. Hines, commander, First Brigade; Lieutenant Colonel Marshall, assistant chief of staff; at Beauvais, June, 1918.

Major General Robert L. Bullard and his staff gather at Gondrecourt on January 17, 1918, the day before moving First Division headquarters to Menil-la-Tour in the Ansauville subsector. Marshall is third and Bullard is fourth from the left in the front row.

*Major General William L. Sibert, First
Division commander, June, 1917.*

Lieutenant General Hunter Liggett.

General John J. Pershing.

Brigadier General Malin Craig.

Lieutenant General Robert L. Bullard.

Watercolors by Joseph Cummings Chase
of some of the men with whom Marshall was associated.

Left to right: *Captain Sidney Fish (one of General Allen's aides), Marshall, and Major General Henry T. Allen, at Montigny-sur-Aube, December, 1918. The handwriting on the photograph is Marshall's.*

Marshall in the Operations Section office at First Army headquarters, Bar-sur-Aube, January 4, 1919.

To Colonel William M. Fassett[1]   July 6, 1918
                                                                [Tartigny], France

My dear Colonel Fassett: I am enclosing herewith a copy of the various orders issued for the relief of this Division by two French divisions, which is now taking place. I believe this will be interesting to you at LANGRES in view of the fact that it is a rather normal relief, arranged hurriedly and in a battle sector.

I am also enclosing copies of a portion of the Plan of Defense, and a map which will give you an idea of our dispositions.

Since seeing you the other day I have had more experience with the employment of the Division arranged with regiments in line each in column of battalions.[2] It has proved a pronounced success for a number of reasons:

—the staff work is much simpler; responsibility for work, tactical dispositions and combat resting with the brigade and regimental commanders;

—reliefs within the Division were carried out without anybody being bothered except the regimental commander concerned, and for him the matter was very simple, involving a minimum of marching;

—raids and similar matters were handled entirely and directly by regimental commanders, who made their own arrangements with the artillery, thus learning to employ artillery as they would have to in a rapid and deep advance, etc.,

—the supply and equipment of each regiment was much simplified. The 3rd line battalions were located at the same place as the supply companies and rear echelons of the headquarters companies. When a battalion came out of the line, it could be cleaned up, reclothed, its records straightened out and everything gotten in shape in the minimum of time. This is a very important factor;

—supply of the troops of the 1st line battalions was much simplified because the regiments occupied narrow fronts and the supply companies were not taxed to the extent they are on a wide front. The salvage question improved tremendously because each battalion had the opportunity of seeing personally the tremendous accumulation of stuff that was brought back to the supply company every day;

—the instruction of troops out of the line was much simplified. A regular course for machine gunners, automatic riflemen, etc., was established at the location of the 3rd line battalions and each unit passed thru these schools during its tour in the 3rd line. The schools were continuous, which is more effective, and could be directly watched by regimental commanders. Also the Division M.G. Officer and Division Staff Officers could keep track of the progress more effectively;

—the Y.M.C.A. and Red Cross were able to concentrate their efforts on the 3rd line battalions and thus contribute more effectively to the rapid refreshing and rejuvenating of the men;

—so far as fighting the division goes I am convinced that this is the best way to handle our large divisions effectively. I believe that had we been arranged in this fashion the entire time we were in the sector, the troops would be in 30 per cent better shape than they now are.

I have not sent other papers down to the school because I did not consider our work as furnishing a sufficiently good model or guide for our people. We were usually required to take up dispositions and carry out movements after a fashion which involved many complications; therefore I have waited until now, when I think I can send you something which is really worth while.   Sincerely yours,

NA/RG 120 (First Division, Historical File)
1. Fassett (U.S.M.A., 1897) had attended Leavenworth a year behind Marshall, who was one of his instructors in 1908-9. He was head of the A.E.F. Staff College at Langres, France.
2. Benjamin F. Caffey, Jr., who assisted Marshall during much of the war—Marshall praised his knowledge and efficiency (*Memoirs,* p. 116)—observed: "The Marshall plan was for the division to attack with four infantry regiments abreast, with each regiment in column of battalions with two companies in assault and two companies in reserve with each company with two platoons in assault and two in support. The third line battalions of the exterior regiments were in division reserve. A regiment of light field artillery (75 mm gun) supported each brigade and the 155 mm howitzer regiment was in general support. In order to keep this formation simple in the minds of the division, it was called the 'normal' attack formation. Colonel Marshall, of course, was aware that there are no normal tactical formations, but he had a difficult problem to solve and he did it. The proof, of course, was the success of the 1st Division at Soissons, St. Mihiel and the Meuse-Argonne." (Brigadier General Caffey to Forrest C. Pogue, January 14, 1961, GCMRL/Research File [World War I].)

To Commanding General, First Corps   July 8, 1918
From Brigadier General Robert C. Davis[1]   [Chaumont], France

Special orders made this date relieve Lieutenant Colonel George C. Marshall from duty with the First Division and direct him report to Chief of Staff AEF for assignment to other duty. On completion of the relief of the First Division from the front line direct Colonel Marshall to comply with this order. Travel directed is necessary in the military service.

NA/RG 120 (GHQ, AG File)
1. Davis (U.S.M.A., 1898) was the adjutant general of the A.E.F.

THE LAST First Division troops left the Cantigny sector on July 8. Marshall remained behind for a day to complete the transition to the French, then motored south to the new headquarters at Chateau Nivillers, near Beauvais.

Marshall had hardly begun to adjust to rear-area life, when on July 12 he received orders to proceed to Chaumont for service with the Operations Section at General Headquarters. "My plans had all been laid to get command of a regiment in the division," Marshall wrote in his *Memoirs,* "and this not only denied me that duty, but removed me from the front." Leaving the division was hard, he wrote. "Bigger problems were to come—but never again that feeling of comradeship which grows out of the intimate relationship among those in immediate contact with the fighting troops." Writing in the early 1920s, Marshall said: "Whatever else was to happen to me—in the war or in the future—could be but a minor incident in my career." (*Memoirs,* pp. 116–18.)

Arriving at Chaumont on the night of July 13, Marshall was given a room in the house of Chief of Operations Fox Conner (U.S.M.A., 1898). Most of the members of the section were old friends. Marshall found the atmosphere they worked in "strange." Their problems and plans were entirely different than those facing the First Division staff. They dealt with ocean tonnage, ports of debarkation, dock construction, tank manufacture, methods of training divisions, and the complexities of inter-Allied politics. "To me this was a different world from that in which I had lived during the past year." (Ibid., p. 121.)

Marshall's first assignment, given to him on his first morning in Chaumont, was to collect as much information as possible regarding the St. Mihiel salient and to begin developing a plan to reduce the salient. (Ibid.) His "Preliminary Study," which assumed four American divisions in assault and three for mopping-up and reserve, was finished by August 6. The operation sought to achieve three general objectives. The first was to "free the main line of the PARIS-NANCY railroad in the vicinity of ST. MIHIEL." The Germans had to be driven back at least fifteen kilometers from the railroad. The second purpose was to "carry out a purely American major offensive before the start of the rainy season in 1918." Consequently, the operation had to begin "by September 15th, if practicable." Finally, the attack would prepare the way for the 1919 offensive, "for which the Operations Section at Chaumont was already planning." (Marshall to Assistant Chief of Staff, G-3 [Fox Conner], August 6, 1918, NA/RG 120 [GHQ, G-3 Reports].)

But the St. Mihiel planning was strongly influenced by British and French successes elsewhere along the front and by inter-Allied politics. The number of divisions available changed constantly, and each change affected the basic conception of the operation. Marshall recalled, "I have always been rather embarrassed by the fact that I submitted a number of different plans—none of them you might say conclusive." (Interview, April 11, 1957.) An August 9 plan envisioned a ten-division drive with French support from the south. The plan, dated August 13, utilized fourteen divisions attacking both faces of the salient. Three days later, Marshall submitted the following seventeen-division plan. ★

REPORT TO THE ASSISTANT CHIEF OF STAFF, G-3   August 16, 1918
Secret   [Chaumont], France

Offensive operation to reduce the ST. MIHIEL SALIENT
and carry our line to include the heights south of GORZE.

1. *STATEMENT OF PROBLEM.*

Such an operation involves the combination of three separate minor operations:

(a) An attack on the southern face of the salient through THIAUCOURT.

(b) An attack on the northern face of the salient through FRESNES.

(c) An attack northward along the heights of the east bank of the MOSELLE.

It is intended in this paper merely to discuss the question of the number of divisions necessary and the general character of each of these three operations.

The penetration to a line including the heights south of GORZE has been imposed as the desired result to be obtained.

2. *GENERAL CONSIDERATIONS.*

The attacks against the south and west face of the salient must be coordinated so that they effectively support each other and converge on a selected point. Each involves a penetration of approximately 20 kilometers.

The attack north along the east bank of the MOSELLE is necessary in order to prevent the enfilading of the right flank of the proposed new line along the heights south of GORZE. It involves an advance of about 8 kilometers.

. . . An operation involving a deep penetration with a limited number of divisions through a very strong defensive organization where the enemy has means of communication which will permit him to rapidly bring up his available reserves, requires that the divisions making the initial rupture of the first and second position should continue on to the final objectives without allowing the enemy time to deploy machine gun detachments and bring up reserves. In this instance the threat of the German divisions cut off in the salient by the pinching out operation must be met by flank guards heavily reinforced with machine guns, and by the reserve divisions. The enemy divisions so cut off will be demoralized by the heavy gas neutralization fire which should be directed on them and by the feeling of having been separated from their own forces. They will be much scattered at the time of the attack and it should not be possible for them to attempt any coordinated action against the rear of our advancing divisions until too late.

3. *OPERATION THROUGH THIAUCOURT.*

A study of an advance through THIAUCOURT to the heights north of the RUPT de MAD has already been made. It was based on a convergent advance on THIAUCOURT from the vicinity of REGNIEVILLE and LAHAYVILLE respectively, the heights west of the MOSELLE and south of PRENY being taken by out-flanking maneuvers. Five divisions were required for the main assault, 1 division in the center was to be employed with a partial penetration and cleaning up mission eventually to form as a reserve, and 2 other divisions were in immediate reserve, i.e.: 8 in all. 2 Army Reserve divisions were to be available for use in emergency or for relief.

With the new objective in view the plan for a convergent attack on

THIAUCOURT ceases to be satisfactory as it would not give a proper direction to the force of the attack. The entire progression should be northeast, except that the right division would have to execute a series of turning movements to clean up the heights south of PRENY.

The left of this advance should come in contact with the right of the advance from FRESNES between SPONVILLE and LACHAUSSEE. The total front of the final objective for the THIAUCOURT operation would, therefore, be about 17 kilometers. To penetrate this front 5 divisions will be required plus 1 division for turning and cleaning up the defenses immediately west of the MOSELLE and a portion of one division for containing and cleaning up the region of BOIS de MONT MARE and BOIS du BEAU VALLON. In addition 2 reserve divisions should be available.

Summary.

>   6 divisions for assault.
>   1 division for cleaning up and reserve.
>   2 divisions for reserve.
>   9 Total.

4. *OPERATION THROUGH FRESNES.*

The limits of the final objective of this operation have already been assumed, the right between SPONVILLE and LACHAUSSEE and the left at BLANZEE. The extensive wooded south of ETAIN is the critical feature of the terrain. It will probably be difficult to conquer and will necessitate considerable maneuvering. It must be taken as otherwise it would afford the enemy a covered approach from which to deliver a counter attack across our line of communications. The remainder of the terrain is more or less flat and dotted with organized villages. It should be possible for tanks. The heights south of LES EPARGES permit the enemy to overlook any operation in the plain to the northeast, but possible artillery activity from this quarter can be sufficiently neutralized by our artillery enfilading the ridge from emplacements within the local salient near LES EPARGES.

To reach the right of the final objective requires an advance of approximately 14 kilometers. The total front of the final objective is 25 kilometers. Once the woods on the left of this line are carried they can be held with a reasonably light force. The progression across the plain of the WOEVRE, if well assisted by tanks, should not prove difficult if the villages are passed by and taken from the rear. It is estimated that a minimum of 4 divisions would be required for the advance into the plain, 1 division for the occupation of the forest west of BRAQUIS and 1 division as a reserve.

Total—6 divisions, minimum force.

5. *OPERATION EAST OF THE MOSELLE.*

To hold the heights south of GORZE without suffering severe losses from enfilading artillery fire and to deprive the enemy of observation points which would enable him to overlook the ravine of the RUPT de MAD from the MOSELLE to beyond ONVILLE, necessitates the conquest of the heights of the east bank of the MOSELLE from our present line north of Hill 369, two kilometers north of ARRY.

To hold safely these heights, it will be necessary to gain a foot hold in the low ground to the east. The terrain involved is difficult, highly organized and defended by the garrison of METZ. There is limited room in which to maneuver. Tanks can not be utilized, except possibly in a small portion of the low ground. Therefore, it would be necessary to precede the infantry advance by at least 1 day of observed artillery fire of destruction.

There is not room for the employment of more than 2 divisions. The heights would probably have to be carried by direct attack along the crests. It is estimated that 2 divisions will be required for this operation.

6. *RESUME.*

Operation through THIAUCOURT	— 9	divisions.
Operation through FRESNES	— 6	divisions.
Operation east of the MOSELLE	— 2	divisions.

Total . . . . . . 17 divisions.

The FRESNES and THIAUCOURT attacks should be launched simultaneously and with the minimum of preliminary artillery preparation.

The operation east of the MOSELLE should commence with violent artillery fire of destruction, starting at the H hour of the attacks west of the MOSELLE. This fire should continue for approximately 24 hours. The first stage of the infantry advance might be carried out at the end of 12 hours, the final advance being started at the end of the 24 hours. . . .[1]

NA/RG 120 (GHQ, G-3 Reports)

1. The attached map and the paragraph describing the map coordinates of the final objective and direction of advance have been omitted.

M Y STATE OF MIND at this period is impossible to describe," Marshall wrote in his *Memoirs.* "I seemed to be getting farther and farther away from the fight, and it was particularly hard to work on a plan and then not be permitted to attend its execution." On August 20, John A. Lejeune (U.S.N.A., 1890), the Marine Corps general commanding the Second Division, personally came to Chaumont to request Marshall's services as commander of the Twenty-third Infantry Regiment in the coming battle. Not only was the request denied, but Marshall was ordered to leave immediately for Neufchateau, where he was to be temporary assistant to Chief of Staff Hugh Drum of the newly formed First Army. (*Memoirs,* p. 125.)

In addition to his heavy load of office work at First Army headquarters,

Marshall had to make frequent visits to the numerous corps and division headquarters to discuss various aspects of the battle plans. Operational secrecy was a frequent topic of discussion. In addition to the sheer magnitude of the enterprise, enthusiastic officers, convinced that their particular job was of momentous importance, and thus an exception to rules governing reconnaissance and travel, made secrecy difficult to maintain. (Ibid., p. 131.) Finally, Marshall wrote the following. ★

MEMORANDUM FOR THE CHIEF OF STAFF,   August 23, 1918
FIRST ARMY   [Neufchateau], France
Secret

Secrecy in preparations for offensive operation.

1. The following measures are suggested as necessary to insure the desired secrecy in preparing for offensive operation:

A. *Regulations governing reconnaissances.*

Hours—Less than 3 kilometers from German first parallel, to be made between dusk and dawn in groups of not to exceed 5, including guides.

Less than 10 kilometers and more than 3 kilometers, to be permitted during daylight by groups of not to exceed 3, including guide.

Vehicles—Automobile circulation to be forbidden, except during hours of darkness, in zone within 7 kilometers of front, and use of side cars to be restricted.

Additional precautions—Officers on reconnaissance within 3 kilometers of front must wear soldier's uniform, including spiral puttee leggins. Leather despatch cases, notebooks, with entries, special maps, etc., will not be carried in this zone. Sam Browne belts will not be worn in divisional sectors.

B. *Corps Control.*

Each Corps Commander will organize a special force, in addition to the usual military police force, to prevent preparations for the attack being made in a manner which might convey information to the enemy of our offensive intentions. The officer in charge of this force and his assistants will inspect all work in progress, observe the circulation and conduct of reconnaissance groups. He will be empowered and directed to take immediate action to correct or stop improperly camouflaged undertakings and undue circulation.

These instructions apply particularly to the construction of artillery or trench mortar emplacements, the construction of signal lines, the repair of roads and trails, the preparation of new dumps (or depots) or the enlargement of existing ones, the rapid circulation of motorcycles on dusty roads, etc.

Corps Commanders are authorized to make specific exceptions to the rules under (A) for particular cases.

C. *Dissemination of Information.* . . .

2. If the foregoing is approved it should be put in force at once, special arrangements being made with the French to permit our Corps Commanders to function in enforcing these regulations over Americans in sectors not now under American Corps control.

Furthermore, it is recommended that visiting from area to area by officers and men of divisions be forbidden.

NA/RG 120 (First Army, Historical File)

To MAJOR GENERAL JOHN L. HINES   September 1, 1918
[Ligny-en-Barrois, France]

My dear General: I am sure no one, not even Mrs. Hines, was more pleased over your promotion than I was, and I regard it as but a step on your way.[1] I had hoped to see you personally to congratulate you, and so delayed writing. Now everything is so uncertain that I must send my congratulations by letter.

I am here on temporary duty helping things along. I do not know how long I will remain—possibly some weeks.

Please do not forget me and put in a word for me some time to get me back to troops. Sincerely yours,

G. C. Marshall, Jr.

LC/J. L. Hines Papers; H

1. Hines (U.S.M.A., 1891) was promoted to major general early in August and given command of the Fourth Division. Prior to this, he had commanded the First Division's Sixteenth Infantry Regiment and then its First Infantry Brigade.

IN PREPARING for the St. Mihiel attack, one of Marshall's chief problems was the extent of the artillery preparation to be made. With little time for elaborate strategems and no heavy tanks, only three options seemed available: (1) fourteen hours of fire in order to break gaps in the barbed wire; (2) five hours of fire, mainly to demoralize the defenders and inspire the attackers; (3) no preparatory fire. As the day of the battle drew closer, Pershing seemed to lean toward the third alternative, a course Marshall considered fraught with potential disaster. (*Memoirs,* pp. 135–36.) Finally, Marshall, and his assistant, Colonel Walter S. Grant (U.S.M.A., 1900), composed a memorandum on the subject. ★

Plan of Attack of First Army, September 12, 1918

The St. Mihiel salient campaign.

MEMORANDUM FOR THE CHIEF OF STAFF,   September 10, 1918
FIRST ARMY   [Ligny-en-Barrois], France

Artillery preparation.

As members of the Operations Sub-section, G-3, 1st Army, we feel it our duty to bring to your attention the following points.

The decision has been made that the artillery preparation for the coming operation will start with the commencement of the barrage, but that plans must be made to put down a 14 hour artillery preparation, so that, if at the last moment it should be deemed advisable to do so, it can readily be done.

In our opinion this 14 hour preparation should be made. The reasons for this are here enumerated.

1. There is no instance in this war where an attack has been made against a position as highly organized as this one without artillery preparation or the assistance of numerous heavy tanks.

2. To attack this position without artillery preparation is taking a gambler's chance—it *may* succeed, but we must not be content with that: for, it *must* succeed.

3. An artillery preparation, considering the amount of artillery at our disposal, can do no harm, but can make the operation easier by shaking the enemy's morale and determination, by putting confidence in our own troops, by causing breaches in trenches and wire, and by putting and keeping hostile batteries out of action.

4. Such preparation will permit a certain amount of registration, which we consider vital.[1]

5. From the moment the first gun is fired interdiction fire can be kept up to prevent the sending forward of any enemy reinforcements or altering his dispositions and can interfere materially with his exercise of command.

6. The artillery at our disposal constitutes a powerful weapon; to refrain from using it up to the maximum possible, without affecting the element of surprise, deprives us of a great advantage.

7. It had been hoped that large tanks would be available for cutting wire. Large tanks have not been forthcoming, and the small number of medium and small tanks are not sufficient for proper wire cutting.

8. Many areas such as woods, etc., should be drenched with gas before our troops are to pass through them, the gas bombardment on these places ceasing several hours before our troops arrive there. If there is no artillery preparation until H hour we will be deprived of the use of gas on those localities where the necessity of gas is the greatest.

9. It has been argued that if the artillery preparation is to commence on D-1 day it should start at daylight, otherwise many batteries, necessarily emplaced in the open, would be exposed to the enemy's view, thus precipitating the artillery phase of the battle. We do not concur in this. Sufficient batteries can be emplaced in reasonably concealed localties to start the preparation at H minus 14 hours, the remaining batteries going into position at H minus 10 hours.

Enemy batteries can not interfere with our guns, however much exposed; our superiority is too great.[2]

W. S. Grant
G. C. Marshall, Jr.

NA/RG 120 (GHQ, First Army Reports)
1. When a gun crew established a new position or prepared for a particular operation, it

would fire a few rounds at selected targets in order to establish the proper ordnance settings for hitting that area. This was called "registration fire."

2. Assistant Chief of Staff Colonel Robert McCleave, one of Marshall's Fort Leavenworth students in 1909–10, wrote at the bottom of the page: "I concur in the above, and recommend that artillery registration be completed just before dark. The fire to continue throughout the night, with the attack at daylight." General Pershing took the second option: five hours of preparation. Marshall later commented, "Whether it was his sound judgment, or the accident of circumstance, I do not know, but his decision exactly met the situation." (*Memoirs,* p. 136.)

O N SEPTEMBER 8, Chief of Staff Hugh Drum called a meeting to hand out new assignments to his staff. General Pershing had agreed to undertake to launch a second offensive on the Meuse-Argonne front, some sixty miles from St. Mihiel, no later than September 25, thirteen days after the first attack. Marshall was assigned the job of planning the transfer of some six hundred thousand men and twenty-seven hundred guns over the three roads between the two fronts. "This appalling proposition rather disturbed my equilibrium," he later wrote. The next few hours stood out in his memory as "the most trying mental ordeal" he experienced during the war. He was fully aware that his reputation hung in the balance. Finally, he dictated the following document (printed in full in his *Memoirs,* pp. 139–42) which he ultimately concluded "represented my best contribution to the war. It was the only official paper I preserved for my personal records and brought home from France." (*Memoirs,* pp. 137–39.) ★

MEMORANDUM [s. Drum]   September 10, 1918
Secret   [Ligny-en-Barrois], France

Release and readjustment of units following
reduction of St. Mihiel Salient.

1. The following information will serve as a guide to Army Corps Commanders during the course of the pending operation, so that they may be prepared to act promptly and without embarrassment upon the receipt of formal orders directing the changes outlined herein.

2. *PLAN OF READJUSTMENT.*

As soon as the advance has terminated, and assuming that a threat of a *heavy* hostile counter-attack does not exist, Corps Commanders will commence the reduction of the number of divisions in line and the regrouping of the divisions so released. The mechanics of this reduction must be foreseen and must be carried out promptly in order to permit the release of the various units indicated hereinafter, by the dates set, for duty in other regions.

The portions of the Army front now occupied by the 82nd Division will probably be taken over by the 8th French Army, releasing that division. The portion of the front from HAUDIOMONT north will probably be taken over by the French. The 1st and 5th Corps, with their corps, troops, will be relieved from duty on the front by D plus 4 and D plus 5 days, respectively, and the 4th U.S. and 2nd Colonial Corps will extend to the right and left, respectively, taking over the front of the 1st and 5th Corps.

3. *UNITS TO BE RELIEVED. . . .*

4. *EVENTUAL DISPOSITIONS FOR DEFENSE OF FRONT. . . .*[1]

NA/RG 120 (First Army, Historical File)

1. The omitted paragraphs (approximately two-thirds of the original document) detailed the schedule for relieving certain organizations, the boundaries between the United States Fourth Corps and the French Second Colonial Corps, and the tentative distribution of divisions along the front.

I T WAS OBVIOUS by the afternoon of the first day's battle (September 12) that the reduction of the St. Mihiel salient was proceeding with greater success than anticipated. Marshall later thought that had the attack been pressed vigorously, the fortress of Metz might have fallen by September 14. (*Memoirs,* pp. 146–47.) Even as the St. Mihiel battle continued, Marshall directed all his attention on the next objective—the concentration on the Meuse-Argonne front. The difficulties he faced were appalling: inadequate roads, insufficient transportation, inexperienced troops. Marshall wrote a memorandum describing the concentration maneuver. (See below, Memorandum for the First Subsection, November 19, 1918.)

On September 17, Marshall was raised to the rank of colonel. Four days later he moved with First Army headquarters northward to Souilly, "a depressing little village at best." He slept but a few hours each day in his tiny billet, spending most of his time at headquarters. (*Memoirs,* p. 158.) The Meuse-Argonne campaign opened with a three-hour artillery barrage in the early hours of September 26. The attack was initially more successful than expected, but by the end of the month the difficult terrain, determined German resistance, and American exhaustion had caused the drive to stall. Pershing ordered a second attack, which Marshall helped to plan, beginning October 4. Again significant progress was followed shortly by continued fierce fighting with little territorial gain. ★

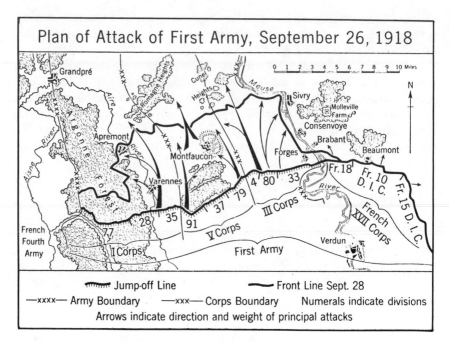

Plan of Attack of First Army, September 26, 1918

Jump-off Line   ━ Front Line Sept. 28
—xxxx— Army Boundary   —xxx— Corps Boundary   Numerals indicate divisions
Arrows indicate direction and weight of principal attacks

The first phase of the Meuse-Argonne campaign.

MEMORANDUM FOR COLONEL   October 13, 1918
ADELBERT DE CHAMBRUN[1]   [Souilly], France

Necessity for Camions.[2]

1. There are now 11 divisions on the active battle front of this Army. These divisions have been engaged as follows:

Three (77, 4, 33) since September 25
Two (32, 3) since September 30
Three (29, 18 Fr., 26 Fr.) since October 5
One (82) since October 7
Two (42, 5) since October 12

Three divisions are in immediate reserve (78, 89 and 26)

One division (80) is moving to the rear to the THIAUCOURT area for rest and refitting.

One division (35) is relieving the 15th Fr. Division in the SOMME DIEUE sector.

Two divisions (1, 91) are in Army Reserve, resting and refitting in the VAVINCOURT and METTANCOURT areas.

One division (90) is being moved north by camion from the TOUL region to the battle front. Lack of camions necessitates this move to be made in two echelons.

2. *PROSPECTIVE MOVEMENTS*

Owing to the exhausted condition of the infantry and the prevalence of colds, influenza, pneumonia and dysentery, the 77th, 4th and 33d Divisions must be withdrawn from the front by October 16th.

The 32d and 3d Divisions must be withdrawn by October 19th or possibly earlier.

3. *LOCAL CONDITIONS*

No adequate shelter for troops exists north of the line LES ISLETTES—CLERMONT—VERDUN. The stretch of the former "No Man's Land" and the country for five kilometers north and south of it, is a devastated region without villages or huts, and traversed by a few and very poor roads. Divisions must be carried south of this devastated region for shelter and rest. The Army Zone lies in a partial salient, which forces all movements north and south through a comparatively narrow stretch of territory. The zone from BAR le DUC north is now congested with troops (except one staging area) and sufficient shelter is not available, bivouacking being the only remedy.

Divisions moving south must be carried into the region near and south of BAR le DUC. To effect these moves by marching or by partial bussing will cause a congestion of the CHAUMONT sur AIRE-NIXEVILLE region, will delay the moves (further exhausting the troops) and will necessitate much bivouacking.

3 [4]. *CONDITION OF THE TROOPS*

The new divisions which have been employed in the fighting between the ARGONNE and the MEUSE have become exhausted physically more quickly than the older divisions, owing to the inexperience of the men, officers and staffs. They must be moved out of the open into adequate shelter in order to quickly rejuvenate them. These moves must be accomplished with a minimum of physical effort and in a minimum of time if the divisions are to participate further in the present battle.

4 [5]. *SUMMARY*

The local conditions described above make the employment of camions for these moves absolutely necessary. Sufficient camions to transport the foot troops of a division will be constantly required for the ensuing week and additional camions for transporting at least 10,000 men will be required for the following week, if the present battle is to be energetically driven home.

NA/RG 120 (First Army, G-3 Reports)

1. Jacques Adelbert de Pineton, Comte de Chambrun, had served since mid-1917 as General Pershing's French aide-de-camp. An honorary American citizen as a consequence of his direct descent from the Marquis de Lafayette, he had known Marshall for some time, having been among those who met General Sibert and his staff at St. Nazaire on June 26, 1917.

2. A *camion* was a "truck" to the Americans and a "lorry" to the British.

FIRST ARMY OPERATIONS SECTION, AUTUMN 1918

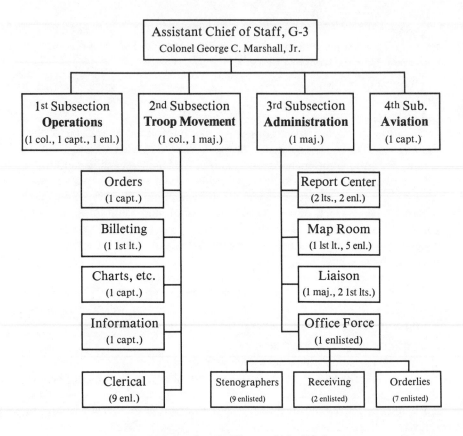

Total Personnel: 17 officers and 36 enlisted
plus 3 enlisted chauffeurs

O RGANIZATIONAL changes in mid-October included Marshall's assignment as assistant chief of staff for Operations of the First Army on the seventeenth. Concerning Marshall and his new job, George Van Horn Moseley commented long afterward: "Remember that in preparation for battle, the Commanding General (in this case that fine, able, modest soul, Hunter Liggett) gives the general plan for the operations, his Chief of Staff co-ordinates the work of all sections of the staff; but it is the Chief of the Third Section, G-3, as we call him, who must work out all the details of the operations, putting them in a clear, practical, workable order which can be understood by the commanders of all subordinate units. The order must be comprehensive, yet not involved. It must appear clear when read in a poor light, in the mud and rain. That was Marshall's job, and he performed it one hundred percent. The troops which maneuvered under his plan always won." (George Van Horn Moseley, "One Soldier's Journey," 2 vols. [unpublished memoir], 2: 32, LC/G.V.H. Moseley Papers.)

The energy of the great American attack, launched on September 26, had been quickly dissipated by the difficult terrain and the stubborn German resistance. By the middle of October, the fighting consisted of numerous detached operations directed toward securing a favorable line of departure for the next general assault. On October 20, Marshall began to prepare plans for an advance all along the front west of the Meuse River. November 1 was the date finally designated for the launching of this operation. Meanwhile, Marshall spent much of his time visiting corps and division headquarters along the front. (*Memoirs,* p. 180.) ★

MEMORANDUM TO THE OFFICERS,   October 27, 1918
G-3 SECTION, FIRST ARMY   [Souilly], France

Secrecy.

1. The Army Commander fears that owing to the long continuation of the present operation officers may gradually become lax in the question of secrecy, as regards handling of important papers and orders, discussing pending operations, etc.[1]

2. The officers of the Section are therefore reminded of the continued importance of preserving secrecy as to our plans and movements. They will see that important orders, etc., are carefully guarded, and that indiscreet conversations among themselves or the members of the office force, are repressed.

G. C. Marshall, Jr.

NA/RG 120 (First Army, Historical File)

1. After October 16, Hunter Liggett commanded the First Army. The Second Army, formally created on October 10, was commanded by Robert Bullard. General Pershing commanded the Group of American Armies.

MEMORANDUM FOR COMMANDING GENERALS,   November 5, 1918
FIRST CORPS AND FIFTH CORPS [s. Drum]   [Souilly], France

Message from Commander in Chief.

1. General Pershing desires that the honor of entering Sedan should fall to the First American Army. He has every confidence that the troops of the 1st Corps,

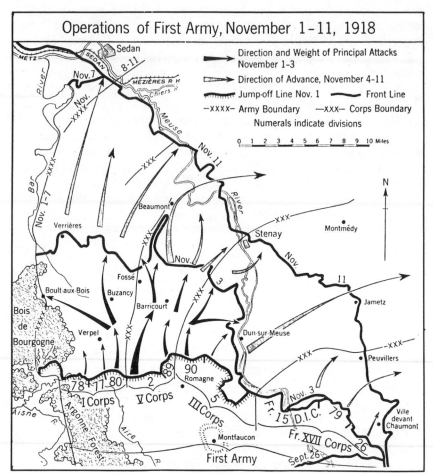

Operations of First Army, November 1-11, 1918

Direction and Weight of Principal Attacks November 1-3

Direction of Advance, November 4-11

Jump-off Line Nov. 1 — **Front Line**

−xxxx− **Army Boundary** —xxx− **Corps Boundary**

Numerals indicate divisions

0 1 2 3 4 5 6 7 8 9 10 Miles

The final phase of the Meuse-Argonne campaign.

assisted on their right by the 5th Corps, will enable him to realize this desire.

2. In transmitting the foregoing message, your attention is invited to the favorable opportunity now existing for pressing our advance throughout the night. Boundaries will not be considered as binding.

G. C. M., Jr.

NA/RG 120 (First Army, G-3 Staff Memos)

MEMORANDUM FOR THE RECORDS OF G-3 SECTION   November 8, 1918
[Souilly], France

Operations of the 1st Army in the direction of SEDAN.

1. Attached hereto is a copy of a memorandum for the Commanding Generals, 1st Corps and 5th Corps, dated November 5, 1918 (G/3 A-137) which was issued about 18:30 hours on November 5th. It was dispatched in written form by the ordinary courier service and was telephoned direct to the 1st and 5th Corps between 18:30 hours and 19 hours on November 5th.[1]

2. Also attached hereto is a memorandum from the Chief of Staff, 1st Army, dated November 7th, regarding the above subject.[2]

3. On November 5th at about 17:30 hours the Assistant Chief of Staff, G-3, G.H.Q. (Gen. Conner) came to the office of the undersigned. He gave to me a message from the Commander in Chief, which is stated in paragraph 1, G-3 Memorandum No. A-137 referred to in paragraph 1 above. The message was verbal and was dictated to me by Gen. Conner.

Paragraph 2 of the above referred to G-3 Memorandum A-137 was drafted by me, excepting the last sentence. Gen. Conner was furnished a draft of the Memorandum as it then existed. Neither the Army Commander nor the Chief of Staff were in their office at this time. About 18 hours the Chief of Staff returned to his office from the front and I presented to him the draft of the Memorandum. He directed the addition of the last sentence of paragraph 2. The Memorandum was then rewritten, telephoned and dispatched as recited in paragraph 1 above.

G. C. Marshall, Jr.

NA/RG 120 (First Army, G-3 Staff Memos)

1. The memorandum referred to is printed immediately above.
2. Not printed.

THE SENTENCE "Boundaries will not be considered as binding" in the November 5 memorandum was intended to mean that the Americans should cross into the sector allotted to the Fourth French Army, whose front line was somewhat behind that of the American First Army. What resulted, however, was a race in which Brigadier General Frank Parker's First Division, attached to Major General Charles P. Summerall's Fifth Corps, marched across the corps boundary into the zone allotted to Brigadier General Douglas MacArthur's Eighty-fourth Infantry Brigade of the Forty-second Division of Major General Joseph T. Dickman's First Corps. Marshall viewed the ensuing recriminations as "senseless. . . . The whole thing to my mind was out of place. The thing was we were succeeding. . . . There's going to be all sorts of turbulence on the battlefield, and this thing was carried back to old animosities. I didn't have much patience with it, but I wasn't the one receiving the animosity." Shortly before his death, Marshall remarked that "they are still fighting" the First versus Forty-second Division battle. (Interview, April 11, 1957.)

By November 9, First Army headquarters was full of rumors of the breakup of the German Army and of armistice terms, but Marshall's time was still absorbed in preparing orders for the constantly changing battlefront, and in preparing for the two great attacks the First Army proposed to launch on November 14 and 15. The armistice on November 11 did not immediately affect the character of Marshall's work. He was still occupied with moving divisions around the American sector of the front and in preparing for advances. But this planning was for the peaceful march into Germany that armistice terms stipulated would begin on November 17. (*Memoirs,* pp. 195–206.) ★

MEMORANDUM   November 12, 1918
Secret   [Souilly], France

Plan of Future Movements.
FUTURE OPERATIONS.

1. Definite instructions have not been received by these headquarters as to future operations. At present the only information at hand is that an advance will be made on November 17th towards the RHINE River, in the general direction LUXEMBORG-COBLENZ. The left of the 1st Army will follow the general line—CARIGNAN-FLORENVILLE-REDANCE. Whether the whole Army, or a part thereof, or only one corps will advance, is not known.

2. In view of the short time available for preparations, the following preliminary steps will be taken, which it is believed will meet any requirements which may be imposed by higher authority.

3. *RE-ARRANGEMENT OF PRESENT CORPS FRONTS.*

The Army Corps will re-adjust their front so as to have only the divisions in line indicated below:

(a) *5th Corps*
77th Division in line;
2nd Division in reserve west of BEAUMONT,
89th Division in reserve near NOUART.

(b) *3rd Corps*
90th and 32nd Divisions in line,

5th Division in reserve west of NANTILLOIS,

1st Division in reserve south and southeast of MONTFAUCON.

42nd Division in reserve near BANTHEVILLE.

(c) *2nd Colonial Corps:*

79th, 6th, and 81st Divisions in line.

15th D.I.C. in reserve west of the MEUSE and north of VERDUN.

10th D.I.C. in reserve south of VERDUN.

26th U.S. Division to pass to Army Reserve in SOUILLY region.

(d) In carrying out the foregoing movements, the 42nd Division will be moved into the zone of the 3rd Corps under orders to be issued by the 3rd Corps in agreement with the 5th Corps.

The movements in the rear zone of the 3rd Corps must not conflict with the march of the 6th Division into the zone of the 2nd C.A.C.

The movement of the 26th U.S. Division out of the zone of the 2nd C.A.C. into the SOUILLY region, will be carried out under orders to be issued by the 2nd C.A.C. in agreement with the G-3 Section, 1st Army.[1]

4. *FORWARD MOVEMENT:*

The following divisions will be prepared to move forward so as to start crossing the present front line early on November 17th, as indicated below:

2nd Division at MOUZON or INOR.

89th Division via DUN-sur-MEUSE.

42nd Division via VILOSNES.

1st Division via CHARNEY.

The following divisions will be prepared to move forward across the present front line on November 19th:

77th Division to follow 2nd Division.

90th Division to follow 89th Division.

32nd Division to follow 42nd Division.

5. *ARMY RESERVES:*

At 12 hours on November 13th the following divisions will be relieved from the corps to which they are now attached and will be attached to the 7th Corps (P.C. at BENOITVAUX).

3rd Division
29th Division
36th Division
78th Division
80th Division

The 26th Division will pass to the 7th Corps upon its arrival in the SOUILLY region.

NA/RG 120 (First Army, Historical File)

1. D.I.C. = division d'infanterie colonial. C.A.C. = corps d'armee colonial.

November 19, 1918
Souilly, France

1. About September 8, General Hugh A. Drum had a conference regarding preparation for the Argonne Operation. At the conclusion of the conference he directed that Col. Monroe C. Kerth take charge of the billeting of divisions arriving on the Argonne front, that Col. Walter S. Grant take charge of the arrangements for taking over command from the French Second Army, of the Argonne front, and that I take charge of the movement of the troops from the St-Mihiel Operation into the zone of the French Second Army—that is, north-west of the line Benoitevaux—Pierrefitte—Naives-devant-Bar.

2. As a preliminary step towards carrying out the movement of the troops, a memorandum was prepared and issued on September 10, Subject: "Reliefs and Readjustments of Units following Reduction of the St-Mihiel Salient." This memorandum arranged for the relief of certain army corps, artillery brigades and divisions, on specified days following D day after the St-Mihiel attack. It designated their assembly points from which they were to be moved to the Argonne front.

While these movements were planned in advance of the battle and covered troops who were to be engaged in the first line of the battle, it developed later that it was possible to carry them out exactly as arranged.

3. In general there were three routes available for the movement of troops from the St-Mihiel front to the Argonne, viz:

(1) via Gironville—Mecrin—Rupt-devant-St-Mihiel—Pierrefitte.

(2) via Trondes—Vertuzey—Commercy—Menil-aux-Bois and Pierrefitte or Lavallee—Naives.

(3) via Toul—Void—Ligny—Bar-le-Duc.

The road from Apremont to St-Mihiel was in the hands of the enemy at the time the first plans for the movement were made and it was not known whether or not it would be passable after control of it had been gained. It proved to be impassable until the movement of the troops was completed.

The two great difficulties in connection with these movements, aside from the uncertainty of knowing when any particular unit could be safely withdrawn from the St-Mihiel battle were:

1st—The movement of the troops across the rear zone of the corps engaged in the St-Mihiel battle during the period when all the roads were congested with the movement forward of ammunition, rations and engineer materiel. Units had to be moved from east of the Moselle across the corps zones.

2d—The limited number of roads available for the movement of the large mass of troops to be transferred to the Argonne front, coupled with the fact that all movements had to be executed entirely under the cover of darkness. The Toul—Void—Bar-le-Duc Road was the motor highway, and the other two roads were employed for the movement of the foot troops and the animal drawn vehicles, except in a few instances where tractor artillery had to be sent over them.

4. The preparation of an ordinary march table for the movements of the troops was not practicable as it was never possible to know over twenty-four hours in advance just what units would be available to put in motion. The artillery brigades destined to be attached to 1st line divisions in the Argonne battle and a large number of French horse 75-mm. regiments were first put in march on the two roads available. The movement of certain reserve divisions by bus and marching was also started.

After initiating the above it became necessary to coordinate all further movements with the movements of the ammunition motor trains and the movements of French divisions being concentrated on the front of the French Fourth Army for the same operation. To accomplish this coordination I would propose each day to Capt. Gorju, C.R.A. [French Army Regulating Commission] officer at Bar-le-Duc, the movements I wished carried out during the next forty-eight hours. He would then compare my proposal with the other movements in prospect and together we would arrive at an adjustment between the two. Based on this arrangement the orders would then be issued to the army corps in the First Army to start certain elements from designated points by designated routes.

To further complicate the problem there were a large number of French units serving in the First Army to be hurriedly transferred to the French Fourth Army.

5. The work of the troop movement officers on duty in the G-3 Section of the I and IV Corps was particularly fine because their problem was a most complicated one; to locate the troops and assemble them at the proper point and put them in march without interference with each other and in accordance with the Army schedules.

Some of the difficulties involved were the following:

Trains could not be obtained for all of the tractor-drawn artillery. We were then confronted with the proposition of moving elements of units which could only travel 3 kilometers an hour while other elements of the same unit could travel 15 kilometers an hour.

Again some tractor artillery could travel 8 kilometers an hour while other portions of its train could travel 15 kilometers an hour.

Solid columns had to be placed on the roads, composed of elements of different divisions, different corps and different armies, all moving at the same time.

The arrangements for the command or the control of these columns were extremely difficult, where it could be arranged.

Camions scheduled to move divisional foot troops would be delayed in arriving at the embussing point, due to some blocks or checks in movement beyond our control, in the zone of the French Fourth Army, for example. The camions had to be used immediately as it was necessary to drive them to their maximum capacity. The resulting movement, taking place at other hours than these arranged for, caused unavoidable crossing of other columns, as it was necessary to route some horse transport via the Toul—Void—Ligny motor road.

Some of the animals in the artillery, both French and American, had become so worn down by the constant movements during the past month that it was very hard to force them through according to any ordinary schedule.

Frequently arrangement would be completed for the movement of certain artillery units, and at the last moment we would learn that some increased activity on the battlefront had made it impossible to withdraw them in time to take up the march. There were one or more instances where units withdrawing suffered such casualties among their horses that their entire schedule of movements had to be changed at the last moment.

The formation of the various columns was always seriously complicated by the necessity of putting certain troops on certain roads in order that they could be conveniently passed into their proper places on the Argonne front. For example, the I Corps units all had to be passed to the region of Les Islettes while units to be assigned to the III Corps were destined for the region just west of Verdun.

While it might have been much more practicable to route a I Corps unit by the northern road, it usually had to be placed on the most southern road in order to avoid crosscutting the columns headed north from the general vicinity of Bar-le-Duc, some of these coming from points south in the training areas.

6. When the various columns reached the line referred to in Par. 1 above, they were taken over by the French Second Army and routed north into their proper positions for the coming battle.

7. Despite the haste with which all the movements had to be carried out, the inexperience of most of the commanders in movements of such density, the condition of the animals and the limitations as to roads, the entire movement was carried out without a single element failing to reach its place on the date scheduled, which was, I understand, one day earlier than Marshall Foch considered possible.

United States Army in the World War, 9: 64–66.

1. The first subsection of First Army's G-3 section was in charge of operations.

ON NOVEMBER 6, Marshall was notified that he was soon to be transferred to an as yet unformed, unnamed army corps and made its chief of staff, normally a brigadier general's position. Only when he arrived in Chaumont on November 19 did he discover that he was responsible for assembling the headquarters staff and special troops for the Eighth Army Corps from units scattered over France. This he accomplished by day and night truck convoys in five days. Marshall also picked the location for the new headquarters, a remodeled, centrally heated, twelfth-century chateau in the city of Montigny, about fifty kilometers west of Chaumont. Marshall moved to Montigny on November 28 or 29, a few days behind the new commander, Major General Henry T. Allen, a colorful cavalryman who had previously led the Ninetieth Division. During December the three divisions (Sixth, Seventy-seventh, and Eighty-first) assigned to the corps arrived and began the strenuous training program mandated by General Headquarters at Chaumont. (*Memoirs,* pp. 205–10.) ★

FROM GENERAL JOHN J. PERSHING   November 29, 1918
                                                 [Chaumont?], France

My dear Colonel Marshall: It gives me great pleasure to inform you that on October 17th I recommended you for promotion to the grade of Brigadier General, basing my recommendation upon the efficiency of your service with the American Expeditionary Forces.

The War Department discontinued all promotions to the grade of General Officer after the signing of the Armistice, and I regret that you will not therefore receive the deserved recognition of your excellent services.   Sincerely yours,

NA/201 File

TRAINING MEMORANDUM   November 30, 1918
                                                 [Montigny, France]

1. Upon arrival in respective areas, Division Commanders will submit a sketch to these headquarters showing the location of all headquarters in their divisions down to and including the battalions.

All headquarters will be marked by appropriate signs.

They will cause reconnaissances to be made in their areas for suitable target ranges, bayonet courses, drill, maneuver and bombing grounds and will construct the same.

A sketch will be submitted to these Headquarters showing the location of these training grounds.

The first day after arriving in the area will be devoted to the cleaning and inspection of arms, equipment, clothing, billets and their surrounding areas.

2. Division Commanders will also prepare and submit to these headquarters training schedules covering a period of four weeks in accordance with G.O. No. 207, G.H.Q., American Expeditionary Forces, Nov. 16, 1918.

A high standard will be required from officers and men, *at all times,* in smartness of clothing, appearance, set up and saluting.

A portion of each day will be devoted to close order drill for disciplinary purposes. In these drills especial stress will be laid upon the setting up exercises. They will cover movements in the school of the soldier, by squads and by platoons.

Especial attention will be given to the alertness, snap and uniformity of commands given by instructors and leaders.

All movements must be practiced and polished until their execution is perfect. Approximation to perfection is not sufficient.

For the purpose of developing speed and smartness the cadence in close order drills will be raised to 128 steps per minute, the length of the pace will be correspondingly reduced.

In moving troops over roads and across fields, columns of squads will be used in order that organizations may be habituated to a formation requiring the minimum road distance. Columns of twos will only be used to pass obstacles, in field exercises and for instruction purposes.

All mounted and horsed units will be carefully instructed in the feeding, grooming and care of animals and in the cleaning of harness, equipment and vehicles.

Mounts and draft animals will be fed five times daily, the forage allowance being divided accordingly.

There will be daily practice in the use of the bayonet and in firing with the rifle, pistol and automatic weapons, service ammunition being used.

When a senior officer approaches an organization at drill or other instructional exercises for the purpose of inspection or observation, the junior will report to him giving name, rank, organization and kind of exercise under execution.

When a junior officer finds himself in the presence of a senior, whom he does not know, he will at once introduce himself by saluting, giving name, rank and organization.

3. Commanding Officers will be judged solely upon the condition and efficiency of their commands, and they will be graded accordingly.

Officers who fail to rise to a sufficiently high standard will be disposed of as heretofore.

All officers will be required to be present with their organizations at drills and other exercises.

4. For the purpose of maintaining a high standard of discipline, punishment will quickly follow offenses and will be proportionate to the offense committed.

NA/RG (Eighth Corps, Historical File)

Marshall's brief association with General Allen's Eighth Corps ended in January, 1919. On the fifth he received orders to report for duty with the Operations Section at General Headquarters, which he did on the fifteenth. Marshall was immediately assigned to collect information and to prepare plans for marching the American Third Army into Germany in the event the peace negotiations in Paris failed. ★

MEMORANDUM FOR THE ASSISTANT   February 10, 1919
CHIEF OF STAFF, G-3[1]   [Chaumont, France]

Study of possible advance of American Troops into Germany.

1. *GENERAL ALLIED PLAN OF ACTION.*

The base of any plan for the possible advance of American forces deeper into German territory must, of necessity, include a general assumption as to the plan of action of the other allied Armies. Under existing circumstances this assumption must be formulated without consulting non-American authorities and can be only a carefully considered guess as to what we believe would be agreed to by all concerned.

If the main purpose of the operation is to gain control of the heart of Germany, that is the region of Berlin, without the necessity of occupying the country generally, the economical and expeditious plan would be to occupy all the North Sea and Baltic ports and to base expeditions on Hamburg and Stettin for a concentric advance on Berlin. The Elbe and Oder rivers would afford excellent facilities for supply. The region bounded by Bremen–Hanover–Brunswick–Magdeburg–Berlin–Stettin could be effectively held by a moderate sized force owing to long stretches of river line and short lines of communication. The present line of the Rhine could then be held as a defensive front with a much reduced force.

Assuming that the occasion for a deeper advance into Germany develops too rapidly to permit of moving troops around to the North Sea and Baltic ports, or that for other reasons a general advance from the present line of the Rhine is considered necessary, the following study is submitted regarding the possible participation by American troops.

2. *ADVANCE FROM THE RHINE.*

The present deployment of the allied forces along the frontier should normally determine their order of battle during the advance and should tend to limit the choice of their respective zones of action.

The Topography of Western Germany (See Map A attached)[2] considered with reference to the location of the present bridge heads, the frontiers of Holland and Austria, the sea boundary to the north including the Kiel Canal, the course of the Elbe River and the location of Berlin, leads to the following conclusions:

(a) The allied initial advance would be conducted on a broad front in a north-easterly direction from Mulhausen to Wesel. A smaller force based on Bremen and Hamburg would effect a junction with the main advance.

(b) The right of the line would be refused from Lake Constance to Leipzig; the left would be advanced until contact was gained with the Baltic Sea in Mecklenburg Bay; the center would rest along the line of the Elbe River, unless the occupation of Berlin became necessary, in which case the left would be further advanced to Stettin.

(c) The ports from Emden to Dantzig would be occupied, and the supply of the center and left of the Armies would ultimately be based upon the ports to the north and would be facilitated by the navigable rivers Weser and Elbe.

3. *PROBABLE AMERICAN ZONE OF ACTION.*

(a) The present American bridge head is too restricted to serve as a suitable base of departure. It extends 32 kilometers along the Rhine and just excludes important roads and railroads. The base of departure should cover the strip from Bonn to the river Lahn, both inclusive, a distance of 62 kilometers. The inclusion of Bonn should not interfere with the British as their main columns would probably advance through Hanover and Munster. The inclusion of the Lahn River should not interfere with the French as there remain to the South numerous routes of advance for their forces.

The axis of the American advance would probably be the line Coblentz–Cassel–Helmstedt–Stendal, an air-line distance of 380 kilometers.

The extent of front to be occupied by American troops at the conclusion of the first stage of the advance (i.e., along the Elbe River), depends upon many factors. However, after a study of the entire front to be held it is believed that the American Army would probably be called upon to cover a front of at least 100 kilometers, and the logical portion appears to be that between Wittenberg and Schonebeck (10 kilometers south of Magdeburg.)

The proposed zone limits are indicated in Map A attached. This zone includes two through railroad lines and sufficient through roads to permit of a well regulated advance.

(b) *Salient Features of the Terrain.*

The zone from Coblentz to Cassel (160 kilometers air line) is rugged, heavily forested country with roads and railroads following circuitous routes. At Cassel the first of a serious of river lines is encountered. The Weser is a navigable stream from Munden to its mouth. The Fulda and the Werra prolong its course to the south and are less of an obstacle.

The general character of the country remains unchanged for the next 100 kilometers east of the Weser. The river Leine intersects the zone before the plain of the Elbe is reached, but is too small to be considered an obstacle. It becomes navigable at Hanover.

South of Brunswick and west of Halbestadt lie the Hartz mountains, covering a rough, forested area blocking 60 kilometers of the width of the zone as it debouches into the low land. In the event of well organized hostile resistance, this region could be developed into a serious obstacle to our advance and would probably have to be turned by an enveloping movement to the north.

The plain of the Elbe presents no particular obstacle, except for the heavy forest areas east of Brunswick. (See memorandum of A.C. of S. G-2 on rivers, hereto attached and marked "B".)

(c) *Enemy Resistance.*

The amount of resistance to our advance which the enemy might be able to offer is entirely problematical and would depend primarily upon the state of mind of the population. In any event he would be forced to operate with practically no airships and would be seriously hampered by lack of motor transport and rail rolling stock. His supply of heavy and light cannon, and minenwerfers, machine guns and rifles, appears to be sufficient for the extent of the Western front on which he would be operating.

The memorandum of the A.C. of S., G-2 hereto attached and marked "C" presents a study of the possibilities of the extent of the hostile resistance which might be encountered.

It appears reasonable to conclude that, in proportion to the frontage and assuming prompt replacements, a moderate sized force equipped with a few heavy guns and a full allotment of light guns, airships and transport, should be able to break down and through the enemies most determined resistance. The police of the country passed through presents another problem which would make heavy demands on our forces unless the complete disarmament of the population could be effectively assured, which seems entirely possible.

4. *TROOPS TO BE EMPLOYED.*

The base of departure is 60 kilometers in breadth. The final frontage to be covered is 100 kilometers. Under existing conditions the advance could be initiated with 1 division for each 20 kilometers of front or 3 divisions in first line. A minimum of 4 divisions would be required on the final front of the advance. The first line divisions should be followed by 2 divisions in second line, two days march (30 kilometers) in rear. One more division should follow the third line, three days march (45 kilometers) in rear of the second line. Truck transportation capable of transporting all the foot troops of one division should be available in rear of the second line. In rear of the third line one division should normally be available for each 100 kilometers of depth, to provide garrison troops.

One division would be required to man the line of communication.

Summary.

1. *When advance had reached Cassel.*

1st line.	3 divisions ⎫	2 army corps.
2nd line	2 divisions ⎭	
3rd line	1 division ⎫	1 army corps.
Garrison troops	1 division ⎭	
	7 divisions	& 3 army corps.

2. *When advance had reached the line of Elbe.*

1st line.	4 divisions ⎫	2 army corps.
2nd line	2 divisions ⎭	
3rd line	1 division	
Garrison Troops	2 divisions	1 army corps.
Communication troops.	1 division	
	10 divisions	3 army corps.

The foregoing is a moderately large force when considered in addition to the necessary corps and army troops, S.O.S. detachments, and possible garrison troops to be left in our present zone west of the Rhine. However, it is about the maximum that would appear to be necessary, and in the event that the advance was made largely because of Bolshevik disturbances, without fear of encountering large organized units of the German Army, the number of divisions could be reduced to 8 and possibly to 6.

5. *LINE OF COMMUNICATION AND SUPPLY.*

Coblentz is the logical point for the advance base of the invading army.

Whether it would be supplied from our S.O.S. in Central France or from Rotterdam would depend entirely upon the availability of the latter point. At the present time Rotterdam appears to be available.

Between Coblentz and Cassel extends one of the most efficient rail lines in Germany, which continues beyond the latter point to Gottingen and there heads north via Hanover for Hamburg. This line would serve as the supply line for the Army until it cleared the Weser. Thereafter Cassel could be organized as the advance base, drawing its supplies from Bremerhaven or Bremen by utlizing both rail and water transportation lines.

Once the Allied lines had cleared the Elbe, the supply of the most advanced divisions could be assured via that river from Hamburg.

G. C. Marshall, Jr.

NA/RG 120 (GHQ, G-3 Reports)

1. Brigadier General Fox Conner.

2. The three appendixes attached to this memorandum are not printed. These were: "A. Philip's Large Scale Strategical War Map of Europe, Central and Eastern Area. B. Memorandums from G-2 regarding Rivers and the Hartz Mountains in proposed zone of advance for American Army into Germany. C. Memorandums from G-2 regarding Strength and Armament of German Army."

MEMORANDUM FOR THE CHIEF OF STAFF,   February 15, 1919
A.E.F. [s. Conner][1]   [Chaumont, France]

German refusal of Armistice Conditions.

1. In compliance with the memorandum of the Deputy Chief of Staff, dated February 13, referring to the Third Section certain questions regarding the above subject for study, the following is submitted.

2. *Questions to be considered.*

In the event that Germany refuses to sign a renewal of the armistice and then assumes a passive attitude leaving the burden of action to the allies:

(a) Will the allies conduct a further invasion of Germany?

(b) If a further invasion ensues, will the American Army participate?

(c) If the armistice is terminated, will the present plan for provisioning Germany be abandoned?

(d) If civil war develops in Germany due to famine, will the allies invade Germany to restore order, or will they limit their efforts to the occupied Germany territory?

3. *Will the Allies conduct a further invasion of Germany?*

When the Allied governments lay down certain conditions to be met by Germany in order that the armistice may be continued and the German government refuses to meet the conditions imposed on her by failing to sign the renewal of the armistice, then the Allied governments find themselves in a position which demands that they take some positive action in order to dominate the situation and maintain their prestige. The particular form of positive action which the allied governments would agree to among themselves, is the question to be discussed herein.

Germany is already in the grip of a rigid blockade and nothing remains without her boundaries which can be seized upon to penalize her for refusing to accede to drastic terms for the renewal of the armistice. More severe terms might be imposed upon her at the Peace Table, but this would be in the nature of negative action. It therefore appears that the Allies would be forced to carry out some form of a further invasion of German territory.

It is certain that both the British and American governments would be very loath to involve their armies in a further advance into Germany, particularly in view of the earnest desire of both governments at the present time to carry out the rapid demobilization of their armies in response to the demands of strong public opinion. It is considered probable that the French government would not be opposed to engaging in a further advance into Germany. The Belgian government may also be inclined to favorably consider an opportunity for bringing more German territory under the control of her armies. An agreement between the foregoing powers as to the course of action to be followed, would undoubtedly be fraught with many difficulties, but it is inconceivable that at the present time they would not present a united front to the German government.

The conclusion is therefore reached that all four of the powers referred to would be obligated to participate in a further invasion of German territory, notwithstanding the fact that such action might complicate the present plans for the rapid demobilization of the Allied armies. The extent to which this invasion would be carried is difficult to surmise at the present time, without a full knowledge of the situation. It would appear that the invasion should be only carried out to such extent as is deemed necessary in order to maintain the present dominant position of the Allied governments and to definitely cripple the power of the German government.

An advance from the Rhine to the line Bremen–Hanover–Cassel–Ulm could be affected by the divisions now occupying the present western front, and would present but few more difficulties to demobilization than are already presented by the occupation of the present bridge heads. The seizure and occupation of the important German sea-ports at Williamshaven, Bremerhaven, Cuxhaven, Hamburg, Kiel, Stettin, Dantzig and Konigsberg could be accomplished by comparatively small naval and land forces and would secure for the Allies control not only of important strategical points, but of German property and manufacturing interests of greater value. The effect of the further invasion and the occupation of sea-ports indicated above would be to secure to the Allies the control of such a portion of German territory with its resources and population, as to render her impotent and at the same time give to the Allies a valuable mortgage on German property.

4. *If a further invasion ensues, will the American Army participate?*

As already indicated in paragraph 3 above, it is believed that the American government would be very loath to engage in a further invasion of Germany, but that under the special situation now existing the government would be obligated to join with the Allies in pursuing the only effective course which appears available.

If the terms to be imposed upon Germany for a renewal of the armistice are so severe as to lead to the belief that the German government may not accept them, the American government seems to be in a position which demands that it either should have refused to acquiesce to the conditions proposed or should be prepared to play its part in imposing the will of the Allied governments on the German nation.

5. *If the armistice is terminated, will the present plan for provisioning Germany be abandoned?*

The termination of the armistice presumes a renewal of hostilities, and even though the German government may remain passive, it is not believed that any plan which contemplates sending provisions into unoccupied German territory could be considered at the present time. The provisioning of the occupied German territory would have to be assured by the Allies, and the provisions would probably have to be supplied by them as soon as the present German supplies in the occupied territory are exhausted.

Unless the action indicated in paragraph 3 above resulted in the German government's decision to acquiesce to the terms imposed for a renewal of the armistice, the conditions in Germany with regard to food would be very liable to produce civil disorders, which might result in a general civil war. Such a denouement would undoubtedly result in the destruction of the material wealth of Germany to such an extent as to render that government incapable, at least for a long period of years, of making the monetary payments which will undoubtedly be demanded of her at the Peace Table. Such a development should therefore be prevented; which means that steps would have to be taken by the Allied governments to insure the provisioning of Germany. Furthermore, such steps could not be taken in the absence of an armistice and previous to the signing of the treaty of peace, unless the Allied governments practically placed all of Germany under military control.

The history of the German people shows them to be law-abiding and opposed to acts of internal violence. Whether or not in the unusual conditions which may exist, following four years of war, the people as a whole would still remain inclined to avoid internal disorders, is impossible to foresee.

6. *If civil war develops in Germany due to famine, will the Allies invade Germany to restore order or will they limit their efforts to the German occupied territory?*

This question has been partially discussed in the foregoing paragraph. A civil war resulting from famine could only be terminated in two ways, either by the extermination of the population or by the relief of the conditions of famine. The Allied governments would undoubtedly have to furnish provisions for Germany. Whether or not they would be involved in an invasion of Germany to restore order would depend entirely upon the character of the civil war. If one side to the conflict was well organized, it might be possible to arrange for the provisioning of the country through medium of this force. If no definite line between the combatants could be drawn, it would be necessary for the Allies to restore order themselves if they desired to prevent the complete destruction of the material wealth of Germany and thus insure for their own people the benefit of the monetary payments which the German government should be required to make.

NA/RG 120 (GHQ, G-3 Reports)

1. Major General James W. McAndrew (U.S.M.A., 1888), A.E.F. chief of staff, had been a student at Fort Leavenworth's School of the Line when Marshall was an instructor, 1909–10. The memorandum was signed for Fox Conner by Colonel Upton Birnie, Jr., (U.S.M.A., 1900) one of Marshall's classmates at Fort Leavenworth, 1906–8. But that Marshall wrote the memo is indicated by his initials at the top right of the first page, a practice which started about this time in the War Department.

As SOON AS the fighting ceased, plans began to sprout that sought to reorganize the army in the light of the war's experiences. At Chaumont, although the Training Section (G-5) had produced a tentative plan by December 6, Fox Conner "recommended that *no* policy for the reorganization of our Army receive the approval of the Commander-in-Chief at this time." There were too many unknown conditions, he told General Pershing. Moreover, it was "unthinkable . . . that any permanent policy will be enacted as law without the Commander-in-Chief's being consulted." (Conner to Pershing, January 9, 1919, NA/RG 120 [GHQ, AG File].)

In Washington, Chief of Staff Peyton March proceeded to write his own bill without consulting Pershing. (Peyton C. March, *The Nation At War* [Garden City, N.Y.: Doubleday, Doran, 1932], pp. 331-33.) March and Secretary of War Newton Baker had Congressman S. Hubert Dent, Jr., of Alabama, chairman of the House Military Committee, introduce the proposal on January 16, 1919. General Pershing sent a copy of the proposed bill to G-5 and to G-3 at Chaumont for comment. Marshall wrote the following for Fox Conner's signature. ★

MEMORANDUM FOR THE CHIEF OF STAFF,   March 16, 1919
A.E.F. [s. Conner]   [Chaumont, France]

H. R. 14560, introduced in the House of
Representatives by Mr. Dent

1. *RESUME OF BILL:*

Provides for Regular Army of 574,625.

Abolishes Inspector General's Department.

Creates: Finance Department,
               Transportation Corps,
               Motor Transport Corps,
               Air Service,
               Tank Corps.

Increases General Staff from 52 to 220 officers, and gives large powers to Chief of Staff and broad field to General Staff Corps, revoking previous restrictions.

Combat troop personnel provided for:
    Infantry—80 regiments,
    Field Artillery—61 regiments,
    Cavalry—29 regiments,
    Engineers—24 regiments.

Staff Corps proportionately increased.

Organization of units left to discretion of President.

Permanent Staff Officers to be recommissioned in Line.

Detail System continued. (4 years Staff, 2 years Line)

Detached Officers list consists of 1022 officers.

"Manchu" Law repealed.

Promotion by selection beyond next to lowest grade.

Original vacancies may be filled in any grade by appointments from within Army or from those who served in this War.

Officers' Reserve Corps perpetuated.

Regular Army and Enlisted Reserve Corps abolished.

Compulsory service or universal training not mentioned.

Three year enlistment period recreated.

2. The Bill is radical in its nature, leaving wide discretionary powers to the President; it makes the General Staff Corps a powerful organization but at the same time creates other Corps and gives all Corps and Departments a large personnel of high rank. The wide latitude accorded the President is the most favorable aspect of the Bill; the most serious weakness is the absence of any provision which connects up the Regular Army with some form of a trained reserve. The bill is evidently a temporary measure.

3. The provision for filling of original vacancies created by this act opens up wide possibilities. It permits the entrance into the Regular Army of men under forty years of age who served during the present War Army. It is possible under the provisions of this Bill to appoint a present first lieutenant of Infantry of the Regular Army to fill an original vacancy as a Colonel of Infantry, Regular Army. If this portion of the bill could be wisely applied, it might prove very beneficial, but would undoubtedly be the source of great discontent and of numerous intrigues.

4. The resume of the bill prepared by the A. C. of S., G-5, with attached tables, is quite complete and leaves nothing to add.

NA/RG 120 (GHQ, AG File)

MEMORANDUM FOR THE DEPUTY   March 20, 1919
CHIEF OF STAFF, A.E.F.   [Chaumont?, France]

Proposal of Brigadier General Evan M. Johnson,
79th Division, regarding lectures.[1]

1. I concur with General Johnson that some action is necessary to bring the personnel of our army to a proper appreciation of what has been accomplished by the American Expeditionary Forces, in order that the petty difficulties, grievances and jealousies may be submerged by a proper appreciation of the

wonderful accomplishments achieved by our military forces in France. To develop in officers this just appreciation of the American effort, it is necessary that they should have a picture of the extent of the organization built up over here, the character of the difficulties overcome and the magnitude of the active operations of our armies.

A lecture tour on which General Drum, Colonel Howe [*Howell*] and myself have been engaged has the foregoing for its purpose, and I believe is accomplishing its object.[2]

2. I think it very important in carrying out any effort to educate our officers along the above lines, that great care should be taken to avoid giving the impression that G.H.Q. is on the defensive and is endeavoring to explain away the various criticisms which are now arising. For this reason I would hardly be in favor of presenting the matter quite after the fashion proposed by General Johnson. I believe the best way to achieve the results desired is to make a plain statement of the facts, covering a period from the arrival of General Pershing himself in France, up to the day of the armistice; first making plain the tremendous task which confronted him because of the lack of any plans or organization, which in itself is the best concrete example of our lack of preparedness, and culminating with a more or less detailed description of the operations of the First and Second Armies and of our divisions on other fronts. From such a talk, officers will unconsciously draw definite and, I believe, just conclusions, which will strongly tend to change their ideas regarding the efficiency of the Regular Army.

NA/RG 120 (GHQ, AG File)

1. Johnson's letter of March 16 to Lieutenant General Robert L. Bullard, Second Army commander, reflected a growing concern among Regular Army officers over what they considered politically motivated "bitter attacks upon army administration and army officers." Johnson wanted picked Regular officers to give lectures to National Army and National Guard units on the "remarkable" results the A.E.F. had achieved despite poor peacetime preparation. Such lectures, he supposed, would help prepare the men, when they returned to the United States, "to do their part in counter-acting any antagonistic sentiment which may be encountered, and to play their part in the creation of a proper system of national defense." (NA/RG 120 [GHQ, AG File].)

2. Brigadier General Hugh Drum, First Army chief of staff, was transferred from the lecturing assignment in mid-April. Colonel Willey Howell, First Army G-2, ceased lecturing in early May, leaving Marshall to finish the series himself. Howell disliked lecturing and thought the troops regarded the talks as "G.H.Q. propaganda." (Howell to Eltinge, May 14, 1919, NA/RG 120 [GHQ, AG File].) However, the commander of the Seventy-ninth Division wrote to request that Marshall deliver his lecture again. "Only a limited number of officers and noncommissioned officers could be present at that time, and they were so favorably impressed by this lecture that all considered it very desirous to have more officers and men in the Division hear the lecture." (Major General Joseph E. Kuhn to the Adjutant General, A.E.F., April 30, 1919, ibid.)

Marshall's lectures were delivered from notes which have been lost. The slides he used are in the National Archives (RG 111). In 1942 a former sergeant and shorthand reporter in the A.E.F. sent Marshall a copy of the record of the lecture given on April 2, 1919, near Montabaur, Germany. (Patrick C. Kelly to Marshall, April 7, 1942, GCMRL/G. C. Marshall Papers [Pentagon Office, Speeches].)

TO MAJOR GENERAL JOHN L. HINES[1]   April 17, 1919
                                                      [Chaumont, France]

My dear General: I returned to Chaumont last night, and the first thing this morning I wish to write and tell you again how very much I appreciated your hospitality and your many kindnesses to me during my first visit to the Rhine. I can see now that I will only have kindly recollections of Germany and the Germans, because of the pleasure you gave me at Neuwied. I have never experienced before such perfect hospitality, and while I must have worn it almost to the bone it seemed genuine to the last moment.

I was sorry not to see you that night at General Smith's party, but when I returned to Treves I was so tired and the hour was so late that I went straight to bed. I think I passed you the next afternoon in Bonn when Drum and myself were heading for Cologne.

I spent two days in Brussels, and that is about all that I can put on paper about my Brussels trip. I even went to see the battlefield of Waterloo, but I am not certain that I saw it. However, I had a wonderful time, and I am a poorer, wiser, and quieter man.

With my warmest regards to you, General King, Chaffee,[2] and all the other members of your very delightful staff, believe me always   Faithfully yours,

                                                      G. C. Marshall, Jr.

LC/J. L. Hines Papers

1. Hines was commanding general of the Third Army Corps, with headquarters at Neuwied, near Coblenz.

2. Brigadier General Campbell King was chief of staff of the Third Corps, and Colonel Adna R. Chaffee (U.S.M.A., 1906) was assistant chief of staff for Operations.

Aide to Pershing

May 1919–August 1924

S PECIAL ORDERS, NO. 116, dated April 26, 1919, directed Colonel George C. Marshall, Jr., to proceed to Metz and report to the Place de la Republique at ten o'clock on the morning of April 30 to receive—along with seventeen other officers, most of whom he had long known—the Legion of Honor of France, degree of officer. Shortly before the ceremony, another medal recipient, Lieutenant Colonel James L. Collins, Sr., (U.S.M.A., 1907) secretary of the General Staff and formerly one of General Pershing's aides, asked Marshall if he would like to become an aide-de-camp to the general. After the ceremony, Marshall said yes. (Major General James L. Collins, Sr., interviewed by Forrest C. Pogue, December 2, 1960, George C. Marshall Research Library, Lexington, Virginia.) The next day, May 1, Marshall joined Pershing's two other aides, Colonel John G. Quekemeyer (U.S.M.A., 1906), a cavalryman from Mississippi, and Major John C. Hughes, a young Princeton University graduate who had volunteered for war duty.

As noted previously, Marshall first attracted Pershing's attention at Gondrecourt in 1917, when the younger officer vigorously defended the First Division against what he considered the general's unjust criticisms. Thereafter, Pershing made it a point to talk to Marshall whenever he visited the division. These encounters gave Marshall some insight into the commander in chief's character. "I have never seen a man who could listen to as much criticism—as long as it was constructive criticism and wasn't just being irritable or something of that sort. You could talk to him like you were discussing somebody in the next country and yet you were talking about him personally. . . . You could say what you pleased as long as it was straight, constructive criticism. And he did not hold it against you for an instant. I never saw another commander that I could do that with. Their sensitivity clouded them up, so it just wouldn't work. I have seen some I could be very frank with, but I never could be frank to the degree that I could with General Pershing." (Interview, April 5, 1957.)

After observing Pershing closely while an aide, Marshall discerned another dimension of the chief's character. "General Pershing as a leader always dominated any gathering where he was. He was a tremendous driver, if necessary; a very kindly, likeable man on off-duty status but very stern on a duty basis." (Interview, April 11, 1957.)

Marshall had plenty of opportunity during the spring and summer of 1919 to observe Pershing in gatherings on- and off-duty. The social demands on the general's time were enormous. Triumphal parades, ceremonies, parties, receptions, and a host of civic spectacles in Europe and later in the United States were considered by their sponsors as incomplete without the American commander's presence. These activities also demanded a large proportion of Marshall's time. In rejecting an attempt by the War Department to have Marshall returned to Washington to strengthen the personnel of Colonel John McAuley Palmer's Special Committee on National Defense Projects and Plans, Pershing responded that Marshall was "a member of my personal staff and can not be spared." (Brigadier General Lytle Brown to the Chief of Staff, June 7, 1919, NA/201 File; March to Pershing, June 10, 1919, and Pershing to March, June 15, 1919, both in NA/RG 120 [AG, Cable Division].) ★

MEMORANDUM FOR THE CHIEF OF STAFF, A.E.F.   May 15, 1919
[Chaumont, France]

Memorial Day Ceremonies

The Commander-in-Chief will arrive by train from Brussels at Dun-sur-Meuse on the morning of May 30th. He will proceed by automobile from Dun-sur-Meuse to the cemetery at Beaumont (southeast of Sedan) arriving at 11 a.m. for the ceremony at that point.

Following the ceremony at Beaumont, he will return to the train for lunch and will then proceed by automobile to the cemetery at Romagne, arriving at 2.30 p.m. for the ceremony at that point. Upon the completion of this last ceremony, he will return to the train and proceed to Chaumont.

The ceremony at the Thiaucourt cemetery will be held at 11 a.m. on the same day, and Major General H. E. Ely, 5th Division, will be designated to conduct it.

The general arrangements for all three of the above ceremonies will be in accordance with memorandum prepared by the Deputy Chief of Staff.

G. C. M., Jr.

NA/RG 120 (GHQ, G-3 Reports)

O N JULY 12, two weeks after the Treaty of Versailles was signed, Pershing closed his Chaumont headquarters and moved with his staff back to American businessman Ogden Mills's Paris mansion at 73 rue de Varenne, where he had stayed during the summer of 1917. Following the Bastille Day (July 14) victory parade, Marshall left with Pershing's party for England. For his wife's benefit, Marshall kept a written record of his experiences on this trip and on two others, a tour of French battlefields (August 1–11) and a tour of Italy (August 16–22). These three interesting documents are published as appendixes to his *Memoirs,* pp. 213–39. Between trips, Marshall began his correspondence on a theme that was to occupy much of his time during the five years he was Pershing's aide: the general's determination to produce a definitive report on the activities of the American First Army. ★

To Brigadier General Hugh A. Drum[1]   August 11, 1919
                                                        [Paris, France]

My dear Drum: General Pershing has just read the "Report of the Commanding General, 1st Army, American Expeditionary Forces: Organization & Operations, 1st Army, A.E.F."

He is not entirely satisfied with that portion of the report which deals with the period from the organization of the army up to Oct. 15th, and he told me to tell you that he should have been consulted with reference to that portion of the report before it was issued.[2]

He proposes rewriting parts 1, 2, 3, and part 4 to paragraph 71, and he desires that all copies of the report which have been issued, be recalled. Will you please take steps to gather in as soon as practicable the copies which have been issued? You undoubtedly have a list of those to whom they were furnished. I will attend to the copies furnished General Pershing, General Conner and myself.

We probably will sail from Brest about September 1st so it will not be possible for you to communicate with me again while I am on this side. However, please have waiting for me in Washington a note acknowledging receipt of this letter and such proposals as you desire to make regarding the re-arrangement of the report so that it will show that a certain portion is the report of General Pershing himself and the remainder is the report of General Liggett.[3]

I am writing a brief note to General Liggett regarding the above but will leave it to you to ascertain his detailed desires in the matter.   Sincerely yours

NA/RG 200 (J. J. Pershing Papers, *Report of the First Army*)

1. Although Marshall addressed him as brigadier general, Drum had reverted to his permanent rank of major on July 31, 1919. Drum had been chief of staff of the First Army from July, 1918, to April, 1919, when he was transferred to the Service of Supply. In July, he returned to the United States and assumed his new post as commandant of Fort Leavenworth's Army School of the Line, from which he was a 1911 honor graduate.

2. Between August 10, 1918, when the organization began its formal operations, and October 15, 1918, Pershing commanded the First Army. On October 16, Hunter Liggett took over the First Army, while Pershing assumed command of the Group of American Armies, which now included the new Second Army under General Bullard.

3. Drum replied with an urgent telegram to Marshall in Paris: "In view of following unable to comply with your request. Records first army were turned in part to G.H.Q., and part to War Department. Believe record distribution army report sent to G.H.Q. distribution included Division and Corps commanders, Assistant Chief of Staff and historical section, G.H.Q., remaining copies filed in army records, probably in War Department. In view of foregoing and considering party signing report [Liggett] suggest inadvisability of modifying same especially if first army records not available for detailed examination as particular care was taken to base report upon first army records." On August 25, Drum also sent Marshall a detailed defense of the report and its issuance. (NA/RG 200 [J. J. Pershing Papers, *Report of the First Army*].)

Marshall apparently found the distribution list. On August 16, 1919, he sent out the first of three mass-mailings trying to recall all copies of the report. A second group of form letters was sent in April, 1920, and a final group in May, 1923.

To Lieutenant General Hunter Liggett   August 11, 1919
                                                        [Paris, France]

My dear General Liggett: General Pershing has just read the report of the Commanding General, 1st Army, and he is not entirely satisfied with that portion of it dealing with the period during which he personally commanded the 1st Army. He proposes re-drafting this portion of the report and I have written to General Drum with reference to the matter and telling him that General Pershing desires the copies of the report already issued to be recalled. I have also asked General Drum to communicate with you direct and learn your desires in the matter of the re-arrangement of the report so as to make a certain portion of it the report of General Pershing himself and the remainder of it your report.

We have just completed this morning a trip over the entire Western Front from Pont-a-Mousson to the English Channel. It was a wonderful opportunity and we were blessed with good weather throughout.

I am addressing this letter to you in care of the War Department but I hope it finds you where you wish to be—in San Francisco.

With my warmest regards, believe me,   Very respectfully and affectionately yours

NA/RG 200 (J. J. Pershing Papers, *Report of the First Army*)

FOLLOWING General Pershing's mid-August, whirlwind tour of Italy— Rome, Venice, the Piave River battlefields, Verona, Milan, and back to Paris in six days—Marshall completed arrangements for leaving France. On September 1, Pershing and his personal party of fifteen boarded the *Leviathan* at Brest. On the morning of the eighth, the ship docked in New York City, and two days later Marshall rode with the two other aides behind Pershing and just ahead of the First Division in the city's mammoth victory parade. The party entrained on the morning of September 12 for Washington, D.C., where they arrived that evening, following a brief stop in Philadelphia. Five days later, on the seventeenth, Marshall again followed Pershing down the capital's Pennsylvania Avenue in the last of the great victory parades.

General Pershing was given special permission to maintain a headquarters in Washington separate from that of Chief of Staff Peyton March. The 105 officers and enlisted men assigned to that post were to assist Pershing in processing the American Expeditionary Forces' records and in writing the final reports. ★

To Major Hugh A. Drum   September 20, 1919
                                          [Washington, D.C.]

My dear Drum:– I am sending you herewith the first draft of the revision of that portion of the Report of the First Army, which covers the period during which General Pershing was in direct command. I am not at all certain that this draft will meet his approval; it was hastily prepared in accordance with the notes he made on the original report.

The General will go over this draft himself within ten days, but I thought it best to send a copy of it to you in order that you might have an opportunity to make such comments and propose such changes as you see fit.

He does not wish to have anything included in his portion of the report which would seem to offer explanations or to be answering criticisms.

That portion of your report which comments on the conferences with Marshal Foch has been changed to agree with the records of these conferences kept by Colonel Boyd in a daily diary and by General Conner.[1] Please make your preliminary suggestions [and] comments as soon as possible and mail them back to me at Headquarters American Expeditionary Forces, Old Land Office Building, Washington, D.C.[2] Sincerely yours,

NA/RG 200 (J. J. Pershing Papers, *Report of the First Army*)

1. Carl Boyd, a close friend and aide to General Pershing, died of pneumonia in Paris, February 12, 1919. It was this position that Marshall was asked to fill. Brigadier General Fox Conner, another of Pershing's good friends, was assistant chief of staff for Operations, G.H.Q., at the time of the August-September conferences with Foch.

2. In his thousand-word reply of September 27, Drum objected to the elimination from Marshall's draft of three key points, each of which, if passed over in silence, might reflect adversely on the American Expeditionary Forces or on Pershing and his staff. First was the supply situation in the First Army's area shortly after the September 26 attack. British and French military writers, Drum observed, "had grasped at the alleged supply failure on our part to criticize the American High Command and Staff." Second, some explanation of the relief from the front in late September of the disorganized Thirty-fifth, Thirty-seventh, and Seventy-ninth Divisions was necessary, not only because of British and French comment, but also because of political repercussions in Congress. Finally, the blame for the partial failure of the October 14 attack should be placed on the commander of the Fifth Division, where it properly belonged, in Drum's opinion, or uninformed observers would attribute the difficulties to causes "which are entirely foreign to the real reasons." (NA/RG 200 [J. J. Pershing Papers, *Report of the First Army*].)

Important as it was, work on the Report of the First Army was of lower priority than the congressional hearings on the army reorganization (Baker-March) bill. Since early 1919, when Secretary of War Newton Baker and Chief of

Staff Peyton March had had the bill submitted, Congress had wrestled with the question of the army's future role. Briefly, the key issues to be addressed were the organization of the army (including the General Staff's status, the chief of staff's powers, and the army's relationship with the National Guard), the army's size (particularly whether it should depend upon universal military training to fill its ranks), and promotion policy.

Between October 7 and 25, Pershing and Marshall relaxed with a small party of friends at the Brandreth, New York, mountain camp owned by Fox Conner's father-in-law. There the two spent part of their time working on the reorganization problem. (Virginia Conner, *What Father Forbad* [Philadelphia: Dorrance, 1951], pp. 88–94; Interview, April 11, 1957.)

General Pershing was scheduled to testify before a combined meeting of the Senate and House military committees on October 31. Returning to Washington for final preparations, on the twenty-ninth and thirtieth Pershing held a series of twenty interviews with various army officials, including the chief of staff, in which he solicited opinions on the reorganization problems. Marshall actively participated in several interviews. (Transcripts of the interviews are in NA/RG 200 [J. J. Pershing Papers, Reorganization—Interviews].) He also secured galley proofs of John McA. Palmer's October 9–10 testimony and studied them with General Pershing. (Marshall to Palmer, March 29, 1935, LC/J. McA. Palmer Papers.)

Regarding Pershing's three days of testimony, Marshall later recalled: "I know the members of Congress were so astonished when he was having his hearings that I sat next to him with General Fox Conner on the other side, that I could interrupt him and talk to him and tell him about something, and he could turn around and tell them. He had no hesitation at all of receiving suggestions or advice from me or from the others about him. It was one of his great strengths that he could listen to these things." (Interview, April 5, 1957.)

During the winter of 1919–20, Marshall accompanied Pershing on a national inspection tour of army installations. Fox Conner, George Van Horn Moseley, and Malin Craig were among the officers Pershing chose to travel with him in his two private railroad cars. After a southern and midwestern swing, Marshall spent Christmas and New Year's with his wife and mother in Atlantic City, New Jersey. Then he was off to Chicago to rejoin the tour of the west and south.

After weeks on the road, when a southern city asked for recommendations on entertainment for the party, the return telegram suggested having pretty girls at the speakers' table and that menu planners eschew chicken and Thousand Island dressing. Moseley later observed, "We had eaten so many chickens that we simply could not look another one in the face. . . . [Thousand Island dressing] was served everywhere, often three times in a single day." (Moseley, "One Soldier's Journey," 2: 15, LC/G.V.H. Moseley Papers.) ★

To the Adjutant General   March 31, 1920
From Major General Charles P. Summerall[1]   Camp Zachary
                                        Taylor, Kentucky

Colonel George C. Marshall, Jr., General Staff.

1. During my service with the First Division, I was intimately associated with Colonel George C. Marshall, Jr., from December 1917 to July 1918. As Operations Officer of the Division, Colonel Marshall was charged with duties of grave responsibility in the training area, in extensive movements of the command and in the operations of the Division in the Ansauville Sector and in the Cantigny Sector. Throughout this period Colonel Marshall displayed high courage, superb loyalty, superior technical skill and thorough mastery of the tactical employment of troops. His tact and sound judgment contributed to the high morale that prevailed in the Division, and he possessed the admiration and confidence of both officers and soldiers. His personality was forceful and appealed to the loyalty and co-operation of every one. He possessed unusual qualities of leadership and administrative ability, and he was conspicuously qualified for the command of a brigade.

2. It is my belief that if he had remained with the Division he would have been recommended and would have received an appointment as a General Officer. I regard him as one of the most efficient officers that I have known and I recommend him for especial consideration for appointment to any grade to which he may be eligible.

C. P. Summerall

NA/201 File

1. Summerall (U.S.M.A., 1892) was commanding the First Division at this time. Between December, 1917, and July, 1918, he had commanded the First Division's First Field Artillery Brigade. Succeeding Bullard, he commanded the division between July and October, 1918, before moving up to corps commands. He returned to the United States and to the First Division in September, 1919.

In his April 11, 1957, interview, Marshall said of "the iron man" Summerall: "He was the nearest approach to the [Stonewall] Jackson type that I saw in the war. And he was a wonder to watch when the fighting was on as a leader. His influence on the men was tremendous, and my admiration for him was very, very great. . . . I never saw anything to beat him on the battlefield. . . . General Summerall was really unconscious of any feeling of fear."

To Major General James W. McAndrew[1]   July 9, 1920
                                    Washington, D.C.

My dear General McAndrew:– Your very nice and much appreciated note of July 7th brought to my mind a matter in which I am much interested, and which seems to me pertains to the General Staff College course.[2] I do not want to bother you with any half baked suggestions, but I have decided that you might be interested in the thought I have in mind.

My observation of the General Staff work in France, particularly at G.H.Q. and in the First Army, and my recent experience at the War Department in connection with Army reorganization, has caused me to feel that one of the most serious troubles in our General Staff has been the failure to follow the proper procedure in determining a policy or a plan, and in stating that policy or plan in such fashion that the various services, boards, or combat staffs could effectively carry out their portion of the plan or policy, or formulate their recommendations.

For example, take the recent problem of the War Plans Division in preparing the plan of reorganization of the Army. The special committee, of which I was a member,[3] found that the recommendations from Leavenworth and from the Infantry and Cavalry Boards were, in a large measure, without value to us because they had not been based on a definite policy of either a large or a small division. Eventually we had to secure what amounted to snap judgment proposals on the interior details of organization.

Another example might be taken from the problem of the First Army, in the middle of August 1918, when it was necessary to call on all the services to submit proposals concerning their phase of the operation against the St. Mihiel Salient. The same thing occurred again in preparation for the Meuse-Argonne attack on September 26th, and again for the attack on November 1st. General Harbord must of had many such situations in the early days of the A.E.F.

My observation has been that in most instances we had no settled method of procedure, and were particularly weak in our method of drafting the instructions which were to serve as a general guide. On the one hand the instructions were frequently too indefinite along certain lines, and on the other hand, were too detailed regarding other matters.

To go back to the first example referred to above, and without my having given the matter any real study, I should think the War Plans Division should have followed some such procedure as this:

First: Have decided what were the basic questions in Army Reorganization. Among these would have been the organization of the Infantry Division. The War Plans Division should then have considered that phase of the problem in a broad manner, securing the best thought from the heads of the Supply Services in the War Department, Chiefs of Arms, and the General Staff College. Having arrived at a tentative conclusion this should have been furnished the Service Schools and the Infantry and other boards, to secure their opinion on the general merits of the proposition. With this data, the War Plans Division should have reconsidered its tentative decision and submitted a definite proposition for final approval of the Chief of Staff.

Second: The policy as to the approximate strength of the division having been definitely settled, the War Plans Division should then have repeated practically the same procedure in working out the details of the divisional organization.[4]

In carrying out the above the most difficult phase of the problem would lie in drafting the guiding instructions in each case. I believe that a great deal of the dissatisfaction with the General Staff has grown out of our weakness in this respect. The services in particular seldom feel that they have been given a fair show, and I am inclined to believe that they seldom have received a properly drafted proposal. You know far better than I do how difficult it is to state a broad general proposition so that the minor participants can properly work into the scheme. We usually oscillate between a too general or too detailed statement.

I do not know whether or not any such course as this is included in your General Staff College training, but I believe that it is highly important, and that we would do well if we could obtain examples of this character of General Staff work from the operations of the German Great General Staff and the French, though I imagine it would be very difficult to secure the exact papers I have in mind.

I hope I have not bored you with this long dissertation, but the matter has so frequently appealed to me as being of major importance that I thought it would be a good thing to bring to your direct attention.[5]   Respectfully yours,

NOTE: On reading this over I find that my remarks about the War Plans Division seem hardly fair to those officers, though they served my purpose for an illustration. They did assume the division proposed by the Superior Board until General Pershing's indorsement rather upset things.

USAMHI/Army War College Papers

1. McAndrew (U.S.M.A., 1888) was commandant of the General Staff College at Washington Barracks, Washington, D.C. As a captain he had been an honor student at the School of the Line in 1909–10, when Marshall was an instructor. He traveled to France in 1917 as a colonel assigned to the First Division's Eighteenth Infantry. Later he was promoted to major general; and he established and was made commandant of the A.E.F.'s General Staff School at Langres, France. In May, 1918, he replaced James G. Harbord as Pershing's chief of staff. In 1919 he returned to the United States and to the General Staff College.

2. McAndrew's letter is not in the Marshall papers.

3. Postwar army reorganization was based on a bill, signed by President Woodrow Wilson on June 4, 1920, amending the National Defense Act of 1916. To implement the new policies, the War Department appointed special boards to prepare plans. In the War Plans Division, a Special Committee of ten officers, including Marshall and Fox Conner, worked to outline new policies for the Regular Army officer corps. (See Special Committee Report, July 8, 1920, NA/RG 200 [J. J. Pershing Papers].)

4. Many A.E.F. officers regarded the huge World War American division of some twenty-eight thousand men—approximately twice the size of European divisions—as clumsy to maneuver and difficult to administer. Beginning during World War I and lasting until the early days of American participation in World War II, army opinion was divided over the relative merits of the large or "square" (four regiment) versus the small or "triangular" (three regiment) division. For a contemporary view on the debate, see Lieutenant Colonel Oliver L. Spaulding, Jr., "Organization Under the New Law," *Field Artillery Journal* 10 (May–June 1920): 273–78.

5. At a July 12 conference with the General Staff College's directors, General McAndrew distributed copies of Marshall's letter. The original Marshall letter has not been found. This version is from one of the copies made for distribution.

To Theodore Roosevelt, Jr.   [July, 1920]
                                                       [Washington, D.C.]

My dear Roosevelt: I have been absent from Washington most of the spring and early summer and it was only after my return a few days ago that I noticed the order citing you for the Distinguished Service Cross. You have my very heartiest and most sincere congratulations on this award, for I really am delighted to learn of this belated but highly deserved recognition of your services.

With no idea of flattery and with absolute honesty I tell you that my observation of most of the fighting in France led me to consider your record as a fighting man one of the most remarkable in the entire A.E.F. Based on personal knowledge of conditions, I consider your conduct as a battalion commander in Picardy during the last week of May and the first week of June, 1918, as among the finest examples of leadership, courage and fortitude that came to my attention during the war.

I do not think I have been prejudiced in your favor because of your peculiar position in France virtually as the representative of your Father's intense desire to serve in battle against Germany. As a matter of fact I opposed promoting you to the grade of lieutenant colonel in January 1918, before we had entered into active service. From the possibly narrower view point of a professional soldier I regarded your career in France as outstanding for high spirit, gallantry and proven ability as an infantry leader under the most trying conditions of the war.[1]

I do not believe I have ever before indulged myself in such frank comments of a pleasant nature to another man as I have in this letter, but I derived so much personal satisfaction as an American from witnessing the manner in which you measured up to the example of your Father, that it is a genuine pleasure to me to express myself so candidly.

Please remember me most cordially to Mrs. Roosevelt, and if either of you are to be in Washington at any time Mrs. Marshall and I hope very much you will give us the pleasure of seeing you.   Faithfully yours,

G. C. Marshall, Jr.

LC/T. Roosevelt Papers

1. Roosevelt, eldest son of former President Theodore Roosevelt, was seven years younger than Marshall. He had been active with his father and General Leonard Wood in establishing the Citizens' Military Training Camp at Plattsburg, New York, in 1915. In April, 1917, he was commissioned a major in the Twenty-sixth Infantry, First Division. He was wounded at the battles of Cantigny and Soissons. Promoted to lieutenant colonel in September, 1918, he led his regiment in the St. Mihiel and Meuse-Argonne campaigns.

Recalling the famous race to Sedan incident of the last days of the war, Marshall commented: "Theodore Roosevelt got in front of his old regiment . . . and pushed on as hard as he could. He had to walk with a staff because he had this knee that had been shot up. I had gotten him back for command of the [regiment], and he was held to be absent without leave from his unit he was assigned to in the south of France. But he was going with his old regiment and making a fine job of leadership. All of this got complicated up on the front, and when he went through the French line, they [the French] were lying down and he barged on through to head for Sedan. They rushed up and protested that it was their sector. 'Well,' he said, 'you aren't advancing.' And he went right along. When they discovered he was Theodore Roosevelt, then they all stood up and cheered him, and he went on ahead.'' (Interview, April 11, 1957.)

After the war, Roosevelt helped to organize the American Legion. At the time of this letter, he was a member of the New York state legislature.

FROM THEODORE ROOSEVELT, JR.   July 14, 1920
                                                 [Oyster Bay, New York?]

My dear Colonel Marshall:[1]   Thank you so much for your letter. I cannot begin to tell you how much I appreciate it. I am putting it aside with my citations and war record to be handed down to the children.

It might interest you to know that in my humble opinion, General Summerall was the biggest troop leader we had in the American army and you were the best tactician. I have quite often expressed this view to people whom I know and you would be pleased and surprised to know how many agree with me.

Mrs. Roosevelt and I will certainly hope to see you and Mrs. Marshall when you get to Washington. Meanwhile, if you two come up around here be sure to come and see us.   With best regards,

LC/T. Roosevelt Papers

1. On June 30, Marshall lost his temporary, wartime rank of colonel and reverted to his permanent grade of captain. He was promoted to major on July 1. Friends, including Pershing, occasionally called him "colonel" for several years.

TO COLONEL JOHN MCA. PALMER   August 3, 1920
                                                 Washington, D.C.

My dear General Palmer: I have been writing some notes of congratulations to the new brigadiers and I have a feeling that I would be leaving the most important thing undone if I did not tell you how very sorry I am, and I believe every one else in the army is, that your splendid services were not officially recognized. Of course we all suspect the reason why, but it is a crime and shame that you are not now a major general. Few men have done so much for the army and therefore the country, as have you, and whether or not you are accorded your just dues, this fact will remain.[1]

With my warmest regards to Mrs. Palmer, Mary and yourself,   Sincerely yours

                                                 G. C. Marshall, Jr.

LC/J. McA. Palmer Papers; H

1. The highest rank Palmer had held up to the time of this letter was that of colonel. He was not promoted to brigadier general until December, 1922. The "reason" Marshall mentions for Palmer's being passed over in 1920 was probably his role in writing the Wadsworth bill which became Congress' alternative to the Baker-March reorganization bill in 1919.

PALMER WAS a casualty in the Pershing-March feud. As early as mid-1919, James Harbord wrote to Pershing from the United States that "the higher officers of the Regular Army are lining up in two general groups," one allied with Chief of Staff Peyton March and another "wearing your A.E.F. brand." (Harbord to Pershing, June 14, 1919, NA/RG 200 [J. J. Pershing Papers, Miscellaneous].) Marshall, although identified with the Pershing faction, was not March's enemy.

In a December 7, 1956, interview, Marshall commented: "I found in going into all the papers afterwards, and in some of the actions which occurred at the time in which I saw General March personally, that he was a master administrator, an executive, with a great weakness of antagonizing everybody and, in particular, in having men about him—one in particular—who were very curt, and almost rude, in their procedure. They operated too much like General March. They needed someone of exactly opposite characteristics as the secretary of the General Staff and in other parts. I admired General March very much in his basic procedure, but I thought he almost ruined himself by his bitterness in his procedure which stuck with him to the last." As he did not join Pershing's staff until the feud was well along, Marshall did not know how much of the disagreement was the A.E.F. commander's fault. "However," he noted, "I think they were both at fault, because it was essential that they get together and they didn't. What saved the situation was Newton Baker."

Marshall, describing Pershing's character in a March 6, 1957, interview, related the following story of an incident which occurred while Pershing was army chief of staff. "There was something came up. General Harbord was deputy chief of staff then, and he brought it to General Pershing and they were going to change this. General Pershing had a way of sending most all of these things into me and nobody knew about it, and all he would put on the paper was 'Colonel M.' Then it was up to me to take a look at it and tell him what I thought. But that was never betrayed outside of the office, that I was put into this position of maybe criticizing my superiors. Well, in this particular case, he had decided in agreement with General Harbord. It was about something that General March had done, and they were changing it, and I thought they were entirely wrong. And when I got the paper with 'Colonel M' on it, I dictated a little memorandum to General Pershing to that effect—why I thought they were wrong and so on.

"General Pershing sent for me and when I came in, he said, 'I don't take to this at all—I don't agree with you.' 'Well,' I said, 'let me have it, General, again, let me have it. I didn't express myself well.' I took it back in there and very carefully drew up my resume of the affair and why I thought it was wrong. He sent for me again and he said, 'I don't accept this. I think Harbord and I are right.' I was very much upset because I thought it was entirely wrong, and I said, 'Well now, General, I have done a poor job on this; let me have that paper again.' So I took it back and rewrote the whole thing to give it a brand new flavor, and then I took it in and handed it to him. He read it, and he put it down and said, 'No!' And as I recall he slapped his hand on the desk, which is something I had never had him do before, and said, 'No, by God, we will do it this way.'

"I got the paper back into my hand—I remember this pretty clearly—I said, 'Now General, just because you hate the guts of General March, you're setting yourself up—and General Harbord, who hates him, too—to do something you know damn well is wrong.' He looked at me and handed me the paper—I didn't have it before—and said, 'Well, have it your own way.' That was the end of this scene where he was bitterly determined to do this, and yet he ended up by saying, 'have it your own way,' which I thought was very remarkable. No prolonged feeling. Nothing. That was the end of the affair. I don't think it was the end of the affair so far as General Harbord was concerned. But General Pershing held no [grudges] at all. He might be very firm at the time, but if you convinced him, that was the end of that. He accepted that and you went ahead." ★

To General John J. Pershing   August 15, 1920
                                           Lexington, Virginia

My dear General: I hope you had a fine time in the mountains but I'm afraid it must have been rather rainy as there seems to have been a wet spell all over the Atlantic States. Schneider writes me you plan to leave for the West on Thursday, but I suppose this will depend on the progress your Board makes.[1] I have been having a fine holiday, riding three or four hours daily through beautiful country. Mrs. Marshall is looking very well and sends you her love. Also Mrs. Coles wishes me to give you her warmest regards.

I find Lexington still excited over your brief visit. You made a tremendous impression on all these people, which means much as they still live somewhat in the Civil War and are painfully conservative. You charmed them all, old and young.[2]

I hope your trip West will be cool, and I know you will thoroughly enjoy Cheyenne and Lincoln. I have written Adamson and Schneider about several matters for your attention before you leave.[3]

As always, I am at your service. With my affectionate regards. Faithfully yours,

G. C. Marshall, Jr.

LC/J. J. Pershing Papers (General Correspondence); H

1. General Pershing headed a board charged with selecting, from among the Reserve and temporary officers who had been retained in the service at the end of the war, those officers who would receive commissions in the Regular Army.

2. Pershing had visited Lexington on June 17–18. Marshall later recalled that "the trip with General Pershing up to the V.M.I. was very interesting and delighted him. . . . I had insisted on his going there because he had gone to West Point [June 14–15] and there were so many V.M.I. men in lead positions in the army." (Interview, April 11, 1957.)

The general also visited Robert E. Lee's tomb at V.M.I.'s neighbor-rival Washington and Lee University, where he was "received in the Washington and Lee Chapel with great ceremony and stood in front of the effigy of General Lee and made his remarks. We immediately received quite a clamor from certain men in Chicago and others who objected to General Pershing going there where Lee was buried. I remember General Pershing left me to answer all the letters. He said, 'You got me to go there, now you attend to the letters objecting to my having gone.' " (Interview, March 6, 1957.)

3. George E. Adamson had been Pershing's private secretary before the war; first commissioned in December, 1917, he was a captain at this time. First Lieutenant John T. Schneider, an artilleryman, joined Pershing's entourage in 1920.

To Brigadier General John S. Mallory[1]   November 5, 1920
[Washington, D.C.?]

My Dear General Mallory,   Last summer during one of our delightful rides I commented on the advice I would give a young officer going to war, based on my observation of what had constituted the success of the outstanding figures in the American Expeditionary Forces, and you asked me to write out what I had said. A discussion with Fox Conner this morning reminded me of my promise to do this, so here it is.

To be a highly successful leader in war four things are essential, assuming that you possess good common sense, have studied your profession and are physically strong.

When conditions are difficult, the command is depressed and everyone seems critical and pessimistic, you must be especially cheerful and optimistic.

When evening comes and all are exhausted, hungry and possibly dispirited, particularly in unfavorable weather at the end of a march or in battle, you must put aside any thought of personal fatigue and display marked energy in looking after the comfort of your organization, inspecting your lines and preparing for tomorrow.

Make a point of extreme loyalty, in thought and deed, to your chiefs personally; and in your efforts to carry out their plans or policies, the less you approve the more energy you must direct to their accomplishment.

The more alarming and disquieting the reports received or the conditions viewed in battle, the more determined must be your attitude. Never ask for the relief of your unit and never hesitate to attack.

I am certain in the belief that the average man who scrupulously follows this course of action is bound to win great success. Few seemed equal to it in this war, but I believe this was due to their failure to realize the importance of so governing their course. Faithfully yours,

G. C. Marshall, *Memoirs*, p. xv.

1. Mallory (U.S.M.A., 1879) had been disabled in the line of duty and discharged in 1918. He was teaching Spanish at V.M.I. at the time of this letter.

To GENERAL JOHN J. PERSHING   December 13, 1920
                                               Washington, D.C.

Dear General: . . . I believe that my trip to Milton and Exeter, particularly the former, may have a good result. Every seat in the Club was taken for the talk on Friday night. They had issued tickets to members and did not open the Club for guests, and I was relieved to see that the house was completely filled, some standing, despite exceedingly bad weather. It proved to be the most sympathetic and responsive audience I have ever encountered and they gave me quite an ovation at the end, though it was apparent they were inspired by a first comprehension of the real achievement of the A.E.F. Most of those present came up to me after the lecture and seemed greatly astonished by my description of what actually had occurred. They all spoke of you and I believe for the first time really appreciated what you had done.

Mrs. Russell was, as usual, delightful, and Mr. Russell quite outdid himself in his efforts to be nice to us.[1] They gave Mrs. Marshall two luncheons, a tea and a supper party, and a friend of theirs gave another tea for her, and just before the lecture the President and Secretary of the Club gave us a big dinner at the clubhouse.

At Exeter we found that Doctor Perry was sick with a bad sore throat and a cold, so we did not see him at all.[2] Mrs. Perry was most hospitable and had all the faculty in for tea the first afternoon and several guests for dinner that night. The combination of older people, little boys and older boys made a very hard audience to talk to but it apparently went off all right. We left Exeter last night, Mrs. Russell having gone up there with us.

Quekemeyer tells me you expect to return to Washington on the 18th or 19th for a few days and then go back to Long Island for Christmas.[3] Mrs. Marshall fully recovered from her temporary indisposition at Carlisle the next morning, and seemed in better shape than any of the others. She cannot stand very much tobacco smoke in a closed room.

We both send you our love.

Marshall

LC/J. J. Pershing Papers (General Correspondence)

1. James and Emily Russell, whom Marshall had met at the outings at Pershing's friend W. Cameron Forbes's "Mansion House" on Naushon Island, Massachusetts, in 1919 and 1920, were friends of Forbes and the Perrys.

2. Lewis Perry was the sixth principal of the Phillips Exeter Academy. Pershing's son, Warren, was enrolled at the academy in Exeter, New Hampshire.

3. Pershing was resting at a rented house in Roslyn, Long Island, near the home of his brother James.

S TORIES of Marshall's fondness for children are numerous. The following is a dispatch to Lewis Perry, Jr., "Colonel Louie," in Exeter, New Hampshire, regarding the winter campaign Marshall had observed there on his recent trip. ★

FIELD ORDERS NO. 1   December 13, 1920
Confidential   [Washington, D.C.]

Par. I: The enemy is badly scared and shows signs of retreating. Molly was last seen in the pantry packing up rations, which indicates a hostile movement.

Par. II: Louie's Army will attack Saturday immediately after breakfast, turning the enemy's left flank by way of the cellar, and endeavoring to capture the hostile commissary supplies in the cake box.

Par. III: The Army will deploy facing the house with its left flank resting on the see-saw and its right abreast of the box where the bicycle lives. Sergeant Major Richards will hold the right of the line. Colonel Louie will occupy the center, and any rookies available will be placed on the left flank.

            The advance will be preceded by a heavy artillery barrage of snow balls, if available, and will press forward despite all hostile resistance until the enemy is captured or driven from the field.

            Lances, shields, guns, revolvers, battle-axes and butcher knives will be carried by the troops. Rations must be captured. Sam Browne belts will be worn.

Par. IV: A first-aid station will be established under the big cedar tree, but seriously wounded may be treated later at Doctor Louie's Drugstore immediately after the charge.

Par. V: General Richards will maintain his Headquarters ten paces in rear of
the center of the line, where messages will reach him.[1]

By Command of GENERAL PERSHING:

G. C. Marshall, Jr.

Chief of Staff

Phillips Exeter Bulletin, May 1978

1. The persons mentioned were: "Molly," one of the Perry's maids; "Sergeant Major
Richards," Lauris P. Richards; "General Richards," Lauris's older brother Frank; and
"Colonel Louie," son of "Doctor Louie," Phillips Exeter Academy's principal.

SOMETIME during 1920, Marshall wrote a brief essay entitled "Profiting By
War Experiences" for the *Infantry Journal* 18 (January 1921): 34–37. He
worried that the typical A.E.F. officer's brief, frenetic, and narrowly cir-
cumscribed service might encourage such men to draw dangerously erroneous
lessons. Conditions on the battle front changed dramatically between the spring
and the autumn of 1918, he noted; moreover, the special conditions which
existed in different sectors of the front necessitated careful study before
presuming to deduce general conclusions regarding tactics and organization.

Infantry officers, Marshall observed, seldom understood the role of machine
guns and field artillery, and frequently misused them. The too frequent
breakdown of communications between units at the front and their various
headquarters bothered him. "Our troops suffered much from the delays involved
in preparing long and complicated orders, due to the failure of the Staff concerned to recognize that speed was more important than technique."

Marshall reminded officers who participated only in the later phases of the war
that tactical mistakes of little consequence then would have proved disastrous if
made when the German Army's morale was high, its reserves were adequate, and
its troops were on the offensive. "What we actually accomplished was a military
miracle, but we must not forget that its conception was based on a knowledge of
the approaching deterioration of the German army, and its lessons must be
studied accordingly. We remain without modern experience in the first phases of
a war and must draw our conclusions from history." ★

TO GENERAL JOHN J. PERSHING   December 23, 1920

Washington, D.C.

My dear General: On several occasions General Wright has spoken to me
about the serious situation which is developing due to the failure of the Senate to
confirm recent Army appointments.[1] He had previously spoken to Quekemeyer
about this and I believe Quekemeyer wrote you. The point of the matter seems to

be this. Some feel that there is a serious danger that the Senate will fail to confirm before its recess and thus throw Army affairs into a very chaotic condition, and incidentally enable a new series of makes[2] to be put through with the new session. Others feel that the confirmations will be made. As you have probably talked this over with Senator Warren, and possibly others in authority, you may know exactly what is going to be done. Of course, in that event, there is nothing more to be said. But if you do not know what Senator Lodge's plans are, I wonder if you would be willing for me to see Senator Wadsworth in an effort to find out.[3]

I think, of course, that it would be very bad business for you to become involved in this affair unless there is a serious possibility of the Senate failing to confirm. However, if there is this serious possibility, then it seems to me the men who played an important part in the A.E.F. and are awaiting the confirmation of their commissions as General officers, will rather expect you to put up a fight for them, which I am sure would be your intention. Quekemeyer thought you might have seen Senator Wadsworth the day before you left the city as he knew you had gone up to the Senate. I will not do anything unless I hear from you.

It is not good practice to mix business and pleasure, but Mrs. Marshall wanted me to find out if you had in mind going to any of the dances that are being given at 2400–16th Street this winter.[4] If so, she wondered if you would have dinner with us on the night of the 6th and attend the dance with us afterwards.

Both send you our love and Christmas greetings.

Marshall

LC/J. J. Pershing Papers (General Correspondence)

1. Major General William M. Wright was executive assistant to the army chief of staff.
2. A "make" was a congressionally confirmed promotion.
3. As part of his efforts to reduce military spending, Henry Cabot Lodge, Sr., Republican from Massachusetts, chairman of the Senate Foreign Relations Committee, was blocking Senate consideration of the War Department's nominations for promotion. James W. Wadsworth, Jr., Republican from New York, was chairman of the Military Affairs Committee.
The "chaotic condition" to which Marshall refers was the necessity of demoting forty-three colonels and lieutenant colonels in order to provide slots for the men not promoted to brigadier and major general who would revert to their permanent, lower ranks. Furthermore, if this happened, some commanding officers would find themselves inferior in rank to some subordinates. Finally, as the *Army and Navy Journal* observed on January 29, 1921, "the 3285 officers of the Regular Army nominated for promotion who will revert to their former ranks should the Senate fail to confirm their nominations are very much disturbed as to where they will rank when again nominated for promotion after March 4."
4. The address of Marshall's Washington apartment, 1919–21.

To Colonel John McA. Palmer

February 25, 1921
Washington, D.C.

My dear General: As soon as your letter came yesterday I tried to make an appointment with Senator W. but found he was just leaving the city to return this A.M. As the appropriation bill for the Army comes up at noon today his

Secretary did not think he would have time to see me before tomorrow morning.[1]

I spend so much of my time doing things for people in whom I have little interest and who I frequently hold in very moderate esteem, that it is a positive or actual pleasure to talk to Senator W. about you. I have not much command of English, but I feel sure I can give him an outline of your services which will impress even him—tho he already knows you so well.

I am so glad you wrote to me frankly and I will derive much satisfaction from anything I may be able to do in your behalf.

I think I would write to General P. if I were in your place. Many have done it and with some success. I understand that Johnson (91st Div.) and Bowley (F.A.) have been nominated for the two existing vacancies, but there is hardly a remote chance that they will be confirmed.[2]

I will write to you as soon as I see Senator Wadsworth.

Mrs. Marshall is in Virginia for a three weeks visit with her mother.

Give my love to Mrs. Palmer and also give me the name of Mary's school in your next letter.   Faithfully yours,

G. C. Marshall, Jr.

LC/J. McA. Palmer Papers; H

1. This letter was not found, but Palmer had been trying to obtain a promotion to brigadier general.

2. Colonel William H. Johnson and Colonel Albert J. Bowley (U.S.M.A., 1897) were nominated to be brigadier generals by President Wilson on February 23, 1921. The third session of the Sixty-sixth Congress failed to act on any promotions to general officer before the session ended on March 4, 1921.

To Mrs. George C. Marshall, Sr.   March 7, 1921
                                                    Washington, D.C.

Dear Mother: That there may be some written record of our business relations in case anything sudden should happen to me, I am writing to advise you that I purchased for you, in my name, on the 4th inst., fifty (50) shares of Pure Oil stock at $33.00 per share.

The transaction stands as follows: To facilitate the purchase of the stock I took one hundred (100) shares,—fifty for you and fifty for me, and signed a note at the Second National Bank here, for $3315.00, which covers the cost of the shares plus the brokerage commission. In addition to my note the bank holds your two bonds as collateral and will also hold the hundred shares of stock as collateral. The loan is at 7%.

My intention is to hold your fifty shares until they increase somewhat in value, and more particularly, until your bonds increase in value. At present they (bonds) are worth exactly 77% of their original value. I think there is a possibility that by summer they may be worth about 85% of par, and the shares of stock should also increase in value proportionately. When this developes I will sell twenty-five

(25) of the shares and transfer twenty-five (25) more to you, remitting the balance from the transaction in cash, after the sale of the bonds. I will take care of the interest and everything, on the loan and will settle this all when I close out the affair.

As this is a business letter I will not complicate it with anything else, except to say that I leave for Boston tonight to be gone until about the 12th. With much love, your devoted son

G. C. Marshall, Jr.

Lily still in Lexington.
I enclose a piece of poetry I did for little Rose Page.[1]

GCMRL/M. M. Singer Papers; T

1. The complimentary close and the last two lines were added in Marshall's hand. Rose Page, ten-year-old youngest child of Dr. Thomas Walker Page, formerly a professor at the University of Virginia and since 1918 a member of the United States Tariff Commission, was one of the few children living in Marshall's building. Her descriptions of Marshall and of 2400 Sixteenth Street, N.W., are in Rose Page Wilson, *General Marshall Remembered* (Englewood Cliffs, N.J.: Prentice-Hall, 1968).

The following poem, handwritten on two- by three-inch pieces of paper, and found in the Rose Page Wilson papers at the Marshall Library, was probably the one Marshall mentions.

I

A little girl I strive to please
Is very shy, but likes to tease
And tell all sorts of funny jokes
about all kinds of curious folks.

II

She likes to ride and dance and coast
But better still to butter toast
and smear it deep with honey sweet
and sit and eat and eat and eat.

III

I think some time along in spring
She'l eat so much of everything
Her dresses all will spread and split
and open out to make a fit.

IV

And then perhaps she'l look right thin
with strips of dress and streaks of skin
I think she'l look real odd like that
With nothing whole except her hat.

To Colonel John McA. Palmer

April 15, 1921
Washington, D.C.

My dear Colonel: I want you to know how sorry I was not to find your name in the list of renominations and I can only hope that sooner or later you will receive your just dues.[1]

Yesterday I handed your letter to the General and had a talk with him about it before he read it.[2] Attached hereto is his note when he sent it back to me; my note in reply to his; and his final remark.[3] From this you will see that he proposes using his influence to have you detailed as you desire. I will keep you advised as to what is happening. Please return the slip so that I may attach it to your letter for our record.

I was delighted to see you and Mrs. Palmer the other day. Please give her my love, keeping a fair share for yourself. Faithfully yours,

Marshall

LC/J. McA. Palmer Papers

1. On March 10, 1921, Pershing submitted a list of fourteen men to be promoted to major general and twenty-eight to brigadier general. These nominations covered the total number of vacancies expected during 1921. Palmer's name was on a "Supplementary List" with four others recommended for brigadier. (Pershing to Weeks, March 10, 1921, NA/RG 200 [J. J. Pershing Papers].)

2. Palmer, in a letter to General Pershing dated April 4, 1921, suggested that he use his writing talents to help solve the country's confusion over military policy. He hoped to do for the army what Alfred T. Mahan had done for the navy in the 1890s: develop "a philosophy of military organization, at once satisfactory to the practical soldier and in harmony with our traditional political ideals."

Given the leisure, Palmer wrote, he would produce some articles for the popular press aimed at influencing national military policy and later a brief history of the army as a political institution. But he was financially unable to retire from the army. "Under these circumstances, I have decided to ask you whether if you think my aim a useful one, you will not arrange to have me placed on special duty in Washington, under your orders or in some other capacity for a time, so that I can have an opportunity to work up my material with access to the Staff College Library." (Palmer to Pershing, April 4, 1921, LC/J. McA. Palmer Papers.)

3. Pershing noted that Palmer would be of greater service in the army than as a civilian. To Marshall's query—"Will you use your influence to have him detailed to duty as he suggests?"—Pershing responded, "Yes." (Pershing to Marshall, April 14, 1921, ibid.)

To Colonel John McA. Palmer   May 2, 1921
                                              Washington, D.C.

My dear Colonel Palmer: My own absence from the city during most of the past ten days and General Pershings absence for a week at the White Sulphur,[1] has caused me to delay in answering your last letter.

You paid me the highest compliment I have ever received, and coming from you makes me value it all the more, so I want you to know how much I appreciate your good opinion and particularly your gracious method of telling me of it.[2]

General Pershing has not taken any action in your case, but I think he is waiting until his own status has been more definitely settled and the new Chief of Staff announced. As soon as these two things are cleared up I will remind him, at his request, of the matter and he then intends to have it settled if possible as you desire.[3]

Mrs. Marshall and I have been off on two motor trips recently, one up into Penna, thru Gettysburg, and one down into the Shenandoah Valley. The country is beautiful and it recalled my staff ride thru the same section in 1908.

Give our love to Mrs. Palmer and keep a generous share for yourself. I have not told her of my modern method of greeting the cook!   Faithfully yours,

G. C. Marshall, Jr.

LC/J. McA. Palmer Papers; H

1. White Sulphur Springs resort in West Virginia.

2. Replying to Marshall's letter of April 15, Palmer wrote that he was "delighted to know that my proposal meets with the General's active approval. I am more than grateful to you for

your friendly interest in bringing the matter so formally to his attention. I feel that you are giving me material help toward an opportunity for successful life work, and if I should meet with any success I will find no more gratifying use of it than in helping a little toward making your merits more widely known and recognized. For I believe you know that ever since I was one of your elderly pupils at Leavenworth I have considered you one of the real leaders of progress in the army. I know nobody in whom endowments of intellect, character, courage and rare tact are more abundantly provided and more perfectly balanced.'' (Palmer to Marshall, April 17, 1921, LC/J. McA. Palmer Papers.)

3. On May 6 orders were issued instructing Palmer to report for duty with General Pershing's staff.

O N MAY 13, 1921, after weeks of stories and rumors in the newspapers regarding General Pershing's future role, the new secretary of war, Naval Academy graduate (1877) John W. Weeks, announced that Pershing was to be army chief of staff beginning July 1. For Marshall this meant not only more office work, but a change of homes. He moved from 2400 Sixteenth Street, Washington, across the river to Quarters No. 3—near the chief of staff's No. 1—Fort Myer, Virginia, where he was to remain until he left for foreign duty in mid-1924.

General Pershing sailed for France, on September 13, with a commission from the president to lay a Congressional Medal of Honor on the graves of the Unknown Soldiers in Paris and London. Marshall and Major General James G. Harbord, the deputy chief of staff, ran the office until Pershing's return on October 28.

France's Marshal Ferdinand Foch, former commander in chief of the Allied armies, also arrived in the United States on October 28. Marshall accompanied Pershing and Foch on the trip to the American Legion convention in Kansas City, Missouri, on November 1, and to the ceremony of entombment for the Unknown Soldier at Arlington National Cemetery, November 11. ★

To Major General Edward W. Nichols   November 16, 1921
                                                        Washington, D.C.

My dear General Nichols: While I was in Philadelphia yesterday attending the banquet in honor of Marshal Foch, I had another interview regarding his visit to the V.M.I. I now find that it has proven impossible for him to arrange a visit to Lexington. He stops in Richmond and from there goes direct to the northwest, practically without pause. I made every effort to point out the many historic reasons why he should be taken to Lexington, but found that the time element was mandatory and that it was wholly out of the question to secure a change in his arranged schedule.

I am very sorry that he will not have the opportunity to see the Cadet Corps, and I know you all will be even more sorry that you cannot have the pleasure of entertaining a Marshal of France.

With my warmest regards to Mrs. Nichols and yourself, Faithfully yours,

G. C. Marshall, Jr.

VMI/Alumni File

TO BRIGADIER GENERAL CHARLES G. DAWES[1] February 7, 1922
Washington, D.C.

My dear General: I have just learned something of the result of your giving Mrs. Marshall a Victrola Record of your Melody, as played by Fritz Kreisler, and I thought you might be interested. She received it in Lexington and several of her friends there heard it played. Out of this developed orders for fifteen of the records, so far as she knows.[2]

One case is particularly interesting to me. Doctor Hunley, Professor of Economics at the College at Lexington, was so pleased with the record that he sent one to his mother in Baltimore.[3] She is a very sweet little old lady, who is blind. So charmed was she with the record, that she had her son procure nine more to send to her friends.

As a contrast to the public interest in you because of your financial and business views, I thought this might be a pleasant change. Faithfully yours,

G. C. Marshall, Jr.

NU/C. G. Dawes Papers

1. Prior to the World War a leading Chicago banker, and from August, 1917, to June, 1919, general purchasing agent for the A.E.F., Dawes was director of the recently created United States Bureau of the Budget from June, 1921, through June, 1922. "It lost its rather dominating power when he moved out," Marshall remarked in his March 6, 1957, interview, "but it still became a very influential and dependable bureau. . . . I got a pretty good insight into the thing because he would come in and talk about it afterwards and before these affairs to General Pershing, and he talked to me because he was so full of it. He talked every time he sat down about these things, and he would sit in my office and talk to me sometimes by the hour."

2. An accomplished, self-taught musician, Dawes had composed his "Melody in A Major" in 1911. Violinist-composer Fritz Kreisler added it to his repertoire in 1922.

3. William M. Hunley had been professor of economics and political science at V.M.I. since 1915.

TO MAJOR GENERAL EDWARD W. NICHOLS June 26, 1922
Washington, D.C.

My dear General: I was very sorry not to see you when you were recently in Washington. Lily, I believe, had a telephone conversation with you, but I missed out entirely. I understood from her that you wished to secure the detail of Arthur

Shipp as Commandant for the term beginning 1923.[1] She understood you to say that you had applied for him at the Office of the Chief of Infantry, and wished me to do whatever I could to insure the detail. Will you please let me know if this is correct, that I may act accordingly.

I read with a great deal of interest of the fine turnout you had at finals this year. Colonel Cootes[2] and myself had hoped to aeroplane up to Lexington, but my recovery from an operation to have my tonsils removed was too slow to permit my running around the country at that time.

Lily will probably be in Lexington in August, and I may take a horseback trip and ride up there if I do not accompany General Pershing to Alaska, which I hope I will not have to do.

Last week I was nominated for promotion to the grade of Lieutenant Colonel, but the Senate Military Committee decided, in view of the drastic reduction in the officer strength, not to confirm any of the nominations, many of which had been pending since last August. The net result is that I will have to wait an indefinite time from a year to four or five years, before I again acquire a vacancy.

With my warmest regards to Mrs. Nichols and yourself,   Faithfully yours,

G. C. Marshall, Jr.

VMI/Alumni File

1. Arthur M. Shipp, who graduated from Fort Leavenworth's School of the Line in 1910, had risen to temporary colonel during the war in Europe. At this time he was a lieutenant colonel of Infantry.

2. Lieutenant Colonel Harry N. Cootes, a cavalryman, had attended V.M.I. for two years as a member of the class of 1896.

To Major General Edward W. Nichols   July 8, 1922
                                                    Washington, D.C.

My dear General: I appreciate more than I can tell you your continued desire to have me at V.M.I., and I am exceedingly sorry that I do not think it would be possible to arrange this detail.[1] Under the law, I have to go to troops in a year and a half. Furthermore, I have been trying to get a release from General Pershing for some time in order that I might return to troops. I have been held on detail for so many years that it is quite essential for me to spend a long time with troops, and as there are now so few organizations in the army and so many officers in proportion to the number of organizations, it is essential that I get in my tour with troops as soon as possible; but as I stated before, the law would make my detail impossible.

I do not know at this time just what can be done about Arthur Shipp, but General Farnsworth, of course, could give you a better idea than I can. However, if it is your wish, as I assume it is, I shall leave no stone unturned to secure his detail.

I had dinner with Locke last night and he told me a great deal about finals and what a splendid artillery and cavalry drill the Corps put out.[2] It is a matter of great regret to me that I was not present this year, as I certainly will be next year.

With warmest regards to Mrs. Nichols and yourself, and with my very sincere thanks for your offer to take me,   Faithfully yours,

G. C. Marshall, Jr.

VMI/Alumni File

1. Nichols's letter to Marshall dated July 4, stated that half the cadets at the V.M.I. were in the Infantry R.O.T.C. unit and that this unit was "the more valuable from the standpoint of discipline and we wish to foster it." The best way to do this was to appoint an infantryman as commandant and professor of military science and tactics. Major General Charles S. Farnsworth (U.S.M.A., 1887), the chief of Infantry and former pupil of Marshall's at the School of the Line (1908–9), "will help me in this. My preference is in the order of their names: (a) George C. Marshall. (b) Arthur M. Shipp. Can you help me?" (Nichols to Marshall, July 4, 1922, VMI/RG 2.)

2. Lieutenant Colonel Morris E. Locke, Field Artillery, was a member of the General Staff at this time.

To the Adjutant General   July 7, 1922
From Major General David C. Shanks   Washington, D.C.

Services of Major George C. Marshall, Jr.

I. Since October, 1921, the Board of officers of which I am President has been engaged in making a study of the subject of promotion and the arrangement of officers on the single list. This board was appointed by the War Department upon the request of the Senate Military Committee.[1]

II. Major George C. Marshall, Jr., was recorder of this board, and upon him fell the important duties connected with securing, tabulating and preparing the voluminous records required by the board in the prosecution of its work. There were numerous classes of officers who would be affected either favorably or adversely by the various changes in the law proposed for consideration of the board. These changes were naturally suggested to the board by representatives of those classes of officers who would benefit from the changes which they proposed. Upon Major Marshall devolved the duty of seeking out and bringing before the board representatives of those classes of officers who would be adversely affected.

III. In all of the onerous duties outlined above as well as in the preparation of its final report Major Marshall showed a grasp, an ability and an energy which were simply invaluable to the board. The Board therefore desires to place on official record its appreciation of Major Marshall's services, and requests that a copy of this letter be filed with his official record.

David C. Shanks

NA/201 File

1. Always a subject of great concern, promotion policy was the focus of considerable

contention both before and after the passage of the reorganization act of June 4, 1920, particularly as reorganization was combined with the necessity of reducing the officer corps to
peacetime levels. Before 1890, officers normally served with the same regiment for most of
their careers; promotion was slow, erratic, and from within the regiment only. In 1890, the
army adopted a system of promotion by branch, thereby equalizing the waiting time among all
regiments of a particular branch. Cavalry and Infantry continued to lag behind Field Artillery,
Coast Artillery, and Engineer regiments in promotion rate. The question of creating a single
list of officers—distributing promotions among all eligible officers, regardless of branch—was
a point of contention between General Pershing, who favored the single list, and General
March, who supported a modified branch promotion system. Whether by branch or by single
list, promotion in peacetime was strictly by seniority.

In response to numerous complaints of inequities resulting from the 1920 reorganization act,
Senator James W. Wadsworth wrote to Secretary of War Weeks on September 28, 1921, to
request that the War Department "detail a committee of officers to make a new, fresh study of
the whole question" of the promotion list. The four men appointed to the board, in addition to
Major General David C. Shanks (U.S.M.A., 1884), were Colonel Charles H. Martin
(U.S.M.A., 1887), Colonel Sherman Moreland, Major George C. Marshall, Jr., and Major
Raymond S. Bamberger. The board met more than thirty times between October 17, 1921, and
May 4, 1922, to hear witnesses and to discuss letters received from officers reporting injustices
before concluding that the single list should be maintained. Records pertaining to the Shanks
Board are in NA/RG 407 decimal files 210 and 334.

LECTURE, ARMY WAR COLLEGE   September 19, 1922
Confidential   [Washington, D.C.]

LECTURE, ARMY WAR COLLEGE   September 19, 1922
Confidential   [Washington, D.C.]

The Development of the General Staff[1]

In studying the staff organization of the different armies it is important to
observe to what extent the character of government in each country has been a
factor in determining the status of the general staff. Its relationship to the
government and to the army has also, in a measure, depended on whether it was
the result of slow growth or sprang into full being by legislative enactment or
executive order. . . .

GERMAN GENERAL STAFF . . .

FRENCH GENERAL STAFF . . .

BRITISH GENERAL STAFF . . .

AMERICAN GENERAL STAFF . . .

CHANGES DURING THE WORLD WAR . . .

SERVICE ON THE GENERAL STAFF

The foregoing constitutes rather a trite statement regarding the highest
echelons of the General Staffs mentioned, with which probably all of you were
intimately familiar. It therefore appears appropriate to conclude this discussion
by considering the difficulties experienced by our General Staff officers in France
and in the War Department, and drawing the most obvious conclusions from this
evidence.

214

A.E.F. GENERAL STAFF:

The bulk of our General Staff officers with the field forces in France were suddenly thrown into the great St. Mihiel and Meuse-Argonne operations for their first battle experience. Many had not previous practical experience, and most had had but three months' instruction at Langres. Under the circumstances they rose to their great responsibilities in an admirable manner, but their lack of adequate training and experience, together with their sudden immersion in a tremendous and prolonged conflict, developed weaknesses which intimately affected the troops, and therefore seem worthy of comment.

A certain, and not inconsiderable, number of officers became depressed or seriously irritated by the frequent necessity of carrying through plans which did not fully meet their approval. This state of mind directly and adversely affected the efficiency of their work, to the manifest disadvantage of the troops. In some instances this condition had a marked effect on the operations of the units concerned. The half-hearted and pessimistic feelings of the General Staff officer was reflected throughout the command.

Another phase was the disorganizing and disheartening effect on some staff officers of frequent changes in orders. Just as they would complete the preparation of the necessary plans and orders for carrying into effect instructions from some higher command, a change of plan would be announced, and this procedure might be repeated several times. I know from personal experience of instructions being changed five times, each occasion demanding a material readjustment of orders already issued. Many officers broke under the strain of these conditions, losing confidence in those above them and developing a highly irritable and nervous mental state. They then ceased to operate efficiently.

Other General Staff officers exhibited that lack of intimate personal knowledge of the marching, billeting and fighting of the troops which makes it impossible to prepare orders and instructions without causing complications, unnecessary hardships and unfavorable battle conditions for the combat organizations. Failure to recognize the time element required for the study and preparation of orders and their transmission through the successive echelons down to the corporals squad, was the most serious failing of many of our hastily trained General Staff officers. They frequently *themselves* absorbed all the available time in the preparation of orders, which could not and did not reach the troops in time for execution. Under the circumstances the latter did the best they could. Too frequently the regimental, battalion and company officers had to exhaust and dangerously expose themselves in striving to communicate delayed instructions to the troops. Poorly coordinated and partially understood operations would result. In the records of the Historical Branch, what may appear to be a model order is often the worst example, having required so much time in preparation that its directions never reached the fighting battalions.

These failings and deficiencies were inevitable, and I doubt if any group of officers similarly placed and without the resourceful and independent characteristics of the American, could have approximated the splendid service our men rendered.

From all this it would seem, however, that to be an efficient General Staff officer with combat forces, a man must possess, in addition to specific General Staff training, certain personal characteristics, and an intimate knowledge of the troops he serves.

He must be able, enthusiastically, loyally and energetically, to carry through orders and instructions which do not meet his approval fifty percent of the time.

He must understand that in large operations frequent changes in orders is the normal and unavoidable condition, and must be accepted with equanimity.

He must ever be conscious of the vital time factor and must govern his work accordingly.

And he must know by actual experience (not mere observation) how the troops live, march and fight.

WAR DEPARTMENT GENERAL STAFF:

In serving on the War Department General Staff as now organized, three considerations seem of especial importance to the individual,—the method for exercising the supervisory and coordinating functions, the necessity for perfect cooperation, and the extreme importance of maintaining a sympathetic understanding with the other elements of the Army.

Many difficulties which have developed in the past, undoubtedly arose from the method of exercising the coordinating and supervisory functions, which in Mr. Root's original conception, were intended to be reserved to the Chief of Staff alone. Here we differ from the Great German General Staff, which did not concern itself with routine business and therefore, did not, as it were, tread on the toes of the several branches and services of the army. It planned campaigns, determined the correct tactical organization and indoctrinated the army—the last probably being the most important.

The weakness in our new system, if any, lies in the possibility of the personnel of the first four sections becoming engrossed in their coordinating and supervisory functions, at the expense of war plans and tactical doctrines. The Fifth Section, or War Plans Division,[2] has not the possibility of this weakness, and the calls it must make on the other divisions should constitute a powerful urge towards the maintenance by them of effective war plans.

It is but an example of one of the most common reactions of human nature that the personnel of the permanent services, long established in the War Department, should consciously or unconsciously appear resentful of the powerful coordinating control vested in the comparatively new General Staff, whose officers arrive in Washington without intimate knowledge of the traditions of the War Department, so recently the epitome of bureaucratic administration.

The success of the War Department General Staff, however, is believed to depend primarily on the diligent efforts of its membership to promote a spirit of cooperation and, most important of all, to develop and maintain a sympathetic attitude of understanding with the services and line of the Army.

The General Staff officer of a division is judged, and judges himself, by what the division accomplishes. Daily he is impressed by the necessity of complete cooperation within the division and a sympathetic understanding between the staff and the troops. He knows that whatever his powers may be, they are not sufficient to overcome the evil effects of a critical and resentful attitude on the part of the staff and troops. He is aware of the vital importance of maintaining a spirit of good will and generous understanding among the officers of the command. He realizes the battle cannot be won without an harmonious, united effort.

Unfortunately, when the same officer takes a desk in the War Department, he is removed from this intimate relation with the organization he serves, that is, the Army as a whole. Burdened with the daily routine, he may easily lose sight of the ultimate mission. Soon out of close personal touch with the services and troops, and without the immediate tests of campaign to measure the quality of the machine, he is apt to give too little consideration to the personal factor. In a position where, indirectly, he can wield great power without the possibility of having the results of his decisions weighed tomorrow, he at times, and unconsciously, proceeds in an impersonal, arbitrary manner.

There can be no question but that if the staff of a division is out of harmony with the services and troops, it is a failure—and the same should hold true for the War Department General Staff. The conditions in the latter are such that it is dangerously easy for the officer personnel to lose touch with the services and troops, and to misunderstand the latter's point of view. Therefore, it would appear that the most important function of the General Staff is to promote a spirit of harmony, cooperation and understanding throughout the Army. If it does not accomplish this, nine-tenths of its value is lost.

GCMRL/G. C. Marshall Papers (Pentagon Office, Speeches)

1. Marshall had delivered a version of this lecture at the War College on September 3, 1921. In that earlier presentation he said: "In this discussion, little has been presented which has not been drawn from well-known sources. Numerous details regarding the German war staff were secured by Major Harry L. Hodges. Much has been a direct quotation from Von Schellendorff, and, in particular, from a memorandum prepared in the War College Division prior to the World War, which was largely the creation of Colonel John McA. Palmer."

The portion of the lecture printed here represents the one-quarter Marshall contributed from his own experiences. For his 1922 lecture, he cut several paragraphs of historical and detailed explanatory material from the 1921 version and added the section entitled "War Department General Staff."

2. Marshall had previously noted that the War Department General Staff was subdivided into five sections: Personnel (G-1), Intelligence (G-2), Operations (G-3), Supply (G-4), and War Plans Division.

MEMORANDUM FOR GENERAL PERSHING   January 15, 1923
Washington, D.C.

With regard to the proposal for reviewing military textbooks in the Historical Section, I fear that some of the public education officials who are pacifistic in their feelings, would seize upon a letter of the character suggested, as a basis for accusing the Army, and more particularly, the General Staff, of endeavoring to mold public opinion along militaristic lines. Once a book has been printed, its author and the publisher would undoubtedly actively resent unfavorable reviews by the War Department. Being a Governmental agency, political pressure and attack could easily be incited. The same result cannot follow in the case of unfavorable reviews by individuals.[1]

I am not now able to suggest a method of handling this matter. If the writers of textbooks could be induced to take advantage of the facilities of the Historical Section, improvement in the treatment of our war incidents might be made.

G. C. M.

GCMRL/G. C. Marshall Papers (Pentagon Office, Selected)

1. In the late autumn of 1922, General Pershing became concerned by the criticisms being voiced by various individuals and patriotic organizations regarding the treatment of military matters in various American history textbooks. He ordered the Historical Section of the War College to study and to submit a recommendation on the matter. Colonel Oliver L. Spaulding, Jr., chief of the Historical Section, responded in December by recommending that the adjutant general of the army send a letter to the superintendent of public instruction in each state, territory, the Philippine Islands, and the District of Columbia, offering to provide "upon request from proper authority, reviews of books, analyzing them from a military point of view and furnishing simple statements as to the accuracy of their presentation of facts." (Spaulding [s. Major General E. F. McGlachlin] to Pershing, December 22, 1922, GCMRL/G. C. Marshall Papers [Pentagon Office, Selected].)

TO MAJOR GENERAL EDWARD W. NICHOLS   January 31, 1923
Washington, D.C.

My dear General Nichols: I have delayed in answering your note until General Pershing's plans for February had somewhat cleared up. I am assuming that the talk you desire would have to be made on Friday evening. Saturday night, of course, would be more convenient for me, but Lily tells me these affairs are scheduled for Friday.

If agreeable to you, I could leave here Friday morning so as to arrive in Lexington at 6:30 Friday evening, February 23rd. In confirming this proposal or suggesting some other date, will you please give me some details of the general character of these talks, —usual length, are lantern slides ever used, your idea of what I should talk about.

Lily appreciates very much the invitation from Mrs. Nichols and yourself, but she will not be able to accompany me as her mother is now with us.   Faithfully yours,

G. C. Marshall, Jr.

VMI/Alumni File

To Major General Edward W. Nichols   February 5, 1923
                                                      Washington, D.C.

My dear General: Thank you for your prompt reply to my letter of January 31st. Now that I understand how these talks are arranged, I will follow your suggestion by having no topic and simply speaking informally to the Corps. Twelve o'clock Noon of Saturday the 24th will be satisfactory to me and I will arrive at 6:30 the previous evening. While I have not looked up the trains yet, I think there is one out of Lexington about four o'clock for Staunton, and if so I will take that and then come up to Washington on the C. & O.,[1] as I must be back as soon as possible.

I leave Friday for New England to talk before the National Association of Headmasters of Boys' Preparatory Schools, at a dinner in Boston on the 10th. Also to make two other talks, not so important. As I have no idea what I am going to say at any of them, my state of mind this week is not very pleasant.   Faithfully yours,

G. C. Marshall, Jr.

VMI/Alumni File
   1. Chesapeake and Ohio Railroad.

Speech[1]   [February 10, 1923]
                                                      Boston [Massachusetts]

When Doctor Perry graciously honored me with an invitation to address the members of the Headmasters Association I was much complimented but very loathe to accept the undertaking. You know, Army officers below the grade of Brigadier General seldom have experience in making after-dinner speeches, and I might add, that our Generals frequently offer proof of this assertion. But the opportunity to talk to you gentlemen who are in such close touch with the young men of the country and who exert such a profound influence on their minds during the formative period, made it seem highly desirable that I should accept Doctor Perry's invitation and do my best to tell you something of the War Department's plans and hopes, and particularly of its interest in developing good citizenship. . . .[2]

Immediately following the termination of war, the public mind centers on the tragedies involved. All are thinking of the recent sacrifices of life, which always have been due in a serious measure to a lack of methodical preparation. Therefore, the legislators are in a frame of mind to recognize our military necessities and they draft their laws accordingly. Then comes a new thought dominating all minds, the war debt, high taxes and their reduction. Economy is demanded by public opinion; everyone loathes war; and a reduction of the military establishment is the easiest political makeshift for immediate retrenchment. So the cycle is completed and we are moving today into the same predicament in which war has always found us.

You gentlemen I believe, are intimately concerned with these passing and contradictory phases of public opinion and you can undoubtedly render a very great service in this matter. To explain—I doubt if as many as 5% of our men study history after they leave school. Therefore, the textbook they use and the manner in which they are taught finally determines their knowledge of American and world history. From their number a few are chosen to represent them in Congress. If it is agreed that the average politician is seldom a student, then one can understand the inconsistencies of legislation regarding national policies concerned with our international relations. It is hard to believe that a man familiar with the history of the centuries could fail to guide his course somewhat by the lessons of the past. As a matter of fact, many of our legislators have premised their decisions on impressions retained from schooling in biased histories, poorly taught and devoid of reference to the conclusions to be drawn from the recorded events.

In this connection the prediction is ventured, that more of our future school boys will know the date of the declaration of war against Germany than will learn that a year elapsed before an American soldier could attack the enemy. Almost none of them will be given any idea of the deplorable situation in which we found ourselves and the reasons for it existing. They will leave school knowing how long the war lasted, how many men were engaged, who were the principal figures, how gallantly our men fought at Cantigny, Chateau Thierry, St. Mihiel and in the Meuse-Argonne; the billions expended and the thousands who died will probably figure in many examination papers; but do you think that much will be known of the real plight in which General Pershing found himself landing on foreign soil, three thousand miles from home without an organization, even on paper, without a plan and without a gun? How many will cogitate on the national dilemma in which we would have found ourselves had our enemy been free to attack us in the first month and not been held at arm's length by our Allies?

Let us analyze this a little further. You gentlemen are representative of the most highly educated and cultured class in America. Are you familiar with

Washington's difficulties with the Continental Congress over the maintenance of his army of the Revolution? Do you remember any of the cautions that he pointed out to the coming American? Are the many humiliating incidents of the land fighting in 1812–13 clear in your mind and more particularly the reasons for them? Do you know why the Union armies were so unfortunate during the early days of the Civil War and the Confederate armies so frequently successful? Have you ever read how most of the State Volunteer troops had to be returned from the Philippine Islands, leaving a small contingent of the Regular Army actually besieged in Manila?

History is filled—in fact, it almost consists, of remarkable repetitions. General Pershing the other day called attention to the fact that during the long period of the Roman Peace protective garrisons were maintained by Roman Legions stationed at Cologne, Coblenz and Mayence, with a reserve of ten thousand at Treves. Eighteen hundred years later, during the recent Peace Conference in Paris, British soldiers were stationed at Cologne, Americans at Coblenz, and French at Mayence, with a general reserve at Treves, which incidentally was his, General Pershing's, Advance Headquarters. Certainly here is a remarkable repetition. If there are any lessons to be drawn from it, would not that be more important knowledge to be implanted in the minds of our future citizens than an extensive collection of dates, names and places?

About a year ago I had occasion to re-read the Life of General Philip Sheridan. He was one of the five men to hold the highest rank in our Army—Washington being the first and General Pershing the last. After the Civil War Sheridan was sent to Europe to observe the operations of the German Army then invading France. He joined the Emperor William on the eve of Gravelotte. In Bismarck's carriage he rode into Pont-a-Mousson—now that was the right flank of General Pershing's army at St. Mihiel. From there he followed the Prussians through Commercy to Bar-le-Duc—that was the principal route in the movement of the American troops from the St. Mihiel salient to the Meuse-Argonne. In Bar-le-Duc he watched the Bavarians turn northward and he followed them to Clermont—that was the exact axis of the advance of the American troops deploying against the Germans in the Argonne Forest. He slept in each of these towns I have mentioned and continued on to his next billet in Grand Pre, still on the axis of the advance of our victorious troops who had cleared the Argonne of the enemy.

And now comes what is to me the most remarkable coincidence. From Grand Pre he followed the victorious Germans through the Foret de Dieulet into Beaumont, where they surprised a French division in its billets and captured practically the entire force. Our Second Division advanced at night through that same forest and captured Germans—not Frenchmen—at breakfast in Beaumont. Sheridan pushed on with the entourage of the Emperor William and from the crest of a hill just south of Wadelincourt looked down into Sedan where the French Army had been cornered, but not yet captured. He stood on the same hill from which the troops of the Sixteenth Regular Infantry of the First Division looked at the retreating German forces in Sedan on the morning of November 7, 1918, four days before the Armistice. Possibly there is a lesson in this. In any event it goes to prove that the friend of today may be the enemy of tomorrow, and that the road over which one advances to victory might be the identical route of withdrawal in defeat.

GCMRL/G. C. Marshall Papers (Pentagon Office, Speeches)

1. Marshall extensively edited the original typewritten document. The edited version is printed here.

2. Omitted here are 275 words tracing the history of the policy of rapidly expanding the United States Army during each war and severely reducing it afterwards.

MEMORANDUM FOR COLONEL   March 5, 1923
OLIVER L. SPAULDING, JR.   [Washington, D.C.]

The reviews that have recently been made of school textbooks on history have aroused General Pershing's interest,[1] and he is searching for some politic method of securing more accurate accounts and instructive lessons regarding the military episodes.

Will you be good enough to give me a little informal statement regarding the Army's connection with the American (?) Historical Association. As I recall, you and Colonel Conger and General McAndrew were connected with this Association; Dr. Johnson of Harvard, being one of the leading members.[2] Just what is the purpose of the Association and does it furnish a medium for reaching the writers and publishers of historical textbooks.

GCMRL/G. C. Marshall Papers (Pentagon Office, Selected)

1. One of the textbooks reviewed was David Saville Muzzey's *An American History* (revised edition, 1920). The reviewer commented that on military history, Muzzey's interest, knowledge, and judgment were "slight," and the "instances of erroneous statement or false emphasis are numerous." The reviewer's chief objection was that the book tended to give the Americans greater credit for military organization, efficiency, and success than was deserved. (Inclosure in McGlachlin to Marshall, January 30, 1923, GCMRL/G. C. Marshall Papers [Pentagon Office, Selected].)

2. Colonel Arthur L. Conger, who had graduated from Harvard University with a liberal arts degree in 1894, had been a year ahead of Marshall as a student at Fort Leavenworth. Major General James W. McAndrew, former commandant of the General Staff College, had died April 30, 1922. R. M. Johnson was a Harvard professor of history who sometimes lectured at the Army War College.

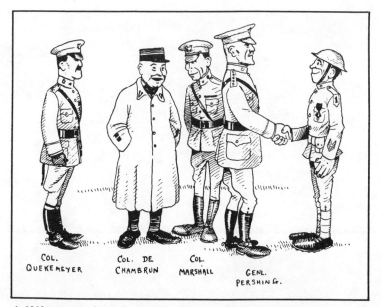

COL.
QUEKEMEYER

COL. DE
CHAMBRUN

COL.
MARSHALL

GENL.
PERSHING.

A 1919 cartoon shows General Pershing awarding the Distinguished Service Cross to a First Division private.

Marshall (left) watches General Pershing award Private Edward Adams the Distinguished Service Cross, at Chaumont, France, May 31, 1919.

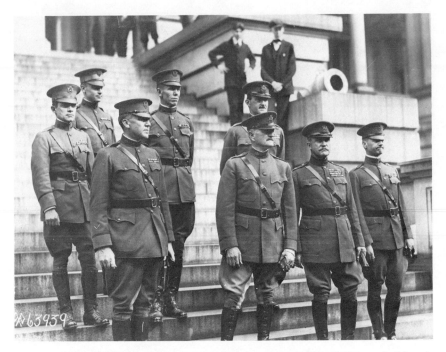

General Pershing and his staff pose on the steps of the State-War-Navy Building in Washington, D.C., September 23, 1919. Left to right are: Colonel Aristides Moreno, Lieutenant Colonel Albert S. Kuegle, Major General Fox Conner, Colonel George C. Marshall, Jr., General John J. Pershing, Colonel John G. Quekemeyer, Major General Andre Brewster, Brigadier General Robert C. Davis.

Pershing and Marshall during their tour of French battlefields, August, 1919.

Colonel George C. Marshall, 1919.

Lily Marshall, about 1919.

On inspection tours, General Pershing and his staff traveled in private cars attached to passenger trains. He is shown here with Marshall in Texas, May, 1922.

225

General Pershing and Colonel Marshall stand beside the grave of Major General Thomas J. ("Stonewall") Jackson in Lexington, Virginia, June 18, 1920.

FROM GENERAL JOHN J. PERSHING   March 7, 1923
                                                        Washington, D.C.

Dear Colonel Marshall: I wish you would make a brief study of the various difficulties that were met in the Draft Law from the time we entered the war up until the Armistice. I recall very distinctly that when Mr. Baker was in France in the spring of 1918 I insisted that the number of troops we were likely to need be called out immediately, when he rather contended that we should not take men away from work on the farms until it was absolutely necessary. Of course, at that time we did not know how much sea transportation would be available and no doubt this influenced the War Department, under his direction, to delay making these calls. The result, of course, might have been very disastrous, and I think he made an error in this respect.

                                                              J. J. P.

NA/RG 200 (J. J. Pershing Papers, Miscellaneous)

MEMORANDUM FOR GENERAL PERSHING   April 9, 1923
                                                        Washington, D.C.

Preliminary study concerning rate of drafting men
during first six months of 1918.

An endeavor to justify any conclusion regarding the maximum rate at which men might properly have been drafted in the first half of 1918, involves a variety of considerations, the principal of which are:

Quartermaster Supplies obtainable, principally clothing and shoes.

Available shelter in the United States.

Rate of shipment of troops to Europe, which involved:

Troop and cargo tonnage.

Tonnage for nitrates from Chile.

Allies' obligations to supply A.E.F.

Vacating of cantonments.

Excessive drafts of colored troops.

Removal of young men from farms and essential industries.

The available records of the War Department are inadequate at the present time to an exact understanding of the conditions in 1918. It has not yet been possible to find the War Program approved April 29th, and promulgated April 30th. Many other important papers cannot be located in the files.

In general, it is apparent that at the end of January, General Goethals was strongly of the view that the then program of drafting men was too large; that the supply situation from a procurement standpoint, was most serious; that sufficient tonnage could not be obtained for shipment of troops abroad; that if the tonnage was available, the port and railroad situation in France would prevent sufficiently rapid unloading and evacuation of supplies.[1] His views were shared by Mr. Charles Day and Mr. P.A.S. Franklin, of the Emergency Fleet Corporation, both members of the War Council.[2] General Goethals opposed any further drafts until supplies could be assembled and Mr. Thorne, his Assistant, definitely recommended no further draft calls until June, 1918. . . . General Goethals made a point of the excessive requirements of General Pershing's "upkeep" tables for supplies and cites the example of overcoats. (See Memorandum of General Goethals, February 7th.)

General Jervey in a memorandum of February 18th, Page 3, to the Chief of Staff,[3] stated the reasons against *calling a new draft in April,* to be:

Shortage of wool uniforms and other winter equipment.

Further congestion of inland transportation and freight.

Further dispersion of equipment already short.

Further congestion of camps where tentage is short and supply of cotton duck needed for other purposes.

Disturbance in industrial and agricultural activities during the spring and summer without just cause.

Unwise expansion of a program whose full accomplishment is probably doomed or much delayed by the limitations of overseas transportation.

He then definitely recommended a reduction in the draft program approved of February 7th, to the figures given for February 25th.

The Chief of Staff in approving General Jervey's memorandum of February 18th, stated the following general principles to be observed:

"1. That when practicable it is desired to give men about six months training before being sent abroad.

2. That it is not desired to draft men until they can be clothed and equipped.

3. That it is not desired to draft men until they are necessary, in order to interfere as little as possible with the carrying on of civil pursuits."

Month[4]	January 21st Draft Program*	February 25th Draft Program**	Program Actually Carried Out***
February	185,000	85,000	90,000
March	100,000	85,000	135,000
April	110,000	50,000	180,000
May	100,000	60,000	375,000
June	100,000	90,000	300,000
July	100,000	250,000	400,000
August	110,000	150,000	280,000
September	140,000	50,000	260,000
October	140,000	50,000	None
November	130,000	50,000	None
December	130,000	50,000	None

*Refer to Memorandum of General Goethals, dated February 7th.
**Refer to Memorandum of Chief of Staff, dated February 25th.
***Approximate.

With the arrival of General March came a vigorous impulse and a dominant optimism,[5] which resulted after the arrival of General Pershing's Cablegram of April 24th (No. 990–S, copy hereto attached),[6] in a complete revision of the war program, bringing about the great troop shipments to Europe in May, June, July and August. Unfortunately, this program cannot be located, and Major Phoenix, now in the State Department, who was Recorder of the War Council at this time, believes that there was no formal program other than General Pershing's cablegram.[7] This is not probable, as a more detailed and inclusive statement to the various services of the War Department would have been necessary than was contained in this cable.

Throughout the heavy shipments abroad, it is apparent that the civilian members of the War Council, the Director of Purchase, Storage and Traffic, and the Chief of Ordnance (General Crozier),[8] were fearful of the consequences, and that the Secretary of War and General March were optimistic and determined, Mr. Baker openly accepting the risks involved.

Nothing has been found specifically indicating why more men were not drafted in the *late* spring, unless it was the difficulty of securing sufficient woolen clothing. Major Phoenix, above referred to, stated that the Secretary himself, consistently opposed further increases in the draft, and without giving his reasons. Apropos of this, Major Phoenix furnished me a copy of a secret memorandum for the War Council, (hereto attached), prepared by him on May 9th, for the purpose of showing that unless more men were drafted there would be a serious shortage of infantry and machine gun units in the United States.

Members of the War Council continually expressed concern over the port and railroad situation in France. On one occasion General March reminded them that General Pershing was undoubtedly as alert to this situation as they were and would solve it. The members of the Council were also concerned with the nitrate situation, which was being pressed by Mr. Baruch.[9] The amount of tonnage required for nitrate shipments was exceedingly large and more was constantly being demanded.

General Wood, Acting Quartermaster General,[10] in a memorandum of June 17th (attached), to the Chief of Staff, gives an interesting outline of the supply situation in view of the tremendous increase in drafts.

I am unable to form an opinion from consideration of the available records, as to whether or not the War Department would have been justified in drafting men more rapidly in April, May and June, but I am of the opinion that the Secretary's advisors were unduly pessimistic in February and March, and prevailed upon him to adopt too conservative a course. However, this latter view probably does not sufficiently take into account the tremendous change in the shipping outlook and Allied supply prospects, created by the crisis of March 21st–April 3rd, (first German offensive).

When one considers the inevitable confusion incident to coordinating industries in the United States, training, shelter, and shipping, it is surprising that the demands from the A.E.F. were met to the extent they were, and any qualms the Secretary of War may have entertained over further increasing the draft, are not surprising, particularly since he and his Chief of Staff, apparently, were the only optimistic members of the War Council.

G. C. M.

NA/RG 200 (J. J. Pershing Papers, Miscellaneous)

1. Major General George W. Goethals (U.S.M.A., 1880), the man in charge of the construction of the Panama Canal, commanded the War Department's Storage and Traffic (later Purchase, Storage and Traffic) Division between December 28, 1917, and March 1, 1919.

2. The War Council was created on December 20, 1917, as an instrument for improving coordination of the work of the various War Department supply bureaus. Theoretically only an advisory committee, the presence of the secretary of war, the assistant secretary, the army chief of staff, and the heads of the major War Department bureaus, gave the council great power to act. The council met nearly every day during the first half of 1918. On Wednesdays shipping matters were discussed, and the secretary of the navy, chairman of the War Industries Board, chairman of the Shipping Board, director-general of the Emergency Fleet Corporation, and the chairman of the War Trade Board attended or sent representatives. The council was dissolved July 8, 1918.

3. Major General Henry Jervey (U.S.M.A., 1888) was director of the War Department's Operations Division between December 12, 1917, and August 31, 1921. Tasker H. Bliss was army chief of staff until May 20, 1918.

4. This table was in somewhat different form on the typed original.

5. Peyton C. March became army chief of staff on May 20, 1918.

6. None of the attachments were with the original in the file.

7. Spencer Phoenix was a drafting officer in the State Department's Office of the Economic Advisor.

8. Major General William Crozier was chief of Ordnance, November 22, 1901, to July 15, 1918.

9. Bernard M. Baruch, a wealthy stockbroker, had been chairman of the War Industries Board.

10. Brigadier General Robert E. Wood (U.S.M.A., 1900) was acting quartermaster general from December 20, 1917, to February 12, 1919.

To GENERAL JOHN J. PERSHING   June 22, 1923
                                              Washington, D.C.

My dear General: Captain Adamson, after his talk with you on the 'phone Wednesday, gave me your message regarding preparation of draft for your remarks at the Army War College. It is rather a coincidence that he should have told me this just as I was completing the correction of the last paragraph to the first draft of this proposed speech. There is attached my best effort, which I hope will serve as a base of departure for you. I could not make it run smoothly to my satisfaction, nor could I find apt expressions for the ideas I wished to convey. But I do think that this will be an important opportunity to dwell on the points I have endeavored to make in my draft.

Every day I am surprised to learn how little many of the officers realize what our principal mission is in the new scheme of things. I think you would find this the case among the members of the present class of the Army War College, even though they have had an opportunity to come in contact with the plans of the War Department during the past year. I find officials of the Reserve Officers' organization quite ignorant of the goal toward which we are driving. They only see the problems and petty ambitions of the officers now in the Reserve Corps who served in the World War and do not visualize a Reserve Corps made up of well instructed graduates from the R.O.T.C. units, and to a certain extent, from C.M.T.C. graduates. They want the regulations to fit the present abnormal make-up of the Reserve Corps rather than the organization made up from those who entered in the normal manner from the bottom. The same misunderstandings and complete failure to look ahead affect the views of the officers in the National Guard. Therefore, I think it quite important for you personally to impress the graduates of this year's class of the War College with your views on this subject, which will be quoted in all the service papers for the benefit of other officers of the Army.

I know you must be having a fine time at Naushon, and I can picture the delightful rides, picnics, swims and evening parties. Please remember me to my friends there of other summers.   Faithfully yours,

LC/J. J. Pershing Papers (Speeches)

MEMORANDUM FOR GENERAL PERSHING   [June 22, 1923]
                                                   [Washington, D.C.]

Address at Army War College Graduation Exercises.[1]

General McGlachlin, Members of the Faculty and Graduating Class:
It is a distinct personal pleasure for me to participate in the closing exercises of this year's course at the Army War College. Furthermore, I regard this as an important official duty. It marks the culmination of our military educational system, which for the first time is a coordinated whole, and probably the most effective in the world, as it should be. For in no other army is it so imperative that the officers of the permanent establishment be highly perfected specialists, prepared to serve as instructors and leaders for the citizen forces which are to fight our wars. The one time role of a Regular Army officer has passed with the Indian Campaigns and the acquirement of colonial possessions. Our mission today is definite, yet so broad that few, if any, have been able to visualize the possibilities of the new fields opened up by the military policy now on the statute books.

I wish especially to emphasize the necessity for broad vision in study or work concerned with the development of our military policy. The economic, political and purely defensive factors are as yet but dimly realized. I often find myself wondering today why we thought as we did yesterday, only to be similarly amazed tomorrow that we saw so few of the possibilities today. There are officers, fortunately in constantly diminishing number, who cannot turn their minds from concentration on a diminutive Regular Army, successfully and gallantly fighting the country's battles, as in Cuba and the Philippines, or serving at isolated stations along the Mexican border. Those days have not entirely passed and probably never will, but they are now of secondary importance in the general scheme of National Defense.

This month the first basic and practical plan for the mobilization of our war forces for a maximum effort was completed. Before Congress laid a definite foundation by specifying the character and composition of our war army, the development of a workable scheme was impossible. The plan of mobilization is in its infancy, but a few days old. Many of you will be personally involved in the improvement of this keystone to our arrangements for the National Defense. The mere plan, however, is valueless without a corresponding development of the instruments upon which it is founded,—the leadership of the Regular Army, the expansion and improvement of the National Guard, and the rapid development of the Organized Reserves. The admirable educational system of the army provides training for our role of leadership; but the loyal and enthusiastic efforts of the Regular Army officer are a prerequisite to success.

You have had a great opportunity these past ten months and I am delighted to learn from General McGlachlin how well you have availed yourselves of it. A new standard has been set this year, which is most gratifying, but it must be surpassed in each succeeding year. The other day the War College was referred to as one of the greatest centers of culture in the United States. To the uninformed, which includes practically everyone except those immediately connected with the institution, this would seem an absurd claim. Yet I believe there is foundation for such a statement, and it is but evidence of the breadth of vision essential to the efficient Army officer of today.

You gentlemen are leaving the War College at a most auspicious moment. The General Staff has now digested the lessons of the World War and the earlier years of its development. Today it is a wonderfully effective machine, admirably arranged to carry out its mission. The Citizen Army has made a beginning, a period of troubled misunderstandings and narrow vision. It is now a lusty infant but facing the usual vicissitudes of that period. The task awaiting in your new assignments is to carry forward this work, to inspire yourselves, your associates and every part of this huge machine for the National Defense, with a democratic spirit of cooperation and common understanding.

In serving on the War Department General Staff or at Corps Area Headquarters, it is difficult to avoid a detached and impersonal attitude which soon carries one out of sympathy with the subordinate organizations and especially with the humble individual worker in the ranks. It is hard for the man at a desk to see with the eye of a troop commander or of a business man struggling with self-imposed duties as an officer of the National Guard or Reserve Corps.

Unintentionally a breach is created, which rapidly widens. It is the special duty of the Regular Army officer to close this breach. As a matter of truth, the establishment of a sympathetic understanding is more important than the performance of any routine duties.

I congratulate the members of the class on the splendid work just completed, and the faculty on the excellence of its contribution to the success of this institution. Finally, I wish to express to General McGlachlin, both officially and personally, my deep appreciation of his leadership of the Army War College during the past two years. It is a matter of profound regret to all of us that he has chosen a new field. It is a serious loss to the Army that an officer of such high rank and brilliant attainments should withdraw from active participation in military affairs. He will carry with him our affectionate good wishes and high esteem.[2]

LC/J. J. Pershing Papers (Speeches)

1. General Pershing's address was delivered on June 28. To Marshall's draft he added four paragraphs of introduction concerning the recent reorganization of the army's educational system and two paragaraphs on the role of the citizen-soldier.

2. Major General Edward F. McGlachlin (U.S.M.A., 1889) retired effective November 2, 1923.

TO ROSE PAGE   August 4, 1923
                              President Harding's Funeral Train

My dear Rose   This will be a hard letter to read, for it is a very hard letter to write, because the train shakes a good bit. I left San Francisco yesterday, very suddenly, to accompany General Pershing on the President's special train taking Mr. Harding's body back to Washington. So this is a very sad journey, though a very impressive one. At all the stations day or night the people, the very kind hearted and sympathetic people of America, stand in long silent lines, bareheaded. The boy and girl scouts, the veterans of our wars and the local military organizations, with their flags hung with mourning streamers, salute as the train rolls by without pause. In the observation vestibule at the rear, a guard of four soldiers, sailors and marines stand motionless on guard around the casket. It is all very solemn and impressive and will grow more so as we reach the more thickly populated country east of Kansas. The silence of the motionless throngs, the steady and uninterrupted progress of the train and the bared heads of the humblest workers along the railroad, marks this journey apart from all others I have taken.

Wednesday afternoon [August 1] General Pershing and I motored 150 miles from Monterey to San Francisco, arriving about eight o clock. We called immediately on Mrs. Harding to inquire about the President. She was very cheerful and optimistic. The following evening, a short period after his sudden death, I sat in the same room listening to a meeting of four members of the President's cabinet to determine what should be done.

This is not a very cheerful letter, Rosey, but I think you will be interested in what I have written.   With much love,

G. C. M.

GCMRL/R. P. Wilson Papers; H

To Mrs. Thomas B. Coles[1]   [September 2, 1923]
From Elizabeth Coles Marshall   Fort Myer, Virginia

Dearest Aunt Lot-   . . . Mud [Mother] & I have been having a very quiet, happy summer together— You know George had started for a 5 weeks Inspection trip & when they had gotten around the loop as far as San Francisco (they had only been gone two weeks) the President died- & Genl. Pershing & George came back on the "funeral train"- George has been on a short trip or two since then- & goes away next week on a motor trip with the General to Greensburg Penn (where G's sister, Marie, lives.)

Miss Pershing[2] is now visiting the General & they both want me to go on the trip too- but I believe it will be a very trying & tiring one from the hectic programme mapped out (all sorts of hot old receptions etc.) & frankly, I can't see much fun in it so I've declined- It's not my idea of a good time- I have enough of that sort of thing in winter—

I'm going to make Mud stay with me until George comes back from Greensburg— Then she says she must go back to Lex[ington] & get things straightened up there before she returns to me here for the winter.—

I will run down there for a week or so & pay a little visit & bring her back with me, before Xmas—

I have a grand cellar packed *full* of furnace coal, enough to last all winter- & poor little Mud hasn't a *lump* in Lex- So I want her here with me safe & warm- before real winter sets in—

I do wish this little house of mine was larger! Of course I *adore* having Mud with me- but I just have the *one* guestroom- & so I'm terribly handicapped- Before Mud comes back- though- Aunt Lot- I do want you & Sharley to pay me a little visit— I've wanted you ever since we have been at Myer, but there seemed to be a perpetual guest in my one little guest chamber! . . .

This is our last winter here, you know- as, a year from now, we expect to go to *China!* (for 3 years.)

George feels he has to go back to troops, for the good of his career- & he has picked China as the place of all others he prefers to go—

I want to take Mud with me, for I'd be wretched if I left her behind—

A lot of our friends are over there– & *all* are wild about it– One of my friends now in Tien Sien (they call it *Tin Sin*) says she has *nine* servants, for the price of *one*, in the States—

Everyone over there lives in the most unbelievable luxury. Beautiful houses— wonderful food—& tremendously gay & interesting. Mud feels a little sceptical but I tell her she has got to be a sport & come along!

It's so nice that George is once more called "Colonel" & this time, not through courtesy but because his promotion has really come—[3] The slump, after the war, was a bit trying.

George is looking perfectly *fine*— He is exercising a lot- He is in the saddle every morning at seven o'clock & rides til 8[30]— Then every day he has a swim in the "Tidal Basin"- & tennis before dinner each evening— He's hard as nails & black as an Indian. I've never seen him looking better— . . .

I hope "Timmie" is feeling all rested & set up by the country— There's nothing like it- & it's the dream of my life- & Geo's- to own a country place- We hope to do it one of these days— He wants to go to California for his- but I think I prefer the East—

Mud sends you lots of love- She looks well- & seems perfectly happy here with me—

We have our three meals a day out on the porch— It is all awninged & I have it furnished in wicker & chintz, with oval matting rugs etc- & its just like a room— We have not eaten our meals indoors for nearly *4* months!

. . . As ever Devotedly

Lily

GCMRL/Research File (Family); H

1. Mrs. Coles, "Aunt Lot," was Charlotte Berkeley Coles, wife of U.S. Steel Corporation Vice-President Thomas B. Coles. Mrs. Marshall's mother (born Elizabeth Chiles Pendleton) had married Walter Coles III, Thomas's brother. The Thomas Coles family lived in New York City, but frequently visited the family home of "Woodville" in Albemarle County, Virginia.

2. General Pershing's sister May.

3. Marshall was promoted to lieutenant colonel effective August 21.

LECTURE, ARMY WAR COLLEGE[1]   September 10, 1923
Washington, D.C.

The Development of the National Army.

General Ely has asked me to talk informally on the development of the National Army.[2] He wished me to give you the result of my own observations while on duty in the War Department and on inspection trips with General Pershing during the past three years.

It has seemed to me that the preliminary development of our military policy, or the National Army, has had three phases. In the beginning General Pershing

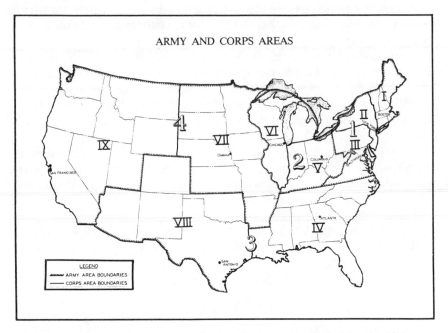

ARMY AND CORPS AREAS

Nine corps areas of substantially equal populations were established by the 1920 army reorganization act. These headquarters were charged with army administration, training, and National Guard and Reserve activities. The Field Army designations shown above were created in 1932.

was concerned with the reorganization of the General Staff on what he felt would be an enduring basis, not liable to disruption on the declaration of war. Immediately following this, his attention appeared to be directed towards the indoctrination of the General Staff and the War Department with a clear conception of the new order of things; then the Corps Area Commanders and their staffs; and finally, the Regular Army as a whole. The second phase involved the education of the National Guard and Reserve Officers in their positions and duties in this new scheme of things, and the development of the R.O.T.C. and C.M.T.C. The final phase came this summer, when he endeavored to draw to an intelligent support of the military establishment, the Members of Congress, the Chief Executives of States, the businessmen of the communities and the public generally.

It may not seem to you that the education of the Regular Army in its new duties and responsibilities presented a serious problem. As a matter of fact, I believe this has been the most difficult task of all. And it is natural that it should have been, because the present mission of the Regular Establishment is so utterly different from what it has ever been in the past, that a comparatively long time would necessarily be required to change the viewpoint of the personnel, particularly, those long in the service and accustomed to a radically different conception of our mission. . . .

In anticipation of some of the matters to be discussed later, I might say now that the greatest change observed last summer was in the viewpoint of the Regular officers, which seemed in a large measure responsible for the unusual excellence of the results obtained, as compared with those of the two previous years.

As a background for a discussion regarding the future possibilities in the development of the National Army, I will briefly outline the present status of the three components:

REGULAR ARMY:

. . . As the principal mission of the Regular Army in the United States is the training of the citizen forces, it is unfortunate that the largest concentration of Regular troops should have to be in the Area of least density of population, which is along the Mexican border. With the recognition of Mexico and the stabilization of that country, it might be possible gradually to reduce the garrison in the Eighth Corps Area if shelter for the troops could be obtained elsewhere. Such a re-arrangement will, of course, be determined primarily by political considerations, and undoubtedly would be vigorously opposed by the citizens along the southern frontier for reasons which need not be commented on here.

Vexing problems of the Regular Army within the United States at the present time are recruiting, due largely to the enforced abolishment of a well established Recruiting Service, and the proper training each summer of large numbers of young men with a minimum number of Regular troops. This last makes it exceedingly difficult to give the Regular organizations that training which is essential if they are to be the models for the citizen components.

NATIONAL GUARD:

The development of the National Guard has been most encouraging, tho' there has been practically no change in its strength in the past year, of approximately 160,000. This failure in growth is largely due to the expiration of three-year enlistments. Six Infantry divisions are complete, except as to Air Service, and eight more will probably be recognized within twelve months. There are to be eighteen in all, and four cavalry divisions. All but one are more than 50% complete. It is expected that before the end of the present fiscal year all organizations required to bring the National Guard to the agreed upon strength of 250,000 will be in process of organization. The present appropriation for this force is thirty million dollars ($30,000,000.)

The great change in the National Guard from the pre-war organization is in equipment and the quality of the officer personnel. The present Guard is thoroughly equipped for its preliminary war mission, except in those essentials not absolutely necessary for peace training, and which would be readily obtainable on the outbreak of war. Horses are the most important item of this nature. The great improvement in the quality of the officers was very noticeable this summer and was frequently commented upon by Governors and their Adjutant Generals. In certain sections of the country which heretofore have had a very weak organization, we found not a marked, but a remarkable improvement, the troops comparing favorably with the best of State troops prior to 1917. The recruitment of the National Guard near large cities has been more difficult than elsewhere, due to strong feelings regarding labor questions and similar matters. There it has been found advisable to confine enlistments to very young men. It appears that in those sections of the country where the bulk of the population is of pure American stock, the development of the National Guard is proceeding most rapidly. An exception to this, of course, is the 27th Division in New York State, though many of its units are drawn from the rural districts. . . .

ORGANIZED RESERVES:

It is in the domain of the Organized Reserves that we reach a new field, without established precedents to guide us. There are now 77,000 officers in the Reserve Corps, the majority of whom are assigned to organizations in 27 infantry and 6 cavalry divisions. Twenty-six of these divisions are more than 60% completed as to officer assignments. One division has only 32% of its officer personnel, due to recent re-allocation of unit areas. In addition, there are 439 separate regiments, largely corps and army troops. It is unfortunate that paucity of funds only permitted 6,000 Reserve Officers to be called out for training this year.

The potential strength of this force is probably not appreciated except by those officers now on duty with it who are also familiar with the struggles of the War Department in 1917. When one pauses to recall that our first war measure was the opening of the training camps for officers on May 15, 1917, and that this was not followed by the assembly of the National Army commands until September of that year, and that the newly created officers were even then without experience in the training of men;—and then if one can picture the situation today, and by that I mean this morning,—the change already brought about is so vast as to be difficult of comprehension. Twenty-six infantry and six cavalry divisons are organized today with a sufficient officer strength of men largely experienced in actual warfare, or very well prepared through the R.O.T.C. camps, to undertake the immediate reception of recruits, their equipment and their training. A staff of Regular officers is on the ground to guide and direct. In other words, the machine is ready, with the foremen and general managers in place. A single telegram will set it in motion. Cantonments are unnecessary; even camps may be avoided; non-military supplies can be purchased on the local market.

The serious problem at the present time relates to the method of distributing arms and other distinctly military equipment, to this force. This last, however, need not delay the formation of the units and the preliminary training. As a matter of fact, this difficulty is not believed to be nearly so serious as might be imagined. If the number and location of the railheads for each divisional area are carefully determined in time of peace, the various organizations will undoubtedly find means of transporting their supplies and equipment without burdening division and corps staffs with this problem. In war time many things are possible which would be impracticable in time of peace, and the war spirit of each community can be relied upon to furnish every assistance within its power.

Think how different our position would have been at the time of our entry into the World War if we had had the present machine at our disposal. It is decentralized, has the necessary men who know at least the preliminaries of their job. It has the direct guidance of trained General Staff officers of the Regular Army,—and yet the total appropriation for this force, which will form approximately seventy-five percent of our war army, is only $1,755,000.

ARMY CORPS:. . .

AUXILIARIES:

As auxiliaries, in effect, to the National Army, are the Reserve Officer Training Corps units and the Citizen Military Training Camps. Their membership, of course, is not in the military service of the United States, but they represent so direct a contribution to the strength of the Army that they may well be considered to all intents and purposes as a part of it.

During the past year there were 104,000 students enrolled in the R.O.T.C., of whom about 7,000 attended camps this summer. $3,100,000 was appropriated for this activity. As to results, we are just reaching the period of material dividends, if measured in the number appointed Second Lieutenants in the Officers' Reserve Corps. In round numbers, 200 received commissions in 1920; 1,000 the next year; 2,200 the next, and this year 3,100. In addition, there were almost a thousand who qualified, but are yet under age. The possibilities of this school for training lieutenants is great. 126 colleges maintain these units; 52 academies; and 47 high schools. The number of graduates who qualify for commissions will materially increase and should provide a steady flow of fine officer material for the Reserve Corps and the National Guard.

These men have not qualified through a short intensive course, as in the old training camps, where it was impossible for the student to absorb all of the instruction attempted. On the contrary, they have had at least three years of training and preparation in which to absorb the instruction provided for them, including at least one summer camp of six weeks. The product of this system of instruction should be far superior to that of the hasty methods followed prior to and during the World War.

The extent of this development is quite surprising. For example, in the University of Illinois there are 2,500 R.O.T.C. students and 22 Regular officers instructing them. Of course, in the essentially military schools, there are many other large groups, but it is in the civil institutions that remarkable progress has been made, particularly in winning the sympathetic cooperation of the heads of colleges and their staffs of professors and instructors.

The Citizen Military Training camps provide a channel to a commission for the young man who cannot afford to go to college or attend a military academy. They also provide a prolific source of advantageous publicity for the National Defense. Four summer camps are involved in this course, but naturally the results will never be so satisfactory as in the R.O.T.C. units.

There were approximately 25,000 students in camp this summer, with a total appropriation of $2,000,000. In all but three Corps Areas, the allotment of students was exceeded, and in these three, special difficulties interfered with the recruiting, particularly in Wisconsin, for example, where a carefully organized effort was made in opposition to the camps.

There has not been sufficient time to produce a material number of graduates from these camps. Approximately 1,700 attended the Blue or final Course this year, and 1,500 are estimated to have successfully completed it.

MOBILIZATION:. . .

FUTURE DEVELOPMENT:

Now as to the future development of this machine. So far as concerns the Regular Army, we know what we have and the difficulties of maintaining it. We know what additions we hope Congress will give us, and the even greater difficulty of securing them.

The question of shelter is gradually being settled, but few troops remaining in cantonments. The more advantageous location of units depends upon the appropriation of funds for new construction in the desired localities. The principal task of the Regular Army is the development of the most economical scheme so far as time and effort is concerned, of carrying out the training of the citizen forces. This will be discussed later in connection with the Reserve Corps.

The peril of the Regular Army appears to lie in the fact that so few of its officers can be given experience in the actual command of troops. Prior to 1916, about 80% of the officers were on troop duty. The knowledge of commanding and leading men was our great asset, which enabled us to overcome an almost equal lack of knowledge of the higher machinery of assembling armies and deploying them on battle fields. Today the situation is exactly reversed. About 75% of the officer personnel in the higher grades and possibly in the lower grades, is not on regimental duty, and opportunities of acquiring experience in the art of exercising command are rare. A Colonel of Infantry today cannot expect to have a regiment for more than about two years in ten or twelve of service. Without careful management, it is conceivable that we might reach a point where the most experienced regimental officers will be in the National Guard and not in the Regular Army. The consequent loss of prestige would be fatal to the leadership of the latter force. The small number of units at our disposal and the tremendous number of tasks away from troops imposed by our present military policy, make this issue appear to me the most serious confronting the Regular Army today. If we specialize on the development of a few men as battalion and regimental commanders we will be unable to furnish efficient instructors and, in many cases, virtual commanders for the units of the Reserve Corps and to assist the National Guard. An officer without adequate practical experience in the command of men has no place as instructor of the R.O.T.C. students at our colleges or in the summer training camps. He is not an asset on the General Staff or in the Office of a Chief of Arm. If he be utilized in the Inspector General's Department, he would be put in the position of inspecting those who were efficient in the command of troops. The problem is a very difficult one.

In the training of the citizen forces, the future development of the Regular Army is largely a question of a state of mind. We are attempting a new mission, a new problem, utterly different from that of the past. We are dealing directly with the civil population which necessitates a thoroughly sympathetic and comprehensive understanding of the civilian viewpoint. We are very limited as to time and also as to funds. We are training men who volunteer their services as a side line to their business and ordinary occupations in life. By every dictum of the law and plan of the War Department we are frankly engaged in creating a citizen force to fight our battles, rather than a small, highly trained, professional army to campaign in Mexico, Cuba or the Philippines. If we fail in the development of a citizen army we will be impotent in the first year of a major war.

It takes time to arrive at this new viewpoint, and more time to renew intimate contacts with the civil population. The officer who has devoted most of his life to training a man, over a period of two or three years, who is absolutely subject to his authority, is treading on virgin soil.

In going about the country with General Pershing two years ago, we saw Regular Army officers struggling with this new problem, some very half-heartedly. A year later we found them carrying out the orders of the War Department with more uniformity. But this summer, the more experienced had come to visualize our new mission and the dominant part it was to play in the career of a Regular Army Officer. They had arrived at a new state of mind and what they were accomplishing was truly remarkable. Around the corner, however, we found other individuals who continued to believe solely in a professional army, blindly hoping for a larger one, and who antagonized the civilian instead of winning his support. It is apparent that once the Regular adjusts himself to this new conception of duty, amazingly satisfactory results can be obtained. It hinges on his state of mind.

NATIONAL GUARD:

. . . It is in the cooperation of the National Guard and the Organized Reserves that a new field has been opened with many possibilities for effective results. This can be discussed more conveniently in connection with the Reserve Corps. The principal point to be realized is the fact that the National Guard now constitutes about 80% of the first line of defense within the continental limits of the United States. It, therefore, demands our best efforts, in connection with the State Officials, to promote its efficiency.

ORGANIZED RESERVES:

It is in the methods to be followed in the training of the Organized Reserves that we have an entirely new problem for which numerous solutions have been offered. Up to the present time it has been necessary to deal with this corps of officers as individuals. Small appropriations have made it impossible to call out more than nine or ten percent for yearly training. Correspondence courses are as yet in a formative state. The personnel is abnormal, consisting largely of veterans of the World War who received their initial commissions in the higher grades rather than as second lieutenants. These men have really been the promoters of the new organization and have had to be treated as such. The systematic development of the Reserve Corps, however, depends upon the reception of annual increments of second lieutenants from the R.O.T.C. and C.M.T.C. It is on such a development that the corps must be built and in building up the organization consideration of the demands and requirements of the present abnormal personnel must be treated as a passing phase, though a vitally important one.

As an economic proposition the return on the money invested is many-fold greater than for the other categories of troops. The present system of training reaches but few officers and is entirely theoretical. It does not hold the interest of the larger portion of the corps. Some other method must be followed and more adequate appropriations demanded. . . .

The student training camps in the summer afford an interesting possibility for the development of the Reserve Corps. At the present time the resources of the Regular Army in personnel are heavily taxed to provide instructors and overhead for these camps. The training of the first year men is identical with the problem which will confront the Reserve Officer in the first weeks of his service in the event of war. It has, therefore, been proposed that the young training camp students form the second, third and fourth platoons of Regular organizations; that regiments or battalions of the Organized Reserves be called to camp as such and superimposed on these Regular organizations; that the preliminary training of the first two days be handled exclusively by Regular officers, but that gradually they be withdrawn from active participation, permitting the reserve unit to carry on the instruction through the elementary school of the soldier. As the program progressed the tour of the Reserve organization would expire and the Regular personnel would carry on, having the benefit of handling their units at war strength, and those officers of the Reserve who were aspirants for advancement could be retained, with or without pay, until the end of the month.

Such a system has certain decided advantages. It effects a greater economy in time, the R.O.T.C. and C.M.T.C. camps being combined in one period instead of extending over the entire summer; it avoids the necessity of creating temporary organizations with the consequent demand for administrative overhead; it enables the Reserve organizations to be handled as units rather than as individuals, and affords an opportunity for the prompt elimination of those officers who fail to demonstrate their ability to handle their organizations. In other words, it determines today whether or not the Reserve officer is qualified to organize and train his unit during the period of mobilization. It enables the Regular Army to complete its training task in a minimum of time and provides war strength organizations.

Of course, many objections have been offered, the most serious probably being the possibility that the training received by the young students would not be as effective as when under the exclusive control of a Regular officer. I doubt the importance of this objection. The Regular Officer would start and complete the training and would be in constant supervision during the period in which the temporary control had passed to the Reserve officer. The latter is not fed up on such work and consequently will approach it with enthusiasm; he has more to gain or lose than the Regular officer. As a matter of fact, Reserve officers were on duty with C.M.T.C. companies throughout the country this summer and no unfavorable comments were heard. As the corps develops the junior officers will be thoroughly experienced in training camp work, as they will all be graduates of such camps. On the whole, this seems the most effective proposal offered.

Reference has already been made to the fact that during the past three years the War Department has been compelled to deal with the personnel of the Reserve Corps as individuals. The time has now arrived when we must deal with organizations through their commanders. This holds out many interesting possibilities, particularly for the winter period. The officers of the Corps complain that so little is demanded of them that their interest is not sustained. . . .

Valuable assistance can be and already has been rendered the Reserve Corps by the National Guard authorities. The use of armories, temporary assignments of Reserve officers to fill temporary vacancies in National Guard organizations, and the use of horses and other non-personal equipment. The Reserve Corps can be of assistance to the National Guard in many ways, and nearby Regular organizations are in a position to offer much in the way of help.

The strength at which the Officers' Reserve Corps should be maintained remains something of an open question and this, in turn, leaves undecided the extent to which the R.O.T.C. and C.M.T.C. are to be developed. The minimum number of Reserve officers sufficient to meet the initial requirements of mobilization, appears to me to be the desirable figure, whatever it is. The larger this Corps, the more difficult it will be to train its personnel, as the funds available will always be very limited. It is thought by many that a corps of 50,000 apparently well trained officers, is distinctly more of an asset than a much larger force of less individual efficiency. The great problem at present is to arrive at a definite policy regarding the method of developing the Reserve organizations. We have been experimenting for three years and the time has come to reach a decision.

USAMHI/Army War College Papers

1. In a letter dated November 23, 1923, to Colonel George S. Simonds, War College assistant commandant since May 10, 1922, Marshall wrote: "[Lieutenant Colonel Upton] Birnie has pressed me to prepare in written form the talk I gave at the War College in September. While reluctant to spread out in written form the very free and personal comments made by me at that time, I have undertaken to do this and am enclosing the manuscript. Its preparation has necessarily been hastily undertaken and should any palpable errors be noticed, please do not hesitate to make the necessary corrections." (USAMHI/Army War College Papers.)

Approximately two-thirds of this lecture is printed here. The deleted portions include a quotation from General Pershing's June 28, 1923, War College graduation speech, three paragraphs of technical details which Marshall noted were "more or less quotations from a paper prepared by General [John McA.] Palmer," and discussions of the distribution of troops within the United States, the development of National Guard reserves, the future of the National Guard, new regulations affecting the Organized Reserves, National Guard–Reserve relations, and a summary of the mobilization and concentration plans in the event of a major emergency.

2. Major General Hanson E. Ely had been Army War College commandant since July 1, 1923.

To Brigadier General John McA. Palmer   October 26, 1923
                                                          Washington, D.C.

My dear General John: . . . As you have no doubt seen in the papers, General Pershing sailed for France last Saturday on the "Leviathan."[1] We got him off without anything getting into the papers until after the boat had left the dock. It was a pretty strenuous affair cleaning up business in the War Department without the knowledge of his purpose getting to more than two or three individuals. He took Mrs. Butler with him.[2] She will return on November 20th and the General expects to remain from two to four months. He hopes to work on his book but has some doubts as to whether he will manage this as he really needs a period of complete relaxation and the south of France in the winter or even Paris afford delightful opportunities for this purpose. I don't believe he autographed the photograph you desired before his departure, but it will be done as soon as he returns. I have just been working on his annual report as Chief of Staff, which he had no time to consider before his departure so has embarrassed me with the responsibility for what he is to say.

We have retired the faithful Ford in favor of an Oakland sedan, with the result that I now go home on the street car, Mrs. Marshall doing all the riding. She is quite delighted with this raise in the world, but will spend the remainder of the year counting pennies.

We intend to motor up to New York for the Army-Navy game as the General wishes me to act as host, in his absence, to the guests he has invited to sit in his box. I think we will run over to Atlantic City on our way back to see my mother.

Please write often and give me the benefit of your viewpoint as to duty with troops, and also what you and Mrs. Palmer are doing.[3]

With my love to you both,   Faithfully yours,

Marshall

LC/J. McA. Palmer Papers

1. Omitted here are 120 words acknowledging receipt of an October 25 letter from Palmer (which was not found in the Palmer papers) and telling of changes of duty for several mutual friends. General Pershing's trip to France was partly a vacation and partly in connection with his position as chairman of the newly created American Battle Monuments Commission.

2. Mary Elizabeth ("Bessie") Pershing Butler was one of General Pershing's sisters.

3. Palmer had recently been assigned to command the Infantry at Fort William D. Davis, Gatun, Canal Zone.

BETWEEN October 20, 1923, and April 3, 1924, General Pershing was absent from his desk in the War Department. During the general's stay in France, Marshall sent him at least one private letter or memorandum per week to keep him apprised of events in the War Department and in Washington, to supply him with information for his memoirs, and to keep him posted on such personal matters as Warren Pershing's schooling and the rental of the general's Washington apartment. The letters to Pershing on the succeeding pages represent approximately one-sixth of the nearly fifteen thousand words Marshall mailed during the general's trip. ★

TO GENERAL JOHN J. PERSHING   November 15, 1923
                                               Washington, D.C.

My dear General: . . . I had hoped in this letter to tell you the status of your Annual Report but unfortunately, cannot yet do so. I re-drafted the Report and had General Wells go over it. He proposed some changes on the ground that I had been too moderate. I made these changes and submitted my original draft and the new one to General Martin. He was in agreement with General Wells' idea. General Hines has had both drafts for the past ten days but has not yet been able to go over them.[1] He promised me this morning that he would try to do this today. As soon as the matter is settled, I will send you the final draft.

Major Thompson has just received a letter from Penfield of the National Defense Society,[2] with a proposal that that organization arrange to give you a dinner on your arrival in New York, in order that you might make a public statement under such auspices. Penfield goes on to say—"Such a dinner can serve an additional purpose, in that I would get together in the form of a Reception Committee, representatives from all patriotic, civic, social and fraternal societies and organizations in this territory."

Other proposals of this sort will undoubtedly be made and I wish you would think the matter over and let me have your views in order that the proper steering may be done over here. I had not thought about this until Penfield's letter came this morning, but my first reaction is that as you went abroad in the capacity of a private citizen, you should return under the same cloak and have nothing to say apropos of your trip at that time. It is conceivable, in fact rather probable, that a very elaborate reception will be proposed for your arrival in New York. Certainly there will be an unusual opportunity to launch any public statement you might have to make. If you said nothing about your observations abroad and merely talked on the National Defense, the omission of the former would tend to emphasize the latter. However almost anything you did at that time would be examined into and given some construction by those who fear you as a Presidential candidate and also by those friends who desire to have you such. This angle makes the matter a rather delicate one and deserving of some forethought, especially as we have had a succession of verbose Senators returning from cursory examinations of the European situation.

I have heard from Roger Scaife regarding the publication of your Memoirs. His reply was not direct to my question regarding, primarily, the best time for the publication of the serial story.[3] . . .   Faithfully yours,

G. C. Marshall, Jr.

LC/J. J. Pershing Papers (General Correspondence)

1. Brigadier General Briant H. Wells (U.S.M.A., 1894) had been the War Department's assistant chief of staff, G-1, between September 1, 1921, and October 31, 1923. Brigadier General Charles H. Martin replaced Wells in that position. Major General John L. Hines had been deputy chief of staff since December 5, 1922.

2. Major Charles F. Thompson (U.S.M.A., 1904) was a member of the General Staff. Clarence M. Penfield was executive secretary of the American Defense Society.

3. Marshall quotes a letter from Roger L. Scaife, a director of the Houghton Mifflin publishing house, regarding the memoirs. In it Scaife notes, "It is just possible that it might have a bigger success five years from now than at the present, for we are rather in the doldrums as far as war literature is concerned." Marshall was also in contact with Churchill Williams of the *Saturday Evening Post* regarding possible serialization of the memoirs.

Approximately one-third of this letter is printed here. In addition to the Scaife letter, omitted paragraphs include mentions of Marshall's trip to Louisville, Kentucky, Warren Pershing's activities, arrangements for the general's return, and the busy schedule in the office.

To Major Aristides Moreno[1]   December 21, 1923
                                                          Washington, D.C.

My dear Moreno: Herewith is my copy of the page proof of the First Army
Report. Under our arrangement you were to enter the proposed changes to the
page proof on your copy. There have been so many changes and corrections that
I have had to make, that I wish you would let me see yours after you have the
proof ready to go to Leavenworth. Otherwise, it should be returned here,
because I cannot take any chance on some mistake going through. You might
misunderstand my proposed changes, etc. You will notice quite an alteration in
Appendix D. These, if you will remember, were to be carefully checked at
Leavenworth, but you will notice that they not only omitted a whole page of
copy, but also they printed in the Index with the old page references. I have
straightened this out so that I think you will understand how it is to be finished
up.
     Do you think it safe to have this printed without another re-check? I would
hate to have another delay, but unless we can be very certain of a careful re-check
at Leavenworth, I hesitate to commit myself to the final printing. Another thing,
as I did not have the last corrected galley proof I could not check the changes
thereon proposed. I do not believe you have this either.   Faithfully yours,

                                                          Marshall

NA/RG 200 (J. J. Pershing Papers, *Report of the First Army*)
     1. At this time, Moreno (V.M.I., 1899) was at the Army War College. Previously he had
been at Fort Leavenworth's School of the Line (1921–22) and Command and General Staff
School (1922–23).

Memorandum for General Pershing   January 3, 1924
                                                          Washington, D.C.

Attached are my notes regarding the Y.M.C.A.[1] They have been collected
from Carter's report to G-1, and from volumes published by the Y.M.C.A. I
have given you rather a mass of figures, not with any idea that you would use
them as such, but for the purpose of making the picture of tremendous and
diverse activities and obligations of the Y in the A.E.F.
     I have always felt that the Y.M.C.A. was most unfairly treated by the Army
and by public opinion, and that this was largely due, not only to a complete
misunderstanding by the soldiers of the task assigned to the Y by you and the
limitations (tonnage) imposed in connection with carrying out that task, but
especially to a comparison with the limited and optional activities of the Knights
of Columbus, Salvation Army, and the Jewish Welfare Board.[2]

                                                          G. C. Marshall, Jr.

LC/J. J. Pershing Papers (General Correspondence)

1. The notes on the Young Men's Christian Association are not attached to the file copy in the Pershing papers.

2. Marshall made similar statements concerning the Young Men's Christian Association's war activities in his *Memoirs,* p. 21, and his interview of April 5, 1957.

TO BRIGADIER GENERAL JOHN MCA. PALMER   January 11, 1924
                                                        Washington, D.C.

My dear General John: . . .[1] As luck would have it, a request came from the General just after Christmas, which required a tremendous amount of work on my part and also considerable haste, as he desired the data as quickly as possible. This pretty well filled my holiday period, but fortunately, I had gone to Atlantic City the day before Christmas to spend two days with my mother. I am enclosing a very poor Kodak of the Marshall establishment with a few additions. Unfortunately, Joe, the furnace boy, is absent. It might interest you to know that he is the son of the cook, about thirteen years old, and as a side-line had a job nearby at the Club, but the wife of the Filipino who runs the mess there, hit Joe in the stomach with a hammer on New Year's Day, and he now works exclusively for me.

There are no indications of when the General will return, but I imagine it will be the latter part of February or March. He has an apartment near the Bois and rides in the park almost every day. From the demands he is making for data, he is evidently working quite hard on his memoirs, but General Dawes' arrival in Paris may divert him from this task.[2]

We had a very busy time during the Holidays, going out almost every night. Mrs. Marshall has formed the habit of going home at ten o'clock, usually with Mrs. Hines, leaving me to dance until the last minute and usually bring General Hines home. Sort of a Jack Spratt arrangement.

I am riding every day for longer periods than heretofore, so I have kept in very good physical trim. This afternoon I am taking [Hugh] Drum out for a ride. He was in a few minutes ago to say that the weather was rather threatening, it certainly would be muddy, and he had not ridden for two months; but I gave him no satisfaction and he is in for about fifteen or twenty miles. However, there will be several ladies in the party, which should divert his thoughts from the seat of his breeches.

I find my position on the Foreign Service Roster is receding with each promotion to Lieutenant Colonel, so there is no prospect of my getting such duty unless I can secure a special exception. In any event, I intend to make a formal request of the General to release me in September.

With my love to Mrs. Palmer and yourself,   Affectionately,

                                                        George

LC/J. McA. Palmer Papers

1. Three paragraphs were omitted in which Marshall mentioned maneuvers in Panama, a photograph of Palmer, and praise of Palmer by Senator Wadsworth and others.

2. Regarding the progress he was making in writing his memoirs, Pershing wrote Marshall on January 9, 1924, that "it could not be published before next fall because it could not possibly be gotten ready, and I get so low in my mind at times that I doubt if it will ever be ready. This happens to be one of the times. I have just remarked to Madame Despecher who is taking this dictation that I would rather fight four wars than write the history of one." (LC/J. J. Pershing Papers [General Correspondence].)

To General John J. Pershing

January 18, 1924
Washington, D.C.

My dear General: I was in Baltimore the night of the 10th to talk to the Reserve and National Guard officers on the Mobilization of the Citizen Army. Several officers from the Third Corps Area Staff were there, and my mode or style of address was considerably cramped by the presence in the front row of General Muir.[1] However, the talk seemed to create a favorable reaction.

On Monday, the 14th, I left for Culver at General Gignilliat's invitation, and on the following day talked to the Corps of Cadets and the faculty, on The Organization and Operations of the American Expeditionary Forces, inspected the school, reviewed the Corps of Cadets, and that evening talked to the First Class and the faculty on matters pertaining to the R.O.T.C., Reserve Corps, Citizen Army, and the effect of our school histories and methods of teaching them, on the National Defense.[2] I had a very busy day there and was much impressed by the institution. They all are still enthusiastic over your brief visit. Tuesday night General and Mrs. Gignilliat gave me a dinner, followed by a dance. I left the next morning for Washington, arriving here yesterday.

On my return I found your two notes with the Plates for the band uniforms, and I have sent the Quartermaster General a memorandum regarding the making of a model cap and uniform in accordance with your instructions. I will keep you advised of developments. I also received your note regarding the tailor-made uniforms for enlisted men and am now checking up on that and will send you the data tomorrow or next day. I plan to inspect one unit in the uniform, but I do not think they have been received yet,[3] for it was only about three weeks ago that we were able to get in our orders for the men in your detachment. General Hines is now absent, but I will bring up these uniform questions with him as soon as he returns.

Your messages regarding the Christmas cablegram, condolences to General Hart, etc., will be delivered.[4] I intend taking the liberty of telling General Wells what you had to say about the boots.[5]

Now as to the date of your return to the United States, the bill before Congress regarding your status on the active list, and the possibility of your resigning as

Chief of Staff. I have been following the bill in Congress and up to the present time have not received a very definite reaction. There seems to be no possibility regarding its failure of passage by practically unanimous vote in the Senate, but the attitude of the House of Representatives is not clear. There has been some talk about the danger of establishing a precedent which might be harmful in the future; and there have been references to the adverse effect of Admiral Dewey's conservative attitude during the latter years of his life. However, I am inclined to the belief that the points just mentioned, have been advanced to disguise other motives; for example, the hostility of the New England group. This, however, I have not been able to verify. It has been my intention to "let Nature take its course" for a time, and then if it did not appear that the bill would be pressed for passage or would be passed by practically a unanimous vote, I intended, without your knowledge, to bring pressure to bear in the proper quarters through the medium of every warm supporter of yours I know in the United States. I feel certain that it would be possible for me to force this bill through by a highly complimentary vote, and I feel that nothing else should be tolerated, the bill having once been introduced.

In view of the foregoing, it seems to me that your absence in Europe places you in a good strategical position at this time, and if at all practicable, you should not return until this legislative matter has been cleared up. I cannot see any urgent reason why you should return to this country within the next two or three months, but as soon as General Hines returns from Panama, I will talk over the matter with him;—confidentially of course, and without disclosing anything regarding your letters to me and mine to you.

As to your resignation as Chief of Staff immediately upon the passage of this bill, I am not prepared to give you my opinion at this time, as this particular thought had not occurred to me until your letter arrived, and I will want some time to consider the matter.[6]

The plans for the maneuvers or test mobilization (National Defense Day), are going forward apparently in good shape and according to your ideas. Drum has immediate control of the affair and you can depend upon its energetic development under his direction and his resourcefulness in finding ways and means.[7] The Secretary of War formally approved the project about two weeks ago. I will send you a copy of the formal instructions to the various Sections of the Staff and the Chiefs of Arms or Services as soon as it is issued, which will probably be within two or three days.

I just sent back to Leavenworth this morning the final check of the page proof of the First Army Report. They will probably begin printing for publication in a week or ten days. If any errors develop in the published report I will be sick at heart, for we have taken infinite care in checking over the last two page proofs. If none develop, I will feel vastly relieved to have this out of the way.

I am delighted that you have worked so hard on your Memoirs, and your dissatisfaction with what you have done is but a normal reaction for you. The longer you work on it, undoubtedly the less you will be pleased with it, because the monotony of the operation will dishearten any one.   Affectionately,

G. C. Marshall, Jr.

LC/J. J. Pershing Papers (General Correspondence)

1. Major General Charles H. Muir (U.S.M.A., 1885) commanded the Third Corps Area.

2. Brigadier General Leigh R. Gignilliat (V.M.I., 1895) had been superintendent of Culver Military Academy, Culver, Indiana, since 1910. During the war one of his assignments had been to the General Staff at A.E.F. General Headquarters at Chaumont, France. Since 1921 he had commanded the Reserve Corps' 168th Infantry.

Marshall's talk to the first classmen and faculty was a longer version of his lecture given on February 10, 1923, printed above.·

3. In the margin beside this sentence, Marshall wrote: "They have not been received yet."

4. The sister of Major General William H. Hart, the quartermaster general, was buried December 7, 1923.

5. Brigadier General Briant H. Wells, commandant of the Infantry School, Fort Benning, Georgia, had irritated American bootmakers by suggesting to his officers that they order their boots from London's Peal and Company. Marshall remarked: "The next time I imagine he will do the thing less directly." (Marshall to Pershing, December 7, 1923, LC/J. J. Pershing Papers [General Correspondence].) Pershing responded: "I am glad that Wells took up the question of boots even at the expense of bringing down upon his head the wrath of American bootmakers who are generally speaking far inferior to the people over here." (Pershing to Marshall, January 2, 1924, ibid.)

6. "Confidentially," Pershing wrote to Marshall on January 2, 1924, "if this new provision to retain me on active service should prevail, it seems to me that I should resign as Chief of Staff at once unless there appears some very grave reason for not doing so." Pershing solicited Marshall's views on this and on the advisability of staying longer in France. (Ibid.)

7. Brigadier General Hugh A. Drum had become assistant chief of staff, G-3, on December 4, 1923.

TO GENERAL JOHN J. PERSHING

January 23, 1924
Washington, D.C.

My dear General: General Helmick is concerned over the fact that the curriculum at West Point does not include, in his opinion, an appropriate course on leadership. He has been in communication with General Sladen regarding this, and also with Colonel Stewart, and while the latter plans to give certain instruction in leadership and command to the First Class, General Helmick feels that the matter has not been given the consideration its importance merits.[1]

Colonel Stewart proposes to devote some time early in the First Class year to short talks on the different phases of leadership and command, these to be followed by opportunities for the First Class men to put into practice the matter brought out by the talks. He hopes that the series of talks, followed by practical application, will fit the First Class men to act as assistant instructors in the various drills in military subjects and as cadet officers and non-commissioned officers, and plans to conclude this applicatory series with one or two lectures summing up the whole subject.

General Helmick thinks that Colonel Stewart's proposal is good, but he does not feel that it fully meets the necessities of the case. He has in mind that there should be a carefully prepared course at the Military Academy for the Second and First Classes, which would cover the considerations pertaining to the management of men in garrison, camp, campaign and battle, particularly the last. He has in mind training the cadets in how to handle young Americans, recruits and training camps students; how to win their loyalty and secure their earnest and energetic cooperation; how to get the most out of men on the march; and how best to exercise command and control under distressing circumstances of fatigue, living conditions, weather and danger; how to inspire them in battle; and particularly, how to maintain the offensive and aggressive spirit, despite fatigue, casualties and hostile resistance. The course would necessarily involve something of a study of psychology.

The difficulty seems to be that in order to initiate such a course, time would have to be taken from other subjects. At present the hours are filled apparently to the limit, and of course any proposal to reduce the number of hours accorded to mathematics, or history, or philosophy, would be opposed.

I doubt if this is an appropriate subject to bring up with you while you are abroad, but I thought it might happen that you would write to General Sladen regarding his advancement and if so, assuming that you agree with General Helmick, a word or two on this matter would have considerable weight, particularly if you indicated something of what you meant by a course in leadership. Up to the present time I think they have done little more than teach a cadet how to give commands and to look firm and inexorable, and this, I believe has been one of the weaknesses of West Point. The cadet has largely had to find his knowledge of leadership and command from what he has seen of the disciplining of 'plebes' and the exacting and strict supervision of his own tactical officers. The results of this system showed themselves in the handling of our National Army, where officers who had not had the benefit of experience in a voluntary camp of the Plattsburg type, failed to get the most out of our young Americans, and too frequently aroused their lasting animosity.   Affectionately,

G. C. Marshall, Jr.

LC/J. J. Pershing Papers (General Correspondence)

1. Major General Eli A. Helmick (U.S.M.A., 1888) was the army inspector general. Fred W. Sladen (U.S.M.A., 1890), superintendent of the United States Military Academy, had been promoted to major general effective January 19, 1924. Colonel Merch B. Stewart (U.S.M.A., 1896) was commandant of cadets.

To General John J. Pershing   January 26, 1924
                                               Washington, D.C.

My dear General: The Duncan Major case has taken a nasty slant, which is not only regrettable, but bodes no good for anybody concerned. Apparently, following the favorable report of the Military Committee for Major's confirmation, there was to be a discussion on the floor of the Senate, but it was assumed that this would be merely an opportunity for those who pose as the supporters of the New England soldiery, to clear their skirts of any charge of indifference. However, on Sunday the 20th, the Boston Herald came out with an article quoting from Colonel Hunt's brief in representing Major's case before the Military Committee in the spring of 1922. The publication of this paper has tended, as was undoubtedly intended, to arouse and line up New England opinion on the grounds that the efficiency of the Yankee Division had been assailed and its record besmirched. I understand that letters and telegrams have poured in on the Senators, demanding the defeat of Major's confirmation on the floor of the Senate. Senator Lodge has been collecting information yesterday and this morning regarding the record of the 26th Division, which I presume he will use in a speech. Mr. Weeks, according to General Davis, is worried, as is also Senator Wadsworth. The latter addressed a letter to Major, asking him if he had any knowledge of how Colonel Hunt's brief became public. Major replied that he knew nothing about it and stated specifically that he had had no part in giving it publicity. I am sending you clippings from the Boston Herald, which will give you the New England slant, and I will keep you advised of what happens, but it is apparent that on next Tuesday in executive session, a very bitter battle is to be waged over this case. The precedent of passing over officers who have been nominated, established in the cases of General Davis, Colonel Drum and Colonel Peck, I am afraid is going to bear rather evil fruit.[1]   Faithfully yours,

G. C. Marshall, Jr.

LC/J. J. Pershing Papers (General Correspondence)

1. Duncan K. Major, Jr., (U.S.M.A., 1899) had been nominated to the rank of colonel. He had been chief of staff of the Twenty-sixth ("Yankee") Division (National Guard) between April, 1918, and January, 1919. Many of the division's National Guard officers had believed that Regular Army officers, particularly Pershing and his staff at A.E.F. Headquarters, discriminated against the Guard. This feeling peaked when the division's popular commander, Major General Clarence R. Edwards (U.S.M.A., 1883), was removed from command effective October 24, 1918, and several other senior commanders were likewise removed shortly thereafter. Three histories appeared shortly after the war which defended the division and its leaders with varying degrees of vehemence: Harry A. Benwell, *History of the Yankee Division* (Boston: Cornhill, 1919); Frank P. Sibley, *With the Yankee Division in France* (Boston: Little, Brown, 1919); Emerson Gifford Taylor, *New England in France, 1917-1919: A History of the Twenty-Sixth Division U.S.A.* (Boston: Houghton Mifflin, 1920). Taylor said of Major: "A most efficient executive, this officer often achieved results by methods somewhat at variance with the principles ordinarily accepted as regulating the daily relations between a Chief of Staff and those about him." (P. 139.)

In the postscript to a letter dated January 23, 1924, Marshall told Pershing: "I understand that today the question of the confirmation of Duncan Major will be debated in an open session of the Senate and that a very warm argument is anticipated, though the Massachusetts people have no chance of success and merely desire the publicity." (LC/J. J. Pershing Papers [General Correspondence].)

To Major General Hunter Liggett   February 11, 1924
                                                         [Washington, D.C.]

My dear General Liggett: Your note of February 2nd has come and I have
notified the people at Leavenworth to specially bind copies of the First Army
Report for Senator Wadsworth and Mr. Kahn, with their names and positions
embossed on the cover.[1] As you expressed no other desire, I have taken the
liberty of notifying the Book Department to send you direct, four full leather
bound copies, eight half leather, and twelve cloth bound copies of the Report,
because I feel certain that there will probably be people to whom you might wish
to give them from time to time. Should this lot not prove sufficient for your
wants, please let me know and I will arrange for additional copies.

It will be a matter of great relief to me when this Report is out of the way and I
will also be very glad when it becomes a document available to the public, so that
the splendid achievements of the Army and its Commanders may become
generally known, which is not now the case.

I hear reports regarding you from time to time from officers of the Ninth
Corps Area, and I am happy to know that you continue in such excellent health,
and that Mrs. Liggett is also well.[2] Of course, you have selected the choice
climate of the United States in my opinion, and have placed your lives among so
many agreeable people. Of all the cities, I believe I would prefer to live in San
Francisco, but my real inclination is for the country.

When I start out on my morning ride before breakfast, I almost invariably
think of you and Fort McKinley, especially on those days when I happen to see
your old orderly, Hall, as I did last Saturday morning. He is on duty in the
colored troop which runs the saddle horses for the War College and officers on
duty in Washington. He seems to be doing very well, but complains that there are
so many old soldiers in the outfit that he holds no hopes for promotion. He is a
distinguished private.

General Pershing has been working rather hard in Paris on his Memoirs, but I
had a note from him a couple of days ago, written from Monte Carlo, where he
is spending a week or two. I imagine he will return to this country the early part
of March.

The other night at a small stag dinner, Senator Wadsworth had quite a bit to
say regarding your advancement to the grade of Lieutenant General. He brought
the matter up himself in connection with some vagary of legislation which he had
been discussing. Senator Wadsworth feels very strongly regarding the failure of
the Government to advance you and freely damns all those in Congress who leap
to their feet in pretentious defense of the rights and dues of the simple soldier,
whenever anything is said about appropriate appreciation of the services of the
out-standing men of whom you are the leading example. According to him, there
is a crowd of men on the Hill playing for votes in connection with the bonus,
who oppose anything that does not pay so many hundreds of dollars a month to

the soldiers. He has apparently honestly tried in every way to do what he feels is not only the right thing, but the only fitting thing in your case, but has found himself opposed right and left by the demagogue type now so prevalent. However, he has not by any means given up hope and they all seem to feel that if this bonus thing is cleared up one way or the other during this session, then there may be some decency in connection with military legislation.

I just had a long letter this morning from Malin Craig, who is apparently doing things at Corregidor.[3] As usual, he has something more than nice to say of you.

With my affectionate regards to Mrs. Liggett and yourself,   Faithfully yours,

NA/RG 200 (J. J. Pershing Papers, *Report of the First Army*)

1. Marshall had written Liggett on January 25 to ask if the general knew of anyone not on the distribution list who should receive the expensively bound version of the report. Wadsworth was chairman of the Senate Military Affairs Committee. Julius Kahn, Republican of California's Fourth District (San Francisco), was chairman of the House Military Affairs Committee.

2. The Liggetts lived in San Francisco. The Ninth Corps Area included not only California, but also Alaska, Washington, Oregon, Idaho, Montana, Wyoming, Utah, and Nevada.

3. Craig (U.S.M.A., 1898) had been promoted to brigadier general in the Regular Army effective April 28, 1921. He was in command of the Coast Artillery District of Manila and Subic Bay in the Philippine Islands.

TO GENERAL JOHN J. PERSHING   February 19, 1924
                                                     Washington, D.C.

Dear General: . . . You will probably have seen from the papers that Duncan Major was confirmed; also that the Executive Session in consideration of his case, lasted two full afternoons. The final vote was 43 to 24, and I am enclosing you the page of the Congressional Record which discloses the vote. Just what occurred during the Executive Session I have not learned definitely, but it is quite apparent that General Edwards' reputation received a severe jolt. I understand, confidentially, that Senator Reed of Pennsylvania, remarked at the conclusion of the sessions, that if as much had been known regarding General Edwards' record at the time of his nomination for a Major Generalcy as was now understood, he would never have been confirmed. Personally, I believe that Senator Walsh wanted the vote to go in Major's favor, but also wished to have it appear that he had made a very desperate fight to prevent confirmation; that his principal desire was to nail General Edwards' record. If my guess is correct, he carried through all three desires.[1]

I talked to Johnson about the preparation of Army candidates for the Olympic Games, and am enclosing a mimeograph of what is being done.[2] I also spoke to General Hines regarding it. They are carefully training Army candidates in various parts of the country for the modern Pentathlon and have about four promising candidates: two at West Point, one at Benning, and one other, I have forgotten where. Each of course, is weak in some department and is receiving special instruction with regard to that. . . .[3] Affectionately yours,

G. C. Marshall, Jr.

LC/J. J. Pershing Papers (General Correspondence)

1. David A. Reed was a Republican and David I. Walsh was a Massachusetts Democrat. Walsh voted against Duncan K. Major's confirmation.

2. Lieutenant Colonel Wait C. Johnson was a General Staff officer. General Pershing had written to Marshall: "We should begin now to make preparation for every single event in which representatives from the Army expect to appear. There is one event to which I think this especially applies, that is the pentathlon which to my mind requires some preparation." (Pershing to Marshall, February 1, 1924, LC/J. J. Pershing Papers [General Correspondence].)

3. Approximately one-third of the letter is printed. The omitted portions referred to Pershing's return and to his apartment, which had been subleased.

To THEODORE ROOSEVELT, JR.   February [21?], 1924
                                                        Washington, D.C.

My dear Roosevelt: I am not informed as to the essential facts in the present chaotic political mess, but it is my very genuine and sincere hope that your future career of public service will not, in any measure, be adversely effected by the customary prejudiced attacks of political opponents.[1]

There has been, it seems to me, too much talk of your name and too little said of your personal record as a patriotic and conspicuously courageous citizen.   Faithfully yours,

G. C. Marshall, Jr.

LC/T. Roosevelt Papers; H

1. At this time Roosevelt's name was being mentioned prominently as a possible Republican candidate for governor of New York. Some Republican politicians objected to his candidacy on the grounds that as assistant secretary of the navy, a position he had held since 1921, Roosevelt was implicated in the Teapot Dome scandal. On February 23, Roosevelt replied to Marshall that he was "in the unfortunate position this time of the innocent bystander on whom certain of the 'bricks' are falling and who cannot defend himself because to do so would hurt one of his friends." (LC/T. Roosevelt Papers.)

To GENERAL JOHN J. PERSHING   February 25, 1924
                                                       Washington, D.C.

My dear General: Mr. Arthur Page and myself had a long conversation on last Thursday here in the War Department and during lunch at the Club.[1] Nothing new came of the interview, except that he made a more definite statement regarding the best time for publication of your Memoirs. He considers the months of October, November, and December to be by far the best periods for publication of such a book. He said that if your volume could not be ready for the book-stands before the end of November, it should be delayed until the following September.

In the copy of the Army & Navy Register which came out last Saturday, I marked for you some comments regarding your bill, written around a recent editorial in the Boston "Transcript." This sort of thing is more or less to be expected from these two sources, though it is very aggravating to have to forgo open comment in order to avoid dignifying it with too much importance. In a note to me on February 19th, General Harbord wrote: "I saw Mr. Stettinius this morning and he talked to me about General Pershing's case.[2] Apparently the proposed legislation for the General has gone to sleep. It would, of course, be unthinkable to have it come up and be seriously combatted or defeated. On the other hand, it cannot very well, with dignity, be withdrawn. I concur with Mr. Stettinius that the best thing that can be · done, in the present state of the Congressional mind, is to let it sleep for a while, trusting to see signs of returning sanity on the part of Congress, which may justify waking it up a little bit later."

I have casually dropped a few hints in certain quarters which I think will work up quite a bit of feeling among the leading officers of the Reserve Corps, and at the proper time I believe these fellows will wish to bring very strong pressure to bear on Congress. I know most of them feel that you are their great hope and that of the Citizen Army movement in the War Department. As soon as this mud-slinging subsides a little bit, we can size up the situation with more assurance.   Affectionately yours,

G. C. Marshall, Jr.

LC/J. J. Pershing Papers (General Correspondence)

1. Arthur W. Page, with whom Marshall had had frequent dealings regarding General Pershing's proposed memoirs, was a member of the publishing firm of Doubleday, Page and Company.

2. Edward R. Stettinius, a banker connected with J. P. Morgan and Company, had held several important positions connected with supplies for the A.E.F., including the post of second assistant secretary of the War Department.

To Major General Hunter Liggett   April 30, 1924
                                                  [Washington, D.C.]

My dear General Liggett: I was very happy to receive your letter of April 22nd and am glad to know that the copies of the First Army Report reached you safely.

As you may have seen in the papers, I am relieved from duty here July 1st and assigned to the 15th Infantry in China. Mrs. Marshall, her mother and myself sail from New York on July 12th, and from San Francisco, August 1st. I am looking forward to seeing you there. I have been struggling to get this detail for the past year and a half and I am delighted that it is finally an accomplished fact, so far as the preliminary orders go. With affectionate regards,   Faithfully yours,

NA/RG 200 (J. J. Pershing Papers, *Report of the First Army*)

MEMORANDUM FOR GENERAL PERSHING   June 3, 1924
                                                        Washington, D.C.

I have read through this translation.[1] It gives an inadequate idea of the American achievements in the war, especially in the Marne salient. The treatment of our operations in the St. Mihiel and the Meuse-Argonne is patronizing in tone, and certainly does not err on the side of over-statement of what we did.

In the description of the Meuse-Argonne operation in conjunction with Gouraud's Fourth Army, it seems to me everything about the latter is stated so as most to impress the reader and is devoid of any criticism, while the description of the First Army's operations is very moderate in regard to achievements and in several instances includes pointed criticisms. No mention is made of the services of American divisions with the Fourth Army, but there is no failure to mention the French divisions with the First American Army. The reader would be led to believe that Gouraud's army acted throughout with great dash and success, while we lagged decidedly behind, but did very well considering the limited amount of training our troops and staffs had had. In the finale of this battle General Fayolle ignores the presence of any American troops between Mouzon and Sedan. He gives the impression that General Maistre controlled your operations as well as those of the Fourth French Army from November 1st to 7th.[2]

I do not think there is anything to be said about this paper and I do not suppose they exaggerate their performances to our disadvantage much, if any more than future American historians will exaggerate our performances to French disadvantage.

My own idea is that we should be scrupulously accurate in recording the achievements of the American army, leaving to the French their propaganda of astute depreciation. Then the historians of the future will take care of the matter.

                                                            G. C. M.

LC/J. J. Pershing Papers (Book File)

1. The Army War College's Historical Section had sent Pershing a copy of the translation of *La Guerre Racontee par Nos Generaux.*

2. Henri J.E. Gouraud commanded the French Fourth Army on Pershing's right during the St. Mihiel and Meuse-Argonne operations. General Marie Emile Fayolle commanded the Armies of the Center. General Paul A.M. Maistre commanded the Group of Armies which included Gouraud's Fourth Army.

MEMORANDUM FOR GENERAL PERSHING   July 9, 1924
                                                  Washington, D.C.

Diary of Col. Marshall.[1]

My dear General: As I told you the day we separated in New York, I have always hesitated in turning over to you this so-called journal of my experiences in France. Knowing what a careful and finished workman you are in such matters, I am very loathe to turn over to you this rough first draft of dictated stuff, which has been done in the midst of constant interruptions. Also, it is extremely personal, because it is intended to be merely a record of what I saw, heard and thought at the time.

So in reading this, please have in mind just how it was done and for what purpose; otherwise, it will seem very egotistical and extremely crude.

LC/J. J. Pershing Papers (General Correspondence)

1. Published as *Memoirs of My Services in the World War, 1917–1918* (Boston: Houghton Mifflin, 1976).

TO GENERAL JOHN J. PERSHING   August 8, 1924
                                               Honolulu, [Hawaii]

My dear General: I have been trying to start this note for an hour without success, as the world and his wife seem to have boarded the boat to say good-byes. We are to sail in a few minutes, so I only have time remaining for a very brief note.

Your wireless message was deeply appreciated.[1] Incidentally, it electrified the ship and quite dignified me. The Captain, the Quartermaster, and numerous minor officials all had to inquire as to its safe delivery to me. Evidently there is no secrecy observed by the operators in such circumstances.

General Summerall has been delightful to me. He placed his limousine and aide at my disposal and we have motored all over the Island. Had lunch with the Summeralls at the Moana [Hotel] yesterday.

Our trip has been delightful, quiet seas throughout and fair weather. Conner gave me quite a party in Panama—lots of champagne.[2]

I am sorry I could not have been in New York to welcome you home. No words can express the regret and loss I feel at the termination of my service with you. Few men in life have such opportunities and almost none, I believe, such a

delightful association as was mine with you. May all good things be yours—
Goodbye. Affectionately,

Marshall

LC/J. J. Pershing Papers (General Correspondence); H
1. On August 2, the day following the U.S.A.T. *Thomas*'s departure from San Francisco,
General Pershing sent the following message: "Au revoir affectionately."
2. Major General Charles P. Summerall commanded the Hawaiian Department. Brigadier
General Fox Conner commanded Camp Gaillard in the Canal Zone.

Tientsin, China

September 1924–June 1927

S UNDAY, September 7, the day the Army Transport *Thomas* brought the Marshalls to the Chinese port of Chinwangtao, was an anniversary of importance to the lieutenant colonel, his wife, and his mother-in-law. On that date in 1901, China and the foreign powers who had suppressed the Boxer Rebellion signed the Boxer Protocols, one of which recognized the foreigners' right to occupy certain points along the railway leading from Peking to the sea: to keep open a line of communication to the diplomatic missions in the capital, and to protect the lives and property of their various citizens in the event of a renewal of antiforeign violence. Following the 1911 revolution in China, the United States sent elements of the Fifteenth Infantry to join the other foreign contingents in Tientsin, an industrial city of nearly one million inhabitants and a sizable foreign community on the Peking-Mukden Railroad.

About one thousand officers and men served in the "United States Army Forces in China," as the command was officially called after July 1, 1924. The China assignment was considered one of the best in the army. The American troops there were better dressed and fed than at perhaps any other post; morale was consistently high. Major General Eli A. Helmick, the army inspector general, commented in his 1925 report that "the 15th Infantry in China is a fine, well-trained body of soldiers, upholding the best traditions of our Army and a credit to our country." (Helmick to the Chief of Staff, October 22, 1925, NA/RG 159 [Reports].)

Officers lived in rented houses and usually had Chinese servants. Altogether, the five servants the average officer employed cost perhaps forty or fifty United States dollars per month. Marshall's pay and allowances amounted to just over sixty-eight hundred dollars in 1924–25. But a published essay on the "Conditions of Service in China" warned prospective applicants that they were not getting duty in paradise. "The prevailing idea that in China one can live like a prince-of-the-blood on the pay of a second lieutenant has as much foundation of fact as the theory that two can live as cheaply as one. It is true that many things which go to make up the family budget are cheaper here than at home, but the low cost of living features of service in China has been greatly exaggerated. Here, as elsewhere, the average officer spends all he gets, the difference being that here he lives on a higher scale. Also, in the course of a tour in China his wife, if he has one, invariably accumulates a rather impressive store of rugs, silver, linen, lingerie, embroideries and other impedimenta that would be utterly beyond his means if priced on Fifth Avenue." (*Infantry Journal* 29 [August 1926]: 171.)

The Fifteenth Infantry's mission was to protect American lives and property against antiforeign activities of the Boxer Rebellion kind. But since 1920 the various factions in China had moved rapidly to reorganize, enlarge, modernize, and professionalize their armed forces. The military operations mounted in China during Marshall's tour of duty were of a radically different nature than the Fifteenth Infantry was expected to meet. By January, 1926, the commander of the Army Forces in China, Brigadier General William D. Connor (U.S.M.A.,

1897), was recommending a reassessment of the army's role. "The other garrisons all have concessions in Tientsin which they can pretend they are here to protect, which gives them a reason for being here, and to which they can withdraw, if necessary, and maintain a relatively dignified position. The American status is entirely different from that of any other nation. We alone have no concession. We alone live and operate in purely Chinese territory, and we alone have no other reason for being here if the [1901] Protocol is not to be enforced. The only place to which we can withdraw is to our own country." (Connor to TAG, January 22, 1926, NA/RG 94 [370.22, China].)

Marshall reported for duty just after the previous regimental commander, his old friend Brigadier General Campbell King, had left and prior to the arrival of Colonel William K. Naylor, formerly the War Department's director of military intelligence. From September 8 until November 21, 1924, command of the Fifteenth Infantry devolved upon Marshall.

At this time the various factions of *tuchuns* (a term usually translated into English as *warlord*) began another round of armed struggles. Tientsin and Peking lay within what was then the province of Chihli. The Chihli faction, under the leadership of Wu P'ei-fu, was then dominant in north and central China, and its strength and policies threatened the Fengtien faction which controlled Manchuria under the leadership of Chang Tso-lin. The day Marshall disembarked at Chinwangtao, September 7, Chang announced the mobilization of his troops against Wu's forces. ★

TO GENERAL JOHN J. PERSHING   September 18, 1924
                                               Tientsin, China

My dear General: I got off a long delayed cable to you three days ago. On Sept. 12th and 13th I was down with a peculiar form of Chinese grippe, which seems to attack all new arrivals, so I did not then send you some word on the day of your retirement.[1] It is impossible for me to picture you in any but the most active role. In fact I know that you will promptly find some outlet for your driving energy, but I do hope you find interests that will make for your happiness and contentment. You more deserve a rest than any other American, but probably will care nothing for such an opportunity.

We are in the midst of a Chinese civil war. The port at which I landed ten days ago, Ching wang tao, was bombed yesterday, and eight miles to the north at Shan hai kuan fighting is reported to have started this morning. I have one company at the coal mines at Tong shan, and had to send some additional men and a car load of grenades, stokes mortar amm. and extra rifles up there yesterday. Thousands of Chinese troops have passed thru here daily for a week or more and the railroad is practically blocked with trains for a hundred miles

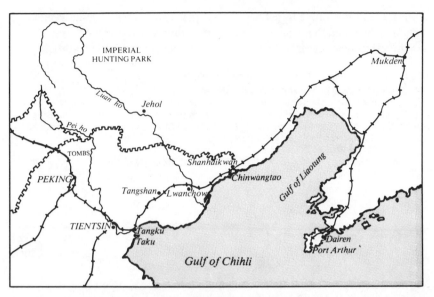

Northeast China, 1924–27.

south of Shan hai kuan. It is reported that the Chinese city of Tientsin goes under marshal law tonight.[2] Altogether I find things very interesting. The regiment has a selected personnel of officers and it is a pleasure to work with them. But I must confess that I have a hard time remembering that every thing I do is not being done directly for you. My five years with you will always remain the unique experience of my career. I knew I would treasure the recollection of that service, but not until I actually landed here and took up these new duties—not until then did I realize how much my long association with you was going to mean to me and how deeply I will miss it. Nothing at this time could appeal to me more than this assignment and I look forward to three years of valuable professional experience and pleasant relations socially.

We have not yet gotten settled in a house as the quarters I am leasing will not be available until the end of the month. Meanwhile we are at the Astor House.[3] Mrs. Marshall and her mother made the trip in good shape, but will be delighted to get organized in a home of our own. Gen. Conner [*Connor*] looks well and just now is very busy with frequent meetings of the several commanders regarding the present unsettled conditions. The regiment with the hospital, Q.M. & C., is organized as a post under my command and Gen. C. and his staff devote themselves to outside affairs, except for the annual tactical inspections.

Please send me a note to tell me of your plans and prospective movements. I am much interested to learn your decision regarding Warren's schooling.[4]

With affectionate regards, believe me, always at your service, Faithfully
Marshall

LC/J. J. Pershing Papers (General Correspondence); H

1. General Pershing retired at noon on September 13, 1924.
2. Tientsin was divided into the Native City and the Concessions: British, Japanese, Italian, and French. The walled American Compound consisted of leased structures covering one square block in the "First Special Area" (the name given the former German Concession), which was administered by a special Chinese bureau.
3. A hotel in the British Concession.
4. Warren Pershing was enrolled at the Institut Carnal, Rolle, Switzerland.

To Major General John L. Hines   September 21, 1924
                                                                        Tientsin, China

My dear General: This note of congratulations will reach you long after your appointment as Chief of Staff;[1] not at all like the telephonic congratulations I used to have occasion to give you so often in old A.E.F. days. As a matter of fact, your appointment had been accepted so long as an assured affair that it came to everyone much as a matter of course. But I am delighted that there was no unexpected hitch and that you are actually at the head of the Army. Your numerous promotions have given me, I am sure, almost as much pleasure as they have to you—because it is not often in the Army that advancements go where they are so richly deserved as in your particular case.

I have landed here quite in the middle of things, as it were. If we had docked at Ching wang tao five days later we would probably have been unable to make the trip up to Tientsin, as the railroad has been literally blocked with Chinese troop movements. The remainder of the foreign summer colony near Ching wang tao are being moved out by boats furnished by the big coal company.[2]

More than 50,000 troops have passed thru here headed for Shan hai kuan. As they usually hold on to their trains, all the sidings are blocked and portions of the main line tracks. Last evening some undisciplined soldiers of the Chinese 9th Division sort of took over the Central Station in Tientsin and killed one of the station officials. The company of the 15th Inf. located at Tong shan has a Chinese division settled around it.[3] Two days ago I sent up to it some additional men, an officer and the required grenade and mortar ammunition. With aeroplane bombing at Shanhaikuan and Ching wang tao and the other disruptions and disturbances, it smacks much the old war time atmosphere.

No one ventures to predict just what is to happen. Chinese methods are too devious for foreign penetration. The trusted body guard of Wu pei fu (the military mogul out here), the 3ᵈ Division, which he has held around him in Pekin, is today passing north thru Tientsin. None of the foreigners can predict what this means, as they can not understand why Wu would risk personal separation from this trusted force.

I did not intend to bore you with so much of this local situation. It will all have changed long before this letter reaches you. General Conner is very busy with the other Commanders and, I think, has very sound views and somewhat dominates matters despite the fact that he is junior to the Japanese C.O.

Mrs. Marshall and Mrs. Coles are only partially aware of the present situation. Their minds are centered on househunting. We are living at the Astor Hotel at present but hope to get settled by Oct. 15ᵗʰ which will be a comfort to us all. The weather has been perfect.

I am delighted with the regiment. The officers seem to be much above the average personnel and the work and problem is very interesting.

Give my love to Mrs. Hines and believe me always,   Faithfully yrs.

G. C. Marshall, Jr.

LC/J. L. Hines Papers; H

1. Hines became army chief of staff on September 14.

2. The Kailan Mining Administration (K.M.A.) was a British-Belgian-Chinese combine. During the hot, rainy months from May through September, the foreign military commands at Tientsin maintained summer training camps on the beaches near the K.M.A.'s deepwater port of Chinwangtao. Between 1923 and 1927, the Fifteenth Infantry leased a camp site at Nan Ta Ssu from the K.M.A.

3. Rifle companies alternated six-month tours of duty guarding the locomotive and car shops of the Peking-Mukden Railroad at Tangshan, a city of approximately sixty thousand inhabitants, eighty-five miles from Tientsin.

TELEGRAM TO CAPTAIN HENRY H. DABNEY   October 23, 1924
[Tientsin, China]

Lieut. Boyles[1] and one squad leave here Friday to join you Stop (Remainder of message to be in code) Confidential Pekin and two Army field commanders have turned over against Wu period[2] Crisis probable on front Friday and for you possibly on Saturday period

Marshall

NA/RG 407 (371.1, China); H

1. Dabney (U.S.M.A., 1915) commanded Company K at Tangshan. First Lieutenant Clifford H. Boyles commanded a squad of Company F.

2. Wu intended to check the Fengtien forces by holding the Shanhaikwan area. To meet Chang Tso-lin's flank attack through Jehol, Wu ordered Feng Yu-hsiang (sometimes called the "Christian General") and Wang Huai-ching into Jehol. Feng, however, decided to switch sides, and on October 22–23 moved his army to Peking and took control of the capital, threatening to isolate Wu's forces in northeastern Chihli.

MEMORANDUM TO THE ADJUTANT[1]   October 25, 1924
                                                                [Tientsin, China]

1 corporal and 5 men will be sent to East Tientsin station to report to Mr. Ritchie, Ry. transportation superintendent, at 5 P.M. today. An officer will be sent by us to the station to see that the corporal locates Mr. Ritchie and understands Mr. R's instructions.

These men are to guard some coaches which are being collected to transport 250 marines to Pekin Monday morning. They are to prevent the coaches designated by Mr. R., from being diverted to some other use. They will *not shoot* except in self defense.

Prepare a concise statement of instructions for the use of the corporal.

————

The International train will not go out Sunday, but is expected to go out Monday.[2]

————

Lt. Depass' instructions will come over from Hqs. A.F.C. about 2 P.M. See that he gets his copy and also a copy of the instructions for the officer in charge of the International train.[3]

                                                                        G. C. M.

NA/RG 407 (371.2, China); H
   1. Captain William B. Tuttle.
   2. The 1901 Protocol granted the foreign nations the right to insure free access from the capital to the sea by rail in the event that railroad officials were unable to maintain it. To accomplish this, after October 14, the Allied or International Train was created to travel between Peking and Shanhaikwan, guarded by detachments of twelve men and one officer from each of the four garrisons. According to an essay on this particular trip (October 28 to November 4) in the *15th Infantry Annual, 1924–25* (Tientsin: Tientsin Press, 1925), this train "had the opportunity of witnessing more of the civil war than any of the others that made the run, passing through the lines at a time when history was being made over night." (P. 135.)
   3. First Lieutenant Morris B. DePass, Jr., Company I.

G ENERAL FENG'S defection demoralized the Chihli forces, who were then smashed in a series of engagements between the cities of Shanhaikwan and Tangshan in late October. Wu withdrew to Tientsin, collected what remained of his best divisions, and left North China by ship from Taku. As both the defeated and the victorious troops converged on Tientsin, the small foreign military contingents stood guard to keep the armed Chinese soldiers out of the Concession area without provoking a fight. By the second week of November, fighting had largely given way to negotiations among the victorious factions. ★

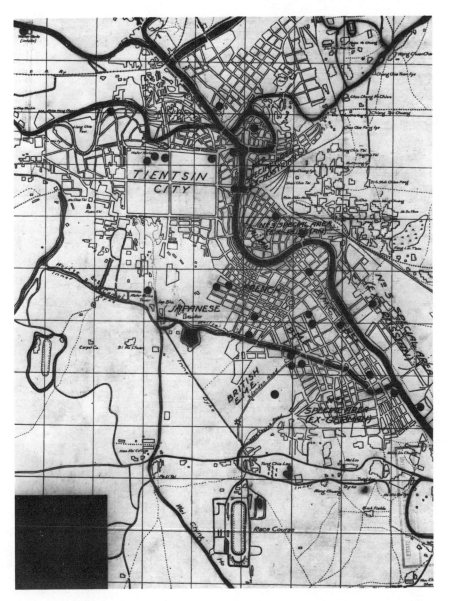

Map of Tientsin (1927) showing waterworks and power and fire stations.

FROM BRIGADIER GENERAL WILLIAM D. CONNOR   November 22, 1924
                                                          Tientsin, China

Commendation.

1. I desire to express to you my gratification at the prompt and efficient manner in which you took the necessary measures to meet the varied and changing situations confronting your Command during these past six weeks of Chinese Civil War.

2. The handling of your Command was especially commendable in that you had but recently arrived at this station and had had only a short time in which to familiarize yourself with the local plans and problems, which, by their peculiar nature, required unusual tact, patience, and foresight in bringing about their successful solution.

NA/201 File

TO JOHN C. HUGHES[1]   January 2, 1925
                                                          Tientsin, China

My dear Johnnie: The morning before Xmas I had all the officers assembled for some purpose, when a cablegram was handed to me. You gave me quite a thrill with your Xmas message and I can not begin to tell you how much Mrs. Marshall and I appreciated it and especially, your thinking to send it. You know, when one is well on the other side of the Earth, evidence that friends continue to remember them evokes a great impression.

I have been exceptionally busy since my arrival. The first two months we were engaged in a modified form of field service,—outposts, patrols, detachments guarding bridges, r r shops, &c. Two of my companies were in the midst of heavy fighting and many of the officers carried out their missions guarding bridges, putting thru trains &c., with guns or knives pointed at their stomachs. Nevertheless we got thru without untoward event and I snaffled a nice letter of commendation out of the affair which is worth my three years in China. More than 100,000 Chinese troops passed thru Tientsin, at least half of them pausing here for a day, week or longer. Equipment very modern. Discipline fair in one army and rigid in the victorious. We disarmed and collected hundreds of the disorganized defeated force.

Write to me some time of things American and New Yorky. Especially of Mrs. Hughes and yourself. With warmest regards to both of you.   Faithfully yrs,

G. C. Marshall, Jr.

GCMRL/J. C. Hughes Papers; H

1. Formerly one of General Pershing's aides, Hughes had resigned from the army, after returning with Pershing and his staff to the United States in 1919, and had become a business executive in New York City.

To Lieutenant Colonel Hjalmer Erickson[1]   January 29, 1925
                                                     Tientsin, China

. . . I was very lucky in arriving here just one week before the Civil War broke out in North China. Before I had learned my way about town and around the military compound, we were involved in meeting constantly changing situations growing out of the Chinese factional war. My daily morning ride for exercise I had always taken in Washington, was here converted to the inspection of a four mile outpost line which we established three miles south of the compound, also in patrolling a little for my own information. Detachments of the regiment along the railroad had some very exciting moments during the "pursuit-retreat-route" stage or phase of the campaign. We disarmed and collected hundreds of the defeated soldiers on our outpost line.

In all, more than 100,000 soldiers passed through Tientsin north or south, by rail, marching and on the Pei Ho in 3,000 ton steamers. Most of these paused here for from a day to a week. The retreating Wu P'ei-fu forces largely disintegrated in this immediate vicinity and for a time constituted our most serious problem.

You ask me some questions about equipment, marching, etc. Almost all your questions are answered in detail in the reports of the several American officers, language students, attaches or detached officers from this regiment, who were observers, which should be on file in the War Department G-2 office. Nevertheless, I will try and give you some rough details.

Discipline and tactical knowledge—estimated by one of our regimental officers who saw fighting two years ago and recently, as 100% improvement over two years ago in Wu P'ei-fu troops. Manchurian forces much higher discipline and better instruction than China proper forces.

Equipment (i.e. arms and ordnance materiel)—Most modern, including signal equipment. Hospitalization and field surgery, etc., considerably behind other matters.

Fighting power—Seems to depend mostly on leadership and ability to secure pay for troops. Men at times seem quite indifferent to fire, even shell fire. Leadership is evidently improving a great deal each year. Several divisions, picked troops, have given such unmistakable evidences of their superiority that all leaders, consciously or unconsciously strive for same standard. A strong man combining the qualities of statesman, politician and military chief, can build up an army in China that would make foreign influence an extremely difficult, if not perilous affair inland. (I am considering only the "fighting power" element.)

Marching is apparently a strong point of these troops—they are reported to have covered long distances, about 35 miles in one case, *I believe, as a division* in one day. If so, that's most unusual.

Transportation—Chinese carts of two to three mules or ponies—about three or four to a company of 150 men—mostly carrying ammunition. As they seize any carts they desire, it is impossible to give exact figures. Some had many, some had but few.

Railroads—they misuse terribly. Here is apparently their greatest technical weakness. They overload trains with men, pony cars and supplies. They will sometimes put double the normal number of cars in one train and add one or two engines. Once troops get a train, they will seldom release it if they can avoid it—apparently to have it handy for the return trip.

Like our generals with motor cars, each Chinese general endeavors to rank for a special train of heavy pullmans and a diner. He will object to switching his train of cars off the main line track, even tho he intends to remain for hours or even a day at a point. All troop commanders terrorize the railroad employees and therefore disorganize traffic, usually completely blocking it. In one serious situation we had to deal with near Tientsin, about 15 or 20 long, overloaded trains were blocked on a double track main line, all headed the same way, water and coal exhausted in locomotives and many fire boxes burned out.

Organization—The following is the approximate organization of some of Wu P'ei-fu's divisions:

> 4 Infantry regts. (2 brigades) of three bns. each.
>> Bns. of four rifle companies of about 150 men.
> 1 or 2 M. G. companies.
> Arty.—1 btry. of howitzers
>> 2 btrys. of 75's $\big\}$ or the reverse
>> 1 btry. of Mountain guns
> 1 co. trench mortars, sometimes with 1 pdrs.
> Signal detachment, fairly well equipped.
> 1 squadron of 4 troops of cavalry—ponies.

These details of organization you can get accurately from formal reports.

Impedimenta—They have a decided advantage over us in simplicity and lightness. Canvas watering troughs; folding fire can with two nested bowls for entire company cooking outfit. Ration, the ideal so far as economy of space, simplicity of preparation, cheapness, etc., are concerned. A Chinese soldier will go farther on a dough ball than an American soldier on a full ration and his Y.M.C.A. or Red Cross "hot chocolate" et ceteras.

Trench mortars—The Manchurian troops had specialized in use of these, due to the influence of an Englishman named Sutton—now a general in Chang Tso-lin's army. (Incidentally the day Sutton arrived in Tientsin with Chang Tso-lin and his victorious army, he, Sutton, received word that he had won the Shanghai Race Meet Grand Sweep $240,000 net—all for a $10.00 ticket.) . . .

USAMHI/Library

1. Erickson had retired in October, 1923, as a result of disability in the line of duty. This version of Marshall's letter is from the United States Army Military History Institute Library where it is catalogued as "Notes on Chinese Troops and Equipment. Extracts from letter, Colonel George Marshall to Colonel Erickson, dates Tientsin, China, January 29, 1925."

To General John J. Pershing   January 30, 1925
                                               Tientsin, China

Dear General: Knowing how little time you have at your own disposal, particularly between a return from Europe and departure for a long voyage to So. America,[1] I appreciated tremendously your long letter of November 18th with an account of your arrangements in the War Department and your plans. I was glad to have Warren's address and I wrote him something of what was going on in China that I thought might interest him.

I grow more and more satisfied with service in China. The officers of the regiment rate unusually high—as do their wives—and the training and school work is very interesting. They do a tremendous amount of athletics—soccer, rugby and American foot ball, basket and base ball, ice hockey, field sports, boxing and wrestling, &c. Most of the officers excell in one or more sports and several are outstanding stars. Just now we get a great deal of exercise and amusement out of our ice rink. They had not taken up skating for several years, so I got a big covered rink built, electric lights installed, warmed dressing rooms and a band room included, and we have fine sport. Three evenings a week we have music for the skating. Occasionally we have ice carnivals or ice athletic sports.

The war situation quieted down the latter part of November, but while it lasted we had very interesting work, which we really utilized as a training affair and polished up on all the details.

Today is "pay day" and we are up against the problem of cheap liquor and cheaper women,—Chinese, Japanese, Russian and Korean. I am relearning much about the practical side of handling men, but it seems much the same old problem. It is in administration that I find the greatest changes,—also in the thoroughness of the training.

With only five months of experience to judge from, I am more and more firmly of the opinion I held in the War Department, that our equipment, administrative proceedure and training requirements are all too complicated for anything but a purely professional army. I find the officers are highly developed in the technical handling or functioning of weapons, in target practice, in bayonet combat and in the special and intricate details of paper work or administration generally, *but* that when it comes to simple tactical problems, the actual details of troop leading, they all fall far below the standards they set in other matters. I suppose this is due to the fact that the application of the principles of troop leading and tactics is largely a matter of judgement, therefore the War Department, thru its inspectors and overseers, is more exacting about those questions which are matters of fact and can be determined in figures or percentages—or in matters of administration.

I have seen several references in local papers to your tour of South America. You must have had a splendid series of welcomes and a very interesting trip.

Quek and Peter, no doubt had a fine time. I am sorry to hear that the latter intends to resign.[2]

I will be interested to hear how much work you have done on your book. Probably not much while traveling. But in Europe you will get down again to hard work.

I am coming along well in my Chinese. So far they only have prepared 75 of what they call lessons. I have reached No. 60, tho I started almost a year behind those who have just arrived at 75. Evidently my Chinese will be much better than my French.

I repeat again, how very much I appreciated your two letters.[3] Please don't forget me when ever you feel in the mood to dictate.   Affectionately yours,

G. C. Marshall, Jr.

LC/J. J. Pershing Papers (General Correspondence); H

1. Pershing had been in Europe during October and November, 1924. When the general returned to the United States, President Coolidge asked him to make a tour of Latin America, beginning with the celebration of the Battle of Ayacucho (December 9, 1824) in Lima, Peru. Pershing's party traveled aboard the battleship U.S.S. *Utah.* They returned to the United States in mid-March, 1925.

2. Pershing's former aides, Colonel John G. ("Quek") Quekemeyer and Major Edward R. ("Peter") Bowditch, Jr., had rejoined the general for the Latin American trip.

3. Pershing's letters of October 2 and November 18, 1924, are in LC/J. J. Pershing Papers (General Correspondence).

TO GENERAL JOHN J. PERSHING   March 17, 1925
                                                               Tientsin, China

My dear General: We were much concerned to read in the wireless news that you had been ill in Cuba. However, I am hoping it was merely some mild stomach trouble brought on by too many banquets.[1] Since the first press notice we have read that you had recovered and were again attending official functions. Juding from the trips I have taken with you, I imagine your recent tour was the most strenuous of your experience.

Things go on here without any special excitements, tho it looks as tho there might be trouble again this summer. But out here you can rarely judge by surface or apparent conditions. The real scheming is entirely beneath the surface; apparent foes are intriguing friends, and friends are doubtful propositions. So far as I can judge, the various provinces run almost independent of Pekin and all government is nothing more than martial law. They permit the courts or officials to function or they ignore them and take arbitrary action just as they, meaning the momentarily "top" men, deem best for their purpose. Nothing is safe from seizure or confiscation. Personal liberty is always in jeopardy.

I think I made a wise decision in selecting China for station as there appear to be more prospects for interesting events here than elsewhere. I have done my best to perfect myself in Chinese and last week caught up with the first class to start Chinese instruction in February, 1924. At my present rate I should be well ahead of them in another month. Yesterday, while conducting a summary court trial, I drew a Chinese witness who could not speak or understand English. Rather than hold over the case until an interpreter could be secured, I took his testimony in Chinese and did not have very much trouble in handling him. If any one had told me last summer that I would soon be able to grunt and whine intelligible Chinese I would have ridiculed the idea.

We are now having interesting little maneuvers based on our local defense plan. I have steared clear of "Red" and "Blue" states and all circumstances and situations not probable in any difficulties out here.[2]

With affectionate regards from Mrs. Marshall and myself,   Faithfully yours,

G. C. Marshall, Jr.

LC/J. J. Pershing Papers (General Correspondence); H

1. In a letter dated May 29, 1925, Pershing told Marshall that he had had "a very bad case of amoebic dysentery." (LC/J. J. Pershing Papers [General Correspondence].)

2. It was common United States Army practice for the opposing forces in war games and maneuvers to be designated by colors. For example, see the Brown Force versus White Force maneuver in the Philippine Islands in January, 1914, above.

To General John J. Pershing   April 22, 1925
                                              Tientsin, China

My dear General: I had a letter from Bowditch last week, written on the Utah telling me something of the details of your South American tour. Your trip must have been a wonderful experience, both from the sight seeing point of view and the wonderful ovation accorded you.[1]

We are receiving very contorted reports of General Dawes' affairs, particularly with regard to his absence on the day of the Warren confirmation vote.[2] I would like to hear his side. Incidentally, I noticed yesterday that Pure Oil was up to thirty-nine. Mr. Stettinius fortunately, has held on to two hundred shares of my stock, and still more fortunately, he sold for me some other stock that had gone from forty-one to eighty,—sold it at the last figure and immediately thereafter it dropped to seventy-one. I am not rich, but at least I am not scared to death.[3]

This morning we completed the first examination attempted in the Chinese language school and I was much gratified to learn that I came out in the first section, composed of the nine students most advanced of those who started in February, 1924. In about three more months I will be ready for a Chinese war. As it is now, I can discuss treaty rights and related subjects with a fair degree of fluency. Last night my Chinese teacher arrived at the house looking very badly, and said that he was too sick to give me a lesson and had only come out because he was on his way to see a Chinese doctor. It was apparent to me that he had the beginning of a case of grippe—severe headache, aching bones and chills. Somewhat against his will, I made him sit down, took his pulse and then gave him the usual pills and capsules, finishing the treatment with an over-dose of castor oil. He seemed delighted to get out of the house, but this morning reported to me that I was a wonderful doctor, *but,* "Please what was in that last drink you gave me, I had a very bad night and I am surprised I feel so well this morning."

I rather expect to learn soon that you have gone to France, and I hope you are able to get down to work on your memoirs. Roger Scaife and General Carter wrote me that General Bullard and General Liggett were both publishing books. Am curious to see what they are like.

With warm regards to your sisters when you see them, believe me, always, Faithfully yours,

G. C. Marshall, Jr.

LC/J. J. Pershing Papers (General Correspondence)

1. Pershing replied: "I think that from the standpoint of international relations it was very beneficial. Without exception the people in the various capitals in South America and other places were most cordial and oftentimes very enthusiastic in their reception to our party." (Pershing to Marshall, May 29, 1925, LC/J. J. Pershing Papers [General Correspondence].)

2. Newly inaugurated Vice-President Charles G. Dawes's sharply critical public statements on certain Senate rules, particularly those permissive of filibustering, had earned him considerable criticism from some senators. (See Dawes, *Notes as Vice President, 1928–1929* [Boston: Little, Brown, 1935], pp. 54–71.)

"My own private opinion," Pershing observed, "is that he has set up a straw man to knock down principally for the purpose of getting himself talked about, and to have an excuse to travel around the country carrying his fight into various states where senators are to be re-elected. He seems not to discriminate between Republican and Democratic senators and as the Republicans' chances for retaining control of the Senate are very slim, Dawes is getting himself into quite a little bit of hot water with the party on this account. However, it is amusing to stand on the side lines and see these people play politics." (Pershing to Marshall, May 29, 1925, LC/J. J. Pershing Papers [General Correspondence].)

On March 10 the Senate had defeated, 40 to 40, the nomination by President Coolidge of C. B. Warren to be attorney general. Dawes arrived in the Senate chamber too late to cast the deciding vote in Warren's favor. Coolidge attempted to raise the point of separation of legislative and executive branch powers, but Warren was rejected again on March 16.

3. On Marshall's Pure Oil stock, see above, pp. 207–8.

To Major General John L. Hines   June 6, 1925
Tientsin, China

My dear General: The entire family was very grateful for your long newsy letter, and all of us were delighted that you had gotten back in good shape again. I suppose you had just reached Washington after your Hawaiian trip; I am sorry you could not have continued westward as far as China, for I think we have more of interest out here at present than you could have found in Hawaii. As a matter of fact, during the last few days a serious anti-foreign sentiment has developed due to the Shanghai student movement and its consequences. To a certain extent, it matters little what the justice or injustice of the affair happens to be. The fact is, that regardless of the merits of the case, the Shanghai student riot has caused a widespread and, as a rule, unreasoning anti-foreign feeling to develop. I suppose it will die down but it must be accepted as a forerunner of definite demands by China for the removal or at least modification of many provisions of the present treaties.[1]

There would be absolute justice in these demands of the Chinese, if they had any form of stable government to guarantee the fulfillment of their obligations under more normal treaty relations. But, unfortunately, there is neither a central nor a stable government; there are merely strong men, or clever men, temporarily acting virtually as dictators. If there was a single outstanding individual who was, throughout China, accepted or feared as a dictator, the situation would be vastly improved. But at present, no one seems to know just who is on top of the heap, Chang Tso-lin, or the present president, or the Christian General, Feng. It appears as if the first named would soon out-maneuver the others, but it is probable the course of these maneuvers will involve heavy fighting in the fall or next spring. I know all this is probably of small interest to you, but it makes life very interesting for us out here.

I have finally trained a Mongolian pony up into a delightful riding animal and do eight to twelve miles every morning, and at least one mile at top speed on the race course. Sundays, of course, I get in twenty or twenty-five miles, so it is much like our riding program at Myer. The past month, tennis has occupied my attention in the late afternoon. The American Tennis Club is convenient and delightfully sociable.

King is probably with you now,[2] and I suppose Mrs. King and the children are delighted to be in Washington, but I imagine he would have preferred command of a post, aside from the personal pleasure of association with you. He certainly made a delightful impression on everyone out here. I found every officer filled with loyal admiration for him.

I am more and more pleased with my choice of station and duty. It suits me perfectly, and the most disagreeable duty here is preferable to desk duty. Of course, I keenly miss the daily association with General Pershing, but I am happy in having a rest from travel, and in doing duty with troops. I am getting to be quite a Chinaman now and will have completed the two and one-half year course by the middle of the coming August.

Give my love to Mrs. Hines. Believe me always,[3]   Faithfully yours,

G. C. Marshall, Jr.

LC/J. L. Hines Papers

1. Long-festering labor unrest in Shanghai culminated in a massive demonstration on May 30, 1925. A clash developed between demonstrators and the foreign-controlled police of the International Settlement. Police shot into the crowd, killing several persons and wounding dozens of others. This shooting was called the May Thirtieth Incident or the Nanking Road Massacre. The incident provoked strikes and boycotts of foreign goods, particularly in central and south China.

2. Campbell King commanded the Fifteenth Infantry between April 12, 1923, and July 23, 1924. On this latter date he was commissioned a brigadier general and assigned to the

Philippine Department. In May, 1925, he returned to the United States to assume the position of assistant chief of staff, G-1.

3. The typed version had "honestly" instead of "always." Marshall scratched out the former word, inserted an asterisk and wrote: "My clerk evidently doubts the sincerity of my usual endings."

To Major General John L. Hines   June 25, 1925
                                                              Tientsin, China

Dear General: I am deliberately stepping out of prescribed channels to bring a matter to your personal attention. Attached is a draft of a paragraph prepared by me for the annual Post Report. Please read it through and believe that I have deliberately understated the case.

The greatest change or shock I experienced on returning to troops, was in the post war method of administering justice. During the months I commanded the Post and Regiment, I continued unaware of what these changes really meant, but since I have investigated and listened to battalion commanders investigate numberless cases, and since I have been President of the one General Courts-Martial, of all Special Courts-Martials and also Summary Court Officer, my understanding of the situation has completely changed.

In brief, Ansell has imposed a harmful system on the Army.[1] Unfortunately, practically all of our Judge Advocates are men without troop duty experience, and whose point of view is not at all that of a soldier. Also, none of the line officers who have commanded regiments and higher units since 1920 can appreciate the vicious phases of the present system. Only by sitting in with it can one understand.

The officers out here work harder than any other group with troops I have ever seen, yet we can only with difficulty find time for brief periods of training or schools where assemblies in large groups are desirable. The administrative work is also a heavy handicap on training, but I have not yet acquired a sufficiently detailed knowledge of its various phases to express a sound opinion in the matter.

But as to the system of administering of justice—we are deliberately squelching the soldierly spirit and developing a tribe of legal quibblers, and both at the expense of troop training. It is very depressing.

Pardon my bothering you in this way, but my purpose is impersonal and a desire to serve.   Faithfully yours,

                                                              G. C. Marshall, Jr.

[Inclosure]
DRAFT COPY[2]

Courts-Martial:
Including the Sub-Post of Tongshan and the rifle camp at Nan Ta Ssu, the following trials were held (to June 20, 1925):

	Convicted	Acquitted	Total
General Courts-Martial	14*	0	14
Special Courts-Martial	54	3	57
Summary Courts-Martial	181	9	190

In this connection it is deemed important to comment on the present methods of administering justice in the army. Supposedly for the fuller protection of the rights of the accused, an elaborate system of preliminary investigations is required, and in the trial of a case, a complicated procedure is followed and a rather strict adherence to technical rules of evidence is enforced. It is believed that, in general, the changes in method imposed since 1918 react to the disadvantage of the military establishment and, in certain particulars, to a material extent.

The present system seriously interferes with the major business or problem of preparing the troops for field service (discipline, morale, schools, garrison and field training, all included). An honest compliance with regulations governing preliminary investigations absorbs so heavy a percentage of the time of the field officers of a command, that they are prevented from exercising that supervision or control over troop training and schools of instruction, which is their normal function; the presence of the witnesses at these investigations for the period required in order to reduce their evidence to a concise written statement, is also prejudicial to troop training; and the cumbersome procedure of a general court-martial absorbs the time of what appears to be too large a number of officers for too long a period, without advantage to the administration of justice.

A very conservative estimate of the average number of officer and man hours absorbed by investigations, court procedure, etc., for each separate case is as follows:

	Officer hours	Man hours
General Courts-Martial	65*	30
Special Courts-Martial	23	20
Summary Courts-Martial	4	8

Based on the foregoing estimate, the courts-martial proceedings of this small command for the preceding twelve months occupied 2981 officer hours and 3080 man hours. Assuming an undesirable enlisted man is eliminated by dishonorable discharge, following four summary court and one special courts-martial conviction, the total of officer and man hours lost from purely military duties are estimated as 99 officer hours and 75 man hours. In other words, three or four consistent offenders in a regiment can have an important and unfortunate effect on the training of that regiment, especially when it is remembered that lack of thoroughness in purely military instruction is often passed over because not detected, while mistakes or omissions of routine in administering justice are promptly dealt with in a disciplinary way.

From the view point of the accused, it is believed that the present involved procedure in special and, particularly in general courts-martial, either reacts to his disadvantage through the unavoidable effect on the court of monotonous repetitions of what soon become meaningless formalities, or to the advantage of the accused when technical objections and the morale effect of purely technical rulings by higher authority invariably cause a few members of a court to turn away from the clearly apparent facts and allow the accused to find protection under some meticulous application of American rules of evidence for criminal law procedure, which are now the subject of increasingly unfavorable public opinion.

Court-Martial practice and procedure in the Regular Establishment prior to 1918, it is believed, brought out the facts, and justice was administered accordingly. Under the present system, the real issue is frequently befogged in the ineffective form of ceremony and quibbling over minutia, while the training of the troops suffers materially. The purpose of the peace time army is being seriously interfered with by the methods now imposed for performing the incidental obligation of administering justice to individuals.

It is recommended that the present system of investigating charges be simplified and left more to the discretion of the convening authority; that the formalities of court procedure and record be simplified; and that the present policy of insistence upon extreme technical observance of the rules of evidence be moderated more in accord with past military court procedure.

LC/J. L. Hines Papers

1. Brigadier General Samuel T. Ansell (U.S.M.A., 1899) had been acting army judge advocate general during 1917–18. He inaugurated a movement resulting in the reformation of the army court-martial system and the adoption of liberalized articles of war. The changes were enacted into law in chapter two of the army reorganization act of June 4, 1920. The basic changes from the previous (1917) code are listed on pp. viii–x of U.S., War Department, Office of the Judge Advocate General, *A Manual for Courts-Martial* (Washington, D.C.: Government Printing Office, 1920). In particular, the new Articles of War, 70, made the preliminary investigation of charges more strict than previously, and a requirement was added that the accused could have full opportunity to cross-examine witnesses at the preliminary examination.

2. Marshall added the asterisks in the tables and a handwritten note at the top of the inclosure: "I have ignored on[e] G.C.M. [General Court-Martial] which took up over 650 officer hours."

To John C. Hughes   July 18, 1925
                                                                   Tientsin, China

My dear Johnnie: A considerable amount of water has gone under the bridge since your Xmas cable surprised me. Out here we blow hot and cold with little pause between currents. One day all is lovely and we pursue a most attractive social round, the next we are in a turmoil of threatening anti-foreign agitations of the Chinese. It all serves to make the time fly and to keep us interested in preparing the troops for possible eventualities. I am doing a great deal of riding and tennis this summer. My ponies have turned out beautifully. Every morning at 6 o'clock several of us meet near my house, ride 3 miles across country to the race Club (which, by the way is really a magnificent establishment, the most pretentious, except Long Champs, I have seen) and have a mile or mile and a half contest on the track, then some casual trot and walk for a bit and home again 3 miles to bath and breakfast. I am becoming a fairly good Jockey, only my weight puts me out of the normal racing class. Some days we ride entirely across country, and there are lots of ditches and mud dikes for excitement.

Evenings at six comes tennis at the American Club, a very sociable and pleasant gathering place. We play until eight, dining normally at eight thirty.

You would envy me my boy. He is perfect as a valet, presses and cleans beautifully, has everything arranged to save me every motion and anticipates every desire. While he can speak English I confine myself, for practice, to Chinese in talking to him. Now I can carry on a casual conversation in Chinese with far, far less difficulty than I ever could manage in French. And I can understand even the wranglings and squabbles of the coolies and rickshaw men.

I have spent one very delightful period at our Camp on the beach 160 miles from here where we have our target range. Bathing, riding and shooting occupies the time. Most of the women spend the entire summer there. I go again tomorrow for ten days to supervise the field firing exercises.

Mrs. Marshall and her mother have grown very fond of China. We have a comfortable, modern house, a good chauffeur and excellent house servants.

Please remember me to Mrs. Hughes, and believe me,   Faithfully yours

G. C. Marshall, Jr.

GCMRL/J. C. Hughes Papers; H

TO GENERAL JOHN J. PERSHING   October 30, 1925
                                                               Tientsin, China

Dear General: Your letter of July 15th reached me after a long delay somewhere en route, probably here in China. I am very sorry to have seemed so dilatory in replying.

Your desires regarding Martin Egan and myself handling your Memoirs and Adamson and myself supervising the disposition of certain official papers and manuscripts, will be followed out by me to the letter. I am much gratified to feel that you have such confidence in my judgement and should these tasks ever fall to me I will give to them my best effort.[1]

It seems absurd to talk of such an eventuality, as I look to you to far outdistance Senator Warren in continuing physical activity and energy,[2] provided you do not permit the Washington official social whirl to demand of your time to the exclusion of outdoor relaxation.

I have seen nothing in the papers recently about Arica affairs, so I suppose matters are moving along without undue violence.[3] I certainly hope so.

Out here the pot boils over and appears to grow daily more involved. An American gun boat with Marines is due here today to reinforce our garrison for the defense of the Tientsin concessions and this possible port of entry. No one, official Pekin or elsewhere, knows just what the present situation is leading to. There are three military leaders now in the field and their possible alignment with or against each other is continuing to be a matter of conjecture. Fighting has started, south of this province, but reports are too conflicting to judge of results.[4]

Recently I spent a week in Pekin with Mrs. Marshall. We dined with the Minister & Mrs MacMurray and young Robert Bacon and his wife.[5] The latter couple we dined with again the one night they were in Tientsin.

During dinner two evenings ago a telephone message from Doctor Heiser (Ex Philippine Health official) arrived.[6] I picked him up at the hotel and he spent the evening with us, boarding his boat for Shanghai at midnight. He is on a trip around the world, due to reach New York next June, and now en route for Manila. We had a very pleasant evening over recollections of Naushon Island days—particularly the boat race—, and he gave me news of Governor Forbes, Bowditch and many others.

My Chinese has progressed far beyond my knowledge of French or Spanish, and is very useful. It will be a great asset to me if real trouble develops out here.

Mrs. Marshall and Mrs. Coles are both well, and happy in enjoyment of China.

With affectionate regards, believe me always,   Faithfully yours,

G. C. Marshall, Jr.

My best to Quek.

LC/J. J. Pershing Papers (General Correspondence); H

1. To Marshall and Egan, Pershing left "the completion and handling of my memoirs and the disposition of the funds, of course under the executor." He directed that Marshall and Adamson "go through my files and destroy any worthless correspondence, preserving the rest to be turned over to Warren, and handling anything that might be considered worthy of publication." (Pershing to Marshall, July 15, 1925, LC/J. J. Pershing Papers [General Correspondence].)

Martin Egan, a former war correspondent in the Philippine Insurrection and later editor of the *Manila Times* (1908–13), had been a civilian aide to Pershing in 1918. Since 1914, Egan had been a member of the staff of J. P. Morgan and Company of New York.

2. Senator Francis E. Warren, Pershing's father-in-law, was eighty-one years old. In 1924 he had been reelected to the United States Senate seat from Wyoming he had held since 1890.

3. In mid-July, Pershing had sailed for South America to serve on the commission attempting to resolve a dispute festering since 1883 between Chile and Peru over ownership of the provinces of Tacna and Arica. Pershing's mission failed, and he returned to the United States in late February, 1926.

4. Sun Ch'uan-fang, tuchun of Chekiang province and formerly an ally of Wu P'ei-fu, marched his troops into Shanghai on October 17 and began moving northward toward Shantung. Feng and Chang, meanwhile, maneuvered for position in Jehol and Chihli.

5. John Van A. MacMurray, an expert on Far Eastern affairs and formerly an assistant secretary of state, became United States minister to China on April 9, 1925. Robert L. Bacon,

at this time a Republican congressman from the First District of New York and a Reserve colonel in the Field Artillery, was the son of Robert Bacon, former ambassador to France (1909–12) and member of General Pershing's staff at Chaumont.

6. Victor G. Heiser had been chief quarantine officer and director of health in the Philippines, 1903–15. At this time he was a director of the Rockefeller Foundation's International Health Board.

To Major General John L. Hines   December 23, 1925
                                                  Tientsin, China

My dear General: Your letter, which came a long time back, was tremendously appreciated by Mrs. Marshall and myself. But I purposely did not acknowledge earlier because I know something of the volume of your correspondence, and did not wish to become a portion of that burden. However, this is a Xmas letter to recall that historic and cheerful period of Gondrecourt and Demange-aux-eaux. That seems a long time ago, which it was; but, if the steam heat and ladies of the family were eliminated, today in China is not so very different from that earlier period. The daily sound of the guns booming is the same and has continued for two weeks;[1] the exciting rumors are of the same nature; the young officers are pulling on the leash in the same old way to get the detail for the International Train or for patrols going in the apparent direction of trouble; even the struggle to procure turkeys for the Christmas dinner is the same. A wireless has just been despatched to our isolated company at Tongshan, 85 miles away, that with the turning back of the International Train last night before it reached Taku or Tongku, under threat of bombardment, the hope of sending them their Xmas turkeys has gone glimmering, and the local purchase of chickens is authorized.

My enjoyment of service out here grows with each month. The work is interesting, the conditions exciting and the time flies. Mrs. Coles and Mrs. Marshall also like it, especially the shopping.

Some day will you do a little favor for me? When you are riding near that farm house where all the orphan kids hold out,[2] will you stop long enough to give that very kindly and motherly woman my regards—and any of the children who were there in my time. They were a nice, wholesome lot and I would like them to feel that I had not forgotten their existence.

With my affectionate regards to Mrs. Hines and you,   Faithfully yours,

G. C. Marshall, Jr.

LC/J. L. Hines Papers; H

1. General Feng had made an agreement with one of Chang's disaffected subordinates, Kuo Sung-ling, who commanded some of the Fengtien army's best troops. On November 27, Kuo and Feng declared war on Chang. Kuo moved toward Mukden, but was defeated and executed on December 23. Feng attacked the Fengtien garrison at Tientsin.

2. Presumably, Marshall was referring to a house in the Fort Myer, Virginia, area.

TO BRIGADIER GENERAL JOHN MCA. PALMER   December 31, 1925
Tientsin, China

My dear Old John: Your letter of two days ago brought me the first news of your prospective retirement, and while I think it decidedly the wise thing to do, it makes me very sad to feel that you and I are not to serve together again. I never expect to enjoy another relationship like ours—official and personal; but while the chance of a renewal of the former is gone, I purpose, with your consent, to look forward to much more of the latter in the future.

I am assuming that all you need to put you back in good shape is a philosophic calm, much fishing and proper contemplation of the duties and responsibilities of a grand-father. What I am particularly interested to know, is where Mrs. Palmer and you propose to locate. I hope in Washington.

Time out here has flown of late, with the sounds of battle in our ears for more than a week and the final confusion incident to the capture of Tientsin by the Peoples Army on Xmas day.[1] Early that morning on the great plain seven miles south of the ex German Concession, I witnessed a tragic sight. Galloping across country with three mounted men, I encountered hundreds of women and children fleeing from the villages further south, which had been pillaged and ravaged during the night by the retreating soldiery of Li Ching Lin.

The usual refugee who has congested the roads leading into the foreign lines during the past three weeks, is a sad spectacle, but the donkies, carts and household belongings are usually with him. But these little groups had nothing. The thermometer was only a few degrees above zero, the wind keen and piercing and the ground hard with frost. Overhead the sky was a brilliant blue and the sun shone; but to those pathetic little groups it must have been a black, calamatous day. Their heavy clothing was gone, shoes often missing, babies crying. None would look at me or listen to my attempts at reassurance. They resembled animals hunted to exhaustion, and paralyzed by fear. And this was Xmas morning in the Year of our Lord 1925!

The long camel trains of artillery and supplies, which accompanied the troops from outer Mongolia, and the troops of cavalry on shaggy Mongolian ponies, made very picturesque sights. We had many difficult contacts with the victors, but came through without precipitating a crisis. I had command of the regiment during this period, as Naylor was sick, so it gave me an interesting problem until two days ago. I did about 25 miles a day on my poney, making early morning and late evening surveys of the daily situations. It was good fun and instructive.

I heard from Captain Jones that he had been unable to locate the Japanese plates and had left the money with the Q. M. at Nagasaki for him to get them. This, the latter was unable to do, so he returned the money to Jones at Benning, and he advises me that he sent it on to you.

Today is my 45th birthday. I'm no longer of the "Young Turk" party. Isn't that sad after the bombast and assurance of our Leavenworth days of Army reformation. With every wish for your contentment, health and happiness in the New Year and my love to Mrs. Palmer and you,   Affectionately,

Marshall

LC/J. McA. Palmer Papers; H

1. Feng Yu-hsiang labeled his army the Kuominchun, or National People's Army. His army defeated the Fengtien garrison under the command of Li Ching-lin.

To General John J. Pershing   March 17, 1926
                                               Tientsin, China

My Dear General: The wireless you were good enough to send me came as a great shock. No one had seemed more vigorous and healthy, more destined for a long life, than poor Quekemeyer. Blessed with a splendid physique, clean and wholesome in his life, it is impossible to grasp the tragedy of his sudden death.[1] A fatal accident, at polo for example, would not have been quite such a shock.

We can only conjecture as to what happened, but I imagine it started with flu and ran on into pneumonia. He probably delayed too long in going to bed! We had a similar case here Xmas week,—a Major Dabney who refused to give up during the serious period of the fighting around Tientsin. I felt very badly in his case, having sent him out with the mounted detachment on Xmas day during an ugly mixup with the victorious Chinese forces. He was sick at the time, but would not admit it.[2]

We feel especially distressed over Quekemeyer's mother. He evidently was always a strong support to her, not to mention his brothers, and his sudden death must have struck her a hard blow. I am writing to her in care of Adamson.

I have been much concerned over the reports of your health, but have reassured myself in the belief that the trouble is but a continuation of your dental tribulations, and will soon be rectified at Walter Reed [Hospital]. But please write, or have Adamson write and tell me the facts. Your long stay at Arica must have been a combination of monotony and heavy strain. I am very glad you are home again.

To go back to Quekemeyer. It is very hard to understand why a man of his type should have been cut off so young, while the many worthless or evilly disposed, are allowed to live; and it seems particularly tragic that the end should have come just as he started on a job that must have been much to his liking. Quekemeyer was a fine fellow in every way. A man of high ideals, clean morally and physically, ambitious, attractive, forcible and capable. You can judge his worth better than any one else; and I know how much you will miss his fine loyalty and intimate companionship.

We are still in a difficult situation out here—patrols, outposts, etc.; and today our gun boat with the British, Japanese, French and Italian left here for Taku to enforce the ultimatum regarding the blocking of the mouth of the river. This is the first definite stand the foreign governments have taken, and their previous "over lookings" may now prove costly.[3]

Colonel Newell recently arrived to take command of the 15th. After a week's observation, he wrote to General Robert Allen that in his thirty-three years of service this was the finest regiment he had ever seen—Army or Marines.[4]

Mrs. Marshall joins me in affectionate regards and the hope that you are again in the best of health, pleasantly occupied and happy.   Faithfully Yours,

G. C. Marshall, Jr.

LC/J. J. Pershing Papers (General Correspondence)

1. John G. Quekemeyer, who recently had been appointed commandant at the United States Military Academy, died at West Point of pneumonia on February 28, 1926. His mother died the next day.

2. Henry H. Dabney died on January 4, 1926.

3. Following his successful capture of Tientsin in December, 1925, Feng Yu-hsiang posted troops at the forts at Taku, which guarded the river access to Tientsin, to defend his flank against Fengtien troops. When the troops were ordered to withdraw, they fired on several foreign vessels, including some Japanese gunboats, in violation of the 1901 Protocol. The foreign powers, making a major issue of the affair, presented President Tuan Ch'i-jui with an ultimatum on March 16, demanding that the government of China stop all preparations for war in the Tientsin-Taku region.

4. Isaac Newell (U.S.M.A., 1896). Major General Robert H. Allen was the chief of Infantry.

To General John J. Pershing   August 25, 1926
Tientsin, China

My dear General: I see by the papers you have been spending the summer in Europe, which I suppose means Paris. There has been no mention in the press of when you might be returning home.

Things go on with me out here much as usual. I really am having a fine time and thoroughly enjoy the life. In ten days I will have completed my first two years in China, and the remaining ten or twelve months will probably fly by. It hardly seems one year since I first came to Tientsin.

The social life here has changed a little since the completion of a Country Club last October. It is sort of an addition to the rich and prosperous Race Club, and has quickly become the focus of almost all social activities. The building is very pretentious (after the style and size of the War College) and is run on a generous scale. They have twelve tennis courts, all croweded each evening, a large and beautifully appointed pool which is usually pretty full from five to eight o'clock each evening, large ball room, out door dancing platform with pavillions, permanent orchestra, tea rooms and terraces, large dining room and a bar as busy as a bee hive. The charges are ridiculously small and, of course, there are swarms of servants at ones beck and call.

We are now doing a great deal of riding in the regiment. We have a mounted detachment of forty on Mongolian ponies, that is a very sporty looking cavalry

A portion of the American Compound (the "Mei-Kuo Ying-P'an" to the Chinese).

Chang Tso-lin pays an official call on Brigadier General William D. Connor, perhaps during the November 11–16, 1924, conference of victors in Tientsin.

Marshall; Eleanor Harding (wife of Major Edwin F.); Major Walter C. Gullion (adjutant general, American Forces in China); Helen McCunniff (wife of Major Dennis E.); and May Tuttle (wife of Captain William B.); at Nan Ta Ssu, 1926.

Captain Frank B. Hayne and Lieutenant Colonel George C. Marshall, Jr., hunting at Nan Ta Ssu, October, 1926.

"Happy" and Marshall at Nan Ta Ssu, 1925.

Marshall on one of the regiment's Mongolian ponies at Nan Ta Ssu.

Major Edwin F. Harding and Colonel Marshall at Tientsin, 1927.

Lily Marshall at the Tientsin Railroad Station, September 20, 1926.

━[P R O G R A M]━

MA TUAN FU

—: PRESENTS :—

THE CHINESE OPERA

IN ONE ACT

"AT THE CUSTOMS"

BOOK WRITTEN BY MA TUAN FU
LYRICS COMPOSED BY MA TUAN FU
MUSIC SNITCHED BY MA TUAN FU

Newell Auditorium
TIENTSIN, :-: :-: :-: CHINA.

MAY 4, 1927

15th Inf. 4-30-27—100.

STILL GOING STRONG

NEWELL'S CHAMPAGNE PUNCH

MAY IT CONTINUE TO HOLD OUT !

THE ACTION

Once upon a time an Army transport named the "THOMAS" sailed from Chinwangtao and landed at San Francisco. On board there were army officers and army wives, especially army wives. These wives were typical of any army transport, — sweet, — beautiful, — precious, — but nevertheless wives under the skin.

The play opens as the above mentioned ocean greyhound leaps across the placid water of the Golden Gate. In the offing you see the Cliff House and in the nearing you behold Alcatraz Island. Every detail of the scene is realistically portrayed in the inimitable Chinese manner. In this connection those of our audience who are unlettered in the mysteries of Chinese Art are advised not to attribute the oriental stoicism of Cro Lien Chang the scene shifter to dumbness, — altogether.

The greyhound moves cautiously up to the transport dock at a slow trot and with one flap of his great tail circles to the right, halts, and folds her wings serenely about him.

The gangplank is lowered and then you see —

CORRAL GABLES

THE EXCLUSIVE RESIDENTIAL DISTRICT OF TIENTSIN EXCLUDED TO HOUSEHOLDERS WITH LESS THAN 10 SMALL CHILDREN.

RELIGIOUS ATMOSPHERE
FASHIONABLE
QUIET
HEALTHFUL

THE POST EXCHANGE

IF WE HAVEN'T GOT WHAT YOU WANT, TRY AND GET IT FROM THE COMMISSARY.

JUST RECEIVED: A FINE LINE OF BULL

"AT THE CUSTOMS"

CAST

LUCILLE, CIVILIAN FRIEND OF FLORENCE - - CRO TAI TAI
DICK, LUCILLE'S HUSBAND - - - - - - - HAV LIEN CHANG
PHIL, LIEUT. U. S. A., FLORENCE'S HUSBAND - LY PAI CHANG
FLORENCE, LIEUT. PHIL'S WIFE, - - - - - PA TAI TAI
[Just back from China]
LIZZIE, FLORENCE'S DAUGHTER, AGE 7 - - HAV TAI TAI
DOROTHY, CAPTAIN DENNY'S WIFE, - - - - LEW TAI TAI
[Also just back from China]
DENNY, CAPTAIN U. S. A. - - - - - - - - LEW YING CHANG
[Just back from China]
DECKHAND - - - - - - - - - - - - - HA YING CHANG
CUSTOMS INSPECTOR - - - - - - - - - TUT LIEN CHANG
QUARANTINE OFFICER - - - - - - - - - PA LIEN CHANG
ROOM BOYS - - - - - - - - - -

MUSICAL NUMBER —— "CHINA".

SUNG BY TUT LIEN CHANG AND HIS CELEBRATED CHORUS OF CHINESE YODLERS.

HA YING CHANG POME FACTORY

WHETHER IT BE AN EPIC OR A LIMERIC,
OURS ARE BEST BY TEST

WE CATER ESPECIALLY TO COCKTAIL PARTIES.

*"What is a home
Without a pome"*
— HA YING CHANG.

HOME OFFICE: TIENTSIN, CHINA,
AGENTS IN EL PASO AND NEW YORK.

Playbill for Marshall's (Ma Tuan Fu's) Fifteenth Infantry Organization Day officers' party skit. Ha Ying Chang was Major Edwin F. Harding; Tut Lien Chang was Captain William B. Tuttle.

292

troop. In addition, the officers own about forty five ponies. I have two. Are polo team is much too good for anything around here. In fact, last year we had three teams in the regiment. When I came here there were only twelve ponies in the corral, so you can see there has been quite a change.

Conditions in China are too confused to admit of a reasonably accurate estimate as to what it is all about. Fighting is continuous, but since March has not been closer to Tientsin on our particular stretch of the railroad, than forty miles north west of Pekin.

I have spent most of the summer at our shooting camp on the ocean, 160 miles north east of here. The bathing here is fine, and the riding in the picturesque country nearby, is delightful. I go back again for the final field firing the first of the week.

I was much surprised to receive a letter from Peter Bowditch telling me of his marriage. I do not know who the lady is, but I suppose it is the same one in whom he was interested in the Islands. His letter was very short and rather sketchy, so I could not tell much about the present status of things.

I hear indirectly, through the Russells, about Governor Forbes' Naushon parties. Recently he had his Philippine friends all there together. I know he has pressed you to attend. I have very delightful recollections of amusing days at Naushon, particularly in September 1919, and also of our month in October at Lake Brandreth that same fall. I think, however, that the most relaxing and amusing time was during our "ship-wreck" week at the Candado-Vanderbilt in San Juan.[1]

So far we have not been able to do much traveling because of the continuous civil war with its following of bandits. But we now have several trips on the cards, to be taken poney back with our mounted detachment. One north to the Eastern Tombs, on through the Royal Hunting Park to [Jehol?], and thence down the Lan River on barges to Lanchow, a station on the railroad 100 miles from here. I am very keen to go and I hope the American Minister does not interpose any objections.

Judging from recent pictures of you in the news papers, you must be in fine trim again, and I imagine your summer in France will have been very beneficial. I certainly hope so.

Mrs. Marshall joins me in affectionate regards,   Faithfully yours,

G. C. Marshall, Jr.

LC/J. J. Pershing Papers (General Correspondence); T

1. On May 10, 1920, the U.S.A.T. *Northern Pacific* ran aground while leaving the harbor at San Juan, Puerto Rico.

TO GENERAL JOHN J. PERSHING   December 26, 1926
                                               Tientsin, China

My dear General: Mrs. Marshall and I were delighted to receive your long letter with the news of what you had been doing this past summer. We get occasional briefs of your movements from the newspapers, but these never cover any but official affairs and, therefore, are not very satisfying. I appreciated your taking the time to write me in some detail of how the world has been going with you.

Life out here goes on much the same each year. We are either just out of near trouble with the Chinese or trouble is hovering near us. At present the Cantonese troops are waging very successful warfare in central China and are threatening Shanghai. Officials in Peking have their wind up pretty badly, fearing the Southern part will leap into control of North China any month, through successes in the field and treachery on the part of leaders in this section. They fear that the Kuomingtang (Southerners) will sweep into power and calmly disregard all treaty stipulations as to concessions and extraterritoriality, in the enthusiasm of conquest and in the belief that the Powers are really unwilling to risk actual fighting over the question.[1]

In anticipation of some such unfortunate outcome, I was sent up to Peking two weeks ago, over the road by auto, to determine the condition of the road and look over the bridges. The country is filled with troops and they establish toll gaits at frequent intervals, and generally conduct themselves in a very high handed manner. It never requires more than a spark to set off an explosion. However, I have learnt that these people are really very simple minded in some ways, and a little polite pleasantry and a touch of Chinese polite formality in expression, smooths the way in most instances. My own vocabulary is now sufficient, about 2500 characters, to deal with any ordinary conversation, so I went through without a serious hitch, except that they held me at the East Gate of Peking for an hour. It was rather cold traveling in an open car, with the thermometer down to ten above and a strong wind blowing.

The situation in China is actually more critical this winter than at any time, so the old fellows tell us, since the Boxer days. Business for foreign firms has gone down the hill steadily the past two years and a number of the smaller American firms have closed up shop and gone home. Most of the American business men I met her in 1924 have given up and returned home.

How the Powers should deal with China is a question almost impossible to answer. There has been so much of wrong doing on both sides, so much of shady transaction between a single power and a single party; there is so much of bitter hatred in the hearts of these people and so much of important business interests involved, that a normal solution can never be found. It will be some form of an evolution, and we can only hope that sufficient tact and wisdom will be displayed by foreigners to avoid violent phases during the trying period that is approaching. And yet it is expecting too much to belief that matters can be readjusted quietly and wisely, with continued public pronouncements by politicians such as Borah and Lloyd George. There may be truth in what they say, but you cannot yell such messages at an excited crowd without the danger of violent and unreasoning outbreaks.[2] We have a good example of the difficulties of the problem, here in

Tientsin. Two editors are daily attacking each other in their respective editorial columns, over the proper metod of meeting each new crisis or question. One is an American, the brother of Fox of the Washington Post, and the other is an Englishmen named Woodhead, to whom Martin Egan gave me a letter of introduction. They are 180 degrees apart in their views. Both are here on the ground and both are Anglo-Saxons and better informed that almost any other men in China. The first trouble is, one hates every thing British and the other hates every thing American. Woodhead talks China but is thinking about Shylock and war debts. Fox reacts in the opposite fashion. The Chinese read and rest assured that the foreign powers will never be able to meet on a common agreed upon ground.

Speaking of war debts, the feeling of these Britishers here, also the Belgians to a more polite degree, is so bitter that intercourse with them is too difficult to be attempted. The British officers and the few higher born or bred compatriots of theirs out here, are sufficiently agreeable, but the common run of business men, who make up the bulk of this rather large foreign community, are so openly rude and offensive, that it pays to avoid them unless one is willing to frankly mix it up with them, which an Army officer on foreign service here hardly dares to do. Fortunately we have such a large Army community and such unusually charming people that we have little or no time for outsiders.

I have run off into a lot of local interests that will bore you, I fear, but there is not much else for one out here to write of. I can only ask questions about things at home, and I do not want to tax you in that manner. By the way, what has happened to Adamson? I have written him, enclosed notes for him in letters to you, etc., but not a word. I always knew he was quiet and reserved, but he seems to have gone completely into the silence so far as I am concerned.

The social life with us is very attractive, frequent tea and dinner dances in the beautiful country club, skating parties, riding breakfasts, numerous home parties, amateur theatricals, indoor squash and tennis,—there is something to do every day if one is so disposed. And the young people are a most attractive crowd, far above the average Army garrison, both intellectually and in personal charm. I have two beautiful Mongolian ponies now, tame as kittens, though it took a long time to win their confidence.

By the way, a few weeks ago a note arrived from Cameron Forbes, written at Miyanoshita in Japan, telling me that he would pass through Tientsin with two nieces. He finally arrived and we had him here at our house. He claimed to be in splendid health, except for a temporary "dust" cold, but I did not fancy is looks at all. For one thing, I think he is seriously overexerting. He told me that every morning on the boat at four o'clock he turned out and ran several miles on the deck, followed by other strenuous exercises. His face shows the strain of just such performances. I know I would not go tearing around at any such rate. I take a large amount of exercise every day, but not such violent exercise as running several miles. Squash tennis is pretty lively, especially when I undertake to beat these young fellows, which I usually do, but it is not prolonged like straight running, and you can pause for a needed breath.

The Governor was enroute to Manila, but he told me he had written to General Wood from the States and again from Japan, and had never received any acknowledgement of either letter. He was much concerned, for I think he rather expected to stay with General Wood at the Malacanan. He plans to be in the Islands six weeks. He has been writing a voluminous treatise on the Philippines, with the assistance of Carpenter, who has evidently been staying with him for a long time. He had a trunk locker filled with the manuscript and his references, and wanted to talk of little else, except his most recent play, produced at Naushon last summer. I had some of our young polo players in for dinner, ostensibly to do their duty by the girls, but I drew the Governor out on his polo set up at Norwood, and they sat at his knee entranced. He was much pleased.

I do not imagine he will be a very popular person in the Islands at this particular period, especially if they get the idea he is writing a book on the question. And certainly he will mention it.[3]

I believe I mentioned in one of my letters that Doctor Heiser (?) of the Rockerfeller Tropical Medecine Foundation passed through Tientsin last year and spent an evening with Mrs. Marshall and myself. In fact he talked to us until two in the morning. I took him to his boat and put him to bed. Reilly, ex Rainbow Division, spent some days with me. He was here representing the Hearst papers, and, incidentally, he was actually on the ground in the field at the most dramatic and exciting episode in last year's revolt against Chang Tso lin.[4] He had the thrill of standing with an artillery commander when he heard a loud rumpus in rear, and turning saw a brigade of cavalry charging down on them, the nearest less than 100 yards distant. This cavalry maneuver turned an advance into an instant route, and Chang captured the rebellious leader with his wife and cut both their heads off immediately.

The gentleman you wrote me the letter of introduction for, never turned up. It is possible that he was discouraged by the difficulties of travel in North China and merely touched at Shanghai. A number have done this. In fact, few tourists have attempted to go to Peking since October 1925.

I see by the press despatches that General Dawes wins a peace prize.[5] Good for him. This will give him fine political capital for his future aspirations, which he undoubtedly has. I will write him my congratulations, but I am always in doubt as to what to say to him. He is too busy reading between the lines.

I had a cable two weeks or more ago from General Ely asking if a detail on the War College faculty would be agreeable to me. This is the sixth time I had been asked since 1919 and I accepted. General Wells had asked me to go to Benning in 1924 so that he could have me made assistant commandant there, but I preferred China. Then he wrote to me a year ago and said he would like to arrange for me to take that detail on my return, but before his letter reached me he had been transferred to the W.D. staff. As Collins has never mentioned the matter since he took control,[6] I decided the "bird in the hand" should be my choice, though I had no thought of going to the War College. Mrs. Marshall, however, is radiant over the idea of a beautiful house at Washington Barracks. I suppose this will mean that I sail on the May 10th transport instead of on the following boat, some time in September. When I return I will have had about eleven years foreign service, and as my contemporaries in the field artillery have three or less, I will be well heeled.

This is a very long letter and a most disconnected one. I hope it does not bore you, but you were always very patient with my monologues. Mrs. Marshall and I would have liked to send you a Xmas rememberance, but we could find no way to avoid your having to pay the duty at your end of the line, and that would make a sorry gift.

We send you are affectionate regards with every good wish for you in happiness and health in the New Year.   Faithfully yours,

Marshall

LC/J. J. Pershing Papers (General Correspondence); T

1. In January, 1926, Wu P'ei-fu and Chang Tso-lin reached an agreement to attack Feng Yu-hsiang's forces. On March 22, Feng withdrew from Tientsin, and over the next month established his armies north of Peking. Although Feng then left for a visit to the Soviet Union, his army continued to fight, and in September allied itself with the rising power of Chiang Kai-shek and the Kuomintang.

The Kuomintang, whose power base was in south China's Kwantung province, had long desired to eliminate the tuchuns and to unify the country with a great Northern Expedition. During the spring of 1926, Chiang consolidated his power over the Kuomintang, and in June his National Revolutionary Army began military operations. By the end of 1926, Chiang's forces were consolidating their control over the lower Yangtze River valley. The American reaction to these events is described in U.S., Department of State, *Papers Relating to the Foreign Relations of the United States, 1926,* 2 vols. (Washington, D.C.: Government Printing Office, 1941), 1: 591–743.

2. Senator William E. Borah, chairman of the Foreign Relations Committee, in a speech on November 16, warned the United States and other countries against any imperialistic or forceful policy toward China. David Lloyd George, former Prime Minister of Great Britain (1916–22), in a speech on December 4, sympathized with the Kuomintang movement in China—insisting that it was not a Communist movement, but a struggle to obtain the fundamental rights of any self-respecting nation—and discouraged British involvement.

3. In 1921, President Harding sent Major General Leonard Wood, who assumed office on October 15 as governor-general of the Islands, and former Governor W. Cameron Forbes to the Philippines to make a survey of conditions. Their report recommended that the United States not grant the Islands independence until the Filipinos had had time to absorb the lessons they had received and to master the governmental powers they already possessed. On July 16, 1926, the Philippine legislature unanimously adopted a resolution declaring the Filipino people's desire for immediate independence. The book Marshall mentions is probably *The Philippine Islands,* 2 vols. (Boston: Houghton Mifflin, 1928).

4. Henry J. Reilly (U.S.M.A., 1904), who had commanded the Forty-second (Rainbow) Division's 149th Field Artillery during the World War, was editor and publisher of the *Army and Navy Journal,* 1921–25; and after August, 1925, he was editorial commentator in China for the Hearst newspaper chain.

5. Charles G. Dawes, acting as a private citizen, headed the committee that submitted the

plan which the Reparations Commission adopted; the plan went into effect in September, 1924. He was awarded—jointly with Sir Austen Chamberlain, British Foreign Secretary—the 1925 Nobel Peace Prize for the "Dawes Plan."

6. Brigadier General Edgar T. Collins, a member of the General Staff between 1920 and 1924, had replaced Briant H. Wells as commandant of the Infantry School at Fort Benning, Georgia.

TO BRIGADIER GENERAL WILLIAM H. COCKE[1]   December 26, 1926
Tientsin, China

My dear General: Your letter of October 13th regarding my detail as commandant, is much appreciated, and I regret very much that the uncertain course of mail coming to China should have involved me in this long delay in acknowledging your thought of me in connection with this detail. I am sorry that it is not possible for me to accept, as I am already placed in the War College faculty. General Ely cabled to find out if the assignment would be agreeable to me, and as I replied in the affirmative, the matter is settled.

Until recently I have had no plans for the past year as to what duty I would go on my return home. Administrative desk jobs have always been my pet abominations, but with so few regiments and so many lieutenant colonels, one has little choice. The head of the Infantry School at Benning wanted me to go there in 1924 as Assistant Commandant, but I was intent on serving with a regiment on foreign service. Later he wrote to me ragarding my detail there on returning home, but before his letter arrived he had been transferred and a new commandant installed in his place. Since then I have heard nothing further about the job. General Ely had asked for me at the War College in 1923 and 24, and now that he has again been good enough to express a desire for my services and I have agreed to go, I would not care to attempt a change, particulary as I am not even a graduate of the War College.

One portion of your letter I do not understand. You expressed a desire for me to get in touch with the situation at the Institute with a view to future possibilities. From this I am compelled to infer, though I may be entirely off the trail, that you contemplate withdrawing as superintendent and had me in mind as a possible successor. It would be a tragedy for the Institute to have you drop the reins after the wonderful development you have engineered, and I trust there is no possibility of such action on your part. As for me, I would never consider throwing up my army career for the uncertainties of your job, unless financially independent. My ideas and methods would too probably arouse the restricting hand of a board of visitors, and I would never willing place myself in the position of being wholly dependent financially on their good will. As a retired officer, my status would be a little different, but that does not happen to be the case. This may seem a strange point of view for one accustomed to the restrictions of army life. But it has been my good fortune to have had a number of jobs where I could pursue a pretty independent course, at least I did pursue such a course. Fortunately for me, the results usually justified the methods, though some of the "old boys" seemed to think I was walking the plank, until the seal of approval was stamped on the enterprise. Of course, I made it my business to be as quietly and unobtrusively independent as the work permitted and went always a considerable distance out of my way in order to be considerate of the opinions and persons of the older officers. But this is merely one way of the world.

I am talking very frankly to you of my personal affairs, but I feel that I owe you this frankness in repayment for your expressed interest in me. And I am not unaware that the army holds limited prospects for the officers in my group, as we are barred by law from promotion except by the slow process of seniority. This, however, I think will be altered as the influence of a large group of older officers who have not ploughed very deep or who did not go very far in the war,—as this influence weakens. Congress always lends far more than an ear to "lame ducks" and their cherished and vested rights, and Congress always suspects all others. But as these fellows grow lamer something must be done, even by a reluctant Congress. All this is, of course, most strictly entre nous.

Please be assured that I am deeply appreciative of your desire to have me at the Institute. I will not forget that you remembered me.

My service in China has been delightful, interesting and several times, exciting. Politically it is the most interesting problem in the world today, and the most dangerous. From a military point of view, the service here has been more instructive than any where else in the army these days. This particular regiment has the most remarkably efficient personnel I have ever seen gathered in one group. The officers have all been selected for the detail and the ranks are filled with fine old soldiers. Frequently we find privates who have been regimental sergeants major, and first sergents who were captains and even majors during the war. We have had many contacts with the Chinese troops, some of them fraught with frightful possibilities, but so far we have been able to carry out our mission without provoking the fatal first shot. I think that the ability of every officer to speak Chinese, has saved us. This feature of training out here has grown so important since the rabid change in Chinese feeling regarding foreigners and their governments, that last winter I started classes in Chinese for the men, and we now have a list of about thirty who can talk the language sufficiently to carry on a negotiation regarding their military duties, with the Chinese officers they may happen to come in contact with. We now have more than a hundred soldiers studying Chinese. I can speak far more of this language than I could French at the end of two years in France.

I have already made this reply to your letter a very long affair, but I felt moved to go into some detail in expressing regret that I cannot accept your kind offer. Incidentally, I will make no mention of your having offered me the detail, so you will not be embarassed in offering some other fellow second choice of the position. Mrs. Marshall and her Mother will not mention it in their letters.

They join me in warmest regards to Mrs. Cocke and you, which I might make Xmas greetings today, if they would not be so long in reaching you.   Faithfully yours,

G. C. Marshall, Jr.

VMI/Alumni File; T

1. Cocke (V.M.I., 1894) had been superintendent at the Virginia Military Institute since October 1, 1924.

EXCITEMENT in the foreign communities in China was heightened as the Kuomintang's military successes were accompanied by increasing anti-foreign agitation. Their nerves were further tightened by reports, frequently exaggerated or erroneous, of attacks by Kuomintang troops on foreigners in Nanking. From Peking, United States Minister MacMurray advised the secretary of state on March 31, 1927, that: "The general opinion held by foreigners, among them missionaries of long standing who hitherto have been disposed to place confident reliance upon the good will of Chinese, is that very serious trouble will occur in the Peking and Tientsin area in the not distant future." MacMurray urged Americans to send their women and children out of the country as quickly and as inconspicuously as possible. (U.S., Department of State, *Papers Relating to the Foreign Relations of the United States, 1927,* 3 vols. [Washington, D.C.: Government Printing Office, 1942], 2:99.) ★

REPORT TO BRIGADIER GENERAL JOSEPH C. CASTNER[1]   April 2, 1927
Tientsin, China

Report of Board concerning measures
to be taken in present emergency.[2]

1. Situation: A demonstration of the character threatened would probably be initiated simultaneously in a number of localities. The most probable areas would seem to be the Japanese concession, Italian concession, down town section of British and French concessions and southern end of Ex German concession, in the order named. Efforts to disrupt telephone service and, at night, the electric light system would probably be attempted. While defensive measures would be more difficult at night, the collection of the agitators during hours of darkness would be more easily detected if the native police can be depended on for that purpose.

2. Policy: Any measures taken to meet a disturbance of the character threatened must probably be continued in effect daily for an indefinite period. It is recommended that dependence be placed on the prompt dispatch by truck, horse and foot, of previously designated detachments from the Compound through various portions of the area, with a reserve of two large trucks to be ordered to the section or sections where the situation is known to be serious. Later action to be determined after the situation has developed.

It is recommended that the women and children remain indoors in the event of a disturbance in our area, in order that the streets may be cleared of all Chinese, by fire action if necessary; that if the trouble arises elsewhere and it then appears advisable to concentrate the foreign women and children in our area, that they be collected at the American Compound and, if necessary, quartered in the vacant houses opposite the corral.

It is recommended that detachments sent out to meet a demonstration of the character threatened be given the following general orders:

"Disperse all groups of Chinese. Clear streets of rioters or suspicious characters. Use fire action in self defense or to disperse those opposing you with arms."

3. Detailed Plan: The following detailed plan for carrying the foregoing policy into effect is submitted:

To cover a possible emergency the following is effective this date:

a. Troops at the alert.

One rifle company and one machine gun platoon, 15th Infantry, to remain in Compound constantly. Detail of organizations will be made daily by roster. Troops will be in readiness for instant duty through the twenty-four hour period. Three men who are able to drive Ford trucks will be detailed in addition to the above if they cannot be secured from the organizations detailed.

b. Instructions for the Officer of the Day.

The Officer of the Day will remain in the Compound throughout his tour. When he leaves Regimental Headquarters he will notify the charge of quarters and advise him of his whereabouts. In case of any suspicion of an emergency he will call the nearest officer to the Compound as assistant Officer of the Day. He will also notify the Commanding General; the Regimental Commander and the Chief of Staff, U.S.A.F. in C.

c. Trucks for transportation of troops.

Three commercial trucks and two army trucks will be kept available in the Compound. The three commercial trucks will be used for transportation of patrols at the beginning of any emergency.

The army trucks will be used for transportation of sufficient men and equipment to meet a disturbance, definitely located.

d. Action when Emergency arises.

(1). The senior officer present in the Compound when an emergency arises will take the required action.

(2). When it is reasonably assured that an anti-foreign disturbance has commenced in any part of the city, patrols will be dispatched over the routes indicated on the attached sketch,[3] as follows:

(a). Three patrols of one squad each (six rifles and two automatic rifles) commanded by an officer or sergeant, each conveyed by commercial truck.

(b). A dismounted patrol of one rifle squad.

(c). A mounted patrol of twelve men.

(d). All available military police will be sent out to guard bridges over Weitze Creek, to prevent the entry of Chinese into the Ex-German concession.

(3). The following orders will be given to the above patrols:

"Move rapidly over the route indicated. Disperse all groups of Chinese. Clear streets of rioters or suspicious characters. Use fire action in self-defense or to disperse those who oppose you with arms.

Report back to the Compound on completion of your circuit unless a serious disturbance is encountered. In the latter case suppress the disturbances, communicating full information immediately to the Compound."

(4). At the first indication of any disturbance in the city, the reserve details to be loaded on the two army trucks will stand by. Each detail will consist of:

1 Officer,
1 Sergeant,
2 Rifle squads, 100 rounds per rifle and 420 rounds
  per automatic rifle,
2 Machine gun crews of 3 men each, 2 machine guns,
  1000 rounds per gun.

(5). When a disturbance of any seriousness has been definitely located in the Ex-German concession, one or both army trucks will be sent to the scene of the disturbance. Officers in charge of trucks will be governed by general orders to patrols above, supplemented by additional orders to meet any special situation.

G. C. Marshall, Jr.

NA/RG 407 (370.22, China)

1. Castner had replaced Connor in the autumn of 1925. The next year he was granted permission to consolidate the Fifteenth Infantry command with his own Army Forces in China headquarters, effective December 10, 1926.

2. Marshall was the president of this four-man board which included Major Joseph W. Stilwell (U.S.M.A., 1904), who had arrived in mid-1926 from Fort Leavenworth's Command and General Staff School.

3. Not printed.

REPORT TO BRIGADIER GENERAL JOSEPH C. CASTNER　　April 7, 1927
Tientsin, China

Report of Board on Precautions to be taken
against Mobs and Measures to Suppress them.[1]

1. *Obstacles:* It is proposed that a barbed wire stockade be erected along the line indicated on accompanying sketch. Barbed wire chevaux de frise to be constructed for use in blocking streets and bridges as indicated on sketch and to be stored or stacked in immediate vicinity of places, to be used as work on stockade is commenced. The estimates for the above are attached hereto.

For the present it is proposed that the stockade be guarded against injury and pilferage by native police and occasional mounted patrols.

2. *Troop Dispositions:* When mob demonstrations are threatened, troops to be disposed in accordance with the present emergency plan, a copy of which is attached hereto. In addition, one rifle platoon and one section of machine guns to be dispatched to First Special Area Police Headquarters on Woodrow Wilson Street and quartered there. Troops at the Police Headquarters to be under the command of a Chinese speaking officer.

Mission of troops at Police Headquarters:

To prevent the collapse of the First Special Area police organization by supporting it in the performance of its functions.

3. *Assumption of Control of First Special Area:* At the first indication of inability on the part of the police of the First Special Area to perform their proper functions it is proposed that the complete control of the area be taken over by the U.S. Army Forces in China.

In so far as possible native policemen and officials to be retained to perform their normal duties.

Posters in Chinese proclaiming to the native population the assumption of control by the United States Army Forces in China to be displayed throughout the area. These posters to issue a warning to rioters and reassurance of protection to law-abiding citizens, urging the latter to cooperate for their own safety.

4. *Arming Civilians:* One rifle and one hundred rounds of ammunition to be issued to each responsible male foreigner residing in the First Special Area who applies for same. The offer by the United States Army Forces in China to issue arms and ammunition as above to be given publicity through local agencies (Chamber of Commerce, American Consul, German Consul). Individuals receiving arms to be required to sign a written agreement as follows:

That fire action will only be taken—
  In self defense, or
  In defense of another, or
  In defense of property, or
  When ordered by an officer or non-commissioned
    officer of the U.S. Army.

5. *Action against mobs:* The following general action against mobs is proposed.

  a. The streets to be cleared of all Chinese, except policemen engaged in the performance of their duty.

  b. (1). Where formed mobs are encountered they will be opposed by a skirmish line supported by the bulk of the unit at such a distance as to avoid hand to hand contact with the mob.

(2). Formed mobs to be exhorted to disperse. If they delay, tear gas bombs will be utilized. Thereafter, if the mob attacks, it will be fired into.

(3). Fire action is authorized in self defense and as above. All ranks will be cautioned to utilize every other means to disperse mobs before firing.

NA/RG 407 (370.22, China)
1. The attachments mentioned in this document are not printed here.

To Brigadier General John McA. Palmer   April 25, 1927
                                                          Tientsin, China

My dear General John: Your check for $130.00 came some time ago, but I have been so busy with excursions and alarms and packing up, that I delayed unduly in acknowledging it. You were very thoughtful in sending the money in advance of the tragedy. For tragedy it seems to be. Our last transport group from here paid fines in several instances, up to $1000.00, and practically all paid heavy duties, one officer $2240.00 on what we thought was an ordinary outlay. Several have left their household goods on the docks because of insufficient funds. A one hundred percent inspection was made in New York, everything to the last dish and doily was unpacked,—and incidentally, much linen lost.[1]

If the situation does not cloud up again I sail May 10th. Otherwise, I will not leave until the trouble is over. Mrs. Marshall and her mother go in any event. We proceed overland from Frisco. They go to Virginia and I go direct to Washington where I will see you, if you have not left for the summer.

I am delighted to hear that you are properly launched again in the writing game, and under such pleasing conditions. I know you are happy and I'm sure you will soon be much in the public eye. I wish I could take the remaining dozen bottles of fine champagne reposing in our pantry, and celebrate this renewal of your literary career.

With affectionate regards,   Faithfully yours,

                                                          Marshall

LC/J. McA. Palmer Papers

1. Palmer had sent Marshall $300 the previous autumn to purchase some Chinese rugs. Marshall replied that he had the merchandise. "As to bringing the rugs in. There I am afraid I must fail you, so far as custom charges go. I have to make a military certificate here regarding my freight that every thing has been purchased over a year before my departure and that it is for me. In San Francisco I have to certify or make an affidavit, that my declaration covers no articles intended as gifts or for others. All the foregoing was brought about by the 'in-law' of a Navy fellow who for a time managed a thriving business by purchasing nice things out here and shipping them by government transport to Manila and San Francisco for sale. So, in order to protect us against having our household freight unboxed in Frisco, these certificates were ordered." (Marshall to Palmer, November 16, 1926, LC/J. McA. Palmer Papers.)

Instruction and Command

July 1927–October 1933

THE ARMY WAR COLLEGE—founded in 1903—held its classes in a Stanford White-designed building at the old Washington Barracks in southwest Washington, D.C., a twenty-minute walk from downtown. From its inception, the college was closely allied with the army General Staff and was specially charged with training staff officers and developing war plans. When Major General James W. McAndrew became commandant in 1919, he set out to change the college's image as simply a planning adjunct to the General Staff. He reorganized the curriculum to emphasize academic instruction rather than field problems and to prepare his students for exercising high command. The instructors used lectures, problems, war games, and map maneuvers in their efforts to provide the students with guidance and experience in commanding large units and to develop their decision-making skills.

For Marshall, the new post of War College instructor meant leaving duty with troops for a desk job in the city, a prospect he did not enjoy. Adding to his worries was Lily's health. She had never been robust and had declined alarmingly during the past few months. A leisurely trip across the continent from San Francisco, and several weeks' rest at her mother's home in Lexington, Virginia, had produced no improvement in her condition.

In the latter part of July, John McAuley Palmer lent the Marshalls his Washington apartment while they tried to organize their new white-columned, brick house at the college. Marshall struggled to prepare for the coming school year. But Lily's condition continued to worsen; she soon had to enter Washington's Walter Reed Hospital for medical tests. ★

To General John J. Pershing   August 12, 1927
From Elizabeth C. Marshall   Washington, D.C.

My dear General: As you may imagine George is typing this for me as I am not able to write myself.

I must apologize for the long delay in thanking you for those beautiful flowers, which thrilled both me and my nurse! You were so dear to remember me and your flowers came at a moment when I was much depressed, and they helped me through a hard day.

George has tried to get you on the telephone three or four times, but without success. Finally, last night the operator at the Metropolitan Club informed him that you were no longer living there. Possibly you had not been there on any of the other occasions they had told him you were not in.

I have a brief respite from the Walter Reed, but will have to go back in a few weeks and probably will remain there quite awhile. A heart is a very slow thing to improve, but I pray that I may be back in my own house at the War College before so very long. And I will look forward to seeing you.

The Palmers have been kind enough to allow us to make use of their apartment, but I expect to go down to the War College tomorrow night, as the unpacking has about gotten over the hammer and nail stage. We have two servants established there that we brought from Virginia, and a temporary maid here at the Palmer's.

George tells me you are looking very well, and I want to see you for myself before very long.

With much love, and thanks for your lovely flowers,

Elizabeth C. Marshall [typed]

LC/J. J. Pershing Papers (General Correspondence); T

To Mrs. Thomas B. Coles   August 20, 1927
                                                        Washington, D.C.

My dear Aunt Lottie: Lily wants me to tell you all how very much she appreciates the many letters you have encouraged her with. She really deeply appreciates your kindness, you, Mrs. Knapp and Charlotte for being so kind and thoughtful.[1]

She stayed in the hospital five days and had all the necessary tests. Unfortunately the basal metabolism test showed a reading of seventy six, which is about as high as it well could be. She did not rest at all well in the hospital and ate very little, growing extremely weak. I brought her home in an endeavour to build her up to a point where they would dare operate, and the joy of her new house, the peace and quiet did a great deal for her. She gained nine pounds and when I took her out to the hospital for another metabolism test the count had gone down to twenty six, which is a great improvement. Consequently, they feel that she is in as good a condition for an operation as she probably will be.

Tomorrow, Sunday, I take her back again and they plan to operate Monday or Tuesday. Of course, it will be three or four weeks before she can be expected to show any material improvement, but after that she should be much better.

At present she is so weak that she is unable to sit up by her own effort, and she suffers from an increasing suffocation due to the pressure of the swollen thryoid gland on her wind pipe. She also suffers from paroxisms of coughing for the same reason. All this, we hope will be eliminated by the operation.

Lily has a great deal of courage about the matter, weak as she is. Of course she realizes that without the operation she would never improve and would probably grow steadily worse.

Colonel Keller, who will operate, is considered one of the most skillful in the United States.[2] He has had for some years a standing offer of fifty thousand a year from the Mayos if he will resign from the Army and join their staff. Fortunately for us he has so far chosen to remain in the Army. While Lily was at the

the [*sic*] Walter Reed he had twenty similar cases awaiting his attention. So he is in practice for this particular operation. The scar will be very small and so located that it can easily be hidden by beads. I am very glad of this, for the idea of a disfiguring scar would be a hard blow to Lily.

I will telegraph you how she comes through the ordeal for I know you all will be very anxious to hear.

Since coming down here I have bought a very convenient radio set, The Traveler. It is merely a leather box, the lid of which has the antennae hidden in it. There is no attachment to anything outside the box, and you can move it about from room to room. Lily finds it a great diversion.

Our house seems very lovely to us. Down stairs it has a seven foot wide hall, which widens at the back to twelve feet. The living room and dining room are connected by double slidding doors and a river porch opens off the dining room, which is partially enclosed and entirely screened. It looks over Potomac Park and is a delightful place for meals and reading. There is a small library or den on the first floor, with a lavatory.

The second floor has a rectangular hall about twelve feet wide and fifteen feet long. On one side are two nice bed rooms, connecting, and the rear opens on an enclosed sleeping porch which extends the width of the house. A bath room opens off the front bed room of these two. Across the hall are two more bed rooms, but rather small, the rear opening on the sleeping porch. There is a second bath room reached from the hall, and the door leading to the back steps, also a linen closet.

The third floor has three servant bed rooms and a bath.

Outside, in front there is a brick porch with dividing steps, a part of the porch forming the top landing. A wrought iron railing with brass trimmings encloses the porch. The porch is roofed, with four large white pillars reaching up to the cornice, and a small ornamental balcony off the stair landing with a wrought iron railing. There are flower beds and flowering bushes all around the house. The flowers are very lovely, and in addition they deliver large bunches of cut flowers twice a week from the green house and its gardens. Altogether, it is the pleasantest house we have had in the Army. Our little house at Fort Mason, San Francisco was more charmingly located, but was very small.[3] Here we have a golf course in front of the house and tennis courts close by.

I rather ran of[f] the paper on the last page, but I know you will forgive my erractic typing.

The car runs along smoothly. I had it gone over in the Packard plant, having run it 2400 miles, and they made it purr and eliminated all the small rattles. The noise I was worrying about in one wheel or tire and had the man at Scottsville looking at,[4] develops into a well known defect of a certain issue of Goodyear tires. The trouble is in the tire and cannot be removed, but does no harm.

The War College course opens on September 1st, thereafter I will not have my entire day to devote to Lily, but she will be in the hospital until the middle of

September at the earliest and when I bring her back I hope she will be so much better that she will not require the constant attention she now does.

This has developed into a long rambling letter, but I wanted you all to know how much Lily appreciated the kindness you have shown her by writing so frequently. She is keenly interested in the changes in your house, so please tell her all about the progress you are making.

With love from both of us,   Affectionately,

George

GCMRL/Research File (Family); T'

1. Charlotte was Mrs. Coles's daughter. The editor has been unable to identify Mrs. Knapp.

2. Lieutenant Colonel William L. Keller had been an army surgeon since entering the service, following his graduation from the Medical College of Virginia in 1899.

3. When Marshall was Major General J. Franklin Bell's aide in 1916–17, both men lived at Fort Mason, although the Western Department headquarters was at the Presidio.

4. Scottsville, Virginia, was a small town near the Coles's "Woodville" house in Albemarle County.

TO BRIGADIER GENERAL JOHN MCA. PALMER   August 26, 1927
Washington, D.C.

My dear General John: I have been so closely occupied the past ten days that I have not found a favorable moment to write you something of what has been happening to us. Mrs. Marshall made so much of a temporary improvement duwing the time I had her at your apartment and down here at the War College that Colonel Keller felt he was justified in taking the risk of operating on her. He was reluctant to do this, but it was apparent that she could not be built up into better con[di]tion and that she would probably soon have another slump and a more serious one. So he operated on Monday morning.

The operation was much more serious than he had anticipated as indicated by the X ray photographs, and required about twice the normal time. As they could not give her the usual anesthetic, it had to be local, and the extent of the operation required him to risk gas. Her pulse went up to 170 during the operation, but came down considerably by the following morning.

I was not allowed to see her until Wednesday, and tho they all said she was making a very good recovery, yet to me she seemed in a very serious condition, suffering a great deal and subject to prolonged periods of suffocation. She showed no improvement on Thursday and it was not until yesterday that she seemed to feel any improvement. But they tell me she had a poor night and is not feeling very well today. I am only allowed to see her a few minutes a day, as it is important to keep her absolutely quiet. I go out this afternoon after lunch.

I hope that by tomorrow she will really start to show signs of making a real recovery. While this operation was a hard ordeal for her in her weakened condition and with her heart in very bad shape, yet it was the only means of helping her, and we are thankful that Keller found it possible to undertake the task. He is very skillful and has been unusually good to her, seeing her seven or eight times a day.

I have also been deep in preparation for my work at the College, which unfortunately, starts the first day of the term, next Friday. I have had to crowd about three months study into ten days, and Mrs. Marshall's predicament has made it difficult for me to concentrate.

I gave your book a reading in July but was so distracted by nursing that I could not do it justice. Again a week ago I went through it again, and I want to tell you that I think it the ablest presentation ever put forth by an American Army or Naval officer, in form, English, analysis and conclusions. I will have to read it a third time before I can give you my detailed reactions, but as I see the matter at present I am in agreement with you throughout. I want more time to consider the Naval slant, but my present conclusions are with yours. I am strong for your views on the Regular Army and the Citizen Army. Also for the Department of National Defense.[1]

With reference to the last sentence, I have just had a sample of the impossibility of cooperation between the services even on the smallest matter, when remote from the influence of the Joint Board.[2] The affair was of the smallest importance, but it gave a good sample of the absurdity of the present lack of system. Butler's Marines were to proceed to Tientsin.[3] There was an Army headquarters with all possible data and familiarity regarding the local conditions and terrain. Yet a Marine officer was sent there to make the preliminary reconnaissance and arrangements. He was not sent to our headquarters, and no notification of his coming or intentions was communicated, so far as I know. Our officers attempted to steer him as to the condition of the road to Taku, the housing and camping conditions in Tientsin, but he was there on a completely independent status and tried to do the matter more or less on his own. We could have done everything for him, yet he came unheralded and except for gratutious services, unaided. All of our officers speak Chinese quite well and many of our men, yet there was no request or arrangement for utilizing their helpful services. The Marines tried to put artillery and heavy transport in a recently filled in area bordering on Race Course Road. They were cautioned against it, and went ahead and lost four trucks. Can you beat this for intelligent cooperation. All this is of course, entre nous.

I have no more time at present, but I wanted Mrs. Palmer and you to know about Lily. Your kindly services helped her a great deal to prepare for this ordeal. We shall not forget.

With love to you both,

G. C. M.

LC/J. McA. Palmer Papers; T

1. John McA. Palmer, *Statesmanship or War* (Garden City, N.Y.: Doubleday, Page, 1927). Palmer was particularly interested in proposing ways of adapting the Swiss citizen-army system to the United States without having to adopt universal military training.

2. The Joint Army and Navy Board, usually referred to as the Joint Board, was originally created in 1903 to coordinate military policy and planning. Formally reconstituted in 1919, board members included the army chief of staff, the chief of naval operations, and the heads of their respective operations and planning divisions.

3. As part of the international effort to protect United States and other foreign citizens in China from the mounting antiforeign agitation accompanying Chiang Kai-shek's victories, a United States Marine detachment landed at Shanghai on February 9, 1927. Reinforcements arrived on May 2 with Brigadier General Smedley D. Butler, who took charge of the Third Marine Brigade. In June, Butler took nearly four thousand Marines to Tientsin.

TO MRS. THOMAS B. COLES [September 5–6, 1927]
FROM ELIZABETH C. MARSHALL[1] [Washington, D.C.]

Dearest Aunt Lot, Sharley & Chottie: I have thought of you all *so* much as I have lain here these last two weeks– and no words of mine can ever tell you what a comfort all your letters have been– I have needed all the help & support possible to carry me through the most horrible experience of my entire life– I believe if I had had any notion before hand what it would be like I might not have had the courage to face it—tho' the doctor says I could only have lived a few months if I had *not* had the operation–

As Geo– has no doubt written you– the X Ray had entirely failed to show the really serious phase of my case—that is, that the Thyroid was even going down into my chest cavity– So my operation instead of taking *20* minutes, as they had expected, it took *two hours*–

I was under morphine for five days & nights afterwards.

I had a very close shave the first night—& it was just about 50–50 as to whether my heart could hold out or not– . . .

My days are long now—for Geo's classes have begun at the War College—& he teaches from *9* A.M. til 4.30 P.M- So he doesn't get over here til *6* in the evening– I can't read a word as my eyes feel so weak– so the days are very long– as I cannot move my neck or head– This position day & night becomes very trying– . . .

———

Tuesday
. . . I hope in a few more weeks to be able to go home– That is my one thought—to get *home*– Of course I was never able to do *one thing* towards settling or arranging my house—& Geo. has not tried to do much. He has not unpacked any of the silver & is just sort of picnicing–

I imagine it will be at least Xmas before I will be able to go downstairs but I will be so happy to be alive– I will not be impatient. Towards spring I hope to be very *much* alive & able to take up life where I left off— . . .   Always your devoted & grateful

Lily

GCMRL/Research File (Family); H

1. Mrs. Marshall was writing from Walter Reed Hospital. Approximately one-third of this letter is printed here.

FROM GENERAL JOHN J. PERSHING

October 6, 1927
[Paris, France]

My dear Marshall: The sad news of Mrs. Marshall's passing away was cabled me by Adamson.[1] It occurred while we were in the midst of the week's entertainment of the Legionnaires in Paris. I sent you a brief cable at the moment but it did not begin to express to you my feelings of sympathy at the great loss that has come to you and to your friends.

No one knows better than I what such a bereavement means, and my heart goes out to you very fully at this crisis in your life. It is at such moments that we realize that our reliance must be placed in the Father who rules over us all.[2]

Believe me,   Always affectionately yours,

LC/J. J. Pershing Papers (General Correspondence)

1. Mrs. Marshall died of heart failure at Walter Reed Hospital on September 15.

2. In the early morning hours of August 27, 1915, a fire swept Pershing's quarters at the Presidio of San Francisco, killing his wife and three daughters; only his son, Warren, survived. Pershing was in El Paso, Texas, at the time.

TO GENERAL JOHN J. PERSHING

October 14, 1927
Washington, D.C.

My dear General: Your telegram was deeply appreciated and your letter even more so, and I am very grateful to you for the flowers you sent to Mrs. Marshall. The truth is, the thought of all you had endured gave me heart and hope. But twenty six years of most intimate companionship, something I have known ever since I was a mere boy, leaves me lost in my best efforts to adjust myself to future prospects in life. If I had been given to club life or other intimacies with men outside of athletic diversions, or if there was a campaign on or other pressing duty demanding a concentrated effort, then I think I could do better. However, I will find a way.

Mrs. Marshall was to have left the hospital the following day. She died suddenly, unexpectedly, while in her chair writing to her mother. Two weeks earlier the shock would not have been so great. I will have to be grateful for many years of happiness such as few seem to find.

I have not inquired of Adamson about the date of your return, but I will do so tomorrow. Meanwhile, please understand that I am very grateful for your sympathy.   Faithfully,

G. C. Marshall, Jr.

LC/J. J. Pershing Papers (General Correspondence); H

TO MRS. THOMAS B. COLES   October 26, 1927
                                                         Washington, D.C.

Dear Aunt Lottie: There has been a violent change in my affairs. Yesterday the Chief of Staff appointed me assistant commandant of the Infantry School at Fort Benning, Georgia to replace a man just promoted brigadier general.[1] Benning is near Columbus, Georgia, 125 miles south west of Atlanta. The job is a much better one than my present occupation as there are 600 officers at Benning of whom 450 are students in the school which will be my direct charge. There is a war strength regiment (3500 men) at Benning, also a peace strength regiment, a battalion of artillery, a company of tanks and a squadron of aeroplanes. These troops are for school demonstrations. The house I will occupy was a farm house before the government took over the place in 1918, and it has been steam heated, refloored and generally fixed up. So you see I will lead a country life, which is what I need. They gave me my choice of remaining here, going to Governor's Island, N.Y., as chief of staff of that corps area, or the Benning job. I thought it best professionally and in my present frame of mind to go to Benning.

This terminates my pleasant plans for Thanksgiving, but I hope to stop a night with you enroute by motor. My sister may accompany me to cheer me up on the trip and to settle my new quarters. If she does, can you put us up for a night about a week or ten days from now?

With love to you all,   Affectionately,

George

GCMRL/Research File (Family); H

1. The army chief of staff since November 21, 1926, had been Major General Charles P. Summerall. Marshall was replacing Frank S. Cocheu (U.S.M.A., 1894), whose promotion had become effective on October 18.

TO MRS. THOMAS B. COLES   November 13, 1927
                                                         Fort Benning, Georgia

Dear Aunt Lottie   We had two days of lovely weather and scenery from Woodville to Chattanooga, stopping at Pulaski and at Lenoir. Marie made an ideal traveling companion. Then we had a delightful visit with the Cootes at Ft. Oglethorpe, even tho it rained.[1] But I rode each day. From there to Benning the roads were not so good, but we made it in a day, arriving at 5 P.M.

The next morning at 9 A.M. our freight arrived at the house, and ever since we have slaved from early morn until well after dark, less hours for lunch and dinner with various friends. I have inherited a fine colored orderly who has worked in the house for two years, and a good cook was found for me; in addition I find a Cadillac car and driver goes with the job. The house is the most attractive I have had. Here is a rough sketch.

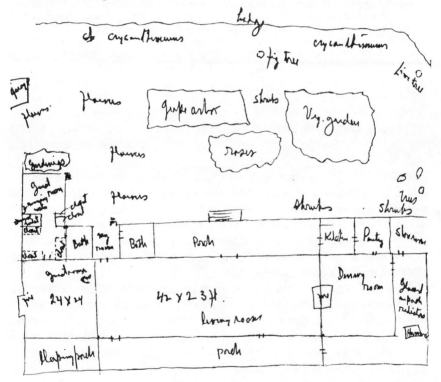

My poor sister has worked so hard she complains bitterly of "misery" in her feet.

We find the house and its surroundings really charming. I commence my riding at 6^{15} in the morning and will explore the wonderful trails they tell me about.

You and Charlotte were very sweet to Marie and gave her a rare treat which she hugely enjoyed. And I am grateful accordingly. I was very glad to be with you on my way to new scenes and surroundings under such changed conditions. It served to me as a warm reassurance that my ties over so many years were not to be entirely disrupted. Thank you for your kindness and thoughtfulness. With love to you both,   Affectionately,

George

GCMRL/Research File (Family); H

1. Lieutenant Colonel Harry N. Cootes, "an old and dear friend" who had attended V.M.I. for two years (1892–94), was serving with a Cavalry regiment at this post in northwest Georgia, near Chattanooga, Tennessee. A few years later, Marshall wrote of Cootes: "He is invariably beloved by all his subordinates and secures their best and happiest efforts. He admires brains and has the ability to spot them. . . . His commands are always very high in morale and splendid in appearance. He makes a remarkably fine impression on civilians and is beloved by many. He is a highly honorable man, completely loyal to his superiors, and [has] done much in the past for the good of the Army." (Marshall to Fox Conner, November 27, 1933, GCMRL/G. C. Marshall Papers [Illinois National Guard].)

To Mrs. Egbert Armstrong[1]   May 16, 1941
                                                         [Washington, D.C.]

Dear Catherine: . . . I am sorry you have been so jostled about of late. Of course these sudden changes are old stuff to me, but I gained experience and acquired a philosophy in more youthful days. I never realized how matter-of-fact one can become in such matters until I took Marie down to Fort Benning, Georgia, with me. She had never moved from the time she had married; I was moving into a new post, and of course a new house—actually old as the hills, 1850, but the nicest one I have ever had.

We arrived after dark, and the next morning, immediately following breakfast with friends, we adjourned to the quarters assigned me. I had directed that the freight be delivered at that hour and that a detail of men be on hand to assist. Dividing the latter into three groups, I put one at uncrating in the yard, one at unwrapping and wiping off, and the third at carrying furniture, boxes and barrels into the house; the barrels were to go on the kitchen porch, the boxes spread out in a glassed-in porch, and the furniture into the rooms I indicated, having given them names in a quick survey with those detailed to the carrying duty. Marie was to sit in the house and merely assist in directing the furniture to the various rooms. Under no circumstances was she to endeavor to arrange it at that time— merely to get it into the right room and out of the line of traffic. The formal arrangement would come at the last hour in the afternoon.

I was out in the yard checking off the crates and boxes, overseeing the un-crating, etc., and directing the carrying party as to what room each item was to go to. A darkey soldier came up to me and said: "Say Colonel, you better go into the house, that lady in there is goin' crazy.'' I found Marie trying to choose a precise spot for some item, with a line of men holding up tons of stuff awaiting her decision. Her only explanation to me for failure to follow my directions was, "I never heard of such a thing!" . . . Faithfully yours,

GCMRL/K. T. Marshall Collection

1. Mrs. Armstrong (born Catharine Lindsey) was a childhood friend from Uniontown, Pennsylvania. Two omitted paragraphs refer to a possible visit by the Armstrongs.

W HEN MARSHALL became assistant commandant of the Infantry School on November 10, 1927, the school was only nine years old. In 1918 three institutions—the Small Arms Firing School at Camp Perry, Ohio; the Machine Gun School at Augusta, Georgia; and the Infantry School at Fort Sill, Oklahoma—were combined and transferred to Camp Benning near Columbus, Georgia. In 1927, the reservation covered over one hundred fifty square miles. The post, where the Infantry School was located, occupied about one percent of the reservation and was about nine miles from the Columbus business district.

According to Army Regulation 350-200 (December 30, 1926), "The objects of the Infantry School are—*a.* to teach in detail the tactics and technique of Infantry and to give a working familiarity with the tactics and technique of associated arms in order to provide competent leaders for all Infantry units and to qualify instructors for the Regular Army, the National Guard, the Organized Reserves, the Reserve Officers' Training Corps, and the Citizens' Military Training Camps; *b.* to train selected enlisted men as technicians and instructors in the duties of enlisted specialists in the Infantry of the Regular Army, the National Guard, and Organized Reserves; *c.* to serve as an agency of the Chief of Infantry in the development and perfection of Infantry tactics and technique."

The commandant at Fort Benning when Marshall arrived was Brigadier General Edgar T. Collins; after May 4, 1929, Marshall's old friend Campbell King held the post. Subordinate to the commandant were the nearly six thousand troops stationed at the post (the Twenty-ninth Infantry, which was used primarily for demonstrations and tests; the Twenty-fourth Infantry, a Negro unit which was used primarily for labor and construction; and numerous special units), the small Department of Experiment, and the Academic Department. Assistant Commandant Marshall directed the Academic Department with a relatively unrestricted hand between November, 1927, and June, 1932.

By the time Marshall took over, the Fort Benning school year was underway. Both the Advanced Course (which usually enrolled between fifty and eighty senior captains and majors) and the Company Officers' Course (which enrolled between one hundred and one hundred fifty lieutenants and captains) began in September and ran through early June. The school also offered short refresher courses for colonels and brigadier generals and instruction for National Guard and Reserve officers, for enlisted specialists, and for horseshoers.

To teach the Academic Department's three to five hundred students, Marshall had a staff of sixty to eighty instructors. In November, 1927, these included one of his former V.M.I. roommates, Lieutenant Colonel Philip B. Peyton, as well as Major James A. Van Fleet, Captain Edward M. Almond, Captain J. Lawton Collins, and Captain Charles L. Bolte. In subsequent years, instructors included men such as Lieutenant Colonel Joseph W. Stilwell, Major Edwin F. Harding, Major Omar N. Bradley, and Major Harold R. Bull. Numerous other men who would eventually attain high army commands were students during the Marshall years at Fort Benning. There were occasional foreign students. One of these— Captain Adolf von Schell, a 1931 Advanced Course graduate—later occupied important posts in Nazi Germany.

One of Marshall's command techniques was to recruit a superior staff, give them their assignments, and leave them alone. If they hesitated, Marshall tried to help; if they failed, he relieved them. Major Omar N. Bradley remarked later: "During the two years I served him as chief of the weapons section in the Infantry School, he sent for me only once to discuss the work of my section. And during that same two-year period he visited me in my office but twice." (Omar N. Bradley, *A Soldier's Story* [New York: Henry Holt, 1951], pp. 19–20.)

Joseph D. Patch, an instructor during Marshall's first year, later wrote: "In my opinion Col. Marshall did more for The Infantry School than anyone who ever served there. We were in a 'slump' and he pulled us out and ran the instruction on a realistic and practical basis. His tactical problems were based on real occurrences." (Major General Patch to Forrest C. Pogue, November 4, 1960, GCMRL/Research File [Benning].)

A student in the 1931–32 Company Officers' Course recalled Marshall's teaching technique. "Marshall would make frequent visits to classes in the field and we would, as a group, have an opportunity to hear him explain his views on the problems of the day. I remember occasions when he would outline a tactical situation to a group of students, then select a student and have him give a field order subject to critique by the other students and finally his observations. On one occasion we rode horses cross-country over a 17-mile course and at the end, without previous warning, were told to draw a sketch map of the area covered." The purpose was to force students "to think on their feet." (General George H. Decker to Forrest C. Pogue, November 5, 1964, ibid.)

Marshall took the lead in sponsoring social and recreational activities— particularly those involving horsemanship. Terry de la M. Allen, who as a major attended the 1931–32 Advanced Course, subsequently wrote that Marshall was "greatly interested in the athletic schedules there, including the Officers' Polo Tournaments and the Enlisted Men's Baseball Schedules. When I reported to him, . . . he wanted to know if I came there to work or to play polo. I told him that I hoped to do both." (Major General Allen to Forrest C. Pogue, November 5, 1964, ibid.)

The office files of the Academic Department have apparently been destroyed, as numerous attempts to find them have failed. Documentation for this period depends upon private papers and various files in the National Archives. ★

TO BRIGADIER GENERAL JOHN MCA. PALMER   December 21, 1927
Fort Benning, Georgia

My dear General John,   I have started several times to acknowledge your note with the carbon of your talk before the Union League Club in Chicago. I think the latter is delightfully done and very interesting. In other words it is on a par with your article comparing the problems of Lincoln and Wilson. With your permission I am going to keep the carbon.[1]

I have wanted to write and tell you how I find things here at Benning, but my time has been so completely occupied that there has been no previous opportunity. The place is greatly improved since I saw it in 1924. My quarters are the best I have had in the army; my servants seem most satisfactory; there are excellent horses to ride and beautiful trails to go over; the school is splendidly organized and permeated with a fine spirit, but it has kept me humping to familiarize myself sufficiently with the course to make recommendation which has to be submitted now for next year and to have any affect on the present course before May or June.

If you feel the need of going into retirement for rest or writing, I think my house is just the place for you. You can fish, shoot, find lovely walks, or hunt wildcats. I will write more in detail of my life here after I return from Charlotte [North Carolina], where I am going to be with Mrs. Coles for the holidays. Affectionately yours,

G. C. M.

LC/J. McA. Palmer Papers

1. Palmer spoke at a luncheon given in his honor on November 10, 1927. His subject was President Lincoln's army organization and staffing difficulties in 1861–63 compared with the present superior situation. Had the United States Army been better organized in 1860–61, Palmer said, there would have been no war. "The Civil War came solely because the Southern leaders knew that the adverse ballot majority [the North enjoyed because of its larger population] was not negotiable as a bullet majority." The moral was—preparedness prevents war.

The "article comparing the problems of Lincoln and Wilson," to which Marshall refers, may have been a draft of an essay ultimately to become chapter twenty-seven in Palmer's *Washington, Lincoln, Wilson: Three War Statesmen* (Garden City, N.Y.: Doubleday, Doran, 1930).

To Henry L. Stimson   December 22, 1927
                                                         Fort Benning, Georgia

My dear Governor Stimson,   Last evening a telegram arrived from The Adjutant General inquiring whether I desired to serve as "aide to Mr. Stimson, Governor General, Philippine Islands," stating that it would be necessary for me to join you before sailing from New York January 20th.[1] I telegraphed The Adjutant General that I did not desire the detail but greatly appreciated the invitation.

Necessarily a telegram to The Adjutant General did not afford much opportunity either to explain my action or to express my appreciation. I am deeply grateful to you for honoring me with this opportunity and I am concerned that you should know just what governed my decision.

Since my return this summer from three years in China I served a brief period as instructor at the War College and reported here last month for duty as Assistant Commandant of The Infantry School. General Ely had taken me to the War College and I felt much embarrassed at quitting that job so soon after my arrival there. I would feel even more embarrassed at leaving General Collins here after this brief period and in view of the effort he made to secure my services.

However, there was still another factor which really determined the matter for me. Back in the days when an aide was more or less an operations officer at headquarters, I served as aide-de-camp to General Liggett in the Philippines. On my return to San Francisco I was immediately detailed as aide-de-camp to General J. Franklin Bell. I left his staff to go to France with the First Division. In the Spring of 1919 when the Army Corps of which I was Chief of Staff was about to be demobilized, I was detailed as aide-de-camp to General Pershing. Now if I became an aide for the fourth time I fear, in fact I feel sure, that to the army at large I would be convicted of being only an aide and never a commander. With your familiarity with the service, I feel sure you will understand this point of view, for I wish you to know that I deeply appreciate your doing me the honor of considering me as a possible aide to the Governor General of the Philippines.[2]

With assurances of great respect,   Very sincerely yours,

                                                         G. C. Marshall, Jr.

YU/H. L. Stimson Papers

1. Formerly secretary of war (May, 1911–March, 1913), Stimson had been appointed to the Philippine post following Governor-General Leonard Wood's death on August 7, 1927. Stimson's party did not actually depart until February, 1928.

2. Stimson replied on January 21, 1928, that he could "appreciate perfectly your sound reasons for preferring military duty. I have never forgotten the impression of efficiency you made on me when you came to the school at Langres and I had the pleasure of talking with you as well as listening to your lecture." As a lieutenant colonel in the Seventy-seventh Division's 305th Field Artillery, Stimson had attended the General Staff School at Langres, France, from February to May, 1918. From March 20 to 29, Marshall was at the school lecturing on administration. The two men shared a mess, at least part of that time, and went horseback riding together. (Interview, April 11, 1957.)

MEMORANDUM FOR THE COMMANDANT   December 22, 1927
                                                Fort Benning, Georgia

Passenger Motor Transportation.[1]

1. I recommend that an estimate for the funds itemized below be submitted for the detailed reasons stated thereafter, these funds to be made available at the earliest possible date.

2. *ESTIMATE FOR FUNDS*

    For 11 motor passenger buses, capacity 25 persons. $70,000.00

    For operation of buses (gasoline, oil, tires, and

        minor repairs) for 8½ months a year. 8,000.00

3. Motor passenger transportation is a major need of the Academic Department, The Infantry School. There are two reasons for this requirement.

a. Tactical. The post is located on an edge of the reservation, seventeen miles from the northeastern corner and thirteen miles from the southeastern. With existing means of transportation, about one-half of the available terrain is only occasionally employed in tactical training. The distant terrain is the most desirable for tactical problems, being less wooded and rugged than the ground closer to the post. Also much of the latter is debarred from use in tactical problems because of almost constant firing on the experimental and school ranges. As a result of this situation the tactical instruction at The Infantry School, in my opinion, has suffered materially by reason of its restriction to a very limited and not particularly desirable area with which the instructors have become over-familiar and of which the students soon tire.

Instruction in Infantry tactics in keeping with the importance of this school demands a wide variety of terrain and frequent contact with unfamiliar ground. This is not now the case. To reach the center of the distant plots referred to requires from eleven to fifteen miles by good roads, mostly paved. It is, in my opinion, important that problems in these localities should be the rule rather than the exception. This can be readily arranged if motor passenger transportation is provided. As a matter of fact, it can be more easily arranged than the present system of transporting students by horse or narrow-gauge railroad to the restricted area referred to, because the center of the most desirable area while fifteen miles from Fort Benning is but ten miles distant from Columbus, where all married student officers reside. I understand that at the Field Artillery School such transportation is available in the form of reconnaissance cars, which are in almost daily use.

b. A secondary consideration is the desirability of furnishing transportation for the students from the city of Columbus to the post and return. At present the married student officers at The Infantry School suffer not only the financial and social disadvantages of residence distant from the post, but they are personally obligated to provide their own means of transportation to and from the post six days a week. The average daily distance is slightly over twenty miles and totals for the school term about 4,500 miles. There is a daily train to the post, but as it leaves the city station (approximately two miles from the average student's residence) at 6:00 AM, it cannot be considered a normal service.

The fact that students have been required in the past to bear this burden of transportation expense and great personal inconvenience in pursuing the courses at The Infantry School is not considered a just argument for its further continuance. As a matter of fact, from my personal knowledge of the efforts to secure the Fort Benning reservation in 1919, those then most interested in the matter were forced to ignore at that time any question regarding the complications presented in transporting the students from the city to the post. Every effort was directed towards obtaining the reservation. As a consequence the infantry student officer has had to bear a heavy burden not approximated at any other post in the army. The obligation to furnish this transportation or to furnish quarters on the post is believed to be an obligation of the government. This particular situation has always adversely affected morale among the students, to the disadvantage of the school. It should be remedied.

Dis-regarding the benefits in the tactical instruction at The Infantry School which would undoubtedly result from the acquirement of the motor transportation referred to, and considering the matter only as a temporary, though very partial remedy, to the present lack of government quarters, it is desired to point out that the cost of these motor buses represents only the approximate cost of permanent quarters for about seven officers. Since there are more than 240 officers now living in Columbus to be provided with quarters on the post and there are about 225 temporary quarters on the post which must be abandoned or replaced in the near future, the cost of the motor transportation which would meet in a measure some to [*of*] the difficulties imposed by this situation is a small matter when compared to the large sums which must eventually be made available for quarters.

NA/RG 177 (451, Chief of Infantry)

1. Marshall's memorandum ricocheted through the army hierarchy for nearly six months, accumulating twenty-one indorsements which generally agreed that the request was reasonable. But in the end—owing to declining inventories of vehicles left over from the World War, to inadequate funds, and to insufficient manpower to maintain the vehicles—all Marshall received was permission to take up the idea of training additional enlisted men to improve maintenance on the vehicles already at the school. Probably at Marshall's urging, the Infantry School commandant raised the issue again in June, 1930, and in December, 1931, with similar results.

MEMORANDUM FOR THE COMMANDANT   January 9, 1928
                                                  Fort Benning, Georgia

Selection of Infantry Officers for the Advanced Course,
Infantry School, and for the Command & General Staff School.

1. I suggest that a recommendation be made to the War Department requesting a modification of the present policy governing the selection of student officers for the Advanced Course, Infantry School, and for the Command and General Staff School.[1] It seems to me highly desirable that a limited number of outstanding officers should be given the opportunity of taking the Advanced Course, The Infantry School, or the course at the Command and General Staff School, regardless of present disqualifications as to rank. In principle, the present policy appears the logical method for governing selections for these details, except that it leaves an insufficient loophole for entry of a large class of officers whose present position on the promotion list bears little relation to their military experience and frequently no relation to their qualifications as to military efficiency. That these officers should be barred for many years from entrance into the two schools referred to merely because of a few months difference in service, is not only unfortunate in its effect on morale, but it is especially unfortunate in its effect on the work of such officers in the Company Officers Course at The Infantry School. Considering this question purely from the viewpoint of the efficiency of The Infantry School, the influence of the Academic Board would be greatly strengthened to the manifest advantage of instruction, if, for example, each student in the Company Officers Course realized that a limited number conspicuous for the outstanding quality of their work, would be detailed for the Advanced Course regardless of rank. The same would apply to students in the Advanced Course. There is another slant to this matter, which would also react to the advantage of the school, and to the service in general. Many officers anticipate preferment in obtaining these desirable details largely because of their rank. While it is desirable that the rank of the officer should usually be a preliminary qualification, I think there would be a very wholesome reaction to a policy giving added importance to the individual qualifications of the officer.

2. I have discussed this matter purely from the viewpoint of the efficiency of The Infantry School. There is, however, another consideration which is probably more important. The present promotion situation in the company grades operates directly to the detriment of the efficiency of the army.[2] The War Department is now seeking legal methods for correcting this condition. There are, I believe, other methods not requiring legal sanction which would do much towards increasing the morale of those officers who are rather hopelessly overslaughed on the promotion list. The foregoing proposal is but one of these methods, and from that standpoint alone I believe it worthy of approval. The fact that there are lieutenants, captains, and majors the same age and with almost the same length of service, would seem to indicate that a considerable latitude in selection of officers for advancement thru our educational systems is now desirable. In time of peace the law will always regulate rank. The army, therefore, should be careful to recognize efficiency by giving it the reward and distinction of appropriate consideration. In time of war, necessity makes the

necessary adjustments. The officer, however, should be fitted for this expectancy in peace.

3. I recommend that:

a. Not to exceed 10% of the officers detailed to pursue the Advanced Course be selected from those whose work has been most outstanding in the Company Officers Course, either during the current year or some previous year, regardless of rank.

b. Not to exceed 10% of the officers detailed to pursue the course at the Command and General Staff School be selected from those whose work has been most outstanding in the Advanced Course, The Infantry School, either during the current year or some previous year, regardless of rank.[3]

NA/RG 407 (210.63)

1. The third indorsement to Marshall's memorandum noted that admission to the Advanced Course was limited to field-grade officers (majors and colonels) and to those captains within the first thousand on the promotion list. All who attended had to be less than fifty years old when the course began.

2. A study of the promotion situation made in 1926 noted that it took, on the average, nine years of service to reach the grade of captain and eleven to reach major. But as the "present hump in the personnel of the Army must be taken into account and must be the controlling feature in our promotion system," the study predicted that by 1940 it would take seventeen years to make captain and twenty-three to make major. The positions available in each grade in 1926 were: major, 1,725; captain, 3,450; first lieutenant, 2,667; second lieutenant, 1,571. (Promotion Study for the Office of the Chief of Infantry by Captain John S. Schwab, October 19, 1926, NA/RG 177 [210.2, Chief of Infantry].)

3. General Collins, the commandant, indorsed Marshall's recommendations as "highly desirable." But the chief of Infantry, Major General Robert H. Allen, thought they "would necessitate a radical departure in existing policies governing the details of officers to the various schools." Marshall reiterated his suggestions in the school's *Annual Report* of June 30, 1928.

In a memorandum dated July 1, 1929, Colonel Lorenzo D. Gasser (Office of the Chief of Infantry) stated that Marshall "had repeatedly urged both verbally and in writing" the new selection procedures. "Furthermore, Colonel Marshall brings up the point that if we are to train officers for General Staff positions at the general service school, we must advance materially the opportunities for the younger officers, namely, officers in the grade of lieutenant, to attend this institution, otherwise, in event of war, the present policy of limiting the attendance to the General Staff School of officers of field grade or the senior captains will result, due to the rapid promotion incident to the outbreak of war, to a lack of suitable general staff officers for our divisions. He, therefore, holds that the entire educational program of the Army should be such as to permit the rapid induction of the younger officers of the Army through the special service schools so that they may attend the general service schools at a much younger age and of corresponding lower rank than is permitted at present." (NA/RG 177 [210.6, Chief of Infantry].)

In August, 1929, the new chief of Infantry, Major General Stephen O. Fuqua, approved a rejection of Marshall's proposals. In addition to the large war-created "hump" on the promotion list, a lack of adequate housing for student officers at Fort Benning made it difficult to detail low-paid junior officers there. Moreover, "to select those 'few officers who graduate at the top of their class' might re-introduce into our school system what is known as 'the old Leavenworth competition' element, an undesirable feature which after years of effort has been reduced to a minimum." (Major Elmer F. Rice to Gasser, August 6, 1929, ibid.)

To Brigadier General William H. Cocke   March 4, 1928
                                                         Fort Benning, Georgia

My dear General: I am sorry you and Mrs. Cocke could not arrange to pay me a visit in February as you had partially planned. I had quite counted on seeing you.

I am writing now as a result of a letter just received from Edmund Coles, in Charlotte. He mentioned that Mrs. Coles had received a formal offer for her house several weeks ago and was about to accept it. As he did not mention the Institute, I am wondering if you are aware of this possible transfer. I had rather imagined that her property, due to its location, was an inevitable acquisition of the Institute. This is merely to advise you that the house is about to be sold, in case you have had any idea of securing it for the V.M.I.[1]

I have not yet met your sister's daughter, but I wrote her husband a note asking him to let me know when she arrived that I might have the pleasure of meeting her. The students, married ones, all live in Columbus ten miles from the post, and I have not yet met many of their families, as I am still occupied in making the rounds of more than three hundred calls I owe on the post.

I wish you would tell me something of Mrs. Warren, and the Senator.[2] I have heard nothing of her health for several years.   Faithfully yours,

                                                         G. C. Marshall, Jr.

VMI/Alumni File

1. The Institute purchased the property, which was located immediately outside the school's main gate, in mid-September, 1928.
2. Senator and Mrs. Francis E. Warren.

To General John J. Pershing   June 21, 1928
                                                        Fort Benning, Georgia

My dear General,   I saw in the paper yesterday that you had just returned from Europe and am writing to find out something of your plans for the summer, as I hope to have more of an opportunity to see and talk to you than I did last summer.

I am leaving here the 26th by motor for Washington. Will probably be there only a day or two. Then will either go up to see my mother in Pittsburgh or down to Virginia on a series of visits. In any event I will do both, but in which order I cannot say now. Most of August I expect to be in New England visiting some old friends from Vermont, then at Ethan Allen, and later at Gloucester, and then with Preston Brown[1] and finally the latter part of August with Mrs. Russell on Naushon Island. Of course, all this is merely tentative, as I am not bound to any fixed dates. I had rather expected to sail for Europe on the Leviathan June 19th, but later decided I did not want to do this.

Hope you are in fine shape, and I am looking forward very much to seeing you in Washington. Affectionately yours,

G. C. Marshall, Jr.

LC/J. J. Pershing Papers (General Correspondence); T

1. Major General Preston Brown, commander of the First Corps Area, had been a friend of Marshall since 1910, at least. In his interview of April 4, 1957, Marshall observed that Brown "was famous not only for his efficiency and his vigor, but for his amusing comments which sometimes took the hide off. I had persuaded him to go to Leavenworth—he was very contemptuous of it. We had met together at one of these shoots at the great target range at Camp Perry in Ohio [August, 1910], and I enthused him with the idea of going there. And he put in for it. As he came out either one or two in the course, he did very well, and that marked the beginning of his great progression in the army, which eventually came out to command a division [Third] in the Meuse-Argonne battle."

TO MRS. THOMAS B. COLES   July 20, 1928
                                                              Greensburg, Pennsylvania

Dear Aunt Lot: I reached here this morning after leaving Lexington yesterday at 2 p.m. I found Mud looking much better than of last fall, but tired from house work. I was pretty closely occupied during my stay for Gen. Cocke filled up all my spare moments with business. Here I found Mother in the hospital with a broken hip. She fell over a chair in her room. Apparently she suffers little pain, but the contemplation of future helplessness is disheartening. Marie looks well, but worried.[1] I will probably be here at least ten days, before leaving for New England.

You and Charlotte gave me a very perfect week at Woodville, spoiled me too much, of course, but made life seem very smooth and "pleasant like."

You were so good to me, and I deeply appreciated every thing you said or did. I would have liked to have remained all summer. If it can be arranged, I am going to stop by on my way south.

With my love to you both,   Affectionately,

George

GCMRL/Research File (Family); H

1. Marshall was visiting his sister, Marie Singer. "Mud" was the late Mrs. Marshall's pet name for her mother.

TO BRIGADIER GENERAL JOHN McA. PALMER   September 15, 1928
                                                              Fort Benning, Georgia

My dear John,   Your letter of August 22d pursued me about the country and did not catch up until my return to Fort Benning four days ago. I secured the September Harper's yesterday and read your article on "America's Debt to the German Soldier" last night.[1] It is delightfully written, very informing, and exceedingly pointed as to moral. I am curious to know what reactions you have received regarding it, particularly as to the last paragraph. I wish it were possible for me to present my ideas in the delightful and cultured fashion you do yours.[2]

I was only in Washington one night on my way south the end of August and I stopped at the Farnsboro[3] to see if there was any chance of picking you up to motor down with me, including two or three visits in the country in Virginia. Miss or Mrs. ———, who stays at the phone, I never remember her name, told me you and Mrs. Palmer were in Cambridge. So that idea fell through. Probably you would not have cared to enter Georgia at this hot season of the year, but we would have had an amusing time, I know, on our way down here. I spent five days with General Pershing in the Blue Ridge Mountains, a week at a house party near Upperville, and a couple of days in Albemarle. All of this I know you would have enjoyed.

I was in Boston for three days this summer with Preston Brown, having arrived there after a visit at Fort Ethan Allen, and continued on to Gloucester for two days and then for ten days on Naushon Island, off Woodshole. Just now I am deep in the business of getting started on the new school year, while the painters are wrecking the inside of my house. Benning looks very green after a rainy summer. The new students have almost all arrived.

With affectionate regards to Mrs. Palmer and yourself, believe me always Faithfully yours,

G. C. M.

LC/J. McA. Palmer Papers

1. "America's Debt to a German Soldier: Baron von Steuben and What He Taught Us," *Harper's Magazine* 157(September 1928): 456–66.

2. Palmer's "moral" was more than simply preparedness prevents war. He asserted that effective preparedness in a republic resulted from a citizen army of organized and trained militiamen based upon military training for all able-bodied men of eighteen to twenty years of age. The Regular Army was to be a small, strictly limited organization performing certain continuing duties that could not be performed by citizen-soldiers (e.g., garrisoning frontier posts and providing military instruction and administration in peacetime). The 1920 reorganization bill, Palmer maintained, was a belated attempt to put into practice a system proposed by Baron von Steuben and George Washington in the 1780s.

In the second half of the final paragraph, Palmer wrote: "If our existing organization is not identical in all respects with Washington's, it is because another military system, entirely different in kind, and based upon the idea of an expansible standing army, has gradually developed since the War of 1812. This system, founded upon an exploded interpretation of the Constitution and supported by incomplete and uncritical historical research, still obstructs the development of our traditional military policy as perfected by Washington and as endorsed by all of the soldiers and statesmen who founded our government."

3. Palmer's Washington, D.C., apartment was in the Farnsboro Building at 2129 Florida Avenue, N.W.

October 8, 1928
Fort Benning, Georgia

My dear General, Am sorry that Mrs. Cocke and you cannot plan at this time to pay me a visit this winter. However, I hope you will feel that I would like very much to have you at any time your affairs are so disposed that you feel in the mood for a southern trip.

I saw the game Saturday, which was made difficult for our boys by the extreme heat. Eight of us went up from here to see the game and each one that I heard discuss the game afterwards had very much the same thing to say. I believe it is worth while repeating to you, though it may sound rather tactless.

We got the impression that the team lacked the old spirit which used to mark the playing of the cadets. It also appeared that the coaching system had not been based on quick action and speed, which seem the only logical foundations for light weight teams which are to oppose much heavier ones. Of course, it could be said that the change of climate and the heat had a depressing effect on our men, but my comments apply as forcibly to the first five minutes as they do to the latter half of the game. The Georgia Tech crowd gave more the impression of representing a military organization than did our men: they assembled for signals in a more orderly and prompt fashion; they returned to their playing positions expeditiously and simultaneously; they got off with the ball fast and as a unit. From the start our men straggled back and made a ragged "huddle"; they returned to playing positions in a casual manner; on a number of occasions early in the game I saw cadets standing flat-footed or on their heels just as the ball was snapped. Early in the game we all had the impression that the men going down the field under a kick were not putting out their full speed and did not approach the tackle with an air of determination to get the other man in spite of everything. I heard more than one comment that a player or two went to the bench at a more rapid run then they went down the field to a tackle. Someone said that the style of game was built on a slow start. I don't know the technique of this, but I do know that Georgia had no such system and that it would seem most illogical for any light weight team.

All of us felt very much the same way about the above. I had not seen the team since I played on it twenty-eight years ago, so my judgment might well be very faulty. But others of more recent vintage got the same impression. Our idea of a cadet on the field is one of quick action, speed, and a relentless fighting determination to stop the other fellow or to go forward. This definitely seemed to be lacking, tho climatic conditions or the small size of the squad could be charged as the reason. With the breaks practically all going against Georgia, as they did, I think a more determined cadet team would have secured a draw or possibly would have won by any little extra touch of good fortune.

Like the usual alumnus, I am expressing opinions very freely, but it seems to me with the history of the institute as a background every V.M.I. football team should give the impression of relentless fighters. There was one fat boy, No. 9, who gave all of us this impression. There were one or two others, but we were not able to single them out so well.[1]   Faithfully yours,

G. C. Marshall, Jr.

VMI/Alumni File; T

1. The final score of the football game, which had been played in Atlanta on October 6, was: Georgia Institute of Technology, 13; Virginia Military Institute, 0. Cocke replied that the chief problems were in the coaching and the lack of strong cadet interest. "There doesn't seem very keen desire to win the Georgia Tech game, whereas everyone is exceedingly anxious to win the game against the University of Virginia." (Cocke to Marshall, October 12, 1928, VMI/Alumni File.) On October 20, V.M.I. defeated the University of Virginia 9–0.

MEMORANDUM FOR THE COMMANDANT   November 19, 1928
                                                 Fort Benning, Georgia

Size of Classes at The Infantry School.

1. A reduction in the size of the Advanced and Company-Officers classes now appears desirable from the viewpoint of efficiency of instruction, limited school facilities, and lack of quarters for officers.

a. Efficiency of instruction.

In the majority of subjects it is only practicable for one officer to conduct the instruction. He usually has assistants, but the principal discussion or lecture must be handled by him. The larger the class the more difficult it is to hold the attention of the entire group. This is especially evident in field work and in the poorly ventilated and necessarily crowded assembly halls during cold or hot weather.

The larger the classes the less practicable it is to give students actual experience with the school troops in field exercises. It is believed that important and much needed practical instruction can be given if students have opportunities to participate as troop officers in some of the demonstrations, somewhat after the same manner as at the Field Artillery School.

It is desirable to mount officers for certain field work, especially in order to utilize terrain not otherwise available. The handling of large classes is difficult and the number of mounts now available is insufficient.

It is believed that the officers selected to take the Advanced Course should be of proved efficiency, especially that they should be of the energetic and ambitious type. The presence of individuals lacking in educational qualifications, dull mentally, or who are unambitious slows down instruction to the direct disadvantage of the majority of the students. This also applies to the Company-Officers Class, though not to the same extent. Smaller classes would make it more feasible to confine details as students to the desired type.

b. Limited school facilities and lack of quarters.

The primitive arrangements for conducting indoor instruction are a constant embarrassment to instruction. Badly arranged section or assembly rooms and poor ventilation are factors which directly and adversely affect instruction. The larger the classes the greater the difficulties in these respects.

Sand table methods and map maneuvers are valuable methods of instruction.[1] The present facilities limit these classes of instruction and make it extremely difficult to handle classes of the present size.

The smaller the classes the better the housing facilities in Columbus as to convenience and cost. The present system grows more irksome year by year as living conditions in the army elsewhere stabilize or improve.

2. A discussion as to the advisability of reducing the size of classes necessitates consideration of the probable number of officers available yearly for these details.

Based on the figures available here, practically all officers above the grade of major are graduates of this school or Leavenworth, and a majority of the majors will have completed the Advanced Course in 1929. A large majority of the captains will have completed one of the Benning courses by 1929 and there will be less than 250 to be given the Company-Officers Course. Slightly more than half the first lieutenants will have completed the old basic or the Company-Officers Course by the close of the present school year.

It is evident that there is a sufficiently large number of graduates of Leavenworth or Benning to furnish ample leaven for the remaining personnel of field rank; and the same remark applies to captains and first lieutenants as regards the Company-Officers Course. The time appears to have come to regulate the size of classes with more regard to the flow of promotion and the yearly additions to the officer corps. It is believed that the size of the Advanced and Company-Officers classes should bear a direct relation to the number of officers promoted yearly to the grade of captain and the number of second lieutenants commissioned each year, respectively. This would mean that the Advanced Class should consist of approximately fifty (50) students and the Company-Officers Class of one hundred (100).[2]

3. *Refresher Class.*

The limitations for this course are billets and the desirability of establishing very intimate relations between instructors and students. Not to exceed 12 officers above the grade of major should be detailed for this course.

4. *National-Guard and Reserve Officers Classes.*

The following figures represent the maximum which can be accommodated and handled with efficiency:

Field Officers Class 25
Company-Officers Class. 125

5. *National-Guard Enlisted Specialists Course.*

Not to exceed 50 can be handled efficiently for this course.

6. *Horseshoers Course.*

Not to exceed 20 can be efficiently handled in the practical work of this course with the present plant.

7. In view of the foregoing, the following recommendation is submitted as to the size of classes commencing with the 1929–1930 courses:

Advanced Class. 50
Company-Officers Class. 100
Refresher Class 12
National-Guard and Reserve
Field-Officers Class 25
National-Guard and Reserve
Company-Officers Class. 125
National-Guard Enlisted
Specialists Class. 50
Horseshoers Class 20

8. *Reductions in faculty and enlisted personnel.*

For reasons given in paragraph 1 *a,* a reduction in the number of instructors cannot be made in the same proportion as recommended for classes. However, it is believed that by a reorganization of the Academic Department a reduction in instructors can be secured without loss of efficiency. The faculty board is now considering the matter of reorganization, and definite recommendations will be submitted at an early date.[3]

NA/RG 407 (210.63)

1. A sandtable was a box or curbed table containing sand which was shaped into relief models of terrain for tactical studies.
2. During the 1928–29 school year, attendance in these two courses was: Advanced, 87; Company Officers', 142.
3. General Collins's lengthy first indorsement reinforced and approved Marshall's proposal. After considerable study in the War Department, and with the General Staff's Operations and Training Division's reluctant acquiescence, Marshall's recommendations were accepted, but only for the 1929–30 school year, in late January, 1929.

To BRIGADIER GENERAL JOHN McA. PALMER   December 20, 1928
                                                Fort Benning, Georgia

My dear John,   Chapter 16 is delightful, intensely interesting, and charmingly written. I do not think of any other comment which might be added. You have done a beautiful job of this portion of your book and if the rest is of the same class and standard, it will prove an enduring monument to you.[1]

Not having seen any of the other chapters, except possibly portions of the one which will include Von Steuben's connection with the Revolution, I feel free to make one suggestion. I think it would be wise to present those portions of your ideas which bear directly on the Swiss system, with considerable indirection or, it might better be said, by inference. This has no particular point with regard to the general reader, but it might have considerable effect on the character of the reviews of the book written by army officers. Certain of them will be looking for a particular page on which to hang their hats, and this would undoubtedly be it.

I really was genuinely sorry when I came to the end of your paper, because it does make delightful reading; you have handled your presentation in a very artistic fashion.

I repeat again that I want to have you down here sometime this winter. Do you know General C. D. Rhodes at all well? That is, are you fond of him? I thought I might have the two of you together. If I did, you would have all the opportunity in the world to work that you might desire,—with golf links 200 yards from the house.[2]

With affectionate regards to you and Mrs. Palmer,   Faithfully yours,

G. C. M.

LC/J. McA. Palmer Papers

1. The chapter Marshall read was published as "Lincoln as a Military Dictator," in *Washington, Lincoln, Wilson*.
2. Marshall's friend from Fort Leavenworth days, Charles D. Rhodes, had been promoted to major general effective September 5, 1928.

LECTURE[1]   [n.d.]
[Fort Benning, Georgia]

Development in Tactics.

I have been asked to talk on the latest developments in tactics. This provides a broad subject that might be argued pro and con for a long series of evenings, so an extreme of brevity is necessary. Furthermore, much that I will say is the result of personal observations and represents my personal views, rather than the formal conclusions of the War Department. I offer these views merely as food for thought, in connection with your military studies and training.

To begin with, please keep clearly in mind that I am dealing with the finished product, as it were, and not discussing the preliminary training that is absolutely necessary to the education of a competent officer. Discipline and disciplinary methods, administration, logistics and elementary tactical technique—all matters of your current extension courses—are not the subject of this discussion. I will only invite your attention to the fact that a necessary preliminary for the musician is a painstaking practice of scales before he reaches the point of making music. Exact forms for orders and annexes, road spaces, systems of abbreviations, symbols for troop units, headquarters, dumps, etc., frontages, formations for attack or defense—estimates of the situations, and a multitude of similar matters of technique, are to the officer what scales and similar exercises are to the musician. Exactitude is required in each exercise, until the correct methods become automatic. That is the sort of training you are now undergoing. Later you will be in a position to add or subtract, to amend, or even to depart rather completely from the methods you have learnt—but not until you have thoroughly mastered the elementary technique.

Before commenting on recent tactical developments, I will ask you first to think back to the World War in its fourth year when the American Army appeared on the battlefield. That was a very special form of fighting, one of static or semi-siege warfare. It seemed very complicated because of the elaborate system of fighting sectors into which the front in France had gradually developed—immense masses of artillery, a maze of trenches, barbed-wire and concrete emplacements, thousands of miles of 60-centimeter railroad actually operating on the battlefield, huge dumps of ammunition and supplies, and installations comparable to the public utilities of great cities. Vast and complicated as this set-up appeared to us, it was more or less fixed in place. Our maps showed every enemy trench. We had photographs of his principal emplacements. We usually knew his strength, the location of most of his cannon and machine guns, the numeral and history of his organizations confronting us.

Green troops in a sector therefore had some chance of saving themselves from the full penalty of their errors. Similar failures in warfare of movement would have led to the destruction or temporary disintegration of a command.

In contrast, picture the opening campaign of a war. It is a cloud of uncertainties, haste, rapid movements, congestion on the roads, strange terrain, lack of ammunition and supplies at the right place at the right moment, failures of communications, terrific tests of endurance, and misunderstandings in direct proportion to the inexperience of the officers and the aggressive action of the enemy. Add to this a minimum of preliminary information of the enemy and of his dispositions, poor maps, and a speed of movement or in alteration of the situation, resulting from fast flying planes, fast moving tanks, armored cars, and motor transportation in general. There you have warfare of movement such as swept over Belgium or Northern France in 1914, but at far greater speed. That, gentlemen, is what you are supposed to be preparing for.

Our officers are almost entirely without practical experience in warfare of movement. Their fighting was confined to the final phases of static warfare. Naturally, it is extremely difficult to break away from the conclusions formed in this special type of fighting. Yet the great military problem of the United States is the rapid mobilization and concentration of field armies and their early employment in warfare of movement.

With this in mind, it was observed by many officers in our troop maneuvers at the service schools, that methods of technique practicable in France, were often ineffective in open warfare.

Certain things became glaringly evident. Warfare of movement was a far more difficult matter than static warfare; mistakes were much more easily made and were far more devastating in their result; large scale maps were seldom available and the solution of tactical problems on an ordinary geological survey map or with no map at all required much more skill than when a map of the Gettysburg type was available;[2] long orders were usually impossible of preparation and written orders were infrequently issued; the brief oral or written order required much more of skill than the detailed affair common to the World War; time was always short, delays were usually fatal; directions and boundaries were difficult of arrangement—the latter often impossible of designation; the tactical methods necessary for the controlled employment of partially trained officers and troops were different from those required for veteran personnel. Even the best of regular officers found the problems of warfare of movement extremely difficult to handle. Above all, it was apparent that few had a correct idea of the various applications of the fundamental principle of simplicity.

So far I have generalized. A few specific examples may be helpful. Take, for instance, the preparation of orders. In France in 1918, days, often a month elapsed between the decision to attack a certain front and the actual operation. Detailed orders were prepared long in advance, special maps were lithographed, ammunition and supplies were accumulated, and at times the troops actually rehearsed a specific operation. Naturally, every item of preparation that could be foreseen was carried out in minute detail. Time was not the dominating element. Information of the enemy was complete to a remarkable degree. The real problems were secrecy of preparation and the judicious allotment of dense masses of preliminary and covering fires. Yet even in France, within the fixed sectors assigned to divisions and brigades, the moment the first phase, the first morning's fighting, was completed the real troubles began—no orders or orders received too late, misunderstandings, lack of information regarding the enemy's new dispositions, the human factor exaggerated to the Nth degree. Our troops usually made the initial advance in good form. Later, in the hurly burly or rapidly changing situations, their lack of training demanded an appalling toll of life or limb. We have come to view the quality of our participation through roseate glasses, the stumbling, blunderings, failures, appeals for help, and hopeless confusion of the moment have been forgotten in the single thought of final victory.

Compare this with August 1914. The order for the entire British Expeditionary Force was, on at least one occasion, a single sentence ordering a further retreat! The dominant consideration was the problem of getting that single sentence to all the troops in time. Consider the question of maps on that occasion. A mass of detailed maps of Belgium and Northern France had been provided but their bulk was so large, the movements into new terrain so rapid, and the difficulty of distribution so great, that none were actually made available and motor maps obtained locally were employed. Yet you probably have come to expect a large scale Gettysburg map as a matter of course. Unfortunately, such a map is necessary for the purposes of theoretical instruction in troop leading and the staff work for small units. And the officers concerned in this type of instruction are the very ones who would most frequently have to work without maps or with only the small scale variety.

Another example: Communications in France were matters of elaborate arrangement—ground wireless, air wireless, the buzzer, telephone, runners, and pigeons, the headquarters usually located in dugouts offering rather complete shelter. Picture an Infantry regiment in warfare of movement, entering under cover of darkness, terrain never before seen, and under the necessity of attacking at dawn—machine guns here, howitzers there, first line companies, supports and reserves, communication with the distant artillery to be assured, command posts scattered about in the open, runners fumbling about in the dark, breakfast to be distributed, orders to be delivered. Do you think all this an easy matter as compared to the more deliberate arrangements possible in 1918? Can you imagine long written orders? Do you suppose tired, irritated and nervous officers will misunderstand this or that, or fail to comprehend their full part in the hurried preparations? Four things are necessary to success under these considerations—discipline that triumphs over fatigue and danger, a thorough grasp of the technique involved, and a knowledge of two vitally important matters— real simplicity and correct methods for maintaining control.

Consider another aspect of the problem in warfare of movement. We are all taught how to set up a command post and establish communications. But that has been found not to be the real difficulty. The troublesome question is, when to make a complete set-up, when to lay all our wires. A premature set-up kills the momentum of the movement and expends valuable wire. Yet how do we maintain control without the complete set-up; to what degree do we first establish a command post?

Consider the matter of direction and boundaries. Without a detailed map, a graphic solution is not often possible. How then, will you manage this? Can you think of a substitute for coordinates, named ridges, hills, and rivers, that all can see on the detailed maps?

Let us consider the opening phases of a fight, advance guard or leading detachments driving in the enemy's covering detachments in order to develop the main line of resistance, and something of the hostile dispositions. Machine guns and automatic rifles are much more deadly weapons today than in 1918. We have improved tremendously in our technique for handling them. How quickly then do you think small covering forces could be driven in? How much fighting and time would be required to make certain you were merely opposed by a small group with a few automatic weapons? To what extent would these small actions cause premature deployments, loss of time and loss of direction?

Go further into the fighting, and a very serious problem arises, for which we have not yet found a satisfactory solution. The machine gun opposing you is seldom in your front. It is usually one or two thousand yards off to your flank, completely concealed from view to its front, and well concealed from your view. How will you meet this dilemma? Even after you locate the gun, how will you be able to designate its position for effective artillery fire or trench mortar treatment?

Naturally, the enemy will do all in his power to disguise the layout of his front, and to disarrange the direction of advance of your several units. How will you offset this difficulty?

In all these matters there is one phase of the question that we find exceedingly difficult to treat in theoretical instruction and that is this—when to make decisions, rather than what decision to make. Your tactical problems of necessity are usually confined to a requirement calling for your decision and order. This is not the real difficulty, that is the question of when to make a decision. The situation changes constantly. Do you constantly change or alter your decision? Of course not, but when does the moment arrive when you should decide on a new course of action?

Summing up these various difficulties, it is apparent that the tactics of future periods of warfare of movement, demand a knowledge of how to operate by means of brief, concise oral orders, based on the ground you can see or on maps with very little detail. They require a knowledge of how to maintain control and direction of units necessarily much dispersed. They compel action when very, very little is yet known of the enemy's dispositions. They involve the necessity for very perfect teamwork between the Infantry on the one side and the artillery, aviators and various commanders on the other. They necessitate a high degree of cleverness in locating enemy machine guns and designating their positions for the effective fire of distant units. They compel a constant tactical readiness in security arrangements as well as in battle tactics, in preparation for the sudden appearance of tanks or other mechanized units in front, flank, or rear.

In all these matters speed of thought, speed of action and direction and speed of operation is essential to success.

GCMRL/G. C. Marshall Papers (Pentagon Office, Speeches)

1. This manuscript, which Marshall may have developed from a presentation to a Company Officers' Course, is the only Infantry School lecture preserved in his files.

2. The "Gettysburg map" was a multiple-sheet, detailed topographical map (scale 1:21120) of the area between Gettysburg, Pennsylvania, and Antietam, Maryland, which was commonly used to lay out school tactical problems.

To Brigadier General John McA. Palmer   January 17, 1929
Fort Benning, Georgia

Dear John,   Your letter with enclosures came in the next mail after a note I sent to you.[1] I have read the manuscript and this is my reaction:

Material,—excellent and unusually interesting.

Treatment,—not up to standard of other chapters I have read. My impression is you have played too frequently on the same string and not brought out the points with all your usual finesse, particularly as to your forcible and frequent comments on the promotion aspects. I do not mean to omit this, but it is a decided side issue when compared to the great question of the principles involved as to Confederate and Union methods of distributing officers of the regular establishment.

You should admit that promotions were inevitable considering the small group of regulars at the disposal of the government and the tremendous forces which were to be raised. If you leave this chapter as now written, my guess is that it will come in for a tremendous criticism, not based on the larger aspects of the problem, but directed solely at your personal attitude on the promotion question. This would be an unfortunate diversion of attention and thought from the main thing. I believe you can leave in all the secondary points you make, but do it in a more moderate or indirect fashion, not affording the cast iron "regular" too conspicuous a target, diverting attention from the main issues.[2]

I would be very glad to read the typed copy as you suggest; and I am gratified that you feel my views are of sufficient moment to warrant this procedure. Incidentally, if you have this respect for my judgment, permit me to observe that your own treatment of these coming chapters would probably be greatly benefited by a little less of the desk at the present time and more of fresh air, with the casual comments Rhodes and myself would willingly supply. I got the impression from this last chapter that you have been tied down too long, and I think, apropos of your possible trip here on the completion of the draft of the manuscript, that such a time is a little too late to work in a refreshed point of view, which I am certain would come from a temporary break in your tremendous effort.   Faithfully,

G. C. M.

How's this for cold blooded criticism?[3]

LC/J. McA. Palmer Papers

1. Some time during the second week of January, 1929, Palmer wrote: "You were so good about reading the former samples that I am sending you two more short chapters. These cover the period from Fort Sumter to Bull Run. . . . And now I am going to ask a great favor of you. I hope the typing of the book will begin about a month from now. Can I send the chapters to you like a serial story as they are typed and get your frank verdict? I will not expect you to concur in all of my conclusions but I do want the reaction of a broad, cool mind before I release it to the publishers, and yours is the broadest and coolest that I know." (Rough draft, LC/J. McA. Palmer Papers.)

2. The two chapters Marshall read were probably those printed as "Promotion and Bull Run" and "The Young Napoleon" (i.e., Robert E. Lee). In Palmer's opinion, the federal government's insistence upon expanding the Regular Army and giving its officers rapid promotions to lead the new regiments—rather than using the Regulars to train a "well-regulated militia" in each of the states—squandered the Union's manpower advantage in the

early part of the Civil War. The Confederacy, having no Regular Army, used its trained soldiers and cadets for militia training. The result was that the Confederacy initially had better troops. (*Washington, Lincoln, Wilson,* pp. 187-209.)

3. This sentence was written in Marshall's hand at the bottom of the typed letter.

To Brigadier General William H. Cocke   January 31, 1929
                                                    Fort Benning, Georgia

My dear Cocke,   During the fall and recently I have been asked to review chapters of a book being written by General John McA. Palmer, Retired. He is under contract, I think to the Atlantic Monthly for the serial rights, and to some publisher for the book rights. In it he traces the course of our military policy from its inception with Washington's proposal for a "well regulated militia." He has uncovered some very astonishing facts as a result of a prolonged study of documents in the Congressional Library, and discloses for the first time what actually was Washington's plan and how it was thwarted by state jealousies and later entirely diverted by John C. Calhoun's policy. He further carries the evolution, if it can be called such, of this plan through the vicissitudes of our military and political history to the present day.

The book, in a large measure, presents a summary of the actions of the leading figures and indicates quite clearly their relation to what actually transpired. Washington, Von Steuben, Jefferson, Calhoun, Lincoln, Jefferson Davis, Lee, McClellan, Jackson, and Grant are presented in considerable detail and in a most striking manner. He covers the initial development of the Union and Confederate armies of the Civil War in a most pronounced fashion, showing in an entirely new light the dilemma of Mr. Lincoln and the failure of the War Department and regular army to furnish him with the proper policy. In contrast he gives a most delightful and critical outline of Jefferson Davis' policy and the reasons which lead to its adoption. In connection with this last, he sketches the career of Stonewall Jackson at the V.M.I. and later, and the employment of the V.M.I. cadets in the first training of the Confederate Army for Bull Run, as a demonstration of how the policy should have been met on the northern side. As a consequence, the V.M.I. comes in for considerable and complimentary reference.

Palmer is the most exact and painstaking military student in the army today. He has one of the best brains in the army and is probably among the four or five most cultivated officers. He was largely the author of the present National Defense Act and is given full credit for this by Senator Wadsworth in his introduction to a recently published book by Palmer, "Statesmanship in War." The thought occurred to me that possibly Palmer might be a desirable person to make the principal address at your next graduation exercises. Naturally I have mentioned nothing of this to him, merely submitting it to you as a suggestion.

I am sending some pecans to Mrs. Cocke. I hope she is not overworking in her self-imposed duties at Lexington and in the remodeling of your place on the James.

With warm regards to you both,   Faithfully yours,

G. C. Marshall, Jr.

P.S. Is there any chance of your visiting me this spring?

VMI/Alumni File

To Brigadier General Frank R. McCoy[1]   April 13, 1929
                                                    Fort Benning, Georgia

Dear General,   Thank you for your nice note of April 10th. I am glad to learn from you of Thompson and Ross, not knowing either one of them personally. I had been told that Major Thompson was especially efficient, but knew nothing of Major Ross. What you wrote of them is very reassuring.[2]

Thompson, in particular, has an exceedingly hard job here in connection with the school. There are a great many excellent instructors in equitation in the army, but none within my knowledge have produced anything like the results secured by Major Smith, of the Cavalry, here at Benning. His work has really been unique, in that he has developed a tremendous fondness for riding in practically everyone with whom he has come in contact officially. No one is frightened or scarred up during the early stages, and most of them usually become surprisingly bold cross-country riders. This refers to all of the students, even the most hardened horse-haters, and to about 200 women. The ladies' equitation class has 180 members, and the first two platoons would make the Italian Cavalry envious of their daring riding, particularly up and down slides.[3]

I wish you could stop here enroute to San Antonio. We are making many changes in the teaching of tactics, and particularly of technique, and I think we are developing a very practical system suited to officers who will be responsible for the development of a hastily raised war time force.

As to the post itself, you would hardly recognize the present Benning. The place is growing very lovely in appearance and remarkable in the facilities offered for outdoor diversion. It is a thoroughly well groomed and presentable post with an unusually happy garrison, an entirely different affair from what I saw in 1924 before my departure for China. I have a large and quite delightful house, and excellent servants who are accustomed to guests continuously. I would be *delighted* if you and Mrs. McCoy would pay me a visit on your way to Texas.   Faithfully yours

G. C. Marshall, Jr.

LC/F. R. McCoy Papers
1. Marshall and McCoy had been friends since 1917. During the World War, McCoy had

commanded the 165th Infantry of the Forty-second Division and later a brigade of the Thirty-second Division. Following the war, he held a number of military-diplomatic assignments in Armenia, the Philippine Islands, Japan, and Nicaragua. In 1928 he was appointed a delegate to the Pan-American Conference. At the time Marshall wrote, McCoy was heading a commission investigating the dispute between Paraguay and Bolivia over the Chaco region.

2. McCoy wrote to praise two men who were to be assigned as instructors at the Infantry School: Major John B. Thompson (U.S.M.A., 1914), who was to teach equitation; and Major Frank K. Ross—McCoy's cousin—who was to be an instructor in artillery.

3. Major Henry J.M. Smith, an equitation instructor, was a graduate of the Cavalry School Advanced Course (1924) and the Command and General Staff School (1925). Equitation was a required course for all student officers, but Marshall also encouraged their wives to ride. One student officer later recalled: "The school had a large stable of horses for the use of students, and Marshall was instrumental in promoting riding for the personnel of the post, both male and female. This included riding privileges, horse shows, paper hunts, etc. It was said that Fort Benning was the 'horsiest' post in the Army." (Colonel Charles S. Ritchel to Forrest C. Pogue, October 24, 1960, GCMRL/Research File [Benning].)

To Brigadier General William H. Cocke   April 18, 1929
Fort Benning, Georgia

My dear General,   I am honored with your invitation to deliver the ROTC commissions to the graduating class this year, and am happy to accept.[1] It is very good of Mrs. Cocke to include me as her house guest for that occasion, and I accept with a great deal of pleasure.

I was involved in tentative arrangements for a semi-official trip at this particular time, but I think it will be possible for me to arrange differently, as I am anxious to see the Institute as a going concern before your control ceases.

As to General Lejeune, his appointment appeals to me as an admirable selection. I know him fairly well and believe he will enter into his duties in a very understanding fashion. He is enough of a national figure to be of decided advantage to the Institute, not to mention that his appointment will produce a very solid backing from the entire Marine Corps. Whoever thought of him is long on good judgment.[2]   Faithfully yours,

G. C. Marshall, Jr.

VMI/Alumni File

1. As the date for his "finals" speech on June 15 approached, Marshall wrote: "Just now I don't feel so enthusiastic about your invitation for the 15th. In that connection I am a little in doubt as to just what my role is, but in any event I will make an honest effort to be brief." (Marshall to Cocke, June 8, 1929, VMI/Alumni File.)

Marshall's address, the V.M.I. student newspaper commented, "was one which stirred and inspired, not only the members of the Graduating Class to whom it was delivered, but also the hundreds of parents, friends and alumni who had gathered in the Hall." (*The Cadet,* June 15, 1929.)

2. Major General John A. Lejeune commanded the Second Division, A.E.F., from July 28, 1918, to August 8, 1919, and later the Marine Barracks at Quantico, Virginia. From July 1, 1920, until March 5, 1929, he was commandant of the Marine Corps. On March 16, 1929, the V.M.I. Board of Visitors approved his appointment as superintendent, effective July 1.

To General John J. Pershing

June 28, 1929
Fort Benning, Georgia

Dear General: I saw Adamson in Washington the end of May and he told me you would not return before September. Your stay will be longer than I had counted on. I have been hoping I could write congratulations on your designation as Ambassador, tho I do not know whether or not you would care for the duties. Yet I think you are more admirably equipped for the post than any other citizen. It would be a fine thing for the country to have you in a powerful position there during this particular period. However, I suppose the choice will be one of political considerations rather than "business efficiency", advertising to the contrary notwithstanding.[1]

I have had a very busy spring and feel much in need of a respite, so I am leaving in two days for the Eaton Ranch near Sheridan, Wyoming, to remain there until September 10th.

I was called to Washington by Mr. Davis, who wanted me to go out to Manila with him as prospective Chief of Constabulary, Mr. Stimson having started the business of getting the law amended to repermit army officers to be so detailed. Mr. Stimson had proposed my name, but I declined for several reasons, the most important one that I do not fancy Mr. Davis as a backer in the present difficult situation. Also, that I should keep closer to straight army business at my age.[2]

My sister spent a good bit of the past ten months with me, enjoying Benning tremendously and being a Godsend for me. She left when I went to Washington. June 15th I made the graduation address at the V.M.I. They were good enough to invite me after I turned down the Superintendency,[3] so I accepted and had a hot trip.

Please try and arrange to make me a visit this winter when the climate is most unfavorable in the north and delightful here. I can give you privacy, gaiety, delightful young people, fine horses and pretty constant diversions, as you might elect. Adamson rather led me to feel that you might have come last year if I had pressed harder. Knowing how you are pursued by importunate people, I always try to go easy on invitations, but they are, I believe, more sincere and more warmly supported by a desire to have you, than those more strenuously proposed.

I hope Miss May has recovered from the shock of last winter, tho I know she will find it hard to adjust herself to life in Lincoln without her sister.[4] Please give her my warm regards.

Warren, I understand, is doing very well at Yale. I had thought he was at Boston "Tech".

With affectionate regards,   Faithfully yours,

G. C. Marshall, Jr.

LC/J. J. Pershing Papers (General Correspondence)
   1. The American ambassador to France, Myron T. Herrick, died on March 31, 1929. For a

few weeks there was speculation that General Pershing might be named to succeed him, but the former Republican governor of New Jersey, Walter E. Edge, resigned his United States Senate seat to take the post in November.

In his letter to Marshall, Pershing said: "What you say about my becoming Ambassador is very much appreciated, but as a matter of fact I could not, in the first place, afford it, and in the second place I wouldn't be bothered with the thousand and one details that the Ambassador over here is called upon to handle. Every American who comes to France thinks he has a special call on the Ambassador and feels rather neglected and perhaps insulted if he is not invited to take luncheon or dinner." (Pershing to Marshall, July 13, 1929, LC/J. J. Pershing Papers [General Correspondence].)

2. Dwight F. Davis had been secretary of war between October 14, 1925, and March 5, 1929. His appointment as governor-general in May, replacing Henry L. Stimson, who returned to the United States in March to become secretary of state, was something of a surprise. Davis faced continuing agitation for independence by Filipino leaders. The post Davis offered Marshall carried the rank of brigadier general.

Pershing responded on July 13: "I think you were very wise indeed not to accept Mr. Davis' invitation to go to the Philippines with him. In the first place the climate is enervating and in the second place I could hardly think of a more unsatisfactory person to work with. Your future interest lies in your continued splendid service with the Army. I hope things may come out for you much better in the near future than you now hope." (Ibid.)

3. Cocke presumably made the offer privately. There is no correspondence on this matter in the V.M.I. archives.

4. Mary Pershing Butler died at her home in Lincoln, Nebraska, on December 13, 1928.

To Major General Frank R. McCoy
July 1, 1929
Fort Benning, Georgia

My dear General: Please accept as very sincere and genuine my congratulations on your promotion.[1] No one is more pleased, not even Mrs. McCoy, than I am that you should at last receive this recognition for your years of remarkably efficient service. I am so glad the President chose to pay you the unusual compliment of publicly recommending you to the Secretary of War.

For years I have held you out as a standard of how to combine high efficiency with equal tact in the performance of military duties.

With affectionate regards,   Faithfully yours,

G. C. Marshall, Jr.

LC/F. R. McCoy Papers; H

1. Effective September 4, 1929, McCoy was promoted to major general and given command of the Fourth Corps Area, with headquarters in Atlanta, Georgia. This command area included Fort Benning.

To Brigadier General John McA. Palmer
July 30, 1929
Wolf, Wyoming

Dear John: Your letter reached me here in north western Wyoming in the Big

Horn Mountains. I will be happy and intensely interested in going over your galley proof or ms. Please send it here where I will be until September 10th.

I am having a charming, healthy, delightful, bankrupting time here. This place is unique and they have all been wonderful to me.

It is splendid to find the publishers so impressed and pleased with your book. I will never be happy until one way or another you receive the public recognition to which you are so indisputably entitled.

With all conceit and no modesty, I am an expert on military brains—and you most decidedly have'm.   Affectionately,

G. C. M.

LC/J. McA. Palmer Papers; H

To General John J. Pershing   September 13, 1929
                                                     Fort Benning, Georgia

Dear General: I returned at 10:00 last night after 2½ months absence in Wyoming, and this morning thought of your birthday occurs to me. This letter will be a rather late arrival of congratulations, but no one wishes you more of health, happiness, and years than your humble servant. I was concerned by the last paragraph of your letter to me, which reached me in Wyoming the latter part of July, referring to the fact that your winter attack of flu had left you in need of a summer cure. However, I noticed in the paper that you had been grouse shooting in England, so I suppose you have gotten well back into shape again. I am wondering if you did not join Baruch, as I noticed he had leased a place for this winter.

I was much distressed this summer to miss an opportunity to see Senator Warren. He visited Sheridan, twenty miles from the Eaton Ranch, but there was no prior notice of his visit, and I did not learn of it until after he had left. Naturally I would have liked so much to have seen him again, for it has now been five years since I left Washington. I am going to write him a note, in the hope that he will tell me something of himself and of Mrs. Warren.

I had a delightful summer, gaining back about eleven pounds—I weigh 180 now—and meeting many agreeable, and some distinguished, people. The last ten days the ground was covered with snow, and the air was rather bracing. I rode daily and often twice a day, as did most of the others. General Harries and his wife have a lovely cottage there and turned over one of their rooms to me, so I was quite luxuriously established. Mrs. Harries had a great deal to say about you, complimentary of course.[1]

I am looking forward to the possibility of your spending some time with me this winter. Please, if you come, do not tie yourself up with engagements which will force you to rush back to Washington or elsewhere, for you may find it more restful and agreeable here than you anticipate. Certainly it will give me a great deal of pleasure to have you, and your presence would be of tremendous interest to this large garrison. General and Mrs. Harbord are probably coming over with General and Mrs. Cocke from Augusta immediately after New Year's. I hope their plans turn out this way.

 With affectionate regards and more congratulations, Faithfully yours,

G. C. Marshall, Jr.

LC/J. J. Pershing Papers (General Correspondence)

 1. Major General George H. Harries, a businessman as well as a soldier, had been an important figure in the Service of Supply in France during the World War.

TO BRIGADIER GENERAL JOHN MCA. PALMER[1]   September 17, 1929

Fort Benning, Georgia

Dear John: The manuscript of your new book arrived during my absence on a camping trip in the mountains, and after my return I was pretty much occupied with a number of all-day riding excursions which had been planned to take advantage of the cool days towards the end of the summer. Therefore, I was too sleepy at night to manage much reading, until my last few days.

 I think you have done a beautiful job. I think your Chapter III is a classic, and to a degree which is almost a disadvantage to the remainder of the book. All of the matter is unusually well written, but this one chapter is unique, in my opinion, in the presentation of military matters.

 I took a liberty, unauthorized, but I believe, well advised. Mary Roberts Rinehart's cottage was right close to my cabin. I made an engagement with her for one afternoon and without telling her whose manuscript I was reading, and after a brief resume of what the entire book was about, I read to her Chapter III.[2]

 She had been undoubtedly prepared to be bored with some trite, amateurishly written military discussion. She sat in front of the fire, smoking, while I did my best. When I had finished, she jumped to her feet and exclaimed, "That is magnificent; that is one of the most interesting things I have ever heard. I am thrilled with it." She wanted to read the entire manuscript, but there was no time for that. She button-holed me several times later to discuss it.

 Now my idea in doing this was to get the reaction of a trained writer and a super-expert on publicity, as well as that of a woman, and mother. You may remember that her article in the Saturday Evening Post was one of the most potent weapons used to organize the women behind the administration's effort to pass the Selective Service Act in April 1917. She wrote this from the viewpoint of a mother.[3] It might appeal to her to review, or at least liberally quote, your book, and if she did, I promise you it would be good advertising.

I suggest that you quietly have the publisher send her one of the first copies, without any request for a review.

I hope you do not mind the liberty I took. It probably will not appeal to you as very important one way or the other, but I believe I have a better sense of procedure in this direction than you have.

I just returned Thursday night and my school work opened this morning. General King arrives at noon, General Fuqua tonight; and General Summerall on Thursday. I will be pretty busy.   Affectionately yours,

LC/J. J. Pershing Papers (General Correspondence)

1. To support his request for General Pershing to read the book and write an introduction, Palmer wrote to Marshall on September 20 to say that he was "taking the liberty" of sending a copy of the letter printed here to the general. (LC/J. McA. Palmer Papers.)

2. Marshall meant that he had read the first part of Part III, "Dramatis Personae," which is printed as chapter XV. (See the following letter.)

3. Mary Roberts Rinehart was a well-known author of novels, plays, and nonfiction. During the World War she wrote for the Division of Syndicate Features of the Committee on Public Information (the Creel Committee).

To Brigadier General John McA. Palmer   September 25, 1929
                                                Fort Benning, Georgia

Dear John: I have been having an orientation course for the instructors, two Generals as guests concurrently with five painters doing over bedrooms, 175 newly arrived student officers, and school opening today. So I have been busy.

Your three letters have been received, and I will be very glad to write to General Pershing. However, I fear that I have made an error in my reference to Chapter III. I had in mind the chapter making the presentation of Civil War characters.[1]

Your last note came this morning, asking about sending your manuscript to Mrs. Rinehart. I think it would be better to send her a copy of the printed book,—and without other comment than that it is with the compliments of the author and publisher. If she does not come across, then we can consider other measures for a reawakening of her interest.

I am so busy this morning that I cannot manage a longer note.   Faithfully yours,

G. C. M.

LC/J. McA. Palmer Papers

1. Chapter XV, "Dramatis Personae," gave vignettes of Jefferson Davis, Winfield Scott, William T. Sherman, Robert E. Lee, George B. McClellan, Thomas J. Jackson, Ulysses S. Grant, Nathan Bedford Forrest, John A. Logan, John Brown, and Abraham Lincoln. (Palmer, *Washington, Lincoln, Wilson*, pp. 165–76.)

To Brigadier General John McA. Palmer   October 21, 1929
                                               Fort Benning, Georgia

Dear John: Appendix II came, and before I got around to acknowledging it, I was called away by Mrs. Coles' sudden illness, followed by her death. I am very grateful to you for serving me again as you did last Friday, and I want you to know that I am deeply appreciative.[1] I was sorry that I had no opportunity to talk to you, but even had there been an opportunity I could not have made much use of it.

Naturally I was much interested in Appendix II, and the generous compliment in your postscript was certainly noted. If I could combine the Congress and the War Department in your person, it would be smooth sailing. Your expressed opinion, however, is deeply appreciated.[2]

The essence of the quotation from Washington seems to be that there is a middle ground in the matter, just as there is in almost every plan for the control of human affairs. Unfortunately, the weaker sisters are the loudest talkers, the other end of the list naturally having to maintain a tactful silence.[3]

Please tell Mrs. Palmer how sorry I was not to be able to see more of her, and that I am grateful for her presence on Friday.   Affectionately yours,

                                               G. C. M.

LC/J. McA. Palmer Papers

1. Marshall's mother-in-law, Mrs. Walter (Elizabeth Pendleton) Coles, died in Lexington, Virginia, on October 16. The burial took place in Arlington National Cemetery on Friday, October 18.

2. In Appendix II ("The Problem of Promotion and Its Influence on Military Efficiency and National Policy") Palmer asserted that promotion strictly by seniority meant that only old men attained high rank, and that it was generally necessary to replace them with younger officers when war broke out. Moreover, with opportunities for advancement by merit precluded, officers sought political and legislative support for expanding the Regular Army rather than building a sound military system based upon a small professional force and a "well-regulated militia." (Palmer, *Washington, Lincoln, Wilson,* pp. 397-401.)

Palmer mentioned Fort Leavenworth graduates Marshall and Hugh Drum as representing "a new type in the American Army"—the thoroughly trained General Staff officer. (P. 298.)

3. Palmer's Appendix I quotes in full George Washington's "Sentiments on a Peace Establishment"—inclosed in a letter to Lieutenant Colonel Alexander Hamilton, May 2, 1783. The following passage on promotion by seniority is quoted again at the beginning of Appendix II: "That it is a good general rule admits of no doubt, but that it should be an invariable one, is in my opinion wrong. It cools, if it does not destroy, the incentives to military Pride and Heroic Actions. On the one hand, the sluggard, who keeps within the verge of duty, has nothing to fear. On the other hand, the enterprising spirit has nothing to expect, whereas if promotion was the *sure* reward of Merit, *all* would contend for Rank and the service would be benefited by their struggles for Promotion." (Ibid., p. 397.)

To General John J. Pershing   December 20, 1929
                                               Fort Benning, Georgia

Dear General: This is to carry to you my Xmas greetings and assurances of my loyal devotion. I hope you are in rugged health and happy.

In the papers I noticed you were in Cheyenne at Senator Warren's funeral. I had written to him about a week before he died. His career to me was a wonderful thing, and I always enjoyed being with him. I hope Mrs. Warren is not suffering from her knee trouble.

I was in Washington for one night in October for Mrs. Coles' funeral. She died just a year, lacking two days, after my mothers passing.[1]

I wish I could have you and Warren and your sister here now; it is cool but not cold and the outdoor life delightful. I do hope you will come to me sometime this winter.

Please give my warm regards to Miss May and to Warren, and please always believe me,   Faithfully and affectionately yours,

G. C. Marshall, Jr.

LC/J. J. Pershing Papers (General Correspondence); H

1. Pershing's late wife's father, Senator Francis E. Warren, died on November 24, 1929. Laura Bradford Marshall died on October 25, 1928.

To Cadet Walter S. Grant, Jr.[1]   January 6, 1930
                                                                    Fort Benning, Georgia

Dear Walter: I appreciated your remembering me with a Xmas card. Thank you for the thought.

I saw a class mate of yours at a dance here. He said he lived near you, and in an old room of mine.

I hope your work goes well and that you are in good spirits. Of course January and February are the blue sour months at school and require a little of the philosophical attitude. Saw wood and exercise—and don't sit on the radiator and grouse.   Faithfully yours,

G. C. Marshall, Jr.

GCMRL/W. S. Grant, Jr., Papers; H

1. Young Grant, son of Marshall's wartime comrade, was a first-year man ("rat") at the Virginia Military Institute.

To General John J. Pershing   February 18, 1930
                                                              Fort Benning, Georgia

Dear General: We had a visit yesterday from General Ely. Before leaving last night he asked me to write to you in his behalf, regarding his possible appointment as Chief of Staff. He will have one year to serve after General Summerall's relief, and seems very, very intent on this culmination of his military career.

General Ely stated that apparently the Secretary of War was quite agreeable to the appointment, but was embarrassed by the necessity of explaining to the President the justification for departure from the policy of only appointing a man who could serve a complete tour. It was Ely's hope that you might feel disposed to speak to the Secretary in his behalf, especially in appreciation of the difficulty above mentioned.

Generaly Ely feels that having been a successful head of the Leavenworth schools, a successful head of the War College, and in intimate touch with the War Department throughout this period, he is in a position to take up the burdens of Chief of Staff with a pretty full knowledge of just what they are, and of the policies now in force. He feels that his presence for only a year would not be a deterrent to army development, but under the circumstances, would offer the best guarantee of smooth progression under the existing policies. Furthermore, he states that his appointment would not establish a dangerous precedent, as he is the last (great) troop leader of the World War to pass from regiment to brigade, to division command, all on the battlefield. He feels that he has given evidence in each of the positions filled by him since the war of level-headed and progressive leadership, which has carried with it harmony in the posts or areas under his command, and with regulars, National Guard, and Reserves.

I do not know just what your attitude is in regard to interference in such matters, but I do remember your speaking about Kreger's case, and, I think, summer before last, you said something about Drum. Whatever your attitude, everyone feels that your expressed opinion carries with it tremendous power.[1]

I am sorry not to have had a line from you telling me you were coming down. Mr. Eaton, of the Eaton Ranch, with his wife and a friend, have just been with me for four days. They saw more horses here than they did on the ranch, and more riders.

With affectionate regards,   Faithfully yours,

G. C. Marshall, Jr.

LC/J. J. Pershing Papers (General Correspondence)

1. The army's mandatory retirement age was sixty-four. The normal tour for a chief of arm or the army chief of staff was four years. General Charles P. Summerall would have served four years as chief of staff on November 20, 1930. Major General Hanson E. Ely, who had been Second Corps Area commander since November 30, 1927, was born on November 23, 1867, and would reach retirement age on that date in 1931. Major General Edward A. Kreger, since November 16, 1928, the army judge advocate general, was born on May 31, 1868, and could have served eighteen months before retirement. Major General Hugh A. Drum, who was made army inspector general on January 29, 1930, was born on September 19, 1879, and would not reach retirement age until 1943.

FROM GENERAL JOHN J. PERSHING   February 28, 1930
                                                White Sulphur Springs,
                                                [West Virginia]

My dear Marshall: I have your letter of the eighteenth in which you speak of

General Ely and his ambitions. Of course I should like to see Ely become Chief of Staff as I think he would make a good one, but I am very fearful that it would be establishing a wrong sort of precedent to appoint a man who has only a year to serve. While he may think there are no other cases likely to come up later on, yet should the War Department commit itself to such a policy there certainly would be other cases that we can not now foresee. However, I will have a talk with the Secretary about it and rather feel him out and see what can be done.

It has been a great disappointment to me not to go to Benning as planned. I am sure that if Egan and I could have gone we might have done a lot of good work on my manuscript. As it is, I have not done so very much. I think you have seen the outline as it stands today, but to my mind it needs a great deal more work on it before it is turned loose. Before that time comes, if it ever does, I should like to have you review the manuscript again and give me your comments.

Although I do not write often, you are in my thoughts frequently and I am hoping that some of these days you will come into your own. Everybody that I meet who knows you always speaks in the highest terms, of course, and I think it is only a question of time when you will be repaid for your patience.

Believe me always, with best wishes,   Affectionately yours,

LC/J. J. Pershing Papers (General Correspondence)

To Brigadier General John McA. Palmer   March 21, 1930
Fort Benning, Georgia

Dear John: The book has come and already I have gone through it. First, let me say again that your introduction to the Civil War is a classic,—by far the best piece of writing you have ever done.

The entire book is much more impressive and interesting reading to me than the manuscript. This is natural, but nevertheless I was surprised at the great difference. You have done a truly momentous piece of work. I am gratified that you employed my name in so flattering a manner, but now I rather wish you had not, as it limits my boosting of the book. However, I am having a copy mailed to General LeJeune at the V.M.I., calling his attention to your presentation of Jackson and the Institute.

I would appreciate your giving me some idea of its reception,—reviews, sales, reaction of War Department, etc. With General Pershing's introduction, you have offset much of the quibbling of small minds.

I appreciate deeply your presenting me with this autographed volume, and I am proud to have so cultured and talented a friend.

Some of our active brigadiers are very busy overseeing the cutting of the grass and white-washing of the corral fence. Your work presents an appalling contrast.

With affection and sincere congratulations,   Faithfully yours,

G. C. Marshall, Jr.

LC/J. McA. Palmer Papers

To Captain George E. Adamson   June 23, 1930
Fort Benning, Georgia

Dear Adamson: I am asking again my usual summer favor of you, to have my mail forwarded from your office for a couple of weeks while I move about in the East. Later I am going out to a Ranch for a long stay.

Will you forward my mail (telegrams collect) to me
"Care Mrs. Clifton S. Brown,
Ocean Beach, Fire Island,
New York"
I will appreciate this kindness very much.

I would also appreciate a note telling me of the General's plans. Is Miss May with him. When does he expect to return from abroad.

I hope you and Mrs. Adamson are well—and that you escaped each Crash in the market.   Faithfully yours,

G. C. Marshall, Jr.

LC/J. J. Pershing Papers (General Correspondence); H

K ATHERINE TUPPER BROWN (Mrs. Clifton S. Brown) met Marshall at a small dinner party in Columbus, Georgia, in the spring or early summer of 1929. A widow with three children (Molly, b. July 18, 1912; Clifton, b. January 23, 1914; and Allen, b. June 15, 1916), Mrs. Brown's husband, a Baltimore lawyer, had been murdered in June, 1928, by an irate client.

Born in 1882 in Harrodsburg, Kentucky, she was the daughter of a distinguished Baptist clergyman, Henry Allen Tupper, Jr. After graduating from Hollins College in Virginia, she studied acting in New York at the American Academy of Dramatic Arts. She performed on stage in Europe and the United States, to the displeasure of her father. (Katherine Tupper Marshall, interviewed by Forrest C. Pogue, March 15 and 17, 1961, GCMRL.)

Following their brief meeting, Marshall and Katherine Brown corresponded and met again in Columbus the next spring. She then invited Marshall to visit her summer cottage at Fire Island, New York, in order to acquaint him with her children. (Katherine Tupper Marshall, *Together: Annals of an Army Wife* [New York: Tupper and Love, 1946], p. 3.) ★

The Marshalls' quarters at Fort Screven, Georgia, 1932–33.

Marshall and Mrs. Thomas B. Coles ("Aunt Lottie") at "Woodville," the Coles family home in Albemarle County, Virginia, 1927.

353

Katherine Tupper as "Rosalind" in Shakespeare's "As You Like It," England, 1907.

Mrs. Clifton Brown and her children in 1922: Allen (left), Molly, and Clifton.

Katherine Tupper Marshall, Chicago, 1934.

Marshall, assistant commandant of the Infantry School, about 1930.

The assistant commandant and the department heads of the Infantry School, 1930–31. Front row, left to right: Morrison C. Stayer, Joseph W. Stilwell, George C. Marshall, William F. Freehoff, Edwin F. Harding. Second row: Howard J. Liston, Omar N. Bradley, Emil W. Leard, Fremont B. Hodson.

To General John J. Pershing
September 13, 1930
Fort Benning, Georgia

Dear General: My congratulations and affection go to you on your birthday. I wish I could see you and hear something of what has past since Bluemont the summer of 1928. Each year without untoward slip has added immensely to your prestige. There have been pitfalls without number, but the dignity and modesty of your course has carried you steadily upward in the public mind, from what once appeared to be the summit. Yours must be a great satisfaction.

I feel free to comment because I once saw something of the difficulties. But my admiration has grown with time and perspective.

In August I wrote you from the Big Horn Mountains in Wyoming, addressing my letter to the Embassy in Paris. I had not known of your return until yesterday. I only got back a few days ago myself. In my letter I told you of my approaching marriage to Mrs. Clifton S. Brown of Baltimore, a widow with a daughter of eighteen, a son of seventeen and another of fifteen. The daughter has been abroad since last September. The sons are off to school. Mrs. Brown's brother is a writer, Tristram Tupper. Her sister is a writer and playwright.[1]

We are to be married in Baltimore the afternoon of October 15th. I would count it a great honor if you would stand up with me. The wedding is to be quiet with only family and very intimate friends of hers—no invitations. Please treat the matter as confidential for the present. My sister alone of my family knows anything about it.   With affectionate regards,

G. C. Marshall, Jr.

LC/J. J. Pershing Papers (General Correspondence); H

1. Allene Tupper Wilkes wrote plays, articles, and short stories. Her best-known play was *The Creaking Chair*, in which Tallulah Bankhead made her London debut in 1924.

To Mrs. Thomas B. Coles
September 25, 1930
Fort Benning, Georgia

Dear Aunt Lot: You wrote a very sweet letter, and so did Charlotte. They would have been acknowledged earlier, but I have been overwhelmed with accumulated summer business, the opening of school, shoals of callers from newly arrived personnel, and many letters.

Please do not feel that I am "walking out" on you. To me you will always be my dear Aunt Lot, unless you will it otherwise. And the first time my car touches Virginia soil you will hear the old unannounced toot from the side of the house.

For my exercise I have been gardening violently this last week, getting in the annuals, to insure early blooming next spring. My hands are blisters and raw spots. I swim late in the evening. My love to you all,   Affectionately,

G. C. M.

GCMRL/Research File (Family); H

TO GENERAL JOHN J. PERSHING
October 1, 1930
Fort Benning, Georgia

Dear General: Thanks for your note of congratulations. You were good to write.

I'm afraid I will not get to Washington on my way north. Things are so active here this particular time of year that I am only going up at the last moment and am returning direct the same day I reach Baltimore.

I hope very much you can be with me. I am asking no one else in Washington. Saving yourself, if I include one friend it would be necessary to ask a large number, and we hope to do this thing as quietly as possible.

But you, please try and arrange your plans so that I can have the great pleasure and the honor of your support. If you can meet me at the Belveder[e] Hotel at twelve thirty on the fifteenth, we are to go to a luncheon and then direct to the chapel at two thirty. From there I go to the train for the south. Faithfully yours,

G. C. Marshall, Jr.

LC/J. J. Pershing Papers (General Correspondence); H

TO GENERAL JOHN J. PERSHING
October 20, 1930
Fort Benning, Georgia

My dear General: Your letter has just come, and I will get to work immediately to outline my idea of the great moments of decisions of your leadership in France. I could sketch now approximately what I said in Baltimore, but I wish to give the matter a little more careful study. It will be mailed to you in a few days.

Just now I want to tell you how deeply I appreciate your going over to Baltimore and lending me your support and the distinction of your presence. It was a very gracious act on your part, and both Mrs. Marshall and myself are very grateful to you. We were both sorry that so much publicity was attached to your presence, as it resulted in considerable harassment of you by the press. It developed that a friend of one of the ladies who entertained you, and therefore was expecting you, tipped off the papers. Mrs. Marshall had not expected that there would be any knowledge of this until after your arrival, but it was then too late to prevent your being pursued as you were.[1]

It was a very satisfying thing to me to have even that brief opportunity to talk things over with you. Possibly I was not very coherent or logical in what I was saying at the time, but it moved me a great deal to see you again after such a long period.

Mrs. Marshall is having her first touch of the Army. The business began the night of her arrival—shaking hands on the Commandant's lawn with about

1,000 people at an al fresco reception and dance. She joins me in affectionate regards.   Faithfully yours,

G. C. Marshall, Jr.

LC/J. J. Pershing Papers (General Correspondence)

1. In her memoirs, Mrs. Marshall wrote that when the wedding party arrived at the Emmanuel Episcopal Church, "the chapel was full and a large crowd had gathered on the sidewalk. My friends were greatly outnumbered, I fear, by those curious to see General Pershing. At the [railroad] station after the ceremony the crowd was even larger. This was rather disconcerting to both of us for we had wished to be married quietly." (*Together*, p. 4.)

TO GENERAL JOHN J. PERSHING
October 24, 1930
Fort Benning, Georgia

Dear General,   Attached are my comments on great moments or decisions. Please read them thru *before* continuing further with this note, for I am going to indulge in criticism, in contrast to the typed comments.[1]

Certain things about the A.E.F. I think are open to stricture, yet have never been touched upon. All I have in mind were directly incident to the hard driving tactics which won the war—therefore excusable. But I think it well to have them in mind so that your treatment of the period or events connected with them may be handled accordingly.

The most severe criticism I could launch pertains to the opening of the Meuse-Argonne battle. We refer to it as our greatest and one of the greatest battles in history, determining in winning the war. We point to the great strength of the German position, describe your offer to undertake this most difficult task with fresh young American troops. We dwell on the fact that we had to make the opening fight with but partially trained, and in some instances, wholly inexperienced divisions.

Yet, knowing all this, the staffs of these inexperienced divisions were absolutely scalped a *few* days before the assault, in several cases I believe the day before—*in order that the next class at Langres might start on scheduled time*. The amount of confusion and mismanagement resulting from this was tremendous. A delay of ten days at Langres would have permitted the machine to get well under way—even a week would have helped immeasurably. Students and instructors were demanded and secured.

I always thought General Fox Conner, Hugh Drum and General Nolan should had determinedly opposed General Fisk at this moment, particularly Conner and Nolan. I always thought General McAndrew should have represented the matter to you in strong terms.[2]

No one has ever leveled this criticism at the A.E.F. control, and I have never breathed it to any one. But I think it could be made, especially, by some of the divisions that were seriously mismanaged.

It is rather odd to send you two such contrasting papers as this and the attached memorandum. But I wanted you to be on your guard.

Possibly, probably you do not agree with me in this matter. But I would hate to have some one, with hostile intent, seize upon it.

I hope you can arrange to send me the manuscript. I will go over it immediately on its receipt, and give you my frankest reaction. Affectionately yours,

G. C. Marshall, Jr.

LC/J. J. Pershing Papers (Book File); H

1. Printed below.

2. Brigadier General Fox Conner was assistant chief of staff for Operations (G-3) at A.E.F. General Headquarters from November 8, 1917, to February 3, 1919. Brigadier General Dennis E. Nolan (U.S.M.A., 1896) was assistant chief of staff for Intelligence (G-2) between July 5, 1917, and July 5, 1919. Major General James W. McAndrew was A.E.F. chief of staff from May 6, 1918, to May 27, 1919. Brigadier General Harold B. Fiske (U.S.M.A., 1897), who had been an honor student at Fort Leavenworth's Army School of the Line during Marshall's second year as instructor (1910), was A.E.F. assistant chief of staff for Training (G-5) between February 14, 1918, and July 10, 1919. Brigadier General Hugh A. Drum was chief of staff of Liggett's First Army from August 10, 1918, to April 17, 1919.

MEMORANDUM FOR GENERAL PERSHING   October 24, 1930
                                                   Fort Benning, Georgia

High Points in the A.E.F.

The preliminary decision of July 11, 1917, as set forth in your cablegram of that date, was momentous. Directly from this flowed the vast plans for the foundation and development of the A.E.F. No such conception had ever before been attempted either in peace or war, in business or fighting. That you had the vision to make this beginning, marks your action as one of the great decisions of the A.E.F.[1]

Training for warfare of movement, as directed in the early fall of 1917, was a courageous and far-sighted decision. The long and desperate contest had drawn the Allied commanders too close to the situation day by day, to permit of proper perspective. But, they had three years experience in major warfare and you had none. You were untried and they were veterans. America was sympathetic to the French and British,—terribly critical of our state of unpreparedness. Your position in taking a view directly contrary to the Allied leaders, was precarious. Your action in suppressing the translation of Petain's printed instructions on "The Offensive Training of Large Units", required rare courage. I am inclined to think that had not the German offensive, opening March 21, 1918, conclusively proved the absolute necessity of training our troops for open warfare, you might have been forced from command by Allied pressure on Washington.

Therefore your determination, early in the war, to train our troops for open warfare was one of the great decisions of the A.E.F.

Your action in placing all of our troops at the disposal of General Foch on March 17, 1918, was a tremendous voluntary concession, in view of the embarrassment it was certain to cause you later in forming a distinct American Army. It was clearly the right thing to do, but the previous attitude of the Allied chiefs and their pressure, direct and indirect, to upset your program of organization and training, gave your action the color of a great decision.

The method of initiating the St. Mihiel battle was unique, daring to a remarkable degree and completely successful. Despite the fact that wire entanglements had been the tragedy and stumbling block of all offensives, unless methodically destroyed by artillery fire or torn open by fleets of tanks, and despite the fact that the St. Mihiel front was heavily covered with successive wide bands of wire entanglements, the attack was launched without artillery fire of destruction and without heavy tanks to cut gaps in the wire. Torpedo charges, carried by hand, were employed wherever necessary. A surprise attack was assured by omitting destructive artillery fire. The rapid advance and complete success of the American assault, causes your decision to omit the time consuming and customary preliminaries, to rank as a great one of the A.E.F.

The continuation of offensive assaults in the Meuse-Argonne battle from October 8th to 20th ranks as the greatest exhibition of leadership displayed by you during the war.

With distressingly heavy casualties, disorganized and only partially trained troops, supply troubles of every character due to the devastated zone so hurriedly crossed, inclement and cold weather, flu, stubborn resistance by the enemy on one of the strongest positions of the Western Front, pessimism on all sides and the pleadings to halt the battle made by many of the influential members of the army, you persisted in your determination to force the fighting over all difficulties and objections. This was the most severe test of the war. The British discounted our effort and criticized our methods; the French did the same; both strove to break up our army by securing detachments of troops. Even American high officials outside the army lent themselves to the clamor. Throughout you stood implacable and drove the army to its great assault, commencing November 1st, which reached Sedan, reclaimed the Meuse and brought us to the armistice.

Nothing else in your leadership throughout the war was comparable to this.

LC/J. J. Pershing Papers (Book File)

1. Marshall may be referring to the "Report on Organization" dated July 10, 1917, forwarded to the War Department on July 11. This report stated that a force of one million men was needed in France by the 1918 campaign season, and that ultimately three million would be necessary. This report is printed in *United States Army in the World War, 1917–1919*, 1: 93–106.

To General John J. Pershing   November 24, 1930
                                               Fort Benning, Georgia

My dear General: I have just finished going over the manuscript of your book.[1]
It arrived Thursday morning, and I have given it most of my time since.

Attached are my comments. Naturally they are the result of a hurried survey,
but please keep in mind that they are also the result of hurried dictation. I have
not had the time to be careful in my choice of language or to be very analytical.
As speed was the dominant factor in this matter, if you were to have the
manuscript Tuesday, I have done my best under the circumstances.

In the comments I have found it advisable, for brevity, to state my opinions
flatly, without couching them in a more restrained or tactful fashion. I hope you
will understand this. I am giving you the best I can manage under the circumstances.   Faithfully yours,

[Inclosure]

COMMENTS ON MANUSCRIPT OF GENERAL PERSHING'S MEMOIRS

I will precede comments on specific chapters and pages by some general
observations. In reviewing this manuscript, I have endeavored to go through it
with three points in view:

a. The desire to locate any statements which might give an impression contrary
to the facts.

b. An effort to guess the probable reaction of the ordinary reader to what you
have said.

c. An effort to spot any portion which would give rise to acrimonious debate,
particularly if the incident does not justify such attention.

First half.

I like the first half of the book. It is a very interesting presentation, despite the
necessity for covering many complicated subjects. I do not like the frequency of
criticism, particularly of the War Department. It seems to me the direct criticisms
should be omitted in most instances, your presentation being confined to the
facts; then once or twice spread yourself on a general criticism, with a mere
reference to the accumulative instances justifying criticism.

When your silence, concerning practically everything in the war, is considered,
I think the frequency with which you directly criticize the War Department will
create a poor impression and will weaken your general statements. There is a
great difference between hammering the country at large for a supine adherence
or acquiescense to a policy of unpreparedness and parsimonious appro-

priations—there is a great difference between this and a constant criticism of certain individuals in the War Department, usually unnamed except by designation of positions. In most of the criticisms I have referred to, the paragraph can stand as written with the exception of the complete omission of the critical comment, which usually concludes the paragraph.

There were changes of control in the War Department, before these dates, and the individuals concerned are not definitely indicated. Every one of importance concerned with the war knows of your hostility to General March, just as they know of your hostility to General Edwards. I think it important not to permit your criticisms to confuse the public as to whom they are directed. I think it very important that your criticisms do not in any way reflect on Mr. Baker. Though we have a hundred more wars, I do not think we will ever be so lucky in the choice of a Secretary. I cannot conceive of any future field commander ever being accorded the support you received. I know you disagreed strongly with him on certain phases of the decisions, particularly regarding the draft during the spring of 1918. You may remember you had me make a rather lengthy study of the situation at this time.[2] The result of this, so far as concerned my impression, was a tremendous admiration for the courage and force displayed by Mr. Baker and by General March at that time.

I think General March displayed picayunish qualities and personal animosity distressing to find in a man of his outstanding ability. But, to me, the fact remains that there was not another man, saving yourself, and possibly General Wood, who could have filled the terribly difficult position of Chief of Staff in Washington. Wood's personal ambitions would probably have been fatal; March's were not absent, but he did a remarkable job, in my opinion, which you should in no way belittle.

As to the earlier period of the war, the situation of the War Department was almost hopeless, and Mr. Baker could not be expected in a few months to reconstruct a machine loaded with impossibilities and which never had functioned correctly. In my detailed comments referring to one of your criticisms of the General Staff, I suggest that you point out the real difficulty, which was a collection of old officers at the head of every division, who had ceased mental development years before, or had had no opportunity to develop and were literally wholly unacquainted with any of the proper functions of a General Staff.

As to your comments on our allies, I think you might omit several where you attribute the ulterior purposes to some seemingly favorable offer or view of theirs. I believe the general reaction will be better if you leave the statement of facts to the reader without the frequent adverse comments at the conclusion of the paragraphs concerned. Then when you hit, hit hard, leaving no shadow of doubt as to what your criticism is and whom you are criticizing.

Second half.

There is a tendency in your early accounts of troop actions to criticize the units or individuals for affairs or matters of comparatively small importance when compared to what occurred later on, when you usually pass over grave errors or commissions without any adverse comment whatsoever. I have called attention to this in the detailed comments.

I do not like your description of the Meuse-Argonne battle. It is too detailed, I think, for the general reader and not detailed enough for the military student. In endeavoring to mention each town and division and division commander, the battle has been made to appear a confused mass of little events, and from my point of view the big picture has been lost. I realize you wished to mention individuals, but practically every one of those mentioned has already been named in your final report. I think you should have described the battle from a very broad and non-technical point of view, and should have drawn attention to great feats or great difficulties by detailed descriptions of incidents in those sections of the field. November 1st was a great feat; it was the first occasion where the army could operate on equal terms with the other armies as to time of occupation of sectors, special troops; the great barrage, artillery and machine gun, in front of the V Corps was worthy of special comment as to its character; the plunge forward in the center of the army by the center divisions was a splendid feat, in great contrast to the frequent half-baked efforts on other fields; the maintained momentum which carried the army up to the Meuse,—these outstanding characteristics of that fight should be featured. My main objection to the handling of the Meuse-Argonne and, to a smaller extent, to the St. Mihiel, is the submergence of the great facts or feats of the battle under a mass of minor details as to small movements of divisions, names of woods and villages, etc.,—often to the exclusion of details covering efforts of great gallantry. For example, the first phase of the crossing of the Meuse by the 5th Division, the attack of the [October] 4th, 5th, and 6th by the 1st Division, the remarkable endurance of the 4th Division, some units of which remained in the line until the 22d of October, I think. You treat Alexander, of the 77th Division, with a very lenient hand, compared to your occasional strictures of the 26th Division.

Detailed comments.

Chapter II, page 2, first paragraph, last sentence:

Retain comment, but omit direct reference to Chief of Staff.

Either indicate more definitely what the trouble was—senior general staff officers wholly untrained for such duty, faulty arrangement, misunderstanding of army at large of the General Staff, and active resentful hostility of permanent bureaus, hopeless fight of younger General Staff officers as yet inexperienced in General Staff work, etc, etc.

Chapter II [III?], page 11, 1st paragraph:

Change "several engagements" to read "many engagements".

Page 22

Change "inclined to yield" to read "sometimes yielded".

Page 14

"God damn him". This will be featured in all press reviews, as it constitutes news. Will the whole English nation take the slant that you have struck at the character of George V?

Chapter XI, page 1, second paragraph, last sentence:

"Laxity and neglect at home". This should either be qualified with some explanation or considerably moderated. It gives an erroneous impression.

Page 5, first paragraph, end of last sentence:

This particularization seems unnecessary and objectionable. The reaction to it will be unfavorable to you.

Chapter XIII, page 4, last sentence:

I would omit this.

Page 5, first paragraph, last sentence:

I would omit this.

Chapter XVIII, page 19, first paragraph:

The effect or influence of the power of the permanent bureaus had its part, and a decided part, in all considerations by the General Staff.

Chapter XXVI, page 16:

Criticism of the 26th Division is a delicate affair. There is this to be said on the side of the division: A raid was usually, almost invariably, a surprise—by the very nature of the operation. Most raids, I guess about 80%, succeeded for this reason, the local garrison having a small chance against the overwhelming assault, and under the heavy concentration of artillery fire. Furthermore, and especially, Seichprey was one of the most vulnerable spots on the western front. (I labored personally with its defense for several months.) I suggest you pass this affair by without adverse comment. Nothing is gained by the criticism, mild as it is, and the solid animosity of an entire region will certainly be awakened. The game is not worth the candle. (Contrast this criticism with the absence of criticism of the 77th Division at Champigneulles in November. Chapter 49, page 7.)

Chapter XXX, page 3, last paragraph, first two Lines:

Is this a proper charge against the War Department? Could this particular emergency, with its special solution as to shipping certain units, be foreseen?

Chapter XXXII, page 12, last complete paragraph:

"Faulty system of training at home", and end of last sentence. This involves too much of repetition of this criticism and weakens the case. (See also last paragraph of Chapter XXXVIII and main paragraph of Chapter XXXVIV, page 13.)

Page 12, next to the last complete paragraph:

"Lethargy and laxity". This is a correct characterization, but without explanation it is unjust. It refers to battle-worn men, tired and bored to death, war blase officers. What our attitude would have been the fourth year is problematical, but I doubt if it would have been one to praise.

Chapter XXXVI, page 6, first paragraph, next to last sentence:
I again urge that you include "with the French Moroccan Division". It seems unfair and ungenerous to omit reference to this splendid war-worn shock division. Every unit always claimed the one on its flanks was "not up". Personally I think the Moroccans were "up". I hope very much you will make this change. You may remember that we had long discussions regarding it at the time of the preparation of your Final Report.

Chapter XXXVIV, page 3, last complete paragraph:
In view of the dramatic success and powerful influence of the August 8–9 attack, you either should not mention it or should include some words of high praise. Don't give the Allies an opening to attack you as ungenerous and unduly prejudiced.

Chapter XL, page 16, second paragraph:
I don't think you gain by this adverse comment on Liggett. If he deserves this comment, you should shoot Alexander and a couple of others and give General Bullard a pretty hard time.

Chapter XLII, page 11, last paragraph, first sentence:
Omit direct reference to 103d Infantry.

Page 12:
Mention name of commander of 101st Regiment. I think it was a Marine named Barch (?).

Chapter XLIV, page 11, last paragraph:
Did not one brigade of 91st Division remain in line attached to 1st Division?

Page 5, last complete paragraph:
Explanation is due the 28th Division that its sector, half in and half out of Argonne and in a valley dominated by heights, was one of the hardest on the field.

Chapter XLVI, page 4:
You give a brief comment on entry of 1st Division into line. The relief of the 35th by the 1st was one of the crises of the battle. Should it not receive more than a mere reference? The forced march of the units of the 1st Division across country and their pick up of an almost abandoned sector merits some attention. Contrast this with details about more or less unimportant phases.

Chapter XLIX:
I have already commented on your treatment of the attack of November 1st.

Chapter L, page 2, last paragraph:
Why include this inferential stricture on the 26th Division—"Between November 3d and 8th Bamford's 26th Division ＊＊＊ made no attack". Contrast this criticism with serious failures and terrible confusion in the cases of the 3d Division, 5th Division, 77th Division, 79th, and 37th.

Page 2, paragraph 2:
I think more should be said about the opening phase of the gallant and difficult effort to cross the Meuse, the shooting out of the bridges, units isolated on far banks, etc. etc.

LC/J. J. Pershing Papers (Book File)

1. On November 17, Pershing sent Marshall a copy of the manuscript of his memoirs which were later published as *My Experiences in the World War,* 2 vols. (New York: Frederick A. Stokes, 1931). Fox Conner, James G. Harbord, Hugh A. Drum, and several other officers also received all or parts of the manuscript for review and comment.

2. See Marshall's memorandum of April 9, 1923, above.

To GENERAL JOHN J. PERSHING   December 2, 1930
                                                                                       Fort Benning, Georgia

Dear General: Your letter of Sunday, by special delivery, reached me an hour ago.[1] I have just telegraphed you that I can arrive in Washington early Sunday morning, and request orders be issued. By leaving here at 7:00 AM Saturday, I can be in Washington about 9:00 o'clock, I think, on Sunday morning. I should leave Washington late Tuesday night.

As to the various points in your letter: I am sorry my criticisms did not appear constructive, as I tried to indicate in the brief time at my disposal what line it seemed to me you should take.

Taking up the comments in your letter in the order in which you make them:

(1) *References to building up the American Army,*—I think your presentation of this phase of the A.E.F. is excellent, except where you guessed at some hidden motive on the part of the Allies in a seemingly commendable attitude or offer of theirs. There was enough overt persistence, without referring to the hidden efforts.

(2) *Condemnation of the Allies,*—I tried to make clear in my hurried comments that I thought it inadvisable to make such frequent criticisms; rather to state the facts and only ever now and then indulge in a general criticism, based on the numerous facts previously presented. It is the frequent reiteration of criticisms that I think weakens the presentation.

(3) *Details of Allied efforts to thwart our purpose,*—I do not think you have gone too much into those details. It is only that I think you have allowed the critical tone or touch to appear too often.

(4) *Armistice terms,*—Without the text before me, I find it difficult to comment on this. The impression now in my mind is that you handled the Armistice terms in a satisfactory manner.

(5) *Style, English, personal attitude,*—I like the style of the book; it is yours. The English is also very plainly yours, and, as always, of a very high standard. Your personal attitude is what most of my comments were directed towards. You displayed marvelous restraint during the trying days in France,—more restraint, I believe, than any of your staff. You have appeared since the war as a model of restraint, the constant subject of increasingly favorable comment on this admirable attitude. The manuscript presents you in a different light, because of the

frequency of criticisms of the War Department and the Allies. I do not mean that the criticisms in most instances were not deserved. But I think in most instances a statement of the facts should suffice, and your criticisms should be reserved for more general statements or summations from time to time. As to the War Department, it seems to me most of your criticisms should take the form of showing the American people the deplorable plight in which *they*, the people, permitted the country to find itself. Practically all of the errors grew out of this, rather than the acts of omissions of particular individuals. The War Department and army were not organized on a decentralized basis, and the former, as a result, was practically submerged in 1917 under the flood of business that poured in as a result of the centralized set up. But regardless of the efficiency or inefficiency of the main heads of the War Department, it is to be remembered that not only the permanent bureaus but the Democratic Congress violently attacked the General Staff. Chairman Hay, of the Military Committee, as I recall, led in the successful emasculation of the General Staff just prior to our entry into the war.[2] This attitude, the resistance to a properly coordinated War Department in favor of the money spending bureaus, the past refusals to accumulate important war stocks—guns, ammunition, powders, electrical technical equipment, airplanes—marks in my mind the reason for most of the errors committed by individuals and is a proper subject for text for lecturing the American people.

(6) *What is the book worth*,—I think when you finally turn it out the book will be the most valuable historical contribution to the war from the American point of view. But I also think the standard you have set for yourself during, and particularly since the war, demands the same high standard of the book, and I have indicated where I think you have not met this requirement. In most, or at least in many cases, the omission of the last sentence of the paragraph accomplishes what I have in mind.

(7) *The Meuse-Argonne*,—I do not think my comments regarding the Meuse-Argonne necessarily mean a shortening of this portion of the book. There is much to be said about the battle, and there is only the question of what line you choose to take.

All of these points I can go over with you personally, but I am including them here so that you may have an opportunity to consider them before I arrive. In all of this I fully realize that I have put myself in a very difficult position, possibly a questionable position, but I am merely trying to tell you what my impressions are, and I realize that they differ very decidedly from those of many other officers of very high position. I have been both frank and honest, which is the best service I can offer you. I am not pessimistic about the book, but I devoted my attention to those phases which I think might be improved. Practically every one of position who has written about the war has lost somewhat by doing so. I do not want to see this happen to you.   Affectionately yours,

G. C. Marshall, Jr.

LC/J. J. Pershing Papers (General Correspondence)

1. No copy of Pershing's November 30 letter has been found in either the Pershing or the Marshall collections.

2. Congressman James Hay, a Democrat from Virginia, was chairman of the House Committee on Military Affairs. He was instrumental in reducing the size and authority of the General Staff Corps between 1912 and 1916.

To GENERAL JOHN J. PERSHING   December 20, 1930
                                                      Fort Benning, Georgia

Dear General: This carries to you Xmas Greetings and good wishes for all of the New Year from Mrs. Marshall and myself. I have a house full—seven—so it will be a busy holiday. Took the young boy on an eighteen mile wild cat hunt yesterday at 5:30 A.M.

I hope you got off your ms on time and to your satisfaction, and I'm sorry you did not feel like coming down here after the fifteenth. Katherine was much excited over the possibility.

I think the book will make a profound impression and will read splendidly in print. On the train and since my return I have thought over the various points we discussed and I find nothing new to offer. The elimination of a few woods and villages will clear up the Meuse-Argonne, and I am certain will give you a more impressive account of the battle than anyone can turn out for you.

My three days with you, while crowded, were delightful for me, and I only wish I could have loafed a bit and talked things over with you.

My affectionate regards and wishes for your Xmas and the New Year. Faithfully yours,

G. C. Marshall, Jr.

LC/J. J. Pershing Papers (General Correspondence); H

To CAPTAIN LLOYD N. WINTERS[1]   February 26, 1931
                                                      Fort Benning, Georgia

My dear Captain Winters: I am inclosing some comments on the Meuse-Argonne to meet your request. Frankly, I don't like to have much to say publicly. It is all right here in the school in connection with instruction, but your proposition is another matter.

However, I am sending you some brief comments; but please see that they are not published or otherwise distributed, save by you verbally in the delivery of your lecture.

I have no written notes of my talk on the A.E.F.,—never had any. I had to deliver the first talk on twenty-four hours notice, all the daylight time being absorbed in a 400-mile motor ride to Brest, so I was committed without written notes and so continued. I did not hear General Drum's talk and do not know whether or not he had written it up.[2]

Benning has changed considerably this past year,—looks quite a finished place, with new quarters and many paved roads. The school goes along smoothly.

With kind regards,   Faithfully yours,

G. C. Marshall, Jr.

[Inclosure]

Critical reviews of the Meuse-Argonne operation are usually concerned with strategical and larger tactical aspects of the battle. The most instructive phases would seem to be those related to smaller affairs, matters of direction and method within the brigade, and especially in the battalion and the company. However, every lesson should be learned with a clear understanding of the special conditions under which the battle was fought—a tired and outnumbered enemy, unable to strike a heavy counterblow but extraordinarily skillful in the employment of artillery and machine guns; our troops strong and vigorous, but deficient in training and lacking that finesse of troop leadership which comes from experience.

To me, the following were the most instructive aspects of the battle:

The chaotic conditions which usually developed within a few hours of a formal "jump off". Troops could be lined up for a set assault and carried through the first phase in comparatively good order, but as the necessity for local decisions, maneuver, adjustments and cooperation developed the efforts became disorganized or confused to a remarkable degree, and only the courage and determination of the *natural* leaders enabled the troops to press on. Leaders understood how to deploy but seldom how to ploy or regroup their scattered forces without bringing the action to a standstill. Fighting of this character will be normal to open warfare.

The inability of subordinate leaders to achieve a combination of fire and movement. Under the stress of battle headlong attacks were usually launched, and while often successful, heavy losses and disorganization usually robbed the unit of further striking power.

Inability of local leaders to approximate any idea of the situation beyond their immediate flanks. The misunderstandings and unfortunate results, due to the above reason, made tragic history over the entire battlefield. The strain of the fighting was so intense that the brain of leaders seemed a blank to all but the violent impressions of their immediate front.

The small part pure tactics played in the handling of most situations. Local decisions were usually dominated by reasons other than tactical,—fatigue, inability or unwillingness to alter existing dispositions, and response to orders to renew the attack by efforts straight to the front. Yet in our training we usually consider only the tactical problem.

The serious effect of poor arrangements to provide hot food to the fighting line. In the few divisions where the supply of hot food was rigorously required, the more so when the fighting was desperate, troops performed feats utterly beyond those who received cold food or went hungry. The former were able to remain "in the line" for much longer periods, to the great saving of the army reserves being collected to stage a renewed general assault. In prolonged fighting the delivery of food is as important as the maintenance of communications.

The small understanding of the practical proposition of maintaining morale. Few officers understood the fatal effect on their troops of a pessimistic attitude and of criticism of seniors. Where the opposite condition existed the troops often achieved the impossible. Their success was seldom due to tactics or technique, unless it was the technique of leadership. It might truthfully be said that in most instances the performance of the troops could be accurately measured by the mental attitude and bearing of the leaders. It was seldom that a determined, resourceful leader failed. It was seldom that a dispirited or disgruntled or critical leader succeeded. Courage was a common trait, but not fortitude and un-questioned loyalty.

In general, it has seemed to me that we discuss the battle in a large or pon-derous fashion, ignoring those features which really determined the issue in the hundreds of local situations which made up the great operation. Unless we deal with the facts about these, the errors will all be repeated, and to a more serious degree in warfare of movement with an army taking the field in the first month of a war.

GCMRL/L. N. Winters Papers

1. Winters had been a member of the Infantry School's Company Officers' Course, 1929–30. At the time Marshall wrote, Winters was stationed with the Twenty-first Infantry at Schofield Barracks in Hawaii.
2. Concerning Marshall's lecturing, see the above Memorandum for the Deputy Chief of Staff, March 20, 1919.

MEMORANDUM FOR THE INFANTRY BOARD   March 2, 1931
                                                   Fort Benning, Georgia

The following indorsement, regarding the statements in Tables of Organ-ization submitted by the Chief of Field Artillery, is suggested:[1]

1. The frontages given in the first paragraph of the indorsement of the Chief of Field Artillery are correct according to our present view of the four infantry regiment division with the new infantry organization.

2. It is still the opinion of the Infantry Board that its recommendation for a division of three infantry regiments is sound. Furthermore, and in accordance

with the recommendation of the Commandant to the Chief of Infantry in letter of January 21, 1931, it is our opinion that the new infantry battalion and regimental organization should be further studied and experimented with before a final decision is made.[2]

3. With regard to the discussion of the Chief of Field Artillery in the 1st Indorsement of the original communication, the following opinions are submitted:

a. The conclusion of the Chief of Field Artillery that the organic artillery of the division should not be increased and that added artillery power should be secured by reinforcement from corps and army, is concurred in.

b. Under paragraph 5 *b* of the Chief of Field Artillery's indorsement, the statements of disadvantages of appreciably increasing the organic artillery are concurred in so far as they go, but it is believed that a most serious disadvantage has not been mentioned.[3] Experience has shown that if the artillery component of a division is large, it is usually found impracticable to withdraw it from the battle with the infantry when the latter has become exhausted. This results in the organic artillery being separated from its divisional infantry and only returned to it when conditions as to time and space make this possible. With the more frequent movement of the foot soldier by bus than was the practice in France, this separation will be an even more serious matter. Statistics will show that in the latter phase of the Meuse-Argonne battle only four divisions (1st, 2d, 26th and 42d) could be maintained with their organic artillery, and it is understood that even this was managed only through a very special effort in each case. It is a great disadvantage to the infantry to operate with strange artillery. If, in an effort to avoid this condition, the division is given practically all the artillery it is believed that it will require in heavy fighting, the cure will almost certainly result in having none of its organic artillery in succeeding phases of the operation or campaign.

c. As to the discussion of the effect of the present increase in the infantry special weapons, under paragraph 4 of the Chief of Field Artillery's indorsement, the following is submitted: The increase in frontage of the infantry units brought about under the new organization is due primarily to the increase in the automatic fire power per man. We expect the defense to be similarly armed and similarly extended. We believe that the conditions as to infantry against infantry will continue to be a stand-off. As to the artillery requirements of this situation, we believe with the increased frontages any given defensive installation will have more space in which to conceal itself, rather than that there will be more numerous groups so that the interval between them will be as heretofore. Under such conditions we believe that the need will be not so much for more density of artillery fire as for more accurate artillery fire. It would appear that this increased difficulty of locating targets will have to be met largely by infantry special weapons.[4]

d. There is, in our opinion, an additional view of this entire matter which apparently is not given much consideration in the artillery discussion. We are preparing for open warfare primarily, with the additions and subtractions which are imposed by static warfare as secondary considerations. In the opinion of the Board, great masses of artillery not only will not be available for a long time but seldom could be maneuvered in warfare of movement. The ammunition supply, even if available in the zone of the interior, would present an almost impossible problem at the front. It would seem that among the considerations which are to govern the solution of the division artillery problem, should be a judicious decision as to the character of organization which will satisfy conditions to be expected during the first six months of campaign and will be adapted to accommodate the changes which are inevitable as the situation grows static and quantity production of war materiel gets under way.

G. C. Marshall, Jr.

NA/RG 177 (400.112, Chief of Infantry)

1. On November 29, 1930, the Adjutant General's Office had requested that the chief of Field Artillery (Major General Harry G. Bishop) comment on the proposed reorganization of the Infantry division. Bishop replied with a long, detailed indorsement on February 5, 1931. The Office of the Chief of Infantry sent this to the Infantry Board, of which Marshall was an ex-officio member. Marshall's memorandum was accepted with only minor changes as the board's reply of March 7.

2. The "square" divisions that the United States fielded in the World War consisted of approximately twenty-seven thousand men divided into two Infantry brigades of two regiments and one machine gun battalion each, an artillery brigade of three regiments, and special troops and staff. American divisions were nearly twice the size of European divisions, and many officers considered them unwieldy and inflexible. Proposals for change generally centered on some sort of "triangular" division of twelve to sixteen thousand men divided into three Infantry regiments and four Field Artillery battalions. The changes under discussion here maintained the square organization, but they increased Infantry manpower by about twenty-five percent.

3. The disadvantages foreseen by the Office of the Chief of Field Artillery were that "any appreciable increase in the organic artillery [would] greatly decrease the flexibility of the brigade and render the proposed division still more extended and unwieldy." (First Indorsement on TAG to Chief of Field Artillery, November 29, 1930, NA/RG 177 [400.112, Chief of Infantry].)

4. This paragraph was taken from a memorandum by Lieutenant Colonel Joseph W. Stilwell, head of the Infantry School's First Section (i.e., tactics). (Stilwell to the Assistant Commandant, February 26, 1931, ibid.) The chief of Field Artillery, noting numerous instances during the World War when insufficient artillery fire had led to increased Infantry casualties, suggested that in order to maintain a high Field Artillery–Infantry ratio, "a reduction in size of the infantry element of the division might well be considered." (First Indorsement on TAG to Chief of Field Artillery, November 29, 1930, ibid.)

IF HE WAS to retain Marshall's services beyond June 30, 1931, Brigadier General Campbell King had to arrange to circumvent the regulation which stated that officers below the rank of brigadier general had to perform "duty with troops" at least one in every five consecutive years. As Marshall had been on detached service since July 1, 1927, he had to serve with troops by July 1, 1931. Despite efforts by Marshall's predecessor as assistant commandant at the Infantry School, the adjutant general of the army ruled that that position did not constitute troop duty. (See NA/RG 407 [210.45].)

King's solution to the problem was to issue Special Orders, No. 96 (April 25, 1931), attaching Marshall to the Twenty-fourth Infantry, already a part of the post's troop complement, "for duty with troops, in addition to his other duties." Thus, for the next year, Marshall was theoretically the second in command of those troops. ★

To GENERAL JOHN J. PERSHING   December 2, 1931
                                               Fort Benning, Georgia

Dear General: Your letter of November 30th has just been received. I find that there is a copy of the book here in the library, and I will undertake to do as you ask as quickly as possible. Parts of this I have seen in serial form, but only gave them a casual reading.[1]

In a delayed reading of my last copy of Time, I saw a reference to your being ill with a cold in Walter Reed. I hope this is nothing serious, but rather a bit of well advised caution. Your letter evidently was written sometime later, so I take it that you are quite well again.

I have had a very busy fall, as to both official duties and social duties. Mollie has had a young lady visitor for a month and the house has been full of young people. My sister's husband has been with us a month, recuperating from a bad breakdown.[2] He has found Benning a great health resort, having gained ten pounds and refound a vigor for golf and other amusements. Mrs. Marshall and I ride eight to ten miles every afternoon, and I get in tennis and longer rides off and on during the week.

I saw the movies of you at Yorktown, and I have read very complimentary descriptions of the troop display there.[3] I see that Colonel Harry Cootes came in for official commendation. In his particular line he does better than almost anybody I know. He has one faculty which is a rare one,—he knows his own limitations, invariably picks efficient people to help him, and always secures their ardent and affectionate support. Can't you say a word for him towards promotion? I would prefer him to many that have been made,—and he is getting seriously well up in years.

With affectionate regards,   Faithfully yours,

G. C. Marshall, Jr.

LC/J. J. Pershing Papers (General Correspondence)

1. In a letter dated November 30, Pershing wrote Marshall about Frederick Palmer's *Newton D. Baker: America at War,* 2 vols. (New York: Dodd, Mead, 1931). Pershing thought writers such as Palmer were giving the War Department too much credit for winning the war. "Although I have only just glanced through the book, it seems to contain many inaccuracies, implications, unwarranted claims, and special pleadings." As Marshall was well aware of the difficulties the A.E.F. encountered in getting trained men and supplies from the United States, Pershing added, "I would like to have you read this book carefully, between the lines and otherwise, and let me know what, if anything, you find that should be corrected or refuted. I think we must insist on keeping the record straight and not permit an exaggerated impression

to be created of the efficiency and foresight of the Administration, the War Department, the War Secretary, or the Chief of Staff.'' (LC/J. J. Pershing Papers [General Correspondence].)

2. Dr. John J. Singer was a physician from Greensburg, Pennsylvania, who had served as an army surgeon during the World War.

3. General Pershing gave a speech and participated in various ceremonies in connection with the sesquicentennial of the British surrender at Yorktown, Virginia (October 17–19, 1781).

TO CAPTAIN GEORGE E. ADAMSON
December 3, 1931
Fort Benning, Georgia

My dear Adamson: I am inclosing herewith two certificates of 32d Degree Masonry, which the holders hope that General Pershing will honor with his signature. The two men are fine old soldiers, master sergeants, and they would be immensely proud to receive this favor from the General. At his convenience, would you be good enough to see if you can secure his signature?

As these documents are valuable, I have registered them to you, and I would appreciate the same in their return to me. Tell the General I am sorry to bother him with this, but I imagine that he will not mind doing it—in fact, he will rather like it.

I wrote him yesterday regarding Palmer's book on Baker, and you might tell him I have already completed half of the first volume. The remainder will require much closer reading. Faithfully yours,

G. C. Marshall, Jr.

LC/J. J. Pershing Papers (General Correspondence)

TO GENERAL JOHN J. PERSHING
March 28, 1932
Fort Benning, Georgia

Dear General: I am inclosing a letter from General Gignilliat of Culver which is self-explanatory. I will be very glad to help Gignilliat out in the matter, but it seemed to me best to ask for your assistance.

I have in mind several incidents in your life, prior to your entering the Army, which I think would be of the character desired. However, my recollection of the details is hazy, though I have a very clear recollection of your telling me about them. One refers to your taking over the management of the farm when you were sixteen. Another, to your first experiences as a school teacher with a refractory pupil. With the incidents of your army career, I am, naturally, more familiar. Would you care to give me your opinion of what were the high points of your career? Gignilliat need know nothing about my reference of this matter to you.[1]

I learned from one of the service papers that you had been in the hospital for bronchitis, but had left fully recovered. Evidently you were being careful, rather than seriously ill. I am very glad you were taking no chances with the uncertain weather of the late winter and spring. Down here it has been extremely warm and then unseasonably cold, the changes coming very rapidly.

We are very busy getting ready for the Corps Area maneuvers which commence in two weeks and have to be woven somewhat into the school work.

I have succeeded in avoiding a desk and getting an assignment to troops and command of a post,—Fort Screven, Georgia. However small, it at least keeps me away from office work and high theory, and I understand it is a very delightful station.

With affectionate regards,   Faithfully yours,

G. C. Marshall, Jr.

LC/J. J. Pershing Papers (General Correspondence)

1. Gignilliat's letter was not found in the Pershing papers. On April 23, 1932, Pershing replied to Marshall, "I appreciate very much your wish to help Gignilliat and also his desire to comply with the request that he has received from A. N. Marquis, but I have been filled up with business affairs and official matters for the last month and this, with preparations for my spring departure for Europe, has made it impossible to give the matter much consideration." (LC/J. J. Pershing Papers [General Correspondence].)

To Captain Claude M. Adams[1]   June 3, 1932
                                              Fort Benning, Georgia

Dear Captain Adams: I am going to ask you to be kind enough to make some preliminary arrangements before Mrs. Marshall's arrival at Screven. She will probably leave here with the three children on the morning of June 13th, though she may leave earlier if it becomes too hot here. In any event I will telegraph you twenty-four hours in advance.

I would appreciate your securing the items on the attached list and having them in the house, as well as the Muir's maid and a striker available.[2]

If Mrs. Marshall leaves here in the morning she should reach Screven in the middle of the afternoon, and I would like to have the maid and the various things in the house ready for her. I propose sending over a bedding roll by express in order to provide the sheets and blankets.

I know you were good enough to tell her that you and Mrs. Adams will be glad to have her stay with you, or at least take her meals with you. Both of us appreciate this very much, but considering the size of the family, the fact that the maid is already available, the house empty and waiting, and the Quartermaster can usually furnish beds, mattresses, etc., she feels it better to establish herself from the first and enjoy your hospitality later.

I will probably leave here the 15th or 16th, depending on how soon I can make my departure after the van with my household goods has left.

I was very glad to arrange to have my orders changed to June from July. Now nothing interferes with my transfer.   Faithfully yours,

GCMRL/G. C. Marshall Papers (Fort Benning)

1. Adams was a Tennessee native who had risen through the enlisted ranks in his state's National Guard during the World War. Appointed captain in the Regular Army on July 1, 1920, he was acting commandant at Fort Screven at this time.

2. Marshall had made arrangements with the former acting commandant, Major James I. Muir (U.S.M.A., 1910), to employ the Muirs' maid as a cook. A "striker" was an enlisted man who did extra-duty work for an officer for extra pay.

TO MADAME JOUATTE[1]   June 15, 1932
                                                    Fort Benning, Georgia

Dear Madame Jouatte: As I am leaving Fort Benning today and going to a new station, I want to tell you of the change. For the next year at least, I will be at Fort Screven, Georgia. This is a garrison near Savannah, on the ocean.

It has been a long time since I have written to you or heard from you, and I will be very much interested in learning how life has treated you the past two years. Everything has gone well with me, and I certainly hope it has with you.

Here in America we are experiencing a great financial depression. I suppose you feel it in France, but I understand that it is not so bad there yet.

With affectionate regards,   Faithfully yours,

GCMRL/G. C. Marshall Papers (Fort Benning)

1. Marshall had lived with the Jouattes in Gondrecourt, France, from mid-July, 1917, to mid-January, 1918. No earlier correspondence with Mme Jouatte has been found.

FORT SCREVEN, Georgia, until 1924 a Coast Artillery post guarding the only entrance to Savannah Harbor, was the home of one battalion of the Eighth Infantry. Located on Tybee Island, eighteen miles east of Savannah, the post's climate was "delightful except during the extremely damp part of the winter," according to Charles J. Sullivan's *Army Posts and Towns: The Baedeker of the Army* (Burlington, Vt.: Free Press, 1926), p. 142. But because of Fort Screven's isolation, officers were advised that a private car was a necessity and servants were "hard to employ and hard to keep." ★

To Lieutenant Colonel Erle M. Wilson[1]   July 16, 1932
                                              [Fort Screven, Georgia]

Dear Wilson: Thank you for your note about General Parker, the Congressman from this district. You may be certain that I will put the big pot in the little one in his case. I appreciate your tipping me off.[2]

I had been about to write you when your letter came. I wanted to congratulate you upon one of the best jobs I have seen done in the Army. I have looked over everything on the post, familiarized myself with the routine, came to know the members of the garrison, and have met most of the leading people in Savannah. In every respect I find a highly satisfactory condition of affairs. You had developed the post in a remarkable manner and the personnel presents a model of loyal and efficient cooperation. In all directions outside the garrison I find the results of your conduct of affairs in the harmonious and extremely cordial attitude of the civilians.

The new theater opened last week and is a little gem. It is too bad you could not enjoy this result of your far-seeing activities. We are about to start in on the planting scheme for the theater and the club, the grading having been completed. For the past three days the prisoners have been hauling material to make a parking space.

Mrs. Marshall and the children are delighted with the place and are thoroughly enjoying themselves in spite of the heat.

With cordial regards to Mrs. Wilson and yourself,   Faithfully yours,

GCMRL/G. C. Marshall Papers (Fort Screven)

1. Wilson (U.S.M.A., 1904), Marshall's predecessor at Fort Screven, was the executive officer of the War Department's Operations and Training Division (G-3).

2. Wilson had written Marshall on July 8 that Homer C. Parker, former adjutant general of the Georgia National Guard from 1927 until his 1931 election to the United States House of Representatives from the Savannah district, had intimated that he wished to visit Fort Screven following the adjournment of Congress. Parker had fought to prevent further congressional cuts in army strength and had consistently supported preparedness, Wilson said. "I feel that it is to our interests to have him return to Congress for we cannot afford to lose a friend and I also feel that in case he visits Fort Screven any red fire that you may put on or black powder that you may burn may help him with the Savannah citizens." (GCMRL/G. C. Marshall Papers [Fort Screven].)

From Lieutenant Philip E. Gallagher[1]   September 27, 1932
                                              [West Point, New York]

My dear Colonel Marshall: I am attaching a letter requesting my detail to the Command and General Staff School for the course 1933–35.

I don't know exactly what to do. Apparently the doors of both the Staff School and the Advanced Infantry School are closed to me simply because I am a lieutenant. I believe this is wrong. The War Department has no control over my promotion status but they can control the school policy, and I believe that the logical policy to adopt would be one based on length of service (regardless of grade) and the individual's record.

I am mighty anxious to push ahead with others of my age and do wish there was some way to get some responsible person to see my point of view. In a very short time they will be deciding that I am too old to be bothered with and if that takes place in the next few years, I am through as far as a career is concerned. I have finished fifteen years service (one-half of my thirty years). I am still a lieutenant (the Bars Sinister, as we call them, are very irksome after so long a time, but I am used to them and can bear them), but this school business just takes all the fight out of me.

In China you advocated the policy of making lieutenants assume the responsibilities that go with the upper grades so I am in hopes that you still feel that way and will see fit to do something to help me out. . . .   Sincerely yours,

GCMRL/Research File (Fort Screven)

1. Gallagher (U.S.M.A., 1918) had taught at the Infantry School from 1918 to 1922, and had then taken the Company Officers' Course there (1922–23), before his assignment to the Fifteenth Infantry at Tientsin. He served as assistant regimental and post adjutant in Tientsin between April 1, 1925, and April 24, 1926. Returning to the United States in November, 1926, he became assistant professor of tactics at Lafayette College. Since June 26, 1928, he had been an instructor in tactics at the United States Military Academy. He had been a first lieutenant since October 16, 1919.

To Major General Edgar T. Collins[1]   September 30, 1932
[Fort Screven, Georgia]

Dear General: Attached is a letter from one of the most able officers I know—regardless of rank.[2] I rated him "Superior" *seven* years ago when he was my regimental adjutant, of a crack outfit in China. He is now as old as I was when I was Chief of Staff of an Army Corps.

Recalling the futile efforts you and I together made to give the highly efficient over-slaughed lieutenants a place in the sun,[3] and as this is one of the most glaring cases of the tragic injustice of the present arithmetical policy governing the professional improvement careers of officers who entered the army during the war, I am sending you these papers.

I know General W. D. Connor was strongly and actively in favor of giving efficient older officers of junior rank a chance in the school system, and that you felt the same way; and considering your respective positions today, surely something can be done to crack the ice short of Mr. Hoover taking a hand. Faithfully yours,

GCMRL/Research File (Fort Screven)

1. Collins was commandant at Fort Benning between March 9, 1926, and May 1, 1929. He subsequently held commands in the Philippine Islands and Washington, D.C. At the time of this letter he was assistant chief of staff for Operations and Training at the War Department.

2. The attachment is printed above.

3. On this issue, see Marshall's Memorandum for the Commandant, January 9, 1928, above.

To Lieutenant Philip E. Gallagher[1]   [September 30 (?), 1932]
                                              [Fort Screven, Georgia]

Dear Phil: This is the best I can think of to do for you. I fought this fight four years at Benning—and without success, but it just happens that Col. Buckner was sort of a "go between" in a discussion of this I had with Gen Conner.[2] He did break the jam at the War College. Gen Collins and I attempted to break it for the advanced class. Possibly the fact that Gen. Conner and Buckner and Gen. Collins are all involved officially in this may be more than a coincidence—it may be decisive.[3] Affectionately yours,

                                                        G. C. M.

GCMRL/Research File (Fort Screven); H

1. This letter was handwritten on the carbon copy of the letter printed above.

2. Major General William D. Connor, commandant of the Army War College from December 20, 1927, until April 30, 1932, had been superintendent of the United States Military Academy since May 1, 1932. Lieutenant Colonel Simon B. Buckner, Jr., (U.S.M.A., 1908) had been executive officer, adjutant, and personnel adjutant at the Army War College between July 1, 1929, and July 4, 1932. Since the latter date, Buckner had been assistant to the commandant of cadets at the Military Academy.

3. Early in November, Marshall sent Gallagher Collins's reply to his September 30 letter which stated that they had won a "partial victory" in that first lieutenants were to be eligible for the Command and General Staff School beginning in 1933. (Collins to Marshall, November 4, 1932, GCMRL/Research File [Fort Screven].) Marshall's attached note to Gallagher observed, "You are undoubtedly rated Superior—so you should have a good show for the detail." (Ibid.) War Department Special Orders, No. 82 (April 10, 1933), instructed Gallagher to report to Fort Leavenworth in August for the two-year Command and General Staff School course.

To Major General Stephen O. Fuqua[1]   November 18, 1932
                                              Fort Screven, Georgia

Dear General: I am much embarrassed by a situation which has developed suddenly as a result of the new Leavenworth policy and my recent service at Benning.

Members of the faculty at the Infantry School who served me well and now are eligible for consideration, naturally look to me to indorse them, especially since their new Chief is not familiar with the special services they may have rendered during the past two or three years. I, myself, understand that such details are figured out impersonally from the efficiency records on file in your office, and I have submitted efficiency reports on these men. But, I am not now in the position to put a special indorsement on their applications for a specific detail.

Recently I have received letters from some unusually fine fellows asking, in effect, if there was not some way in which I might express my views on their particular qualifications for the Leavenworth detail. It would be presumptuous for me to write letters to your office requesting special consideration for this or that man, yet I feel a pressing obligation on me in the case of some of these men, to do something to help them because of the unusually fine service they rendered the Infantry School, in general and me in particular, in developing and improving the courses there. For this reason, and with a disturbing understanding of the delicacy of my position, I have decided to list for your eye the men I am referring to, with a statement regarding their recent services at Benning. I hope you will not feel that I am intruding, and that you will understand the motive which has caused me to do this.

Captain W. S. Paul:

Instructor in supply. Superior officer. He contributed in a variety of ways and in a superior manner to the development of the supply course and to questions of supply before the Infantry Board. He is vigorous physically, tactful to a marked degree and popular. Temperamentally, physically and mentally he displays the qualities which mark him as unusually adapted for higher command and staff training.

1st Lieut. Julien E. Raymond:

Instructor in signal communication–radio specialist. A superior officer, very bright and alert. An outstanding instructor at Benning. Capable of performing any task with high efficiency. One of the best and most deserving lieutenants I have met in the Army. Admirably adapted for higher training. A marked example of the junior officer of great ability submerged by the promotion situation. The kind who should be allowed to progress where the law does not forbid.

Captain Russel B. Reynolds:

Very able machine gun instructor. Ambitious, hard working, dependable, strong character.

1st Lieut. Fremont B. Hodson:

Book Shop Officer. Unusual business ability, largely responsible for vigorous development of Book Shop business, and greatly increased profits which enabled us to buy much expensive machinery. A hustler. Tactful, reliable, aggressive. He will be forty in February 1934.

Other officers have appealed to me, but I have confined myself to the most deserving. They will not be informed of the action I have taken.[2]   Faithfully yours,

G. C. Marshall, Jr.

NA/RG 177 (210.632, Chief of Infantry)

1. Fuqua had been chief of Infantry since March, 1929.
2. In the margin of Marshall's letter, someone in the Office of the Chief of Infantry wrote "not on list" beside Raymond's, Reynolds's, and Hodson's names, and "10th alternate" beside Paul's name.

To MAJOR GENERAL STEPHEN O. FUQUA   November 25, 1932
[Fort Screven, Georgia]

Dear Fuqua: Your letter, with the extract from the annual report of The Infantry School, has just come. I appreciate very much your taking this fashion of bringing it to my attention, and I even more appreciate your cordial expressions.[1]

Already Benning seems very far away, and from what Campbell King told me when he was here Tuesday night, it is booming. I will always have a soft place in my heart for Benning. It caught me at my most restless moment, and gave me hundreds of interests, an unlimited field of activity, delightful associates and all outdoors to play in. At a War College desk I thought I would explode. The change to Benning was magical, with its atmosphere of youthful vigor, its absence of ponderosity and its balm of fresh air. I'm not a city boy.   Faithfully yours,

GCMRL/G. C. Marshall Papers (Fort Screven)

1. Fuqua's letter of November 22 quoted the following extract from the Report of the Infantry School for 1931–32: "The closing of this Academic year marks the termination of the four and one-half year tour of Lieutenant Colonel George C. Marshall, Jr., as Assistant Commandant of the school. This report would not be complete without a testimonial to the splendid work that has been accomplished by this officer. Under his direction each year has witnessed a steady and marked improvement in the subject matter covered, as well as the methods of instruction in the school. The present high standard attained is due to his energy, his foresight and his very unusual qualifications." (Fuqua to Marshall, November 22, 1931, GCMRL/G. C. Marshall Papers [Fort Screven].)

To MRS. THOMAS B. COLES   December 27, 1932
[Fort Screven, Georgia]

Dear Aunt Lottie: This note was supposed to have been written the day before Xmas—but was not.

Xmas day Allen was a passenger in an aeroplane crash, and now is in a Savannah hospital with a fractured jaw, a severe concussion, four teeth gone badly lacerated mouth and chin, and severe neck and a shoulder bruises. He will be forced to subsist on liquid diet—thru a tube—for about seven weeks. But we feel that he was saved from a worse fate by a miracle.

Otherwise we had a very happy Xmas, along with the fuss of staging a children's play and doing up 175 presents for the post and neighborhood children.

Katherine's sister is with us this winter. Mollie is here, but Clifton is attempting to do business—first in New York and now in Baltimore.

I promised Mrs. Knapp a remedy I took for neuritis, but I found from my doctor that it would not do in her case.

I hope she is better and that you have escaped flu and colds, which are prevalent here. Charlotte always seems to be the hardy member of the family—probably part constitution and part pluck. I hope she is well and happy.

With my holiday greetings and love to you all,   Affectionately,

G. C. M.

GCMRL/Research File (Family); H

To the Adjutant General   January 9, 1933
                                                  Fort Screven, Georgia

I request that when a vacancy for my promotion occurs that I be nominated under the name George C. Marshall, the present *junior* of my name to be omitted.[1]

G. C. Marshall, Jr.

NA/201 File

1. The request was granted and became effective on January 13, 1933.

To General John J. Pershing   January 24, 1932 [*1933*]
                                                  Fort Screven, Georgia

Dear General: I see references to you frequently in the press since your return from abroad and one picture of you in the Movie.[1] You seem to be in fine shape and I certainly hope this is the case, and that you have avoided this epidemic of flu which has struck hard in the South. The weather here has been mild and delightful all winter—no severe cold and few rains. I ride, play tennis and occasionally fish for diversion, and the family offers me plenty of company.

Mollie (19) is with us and Mrs. Marshall's sister. Allen (16) crashed in an aeroplane Xmas day and now takes nourishment thru a glass tube. He fractured his jaw, cracked a cheek bone, lost four teeth and suffered a severe concussion.

Fortunately, he made a quick recovery, except that his teeth must remain wired together for another four weeks until his jaw bone has healed. Then he can go back to school at Woodbury Forest in Virginia.

I hope Warren is progressing in his business in spite of the depression.[2] If he weathers this gale he should have little to fear in the future.

I went up for my promotion exam in December, but I doubt if a vacancy occurs before June. I find the life here quiet but interesting and agreeable. The personnel are of an unusually high standard and I find it pleasant to again be in close touch with young officers and the men.

I gather from Peter Bowditch's letters that he is having a very hard time financially and with a sick wife. He bitterly regrets having resigned from the army.[3]

General Dawes' troubles as I learned of them thru political speeches, "Time" and the press, seemed a tragic climax to a conspicuous career.[4] I have wanted to write to him, but have hesitated because of ignorance as to his actually situation and because it has been years since I have seen him or heard from him—eight, I believe.

March's book seems to have died in the public mind, murdered by his convincing egotism.[5]

Some one in Savannah told me you had been appointed Grand Marshal of the Inaugural parade. I did not see the account in the paper. This is a fine compliment to you, but I imagine that you do not relish the job.

Baruch seems to be in the middle of things again.[6] He interested me more than most interesting men. I always enjoyed talking to Baruch and Mr. Baker more than any other of the prominent characters of my tour in Washington with you.

This is a long and rambling letter, but I wish you would write me one, equally long with what you are doing and thinking these days.   Affectionately,

G. C. Marshall

LC/J. J. Pershing Papers (General Correspondence); H

1. Marshall presumably saw Pershing's picture in the newsreels. The general had returned from France in late November, 1932.

2. Pershing's son, Warren, had graduated from Yale University in 1931 and was working as a stockbroker in New York City.

3. Major Edward R. Bowditch, Jr., had resigned on April 16, 1925.

4. On January 22, 1932, former Vice-President Charles G. Dawes became president of the new Reconstruction Finance Corporation (R.F.C.), a governmental institution designed to make confidential loans to corporations. Critics attacked the R.F.C.'s lending policies as favoring the wealthy and the large corporations. On June 6, 1932, Dawes suddenly resigned from the R.F.C. A few days later he returned to Chicago to take control of the Central Republic Bank and Trust Company—popularly called the "Dawes Bank"—which was experiencing financial difficulty, as were all Chicago banks. On June 27 the R.F.C., to prevent the bank's failure, committed itself to lend it ninety million dollars. (Jesse H. Jones, *Fifty Billion Dollars: My Thirteen Years with the RFC, 1932–1945* [New York: Macmillan, 1951], pp. 72–81.)

When the R.F.C.'s lending policies—and the Dawes loan in particular—were made public in July, 1932, criticism of the R.F.C., of Dawes, and of the Hoover Administration increased. In midwestern states, the Dawes loan caused the Republican party "heavy damage." On

November 4, four days before the election, President Hoover made a "spirited and at times dramatic defense" of the loan in a St. Louis, Missouri, speech. ("National Affairs," *Time* 20 [November 14, 1932]: 10.)

Despite the R.F.C. loan, in October the Dawes bank was forced to reorganize as the City National Bank and Trust Company. ("Still Open Dawes," *Time* 20 [October 17, 1932]: 47.)

5. Former Chief of Staff Peyton C. March had written *The Nation At War* (Garden City, N.Y.: Doubleday, Doran, 1932).

6. Bernard M. Baruch had been active during the 1932 election campaign as an economic advisor to Franklin D. Roosevelt. Following the election, as Baruch later recalled, rumors of his influence with the new administration and reports that he would be appointed to some significant government position were common for months. (Bernard M. Baruch, *Baruch: The Public Years* [New York: Holt, Rinehart and Winston, 1960], pp. 249–50.)

To Captain Frank B. Hayne[1]

[February 7 (?), 1933]
Fort Screven, Georgia

My dear Frank: I was really glad to get your letter with its news of you and Ann and her parents, but I am awfully sorry you are depressed and terribly sorry (poor English) to learn of Mr. Dulany's trouble.

As to your Machine Gun proposition—any one who will really simplify anything concerning our weapon technique, tactics, &c., so as to permit more ready understanding by citizen soldiers and more rapid training by war levys, performs a very valuable service.

I am not familiar with all the M.G. complications, but I am familiar with the general complexity and poor presentations on all counts. I made war on this constantly at Benning, and while I could not materially change the T.R.'s I did massacre the school system of presentations and technique. I know we lopped off over 40% of the M.G. papers and presentation.

The troubles in all these things are basic and have their root in Washington. The very method or manner in which the manuals are presented is, in my opinion, a fatal fault. All should be clearly divided into two parts—the first including *only* what the citizen soldier *must* know *prior* to mobilization, the second part, what he must start to learn immediately on threatened mobilization. The professional soldier must know it all. There the system of publication, or arrangement I believe is faulty. There should be one detailed manual and only one—the platoon chief's. It would cover individual, squad section and platoon, with all necessary details. Company, battalion, regiment and brigade should be combined in one manual as general in statement as the field service regulations.

The annual inspection is on now and I am very busy. I will probably be in Washington at the A. & N. Club o[n] March 3 to 5th on a meeting of the Mershon Board—Colonel Robbins of Iowa (former asst. Sec. of War), Gen. Gignilliat of Culver and myself. The Secretary of the Board picked inauguration as a good time and has engaged our rooms already.[2] I will see the Dulanys then, and I hope you and Ann. I suppose I will see you parade.

With affectionate regards to you both,   Faithfully yours,

G. C. M.

GCMRL/F. B. Hayne Papers; H

1. Hayne and his wife, Ann Dulany Hayne, had been in Tientsin, China, with the Marshalls. At this time, Hayne was in the Thirty-fourth Infantry at Fort George G. Meade, Maryland.

2. The Civilian Military Education Fund (also called the "Mershon Fund"), whose goals were to improve civilian-military relations and to promote civilian military and Reserve officer training, was established by Colonel Ralph D. Mershon, an electrical engineer and inventor. An alumnus of Ohio State University, Mershon had been active in drafting legislation for the Reserve Officers' Training Corps and having it included in the National Defense Act of 1916. Marshall was appointed to the Mershon Fund Board in 1929.

Colonel Charles B. Robbins, an officer in the Iowa National Guard who had seen army service in the Philippines (1898–99) and France (1917–19), and a former assistant secretary of war (1928–29), was chairman of the Mershon Fund's National Committee. Colonel Ralph C. Bishop was the board's secretary.

To GENERAL JOHN J. PERSHING   March 8, 1933
                                               Fort Screven, Georgia

My dear General: After a weeks shooting up country on a big plantation I went direct to Washington expecting to see you. Not until I arrived there did I learn of the change in your plans. I was greatly relieved to find out from Adamson and Colonel Jones that you were not really ill.[1] I had feared flu or grippe was your portion.

It was a great disappointment not to see you. I had counted on it, but did not realize how much until I learnt you were still in Arizona.

Washington was a remarkable looking place. Seemingly, every deserving Democrat in the country was there—streets crowded, hotels overflowing and every crowd sprinkled with the uniforms of governor's staff officers. The parade was Democracy at its blatant best and the simultaneous closing of the banks made plenty of atmosphere for the occasion. The crowds were still looking for you—did not seem to have seen the notices in the papers. As a matter of fact the first notice I saw was in the Army & Navy Register. I think Grayson and his committee must have tried to suppress the news of your absence.[2]

In this connection, I asked Adamson to let me know hereafter of your principal movements and changes of plan. Neither the Columbus, Ga. nor the Savannah papers are worth a damn. They carry very little news outside of local affairs. And I have not cared much about reading papers several days old. As a consequence I get most of my news, and of you, from "Time". I did not know when you returned from France or when you left for the West. As a matter of fact the local paper said you had arrived at Howard Coffin's place on St.

Simeons Island near me.[3] I telephoned and was told you were not there. I did not know you had left the Metropolitan Club until Jones told me.

I do hope this finds you enjoying the sunshine and clean air of Arizona and feeling well.   Affectionately

G. C. Marshall

LC/J. J. Pershing Papers (General Correspondence); H

1. Lieutenant Colonel Glenn I. Jones was a physician on duty at this time in the Office of the Chief of the Air Corps.

2. Rear Admiral Cary T. Grayson, formerly President Wilson's personal physician, was chairman of the Roosevelt inauguration committee.

3. Howard E. Coffin, a businessman and engineer, had been a member of the Advisory Commission of the Council of National Defense from 1916 to 1918, and had held other military advisory posts.

To Major General Edward L. King   March 9, 1933
Fort Screven, Georgia

My dear General: I found your letter regarding Captain Smith, on my return from furlough yesterday. He has told me of your kindness and advice, and he has decided to let the doctors settle the case for him, and expects retirement.[1]

Mrs. Marshall and I spent four days on a big plantation near Augusta, quail shooting, and had fine luck. On my return I left immediately for Washington for a meeting of the Mershon Board—Colonel Robbins of Iowa, General Gignilliat and myself saw the inauguration, and looked for you without success.

The Screven animal column leaves here tomorrow. The troops leave by motor March 25th.[2]

As only two line officers will remain here and Captain Smith may be ordered off before a retiring board, I would like to attend to final C.M.T.C. preparations and post affairs here until time to join the Battalion at Fort Benning just before regimental headquarters is due there.[3] There will only be two hundred odd men, and the battalion commander will be with them. Also the same Captain who commanded them last year and set up the tents at Benning. So there is considerably more I can find for myself to do here until April 5th than there. May I have your permission to report at Benning April 5th,—on my own transportation?

I appreciate your standing invitation at McPherson and wish I could find occasion to accept. However, I will see you soon at the concentration.

I had the new Mayor of Savannah with most of his City Officials, the same from Tybee, the County Commissioners and some of the Chamber of Commerce for a demonstration yesterday, inspection of a barrack, supper with the men and a prize fight. The men put up a splendid show. The civilians furnished the speeches in each mess at supper and the fights (our first here in some years) were excellent amateur affairs. Also the Lord was good to us in weather. A number of the City Officials told me it was the first time they had been on the post in many years, so I feel we did some good, and I know we staged a very clever and interesting show despite the small size of the Command and no music.

This has been too long a letter.   Faithfully yours,

GCMRL/G. C. Marshall Papers (Fort Screven)

1. Captain J. E. Smith, the post's quartermaster, retired in the autumn of 1933 for disability in the line of duty.

2. The Fourth Corps Area maneuvers at Fort Benning were scheduled to begin in early April. The horse- and mule-drawn units carrying equipment and supplies were expected to march the approximately two hundred fifty miles to the maneuver area.

3. Fort Screven was the site of one of the summer Citizens' Military Training Camps.

To Cadet Clarence E. Gooding

March 20, 1933
Fort Screven, Georgia

My dear Gooding: Your letters of February 16th and March 17th have been received. I especially enjoyed your February letter with the interesting items of cadet life and your own progress.[1]

I am sorry not to be able to give you the data requested in your March letter. The demonstration you saw did not involve much in economy of time, as I recall it. On the contrary, I think it was so carefully and methodically done that considerable time was involved. I will endeavor to get you, from Benning the exact data.

This much I can tell you now. The time required to train recruits is variable, depending on several conditions. If the recruit is to serve in a veteran unit the time required can be shortened materially—I would say about 50 percent. If the organization is entirely new except for a few trained N.C.O.'s then the recruit period must be much more thorough, and therefore longer.

Again, if our new drill is used the time required can be very much shortened, again, I believe almost 50 percent. This old drill—as you now have it—required an interminable period.

Another consideration,—if you are dealing with peace time recruits, the time required is materially lengthened over that required for war time recruits. In war you get men of better education, mentally more alert—and all are keen to progress because of the pressure and patriotism of war time.

I will see what data I can locate at Benning.   Faithfully yours,

GCMRL/G. C. Marshall Papers (Fort Screven)

1. Cadet Gooding was a member of the United States Military Academy class of 1936. His February 16 letter is not in the Marshall papers. Gooding had briefly been Marshall's office orderly at Fort Benning. Marshall had helped to secure Gooding's appointment to West Point. His March 17 letter requested information regarding recruit training for an article in the West Point magazine comparing American and German training methods. (See also Marshall to Pershing, June 2, 1936, below.)

To the Commanding General, Fourth Corps Area   March 24, 1933
From Major Thomas W. King[1]   Fort McPherson,
                                               Georgia

Annual Inspection of Fort Screven, Ga.
FY 1933.

. . . VII. *ADEQUACY OF PAY AND ALLOWANCES OF OFFICERS.*[2]

1. With reference to the above, the Commanding Officer states as follows:

"1. Conditions at Fort Screven are abnormal. Cost of living, food stuffs and garrison social requirements are unusually low. The financial situation of the officers is therefore not a fair example for the Army at large.

"2. Those officers most seriously affected by the present rate of pay and allowances may be divided into two classes,—*a* junior officers old in years due to slow promotion, and *b* young officers drawing pay and allowance rates for the first five years of service.

"*a.*   The first group have been benefited by the great decrease in prices generally and they usually have managed to accumulate enough household goods and uniforms so that they can get along with a few replacements each year. But as their children grow older and more numerous their expenses steadily increase. I find that officers in this group at Fort Screven live in reasonable comfort, but those with families are unable to accumulate any reserve and are usually involved in time payments on a car (a necessity here). All are too insecurely established financially to make desirable social contacts with civilians in the same walk of life. All are seriously embarrassed with the problem of educating and meeting the unavoidable expense of their children as they reach high school age. All with families are embarrassed in maintaining reasonable life insurance to safeguard their families.

"*b.*   Young officers in the first pay period live a precarious existence, even here where good quarters are available and the cost of living is very low. Their margin of safety financially is so slender that any untoward event, such as the arrival or sickness of a baby, the breaking down of their car—which is an absolute necessity here—usually plunges them into debt, unless their parents come to the rescue. They are unable to maintain a suitable position in contact with the civilians of the nearby city who occupy a corresponding position, unless they have some outside assistance."[3]

NA/RG 159 (333.1, Fort Screven)

1. King was the assistant inspector general for the Fourth Corps Area.
2. On June 30, 1932, President Hoover signed the Omnibus Economy Bill. Among other stipulations, all military officers were required to take unpaid furloughs totaling thirty days during the 1933 fiscal year. This amounted to a salary reduction of eight and one-third percent of their active duty pay. In addition, all paid leaves were prohibited, and after July 1, 1932, salary increases resulting from promotion or from length of service were prohibited. ("Economy Decisions up to Comptroller General," *Army and Navy Journal,* July 2, 1932.) See also Marshall's Memorandum for General Hammond, April 13, 1934, below.

3. King also noted that "officers who had been promoted and whose services entitled them to enter another pay period since June 30, 1932, felt that they were being unduly discriminated against." In paragraph XXII, King recommended a commendation for Marshall "for the efficient and economical administration of his duties and the high state of morale of his command."

To Theodore Roosevelt, Jr.   March 30, 1933
Fort Screven, Georgia

My dear Roosevelt: Major Ridgway sent me a copy of your annual report on the Philippines.[1] It is one of the few reports of this nature I have ever read with much genuine interest. I want you to accept my congratulations, my tribute of praise on a truly remarkable piece of work. It seems to me you have submitted conclusive evidence of one of the most remarkable exhibitions of colonial government in history, where harmony, efficiency and patriotism prevailed throughout.

    With warm regards to Mrs. Roosevelt and you,   Faithfully yours,

G. C. Marshall

LC/T. Roosevelt Papers; H

    1. Roosevelt had been governor-general of the Philippine Islands since 1932. Matthew B. Ridgway (U.S.M.A., April 1917) was one of Roosevelt's advisors. Ridgway had commanded a company of the Fifteenth Infantry at Tientsin, China, from July 25, 1925, to May 1, 1926. During the 1929–30 academic year, he had been a student at the Infantry School.

To Brigadier General Leigh R. Gignilliat   April 5, 1933
Fort Screven, Georgia

My dear General: I suppose Bishop is sending you copies of his letter to me about the Lehigh Conference, and especially with reference to the subjects for discussion.[1] Will you be good enough to let me know if any of the subjects proposed by P.M.S.&T.'s and not already on our approved list, appeal to you as desirable topics. Also which of our subjects you would then omit.

    One view of yours in particular I would like to have. What do you think of Colonel Parrott's (Princeton) proposal to discuss the handling of pacifists?[2] At present, I am of the opinion that this should only be done informally without a designated plan on our program. It seems to me all publicity on the Conference should indicate unmistakably that we were solely concerned with increasing the teaching and administrative efficiency of the R.O.T.C., and not with combatting its enemies, except by improving the course.   Faithfully yours,

GCMRL/G. C. Marshall Papers (Fort Screven)

    1. The Civilian Military Education Fund was sponsoring a conference on R.O.T.C. at

Lehigh University in Bethlehem, Pennsylvania, May 8-9. No letters from Ralph C. Bishop to Marshall for this period have been found in the Marshall papers.

2. Lieutenant Colonel Roger S. Parrott (U.S.M.A., 1908) had been P.M.S.&T. at Princeton University since 1929. No documents between Parrott and Marshall have been found in the Marshall papers.

I N AN EFFORT to provide temporary relief for unemployed, young, male citizens, President Roosevelt asked Congress on March 31, 1933, "to create a civilian conservation corps to be used in simple work, not interfering with normal employment, and confining itself to forestry, the prevention of soil erosion, flood control and similar projects." Ten days later, the president signed the "Act for the relief of unemployment through the performance of useful public work, and for other purposes." Executive Order No. 6101, issued on April 5, created the agency officially titled Emergency Conservation Work, but best known by its popular name: the C.C.C.—Civilian Conservation Corps. (*The Public Papers and Addresses of Franklin D. Roosevelt,* 13 vols. [New York, 1938-50], 2: 80-81, 107-8.)

"We were en route to Fort Benning for the annual Corps Area Maneuvers," Marshall wrote to a World War acquaintance on March 29, "when the concentration was called off because of the President's emergency employment proposal for 250,000 men." (Marshall to Captain Germain Seligman, March 29, 1933, GCMRL/G. C. Marshall Papers [Fort Screven].) The cancellation was precipitated by Secretary of War George H. Dern's "warning instructions" to the corps area commanders on March 25 to begin preparations to organize, feed, clothe, and house one hundred thousand men for a short period. (Colonel Duncan K. Major, Jr., to TAG, March 25, 1933, NA/RG 407 [324.5, CCC (3-25-33)].)

The army's role was to be of longer duration and of greater extent than anyone initially realized. By early July, 1933, barely three months after enrolling the first man, the C.C.C. had settled 250,000 young men, 25,000 World War veterans, and 25,000 experienced woodsmen in 1,468 camps of approximately 200 men each. (*The Public Papers and Addresses of Franklin D. Roosevelt,* 2: 110.)

To expedite the sudden influx of men, corps areas were divided into C.C.C. districts. While at Fort Screven, Marshall commanded District F: Florida, much of Georgia, and a small part of South Carolina. When he was transferred to Fort Moultrie, he commanded District I: South Carolina.

The new C.C.C. men were sent to Marshall and the other district commanders to be apportioned into companies, housed, fed, clothed, and entertained. The district commander was charged with inspecting and approving potential camp sites and supervising the construction of the camps. Marshall's first group, Company 449, arrived about April 26. By the end of May, he commanded two C.C.C. companies of 406 men at Fort Screven. By the time he left Screven, he had supervised the creation of ten camps housing 1,879 men. When Marshall took command at Fort Moultrie on June 29, District I had a total of eleven C.C.C. camps and 1,915 men. (Weekly Morale Reports, May 1 to June 25, 1933, NA/RG 407 [324.5, CCC (3-25-33)]).)

To handle the C.C.C. mobilization, nearly all normal garrison duties were temporarily suspended. According to one of his assistants at Fort Screven, Marshall "ate, breathed and digested the many C.C.C. problems." (Reuben E. Jenkins to Forrest C. Pogue, October 26, 1960, GCMRL/Research File [Fort Screven].) Writing to Marshall in May, Colonel Laurence Halstead, acting chief of Infantry, doubtless spoke for many Regular Army officers: "This work is onerous and probably distasteful to the Army as it is not exactly military work but I feel that it is the salvation of the Army. In fact, it is my opinion that the Army is the only Governmental agency that was able to handle this proposition. I have noticed a cessation of talk of reducing the Army by four thousand officers since we started in on the conservation work." (Halstead to Marshall, May 26, 1933, GCMRL/G. C. Marshall Papers [Fort Screven].) ★

FROM MAJOR GENERAL EDWARD L. KING[1] April 6, 1933
Fort McPherson, Georgia

Dear Marshall: . . . Sorry we didn't have the maneuvers, but with the labor situation coming on, I felt we should be set to go, and I wanted to be ready for it. The quota for this Corps Area is 7,100, and my general scheme is to establish a camp at Bragg near the textile industries of North and South Carolina; one at Oglethorpe for Chattanooga and vicinity; one at McClellan for the Birmingham area, and one at Pensacola for New Orleans and other points.[2] By reducing the number of camps I am saving overhead and keeping the new men out of small posts and away from the immediate vicinity of large cities as far as possible. The only thing you will have to do about it is the possibility of giving me, if necessary, some of your troops or organizations to send to one or more of these camps to furnish personnel for handling.[3] This, however, I hope to avoid and shall do so if posssible.

My kindest regards to Mrs. Marshall, and the children.

With best wishes, Sincerely yours,

Edw. L. King

GCMRL/G. C. Marshall Papers (Fort Screven)

1. King (U.S.M.A., 1896) commanded the Fourth Corps Area, which included Fort Screven. Approximately sixty percent of this letter is printed here. Omitted are three paragraphs concerning personnel matters.

2. By the end of April, King discovered that the seven thousand were but the first increment of an expected thirty-eight thousand men his corps area was expected to process. (TAG to King, April 28, 1933, NA/RG 407 [324.5, CCC (3-25-33)]).)

3. A story making the rounds at Fort Screven concerning General King's request, as related by First Lieutenant Reuben E. Jenkins, was that Marshall replied: "Leave me my post

surgeon, my commissary officer, my post exchange officer and my adjutant and I will run this command with the First Sergeants; and if worse comes to worst, you can have the adjutant, for the Post Sgt. Major can take over those duties in a pinch.'' Eventually Marshall did have to run Fort Screven with first sergeants. (Jenkins to Forrest C. Pogue, October 26, 1960, GCMRL/ Research File [Fort Screven].)

To Major General Edward L. King   May 26, 1933
                                                    [Fort Screven, Georgia]

My dear General: Paragraph 44, Special Orders 119, War Department, C.S., relieves me from duty here immediately and sends me to Moultrie. I have no information on the date Colonel Allen is relieved at Moultrie. My successor Colonel Abraham, is due here after July 1st.[1]

I do not want to do any thing which might jeopardize my transfer to Moultrie, and so far as my personal affairs are concerned, I can move any day the Quartermaster can provide a van for my freight.

However, there are these official considerations: This is a Forestry District Headquarters. We are deep in establishing Camps, mostly at a considerable distance. My principal assistant Major Matthews is junior to two Majors sent in here for temporary duty.[2] Matthews is fully up to the job of handling the District, the Reception Center and the C.M.T.C., but I doubt the complete success of turning all this over on a moments notice to a casual officer unfamiliar with the Post, the District affairs and our C.M.T.C. problem,—which will require some finesse to handle this year.

Moultrie may be in the same predicament, but it is not yet deep in Forestry Camp Construction, which is no path of roses in a swamp region.

I thought that possibly you might see fit to request delay in my departure from here until after July 1st, or at least might authorize me to delay my departure until the last moment of this fiscal year.

I have one company in Camp at Ocala, Florida, another leaving here tomorrow for Camp at Eastport (near Jacksonville, Florida), a camp ready today at Hinesville, Georgia for a Benning Company (they evidently can't send it immediately), another Camp probably ready Sunday at Homerville, Georgia, for a Georgia Company, another Camp water system, septic tank, etc. is well under way on Sewanee River near Lake City, and work starting today on the Camp at Ocean Pond, Ocala National Forest, near Lake City.

The very few officers I have here have been splendid, each man carries about five jobs, all display fine initiative and I believe, with the absolute minimum of overhead staff, an excellent bit of work has been accomplished. I am now trying to round things out on a more formal basis, and I am ready to put on high speed reconnaissances of new Camp sites when announced, with initiation of most important water and similar installations the same day and hour the reconnaissance officer determines that there is no especial difficulty regarding the proposed camp site.   Faithfully yours,

GCMRL/G. C. Marshall Papers (Fort Screven)

1. Marshall was to take command of the Eighth Infantry Regiment, with headquarters at Fort Moultrie, near Charleston, South Carolina. He was replacing Colonel Gilbert M. Allen, who had been detailed as P.M.S.&T. at the University of Florida. Lieutenant Colonel Clyde R. Abraham (U.S.M.A., 1906), at this time a student at the Army War College, was scheduled to take over as commander at Fort Screven on July 1, 1933. Marshall was to be promoted to colonel effective September 1, 1933.

2. Frederick S. Matthews had entered the Regular Army from the Maryland National Guard in 1917. He was a 1932 graduate of the Command and General Staff School.

To Lieutenant Colonel Clyde R. Abraham   May 26, 1933
[Fort Screven, Georgia]

Dear Abraham: I have been waiting to receive notice of my orders before writing to you—tho I had the Adjutant send you a note. This morning my orders came for Moultrie, tho whether I go immediately or delay for awhile will be settled by General King, as I am deep in the complicated business of building Camps in the Florida-Georgia Swamp areas, as well as running a big CCC Camp here and getting ready to take on an increased sized unit of 500 C.M.T.C. boys June 13th, with reserve officers to handle them.

You will find Screven a charming place to live and in beautiful order, thanks to the long start Erle Wilson gave it. Almost everything has just been repainted, screening et cetera is in excellent shape, lawns, flower beds, et cetera are doing well, new ambulance, new fire engine and material on hand to complete painting and do all repair work for next year. I think I have three new bath room sets to install. The "rum runner" I got ahold of last fall is just being remodeled with all conveniences—a fine fishing, picnic and hunting boat, and able to take an entire Company aboard for training to South Carolina.

Your house will please you. It has had all screening renewed, venetian blinds for porch, and is freshly fresh and nearly new outside—and almost so inside. I know Mrs. Abraham will like it. If I am here when you come there will be a big set [of quarters] empty next door to me for your temporary use.

If there is any other information you want, Please let me know.   Faithfully yours,

GCMRL/G. C. Marshall Papers (Fort Screven)

To General Charles P. Summerall[1]   June 1, 1933
                                                              [Fort Screven, Georgia]

My dear General: Your very gracious note came this morning, and Mrs. Marshall and I are deeply appreciative of your invitation. At present we plan to leave here about June 28th, she and the family to go on a visit while I go thru direct to Fort Moultrie to take over the Forestry work there, which I understand will have developed into a district affair by that time; that is, building and running camps over eastern South Carolina. In that case I would have my hands so full that I could not pause for the great pleasure of a visit with Mrs. Summerall and you.

Here I am busy with several thousand Forestry boys, either on the post or scattered in camps (still under construction) from Ocala, Florida, north to Waycross, Georgia. Between satisfying the Auditor for the War Department and meeting the pressure to proceed at top speed, it has been an interesting and illuminating experience. We have much, very much to learn about simplification and decentralization.

I am looking forward with more pleasure to seeing something of you this coming year, than to any other aspect of my transfer.

With warm regards to you both, and deep appreciation of your offer of hospitality,   Faithfully yours,

GCMRL/G. C. Marshall Papers (Fort Screven)

1. The former army chief of staff (November 21, 1926, to November 20, 1930) had retired at the end of March, 1931. Since September 12, 1931, he had been president of The Citadel, The Military College of South Carolina, at Charleston.

To Lieutenant Colonel Clyde R. Abraham   June 3, 1933
                                                              [Fort Screven, Georgia]

My dear Abraham: Your letter just received.[1] I am slated to leave here June 28 or 29, and I imagine any leave you may have will be cancelled so as to bring you here July 1st, as you will find a big job awaiting you as District Commander. I have six camps now, from Ocala, Florida, to Waycross, Georgia, with 1200 men in them or about to land. I also have 850 CCC men here. By July 1st this district will probably have 3500 men in scattered camps, to supply, inspect and administer, and possibly 500 CCC men in camp here. All this running on a little post headquarters without the addition of a single extra army clerk from outside, means lots of work and supervision.

Moultrie has not yet been given a district, so I suppose I will arrive there in the middle of the throes of trying to establish camps on an economical basis in the low swampy regions along the coast.

I am utilizing these Forestry boys to clear and grade all the formerly inaccessible portions of the reservation and all the adjacent jungle, so that the training area will be tremendously increased, the appearance of things equally improved and the mosquitoes almost eliminated.   Hastily yours,

GCMRL/G. C. Marshall Papers (Fort Screven)
  1. This letter was not found in the Marshall papers.

To Brigadier General Leigh R. Gignilliat   June 3, 1933
[Fort Screven, Georgia]

My dear General,   I have been due to write you and Colonel Robbins an account of the Lehigh conference ever since my return, but have been too deep in Forestry business to find the time.

It seemed to me the conference was a success. All were interested, the committee reports were entered into with fine spirit and Colonel Bishop's arrangements were excellent and also those of Dr. Richardson and Major Green of Lehigh.[1] Judged by the reaction of the army officers the affair was a decided success. While no very positive or conclusive recommendations were forthcoming, yet this was not due to lack of interest. This seemed to indicate that a wide variety of special conditions imposed a variety of ideas, and also that the basic scheme and procedure was sound and had been steadily improving.

I think the money we expended was well worth while and demonstrated the desirability of having these conferences regularly, but with more civilian educators than army officers present.

I received the commencement invitation to Culver and appreciated the courtesy. I would like to attend but that is not possible.

My little post has 900 forestry boys here and 1200 now in camp. I am constructing, supplying and administering camps in Florida and southeast Georgia. This week I will probably be given ten or fifteen more camps to prepare and run in my District, which will mean a total of 5000 CCC men to supply and administer.

June 28th I leave for Fort Moultrie to command that post and the regiment, as my promotion should occur within the next six weeks.

With warm regards,   Faithfully yours,

GCMRL/G. C. Marshall Papers (Fort Screven)
  1. By "Dr. Richardson" Marshall probably meant Charles R. Richards, president of Lehigh University since 1922. Major James O. Green, Jr., (U.S.M.A., April 1917) had been professor of military science and tactics at Lehigh since 1931. Marshall had presided at the May 8–9 R.O.T.C. conference. See Marshall to Lowe, February 13, 1936, below.

To General John J. Pershing   July 11, 1933
                                                        Fort Moultrie, South Carolina

Dear General: I see in the press that you have gone to France. Adamson promised to give me advanced notice of your important moves, but he evidently forgot.

I hope you are feeling strong and are without worries. Certainly Warren's fine progress should be a continuing source of satisfaction. He is a splendid fellow, and I wish I could see what the last few years have done for him.

My last few months at Fort Screven were busy with this Forestry work. I commanded a district and established 4500 young men in camps throughout Florida and southeastern Georgia. Transferred to Moultrie June 30th, I inherited another Forestry district, covering South Carolina. In addition, I have a C.M.T.C. camp starting next week and three N. G. regiments coming into camp here for training. As few regular officers remain, it is hard to manage.

This CCC affair has been a major mobilization and a splendid experience for the War Department and the army. The former has got a lot to learn about decentralization and simplicity. The funds were usually so restricted that operations were hampered as to speed. Apparently all was decentralized, but usually a joker was tucked away somewhere in each lengthy instruction.

Mrs. Marshall and the boys have not arrived yet. They are visiting friends on Pawley's Island near Georgetown, S. C. This has been fortunate, as my house is a mess with thirty five workmen in it. Mollie came here with me, and is struggling with the housekeeping in the midst of confusion. The house is tremendous, and delightfully located, facing the ocean. I hope you honor it and us with a long visit next winter. You would find this restful and climatically ideal for the cold season. And then too, we could find so much to talk over and discuss.

My promotion comes along this month or next,—it has been a long wait for one grade, and for a time I thought the President would make it still longer.

With my prayers for your continued good health,   Affectionately,

                                                              G. C. Marshall

LC/J. J. Pershing Papers (General Correspondence); H

From Major General James F. McKinley[1]   October 3, 1933
                                                          [Washington, D.C.]

My dear Colonel Marshall: Orders will issue shortly assigning you to duty with the Illinois National Guard as Chief of Staff of the 33rd Division, Chicago, Illinois.[2]

General Keehn wrote to General MacArthur asking that he assist him in the selection of an outstanding Infantry colonel for this position. General Keehn is by profession a lawyer and is exceedingly anxious that he have an officer assigned to his Division on whom he can completely rely as to military matters. This position is considered in the War Department as one of great importance. In fact, due to the present economic situation, it might be considered as a critical one.

General MacArthur suggested your name to General Keehn. I know that you will be delighted to hear that he stated to General Keehn that you had no superior among Infantry colonels and that, in view of your outstanding ability, he would not send him any other names unless he, General Keehn, asked that it be done.[3]

I have been told, though I can't vouch for it, that there are emoluments connected with this position.[4]

With kindest regards,   Sincerely yours,

NA/RG 407 (210.65, Office File)

1. McKinley had been the army adjutant general since February 2, 1933.
2. War Department Special Orders, No. 234 (October 7, 1933), ordered Marshall to Chicago.
3. "Suggest Lieutenant Colonel George C. Marshall. He has no superior among Infantry Colonels. Have other names if not satisfactory. He is of such outstanding ability however that I suggest you confer with General Parker with reference to him before proceeding further with the matter." (MacArthur to Keehn, September 28, 1933, NA/RG 407 [210.65, Office File].) Major General Roy D. Keehn commanded the Thirty-third Division, Illinois National Guard. Major General Frank Parker commanded the Sixth Corps Area, which included Illinois, from April 7, 1929, to October 22, 1933. General Douglas MacArthur had been army chief of staff since November 21, 1930.
4. "It was the policy of the Commanding General, 33d Division, to provide an allowance to each of General Marshall's predecessors and his successors, until 1952, to cover the increased costs of living in Chicago, as compared to living on an Army post. These funds, incidentally, were not appropriated funds of the State of Illinois. They were funds belonging to the National Guard Commission, comprised of business men of Chicago who raised and donated the funds for the welfare of the Illinois National Guard for many years." (Major General Leo M. Boyle [adjutant general, state of Illinois] to Forrest C. Pogue, September 28, 1961, GCMRL/Research File [Illinois National Guard].)

To Major General John L. De Witt[1]   October 16, 1933
[Fort Moultrie, South Carolina]

Dear Dewitt: I am leaving here Friday for duty with the Illinois National Guard, after duty with troops since 1924—3 years in China, 5 at Benning, 1 at Screven and four months here. Naturally I have reached some conclusions during those nine years, frequently at variance with my point of view as a staff officer in Washington.

Knowing you well and having the greatest admiration for your ability and your unselfish devotion to duty, I propose singing my troop swan song by listing certain matters connected with the Q.M.C. which do not impress me favorably. Please accept these comments, not as criticisms, but as a desire, an effort to lead to something constructive. They in no way apply to your period of Q.M.

leadership, but are old affairs in my experience, made conspicuous by my long period with troops. I will not attempt much of discussion, merely mentioning the points that impress me as requiring attention, for the benefit of the line of the Army.

Clothing and Equipment.

Why does the Army have to have so much of poor grade or shoddy clothing, as compared to the Navy and Marine Corps? Every soldier has to buy his cotton shirt or he is not allowed at parade.

Flannel shirts are also of very poor quality. Not so with the Marines.

Blankets are of poor quality, generally shoddy. Sheets are short length and soldiers are long.

It ought not to be necessary for officers to send to Marine Corps Depots for cotton shirts, or to depend on the mixed shopping of Post Exchanges for satisfactory shirts.

Khaki shows great improvement.

Coal.

Here, for example, a very soft, small lump or almost dust coal is delivered. This may seem to be an economy, but I doubt it. Certainly it gives infinite trouble, and does not help morale. Freshly painted houses or offices (often heated by stoves) are soot covered after one month of fire. My quarters have just been painted. Already the room in which we have started an open fire is badly marred by coal smoke. The outside of the quarters turn a bilious, dirty mustard color from soft coal smoke. I have had buildings scrubbed, but they tell me it [is] of little use—only temporizing—and I know the small troop personnel cannot afford the men for this purpose. The coal purchases may show an economy, but maintenance requirements is increased and morale is certainly not improved.

Personnel and System.

The clerical or business system in vogue requires a tremendous amount of attention and some skill—certainly experience. It requires more men to maintain a satisfactory paper system than it leaves to serve the garrison. It is so complicated that post commanders can easily be confused as to just what is going on, and their supervision either becomes perfunctory or too close and time consuming.

The Q.M. personnel is usually inadequate, decidedly so at this post. A partial reason is the elaborate clerical work and elaborate reports required, the mass of requisitions seemingly necessary, etc, etc. Part of the trouble, I know, is due to legal requirements—but not all.

I have come to feel that if my Q.M. seems to have all his papers in proper shape, then I will find he gives little time to his real business of doing his part by the post and garrison. If he does the latter well, then I am suspicious about the state of his records, warehouses, etc. Few men can manage both phases satisfactorily. Therefore, the system would appear to be faulty.

All this is probably old stuff to you, but what I can not understand is why the Navy and Marine Corps seem always to be able to do better in this clothing matter, year after year, ever since I have been in the Army. I know they have more money, because they are more popular with Congress and I believe they are less rigidly held to account for the details of their expenditures, but even this would not appear to excuse their tremendous advantage over us in the way of uniform materials and cut of garments.   Faithfully yours,

GCMRL/G. C. Marshall Papers (Fort Moultrie)

1. De Witt had been quartermaster general of the army since February 3, 1930. He had been a fellow student of Marshall's at the Infantry and Cavalry School in 1906-7. During the World War, De Witt served as assistant chief of staff for supply (G-4) for the A.E.F.'s First Corps (February-July, 1918) and First Army (August, 1918-January, 1919). Between 1919 and 1924 he was a member of the War Department General Staff.

Illinois National Guard

October 1933–October 1936

THE CHICAGO ASSIGNMENT came as an unwelcome surprise. The Marshalls had just finished redecorating their large house at Fort Moultrie and expected to remain there at least two years. Moreover, Marshall was reluctant to leave duty with troops for a desk job in a large city. Making a rare request for special consideration, he wrote to Chief of Staff MacArthur for permission to remain with his regiment. Another long period of detached service, he feared, following so closely on detached service at the War College and the Infantry School, might be fatal to his career. (K. T. Marshall, *Together*, pp. 17–18.)

The orders stood, however, and on October 20, 1933, the Marshalls left the regiment for Chicago to look for a place to live. Seven days later, Marshall reported for duty as senior instructor with the Illinois National Guard. Mrs. Marshall observed that during their first months in Chicago, "George had a grey, drawn look which I had never seen before, and have seldom seen since." (Ibid., p. 18.)

The Illinois National Guard consisted of the Thirty-third Division and attached troops—nearly ten thousand men, of whom more than half resided in and around Chicago. In addition to their two weeks of field training each summer, the Guardsmen met once each week in their armories; officers and non-commissioned officers usually worked one or two additional evenings per week. Besides armory drills, there was instruction in weapons, gunnery, motor mechanics, engineering, electrical communications, supply methods, tactical map problems, and plans for mobilization in war and for local emergencies. (*Illinois Guardsman* 2 [March 1935]: 22–23.)

The Illinois National Guard's commander, Roy D. Keehn, was a politically well-connected attorney for the Hearst newspapers in Chicago who had been a lieutenant colonel in the Judge Advocate General's Department prior to his promotion to major general in 1929. The Regular Army officers assigned to the division were frequently critical of the division's technical ignorance and lack of efficiency. But, one former instructor recalled, any Regular who tried to "buck the National Guard in any way" ran the risk of being "reported as non-cooperative, transferred, and on a poor status with the War Department." (Colonel Charles S. Ritchel, "My Recollections of General George C. Marshall," n.d. [1960?], GCMRL/Research File [Illinois National Guard].)

Prior to Marshall's arrival, another former instructor wrote, "the units of the Illinois National Guard were content with some close order drill, limited firing practice, 'spit and polish' and near 100% attendance at Armory Inspections and Summer Camps." (Colonel Arthur Pickens to Forrest C. Pogue, November 13, 1960, ibid.) Both instructors agreed that Marshall soon impressed upon General Keehn and his subordinate officers the need for schools of instruction, tactical exercises, and war games to aid in getting the division combat-ready. ★

To Major General Frank R. McCoy   November 3, 1933
                                                   Chicago, Illinois

Dear General: I found your letter on my arrival in Chicago a few days ago. It had been forwarded from Moultrie. I was delighted to hear from you and am looking forward to an opportunity for a heart-to-heart talk.

My coming here was a sudden and unexpected affair—arranged personally between Gen. MacArthur and General Keehn. I will enclose my correspondence with General MacArthur which will explain matters.[1]

Just now Mrs. Marshall and I are hunting industriously for living quarters. We strongly favor the near north side—but our purse strings do not. We are temporarily living at a hotel near the Drake—directly in rear of the Lake Shore Athletic Club.

Naturally I miss the genial and gentle surroundings of Charleston and South Carolina. I had fixed Moultrie up quite a bit, and our quarters were lovely—all done over, and made white wood work inside. I never expect to have a more delightful home. The CCC camps and boys in S.C. were in a fine state and I was set for a fall of wonderful hunting. We will have to cultivate our tastes to city life.

The children—those not at school—join us the end of the month. We hope to be settled by that time.

There are no two people we would so much like to see as you and Mrs. McCoy. Think you both are Mrs. Marshall's choice of all she has seen of the Army..

With affectionate regards,   Faithfully yours,

                                                   G. C. Marshall

LC/F. R. McCoy Papers; H

1. McCoy took command of the Seventh Corps Area, whose headquarters were in Omaha, Nebraska, on October 1, 1933. Marshall's correspondence with MacArthur regarding the Chicago assignment has not been found. McCoy's reply indicated that he returned the correspondence. (McCoy to Marshall, November 9, 1933, LC/F. R. McCoy Papers.)

To General John J. Pershing   November 13, 1933
                                                   Chicago, Illinois

Dear General: Your nice and thoughtful note of congratulations followed me from Ft. Moultrie to Chicago. I came here on unexpected and sudden orders, to my complete surprise. An anticipated critical situation this winter with the hungry, and the striking coal miners caused my selection. I tried to remain at Moultrie, where I had only been established four months, but without success. There, I had a regiment, 4000 CCC men throughout South Carolina and rather complete independence. Gen. MacArthur wrote me in a very sympathetic manner, but it was "back to staff duty" for me. I seem fated.

We have not yet gotten settled, but I have signed a lease for an apartment on the "close in" North Side, about three blocks south of the Drake Hotel.

I spent Sunday a week ago with General Dawes. He seems very quiet, compared to his old assertive self. I know he must have suffered terribly the blow to his prestige.[1]

Mrs. Marshall motored out with me. The children (less Allen in school in Virginia) motor out next week from Baltimore.

City life is a great and depressing contrast to the delightful existence of my past few years on a post with troops. I suppose I will grow accustomed to it in time. Fortunately I can walk to and from my office in twenty five to thirty minutes, and an armory with horses is only a block distant.

I appreciated your letter very much, and I hope you are in fine shape. Affectionately,

G. C. Marshall

LC/J. J. Pershing Papers (General Correspondence); H

1. See Marshall to Pershing, January 24, 1933, note 4, above.

To JAMES F. BYRNES[1]   November 17, 1933
[Chicago, Illinois]

My dear Senator: Your note of congratulations on my promotion, written at sea, was received with deep appreciation. I was much impressed with your thoughtful and gracious action in remembering me in this fashion. It was gratifying to know that you had me in mind.

When you were on Sullivan's Island I had no idea that my tour of duty there would only last four months.[2] I had every reason to expect two years with the 8th Infantry. But because of threatened civic disorders out here, strikes and unemployment, I was suddenly transferred to this assignment.

I had found many friends in Charleston during my short stay, and I had become intensely interested in the CCC Camps of South Carolina—not to mention the hunting prospects for this fall. I think we had the finest lot of young men and the best Camps in the entire Country. Certainly everything I have heard elsewhere would indicate that our type of men, our standards of discipline, our organizational spirit and our Camps were on a much higher plane.

I was very sorry to leave South Carolina, and I regret to feel that next summer Mrs. Marshall and I will not have some pleasant days on fishing expeditions with Mrs. Byrnes and yourself. I hope you are fully recovered and fit for the hard winter in Washington which undoubtedly is before you.

With warm regards from Mrs. Marshall and myself to you both,   Faithfully yours,

GCMRL/G. C. Marshall Papers (Illinois National Guard)

1. Byrnes, Democratic congressman from South Carolina (1911–25), had been elected to the United States Senate for the 1931–37 term.
2. Fort Moultrie is located on Sullivans Island at the mouth of Charleston Harbor, South Carolina.

To Major General Edward Croft[1]   November 28, 1933
[Chicago, Illinois]

My dear General: I have been intending for sometime to express to you my regret that my services with a regiment were so suddenly terminated, but getting settled in a new job and in an apartment has delayed me. I have never been so reluctant to leave a job in the Army as I was to give up command at Moultrie, along with the South Carolina CCC. It was all intensely interesting, and I found it a delightful experience in every respect.

In your note to me last spring you expressed some curiosity about the conclusions I had drawn regarding training conditions and methods at a small post. I did come to several definite conclusions, and I was able at each of two posts to increase the turnout considerably and engage in very interesting work. I found several factors influenced the matter. In the first place, it seemed to me that my main function was to protect the troops against my staff; to organize fatigue on the basis of working parties for definite tasks assigned to companies; to require the services (Q.M. in particular) to foresee jobs well in advance and for my headquarters to assign those jobs as jobs to company commanders, the men, methods, tools and other means being the problem of that officer; to permit no fatigue work in the mornings except as emergency propositions with my express approval; to arrange special duty details myself (almost) day to day, to fit in with training work; to get big turnouts in the late afternoon for evening and all night exercises, every one being back in the post by 8:00 A.M., etc., etc.

I found the routine training programs too ponderous and elaborate for the constantly changing requirements of garrison life. Instead, we decided the rough priorities for what we wanted to do and I personally adjusted and readjusted post requirements and training hours to secure the largest turnout with the least disturbance of post affairs. I found my daily task lay in coordinating these factors to meet the desired end, and it appeared that detailed programs prepared in advance usually defeated themselves because of the constant development of unexpected demands. I insisted on men being given furloughs throughout part of the summer reserve training, and even during target practice, then I allowed no furloughs November 1 to December 20 and February 1 to March 30th. In this way all the men were present for bayonet, grenade, anti-aircraft and rifle company machine gun practice, as well as for tactical exercises. Rifle companies were always combined for close order drill and first sergeants were the close order drill masters. The officers I kept busy at other tasks, plus their company administration. All in all we had very little on paper, but we knew where we were going and seized every opportunity for a good attendance enroute. I did not intend to go into such details to such boring length, but I was deeply interested in the results.

My senior assistant here is Lieutenant Colonel Joseph C. Hatie, Infantry. He is unusually efficient and seems to have a positive flare for divisional staff work and harmonizing conflicting people and interests. He is in for the War College, and I can testify that he is very much the desired type.[2]

With warm regards,   Faithfully yours,

GCMRL/G. C. Marshall Papers (Illinois National Guard)

1. Croft—who became chief of Infantry on May 6, 1933—had drafted the list of "outstanding and suitable" men for the Chicago assignment from which the army chief of staff selected Marshall. (Croft to Marshall, December 2, 1933, GCMRL/G. C. Marshall Papers [Illinois National Guard].)

2. Hatie was not detailed to the War College.

To Major General Stuart Heintzelman[1]   December 4, 1933
                                                          [Chicago, Illinois]

Dear General: Since your arrival at Leavenworth I have written you three letters, none of which were mailed. I wrote the first on your assignment as Commandant; spent a great deal of time on it and finally decided I was simply borrowing trouble for myself. Later, the last month I was at Benning, I drafted, and redrafted many times, another letter of the same nature. I carried it to Fort Screven with me and finally came to the same decision and tore it up. Later my feelings again grew too strong and I painstakingly prepared another letter last spring on the eve of the Corps Area maneuvers, but again weakened and decided to let some one else pull the chestnuts out of the fire. But, since coming to Chicago and starting work here with this excellent National Guard Division, I have finally decided to let go and tell you, very confidentially I hope, what I have long wanted to say to you personally.

Briefly, my experience at Benning, especially my observation of two Corps Area maneuvers (about 7000 troops) most of which I was charged with staging, has lead me, not to the opinion, but to the firm conviction that our teaching and system has to be materially modified if we are to avoid a chaotic state of affairs in the first few months of a campaign with a major power. I think we have the best school system in the world, but I also think we are suffering acutely from a lack of practical experience in anything approximating warfare of movement at the outset of a campaign, with inexperienced officers and hastily recruited-up-to-war-strength organizations.

I might premise most of my observations on a preliminary statement of several personal beliefs, namely:

a. That the tactics and leadership of partially trained troops, is a much, much more difficult problem than for veteran organizations of full war strength. And that a different or much modified technique is required.

b. That handling troops with small scale and commercial maps—or no maps except the automobile type—is a much more difficult problem than doing the same thing with a Gettysburg map. And that a different technique is required.

c. That warfare of movement, except where the situation has temporarily stabilized for a day or more preliminary to a great assault, does not admit of orders one half or even one fourth as long as those turned out in our schools. And that, the shorter order, especially if oral, is a much more difficult problem than the elaborate, detailed order of the Gettysburg map variety. (We learnt that the modern German divisions are sometimes deployed on oral orders).

d. That the lack of troops, the infrequency of prolonged maneuvers, the tremendous number of desk jobs or non-command jobs now prevalent in the Regular Army, and the frequency of pure command post training, has led us into theoretical misconceptions that do not hold water in the actual business of handling large bodies of troops in protracted maneuvers.

I will briefly cite, in fragmentary fashion, a few of my experiences at Benning that led me to an almost complete revamping of the instruction and technique at that school. All of this I had to do quietly and gradually, because I felt so much opposition would be met on the outside that I would be thwarted in my purpose. General Collins and General Campbell King were in complete agreement with me, and both felt that general service publicity might bolt the business. Also, we had to educate our local constituency first, particularly the faculty, in order to have the necessary backing. In other words, we bored from within without cessation during my five years at Benning.

I found it next to impossible to convince instructors long absent from troops and steeped in school technique, of the urgent necessity for simplifying matters, no matter how great their war experience, and no matter how loyal they were. They had become unconscious creatures of technique, and lived in the experiences of the fourth year of a war. I made very little progress with these fellows until I stopped all rehearsed demonstrations of tactics, introduced a number of free maneuvers into the course and, finally, placed instructors in command in maneuvers, with all the Corps Area troops, and let them commit errors, some so gross as to be almost amusing, in their blind following of technique. I then endeavored to secure all replacements for the faculty from officers returning from foreign service where there were plenty of troops. This, even to the point of putting men in the tactical section who had not graduated from the Advanced Course or from Leavenworth. Incidentally, I found that the meticulous marking or grading methods caused instructors to draft problems from the view point of uniform and exact grading, rather than entirely with a view to getting across a certain lesson or example—tho they never would admit, or even seem to realize this.

I found that the technique and practices developed at Benning and Leavenworth would practically halt the development of an open warfare situation, apparently requiring an armistice or some understanding with a complacent enemy.

It was evident in many things that the real problem, the real difficulty, usually was not comprehended until too late. For instance, as a small example, all knew how to set up a command post but few understood the real problem, how to avoid a complete set up until the proper moment had arrived. The momentum of an operation was usually killed by the premature setting up of complete command posts. Or, prolonged thought would be given to reaching a tactical decision on purely tactical grounds, when the difficulties of execution or some entirely non-tactical matter, were the real dominant factors.

I found that the ordinary form of our tactical problems committed two deadly sins, relieving the student from the greatest difficulties of his tactical task in warfare of movement. The information of the enemy was about 80% too complete. And, the requirement called for his decision at a pictured moment, when the real problem is usually, *when* to make a decision, and not, *what* the decision should be.

I found no single officer in the entire Corps Area, including the school, ever found time or the map facilities to produce an order in the maneuvers one quarter of the length of a school order in similar situation—and all lacked the technique for preparing the briefer order, which requires much more skill than the voluminous, stereotyped variety.

I found the estimate of the situation had been so restricted to purely tactical questions and governed by so special a technique, suitable for such situations, that officers seldom properly estimated any situation or problem other than the tactical. They had been indoctrinated to the exclusion of orderly thinking habits regarding other matters (not involving the terrain, the enemy, etc.) where rapidity of thought was essential.

In the Corps Area maneuvers the mistakes were so numerous, and often so gross, that a critique was extremely difficult to handle with tact. Staff officers of brilliant reputation in the Army, graduates of Leavenworth and the War College, former instructors at those schools, committed errors so remarkable that it plainly indicated our school system had failed to make clear the real difficulties to be anticipated and surmounted in warfare of movement. The individual sank in a sea of paper, maps, tables and elaborate technique. Or, if he attempted to shorten the working method he confused everything because of lack of training in the more difficult—the simpler methods. Like women's clothes, the simpler the dress the more expensive the garment.

Now, if this was the case with highly trained officers and exceptionally trained troops, what will be the case in the event of a major mobilization and an immediate campaign, with partially trained national guard and theoretically trained reserve officers? I insist we must get down to the essentials, make clear the real difficulties, and expunge the bunk, complications and ponderosities; we must concentrate on registering in men's minds certain vital considerations, instead of a mass of less important details. We must develop a technique and methods so simple and so brief that the citizen officer of good common sense can readily grasp the idea.

The first "skin sheet" I checked at Benning had sixty-eight cuts. I limited it to twelve cuts, and later would not allow but two or three major cuts—the minor corrections being solely for the information of the student.[2] One of the first problems I checked over started with a matter of Army Corps, and at the bottom of the third page I found it was a problem for a communication platoon. I limited this situation to six inches of typed space.

Witness the mass of documents and the months of work a Corp Area staff puts up for an Army Command Post Exercise, all of which could be cut 50% and the benefits of the exercise actually increased. But they are proud of the mimeographs!

I found the Infantry School mimeograph on supply was a prized document covering one hundred and twenty pages. After futile efforts to shorten and simplify it, I caused the entire thing to be thrown out and restricted the new pamphlet to ten pages. I required the supply procedure to be demonstrated completely on the ground. This took one and one-half days the first time and two and one-half hours when I left. The course became the most popular and effective in the school and worked a complete metamorphosis in the 29th Infantry in the field. Every cut or simplicity I imposed at Benning was opposed, often violently. And I think I am accurate in saying that all were enthusiastically approved once they were in effect.

I never got the G-2 business anywhere near what I thought it ought to be—generally, it was an elaborate, impracticable collection of data. I read a G-2 solution of a Leavenworth problem—before your time—in a situation depicting the *second day* of a war (on one of those damned river lines marking the boundary between Red and Blue states) in which fighting had occurred all day. The G-2 effort was *four*, small typed, printed pages! Imagine the tired distraught Division Commander the second day of a war, the first time under fire, trying to pore through such a report—if it ever could have been prepared—to find the meat of the matter.

I am dealing with this in a very fragmentary, disconnected fashion, but if I give you a general impression of any differences with the existing system I will have accomplished my purpose. I feel sure that if, say, every other year or every third year, your instructors could go through protracted divisional maneuvers, a few of them in command or top staff positions, the Leavenworth technique would automatically be simplified year after year until it was perfectly adapted to the practical business of open warfare, partially trained troops and citizen officers.

At first I found my Instructors did not even want to go to Corps Area maneuvers at Camp Jackson near Columbia [South Carolina]. They preferred the even tenor of their theoretical ways. But, I must say now, that I think the faculty at Benning the last three years I was there was composed of the most brilliant, interesting and thoroughly competent collection of men I have ever been associated with. We all learned together, but we had a devil of a time getting started. We never got to the point of teaching tactics as General Morrison taught it[3]—most of our supposed tactical instruction fell into the domain of technique.

It appears to me that Leavenworth should specialize on the tactics and technique specifically adapted to—

> Partially trained troops;
> Partially trained officers;
> Mixed strength of organizations and lack of special troops;
> and the first six months of a major war.

If this be thoroughly understood, there would be no difficulty whatever about handling veterans, static situations, unlimited ammunition supply and equipment, detailed maps instead of Geological Survey maps or similar affairs of commercial production. Honest to goodness simplicity would be achieved.

Now, having expressed myself far too freely, injected myself into the business of a Major General, and laid myself open to all kinds of trouble, I will close by saying this: I do not believe there is another General officer in the Army I would have chanced this letter with, except yourself. I ask you to consider it for your eye only. I do not want you to trouble to acknowledge it, or commit yourself to any expression regarding it. But simply believe that only my intense interest in the field efficiency of the national army has caused me finally to put myself on paper to the Commandant of Leavenworth.

This is not the carefully prepared production that any of the three previous drafts were. It is a first run of my pencil, and must go as first written. I have too little time and clerical assistance to do otherwise.   Faithfully yours,

GCMRL/G. C. Marshall Papers (Illinois National Guard)

1. Heintzelman (U.S.M.A., 1899) and Marshall had known one another since the World War, when the former served in the Operations Division at A.E.F. General Headquarters (July, 1917, to January, 1918); as assistant chief of staff for Operations at First Corps headquarters (January to June, 1918); and as chief of staff for the Fourth Corps (June to September, 1918) and Second Army (September, 1918, to April, 1919). During the period Marshall was in Washington as aide to General Pershing, Heintzelman served in the War Department as assistant chief of staff for Intelligence (September, 1921, to November, 1922) and as assistant chief of staff for Logistics (November, 1922, to November, 1923). He had been commandant of the Command and General Staff School at Fort Leavenworth since 1929.

2. The "skin sheet" or grade report sheet for students' problems in military schools traditionally showed many minute "cuts" in grade for small errors. When Marshall was a student at Fort Leavenworth, grading was frequently carried out to hundredths of a point. See Marshall's grade report of July 1, 1907, above.

3. For Marshall's views of Major General John F. Morrison, see Marshall to Lentz, October 2, 1935, above, pp. 45–47.

To Major General Stuart Heintzelman   December 18, 1933
[Chicago, Illinois]

Dear General: I appreciate the generous manner in which you received my comments. I do not mind your showing the letter to Burtt, but please ask him to protect my interests by not quoting my free handed criticisms and general statements.[1] A single sentence could be used against me with deadly effect, as depreciating the splendid work of Leavenworth, or trying to tear down the wonderful system which has been built up. That, of course, is far from my purpose, but ardent supporters of the present methods will never take kindly to my criticisms.

I would like to talk this matter over personally, and possibly I can arrange to fly over some time and see you.

Meanwhile, I am taking the liberty of commenting on a point mentioned in your letter, referring to the use of detailed maps when "we cannot look at the ground."[2] I think this aspect should be considered:

In warfare of movement division or corps staffs will seldom have time or opportunity to see the ground except from a plane. They will usually have to work from small scale maps. They may secure a mosaic in time, but they will be under the necessity of drafting instructions to be used by the lower echelons with reference to the small scale map, or no map at all. The assertion that the Air Service can quickly give us prints in large quantities needs to be taken with a large dose of salt. There are too many "ifs"—if the weather permits, if the enemy aviation permits, if the photographic planes are available, if the printing can be managed on the field on that day at the speed claimed,—*and if the distribution can be managed.* If you get your mosaics, fine! But the hard thing to learn is how to manage without them. If that is understood, then there is little necessity to teach officers how to utilize the mosaic—or detailed maps—for that is an easy technique.

It always appears to me that we stress the easy and infrequent things to do, and give little attention to the hard things to learn, which will be the normal requirement at the outset of operations.

I talk a great deal of maps, because they have played a tremendous part in the development of our technique.

Early in my stay at Benning I accompanied two Instructors out with the class for a terrain exercise in a battalion engagement during the development phase of an action, where the hostile dispositions and intentions were not clear. A large scale map was used. After the students had dispersed to work on their solutions, I asked the Instructors to put away their maps and solve the problem for me on the basis of no maps available. They were at a complete loss for a workable method (or technique) to handle the affair, and were two hours preparing a solution—a very poor one. Fifteen minutes should have sufficed.

I saw this sort of thing times without number, and these were Leavenworth men. Finally, I required the use of the Geological Survey Map—except in a few special cases. A wail went up, and remained up until the faculty developed a suitable technique for such scant means of reference. The point I am trying to make is, they had no positive method for the line along which they should have been most skillful. On the contrary, they were skillful in meeting the exceptional situation—which happens to be the easiest to manage.

A letter yesterday brought to mind another good illustration. A member of your present second year class wants my help towards the War College. He writes that he stood near the top last year and thinks he will be the "top" this year. Also, he states that he stood first at Benning. I knew this last, because the week after I reached Tientsin I took the regiment out into the country on a maneuver. This fellow commanded a company, and to him fell the task of enveloping the hostile flank. Nothing happened. Time passed, and the situation finally died. I found this officer on the bank of a canal trying to draft a written order for seventy men, and completely stuck because he could not tie the order to the limited data on the blue print of General Van Deman's sketch of the terrain. I learnt that he had stood first at Benning, and I then and there formed an intense desire to get my hands on Benning. The man was no fool, but he had been taught an absurd system, which proved futile the moment a normal situation of warfare of movement arose.

Take the intimate details of the Battle of Ethe, or of Lodtz, and what do you find.

The original British Expeditionary Force was furnished detailed maps of Belgium and Northern France. But the mass of the maps was so great and the movements of the forces so sudden and covered so much terrain, that the maps were never distributed and the famous retreat was carried through on automobile maps procured locally. A single sentence sometimes sufficed for the order of the day. The real problem was to get the order to the units in time.

The German Offensive of March 21, 1918, ran the French off their customary maps, and when the 1st Division arrived there weeks later, only the small scale hachured map was available. And this was in the fourth year of a war.

My contention is, that our methods and technique below the Army Corps, should be specifically adapted to partially trained officers and men, incomplete divisional units, and to the conditions common to warfare of movement in the first phases of a campaign. Master that, and the rest is simple.

I think I could anticipate every argument your faculty would present to meet my proposals. I've heard them stated, recited and sung by the Leavenworth men at Benning. I went to Leavenworth and talked to General Brees and Colonel Byroade.[3] We did not agree. But I'm certain that if they had seen what I had had the opportunity of seeing, they would have disagreed with themselves.

One more point. I found that the splendid, fighting battalion commanders of the old First Division, who were largely represented at Benning, seemed to have completely forgotten—if they ever realized—the crude, stumbling performances and countless errors of our first year in France. They only recalled, in putting their experiences into the development of school technique, the skillful performances at St. Mihiel or in the Argonne. This presented the most difficult and embarrassing obstacle to my efforts.

Benning has yet a long way to go in the improvement of its methods to meet our National Defense problem. I think the Mailing List marks its greatest improvement.[4] It now has readers where formerly it only had subscribers. Its small problems make the real picture of a battle. It is being used throughout the country by National Guard and Reservists, and not filed or dumped into the waste basket.

Forgive me for my persistent repetition of a single theme. It's so hard to put on paper the hundred angles of this subject.   Faithfully yours,

GCMRL/G. C. Marshall Papers (Illinois National Guard)

1. Heintzelman had asked Marshall to allow him to show the December 4 letter to Colonel Wilson B. Burtt (U.S.M.A., 1899), the assistant commandant. (Heintzelman to Marshall, December 4, 1933, GCMRL/G. C. Marshall Papers [Illinois National Guard].)

2. Heintzelman had written: "In general, I may say, I thoroughly agree with the fundamental ideas you present. As to some of them, we have been struggling to carry them out. As to others, there are difficulties as to details. And, in some cases, the mechanics of instruction here make it impossible, or at least seem to us inadvisable. For example, when we cannot look at the ground we must use the best maps we can get. In some of the work about here where the classes can be taken to the ground we forbid the use of any maps except those furnished and limit the data thereon as, for example, one or two use Air Corps photographic mosaics and maps that only give roads and stream lines." (Ibid.)

3. Brigadier General Herbert J. Brees—an honor graduate of the Infantry and Cavalry School (1903), and a graduate of the Staff College (1905) and the Army War College (1907)—had been an instructor at Fort Leavenworth (1919–20, 1925–29). Colonel George L. Byroade—an honor graduate of the School of the Line (1922) and graduate of the General Staff School (1923)—had also been an instructor at Fort Leavenworth (1925–31).

4. The Infantry School's *Mailing List*, published semiannually, consisted of a compilation of instructional matter on infantry tactics.

To Brigadier General Leigh R. Gignilliat   February 14, 1934
[Chicago, Illinois]

Dear General: I am inclosing a letter to me from Mr. Mershon of February 8th, and a letter to me from Colonel Robbins with reference to Mr. Mershon's letter.[1]

In acknowledgment of a Christmas greeting note to Mr. Mershon, in which I made some reference to the important benefits, which had resulted from his generous contributions, I received a rather lengthy letter from him expressing gratification over the fact that I thought positive good had been accomplished. In this letter he discussed the propriety of preparing a booklet describing the fund, with the view to securing other financial support. He did not wish his name to be brought to the front anyway.[2]

As our Committee was meeting here that same week I acknowledged his letter and told him that the matter of the booklet would be discussed at the meeting and a recommendation made to him. I also went into some detail in explaining an important part I thought the Committee, through his fund, had played in saving the situation for the ROTC and CMTC, as well as promoting considerably the professional standards of the ROTC through a pamphlet and through the Lehigh meeting. In this letter, of which Colonel Robbins has my copy, I commented on the difficulties of preparing a pamphlet about the fund without, of necessity, giving prominence to Mr. Mershon's part in the matter. I also expressed some doubt as to whether we were ready at this time to propose a definite policy for the expenditure of a large additional amount.

Mr. Mershon's letter, which I am inclosing, gives in considerable detail his reaction at the present time. I imagine that these are the result of a combination of two influences—his major interest in the CMTC and the serious depreciation of all utility stocks of public utility holdings.

The effect of his letter on me has rather been to crystallize for the first time in my mind what, at least at the moment, seems to me a legitimate and important use of a continuing fund in connection with the civilian-military education of the general public. I believe that his idea can best be served by setting up a permanent office, very much as we have at present, controlled by a Committee very much as exists at present, to function as a continual guard against the emasculation of the CMTC (and incidentally the ROTC) phase of military training, and to exert a continuing influence to secure the increase of the CMTC until it represents the most important phase, in point of size, of our military construction program.

The Regular Army has a headquarters from which to fight its own battles, however ineffective it may be politically; the National Guard has a solid backing to protect its future interests; the Reserve Corps is developing almost as much permanent strength from political pressure as the National Guard; the ROTC has at least the various college heads and the PMS&Ts to represent its interest. The CMTC is the only phase of our military training program which is not continuing throughout the year and has very little positive backing. Therefore, such a Committee, as I have described, would remain a continuing force to safeguard the existence and to promote the development of the CMTC.[3]

When I started this letter, I did not intend to go into any proposals, but merely to forward to you the attached communications as suggested by Colonel Robbins.

I hope your rest in the Arizona climate has been beneficial and that you have acquired some of those pounds that both you and I always seemed to lack.

With warmest regards.   Faithfully yours,

GCMRL/G. C. Marshall Papers (Illinois National Guard)

1. Neither letter was found in the Marshall papers.

2. Marshall, Gignilliat, and Charles B. Robbins, members of the Civilian Military Education Fund's National Committee, which Ralph D. Mershon supported financially, had met in

Chicago on January 14. Prior to the meeting, Marshall had asked General Pershing to send "a little personal note to Mr. Mershon commenting favorably on his efforts in behalf of civilian-military education. . . . Mr. Mershon seems to be a very mild, unobtrusive person, with a great desire to be helpful—to the extent of his entire fortune." Pershing agreed to send the note. (Marshall to Pershing, January 8, 1934; Pershing to Marshall, January 12, 1934, LC/J. J. Pershing Papers [General Correspondence].)

3. In 1933 Congress reduced the C.M.T.C. appropriation for summer camps to one million dollars—less than half the sum granted in previous years. The number of men who could be trained was reduced accordingly.

TO GENERAL JOHN J. PERSHING   February 23, 1934
                                                                 Chicago, Illinois

Dear General: I am not at all certain of your correct address but I imagine any letter addressed to you in Arizona will reach you. I saw a note in the paper that you had gone to the south west for the remainder of the winter, and I was relieved to learn that you had decided to avoid disagreeable phases of a winter in Washington.

Out here it is very cold today, and has been colder. Sudden changes are the curse of the climate, and we had one of forty two degrees in ten hours a few weeks ago. I never know what costume I should wear to the office. As I walk down and back, the question of a heavy or light overcoat and woolen or leather gloves, is a problem. I envy you the beautiful Arizona winter days. My sister spent several months there three years ago and loved it.

Just now we are all interested in the air mail affair. The Army has taken over our National Guard hangars and offices. I was out there yesterday just after they learnt of the death of one of their pilots. They only have young fellows inexperienced in night flying, unfamiliar with the necessary modern instruments, and comparatively untrained in blind flying. I think the personnel here only averages a half-hour of blind flying.[1]

I have been trying to get them to take over our National Guard pilots. They are graduates of the blind flying course and have flown all the mail routes out of Chicago at night and many times by day.

Another thing, the air service is endeavoring to handle all their staff work, administrative work, with their own personnel, which seems wholly insufficient. A great deal of the work could be better done by other Army officers trained in such administrative tasks. It worried me to see the state of things yesterday.

I am not seeing very much of General Dawes. I really am a little embarassed. He seems to me so tragic. And I know he must be exceedingly sensitive. I think, if the Exposition pays out this summer, that will buck up his morale tremendously, as he will feel responsible for the financial involvements, and if the underwriters get all their money back it will be a triumph for these days, when all other investments realize but a portion of the original amounts.[2] Ever so often the papers carry some comment on his bank relations with the Federal government. Two Sundays ago the Tribune gave a page, with photographs, to the tragedies among the former high and mighty, in the depression. Most of the writeups referred to instances of suicide, but Dawes was included in the presentation. I know such things must open every wound. He does not react with his old dash. I made some reference to an article in "Time" the other day—having no connection with him or the depression. He remarked, in rather a pathetic tone for him, "I don't know why it is but they (Time) always hammer me".

Take good care of yourself.   Affectionately,

G. C. Marshall

LC/J. J. Pershing Papers (General Correspondence); H

1. Allegations of fraud by private airmail contractors caused the Roosevelt Administration to cancel all such contracts, effective February 19, 1934, and to order the Army Air Corps to haul the airmail. The events surrounding this decision and its repercussions are discussed by the chief of the Air Corps at that time, Major General Benjamin D. Foulois, in his memoirs, *From the Wright Brothers to the Astronauts*, pp. 235–61.

2. Since 1929, Charles G. Dawes had been chairman of the finance committee for the international exposition—officially titled "A Century of Progress"—which commemorated the city of Chicago's first centenary. The exposition, which ran from May 26 through November 13, 1933, was considered successful enough by its backers to reopen for the 1934 season (May 26 to October 30).

To COLONEL CHARLES C. HAFFNER, JR.[1]   March 29, 1934
[Chicago, Illinois]

My dear Colonel Haffner: Thank you for the copy of The Cannoneer and Driver, which I found on my return to the office from an extended leave to Thomasville, Georgia. I have read with considerable interest your editorial, or comments, on "Loyalty" and I wondered how carefully this would be read by the officers and to what extent it would be taken to heart.

After some experience, particularly in war and in the War Department, I have come to believe that this is by all odds the most important attribute of an organization. With it almost anything is possible. Without it you really do not have a military organization. The principal trouble is, officers seldom realize when they are being disloyal, and it is the accumulation of small disloyalties, however conscious, that break down the military fibre of a unit.   Faithfully yours,

GCMRL/G. C. Marshall Papers (Illinois National Guard)

1. Haffner commanded the Illinois National Guard's 124th Field Artillery Regiment, which had its headquarters in Chicago.

SPEECH ON THE ILLINOIS NATIONAL GUARD   [Spring ?] 1934
                                                     Chicago, [Illinois]

In accepting your invitation I was moved not only by appreciation of your courtesy in inviting me, but also by General Keehn's desire for me to comment on my impressions of the Illinois National Guard, in view of my recent assignment to duty here and previous unfamiliarity with this military organization.

I came to Chicago last fall, a stranger to the community and a novice to my duties as Senior Instructor for the Guard. But I have learned a great deal in the past ____ months,[1] and I am inclined to think that some of the things I have learned are matters of interest to the citizens of the State, and especially to the influential members of the community like yourselves.

Because I am an officer of the Regular Establishment, does not mean that my interests and ideas lie in a field remote from those of the National Guard. It is a fact that the better informed an Army officer is, the more he is impressed with the vital importance of the National Guard, and the critical importance of its state of efficiency.

You know—or more possibly, you don't know—that we have fewer Regular troops in the United States today than twenty years ago, and unfortunately most of our organizations are stationed in the sparsely settled districts along the Rio Grande, or where shelter happens to be available, near the summit of the Rocky Mountains, for instance. All our combat troops in this country could be given reserve seats in your great stadium. A big-league ball park could accommodate them. There are more Regular soldiers in this country, but they are of the non-combat type—such as medical personnel, ordnance, and quartermaster men, telegraph and telephone operators, clerks, chauffeurs, teamsters and mechanics. Before the World War most of these duties were performed by civilian employees. Today they are included in the total enlisted strength of the Army you see referred to in the statements of the Federal Budget.

I have referred to this phase of the situation in order to make clear the position of the National Guard in this country. In brief, the Guard constitutes almost our entire first line of defense. Our war army would eventually consist of about five percent Regular troops, twenty percent National Guard, and seventy-five percent of men obtained by selective conscription and officered by the Reserves. It is apparent that with so few Regular troops, our dependence in the first months of trouble must rest principally on the State forces called into the Federal Service.

Now just what does this mean? If you admit that in another National emergency involving war, America will have to depend strictly on herself and will not be free to prepare behind the skirts of an ally—that is, a country not in our debt—then you must in turn accept the prospect of having our State troops sent to the theatre of operations in the first few days of war, and there immediately committed to action. This would be in decided contrast to the last war, where the

Thirty-third Division, for example, was not employed as a division until seventeen months after our declaration of war, and even then there was never a time nor opportunity to arrange for its artillery brigade to join it.

Another consideration heavily colors this picture. The last War while the greatest war, had become a highly stablized war when we entered. Such warfare is far simpler in its requirements of troop training than warfare of movement, such as occurred in August and September of 1914. More complicated materiel is required, but far less of troop training. Units fought in what amounted to a slot or carefully defined section of the great front. Extended reconnaissance, preliminary engagements, uncertainties regarding the enemy—these complications were not inflicted on the troops. Organizations merely moved into a carefully delimited sector of a vast military setup, closely confronted by an enemy in fixed place, whose every trench and position had been photographed and studied by experts. Warfare of movement is about as complicated, in contrast to this character of fighting, as the double reverse-forward pass play of modern football would be in comparison to the old-fashioned line buck of thirty years ago.

The rapidity of movement incident to modern motor transport and the development of fast planes, fast tanks and radio communications, add greatly to the difficulties. Warfare of movement—what we must expect at the outset of a campaign, what the National Guard must bear the brunt of—requires skilled officers, trained non-commissioned officers and a very high standard of discipline. The troops must be able to survive terrific and prolonged physical exertion, intermittent meals and unavoidable confusion. Fortitude of the highest order is essential; unquestioned loyalty, despite losses, failures and misfortunes, is absolutely necessary. And the point I am trying to make clear is, the troops of the Guard must be prepared this week to undertake such service next week. Conscription by selective service could not produce effective troops for many months. The Regular Army is entirely inadequate. Therefore the National Guard must be ready.

So, there is always before us the yearly problem of promoting the efficiency of the Guard. Armory training once a week affords the only opportunity during all of the year, except the two weeks the troops are sent to camp in the summer, paid and supplied by the Federal Government.

What was expected of the Guard twenty years ago is no criterion of what is demanded today. Your security before the world depends in a large measure on the efficiency of the Guard, and your support and the public understanding of the situation, is essential to that efficiency.

Service in the Guard is still voluntary, but it lacks the old inducements of a few simple drills, numerous showy parades and a club-like organization. Today the Federal Government requires certain standards of training in a multiplicity of highly technical matters. The Infantry soldier no longer confines his efforts to shooting a rifle, drill movements and parades. He must understand the complications of light machine guns, heavy machine guns and their indirect fire, grenades, one-pounder cannon, six-inch mortars, and almost everything electrical but television. He must be geared into an elaborate and much scattered team. The Division requires six-inch artillery, eight-inch howitzers, tanks, aeroplanes, gas defense, draft horses, trucks, mounted work, elaborate electrical communications, and many other matters. Marching in single column this massive divisional organization would cover ____ miles² of road space. All this means work, hard work, with little time for the splashy display features of soldiering common to the past.

Business men, sometimes those very prominent in the world, are often indifferent to the affairs of the Guard. A few may even be contemptuous of its military importance, at least cold to matters concerned with its moral support. Only ignorance of the real situation permits this attitude, unless the individual is equally indifferent to fire, theft and life insurance, and police measures to protect his home and family. Such an attitude of indifference to the Guard could not well be based on a belief in the desirability of a large standing army, for such an army is an economic impossibility in this country, even if it were not completely out of keeping with democratic ideals.

There is another and much more intimate relationship of the Guard with your interests. The past three years have given us a glimpse of serious possibilities, under the duress of a great economic depression. Strikes, fomented unrest among vast numbers of unemployed, Bonus armies, numerous "shirt" movements, and other indications of an abnormal state of "nerves" in the world, have caused citizens to worry or to flinch before the possibilities of chaotic conditions. Here and there in the country the ordinary power of the civil authorities has been temporarily overwhelmed or has merely broken down. In view of these possibilities, what have you to depend on for the orderly continuance of affairs in Illinois?

You have your National Guard, ready today, every plan prepared and carefully studied, to meet instantly the call of the Governor, to suppress disorders and restore and maintain the peace. Every man knows his place, every officer and non-commissioned officer knows his duty—and a very distasteful duty it would be—to safeguard your welfare and that of your family and community, in the shortest possible number of hours. You would undoubtedly welcome such help in an emergency; it would meet your enthusiastic approval. But, gentlemen, there is absolutely necessary to the efficiency of such a plan, your understanding, your sympathetic and your appreciative support of those officers and men who give so freely of their time in your direct interest.

Speaking impersonally, as a regular officer, the work required of these men is hard work—often monotonous work. As the representative of the Federal Government, I am responsible for many of the least enjoyable features of that work. Being an officer of the National Guard in Illinois involves a serious obligation on a man's time, a very serious obligation regarding possible duties, particularly those distasteful and dangerous duties in the suppression of domestic disorders. That officer is, therefore, entitled to your active support and evident approval, and from a purely selfish point of view, your personal interests demand that support and approval.

I have been impressed by the general efficiency of the Illinois National Guard. I have been profoundly impressed by the tremendous amount of work General Keehn and his officers have done in preparation for any serious domestic emergency which might develop within the State. I feel free to assure you that you are fortunate in possessing this strong arm behind the ordinary peace processes of the civil authorities, and behind the law and the courts. In my investigation of the efficiency of the preparations of the Guard to support the civil authorities in the maintenance of peace, I have found a fine attitude of idealism, I may call it, on the part of the officers centered in a profound effort to be prepared to do their duty by the State, an attitude completely devoid of political significance regarding this or that consideration, such as corrodes or mutilates so many of our public endeavors. Sincerity and genuine patriotism govern, for which we should all be very thankful.

GCMRL/G. C. Marshall Papers (Pentagon Office, Speeches)

1. The file copy of this speech has a blank line drawn before "months," as printed here. Most likely Marshall presented the speech more than once to civic groups.

2. The file copy of this speech has a blank line drawn before "miles," as printed here.

To Major General George V. H. Moseley[1] April 5, 1934
[Chicago, Illinois]

Dear General: I am very sorry it was my hard luck not to remain in the Fourth Corps Area and serve under you. I spent a year at Screven, but only had four months at Moultrie before the pleasant trend of my duty with a regiment was disrupted.

The C.C.C. in South Carolina was the most interesting problem of my Army career. I built most of the camps in Florida and Southeastern Georgia—had them largely completed before the boys landed—but in South Carolina I had the opportunity both to build the camps and to get in close contact with the boys.

I have never seen a finer group of young men. And the reserve officers did splendidly. These last I gave a preparatory course of three days with the C.C.C. Company at Moultrie, under a reserve officer, and at post headquarters and in the supply depot on the Charleston side of the harbor. Then those destined to command companies were sent through two or three selected camps, for several days at each, so that they had the benefit of seeing the best items of arrangement or management in these camps. When they actually took over command they had the advantage of a rather broad knowledge of the problem, and their prestige with the boys was protected against the unfortunate results of knowing less of the routine and problems than the boys themselves. I made it unmistakably clear to the Captains that their continuance on this duty would depend entirely on the efficiency of their companies, the administration of the camp, excellence of the mess, morale of the men and work done in the woods. I explained that I could not let personal consideration for them and their financial problems or earnest but unsuccessful efforts to perform their duties, carry any weight with me. I would be compelled to protect the interests of 200 boys, rather than one reserve officer. As a result, they uniformly did well and gave me fine, intelligent support.

I picked out sixteen C.C.C. leaders who were R.O.T.C. graduates, and had them all ordered to active duty. These men rendered splendid service.

When you visit Screven or Moultrie there are several officers I would like you to meet and look over with some care. They are all fine men, to be trusted with important jobs.

Major Matthews, battalion commander at Screven.

Major Meyers, Surgeon at Screven—the most effective and expeditious surgeon in handling new drafts that I have come in contact with.

Captain Adams, Adjutant at Moultrie.[2]

All three of these men did the work of the usual dozen officers in helping me through the development of the C.C.C., as well as in post affairs. They are unusual, and can operate with a minimum of red tape, paper and supervision.

With warm regards,   Faithfully yours,

GCMRL/G. C. Marshall Papers (Illinois National Guard)

1. Moseley took command of the Fourth Corps Area on January 13, 1934. Previously he had been commander of the Fifth Corps Area (March 26, 1933, to January 12, 1934) and deputy chief of staff of the army (December 22, 1930, to February 22, 1933).

2. The men mentioned were: Frederick S. Matthews, David A. Myers, and Claude M. Adams.

To Brigadier General John L. De Witt[1]   April 7, 1934
                                                        [Chicago, Illinois]

Dear De Witt: I have waited until the flood of congratulations has somewhat subsided before telling you how greatly pleased I am to see that your fine services have been recognized by passing you on to the list of General officers of the line. My only regret is that they did not do this while you were still Quartermaster General, in order that more promptly you might have been advanced to the grade of Major General.

I was so familiar with what you did in France and fairly well informed as to your services in the War Plans Division later on, that it always seemed to me you had done more and received less recognition than almost any other officer in the Army. Your possible competitor in this class, in my opinion, was General John McA. Palmer. I always felt that to retire him as a Brigadier General was a tragic bit of ingratitude.

Now, I hope in a very short time you will have a Corps Area where you know so well what there is to be done and how to do it.   Faithfully yours,

GCMRL/G. C. Marshall Papers (Illinois National Guard)

1. De Witt had been quartermaster general of the army from February 3, 1930, to February 2, 1934. He was promoted to brigadier general on March 26, 1934, and given command of the First Division's First Brigade.

To MADAME JOUATTE   April 12, 1934
                                                    Chicago, Illinois

Dear Madame Jouatte: I believe my last letter to you was written in June 1932—a long time ago. I was just leaving Fort Benning, Georgia. I went to Fort Screven, Georgia, for one year and in June 1933 moved to Fort Moultrie, on the sea coast at Charleston, South Carolina.

There I had the pleasure of entertaining the French Consul General from Philadelphia and the officers of the French Naval vessel Encastrenaux. I saw an account of their visit with me in the French publication L'Illustration last October, with a photograph.

Unexpectedly, due to the threat of labor disorders, I was moved out here to Chicago, last October. We motored out and spent four days with General Campbell King—you will remember him coming to your house for Thanksgiving and Christmas dinners—in the mountains of North Carolina near Ashville (you must get out your geography and look up these places).

We will probably be here in Chicago for some time.

I hope all goes well with you, that these hard times have not affected you and that you are happy and contented.

Always believe that I have not forgotten you or your many kindnesses to me.   Affectionately yours,

GCMRL/G. C. Marshall Papers (Illinois National Guard); T

MEMORANDUM FOR GENERAL HAMMOND[1]   April 13, 1934
                                                    [Chicago, Illinois]

Governmental treatment of Army as to pay and allowances.

Reductions in Pay.

As of July 1, 1932 Congress reduced the pay of the Army by eight and one third percent (8 ⅓%) and made further reductions in allowances. Furthermore, a ban was placed on increases of pay for promotion or as provided for at stated intervals automatically, regardless of promotion. Later under special authority vested in the President, a cut of fifteen percent (15%) was imposed and the "freeze" on promotions and automatic increases was continued. The basis for these Federal reductions in pay was the amount of the reduction in the cost of living in 1933 as compared to 1926.

Result of reductions.

Considering only the Junior elements of the Army, the second lieutenants and enlisted men, the effect of these reductions was drastic in the extreme, far beyond what would be assumed as the results of a mere 15% cut, below even the cost of living standards of 1908.

For example, a second lieutenant received as pay and ration money $140.60. This was cut to $119.51 or 18.5 percent less than he received 25 years before. The difference in the cost of living between 1908 and 1933 was great. Never the less he was given 18.5 percent less money in 1933 than in that far off period of cheap living.

However, this was not the worse phase of the reduction for these young men. When their salary was set by the Pay Act of 1922 they were purposely given less money than in 1908 in order that after promotion to first lieutenant or after five years service if promotion was unduly delayed, they should receive sufficient increase to permit them to marry. This without increasing the total pay of the Army. The reductions of 1932 and 1933 prohibited increases for promotion or after five years service, with the result that these young men, most of whom married during their fourth year of service with the then legal certainty of a material increase in pay, found themselves after six years of service drawing 42 percent less money than the Government had promised them. Officers with wives and one or two children were required to maintain themselves on $119.51 a month, 30.4 percent less than they would have received 25 years earlier.

In the case of the private soldier the full effect of the reductions was equally drastic. A private who was a good enough soldier to qualify as expert rifleman, suffered a reduction of 33.3 percent in monthly pay. On a yearly basis, including his clothing and reenlistment allowances, his reduction was 44.7 percent.

The Sergeants received a total cut of about 23 percent and the Master Sergeants 20 percent.

Comparison with other Government Services.

The Navy and Marine Corps received the same general reduction as the Army. All these services had previously been denied the large increases given the Civil Service, the Diplomatic and Consular Service, the Congressmen and high government officials. As a result, with only about ten percent increase in pay since 1908, the Army was cut in general, far below the standard of 1908. While the Diplomatic Service, for instance, still held an increase, after the cut, of more than 150 percent. Congressional pay was only cut 15 percent, following an increase in 1928 of 33 percent. The Postmen were left with more than a 6 percent increase over their 1908 standard of pay.

Special status of military personnel.

The heavy reductions imposed on the military-naval officers and men should be considered in the light of their special relation to the Federal government. They cannot resign; they must present a certain standard of appearance no matter how closely pressed they may be financially; they must accept the added expenses of moves and special service; they constitute the government's final backing in the event of grave emergencies; they must hazard their lives in the government service, with no choice of resigning if they do not care to serve. Yet on these servants the Federal government imposed its most drastic program of economy, and at a time when it was demanding more of the Army to meet the special requirements of the New Deal, than of any other branch of the government.

The Army put over the CCC for the government after the inability of the originally designated agencies to handle the problem, had become evident. Officers and men were suddenly scattered in 1400 Camps throughout the United States, under the necessity of maintaining their families in one place and themselves in another. The wives and children of married soldiers were often without funds for food and rent. Corporals of years of service found themselves first sergeants of CCC companies, every man of these companies receiving as much or more money than the first sergeant. Regular soldiers in large numbers found themselves unable to continue allotments of $10.00 a month to their parents, while CCC boys, picked off the streets, were enabled to contribute from $25.00 to $40.00 a month to their families.

The regular soldier had no choice of post or duty. The CCC boy was free to terminate his connection with the government any time. He could not be worked more than six hours a day. The regular in the CCC Camp was usually on duty twelve hours a day.

Despite the inequalities and injustice of this arrangement, the regular soldiers gave their earnest and most efficient services to make the CCC a success it has been.

Present Status.

Congress recently restored 5 percent pay and provided for a further increase of 5 percent July 1st. The ban on pay for promotion was lifted, but the prohibition against automatic increases remains in force. This last continues the heaviest cut imposed on second lieutenants of more than four years service.

The elimination of reenlistment allowances, and the cut in clothing allowances remains in force. Extra pay for marksmanship has been partially restored—no marksman or sharpshooter pay allowed, but one year in three an expert rifleman will receive $5.00 per month. Similar adjustments have been made for the Artillery, etc.

GCMRL/G. C. Marshall Papers (Illinois National Guard)

1. Brigadier General Thomas S. Hammond commanded the Illinois National Guard's Sixty-sixth Infantry Brigade, with headquarters in Chicago.

To Major General Fox Conner[1]   April 25, 1934
                                                  [Chicago, Illinois]

Dear General: I have just read your note of April 23rd regarding the book on the A.E.F. In the same mail I received a letter from Roger Scaife, telling me of his luncheon with you but not indicating that he had been doing a little business as well as lunching.

My suggestion to him to meet you was on the basis that you might be very helpful in your comments on various writers who deal with the World War period and wish to get themselves published. I did not have in mind that you might weaken on the writing business but I am delighted to learn that you will undertake such a task.[2]

However, to be perfectly frank, I do not think such a book as you propose in your note would be of great interest unless it were a very honest statement of the facts. This would mean that "many toes would be tread on" and much "yapping" would result. Just how pleasant you would find this aspect I do not know. But I am certain that a restrained discussion of the presentation, avoiding a plain statement of the facts concerning the delicate issues, would not gain many readers.

With your literary ability, your general military knowledge and your comprehensive knowledge of affairs in France, coupled with your ability to reduce things to their simplicities, you are better prepared to write such a book than any one else I know in the Army.

I am turning the matter over in my mind and will write you in a day or two with suggestions along the lines you requested me.

I spent the morning here with General Pershing a week ago, and Dawes and Mrs. Marshall came in for lunch. He seemed in fine spirits but had just recovered from a heavy cold in Lincoln and has little left of his former sturdiness, except in carriage and character.   Faithfully yours,

GCMRL/G. C. Marshall Papers (Illinois National Guard)

1. Conner had commanded the First Corps Area since October 7, 1930. Promoted to major general (October 20, 1925), Conner had served in the War Department as acting chief of staff, G-4 (1924–26), and as deputy chief of staff (1926–27); then he commanded the First Division (1927) and the Hawaiian Department (1928–30).

2. Scaife had recently become vice-president and director of the Boston, Massachusetts, publishing house, Little, Brown and Company. In his April 23 letter to Marshall, Conner said that Scaife wanted him to write a book on the General Staff at A.E.F. General Headquarters. "I do not quite visualize just how that is to be accomplished. What would be some of the Chapter Headings and how should the Staff rather than the Command viewpoint be emphasized?. . . Please give me some advice. I need it badly." (Conner to Marshall, April 23, 1934, GCMRL/G. C. Marshall Papers [Illinois National Guard].)

To Major General Fox Conner   May 12, 1934
[Chicago, Illinois]

Dear General: I have hesitated to send you my suggestions regarding Chapter Headings and other ideas for your book, because up to the present time I have not come to any satisfactory conclusion. However, I have decided to send on to you my first outline as a basis for any discussion you care to have with me on the subject. It is a little hard to make clear my tentative idea without rather copious notes under each heading, but I will endeavor to indicate what I first had in mind, by a few brief hints:

I—The Small Beginning.
A picture illustrating the minute size of this staff, the character of its personnel, the initial ideas of some of its leading members, presenting a basis of comparison for the tremendous developments which followed.

II—The Speed of Developments.
A graphic description of the approach of the staff to the tremendous decisions which had to be made during the Summer and early Fall of 1917.

III—Delegated Authority.
Much that might come under II and IV would be covered in this Chapter as illustrations of the point that I think of important interest that you should make. I have in mind a clear picture of the remarkable extent to which General Pershing delegated authority to various trusted individuals of his staff, in contrast to the practice of the English and the French, and also despite the fact that he managed to retain an absolute dominance over the entire situation which seemed never to be questioned by any individual, however dominant the latter's personality. I think this is one of the most interesting aspects of the A.E.F. staff, and the one which is least understood in America.

IV—Relations with the French.
While the subject of this Chapter will find a place in almost every other chapter of your book, I think that one chapter should be specifically devoted to a presentation of this matter, however many references there may be in other portions of the book.

V—Relations with the British.

I am not so certain that this should be a separate chapter. Probably it would be better to have included it under IV.

VI—Relations with Washington.

I first had this "Troubles with Washington". It seems to me this should be given special treatment though it must be referred to in other chapters.

VII—The Selection of Subordinate Leaders.

By this I mean a description and a discussion of the problems concerned connected with the selection of the leading officers of the command and staff. You can make your book a best seller on what you write under this heading. However, I did not have in mind that you would go that far, but I think there is a great deal of tremendous interest and instruction that could be covered under this heading. There is the situation where General Pershing of necessity was first rather confined to a test of his own contemporaries, almost none of whom had had anything like his opportunity for development as great organizers and leaders; then his gradual moves to put the vigorous, able, determined men in control positions; and the further possibilities as to what would have been the situation in this respect in the Spring of 1919. Almost a book could be written under this heading.

VIII—The Expansion into Field Armies.

Nothing that has yet appeared in print gives anything like an adequate picture of what it meant to progress from the organization of a single corps in July to the development of two Field Armies by October 12, 1918. The limitations through lack of special troops (through no fault of ours), creating of a number of corps and two huge Army staffs, the take-over of highly stabilized and immensely complicated sections of the front simultaneously with the initiation of major operations—all of these things are so much Greek at the present time to the people in this country and to most of the members of the A.E.F.

General Pershing's descriptions in his book do not make this picture at all. As a matter of fact, there is hardly a General officer in our Army today who really understands the real magnitude of what I am referring to here. How many automatically realize that there were more special Army troops required for each Army than the total of Meade's Army at Gettysburg, or that the full complement of corps special troops almost outnumbered Meade's and Lee's combined armies.

Under this heading could come a very interesting discussion of the peculiar situation which developed—and which used to drive you frantic—while General Pershing combined the command of the Field Army with his duties as Commander-in-Chief. This followed by the almost amusing reversal of things the day after he relinquished command of the First Army. Even the most serious movie always includes its lighter touches, and I have to laugh when I think of your diatribes prior to October 12th and a few drums clamoring immediately after October 12th.

IX —The St. Mihiel.

X —The Meuse-Argonne.

XI —On the British Front.

XII—The French Attitude After The Armistice.

Here again you can make your book a best seller if you tell the truth about what happened. Certainly this merits a considerable discussion.

I have had in mind, under the headings I have given, that in one sense your book would not have an exact chronological study of a staff. Rather, that it should be a discussion of various phases of the activities of the A.E.F. as concerned GHQ. What are the most interesting phases or subjects which are debatable. I am merely trying to give you my reaction.   Faithfully yours,

P.S. I hope you and General Brown did not eliminate me on your recent visit to Washington.[1]

GCMRL/G. C. Marshall Papers (Illinois National Guard)

1. The book Marshall outlined was never written. Conner and Major General Preston Brown, commander of the Sixth Corps Area, were members of the Eligible List Board. This board, composed of at least five major generals, was appointed by confidential War Department special orders. It met annually—in this case, on December 20, 1933—to select colonels to be placed on the list of those eligible for promotion to brigadier general.

TO COLONEL RALPH D. MERSHON   May 21, 1934
                                               [Chicago, Illinois]

My dear Colonel Mershon: I have just returned from the R.O.T.C. Conference at Purdue, which your Committee arranged. In the unavoidable absence of Colonel Robbins and General Gignilliat I had to preside. A list of those attending is attached.[1]

A full report on the affair will, of course, be sent to you by Colonel Bishop but I thought you would be interested to get an early impression of how the Conference went off. To me it seemed a much more profitable and satisfactory gathering than at Lehigh last year. Of course, we knew a little better how to arrange and stage manage the affair, and many of the army officers attending, and some of the professors, had read the report of the Lehigh meeting.

This time I arranged to have college deans function as chairman of every committee, and towards the close of the committees' private discussions I emphasized our desire for the views of the college deans rather than for those of the army officers. These committees took their work very seriously and gathered in committee conferences at every opportunity. For instance, on the first evening after a dinner at which fifty members of the Purdue faculty were present, and where we were so fortunate as to have two unusually fine after dinner talkers— far above the usual standard, some of the committees pursued their discussion until one in the morning. Some turned out at an early hour the following morning and got in a hour's additional committee debate before the general session opened at 9:30.

A number of the college presidents, or deans, expressed to me their enthusiasm for the benefits they had received from this conference. In general, their various statements reflected this view—that they had arrived with an interest in the R.O.T.C. thinking they knew a great deal about the activities, and they found that their knowledge was exceedingly superficial and that they were leaving with a broader understanding and assurance that with the knowledge they had attained they could do a great deal for the protection, or the maintenance, or the improvement of their local R.O.T.C. units. They had all heard the expression of a great many points of view. They heard how various difficulties were quite satisfactorily met in various institutions. They were often astonished to learn how completely the R.O.T.C. activity had been integrated into college affairs, whereas in their own institutions this was not the case. Altogether, they acquired a mass of valuable information which I am sure will be very helpful in the faculty attitude of their particular colleges or universities regarding the R.O.T.C.

For the Army officers, the conference was a tremendous help,—both as to the information they had derived from the experiences and views of others and also particularly because they felt the faculty representative of their own institution would return home prepared to support them strongly and intelligently before the faculty regarding any proper proposal made.

I was tremendously encouraged by the apparent success of this conference. At Lehigh I thought it was an excellent thing. But at Purdue the affair ran off in such a fashion that it impressed me as possibly being a tremendous factor in general improvement of R.O.T.C. conditions in this general section of the West.

The officials of Purdue were most cordial in their hospitality, and all displayed a great interest in the affair. I am very sorry you could not be present, particularly as this is a technical institution and most of its activities are directed along lines which would be of direct interest to you. The turnout of the local R.O.T.C. unit was an unusually fine demonstration of what can be done to bring about the very thing you have had in mind regarding development of young men. I was very much impressed with the splendid showing made by these boys, and it is hard to believe all this had been managed in a very restricted number of hours.

I think Colonel Robbins and General Gignilliat are planning to have a meeting of the Committee to consider some of the points brought up in your letter to me, shortly after the close of Culver, that is in June. General Gignilliat has returned from the Southwest much improved. He arrived in Purdue at Noon of the last day, field inspections having prevented his leaving Culver the day before. Therefore, he had an opportunity to see something of the Conference, and the members had the fortunate opportunity of meeting him and hearing him talk. Faithfully yours,

GCMRL/G. C. Marshall Papers (Illinois National Guard)

1. The conference was held May 18–19 at Purdue University, West Lafayette, Indiana. The list of persons attending was not found with the file copy printed here.

TO MADAME JOUATTE

June 1, 1934
Chicago, Illinois

My dear Madame Jouatte: I was greatly distressed to learn of M. Jouatte's death last Fall. You have my deep sympathy and condolences. Your son's marriage leaves you very lonely, indeed, and I hate to think of this great change in your life.

We are in the midst of a World's Fair or Exposition here in Chicago, which opened last Saturday. 140,000 people attended the first day. Yesterday 500,000 children—and some older people visited the Fair. This will continue all Summer, so Chicago will be a very busy place. Today it is hot, the hottest in many years, and a lack of rain since February has ruined the farmers crops over all this western country, far up into Canada. The lack of grass and a strong wind produced a great dust storm in early May, that started in middle Canada, traveled 1200 miles to Chicago and turned day into dusk, and blew on 800 miles to New York and Washington. This has never happened before in the history of this Country.

I will send you some pictures of the Fair.

With my sympathy and affectionate regards,   Faithfully yours,

GCMRL/G. C. Marshall Papers (Illinois National Guard); T

REPORT TO THE COMMANDING GENERAL,
SIXTH CORPS AREA[1]

June 19, 1934
Chicago, Illinois

1. The following detailed report on the Illinois National Guard is submitted:

2. *a. Organization and Administration.*

No comments. Generally up to a satisfactory standard.

The 33d Division lacks portions of its heavy artillery, Medical Regiment and Q.M. Trains that should be provided at an early date, to render the Division more effective for immediate use in a theatre of operation.

    b. Command and Administration.

    (1) Command,—Generally of a high standard of leadership, except in a few cases now being adjusted. Evidence of steady improvement in the quality of command.

    (2) *Administration,*—Generally satisfactory. Improvement shown in handling routine business.

    (3) *Federal Inspection,*—For the first time in years not a unit received an "unsatisfactory" rating.

    c. Equipment.

    Equipment in excellent shape, except as to war time motor vehicles and tanks. Clothing has suffered from reduced maintenance allowances, and from a long period of strike duty for a number of units.[2]

    d. Housing and Care of Property.

    Superior at present. The general renovation and improvement of all armories—especially of storerooms—through the labor and funds provided by the C.W.A., has placed every thing on an exceptionally favorable basis. Approximately $1,500,000 of C.W.A. funds were expended on armories and target ranges.[3]

    3. *Efficiency* as compared to preceding year.

    Improvement apparent in training and quality of officer personnel. Probably a loss of efficiency in enlisted personnel, due to reduction in pay drills and the effect on morale of unemployment. However, the elaborate C.W.A. program for the Illinois National Guard, which provided many special jobs as paymasters and pay guards, and aroused active interest in the general improvement of all armory plants, probably offset much of the ill effect of reduced pay and pay drills and the situation as to unemployment.

    4. *a. Strong Points.*

    (1) High Morale.

    (2) Confidence in ability to handle difficult tasks, due to recognized ability and World War experience of most of the officers in important command and staff positions.

    (3) Progressive work in Army Extension Courses.

    (4) High standard of efficiency of field artillery units and of Engineers.

    (5) Excellence of practical plans for meeting domestic disturbances, and intimate familiarity of officers with these plans.

    b. Weak Points.

    (1) Casual attitude of some subordinate headquarters in carrying out routine instructions.

    (2) Tendency to make staffs the dumping ground for the less effective officers. This is being rapidly overcome in some staffs, but there remain examples of weak staff organizations.

    (3) Infantry tactical training in general, and in communication and staff work in particular.

Corrective measures are being taken, but the problem is a very difficult one to solve satisfactorily with so limited a period for field training.

(4) Excessive turn over in enlisted personnel, especially in infantry units.

(5) Low attendance of certain units at drills.

5. *Suggestions and Recommendations.*

National Guard administration and training usually suffers from an over dose of paper. The essential requirements are drowned in a mass of less important matters presented in instructions, programs and schedules. It is important when dealing with busy men, not to flood them with literature for their instruction or guidance. This should be held to a minimum, and strict compliance with the instructions then required. Many of the deficiencies or weaknesses seemingly inherent in the National Guard are largely due in my opinion, to an unwise policy which produces voluminous papers and promotes paper work, breeding a generally careless attitude on the part of the recipients. Regular Army efficiency can survive such administrative burdens, but the National Guard officer, with the limited time for military matters at his disposal, is seriously and adversely effected.

NA/RG 394 (Sixth Corps Area, Illinois National Guard)

1. Marshall's report on the Illinois National Guard for the fiscal year ending June 30, 1934, submitted to Major General Preston Brown, Sixth Corps Area commander.

2. Years of declining standards of living, conflicts between labor and management, and factional fighting within the United Mine Workers Union in the Illinois coal fields had culminated in violence in August, 1932, and the calling out of units of the Illinois National Guard. Strikes continued into 1933.

3. The Civil Works Administration (C.W.A.), headed by Harry L. Hopkins, was created in the late autumn of 1933 to give temporary employment to some four million unemployed persons during the winter of 1933–34. The C.W.A. lasted approximately three and one-half months; then it was absorbed into the Federal Emergency Relief Administration.

To General John J. Pershing   September 5, 1934
                 Fort Monmouth, New Jersey

Dear General– I am writing from the Army Command Post of the CPX, in an atmosphere not so very different from Souilly or Ligny en Barrois sixteen years ago, to send my congratulations on your birthday. I hope this reaches you on that day—it should if the boat schedule for mails is to be believed.[1] My affectionate greetings and my most sincere wishes for your continued health and happiness go with this letter. It's too bad you could not have appeared here on your birthday to receive the personal congratulations of the host of your old subordinates who are engaged in this problem.

My family is on Fire Island off Long Island, where I go for a week on leaving here. Molly sailed August 30th on a Dollar boat for San Francisco via Havana and Panama—enroute to Hawaii, China for six months, and on round the world. She will be gone a year. The youngest boy goes to University of Virginia this fall. His brother is doing real estate in Chicago.

I have been busy with troop maneuvers this summer, ending up in a division march towards Chicago, entrainment, bivouac in Grant Park in front of the Loop and review in the Fair of 10,000.

My congratulations again, which go with my prayer for your celebration of many more birthdays in which to receive the honors and plaudits of the constantly increasing number who realize the magnitude of your achievements. Affectionately yours,

G. C. Marshall

LC/J. J. Pershing Papers (General Correspondence); H

1. Pershing replied from Paris that he had "just returned from Vittel, where I have been taking my annual cure." (Pershing to Marshall, September 20, 1934, GCMRL/G. C. Marshall Papers [Illinois National Guard].)

To the Ford Motor Company   September 22, 1934
                                                [Chicago, Illinois]

Defective Car.

Gentlemen: In October 1933 I purchased a Tudor Sedan V-8, Motor No. 18–456524, from your agent in Charleston, S.C. For 500 miles the car was driven 25 or less miles per hour and carefully lubricated. Up to 1,000 miles it was driven at 35 or less miles per hour. Every reasonable care was taken.

At 3,200 miles, while enroute from Chicago to Georgia, a valve spring broke and a bearing burned out. This occurred near Rockville, Indiana on a Sunday. The Buick agency towed in my car and repaired the damage. I tried to reach the Ford agency by telephone, without success, and was compelled to seek aid elsewhere. I was delayed overnight eighteen hours and put to that extra expense and a bill for $12.00 for the work.

On the same trip, in the mountains of West Virginia in a blizzard, the gasoline pump failed, and left me stalled for three hours before I could get assistance. A friendly car pushed me until the motor, of itself, picked up. The same thing occurred again the next day near a small Ford agency on the Lincoln highway in eastern Indiana. After two hours work on the gasoline pump, it was gotten to work. It failed again in Fort Wayne and your agency there worked for two hours on it, at my expense. It failed again, after dark, during a heavy snow storm, as I approached Chicago—on the same trip. A motorist pushed my car for half a mile and it started up. All this trouble on one trip.

In Chicago I noticed a low knock. Your agency on Lake Street, Chicago, examined the car twice and reported nothing the matter. Finally, in Rockford, Illinois, your agent found the right front wheel hub defective and replaced the hub, curing the noise. On my next trip—just completed—a connecting rod bearing or part broke. Your agent at Butler, Pennsylvania, repaired this for $8.10. It occurred in the evening. The mechanic told me the oil was thin and badly burned—it had been changed 450 miles back; that evidently the piston fittings were defectively adjusted. He endorsed his finding on the back of the bill (inclosed herewith).

The car uses one quart of oil (the best grade) each hundred miles. The oil must be changed every 500 miles or less as it is burned out by that time.

This car has given continuous trouble. It quite evidently is a defective car. It has been a continuous expense and has failed me invariably at critical times. I have owned Fords off and on since 1913. I understand the care of motors and the importance of lubrication. I have never been in trouble on the road *but once* before buying this car.

I feel that your company owes me some adjustment in this matter, and I, accordingly, am submitting this statement of the case for your consideration.[1]   Very truly yours,

GCMRL/G. C. Marshall Papers (Illinois National Guard)

1. The Ford Motor Company's reply was not found in the Ford archives. Marshall sold the troublesome automobile in November. He purchased another Ford the following spring.

TO COLONEL CHARLES W. WEEKS   October 11, 1934
                                               [Chicago, Illinois]

Dear Charlie: I received my copy of the Volume VIII of the Mailing List yesterday, with the subscription cards and form letter.[1] Already I have called the attention of all my Instructors to the importance of having their companies subscribe, as well as the officers. I found infantry officers who had been at Benning when the new type mailing list was first issued, and had since gone through Leavenworth, had never seen a copy until they received Volume VIII.

In connection with this matter, I would like to express myself very frankly. Long experience in tinkering with new ideas or methods in the Army has schooled me to ignore completely what happens after I leave the scene of each endeavor. I seldom ever inquire, and thus avoid all disappointment or discouragement. This Mailing List has been an exception in my experience. I was so deeply impressed with the necessity of vitalizing the old List and making it of genuine practical help to the National Guard and the Reserves, and I encountered so much of resistance or lack of enthusiasm in the faculty to a change of method and in the production of material, that I was really worried for fear the Mailing List would suffer a complete relapse.

Now, in Volume VIII, I find my brightest hopes realized. In quality of paper, binding, particularly in type and printing, in lithographing, in the excellence and simplicity of the drawings, in the selection and quality of the contents—this volume is a very fine production. A Colonel of the Guard, who is Vice President of the largest publishing company in the West, could not understand how the Infantry School could produce such a finished volume and at such an absurdly low price.[2]

Please accept my congratulations, and please tell your young men who did the mechanical work of preparing the back, that I greatly admire the job. Leavenworth had better look closely to its laurels. (I hope you send General Heintzelman—personally—a copy).

With warm regards.   Faithfully yours,

GCMRL/G. C. Marshall Papers (Illinois National Guard)

1. Weeks succeeded Marshall as head of the Infantry School at Fort Benning. The school's *Mailing List,* which was prepared under Weeks's supervision, described itself as "a semi-annual publication containing the latest thought on Infantry."

2. Colonel Charles C. Haffner, Jr., commander of the 124th Field Artillery Regiment, was associated with the R. R. Donnelley and Sons publishing company.

To Major General George V. H. Moseley   October 29, 1934
[Chicago, Illinois]

Dear General: I received your note of October 22nd, and have gone over your discussion of Training Methods very carefully.[1] I agree with you in practically every thing you said. Sometimes a little more vigorously than you put the matter. But it is delightful to find a Corps Area Commander so keenly on the job regarding these basic matters.

I spent the five years of my stay at Benning trying to make the practical dominate the theoretical, trying to compress five pages of technique into a single paragraph of practical direction.

Since coming to the National Guard I have been more than ever impressed with the near futility of drowning everybody in an elaborate technique of forms and fashions, all going back to static warfare as a basis. I have had long correspondence with General Heintzelman on this subject. He seems to agree with me, but the difficulty is putting it over.

I suppose our entire trouble rests on the fact that we do not have large forces to maneuver frequently each year. Certainly no country that concentrates yearly large bodies of troops, would evolve the staff methods that have been grafted on to our paper army. It fell to me in the World War to actually write more detail orders, and to actually prepare orders for large forces, than I believe any other officer in the Army, but what may have been the right method over there is certainly not the right practice for the first two or three months of a war with partially trained troops.

I appreciate your comment regarding my future, and I am very sorry you are not in the position to bring it about.[2]   Faithfully yours,

GCMRL/G. C. Marshall Papers (Illinois National Guard)

1. Moseley, who had recently seen Marshall at the National Guard convention in Nashville, Tennessee, inclosed in his October 22 letter some remarks on training he had made to the War Department. The inclosure is not in the Marshall papers.

2. Moseley ended his October 22 letter by saying: "I hope you will guard your health carefully for if there is any justice in this man's army, there must be much in the future for you." (GCMRL/G. C. Marshall Papers [Illinois National Guard].)

To First Lieutenant Charles T. Lanham[1]   October 29, 1934
                                                       [Chicago, Illinois]

Dear Lanham: I appreciated your letter of October 25th very much and was much interested in all you had to say. The fact that you young men are concerned over my advancement is very gratifying to me—more so than a similar interest from older officers would impress me.[2]

As to the Mailing List.—The reason I wrote as I did to Colonel Weeks was not merely to compliment him on Volume VIII, but more especially because I feared exactly the condition you describe.[3] The situation during the development of this new form of Mailing List was similar to the present difficulty—only I was very fortunate in having some highly competent men to carry out my ideas. It is exceedingly hard to break in on the standardized instruction of courses in tactics and technique. I am having the same difficulty here, but have more freedom of action.

It is fine that "Infantry in Battle" is going over in such good style. Harding sent me Liddell Hart's comments,[4] but I have not seen any other review. I proposed to him that he have Fred Palmer write a review for the New York Times. I do not know whether this is the review you refer to or not.

As to your unhappiness at Leavenworth, go pretty easy on that.[5] An able officer of low rank has a hard battle to fight, particularly with himself. Do not let this effect your morale, because you can never tell what moment the "worm turns." I have had plenty of experience at this business, and have watched many sink in mental irritation over the depressing outlook. Keep your wits about you and your eyes open; keep on working hard; sooner or later the opportunity will present itself, and then you must be prepared both tactically and temperamentally to profit by it.   Faithfully yours,

GCMRL/G. C. Marshall Papers (Illinois National Guard)

1. Lanham (U.S.M.A., 1924) was a member of the Infantry School's Company Officers' Course, 1931–32. During the 1932–33 and 1933–34 school years, he was an instructor in military history and the editor of school publications. He edited *Infantry in Battle* (Washington, D.C.: Infantry Journal, 1934), for which Marshall wrote the introduction, and

volume eight of the Infantry School *Mailing List.* Since June, 1934, he had been stationed at Fort Leavenworth with the Seventeenth Infantry.

2. "Your many prophets throughout the service are becoming a bit restive at the War Department's delinquency in giving you your first star," Lanham wrote in his October 25 letter. "The 'old guard' at Benning never allowed you more than a year in your present grade. I think we are far more chagrined at this inexcusable delay than you." (Lanham to Marshall, October 25, 1934, GCMRL/G. C. Marshall Papers [Illinois National Guard].)

3. It was difficult to obtain essays for the *Mailing List,* Lanham observed, because they were printed without identifying the author. As a result, the editor frequently had to write most of the contents. Some kind of author recognition was essential; but the individual writer could not be identified because "if a lieutenant signed an article many an officer of field rank would never read it." Unless something was done soon, the *Mailing List* would "shortly become moribund." (Ibid.)

4. Captain Basil H. Liddell Hart was a well-known military correspondent for the London *Daily Telegraph* and the author of numerous books on military subjects.

5. Lanham said that he had asked for the Fort Leavenworth assignment "believing it was a stepping stone to school. I have revised that opinion. Unless one is a student or a member of the faculty here one is considered to be several theosophic planes lower than an ass. At least that is my impression. And it certainly does neither professional ardor nor the ego any good." (Ibid.)

To Lieutenant Colonel Edwin F. Harding[1]   October 31, 1934
                                                                                        [Chicago, Illinois]

Dear Harding: My congratulations on your promotion which I see has been in effect for some weeks. I suppose Eleanor is pleased to be "Colonel's lady," even if this promotion does not promote her from the kitchen to the living room.

I had a long letter from Lanham the other day, inspired by a copy he had received of a complimentary letter I wrote Colonel Weeks on Volume VIII of the Mailing List. Lanham seems terribly depressed in his Leavenworth station and very restless over lack of opportunity—and, I suppose, the fact that he is an unknown in that concentration of brain power. I tried to counsel a little patience, and warned him against the pessimistic attitude, because one can never tell when the real opportunity is going to develop. I think I will write General Heintzelman about it to see if I cannot get him attached to the faculty, at least on a part time basis.

Whenever I am conniving to get these young fellows with genuine ability put in a suitable setting, I deplore the fact I have not gained a position of sufficient power to do what I think should be done. I am awfully tired of seeing mediocrity placed in key positions, with brilliancy and talent damned by lack of rank to obscurity. There are so many junior officers of tremendous ability whose qualities the service is losing all advantage of that it is really tragic.

With my love to Eleanor and you, and the youngest lady,   Faithfully yours,

GCMRL/G. C. Marshall Papers (Illinois National Guard)

1. Harding (U.S.M.A., 1909) had been acting commander of the Fifteenth Infantry at Tientsin, China, when Marshall arrived in September, 1924. He and his wife, Eleanor, sailed for the United States with the Marshalls in May, 1927. Harding was a student at the Infantry School when Marshall arrived in the autumn of 1927. Following a year as a student at Fort Leavenworth's Command and General Staff School (1928-29), Harding returned to the Infantry School as an instructor and the chief of the Fourth Section—which taught military history, among other things—between September, 1929, and June, 1933. After spending the 1933-34 academic year at the Army War College, he was assigned to the Office of the Chief of Infantry and made the editor of the *Infantry Journal*.

To Major General Stuart Heintzelman   October 31, 1934
[Chicago, Illinois]

Dear Heintzelman: You have a Lieutenant on the Post, I think he is assigned to the battalion there, who has genuine ability of a high order and has had a great deal of experience along the lines that Leavenworth requires. I am referring to Charles T. Lanham, Infantry.

I placed Lanham in the Historical and Editorial Section at Benning. He edited "Infantry in Battle," a copy of which I sent you. Volume VIII, the most recent issue of the Benning Mailing List, was edited by him and most of the material prepared by him. If you will scan this book, you can gain some idea of his ability along these lines. He understands the business of putting technical military matter into a form acceptable to the citizen soldier. He is thoroughly dependable and a very hard worker. Unfortunately, like quite a few other brilliant young men I know, he is damned by lack of rank.

If you know nothing of Lanham, I am asking you to send for him some time and talk to him. I know it would be a great encouragement to him to feel that he was not a complete nonentity at Fort Leavenworth, and you have the touch that carries inspiration.

Incidentally, "Infantry in Battle" has received some wonderful reviews in England.[1] The British Quarterly, I believe, characterized it as the most important military text since 1874, which is going some. Liddell Hart quotes the commander of the British First Division at the maneuvers last Summer, as saying it is the finest infantry text in his experience, and that it was the only book he took with him on maneuvers.   Faithfully yours,

GCMRL/G. C. Marshall Papers (Illinois National Guard)

1. *Infantry in Battle* was also praised by German military critics. It was translated into German and Spanish.

To Major General Stuart Heintzelman   November 5, 1934
[Chicago, Illinois]

My dear General: The diploma awarding me the degree of Doctor of Philosophy of the Command and General Staff College or the University of Leavenworth as the Latin phrases it, has been received. I must admit that a little time was required to secure an accurate translation. However distinguished I may be as a philosopher, it was painfully evident that little Latin still lurked in my head.

I feel signally honored and highly complimented by this award, the more so when I read the signatures of authentification, especially that of Praeses Commandant.

The formality and completeness of the document makes it so impressive that I am in doubt as to the finality of the award. But whether a generous and delightful gesture recording your similar gesture of June 15th, or the genuine article, I am deeply grateful and shall prize this diploma as evidence of a high point in my Army career.   Faithfully yours,

GCMRL/G. C. Marshall Papers (Illinois National Guard)

To Major General Charles H. Martin[1]   November 7, 1934
[Chicago, Illinois]

Dear General: I read a few minutes ago with great delight of your election as Governor of Oregon. Mere congratulations would be a mild expression of my feelings.

When you were in Congress I had in mind writing to you on several occasions but always postponed doing so, with the expectation of calling on you personally in Washington. But I never had the opportunity to call, and thus failed to communicate with you in any manner.

To me your splendid career in civil life is one of those few cases where the genuinely fine character receives something of the success deserved. I greatly admired your attitude and efficiency during your Army career in Washington, and I was gratified by the evidences of friendship you gave me.

The contrast between your unselfish bearings and the self seeking scheming of so many others, made a deep impression on my mind. You and old John Palmer were the two seniors whose advancement personally concerned me. In Palmer's case I bearded Mr. Weeks in his den—and evidently acquired his active dislike, as well, I suspect, as a somewhat critical attitude on the part of General Pershing for injecting myself into his business.

It is probably an impropriety to tell you now that I had it out with General Pershing in 1920 over your priority rights for promotion, because there was a

Marshall's diploma from the "University of Leavenworth," June 15, 1934.

long list of obtrusive people clamoring for their own advancement, while you remained utterly silent. It may be bad taste to mention this, but I really am boasting of my own discernment, so completely justified by your subsequent career.

Please make my compliments to Mrs. Martin, and believe me very,   Faithfully yours,

GCMRL/G. C. Marshall Papers (Illinois National Guard)

1. Martin had retired from active duty in 1927. In 1930 he was elected to Congress (Oregon, Third District, Democrat), and reelected in 1932.

To Major General Hugh A. Drum[1]
                      November 7, 1934
                                  [Chicago, Illinois]

Dear Drum: I wish to take up with you, very confidentially, a matter that I think is of some importance. Major General Roy D. Keehn of Chicago, commanding the 33d Division, was recently elected President of the National Guard Association, and as such is duty bound to represent the interests of that Association before the War Department and Congress, as expressed in a number of directive resolutions passed at the Nashville Convention in October.

General Keehn has had little part in the Association and is comparatively unfamiliar with the methods which have been pursued by the legislative committees of the Association in the past, and with the leading actors in the Association. As a matter of fact, I don't think the latter regard him in a particularly friendly light, though they accepted him as President for this year.

General Keehn makes no pretense of knowing much about the technical business of soldiering. He professes to know nothing, and is too modest and self effacing in these matters, if anything. But as a leader of men, a driver, a man who gets things done, of large vision, and of great influence, he is a very strong character. He has only participated once in National Guard affairs in Washington, and that was in connection with the limitations on Armory Drills, in which I believe he played the dominant part after it became evident that the committee was without ideas or means to get action.

Knowing the misunderstandings and difficulties that often blossom between the War Department's necessities and the National Guard desires, and the capital which some usually make of these incidents, I am particularly anxious for General Keehn to have a direct personal contact with some one in a key position on the War Department General Staff. I do not want him to have to depend solely on information and views filtering out through the National Guard Bureau. I want him to know some one in the War Department of position and power, with whom he can talk things over informally, get the War Department's position straight in his own mind and make clear the practical aspect of the National Guard situation.

For these reasons, I hope you will take the time to meet General Keehn when he is in Washington, and let him know you. He probably goes to Washington the week of November 19th, and I would like to have him call you up and have you lunch with him.

General Keehn knows General MacArthur and will undoubtedly call on him, but I am concerned to have you meet him, and have him meet you. He is a fighter, but he is frank and straightforward and without guile. His interest is purely impersonal and entirely directed to the improvement of the Guard. He has no irons in the fire. The one positive view he put forward at Nashville, in his only and exceedingly brief impromptu speech, was to the effect that the Regular Army, the National Guard and the Reserves should get together in a genuine spirit of harmony and cooperation for the common good of the Army. You and he together can do much to bring this about.

Please let me know if a meeting such as I suggest is agreeable to you. Faithfully yours,

P.S. The sub-marginal land business has gone through many adjustments, and General Keehn has succeeded in getting the Government land experts to locate a new tract, suitable for an artillery range, and submit a full report on it. He has arranged with Farley to get some action on this report while he is in Washington.[2]

GCMRL/G. C. Marshall Papers (Illinois National Guard)

1. At this time Drum was army deputy chief of staff.
2. James A. Farley had managed President Roosevelt's 1932 campaign and was at this time the postmaster general of the United States and the chairman of the Democratic National Committee.

To Major General George V. H. Moseley   November 12, 1934
[Chicago, Illinois]

Dear General: You were certainly a peach to interest yourself voluntarily on my promotion by talking to the Secretary of War about it. I cannot tell you how much I appreciate the way you have always seemed to have me and my interest in mind. Whatever may happen I can have the very satisfactory feeling that you will put the seal of your approval on my record.

Naturally I will treat what you have told me as most confidential, and I can but hope that Mr. Dern did more than listen pleasantly. Please believe me I am very grateful to you.[1]   Faithfully yours,

GCMRL/G. C. Marshall Papers (Illinois National Guard)

1. Marshall had previously written to Major General Briant H. Wells on the occasion of the general's retirement: "General Brown's sudden retirement the other day was another blow. If this keeps up, I won't have a friend left on the Active List." (Marshall to Wells, October 31, 1934, GCMRL/G. C. Marshall Papers [Illinois National Guard].)

Writing to Major General Preston Brown, Marshall observed: "A letter came from Moseley this morning in which he was good enough to tell me that he had made a long talk to Secretary [of War George H.] Dern in Atlanta last Tuesday on the question of the type of men who have been selected for promotion and had interested Mr. Dern in my case. From having seen the Secretary at Fort Monmouth, I am inclined to think he merely listens pleasantly regarding military matters. At any rate I am much beholden to General Moseley for his friendly interest." (Marshall to Brown, November 12, 1934, ibid.)

To Major General Johnson Hagood[1]   November 13, 1934
[Chicago, Illinois]

Dear General: I can't begin to tell you how much I appreciate the fine thing you did for me in proposing my promotion to the Secretary of War. The fact that you did it in the particular manner you describe makes me all the more grateful to you for such marked interest in my career. Naturally I have never forgotten the efficiency report you rendered on me at the termination of our first service together, in 1916, at Fort Douglas, Utah.[2] I recall that you then recommended me for advancement to the grade of Brigadier General, remarking in your recommendation that you did this despite the fact I was eighteen hundred files your junior. Now again you step to "bat" in my behalf, though this time I was not even under your command. I deeply appreciate your action.

By an odd coincidence a letter came to me from General Moseley in the same mail with yours, in which he informs me that the Secretary of War stopped with him over night and he, Moseley, wanted me to know that he urged on Mr. Dern that I be promoted immediately. It seems rather odd, and very fortunate for me, that you should have picked up the Secretary on his next stop and mentioned my name.

With my most sincere thanks,   Faithfully yours,

GCMRL/G. C. Marshall Papers (Illinois National Guard)
 1. Hagood had commanded the Eighth Corps Area since 1933.
 2. See Marshall to Major General Edward W. Nichols, May 27, 1917, note, above.

To General John J. Pershing   November 19, 1934
                                               Chicago, Illinois

Dear General: I am enclosing two letters which are self explanatory. Two or three BG vacancies now exist. I want one of them. As I will soon be 54 I must get started if I am going anywhere in the Army.

Up to this moment I have made no move of any kind. Moseley's and Hagood's recommendations were unsolicited. I have written to no one regarding promotion, but have received numerous letters on the subject.

I would appreciate your bringing my name to the attention of Mr. Dern, and I would appreciate your merely requesting him to send for my efficiency reports since 1915 and allowing them to decide the issue.

In your files there is a volume listing the recommendations for general officers made in France after the armistice. These recommendations were never placed in the War Department files. Consequently, recommendations of me by Generals Liggett, Bullard, Hines, Summerall and others do not appear in my 201 file. I would appreciate your having Adamson place these in circulation.

I am determined not to exert political influence in my effort to be recognized, and I do not want to follow the usual course of writing to a number of senior officers soliciting letters from them, though a number have offered their services without solicitation by me. Such letters as a rule do not mean much, because the

War Department is flooded with them, since few care to offend by declining such requests. I am prepared to gamble on my written record in the War Department before, during and since the war, for I have been told no one else in the list of colonels can match mine.

I have had the discouraging experience of seeing the man I relieved in France as G-3 of the army, promoted years ago, and my assistant as G-3 of the army similarly advanced six years ago. I think I am entitled to some consideration now. But I will confine myself to you.[1]   Faithfully yours,

G. C. Marshall

LC/J. J. Pershing Papers (General Correspondence); H

1. Robert McCleave, who had preceded Marshall as G-3 of the First Army, A.E.F., had been promoted to brigadier general in December, 1929. Stephen O. Fuqua, who had been Marshall's assistant as G-3 in troop movement, had the rank of major general by March, 1929. No reply to this letter has been found in the Pershing or the Marshall papers.

TO COLONEL EDGAR A. FRY[1]   November 19, 1934
                                                              [Chicago, Illinois]

My dear Colonel Fry: I am trying to iron out the difficulties in the way of a program for the middle of next May which we think will give a tremendous boost to the weapon efficiency of the 33d Division. With the assistance of the C.W.A. the target range at Camp Logan, within easy access of seventy-five percent of the State troops, has been placed in excellent condition, and not only has ample facilities in the way of targets, but has excellent facilities for putting five hundred men over night—the State maintaining a mess.

We plan to assemble all the company officers of the Infantry, Cavalry and Engineers at Camp Logan on Thursday night, May 16th, and give them a regular Benning school of arms course until Sunday evening. Rifle and machine gun, one pounder and the Stokes will be fully covered, and a briefer course on the automatic rifle for selected officers, who will also have to take the rifle course. I plan to have fifteen Regular Army Instructors, a similar number of non-commissioned officers and about ten Benning graduates from the National Guard to carry through the affair. This is arranged in May so as to have the officers ready to conduct the firing instruction of their companies in June and July.

I find that, except in a few instances, the actual instruction of enlisted men is very haphazard, as most of the officers have not the ability and knowledge to act as satisfactory instructors. The result is a great deal of the ammunition is absolutely wasted, and from what I have been able to learn most of the combat firing at camp has been a complete waste of ammunition, until last Summer.

To correct this situation several things are necessary. The officers must be thoroughly trained as instructors, which seldom can be managed successfully by the instructor during the armory period of training. The firing must be largely completed before going to camp in August and for two reasons,—there is no time at Camp Grant for known distance firing if we are to make any progress in tactical instruction, and the musketry and combat firing is an absurdity unless the known distance firing has already been carried through. Also, while heretofore they have attempted to scramble through their known distance firing after camp, that is the least likely period for getting the men out.

Now, with all the company officers completely in the hands of a corps of Regular Army Instructors for three days on a fine range, I think we can do wonders to improve the situation, and I purpose having the complete school for machine gun companies and howitzer organizations at Camp Grant this Summer.

The difficulty in the matter is this—your regulations, or rather your Project 11, Program of Expenditures for support of the National Guard, does not permit the expenditure of any money for range-keepers after October 31st. I made a beginning in this matter last June, with the result that the State had to finance the range-keepers for that month. Is there any possibility of getting the small sum necessary for next June? Also, will it be possible for us to make a saving between the middle of September and October 31st—or a longer period—in the 1936 money, to be used in June of 1936?

You had some correspondence with General Black regarding this, when you disallowed last June's expenditures (June 13, 1934, file 230.147, Ill. 34). Faithfully yours,

GCMRL/G. C. Marshall Papers (Illinois National Guard)

1. Fry, once a student of Marshall's at the School of the Line (1908–9), worked in the Office of the Chief of the National Guard Bureau.

SPEECH ON ARMORY TRAINING[1]   [Early 1935?]
                                                          Chicago, Illinois

General Keehn has scheduled me to discuss armory training and the program for next summer. A year ago it would have been very difficult for me, to a certain extent impossible for me to offer many practical suggestions. I would have been compelled to theorize, because I knew little or nothing of the Illinois National Guard, except that I was concerned with operations of the Thirty-third Division in the Meuse-Argonne and checked up on its splendid work by several personal inspections during the battle. . . .

I do not intend to enter into any technical details regarding training. The instructors with your organizations can provide that information. I wish to talk primarily about the mental attitude in which the training is approached, for that determines the results. That represents a fact; training procedure too often merely represents a form.

The present position of the National Guard in this country is practically that of the Regular Army twenty years ago. We have fewer regular troops today and a military problem vastly greater than before the World War. The National Guard, as demonstrated by the recent New Jersey First and Second Army Maneuvers, must be prepared to take the field straight from the armories and troop trains, possibly without a day for ordinary training activities after mobilization. Efficiency must therefore be increased, particularly as regards staffs and commanders from the battalion upwards. No increase in training time is practical of arrangement. Therefore, whatever is to be done must be done within the hours now scheduled.

The practical proposition is, what, if anything, can be done to secure this absolutely necessary increase in efficiency? Is it possible of realization? Yes, it is, decidedly so, but it depends first of all upon your mental attitude, and then on the perfection of certain details.

Take the armory training period as an example, and it is the all important example, because little more can be accomplished in the summer field training, in fact, normally less than was accomplished last summer under its very strenuous schedule.

How can this armory training be so conducted as to produce a positive advance over previous years, in general efficiency? By the effective use of every minute of the available time, everything conducted in a manner to inculcate the military, that soldierly spirit, which breeds dependability.

Probably the most effective disciplinary influence, considering the shortness of the time involved, is the promptness, the exactitude and smartness with which an organization "falls in" for drill. Long close order drills, particularly where the movements are not diversified and every error is not immediately and exactly corrected, do not promote discipline, often are actually destructive of discipline.

If I am right on these points, then the thing to do is carefully to cultivate the habit (and requirement) of getting down to business in a very formal and exact manner, and from that moment to the conclusion of the drill period, have every individual in the armory understand that a soldierly bearing, smartness and military courtesy must govern. If it is a NCO School, don't permit the casual grouping of the men. Have the detachment fall in, march to the room and be reported in a strictly military fashion to the instructor. Don't permit gossipy groups of officers on the floor while someone struggles with drill or instruction. Don't permit first names to be bandied about during that hour-and-a-half. Inculcate every man with the idea that when eight o'clock strikes, all are on military duty and everything is to be done in a military manner.

You want your men to respond promptly to your orders. You cannot do this if you set an example of ignoring the orders you receive. If your staff, or your lieutenants, or even your clerks, know that you treat written instructions or orders from higher up, very casually or entirely ignore them, the entire organization quickly becomes infected with a similar contempt for the sanctity of a military order—and you will reap the whirlwind some day.

The two worst habits, in a military sense, you can follow are to ignore orders from above and issue orders or instructions which you do not require absolute compliance with.

Never give an order—and by this I mean even what you may say informally to a staff officer, or to a clerk—that you do not intend to see carried out. The armory is the place to inculcate that military spirit which makes everything possible. Too often it is the place where the bad habits are developed by example and by carelessness.

You cannot train without planning. You cannot impart instruction without preparation. Training plans in the past have too often been merely so much paper, for which credit was taken as though responsibility for that training had been completely discharged. Instruction has been a failure and a waste of time, due to lack of forethought and preparation.

A common weakness in organizations is poor command and staff technique. Commanders of companies will devote the drill period to problems of administration, leaving the supervision or conduct of training to the lieutenants. The government provides drill pay for instruction work, and administrative pay for another purpose. The latter often submerges or emasculates the former.

Staff officers are too seldom used by commanders for the purposes intended. Each commander has the obligation to train his staff—that is, to use it and not do all the work himself or, more frequently, to absorb himself in administrative work that should have been decentralized among the staff, while he supervised the training.

Gentlemen, you make or break your organization during the armory drill period.

In my opinion there is time for a fifty per cent increase in efficiency without an extra hour or a different type of officer or soldier. And I am not merely of the opinion, I know that the men greatly prefer to belong to a highly disciplined, hard-working, business-like organization. They are proud of it. They boast of it. The stricter the better—within the prescribed hours. Later on comes the social or diversional side. But they should never be mixed with the business end.

It is all in the state of mind, the mental attitude, and not in the lack of time.

If a man is not a leader, there is little that can be done about it. Plans, programs, regulations have no effect. But if he is a leader, and the majority of the commanders must be leaders or they could not have gained their present positions, and he decides that these improvements can be made, they will be made, without a shadow of a doubt. . . .

GCMRL/G. C. Marshall Papers (Pentagon Office, Speeches)

1. Approximately sixty percent of this speech transcript is printed. The omitted portions include a brief summary of Marshall's association with the Illinois National Guard and a recounting of his past experiences with other Guard organizations.

Major General Frank R. McCoy (seated left), Sixth Corps Area commander, watches a special demonstration by a war-strength company in Bell Bowl at Camp Grant, near Rockford, Illinois, August 7, 1935. To McCoy's left are Brigadier General Thomas S. Hammond, Marshall, and Colonel Herbert E. Algeo.

Marshall, "enemy" commander in the 1936 summer maneuvers, is shown conferring with the Sixth Corps headquarters staff: (left to right) Marshall, Colonel Fred R. Brown, Colonel H.C.M. Supplee, Brigadier General Dana T. Merrill (seated), Captain Sarratt T. Haines, and Major Floyd H. Cook.

Marshall and his Twelfth Brigade assistant chiefs of staff at the Michigan maneuvers of 1936.

Marshall (center) directs the March, 1935, Command Post Exercise in the 131st Infantry Armory, Chicago.

Brigadier General John McA. Palmer,
about 1923.

Major General Frank R. McCoy, 1930.

453

Marshall (left) instructs the umpires during the winter, 1936, Illinois National Guard war games in the Chicago vicinity.

Marshall (standing, third from the left) and his Twelfth Brigade staff at the Sixth Corps Area maneuvers near Allegan, Michigan, August 19, 1936. Standing to Marshall's left is Second Army commander Major General Charles E. Kilbourne.

MEMORANDUM FOR THE ADJUTANT GENERAL   January 10, 1935
                                             [Chicago, Illinois]

Reductions in Paper Work.

1. This morning as Senior Instructor for the Illinois National Guard there passed over my desk three "Certificates of Limited Losses," covering small items of equipment and clothing lost during the maneuvers and overland march of last August, by three different organizations. The totals of money value involved were, $19.24, $18.27 and $18.53. Half of those amounts would probably have correctly represented the actual value of the items at the time of their loss, or a total of $28.00. These papers bore 28 signatures, and it was necessary for me to sign my name 12 times, making a total of 40 signatures.

2. I submit that such procedure eventually results in a loss of supervision, rather than a gain. One signature by each party on the original paper should suffice, and would result in more time being devoted by supervisors in checking the items, rather than, as at present, in dashing off a number of signatures on trivial papers in order to be free to attend to more important duties. Approximately 1000 signatures of this particular nature must be made by the Senior Instructor each fiscal year.

3. An amendment to regulations is recommended authorizing a reduction in the number of signatures required on such documents.[1]

GCMRL/G. C. Marshall Papers (Illinois National Guard)
  1. No reply to this memorandum was found in the Marshall papers.

TO MAJOR GENERAL EDWARD CROFT   February 13, 1935
                                       [Chicago, Illinois]

Dear General: Acknowledging your note of February 1st, stating you would be glad to have my ideas relative to the handling of the graduating class from West Point, I had this in mind: I was impressed while at Benning by the fact that the magnificent overhead of reservation, facilities, troops and the school faculty, was not utilized to its full capacity. Each year I noted the splendid affect on the young graduates from West Point of a tour with the 29th Infantry. However, when at Fort Screven and Fort Moultrie, I was honestly horrified by the lack of development—if not the actual deterioration—in the young lieutenants who had reported directly from West Point. They appeared to be from another litter than those sent directly to Benning. I had to make it my personal business to attend to the development of these young men.

With this as a background, my conclusion is that if it be possible, the entire infantry cadre from West Point should be sent directly to Benning. A satisfactory arrangement for such assignment did not occur to me until I learned that you had made the 24th Infantry a combat regiment. That addition of infantry troops in training at Benning appeared to make the solution comparatively simple.

I would handle the matter in this fashion: To give continuity of policy and the necessary efficiency for instruction and demonstration, the commanding officers and Plans and Training Officers of the 29th Infantry, 24th Infantry and Tank regiment should have a three-year tour; lieutenant-colonels, the majors, the captains and one first lieutenant in each company, should have two year tours, vacancies alternating. These lieutenants in particular should be picked men from the classes graduating from Benning. I am a little uncertain as to whether young graduates should go directly to the Tank Regiment, but I am inclined to think they should, despite the disadvantages the tank people would advance.

Now, as to the new second lieutenants. The entire infantry list from West Point should report for duty, at the end of furlough, with one of these three units at Fort Benning, one for each platoon. They would find in command of their platoons their predecessors from the preceding class of West Point, who would remain in command of the platoons for the first two months, while the newly arrived officers were "finding" themselves and receiving preliminary schooling.

To start with the newly arrived officer, he should go through his first two months in understudying his predecessor and in following a course in administration, interior economy of the company, military law, etc. At the end of two months he takes command of the platoon. The second in command of the company, especially selected first lieutenant, has the development of these young men as his particular problem. (There might be two of the veteran lieutenants in a tank company). The captain is busy commanding the company and arranging for the necessary school demonstrations. When a platoon is to give a demonstration early in the year and the young lieutenants are not considered sufficiently able for this purpose, the trained first lieutenant could handle the unit, but to meet the certain objections from members of the weapon section of the school faculty I would say, it is not undesirable to have these young men in command of the demonstration sections of the platoons, because they are just about the type who will have to carry out these missions in time of war—except, presumably, they will be far better trained than their war prototypes, however short the time they have been at Benning.

During the year these young men should follow a system of schools—not regimental as would normally be the case—but handled by the school faculty who are much better prepared to do this and would thus relieve the regimental officers of this time consuming feature. The course for these equivalent-to-regimental schools would be carefully determined so as to fit in with another period of schooling, to follow the termination of fourteen months troop duty.

At the end of the first year, September 1st I suppose, these young men would receive the members of the newly arrived increment from West Point. For two months they would have the morale raising pleasure of being the guides and advisors of the more recent graduates. At the end of this period of two months—or a total of fourteen months on troop duty—the young men would be given a three months course in the school. This particular course could be far in advance of what would ordinarily be the case, because the preceding year of regimental schools—though conducted by the school faculty—would have covered a large number of items which we have always had to give the student of the former company course; and the group would be homogeneous, and uniformly prepared for the work.

At the end of this three months school the young officers should *all* be sent on foreign service where there are plenty of troops, large maneuvers, and definite war problems on ground that a man can see. The completion of the foreign service tour would, to a certain extent, complete the formative period of an officer's service, all of which would have been under the most favorable circumstances for the development of military ambition—fine troops, excellence of instruction, and impressive military surroundings.

I have never felt that we got anything like the full benefit from the maintenance of the war strength 29th Infantry, or from the concentration of infantry, artillery, tanks, etc., at Benning. The scheme I have outlined would certainly operate the factory more nearly at capacity. When Fuqua was Chief of Infantry I tried my best to feature the Refresher Course in some such fashion, because I thought it highly desirable that a number of leading officers of the Army, particularly of other arms and from those on duty in the War Department and at the War College, should have an opportunity to review the work of the schools and witness the actual operations of the combined arms, such as can only be seen in this country, at Fort Benning. I thought that the Refresher class should consist of from 50 to 60 officers. The additional overhead required for this purpose was two or three old buses and drivers, and about five orderlies. To meet the difficulty about mileage expense, I got General Fechet to agree that he would transport these people by airplane, concentrating them at New York, Washington, Chicago and St. Louis and bringing them on from there by transport plane.[1]

I wanted the Chief of Infantry to select and *invite* six or seven of the leading—efficient—National Guard and Reserve officers, men of distinction in civil life, and certain members of the General Staff and a few instructors from the War College. The course to be so arranged that the most interesting part would be during the first ten days, so that the busier members could then return to their duties while the others continued on for the full four weeks. I had the course built up for this specific purpose, and set for the most agreeable and convenient period of the year—November, December—but was never able to secure more than the usual yearly run of colonels enroute to regiments or who had just joined, mostly men too old for my purpose. I was only able to get one or two cavalrymen and no artillerymen or engineers. The trouble seemed to be that they went into the matter rather elaborately, rather as a new policy, and considered all the complications involved. I wanted it done merely as an experiment for one year. If it did not sell itself, then that was just too bad.

If some such scheme as this could have been put through, and I am confident it could have been done, we would now have a large number of officers speaking a common language regarding actual troop operations, all familiar with infantry doctrines and Benning. The larger class could have been handled without practically one hour's extra work by the school faculty and without the expenditure of any money for additional ammunition, etc.

* * * * *

As you can see from the foregoing, I am very much of the opinion that the facilities and opportunities at Benning are not used sufficiently either at the bottom or at the top; and, confidentially of course, I think Benning is so far ahead of the other places that it is a shame not to feature it in every way we infantrymen possibly can arrange for. It is rather hard to get this down on paper with all the various details involved and without opportunity to expand on the various difficulties that would be suggested. But I think I have made my idea fairly clear and submit it for your consideration.   Faithfully yours,

GCMRL/G. C. Marshall Papers (Illinois National Guard)
1. Major General James E. Fechet was chief of the Air Corps from December, 1927, until December, 1931.

To Brigadier General John McA. Palmer   February 21, 1935
                    Chicago, Illinois

Dear John: I should have written you some time back regarding Professor Linn's article on the National Guard, which was largely based on your book. Originally this was prepared to go in the Sunday Magazine supplement of the Hearst papers but when it was found the magazine section was made out so many months ahead that the article would not appear in time to accomplish its purpose, General Keehn, President of the National Guard Association, decided to get it out in pamphlet form. I am sending you a copy of the pamphlet which is self explanatory.[1]

What actually happened was that General Keehn went to Washington for a meeting of the Legislative Committee of the National Guard Association and for a hearing before the Sub Committee on Military Appropriations.[2] He had a copy of the pamphlet handed to each Senator and Congressman, personally delivered copies to the Chief of Staff, Secretary of War and the President, and of course to all the members of the National Guard assembly in Washington. A number of these representatives were desirous of obtaining these pamphlets for distribution within their states, so that they have purchased lots of approximately 500 for such distribution. The National Guard Bureau has already used up about one thousand copies, giving them to writers, press men and others soliciting any information. To date approximately 12,000 copies have been distributed throughout the United States and it appears as though there will be a continued call for additional copies which may run the total up toward 20,000.

The interesting thing is, the House of Representatives will probably pass a resolution shortly urging the President to provide out of the four billion fund enough money to re-fit the National Guard and to make possible the increase desired. At any rate so much pressure has been brought on the Congress that they are anxiously concerned as to how the desires of the National Guard can be met.

I hope the treatment of your data by Professor Linn is acceptable to you. He did his best, and when you consider that he did the work in two afternoons, after having read the book one evening, I think he did a pretty fair job of it—always having in mind it was intended for Hearst newspaper distribution to appeal to that sort of reader. Incidentally, Professor Linn is a pacifist, but I think your book somewhat undid him. At any rate, he is a very amusing fellow, and a great mixer and somewhat of a bonvivant.

I am writing this hastily, with apologies for my long delay.   Affectionately yours,

G. C. Marshall

LC/J. McA. Palmer Papers

1. James W. Linn, English professor at the University of Chicago, wrote a pamphlet entitled "Washington's Lost Plan Revived," which the National Guard Association reprinted as "An Appeal to the 74th Congress by the National Guard Association: Washington's Lost Plan Revived." Marshall had introduced Linn to Palmer's book *Washington, Lincoln, Wilson*.

2. General Keehn testified on January 22, 1935. Excerpts from his testimony are printed in the *Illinois Guardsman* 2 (March 1935): 5, 20.

To Lieutenant Colonel Edwin F. Harding   February 26, 1935
                                                      [Chicago, Illinois]

Dear Harding: When the box of cuts came, so promptly after my note to you, and I looked them over, I must admit I felt apologetic, because I certainly have been imposing on you. Nevertheless, your generous response is deeply appreciated and will not be forgotten. The cover cut came shortly after my return from Washington and I plan to use it probably in the April issue.[1]

I appreciate your generous comments regarding the last issues of the ILLINOIS GUARDSMAN, but you are rather drawing a long bow, in the spirit of friendly encouragement. The truth of the matter is, just at present I am playing the magazine down to the enlisted men, who form 90 per cent of the subscribers. It is rather hard to do this and at the same time get out an issue that would appeal to officers. However, I am gradually headed that way and think in two or three more months I will do much better. Gradually I hope to wash out the triviality of the regimental notes and make this portion of the magazine more a series of articles on what is occurring in the regiment that will be of general interest throughout the Division.

My principal difficulty is to secure any material regarding the down state units, who at the same time are jealous of what appears about the Chicago units. Their attitude is inconsistent, but an important consideration. The reason we apparently favor the Chicago units is, the Colonels are more "houndable."

I imagine you and the Tuttles will have a lively weekend. I wish I could join you.[2]

Katherine, with Mrs. McCoy,[3] is deep in the business of attending auctions. There are rare bargains here in Chicago, BUT the only trouble is, they usually come back with something other than what they went after. We drew a pool table in one of the recent events. I expect to use it after we have retired.

Give my love to Eleanor.   Faithfully,

GCMRL/G. C. Marshall Papers (Illinois National Guard)

1. Marshall had written to Harding, the editor of the *Infantry Journal,* to borrow the printing plates ("cuts") for some illustrations.
2. Major and Mrs. William B. Tuttle were friends from the Tientsin, China, assignment.
3. Major General Frank R. McCoy took command of the Sixth Corps Area, which had its headquarters in Chicago, on February 1, 1935. General and Mrs. McCoy leased the apartment across the hall from the Marshalls.

To Silas H. Strawn[1]   March 12, 1935
                                                        [Chicago, Illinois]

My dear Mr. Strawn: Apropos of our conversation the other night at the Bernay's dinner, I am sending you a copy of the March number of The ILLINOIS GUARDSMAN, in the hope that you will read the editorial on pages 22 and 23.[2] On page 5 you will find extracts from General Keehn's recent testimony before the Military Committee of Congress, which gives some idea of the present problems of the Guard.

Frankly, as a regular officer charged with assisting in the development of efficiency in the State troops, I have been much impressed—and somewhat nonplused—by the general indifference of the citizens of Chicago to the Guard. I was hurriedly sent out here in October 1933 because of the threat of serious disorders by the unemployed, at a time when 150,000 families in Cook County were without work and the legislature had refused or failed to appropriate relief funds. The CWA was then unheard of. To my surprise, I found most of my civilian friends utterly indifferent to the Guard, or almost completely ignorant of its organization, strength, efficiency and importance to the then threatening situation.

I am deeply interested in the development of civilian support and appreciation of these State-Federal troops, as their efficiency is directly influenced by the lack or fact of public interest in their organizations, and their efficiency is a matter of great importance to the National Defense, as well as to the local situation in Illinois.[3]   Faithfully yours,

GCMRL/G. C. Marshall Papers (Illinois National Guard)

1. Strawn was an influential Chicago lawyer and a former president of the United States Chamber of Commerce (1931–32).

2. The editorial ("Chicago and Illinois") restated a theme which had concerned Marshall since he had arrived in Illinois: "What do the business men of Chicago, the bankers and lawyers know of the organization and purpose of the National Guard. It has their remote approval, but how many of them realize its potential importance to the city?"

3. Strawn replied that he was interested in helping, and he and Marshall arranged to meet to discuss the problem. (Strawn to Marshall, March 14, 1935, GCMRL/G. C. Marshall Papers [Illinois National Guard].)

To Brigadier General John McA. Palmer   March 27, 1935
Chicago, Illinois

Dear John: I have just received your letter of March 24th this morning and read it with a great deal of interest.[1]

I have always felt, as you well know, that you received less appreciation for your work than any other individual I have ever known in the Army. I have tried to make it my business when an opportunity offered to square the deal a little.

However, I am rather inclined to think, reading between the lines in your letter, that you did not like Linn's pamphlet. Is this the case, and, if so, what is the trouble?[2]   Faithfully yours,

G. C. Marshall

LC/J. McA. Palmer Papers

1. Palmer's letter was a lengthy and bitter complaint at the lack of recognition that he had received for his part in the 1920 army reorganization bill passed by Congress.

2. Palmer replied, "I was delighted with Professor Linn's splendid article and I am in full sympathy with its argument for National Guard legislation." (Palmer to Marshall, March 30, 1935, GCMRL/G. C. Marshall Papers [Illinois National Guard].)

To Brigadier General John McA. Palmer   March 29, 1935
Chicago, Illinois

Dear John: I have just gotten your letter of March 26th. I did not misunderstand what you said in any degree, and I think you are too prone to paralyzing accuracy. I treat historical facts in a more casual way than you do and suffer less strain in so doing.

461

As a matter of fact, your testimony before the Senate Committee reached *me* in galley proof form almost immediately after you gave it, and I went over it with the General. Later, the next day or the day after as I recall, he testified before the joint Committees. I thought you were right then, I know you are right now. What you have always needed was a manager and a publicity agent, and then a trifling operation in amputation of the conscience. Most people do not require this.[1]

With my love to Mrs. Palmer,   Ever faithfully yours,

G. C. Marshall

LC/J. McA. Palmer Papers

1. Palmer had been instrumental in significantly changing the original Baker-March proposals to Congress in 1919 concerning army reorganization. He had written in a March 24 letter to Marshall that "in the orthodox propaganda, we are given to believe that Congress derived its wisdom from the War Department's official recommendations and from General Pershing, who was still in France, and knew nothing about the plan until he endorsed it later on as a *fait accompli*." Two days later, Palmer wrote to apologize for his "half-cocked" reference to General Pershing. "My letter was perhaps inspired by a sense of injustice. I have been silent about this, but it broke away from me in my fraternal feeling toward you." (Palmer to Marshall, March 24 and March 26, 1935, GCMRL/G. C. Marshall Papers [Illinois National Guard].)

SPEECH ON THE STATE OF THE ARMY[1]   [1935?]

[Chicago, Illinois]

. . . For the first time in our history we have an organized nucleus for a formidable National Army. Its mobilization is planned to the last detail; it is decentralized out of Washington; all its officers are being trained under the guidance of the Regular army; a few telegrams can set the machine in motion; war reserves are strategically located in great depots; plans for the rapid procurement of war supplies have been formulated, down to individual factory layouts in private enterprises for turning their production in a minimum of time to the supply of special equipment not of a standard commercial pattern—the production of these war supplies has been allocated among the industries and factories in accordance with agreements and joint studies by the Army and Navy and the business men themselves. There should be no hodge-podge of half-baked ideas, struggling against the fatal time factor as in 1917 and 18.

But, and here are the points I would like to draw to your special attention—we are up against certain factors that seriously limit our defensive powers and cannot be overcome in the first year of a war. In these we labor under a dreadful disadvantage, compared to other great powers, especially when you consider that it is the humble war recruit—your son or mine—who must pay the price of the present dilemma.

In quality and number we are fabulously rich in man-power. But in this scientific and machine age mere men, in war, are often impotent if the enemy has been progressive. Here are a few examples of what I mean: Certain war materiel requires a long time to manufacture and much of it is vital to success in battle. Tanks, for example. Without tanks and opposing tanks, infantry is almost helpless.

We have the best tank in the world. It was made at Rock Island—but its development required fifteen years of experimentation—the time consumed being largely due to the small amount of money available from year to year.[2] The automobile industry thinks little of spending a million or more on the development of a new type of car, not differing greatly from the standard type. We have had less than a million over fifteen years, for the development of a light- and a medium-weight tank. We now have the model—about thirty have been built—ninety or more are building. But we need hundreds, and if we were thrown into war tomorrow it would be almost a year before our infantry could be protected in its advances by an adequate tank force against machine gun holocausts—not to mention the fact that the British, French, and Italians have developed large tank forces.

The Thirty-third Division here in Illinois has one tank company—in Maywood—a company of unusually high morale and training. It has not a single tank, it may get one lone tank before the year is out—its complement is twenty.

Today I have been talking about the possibilities of the first weeks, the first six months of a war. We started the business of having tanks manufactured in 1917—the man in immediate charge was my intimate friend—my mess mate in France—he was once head of the American Legion. But in spite of all he or others could do—a year and a half after war was declared, there was not an American-made tank in France, and on November 1, 1918, I personally arranged for the entirely available American tank force with our Army, to assist in the great assault of that date—and we had eighteen tanks instead of the 650 deemed necessary—a year and a half after we went to war.

Take our infantry weapons, for example:

Our rifle is a thirty-two-year-old model. Can you picture a 1903 model of an automobile, an airplane or a radio? But that's what our boys are to carry. Why?

We have developed the finest semi-automatic shoulder rifle in the world (that's a typical American boast), approaching the equivalent of a light machine gun, yet weighing no more than our old Springfield rifle. It would be a menace to the lordly swooping airplane, a terror to advancing infantry—and it would take almost a year to put it into quantity production. We need a hundred thousand for the peace strength regular army and National Guard—Congress has appropriated funds for manufacturing 1,500—we need 500,000 for a first issue on mobilization and as many more within six months. Every infantry weapon—rifle, machine gun, automatic small cannon and howitzer or trench mortar, is a World War or earlier model. We need a light machine gun, we need a 50 calibre machine gun for use against tanks and airplanes, we need a long range Stokes mortar. We have the models but not the money for these weapons which would be worth more than their weight in gold on the battle-field to the plodding, sweating, suffering doughboy. For whatever the sensational magazines or press may say—while the next war will undoubtedly start in the air, it will inevitably end in the mud—as usual.

Our air service is far better developed or equipped than any other portion of the army. But our air resisting weapons, anti-aircraft machine guns and cannon equipment is sadly deficient.

Again we have the models, and a few in service. And, again, I hazard the statement that they are the best in the world. But it would require a year or more to produce them after the declaration of war. Meanwhile, ignoring the tribulations and suffering of the men in the field, what would happen in Chicago? An overwhelming demand for antiaircraft protection. But with what? The pitifully few guns, directors, detectors and synchronized searchlights now available, would be insufficient for the Chicago and New York Metropolitan districts, even if we stripped the fighting army of every piece of such equipment. And it takes a year to make it. The development of our anti-air materiel is very interesting but has been given little publicity. The problem was one of multiple complexities. Some method for the instant and simultaneous determination of how high—how far off—in what direction—and flying at what speed, of a plane, and from this the calculation of a direction and new altitude for the plane at a given later moment so that the projectile would meet the speeding plane at a predetermined point and at a split second moment, at which the fuse of the shell was set to burst. All this had to be the calculation and adjustment of approximately a single instant. We have the machines and instruments that do it, with guns automatically aimed and fired with heavy shells, at ranges of eleven miles and up to altitudes of eight miles. Your Illinois Coast Artillery Regiment on Broadway has this equipment. How do they locate the plane at night—more magic, sound detectors automatically influence searchlights, focusing them on the target. The Sperry Gyroscopic Company has played a large part in these matters and we have them in small numbers.

Our Coast defenses have guns up to sixteen inches, firing a 2,340 lb. projectile twenty-eight miles. But again our numbers are limited and production requires long fatal months.

I could go on citing instances of special war materiel which we lack and which probably could not be produced before the end of the first year of a war. A special effort was recently made to secure the necessary funds for complete modernization of our war materiel or equipment—some of the famous four billions was to be spent for the purpose, and for two reasons: It would render our volunteer army so formidable that we would be spared the threat of war, and it would start the heavy industries to work—as almost all of this materiel would come from the steel and iron trades.

This allocation was barred, in the Senate, by a resolution forbidding any of the money to be spent for war-making supplies. So, we continue in the predicament of the past ten years, which grows more serious with each succeeding year.

I am not here to talk about possibilities of war, or about peaceful adjustments. That is not my business. I am discussing an existing condition, with its implications.

The decision rests entirely in the hands of citizens like yourselves—and the penalty, if any, will be paid by citizen-soldiers.

GCMRL/G. C. Marshall Papers (Pentagon Office, Speeches)

1. Charles G. Dawes arranged for Marshall to meet Chicago's leading business and professional men and to speak before various civic organizations. (K. T. Marshall, *Together,* pp. 18-19.) This speech was probably delivered to such a group. Approximately sixty percent of the speech is printed here. In the omitted portion Marshall detailed the number and distribution of Regular Army and National Guard troops.

2. Rock Island Arsenal, located on an island in the Mississippi River near Rock Island, Illinois, was a United States Army research, development, and production facility.

To Lieutenant Colonel Robert W. Davis   April 2, 1935
                                                    [Chicago, Illinois]

Dear Colonel: Your letter of April 1st was in the mail this morning and interested me tremendously.[1] I am so glad you gave me your view of the whole affair, and I am delighted to learn what a great success it was. I had Captain Potter describing the affair to me, when he was in last Saturday.[2] I think you are to be congratulated not only in having put over a fine appearance, but in having done some pioneer work in demonstrating what can be done by scattered units— yours are about as well scattered as any could be, outside of the State of Texas.

The matter interested me greatly, because it strikes at the great weaknesses of the National Guard—poor instructors, who in turn involve the Guard in a tremendous loss of time—aside from the fact that instructional work is inefficiently handled. I am looking forward to the write-up of the affair, because I want to play it up strong in the May issue of the GUARDSMAN. Incidentally, I may find it desirable to insert some portions of your letter to me, if this does not meet your disapproval. The photograph I will use in illustration of the article.

Speaking of the GUARDSMAN, I have heard that there have been numerous instances where my instructors have found whole months issues of the GUARDSMAN stacked up in storerooms and forgotten, company commanders not having seen to delivery to the men. In one case, I believe they found copies covering two months, not one of which had been delivered to the men. Considering that this matter is the particular desire of the Division Commander, represents a display of poor cooperation on the part of the company commander and he would probably fail to a greater degree in the field—because "The Leopard does not change his spots."

Aside from the question of working up interest in the GUARDSMAN, I am more deeply concerned in its usefulness for general instruction purposes in a sugar-coated form. For example, the description of your Cairo School will undoubtedly lead to others of the same kind, just as previous descriptions of certain instructional methods or arrangements have led to their duplication in other units. I find that some of our little crude puzzles, which are merely tactical problems under another name, have stirred up more intelligent study and investigation than hours of routine instruction. So, we are going into a whole page of so-called puzzles.

I hope nothing interferes with the inspection of some of your units in May. I was very sorry that the plan for the end of March fell through, because of engagements General Keehn had to meet in Washington. He is now in California and probably will not be back until about the 10th, and then will probably have to go immediately to Washington in connection with the program for armory construction.

We are having a Critique tomorrow night for the Division Staff and all the field officers in town on the War Game.[3] I am sorry you cannot be here, because I think it will be interesting. I have never seen in tactical problems, or in the field, a situation which so clearly illustrated the possibilities of all methods of leadership by regimental commanders, and I am trying to utilize a discussion of this to make clear what should and what must be done in the field.

Apparently our program for summer camps goes through without any changes over what has already been published in the GUARDSMAN. I am still delayed in preparing the formal program, because we are trying to locate some land within a reasonable distance of [Camp] Grant where a decent maneuver can be held in the middle of the second week.

With my regards to Mrs. Davis, believe me   Faithfully yours,

GCMRL/G. C. Marshall Papers (Illinois National Guard)

1. Davis commanded the 130th Infantry in southern Illinois. His letter explained the regiment's annual school held March 22–24 in Cairo, Illinois. Marshall quoted Davis's letter in "An Infantry Convoy and School for Instructors: 130th Infantry Initiates Winter Use of Trucks," *Illinois Guardsman* 2 (May 1935): 8–9.

2. Captain Harold E. Potter was a Regular Army inspector assigned to the Illinois National Guard.

3. On March 8 the Thirty-third Division and attached troops held a Command Post Exercise in the 131st Infantry armory in Chicago, concluding a combined map problem–war game exercise initiated in the fall and resembling the New Jersey CPX held in September, 1934.

TO COLONEL HUNTER PENDLETON   April 8, 1935
                                               [Chicago, Illinois]

My dear Colonel Pendleton: I have just read the notice in the Alumni News of your retirement in June. Your departure from the faculty will mark a great change at the V.M.I. I fear that with you will go the last trace of the atmosphere I grew up in as a young man.[1]

A "dub" in Chemistry, and not a student at any time, I was not a shining light in your sections. But I carried away with me some very precious, though intangible, assets gained through your example. Later on, from Mrs. Coles and Lily I learned to know you better and to appreciate you more at your true value. Lily admired you tremendously, and with her mother, had a deep affection for both you and Mrs. Pendleton, which I came to share.

I hope you both enjoy good health and that your plans will make for an agreeable and happy period in your retirement. There must be a profound satisfaction in completing an active career, clean in the knowledge that you have exercised a beneficial and a beneficent influence over the lives of thousands of young men, and that you had stood a little higher each year in the admiration and regard of every person with whom you have been associated.

My affectionate regards to you both.   Faithfully yours,

GCMRL/G. C. Marshall Papers (Illinois National Guard)
1. Pendleton was professor of chemistry between 1890 and 1935.

To THE CHICAGO MOTOR COACH COMPANY   April 30, 1935
                                                 [Chicago, Illinois]

Gentlemen: About 9:00 A.M. on April 25th, on a bus (#51, 52 or 53) approaching Jackson Street, I had occasion to notice a particularly courteous and kindly service rendered by the bus driver to a passenger. Going west on Jackson, I noticed other evidences of this same nature.

Since this driver's attitude and methods were in marked contrast to a number of exhibitions of gratuitous rudeness and boorishness I have also observed, I wished to commend him to your attention. Unfortunately, I am not certain that I recall his name and number correctly, but I think the name was "Clayton" and his number was "285." He was a man between 45 and 50, thin type, and wore glasses.

I hope I have identified him correctly, for he is deserving of mention and is an asset to your company.   Very truly,

GCMRL/G. C. Marshall Papers (Illinois National Guard)

To CAPTAIN DAVID D. BARRETT[1]   May 13, 1935
                                                 [Chicago, Illinois]

My dear Barrett: I received your letter of May 7th the other day, and it was not until this morning that the "Primer in the Writing of Chinese Characters" arrived.[2] I was very glad to hear from you and to learn something of what you had been doing, and was delighted to learn that your recent tour in China had been so satisfying in professional interest.

While I have not had an opportunity to do more than merely scan the book, it immediately impressed me as being exceedingly well done, very well set up, and makes me wish that we had had some such text while I was with the 15th Infantry. You have quite evidently done a fine job of it and I congratulate you.

I think it an excellent thing for younger officers to keep their brains whetted up by undertaking tasks of this sort, rather than dropping into the stodgy business of merely carrying out orders. If one does not have some specialty or avocation, the added years mean a decided let down in general tone and efficiency.

I often recall our days at Nan ta Ssu and the year you spent at Benning. And I recall, too, your regret at being sent to R.O.T.C. duty in New York. But since then you have been with troops pretty constantly and although Crook is not desirable climatically, it is a post and you will have plenty of men after July 1st.

I, too, trust that we may serve together again, and I appreciate the nice things you have to say about me.

With warm regards,   Faithfully yours,

GCMRL/G. C. Marshall Papers (Illinois National Guard)

1. Barrett was a graduate of the Infantry School, Company Officers' Course, in 1929. He had served as S-2 (Intelligence Section) with the Fifteenth Infantry in China from the fall of 1931 to the fall of 1934. At the time of his letter, he was serving as regimental S-3 (Operations and Training Section) at Fort Crook, Nebraska. (Barrett to Marshall, May 7, 1935, GCMRL/ G. C. Marshall Papers [Illinois National Guard].)

2. David Dean Barrett, *A Primer in the Writing of Chinese Characters* (Shanghai: Kelly and Walsh, 1934). The work had originally been produced for *The Sentinel*, the official weekly of the United States Army troops stationed in Tientsin, China, to interest the soldiers in the Chinese language. (Ibid.)

MEMORANDUM FOR THE SECRETARY OF WAR   May 24, 1935
FROM PRESIDENT FRANKLIN D. ROOSEVELT   The White House

General Pershing asks very strongly that Colonel George C. Marshall (Infantry) be promoted to Brigadier.

Can we put him on list of next promotions?[1] He is fifty-four years old.

F. D. R.

FDRL/F. D. Roosevelt Papers (PPF 1604)

1. Marshall's name was not placed on the list of next promotions. In a letter thanking General Pershing for mentioning his name to the president, Marshall lamented: "I can but wait—grow older—and hope for a more favorable situation in Washington." (Marshall to Pershing, June 10, 1935, LC/J. J. Pershing Papers [General Correspondence].)

To Lieutenant Colonel Edwin F. Harding   June 22, 1935
[Chicago, Illinois]

Dear Harding: I have just read your letter of June 20th, and am answering it immediately as partial expression of my appreciation for the trouble you have taken and for the value of your criticisms and suggestions about the GUARDS-MAN. Much that you said I already had debated in my own mind, particularly regarding some of the typographical matters, which I had previously discussed with the supposed expert on that subject from the Kable publishing company. Am going to "turn the hose" on him again with your letter as added evidence as to the correctness of my view.[1]

I rather think you were doing a subtle compliment in praising the unsigned articles, guessed I had probably done them, which I had. The trouble has been I had to whack them out in about a half hour each with almost no time for reference or care in preparation. Incidentally, however, these do not interest the bulk of our readers who are enlisted men. The officers like them, but the men don't care much about them—only the illustrations save them. And in most instances the articles are written because I happen to have the illustrations— usually free cuts. The Leavenworth article was purely a filler because I knew I could get the cuts for nothing. I happened to see the description in a book I was reading on Mexico.

I was interested in what you said about the Personalities Here and There. This is the most valuable item in the magazine toward building up subscriptions and interest among the enlisted men. The letters from these men have also had tremendous value in getting the men interested, however foolish some of the letters may seem.

The Regimental Notes, of course, represent our big problem. I think we have improved them in quality about fifty per cent—but that's not saying very much for them. But they are vital to the magazine, as we depend absolutely on the subscriptions of the enlisted personnel. Whenever the notes of the unit are missing, there is a storm of protest, which tells the story. We are under fire continuously for cutting out portions of the notes submitted and I assure you the parts we cut out are uniformly terrific, nevertheless a protest. Anything that we print which is reasonably presentable, that has to do or has been written by an enlisted man goes over big. My problem is to locate men who either have had unusual experiences or have some ability in writing.

I am immensely grateful to you for the trouble you have taken and your letter will really be most helpful. . . .[2]

With warm regards, Affectionately,

GCMRL/G. C. Marshall Papers (Illinois National Guard)

1. Marshall had written to Harding on June 13 requesting his "*frank* opinion" on how the *Illinois Guardsman* compared with the magazines of the California, New York, and Pennsylvania National Guards. Harding replied on June 20 that Illinois was superior to the first but

inferior to the latter two "in certain respects, mostly typographical."

2. The one-third of the letter omitted concerned a mutual friend, Marshall's family vacationing at Fire Island, and Harding's family.

To Colonel Ralph D. Mershon   June 27, 1935
                                                          [Chicago, Illinois]

My dear Colonel Mershon: A copy of Bishop's letter to you on June 25th gives me the first news I had of your operation.[1] I am sorry not to have known of this at the time, but delighted to know that you evidently have made a successful recovery. I certainly hope so, and this note carries my sympathetic interest in your convalescence.

As to the development of affairs with the Civilian Military Education Fund, it appears to me that we are gradually gaining the dominant position of importance or influence in the general field of civilian-military education. The gain during the past winter has been very marked, along with a general reaction to the organized pacifistic-communistic efforts to suppress military training. Here in Chicago yesterday the school board vigorously supported their superintendents proposal to organize a number of new R.O.T.C. units. The Chicago Tribune has been running editorials strongly supporting the R.O.T.C., and the recent legislative investigation of communistic tendencies at the University of Chicago aroused public interest and exerted a favorable influence on the pathetic ROTC unit at that institution. The worm seems to be turning, though during the previous two years things looked blacker than at any time within my recollection.

I therefore think that you have exerted a profound influence, during the most critical [period], on the development of civilian-military training among the young men of the country.

With the hope that your progress continues to be favorable and that you will soon be or already are enjoying excellent health,   Faithfully yours,

GCMRL/G. C. Marshall Papers (Illinois National Guard)

1. No copy of Ralph C. Bishop's letter has been found in the Marshall papers.

To Major General Roy D. Keehn   [August 8, 1935]
                                                          Camp Grant, Illinois

Dear General: I have just come in from the target range. We accomplished by 11:15 A.M. what took us to 4 P.M. last year. The troops, 165th Brigade will eat lunch in camp with their range firing completed. All, a great improvement over last year.

The Machine Gun and Howitzer School (Monday afternoon and Tuesday and Wednesday mornings) went over with a bang. All seemed delighted. Colonel Buchanan much pleased.[1]

The Bell Bowl demonstration Tuesday at 3:30 P.M. went off in great shape, the composite war strength company of the 131st Infantry staging a fine climax in an attack. Major Brown (their instructor) broke a rib in his zeal.

The Command Post Exercise showed a great improvement, and the Division Staff conducted and umpired the entire affair. The staff has done beautifully throughout. I am merely a spectator—except for the hour in Bell Bowl.

General McCoy arrived Tuesday noon and left Wednesday afternoon. He was much impressed, especially with the smooth way things were running and the manner in which the officers and non-coms were carrying themselves in conducting instruction.

A night compass bearing problem for the officers was carried out last night, starting at 8:30 P.M. Some completed their ¾ mile course in the dark by 9:20 P.M. and boarded a truck for camp. A few got lost. DeRoulet's son,[2] I understand, got in at 3:00 A.M. Colonel McKinley covered himself with glory, and a little mud. He made the most accurate course in direction and distance, finishing at 9:45 P.M. Which was a fine thing;—for if a man his age—not in the line—could do it in that fashion, the youngsters were barred from grousing.[3]

Everything is going well, though your presence and direction is sadly missed. Everyone is solicitous in inquiries regarding your improvement, which I understand, has been marked. God knows, it was time you had a decent break and a little freedom from pain.[4]

My prayers go for your rapid recovery.   Faithfully yours

GCMRL/G. C. Marshall Papers (Illinois National Guard)

1. Lieutenant Colonel Kenneth Buchanan commanded the 106th Cavalry Headquarters Troop in Urbana, Illinois.

2. Lieutenant Colonel Alfred De Roulet commanded the Chemical Warfare Section at Thirty-third Division headquarters. His son, First Lieutenant Paul A. De Roulet, served with the 131st Infantry, Company L.

3. Colonel James J. McKinley (b. 1877) served with the 108th Medical Regiment.

4. Keehn had been seriously injured in an automobile accident near Beulah, Wyoming, in July, while vacationing with his family. He was confined to the hospital with a broken left shoulder and a badly damaged right arm which was causing complications due to gangrene. His arm was amputated between the shoulder and elbow on September 1.

To General John J. Pershing   September 8, 1935
                                               Fire Island, New York

Dear General: Congratulations, along with hundreds of others, on your birthday. I was recalling today a birthday dinner we had for you out of the Chevy Chase house in 1920 and how much of a hit my rhymes didn't make. I can't recall your birthday celebration in 1919. It must have been during the New York reception, for I think we were there then. A little later at Naushon I recall some sort of a party, but it must have been too late.

Do you recall those lovely fall days in the Adirondacks? Next Wednesday we motor up to Lake Placid or Saranac to spend a week; and on through Canada to the straits of Mackinaw, and south through Wisconsin to Chicago.

I came east three weeks ago to join Mrs. Marshall and the children—drove the 950 miles straight through without a stop for rest. Made New York City from the Loop in 24 hrs. and a half. During most of July I was at Camp McCoy at Sparta Wisconsin with the Illinois Artillery regiments; and at Camp Grant from Aug. 1 to 18th with the remainder of the division. Was quite pleased with results. They had made a vast improvement since a year ago, and were very proud of themselves. They now recognize the importance of my severity along certain lines.

Mrs. Marshall has been here since June 10th. I sent her on with our colored man. Molly had lan[d]ed from her ten month trip around the world, on June 5th, and had opened the cottage. Allen came up from the University of Virginia at the same time. He "life guards" at thirty bucks a week. Has made ten rescues in the heavy surf. Please arrange to stop over with me in Chicago this fall.

With all my best wishes for you,   Affectionately,

G. C. M.

LC/J. J. Pershing Papers (General Correspondence); H

To MAJOR BENJAMIN F. CAFFEY, JR.   September 19, 1935
                                                    [Chicago, Illinois]

Dear Caffey: Your letter of September 3rd was forwarded to me at Fire Island, New York, and I delayed replying until my return from leave this morning, knowing that you were absent yourself in the West.

I hardly know what advice to give you about the handling of a split staff such as yours. The staff of the 33d Division is almost entirely located in Chicago, which facilitates training.[1]

My problem has been to create a staff team rather than a lot of individuals well up on extension course work or on other problems. Also, I have been struggling with the proposition of overcoming, as it were, the effect of the character of problems given in Leavenworth which dealt with war strength organizations of well trained men, and on a basis not well adapted to the situations common to the first month of the campaign. I have stuck largely to geological survey maps; taking situations similar to those that occurred in the New Jersey CPX with this division; had them work out each detail of their time, the time element being the most important phase of the matter. This has meant teaching them how to do business in a fragmentary fashion; to do the vital things omitting the trimmings; to do everything in the manner that would be necessary in handling the partially trained men and officers they will have to deal with in the beginning of a campaign.

It took me almost a year to lead them to an understanding of what their problem would be at the beginning of a war. All of them could draft extensive type of orders with numerous annexes; none of them could handle situations which had to be treated instantly. I took the New Jersey situation of this division as it arrived there, and placed it on a geological survey map here. We worked it out first as a map problem, later carried it on as a war game—which consisted of a two-sided CPX indoors, 22 command posts set up in one armory. Then this summer on the last day of camp, while they were packing up their tenting, etc., I took them all 18 miles to the site of the war game and worked it out as terrain exercises on the ground. This proved the most profitable part of the whole business, and a splendid lesson in map reading.

The staff of the division is a very good team and they understand pretty well exactly how to handle things during the perspective hurly burly of the first few weeks of a campaign. They all know how fast they must work, how brief the orders must be, how careful the checks and supervision must be, to make things work within the brief time usually available.

I have "ding-donged" on this one situation, which involved detrainment by detachments and being rushed into action until they have a pretty fair understanding of the technique required, and the mishaps to be avoided.

If I can find it I will send you the number of the National Guard magazine which outlined something of the procedure.

This is not a very satisfactory letter, but it will give you some idea of what I have been doing. Now that you are so close, we will be able to see something of each other again.

Give my best regards to Mrs. Caffey and believe me always   Faithfully yours,

GCMRL/G. C. Marshall Papers (Illinois National Guard)

1. Caffey, who had recently been detailed as the instructor for the headquarters of the Thirty-fourth Division (National Guard) at Council Bluffs, Iowa, wrote on September 3 to ask Marshall's "ideas on the scope of instruction for your division, the methods of instruction, etc. What type and kind of instruction do you give your division headquarters company? As a matter of fact, I will be pleased to get any or all information which you think may help me." He was, he observed, "a wanderer in a strange land." (Caffey to Marshall, September 3, 1935, GCMRL/G. C. Marshall Papers [Illinois National Guard].)

To James W. Wadsworth   October 2, 1935
                                                        [Chicago, Illinois]

My dear Senator:[1]   The enclosed pamphlet reached me a few days ago. In it I noticed your letter to Colonel Orvel Johnson regarding John Palmer.[2] This thought occurred to me: In my opinion, Palmer rendered one of the most important services to the Army and to the National Defense of the past fifty years. Few army officers have contributed more to the Government of lasting benefit. Yet, comparatively speaking, he has received literally nothing in the way of reward. Fellows have been made brigadier generals for keeping the grass cut and buildings painted. Others have been promoted and retired major generals for no other reason that I could see except more years and seniority. Yet he was retired as a brigadier.

I know, possibly better than most of his friends, what his weakness is, what has caused people to pass his services by; and I am familiar with the feeling created by portions of his recent books. But the fact remains he made a great contribution to our Government and he has been virtually ignored.

Some time when you are in a position to do so, which I am firm in the belief you will be, please consider the possibility of securing legislation that would register officially governmental recognition of his service.

I have not seen Palmer for eight years and only hear from him occasionally, but knowing the circumstances in his case I have always been impatient to see justice done him.

I had lunch with General McCoy an hour ago—he and I live side by side here in Chicago. Possibly you may know the two others who were at lunch—Mrs. Sidney Cloman and Lawrence Whiting.

I always look forward to the possibility of seeing you. Think I was out of the city when you were here buying cattle last year. I hope I will have better luck next time.   Faithfully yours,

GCMRL/G. C. Marshall Papers (Illinois National Guard)

1. Wadsworth served two terms as senator from New York before being defeated by Democratic party candidate Robert F. Wagner in the 1926 election. He had served in the House of Representatives from the Thirty-ninth District of New York since his election in 1932.

2. This letter was printed in *Washington's National Defense Plan: Address by Brig. Gen. John McAuley Palmer. . .* (Washington, D.C.: Government Printing Office, 1935).

FROM GENERAL JOHN J. PERSHING   October 4, 1935
                                                 Paris, France

My dear Marshall,   . . . I have just received word that you are to be on the next list of Brigadier Generals to be promoted probably in December. The Chief had still intended to make you the Chief of Infantry, but as no one knows when the vacancy will occur, I told him that you would prefer to be in the line, and so it will be done, at least that is the plan at present. Of course we never know what may come up to change the plan, but I feel pretty certain that it is going to happen.[1]

With affectionate regards to Mrs. Marshall and the family, Very sincerely yours,

John J. Pershing

GCMRL/G. C. Marshall Papers (Illinois National Guard)

1. Pershing had written to his friend John C. O'Laughlin—formerly a newspaper correspondent, an associate of President Theodore Roosevelt, and an official of the Republican National Committee (1933-34), and the publisher of the influential *Army and Navy Journal*—to ask that O'Laughlin "put in a good word" for Marshall with Chief of Staff MacArthur, if he found the opportunity. (Pershing to O'Laughlin, August 23, 1935, LC/J. J. Pershing Papers [General Correspondence].) O'Laughlin soon reported that he had spoken with MacArthur, and that the chief of staff thought that Marshall should wait until the chief of Infantry post became available. However, MacArthur agreed to recommend Marshall for promotion to brigadier general on the next list that was sent to Secretary of War Dern. (O'Laughlin to Pershing, September 16, 1935, ibid.)

To Brigadier General John McA. Palmer   [October 14 (?), 1935]

Chicago, Illinois

Dear John: I wrote Wadsworth and received an encouraging reply. In part, he wrote "If he (you) had done nothing else, his work in the revision of the National Defense Act would entitle him to that (major general) distinction." He thought McSwain would be cooperative, but had no way of estimating the reaction of the present Senate Committee. Referred to Sheppard and Roberts being the only two on the committee familiar with the past.[1]

Expressed his willingness "to sound out the situation when Congress reconvenes and, of course, it will be absolutely necessary to persuade the Secretary of War as well as the President to see this matter as we do."

MacArthur pulled in an "oak leaf" for his DSM the other day, so possibly they might go ahead on that line. But that does not pay the bills that the additional pay of a major general retired does, even if it does carry some honor. I should think we could get the "oak leaf" without great difficulty, but I think it would be too bad to short circuit the more material honor.

I will endeavor to keep an oar in this—but, judging from my own career, I am not much of an oarsman.   Hastily and affectionately,

G. C. M.

LC/J. McA. Palmer Papers; H

1. Congressman John J. McSwain, from South Carolina, was chairman of the House Military Committee. Congressman Wadsworth wrote that Senator Morris Sheppard of Texas and "Senator Roberts" (Joseph T. Robinson) of Arkansas were about the only senators who would remember Palmer from 1920. (Wadsworth to Marshall, October 7, 1935, GCMRL/ G. C. Marshall Papers [Illinois National Guard].)

To General John J. Pershing   October 23, 1935
                                                                Chicago, Illinois

Dear General: I just received your letter of October 4th, which was forwarded from Fire Island.

Quite evidently you were thoughtful and kind enough to mention my name to Craig in your note to him of congratulations.[1] I am very grateful, and am much relieved to learn that apparently I will be "in" on some of the makes in the near future. I am particularly glad that you made clear that I prefer the line to the Chief of Infantry job. I want command duty, with the attendant possibilities for the future. I do it much better than desk, administrative work, but it has generally been my fate to draw the latter class of duty.

I was in the mountains with no radio, on your birthday, so did not hear the splendid program in your honor, but I read of it and was told about it, and I saw the numerous fine tributes in the papers. It grows increasingly evident each year that public appreciation and realization of what you did in France, is growing by leaps and bounds. The immense difficulties of the task and your skill and courage in surmounting them, can never be fully understood, even by those close to you. But time is bringing a bountiful harvest of esteem, admiration and affection.

I am back at the job again, and quite busy—tho very tired of desks and city life. We have a young Gordon setter, and I long for a generous reservation with quail and turkey, like Benning.

Our Illinois division commander, Keehn, got smashed up in a motor accident in July, lost his right arm in August and is still struggling for strength and relaxed nerves which will permit him to get some peaceful sleep. He is very pathetic. With my most affectionate regards   Faithfully yours,

                                                                G. C. Marshall

Saw Cameron Forbes two weeks ago. He looks well.

LC/J. J. Pershing Papers (General Correspondence); H

1. Marshall assumed that Pershing was referring to General Malin Craig, who had become army chief of staff on October 2, as "Chief." Pershing, however, was referring to the previous chief of staff, General Douglas MacArthur.

To Major Benjamin F. Caffey, Jr.   October 25, 1935
                                                                [Chicago, Illinois]

My dear Caffey: I was much interested in your letter of October 8th regarding the Fourth Army CPX.[1] What you say is much what I saw in New Jersey September a year ago. As a matter of fact, I have had to be increasingly careful in expressing my views, because they are so antagonistic to what seems to be the thought and practice in the army today. The truth of the matter is, I think you and I had an unusual opportunity to see things in France, over a long enough period of time and through a sufficient variation of situations, to give us a little bit different viewpoint than the average officer. I recall that during the Meuse-Argonne I found my ideas at decided variance from the ideas of most people, and I still find them so.

This question of the liaison at the front, or transmission of information to the rear, has been a special point I have been taking up with the 33d Division this year in preparing for the army maneuvers to be held in this Corps Area next summer. In our maneuvers last summer, in which we had skeleton division staffs on both sides, they followed very much the practice of the First Division at Soisson—with you in an advanced CP, to keep in better touch with what was going on. Also, I had them follow the practice I used to use at Souilly—that is, sending someone to find out what was really going on, and, in particular, to find out if the orders and plans of the Division were practical and could be really carried out.

I know if I have a division in war, I will have around me a group of three or four young officers and about ten sergeants—the latter accomplished communication experts—whose sole business in life will be to keep me informed as to what is actually going on. I know of no other way to meet the situation which is bound to arise, and will be greatly exaggerated in mobile warfare situations, which we have never yet experienced.

I declined an invitation to go to Santa Fe with the National Guard Convention delegates, though I went to Nashville last year. Possibly you went along with your Nebraska people.

With warm regards to Mrs. Caffey and yourself,   Faithfully yours,

GCMRL/G. C. Marshall Papers (Illinois National Guard)

1. Caffey wrote that the Command Post Exercise was "discouraging, indeed, most discouraging, because it resulted in straight frontal attacks for three days or until the Army itself made an envelopment of the enemy north flank with a mechanized cavalry brigade and a motorized infantry brigade; it was discouraging because logistically the movements ordered were impracticable; it was discouraging because of the immense amount of paper work involved." Moreover, Caffey wrote, "I have become rather a 'nut' on the question of commanders getting information of their subordinate units. We know what a difficult time we had in the World War and if it were difficult then, what will it be in a war of movement?" (Caffey to Marshall, October 8, 1935, GCMRL/G. C. Marshall Papers [Illinois National Guard].)

To Major Neil S. Edmond[1]   November 7, 1935
[Chicago, Illinois]

Dear Captain Edmond: I read your letter of November 6th with considerable interest, and glad to note what you are doing.

I will look into the question regarding more trucks for the Service Company in Decatur.[2] Incidentally, you speak of their specializing in motor transport training as much as the gasoline will permit. The greater part of the training does not require the expenditure of gasoline; the officers must be theoretically up on all convoy procedure, as well as securing and issuing rations in the field; the non-commissioned officers must understand all the principles in connection with convoys and maintenance, must be trained in special map reading, to follow routes at night, etc., each one of these companies must be able to function perfectly under campaign conditions next summer, otherwise a lot of the men are going hungry, and this means a great deal of theoretical training.

There is something I would like you to do. While I was in Decatur I looked about the city to find the best open ground to stage a brigade problem, including artillery, etc.—as a matter of fact, it would have to be a Division set-up involving employment of the down-state brigade. I found what seemed to be suitable ground along Lake Decatur. What I want is favorable country close to the city, of which there is a geological or other map showing topography. On this I propose to lay out a problem to be solved by the 65th Brigade Headquarters, and, in turn, based on their solutions, by the 129th and 130th field officers. We will bring artillery into this, possibly engineers and certainly air service. After the work is gotten down to include the regimental commanders and staffs, and the brigade headquarters has received the orders of the artillery regiment supporting them, I hope to arrange for a concentration of the down-state field officers, and plans and training officers at Decatur. If they reach there with two hours left of daylight, it will be possible to go over the actual ground, then return to the armory and make such alterations in their theoretical solution as the ground seems to indicate. After dinner we would go into the critique and some special talks by artillery and air officers.

Do not advertise this proposition, because I do not wish to have it talked about until I have Colonel Culbertson's assent,[3] and I do not wish to take it up with him until I have the problem, and I do not wish to send out the problem until I have the air service take photographs, etc. After you have located the ground that seems best to you, please make a draft of the situation to meet the above.

Am glad you like Decatur.   Faithfully yours,

GCMRL/G. C. Marshall Papers (Illinois National Guard)

1. Edmond, graduate of the Infantry School's Company Officers' Course in 1922 and the Advanced Course in 1930, had been promoted to major on August 1, 1935. He was stationed at Peoria as senior instructor for the 130th Infantry.

2. Major Edmond was on an inspection tour and reported that the Service Company in Decatur requested three more trucks. (Edmond to Marshall, November 6, 1935, GCMRL/G. C. Marshall Papers [Illinois National Guard].)

3. Colonel Albert L. Culbertson commanded the 130th Infantry headquarters at Delavan, Illinois.

To Major Truman Smith[1]   December 16, 1935
                                                            [Chicago, Illinois]

Dear Smith: The little booklet came a few days ago and much surprised me. I
have not yet found anyone who can read German script, so I can only guess at
the introduction. But I will have it translated shortly. What brought about this
translation? I am curious to know, but I imagine you had a hand in it. In any
event, I very much appreciate your sending me the result.[2]

I suppose you and Mrs. Smith will have a delightful Christmas season in
Berlin. It has been a long time since I have seen you and I look back with many
delightful memories to our gatherings three or four years ago. I understand my
old house has been torn down so no trace of that is left.

In your note you speak of that being the hardest job you ever tackled. I would
be interested to know just what your work consists of other than the formalities
which you are obliged to keep up with. I would also be interested to get your
reaction to the present situation, if that is not a dangerous thing for you to
comment on.

With Christmas greetings to both of you from Mrs. Marshall and me, and our
very best wishes for you in the New Year.   Faithfully yours,

GCMRL/G. C. Marshall Papers (Illinois National Guard)

1. Smith, an instructor at the Infantry School when Marshall was assistant commandant,
had reported for duty in August, 1935, as military attache at the United States Embassy in
Berlin. See Smith's reply of January 2, 1936, below.

2. *Infanterie im Kampf* [*Infantry in Battle*] had been published in a two-volume paperback
edition, part of a series of works on military subjects, by Ludwig Voggenreiter Verlag of
Potsdam. "This pamphlet sells for about 40¢ in Germany. I think it is a far better policy to
publish books like this in a cheap edition than in our expensive $3.00 edition which are above
the strength of so many lieutenants." (Smith to Marshall, November 16, 1935, GCMRL/G. C.
Marshall Papers [Illinois National Guard].)

From General John J. Pershing   December 16, 1935
Personal   Washington, D.C.

Dear Marshall: It was very nice to get your letter of November 29th, but I am
not going west through Chicago at this season. My sister is here and she and I
start tomorrow for Arizona, by motor, going down through Virginia, Tennessee,
Arkansas, etc. I thank you very much for the invitation just the same, and am
sorry that I shall not see you.

I do hope that things will come out our way before many months of the New Year have passed, but there is no telling what may happen. It might not be so easy to overturn an established practice of appointing dead timber to the higher positions. However, I had a long talk on this subject with M.C.¹ the other day and he holds exactly my opinion of the absurdity of such a policy. Whether or not he will be able to change it, I do not know. I do know, however, that he is strong for you, and if it is at all possible something will be done. All this, of course, is very confidential. Always affectionately yours,

John J. Pershing

GCMRL/G. C. Marshall Papers (Pentagon Office, Selected)

1. Chief of Staff General Malin Craig.

To MAJOR WALTER S. WOOD   December 20, 1935
                                            [Chicago, Illinois]

Dear Wood: I have just received your letter with further comments regarding the GUARDSMAN. I am very glad to find out how well things have gone.¹

As to the advertising proposition, I think Colonel Davis will receive a letter in the next day or so, proposing that he select an individual to function as advertising solicitor in the southern part of the State on the basis of receiving 25% of collections. We can manage the extra space required by increase of advertising, and I agree with you that if your people are active in getting something for the paper and also seeing activities of that region mentioned in the paper, interest will be stimulated.

Incidentally, you seem to be something of a writer, and I know you have had quite an experience in the National Guard. You must have some positive ideas as to the most efficient and *expeditious* method of winter training for the National Guard. If you have any such idea, I wish you would put it in concrete form so we might publish it in the GUARDSMAN.

I feel at the present time we are still stumbling around trying to find a satisfactory method for training infantry regiments.

The artillery scheme is pretty well cut out and the nature of their service in the field is along such precise lines, in a manner of speaking, that their training system seems quite satisfactory. The same applies to the engineers, medical troops, and even to the special troops. But when it comes to the infantry, I think we are pretty much of a flat fizzle and it is up to the regular officers to devise a more efficient method for producing a genuine combat team.

I spent July in camp with the three artillery regiments and I have seen their work at other times. I followed the Engineers pretty closely and have seen quite a bit of the Medical troops; and when I compare infantry communications with artillery communications, and infantry one pounder and trench mortar technique with artillery gun technique, I am appalled at the contrast. Even more depressing is the contrast between an artillery regimental team and the infantry regimental team. In the infantry they understand the initial deployment and the message center technique and a little about communications; but when it comes to coordinating the special weapons, as well as knowing how to use them in connection with advancing infantry, when it comes to knowing how rear units are led forward, how communications are intended, how effective artillery support is actually secured—weaknesses are tragic. I think this is largely our fault, because I see the same weakness in regular infantry regiments.

I am talking very frankly here, so this letter must be confidential, but am concerned to find a beginning to the solution which I know does not consist of merely learning to recite combat principles.

Think this over.   Faithfully yours,

GCMRL/G. C. Marshall Papers (Illinois National Guard)

1. Wood, a Regular Army instructor with the 130th Infantry, wrote to Marshall on December 11 to pledge the regiment's closer cooperation with the *Illinois Guardsman*. He also inclosed a copy of a letter he had written to the regiment's officers encouraging them to support the magazine and to supply it with information and pictures.

To GENERAL JOHN J. PERSHING   December 27, 1935
                                              Chicago, Illinois

My dear General: Your Xmas wire was received and gave us much pleasure. I was uncertain as to how quickly you would make the trip, so delayed my letter until I knew where you were—and I am guessing that you are at the Arizona Inn, as usual.

I hope you and Miss May had a restful journey, if there is such a thing, and that you reached Tucson in good shape. I envy you that mild winter climate, for it is very cold here, and the streets are glassy and the pavements alternating between snow and ice.

I suppose you saw the "makes", published on Xmas morning. Naturally, I was disappointed after the intimation in your letter from Paris. But your note from Washington prepared me for what happened.[1] I had been told by McCoy last spring that General Craig had protested to the Secretary of War in the fall of 1934 against the type of men being promoted and had named me as the first man to be promoted. For this reason the disappointment was a little greater than it might otherwise have been. Every one of these men just made was junior to me—in position—in France. And, as a matter of fact, most of the brigadiers of the past six years were also in more subordinate positions in the A.E.F. The man I relieved in the Meuse-Argonne was promoted years ago, and my principal assistant was made a major general six years back.[2] I have possessed myself in patience, but now I'm fast getting too old to have any future of importance in the army. This sounds pessimistic, but an approaching birthday—Dec. 31st—rather emphasizes the growing weakness of my position.

Our entire family was together Xmas, the first time since 1931, and we had a gay and noisy time, with a house full of young people.

Katherine had a telegram the other day from Ann Clews, announcing her marriage, that day, to Blumenthal. Yesterday she had a letter from Ann in which she referred to meeting you in Paris. She was visiting Katherine when she became engaged to Clews.[3]

McCoy and I have been playing some squash racquets this winter, and are starting on indoor tennis next week. Exercise is a problem in the city, though my two mile walk to the office—and home again—helps a little.

Dawes has been having Saturday lunch parties at the Chicago Club for eight or ten, featuring any interesting person passing through town. There have been some quite interesting discussions. We are going out to his house for a formal party New Years night. He seems in high spirits, so I suppose financial matters have cleared up a bit.

This is too long a letter and I hope has not bored you.

With affectionate regards and all good wishes for the New Year to Miss May and yourself,   Faithfully yours,

G. C. Marshall

LC/J. J. Pershing Papers (General Correspondence); H

   1. Marshall refers to Pershing's letters of October 4 and December 16 printed above.
   2. See Marshall to Pershing, November 19, 1934, above.
   3. In 1926, Mary Ann Payne of Baltimore, Maryland, had married James B. Clews. In 1935, she married banker George Blumenthal, who had residences in New York City and in Paris.

FROM MAJOR TRUMAN SMITH   January 2, 1936
                                                          Berlin, [Germany]

My dear Colonel Marshall: I had nothing whatever to do with the translation of *Infantry in Battle*. I sent it to you primarily to indicate to you the importance which foreign nations gave to our Benning work. So far as I know, it is the only American work on pure tactics which has ever been translated into German. The book has received high praise from German critics and these criticisms will appear translated at an early date in the Infantry Journal.

You say in your letter you wonder what our work consists of other than formalities. I assure you that the formalities are many, very trying and very boring. They are rather, however, the impediments to work rather than the work itself. The German military expansion is the greatest which the world has ever seen in time of peace. The most powerful if not the largest army and air force in Europe is coming into existence under a strict veil of secrecy. Piercing this veil is proving a difficult task, particularly as the Germans are not furnishing us information in a lump form. We have to dig out each detail bit by bit.

I am fortunate in a very able assistant: Captain James C. Crockett, an infantry officer who was formerly General Preston Brown's aide. He is a real soldier of great ability and capable of the hardest work.

We know already of 31 new types of organization and some 50 new weapons. We are trying to prepare thorough studies of between 10 and 20 pages on each new type of unit in which we present in war college study form the weapons, organization and tactics of each new unit. In each case we visit one of these new types of units for several days, consolidate our personal experiences with the German tactical textbooks on the subjects, and prepare a thorough report which is not only of value to G-2 but which can be used in the service schools. In the last two months we have finished about five and we hope to complete 20 or 25 during 1936.

I have long been very disgusted at the trivial contents of most of the reports received by G-2 from Military Attaches, and am trying my best to set out on new paths. So far the War Department seems very pleased. I hope we can continue to please them.

The military changes here are so profound and so numerous that we have, I am sure, two years more work ahead of us before things get down to normal. When that time comes, I shall apply to come home.

Here are some of the interesting military developments of Germany:

1. The creation of three armored divisions with a total of some 2500 new, speedy and powerful tanks organized into 9 tank regiments.

2. The new motorized rifle regiments.

3. The motorized reconnaissance battalion.

4. The corps and divisional reconnaissance regiments.

5. The motor bicycle companies.

6. The "infantry accompanying" batteries. (a 75^M Howitzer)

7. The 200 or more new anti-tank companies, each equipped with 9 new type armor piercing 37 mm. guns.

8. The radio telephone for infantry artillery liaison.

9. The new and extraordinary 2 cm. anti-aircraft machine guns which I think are the best thing of their sort in the world.

10. The practical abolition of the cavalry.

11. The adoption of the Kampfgruppe: a regiment of infantry and a battalion of field artillery, as the essential battle tactical unit.

12. The abolition of the field gun and its replacement by the 105 mm. howitzer as the standard field piece.

These are but a few of the many military changes coming out of Germany.

By next fall the peace army of about 600,000 men should be ready. Several years, however, will be required before the reserve units are organized, trained and equipped.

As the army is still coming into being, I do not look for any aggressive policy by Germany until the work is finished, and that will not be until about 1939. Germany is preserving strict neutrality between Italy and the League in the Abyssinian dispute.

Major von Schell has become one of the very noted instructors at the German War Academy. The Chief of the General Staff, General Beck, told me the other day that he considered Major von Schell one of the half-dozen finest tactical instructors of the German Army. He seems to have grabbed off for himself about the finest job open to an officer of his length of service: that of operations officer of the new German armored corps (tank corps). He will be transferred to this post in June. He remains a devoted friend of America and is usually detached to accompany any American officer who comes to Berlin. He has written an article on anti-tank tactics which will appear in the Infantry Journal in the spring.

The government here is an astounding combination of good sense, nonsense, brutality and ultra-militarism. No German whom you meet likes it, but it is nevertheless all-powerful. Inasmuch as this government will shortly be backed by one of if not the most powerful army in the world, I look for eventual trouble. Germany is either going to expand in Eastern Europe or the western nations are going to have to stop it. From the way Europe looks now, it wouldn't surprise me at all to find France and England giving Germany a free hand to help herself to Russian territory. Stopping her will cost just about 3,000,000 men. The strength of Germany's position is that she intends to leave France and England strictly alone and she is absolutely respecting the Rhineland neutral zone.

This letter from its contents I beg you to hold confidential.

I am trying in my new job to remain a soldier and to do the best I can in a very difficult situation.

I hope you will get hold from G-2 some of our reports, read them and send me a letter of criticism. I particularly ask you if you would get hold of our reports on the Silesian maneuvers (No. 14,281), the Anti-Tank Company (No. 14,336), and the Minenwerfer Company (No. 14,327). I know G-2 will be glad to let you have them.

With best wishes,   Sincerely,

Truman Smith

GCMRL/G. C. Marshall Papers (Illinois National Guard)

To Major General Roy D. Keehn   January 18, 1936
                                                 [Chicago, Illinois]

My dear General: Roy was just in to see me and spoke of a wire he had received stating that you were improving daily.[1] This is good news, indeed, and I do hope you find relaxation in the Florida sun. Up here there has been little or no sun—sort of a general gloom, and today a snow blizzard seems to be starting up.

General Hammond has been in Washington all week struggling against the Quartermaster General's formal turn down of that heating installation—based on a very adverse report of the civilian engineer who had been causing the trouble.

Lawton came in two days ago, much pleased with his promotion.[2] He said he had wired you the night before. That came as a surprise to me, though, of course, I knew from what you had told me, that he had been working hard to get it.

The 8th Infantry was inspected last Tuesday night. They got a very complete and thorough going over. The inspection of all ordnance by the members of the Ordnance Company was a most successful innovation. The Ordnance fellows were pleased to be in the picture and what they did will be productive of good results—for the regiment and for them.

Colonel Warfield seemed much pleased with the affair, and his people made a creditable showing.[3] The Division Staff put up a much more workmanlike job than last year, and got in their reports the same evening.

The 202nd will be inspected next Tuesday, and I understand they have been making large preparations.

The final choice of Chief of the National Guard Bureau came as a complete surprise. I understand he is an excellent man—though I do not recall having met him. Anyway, you are well out of it.[4]

Governor Horner seems to be making quite a fight. I understand he has a pretty good organization set up in all the down state counties and is assured of their strong support. Boyle told me that the Lake County Chairman told him that Lake County would solidly support Horner, and he thought the other counties would do the same.[5] However, I am in ignorance in such matters, and have little idea of what is actually going on.

General McCoy has made frequent inquiries regarding you. He fully understood your final decision in the matter of the National Guard Bureau.

Mrs. Marshall is well, and she and I have been having long walks in the snow, and in the Forest Preserve south of Des Plaines, on Sunday mornings, exercising an Irish setter puppy—five months old.

With affectionate regards,   Faithfully yours,

GCMRL/G. C. Marshall Papers (Illinois National Guard)

1. Captain Roy D. Keehn, Jr., commanded the elite Black Horse Troop (Troop E) of the 106th Cavalry.

2. On January 14, Colonel Samuel T. Lawton, 122nd Field Artillery, was promoted to brigadier general and assigned to command the 58th Field Artillery Brigade.

3. Colonel William J. Warfield commanded the Eighth Infantry headquarters in Chicago.

4. Keehn had been seriously considered for the post of chief of the National Guard Bureau, but he decided against it. (Malin Craig to Marshall, January 6, 1936, GCMRL/G. C. Marshall Papers [Illinois National Guard].) Major General Albert H. Blanding, commander of the

Thirty-first Division in Florida, became chief of the National Guard Bureau on January 31, 1936.

5. Henry Horner was reelected governor of Illinois for the 1937–41 term. Captain Leo M. Boyle served with the Quartermaster Section at Thirty-third Division headquarters in Chicago.

MEMORANDUM FOR GENERAL McCOY

January 31, 1936
[Chicago, Illinois]

I am sending you, herewith, the basic instructions and preliminary situations for a so-called War Game, which has been enroute since the fall. As both National Guard and Reserve units are involved, I felt that you would be interested in the layout, which comes to a final head on Sunday, March 1st.

I have not enclosed maps, because I did not think you would care to laboriously study the dispositions at this time, but I hope you will run your eye over these papers and get a general idea of the procedure being followed. The area involved is in the vicinity of the Arlington Race Track and southeast of Des Plaines. As it is close to Chicago many officers and some times staffs, have visited the terrain.

Since these memorandums were distributed the various solutions have been received, and the resulting situations from initial contacts—principally cavalry action and artillery fires—have been communicated to the commanders concerned. This procedure has passed through three or four phases already, and the cavalry contacts have grown from patrol actions to a more general engagement between two Red squadrons and a portion of the Blue regiment. The commanders of the reserve infantry organizations have all become involved—though not their troops—as their preliminary reconnaissances carried them partially into the zone of the cavalry activities, and into areas under the Red artillery preparation fire. By mail and by telephone these successive phases have been handled, until we have almost reached the point of infantry contacts.

Colonel Fox, at the Planetarium, commands the Reserve infantry brigade, and seems to have become quite excited over the situations in which he found himself while on his supposed early morning reconnaissance.[1]

GCMRL/G. C. Marshall Papers (Illinois National Guard)

1. Astronomer Philip Fox was the director of Adler Planetarium.

TO LIEUTENANT COLONEL FRANK E. LOWE[1]

February 13, 1936
[Chicago, Illinois]

My dear Colonel Lowe: I have just received your letter of February 11th notifying me of your recommendation for my reappointment on the Advisory

Committee of the Mershon Fund. I appreciate the compliment and the distinction and am happy to accept.

When first made a member of this Committee I was not aware of whom my sponsor had been. As a matter of fact, I thought my appointment had come through the Secretary of War; it was a long time before I learned that my name had been proposed by the head of the Reserve Officers Association.

I was rather dubious about the matter, as I felt that a professional soldier would labor under a considerable disadvantage in the work of the Committee. I still think it would be much better if I were not in the Regular Army, because everything that I may do or say must bear the taint of probable professional prejudice on my part.

I have genuinely enjoyed my work with the Committee, and have derived a considerable amount of satisfaction from what has been accomplished. I have been particularly gratified to find the War Department becoming more acutely conscious of the pros and cons involved in the attitude of college faculties regarding the ROTC, and its instructors.

The regional ROTC conferences attended by large numbers of distinguished educators, were of particular interest to me, and I am inclined to think they did me more good than any one activity of the Committee. I presided over one at Lehigh University in 1933 and another at Purdue in 1934, and regret that we have not been able to stage one in the South and one in the Far West.

With thanks again for your courtesy in proposing my name,   Faithfully yours,

GCMRL/G. C. Marshall Papers (Illinois National Guard)

1. Lowe, a member of the Civilian Military Education Fund's National Committee, was president of the Reserve Officers Association of the United States.

To MAJOR GENERAL ROY D. KEEHN   February 26, 1936
                                                [Chicago, Illinois]

My dear General: I have just finished reading your letter of February 23d (per secretary Kay Keehn[1]—to whom congratulations are extended). Also I have just finished telephone conversation with Corps Area Headquarters and learned that Governor Horner finally has answered General McCoy's telegram of ten days ago requesting his concurrence in the date for the maneuvers.

The adjustment of dates and places has been one of exceeding difficulty. In the first place, and this is most confidential, the Governor of Ohio declined to permit his troops to participate. General McCoy rode along with this impasse for two months, keeping the matter quiet and endeavoring to find out just what the trouble was. While he has not told me, I understand indirectly, that pressure in

Ohio came from the merchants and other business interests connected with Camp Perry, who did not want to lose their summer "take." Finally, however, at the last meeing of the Adjutants General of Ohio, Indiana, Kentucky and West Virginia, which General McCoy attended at Columbus, Ohio, the Adjutant General of Ohio told him that the Governor acquiesced in the participation of the Ohio troops. This I understand—again most indirectly—was due to the tremendous howl that went up from the troops when they found out they were going to be left out. All this has been kept entirely quiet, and I don't think anything is known of it outside of Ohio—which saves embarrassment.

After a long discussion with all the various states, an adjustment was finally reached as to dates. Each Governor was then approached by General McCoy by telegram to secure a definite statement of acquiescence. The wire to Governor Horner reached Springfield the day he left for Florida and his people there would not forward anything to him in Florida. Since his return we could get no answer out of him. Meanwhile, all the other states were wiring Corps Area to make the announcement so they could go ahead with their plans—and particularly so they could inform employers the period for which summer leaves would be desired for the Guard personnel. Also, Washington began pressing General McCoy for an announcement so they could go ahead with their part of the affair. I got Regan,[2] who was in Rockford night before last with a council meeting, to talk to the Governor over the telephone. As a matter of fact, the Governor called him for something else. Regan said he could get no where with the Governor in an understanding of the situation. Yesterday noon he went to Springfield and said he would try to make the picture clear to the Governor and get an answer out of him for General McCoy. This morning Corps Area Headquarters tells me they received letter from General Black conveying the Governor's agreement to the date mentioned.

The training period will commence August 8th. The troops of the Sixth Corps—32nd and 33d Divisions, and a skeleton regular division, will concentrate close to Lake Michigan between Holland and South Haven. After a preliminary period of training within each division, the force will move eastward. The actual details of the maneuver movements have not been sufficiently worked out for a final conclusion to be arrived, but this will now be carried to a head very rapidly and announcements should follow shortly.

I understand the Army Appropriation Bill has cleared the House and will shortly be taken up by the Senate. It carries the necessary amount for these maneuvers; very small, but just what the budget authorities authorized.

I suppose you have been interested in reading about General Hagood's relief from command, following his testimony before a committee of Congress. I notice quite a drastic editorial in the Chicago Tribune on the subject this morning.[3]

The staff had a prolonged meeting Monday night, working out final details of their preparation for the War Game finale on Sunday, March 1st. I think this experiment, and that they will get on Sunday, is going to prove very helpful next summer. This is the first time the Division Staff has carried out all its functions in such an affair, and their interest has been stimulated by the fact that they have an enemy of unknown strength composed of organized reserve units. These last will function in the War Game Sunday. Old Colonel Fox, who presides at the Planetarium, is one of the reserve commanders and has gotten quite excited over the situations in which he has found himself during the preliminary map problem phase of the Game.

It turned very warm here Sunday, and was almost balmy yesterday. Today it is slightly cold but a soft snow has turned into a disagreeable drizzle. Am awfully sorry that you are having such hard luck with the weather but the curse seems to spread over the whole United States. My sister was at Palm Beach for a month in January and February, and could go in bathing only three times. Then she stopped for a visit in North Carolina and struck snow and sleet up there.

If I were you I wouldn't worry about how well you will feel up to the proposition of camp life during maneuvers. There is plenty of time to settle that next June or even July. Don't concern yourself about it now. Your only thought should be concentrated on getting thoroughly strong again, and I am hoping that business considerations have not troubled you too seriously.

With affectionate regards,   Faithfully,

GCMRL/G. C. Marshall Papers (Illinois National Guard); T

1. Roy D. Keehn's daughter.

2. Colonel Lawrence V. Regan was chief of staff at Thirty-third Division headquarters in Chicago.

3. In testifying before a House of Representatives appropriations subcommittee on December 17, 1935, Major General Johnson Hagood complained of the difficulties the army had in maintaining quarters for its troops at a time when there was a great deal of money for Works Progress Administration projects. Referring to the four billion dollars Congress appropriated for the W.P.A. the previous year, Hagood said, "I call it stage money because you can pass it around but you cannot get anything out of it in the end." He added that "much of the stage money is being wasted." Hagood's testimony was published on February 10, 1936. The War Department relieved him of command of the Eighth Corps Area on February 21. Restored to command in April, he retired at the end of May. (*New York Times*, February 11, February 25, and April 14, 1936.) The *Chicago Daily Tribune* editor observed that Hagood had broken the Roosevelt Administration's rule that "the greater the truth, the greater the offense." ("A General is Sent Home," February 26, 1936.)

To Roger L. Scaife   March 16, 1936
                                                                   [Chicago, Illinois]

Dear Roger: Thank you for your detailed letter of March 11th regarding IN-FANTRY IN BATTLE and BATTLE LEADERSHIP. As you say, these books are not a high standard publication; however, our problem has been to get them out as cheaply as possible in order to keep the price down. Both books were printed at Benning, though INFANTRY IN BATTLE was published through the financing of the Infantry Association in Washington.

I realized when I sent them to you that neither was suitable for general sale. What I wanted was for you to glance at some of the chapters of INFANTRY IN BATTLE that you might get some idea of how I eventually managed to get into print the meat of the monographs, of which I spoke to you so long ago. BATTLE LEADERSHIP I had printed, though my name is not mentioned, because the contents represented a very clever presentation of some of the imponderables that play such an important part in battle.[1] Von Schell, the author, was a student officer at Benning, though a veteran of 265 battles in the German Army. Through him I came to know von Blomberg, the present minister of war for Germany.

INFANTRY IN BATTLE has gotten remarkable reviews from the most prominent German military critics and, as I told you, they translated it into German, in Tauchnitz form[2]—a compliment they have paid practically no other army that we know of—so evidently there was some merit to the manner presenting the matter.

I hope your business is booming this winter and that Mrs. Scaife and you are in the best of health. Two years ago we were all at Thomasville [Georgia], and I wish we were there now.

With warmest regards to you both.   Faithfully yours,

GCMRL/G. C. Marshall Papers (Illinois National Guard)
1. Adolf von Schell, *Battle Leadership: Some Personal Experiences of a Junior Officer of the German Army with Observations on Battle Tactics and the Psychological Reactions of Troops in Campaign* (Fort Benning: Benning Herald, [1933]).
2. The Tauchnitz family of printers in Leipzig, Germany, had published numerous highly respected, inexpensive, paperback books of literature since the mid-nineteenth century.

TO COLONEL CAMPBELL B. HODGES[1]   March 16, 1936
[Chicago, Illinois]

My dear Hodges: Spalding's letter with your note has just arrived.[2] You were very good to mention my name in writing to Spalding and he was most generously flattering. What you quote of Mr. Dern's remarks regarding the two of us was naturally very interesting to me, and I am further indebted to you for mentioning my name to the Secretary, which I know you must have done. Such loyal and generous friends as you have been, are pretty rare in this world, and I appreciate tremendously your continuous interest in my welfare. The truth of the matter is, you are so busy thinking about others that you omit all consideration of yourself. Your career, particularly these last ten years, has been increasingly conspicuous.

I hope we will be closer together in our next change of station. Faithfully yours,

GCMRL/G. C. Marshall Papers (Illinois National Guard)

1. Hodges (U.S.M.A., 1903) commanded the Fourteenth Infantry at Fort Davis, Canal Zone. He had recently returned from detached service (September, 1935, to January, 1936) as aide to Secretary of War George H. Dern, who was attending the inauguration of the Commonwealth Government of the Philippine Islands. Hodges's letter stated that the secretary had said several times that a promotion system that had not promoted George Marshall and George Spalding (U.S.M.A., 1901) must be wrong. "I told Mr. Dern that in my opinion you [Marshall] should be made a B.G. at once, and that when next vacancy for C. of S. occurs your name should be among those considered for the job." (Hodges to Marshall, March 4, 1936, GCMRL/G. C. Marshall Papers [Illinois National Guard].)

2. Spalding told Hodges: "You mention George Marshall. I'm sorry he has not been made. Indeed, I am embarrassed to think that I was selected first, as I think he is one of our very great soldiers. I'll do all I can to see that he does not wait long." (Colonel George R. Spalding to Hodges, February 26, 1936, ibid.) Spalding was promoted to brigadier general on May 14, 1936.

To Brigadier General Robert E. Wood[1]   April 9, 1936
                                                     [Chicago, Illinois]

My dear General: The other evening at General McCoy's you made a very interesting statement regarding similarity of your administrative problems with those experienced in the Army. Also, you collaborated a little on the fact that business organization was more or less based on military organization in procedure. I thought what you said, and particularly your reference to daily comparisons in your company, were unusually interesting.

Would you favorably consider writing a little article on this subject to be published in the ILLINOIS GUARDSMAN? Anything from one page up would be gratefully received, and I am sure would be of great interest and even greater practical value. Many of the officers in the Guard feel that military procedure of command and staff is a thing apart from all business practices; and, as a matter of fact, it is one of their greatest weaknesses. For this reason, I think a few words from you would have an important effect.[2]   Faithfully yours,

GCMRL/G. C. Marshall Papers (Illinois National Guard)

1. Wood had retired from the army in 1919 and moved to Chicago where he worked for Montgomery Ward and Company (1919–24) and then for Sears, Roebuck and Company. He became president of Sears on January 1, 1928.

2. No reply to this letter was found in the Marshall papers, and no article by Wood appeared in the *Illinois Guardsman*.

To Colonel John L. Homer   April 15, 1936
                                                           [Chicago, Illinois]

Dear Homer: I see you have been assigned to the office of the chief of your branch.[1] I hope this is an agreeable arrangement; also, that the War College in September is still a possibility. Let me hear from you.

We are packing up preparatory to moving into a furnished house on the Monroe place adjacent to the Dunham Woods Riding Club—forty miles out, near St. Charles.[2] We transfer May 1st and I will become a commuter. I don't like this last much, but the outdoor life in the spring, early summer and fall makes it worth while. Mrs. Marshall and Molly will probably go up to the north woods for July and August, if I can ever persuade Mrs. Marshall. She has no idea of Illinois back country heat in the middle of the summer.

I hope Mrs. Homer is finding life pleasant and interesting in Washington. We often talk of you both.   Faithfully yours,

GCMRL/G. C. Marshall Papers (Illinois National Guard)

1. Homer (U.S.M.A., 1911), formerly an instructor with the Illinois National Guard in Chicago (1929-35), and, at the time Marshall wrote, a student at the Army Industrial College in Washington, D.C., was assigned to the Office of the Chief of Coast Artillery effective July 1, 1936.

2. The Marshalls had been living in an apartment at 190 East Chestnut Street in Chicago. They were moving to a cottage—"ideally situated on an extensive and elaborately organized farm-estate" (Marshall to Major Harold E. Potter, May 27, 1936, GCMRL/G. C. Marshall Papers [Illinois National Guard])—at the White Gate Farm near St. Charles, Illinois. William S. Monroe, a mechanical engineer in Chicago, resided at the farm during the summer.

From General John J. Pershing   May 26, 1936
                                                         [Washington, D.C.]

My dear Marshall: Following up our discussion, I had a conversation here in Washington after my arrival and found that you are positively and definitely on the slate for September. I said that I, of course, realized that you would be, but wondered why it could not have been arranged for you to receive the first appointment instead of being grouped with a half a dozen others who would be senior to you in rank as they probably are ahead of you in the relative standing now. I doubt very much whether this will be done, but it is a possibility. In any event the others to be promoted at that time are so much older than you are that they will probably not stand very much in your way.[1]

I regret that the powers that be could not have seen their way to do this earlier, but with the number of years you have to serve I am sure that you are destined to hold a very high place on the list of general officers before you reach the age of sixty-four.

Please remember me to Mrs. Marshall, and with kindest regards, believe me, always, Yours affectionately,

LC/J. J. Pershing Papers (General Correspondence)

1. The six men to be promoted on October 1 would be ranked as brigadier generals in the same order as their relative positions on the colonel's promotion list. In the April 20, 1936, *Army List and Directory*, these men had the following list positions: George P. Tyner (#157, age 60); William H. Wilson (#179, age 58); Robert McC. Beck, Jr. (#223, age 57); Walter Krueger (#257, age 55); Asa L. Singleton (#258, age 60); George C. Marshall (#294, age 55).

To General John J. Pershing   June 2, 1936
                                                   Chicago, Illinois

Dear General: Thanks a lot for your letter of May 26th and for your continued efforts in my behalf. I do appreciated the trouble you have taken and feel very grateful. I am glad to learn that I am to be in on the September appointments, but naturally am sorry that I have to land so seriously blocked by juniority on the list. Your effort to prevent this is all the more appreciated for that reason.

Your Arlington speech was received and I was very glad to have it, as the press quotations out here were not at length, though they gave you a good write-up.[1] The news reel of you, with the ladies at the "cake ceremony" was excellent of you, and your "asides" went over very effectively with the movie audience.

By the way, I have a favor to ask. When you are handing out diplomas at West Point you will see a cadet named Clarence Gooding, about 120 in standing. I would greatly appreciate your making some personal comment to this young fellow when you hand him his diploma. He was my office orderly at Benning— for only a few months. Having just enlisted, I was greatly impressed with his efficiency, bearing and general intelligence. I found out that he had been trying for West Point and had had no success. Finally he enlisted for this purpose and was refused permission to join the candidates class of men being coached. Without his knowledge, I wrote to his congressman in Texas and got the promise of an appointment if a vacancy occurred. The first alternate dropped out at the eleventh hour and Gooding received his appointment. The principal failed and Gooding passed. He is a fine boy and would be electrified by a personal word from you.[2]

Mrs. Marshall and I greatly enjoyed seeing you here, or rather, in Evanston. I particularly enjoyed my talk with you Monday morning.   Affectionately, and grateful your,

                                                   G. C. Marshall

LC/J. J. Pershing Papers (General Correspondence); H

1. Pershing had given a speech on Memorial Day (May 30) at Arlington National Cemetery.
2. See Marshall to Gooding, March 20, 1933, above.

To Major General Frank R. McCoy   June 15, 1936
                                                    Chicago, Illinois

Dear General: We miss you and Francis [*Frances*] increasingly as time goes on. Not a day passes without regrets being expressed over your transfer.[1] Keehn was deploring it this morning; the Monroes and the Hammonds were doing the same last evening at our place—also the Mersheys [?].

I have been up in Michigan twice with Gen. Kilbourne—last Wednesday and Friday.[2] They were out with us for the afternoon and dinner, last evening. Ridgeway took Peggy to Washington Friday for an operation this week. He came back this morning. I imagine it is serious.

Our bloodhound Ponty, is enjoying the country more than any of us. He roams free all day, pals with a colt—racing all over a pasture with him most of the day. Molly and I are playing tennis with several agreeable couples. My arm is sore but does not pain seriously.

Thick cream, fresh eggs, strawberries fresh from the vines, and lettuce plucked and eaten within the hour, are country pleasures we are enjoying. We live outside the house. Katherine has painted everything but the grass and trees, and gardens vigorously. I wish you were in St. Charles in that lovely house there. It is too bad, but I hope and suppose that you are deeply and agreeably engaged in New York affairs. Why don't you establish a summer CP on Lake George or Champlain?

    With affectionate regards to you both,   Faithfully yours,

                                                    G. C. Marshall

LC/F. R. McCoy Papers; H

1. McCoy commanded the Second Army and Sixth Corps Area until May 1, 1936, when he was transferred to Governors Island, New York, to command the Second Corps Area.

2. On June 1, 1936, Major General Charles E. Kilbourne (V.M.I., 1894) assumed command of the Second Army and the Sixth Corps Area. During the World War he had served with the Eighty-ninth Division in France (May–October, 1918). Kilbourne had taught at the Army War College (1920-24) and had been assistant chief of staff, War Plans Division (August 24, 1932–February 14, 1935).

Report to the Commanding General,   July 27, 1936
Sixth Corps Area   Chicago, Illinois

Report on the Illinois National Guard for
the fiscal year ending June 30, 1936.

1. In compliance with letter on above subject, from the Commanding General, Sixth Corps Area, dated July 18, 1936 (319.1-2 Gen 80 (20)), the following report is submitted:

a. General condition, particularly with respect to:

(1) *Organization and administration.*

(a) The partial organization of the Quartermaster Regiment, which closely followed the recent issue of new motor vehicles, will materially increase the efficiency with which this new method of transport is handled.

(b) New units of the 123d Field Artillery have been organized, partially equipped, and will go to camp for the first time in August.

(c) The quality of newly commissioned officers has steadily improved, due to more rigid requirements for appointment, prompted by the realization of higher commanders that commissions must be given only to those men whose mental growth would continue rather than end with the receipt of a lieutenant's commission.

(d) Administration throughout the State is generally excellent and was the subject of especially favorable comment in reports on the last annual armory inspection.

(e) Particularly gratifying is the fact that officers generally are more careful in reading and more punctilious in complying with instructions from higher authority. This is a distinct and important advance.

(2) *Command and Training.*

During the past year there has been a marked increase in general efficiency, particularly in the following respects:

(a) Special stress has been placed on cooperation between the various arms and services, and this has resulted in a growing realization of the necessity for team-work and much progress in actually accomplishing it. Staffs have become more thoroughly acquainted with the needs and problems of subordinate units and therefore more thoroughly alive to their own responsibilities in connection with the supervision of the administration, supply and training of these units.

(b) Planned group instruction has replaced the old, careless method of trying to follow a unit schedule without regard to the training progress made by the individuals of the unit. The use of this method develops the latent qualities of leadership in junior officers and NCOs and has done more than anything else toward developing sound, well trained company units.

(c) National Guard officers, exclusively, were used as instructors at the three-day School of Small Arms held in June and the results attained were exceptionally fine. Aside from developing these officers as instructors, this policy, which will be continued, has greatly bolstered the morale of all other National Guard officers. Incidentally, it is at the root of every method for increasing the efficiency of the National Guard.

(3) *Equipment.*

(a) Most of the overcoats, raincoats and shelter halves, although whole, are in unserviceable condition, due to age.

(b) The new .22 calibre machine gun will greatly facilitate the training of machine gun units.

(4) *Housing and Care of Property.*

In several rented armories the arrangements are inadequate, but one new armory is in process of construction, and plans are under way for the construction of enough new armories to replace all of these now considered unsatisfactory.

b. Efficiency as compared to the preceding year:

Much improved, with a sound basis established for even greater improvement. This improvement is believed to be basic and lasting, as it concerns the development of able instructors—commissioned and non-commissioned, and the development of efficient staffs—heretofore a great source of weakness.

c. (1) *Outstanding Strong Points:*

Excellent morale.

Planned Group training.

Staff team-work.

Care of property.

Unit administration.

(2) *Outstanding Weak Points:*

Lack of effective personal supervision of training by regimental and higher commanders.

Knowledge and application of instructional methods.

Large turnover in enlisted personnel. This is due this year to sudden increase of employment (coupled with fear of men of asking any favors), and poor instruction by company officers and non-commissioned officers failing to hold interest—this weakness is rapidly being corrected.

d. Suggestions for Improvement.

(1) *Instructors.*

(a) *Employment:* We have found that wherever instructors work as a group, far better results are obtained than from the continued efforts of a single instructor, week in and week out, with the same organization. Where it has been convenient to assemble instructors, as in Cook County (Chicago), important developments in methods of instruction have been obtained. As a result of this experience, it is planned to utilize this system on a more extended scale during the next training year, treating the instructors more as a faculty to introduce the instructional methods of the special service schools as adapted to National Guard conditions. The instructor's routine work with his regiment will be an additional duty, rather than his principal duty. The main effort will be concentrated on preparing National Guard officers and selected non-commissioned officers to instruct in the manner taught at the special service schools.

(b) *Attitude:* Officers on duty with the National Guard often feel isolated; feel that their efforts are not appreciated; and that they are completely out of touch with their corps in the regular army. Whether there is justification for their state of mind or not, I cannot say; but it merits some consideration. A truly efficient instructor with the National Guard does a great deal of good, both for the Guard and for the regular army. He also becomes something of a specialist in the problem of handling the citizen-soldiers in war time. The mediocre instructor lowers the prestige of the regular army and accomplishes little. The poor or lazy instructor does incalculable harm. The time has come, I believe, to require a very high rating of efficiency for senior details with the National Guard, and, so far as possible, for the details in the lower grades. Incidentally, the average of efficiency of the instructors on duty in Illinois is unusually high; and for that very reason the contrast with the mediocre officer is the more glaring and unfortunate.

(c) *Property Inspections:* The employment of instructors in counting and inspecting property seriously interfered with instructional work, and it is not believed that much of importance was accomplished by these inspections. The state officials conduct a very thorough and satisfactory inspection in Illinois.

(d) *Mileage for Instructors:* The increased allotment of funds for travel by instructors during the past year made it possible to greatly increase the value of the instructor to the state. Even so, officers operated at times at their own personal expense. Lack of funds in previous years limited to a serious degree the effectiveness of the instructors. If it can possibly be avoided there should be no cut in mileage allotments; about a twenty percent increase would be desirable.

(2) *Sergeant-Instructors.*

The present situation as to sergeant-instructors is unsatisfactory. In the first place, there are too many outstanding non-commissioned officers of long service and holding difficult positions, for whom promotion prospects seem well nigh hopeless. It does not seem right that men of special and proven talent, holding very responsible positions, should be held down year after year, while other men, lacking the same ability, are promoted solely because of length of service. I, therefore, recommend that sergeant-instructors be removed from the present promotion list, which includes other men on DEML [Detached Enlisted Men's List], and placed on a separate promotion list, as was formerly the case in this Corps.

The other difficulty refers to training. Sergeant-Instructors who remain for more than four years with the National Guard not only get out of touch with training and administrative developments in the regular army, but what is much more serious, they lose the disciplinary attitude of a soldier of the regular army. Refresher courses are good things, but I would personally prefer to see sergeant-instructors returned—in grade—for at least a year of troop duty with the regular army after four years with the Guard. Whether they would be redetailed as sergeant-instructors could be determined later, but they should *not* be returned to the same state.

(3) *Infantry Communication Units.*

Due to the difficulty of maintaining such small units as infantry battalion headquarters companies and the fact that communications training requires exceptional uniformity, thus making it necessary for the battalion and regimental groups to constantly work together, it is believed that morale and efficiency would be greatly increased if all of the communications personnel of an infantry regiment should be included in one company unit, i.e., the regimental headquarters company.

The increasing importance of communications and the high degree of technical and executive proficiency required of communications officers emphasizes the need for giving those officers rank commensurate with their duties. The regimental communications officer should have the rank of captain and battalion officers the rank of first lieutenant.

Increase in grade or higher specialists ratings should be given to the enlisted communications technicians, particularly radio operators.

(4) *Howitzer Companies* (Infantry).

Several adverse factors, stated below, combine to make the maintenance and training of these units very difficult. Improvement will occur as soon as these handicaps are removed.

(a) The howitzer company is allowed three less sergeants than other line units of the same strength. The bad effect of this condition is particularly noticeable where this company is housed with other units.

(b) The allowance of .45 calibre pistol ammunition is wholly inadequate.

(c) No .22 calibre pistols are provided for indoor pistol practice.

(d) No satisfactory sub-calibre device for indoor firing of the howitzer weapons is provided.

(e) The gunners test is too long drawn out, laborious and complicated, with the result that few men of the unit ever become eligible to actually fire the weapons, even when suitable ranges are provided, which is seldom the case. It may be satisfactory for regular army units, but it is very unsatisfactory for the National Guard.

(5) *Training Supervision.*

Regimental and higher commanders should exercise closer personal supervision of training, and they should show more vigor and initiative in correcting deficiencies. Too much of the burden of recruiting and training is placed on the company commander and too much of the business of fault-finding is left to the instructor.

(6) *Qualification Courses.*

(a) A more satisfactory machine gun qualification course should be devised. The present course, using the .22 calibre machine gun, is too easy and it is not a real test of ability to use the weapon.

(b) More insistence should be placed upon exact compliance with regulations governing record practice. There is a wide variance between States with regard to the degree of adherence to these regulations. Under existing conditions a unit firing a record course in exact compliance with regulations is made to appear inferior by comparison with other units which have been more lax in their observance of the rules, when, as a matter of fact, the very reverse may be true. The truth of this statement has been conclusively demonstrated in this State and I am sure that it can be equally well demonstrated elsewhere. Laxity in this respect does much to lower the integrity of the officer corps with resultant loss of potential combat efficiency. The condition is largely due, in my opinion, to the insistent pressure from higher headquarters for high percentages of qualifications. Until this condition is corrected, I am inclined to oppose further listing of units in order of supposed excellence in target practice.

(7) *Instructional Methods.*

The three-day School of Small Arms conducted in Illinois in 1935 and again in 1936 has tremendously improved the general standard of instruction in infantry weapons. Future schools will stress tactics and other phases of training. However, the field is so large and the need so great that I think that the service schools should be requested to prepare some extension courses particularly adapted to the needs of the National Guard. These courses should cover, at least, all of the basic training subjects and the tactics of small units, and should be especially complete with regard to explanation of instructional methods. In preparing them due consideration should be given to the short time available to the National Guard for preparation and presentation. Also, I think it very important that the officers preparing the courses should have had actual experience on duty with the National Guard.

G. C. Marshall

NA/RG 394 (Sixth Corps Area, Illinois National Guard)

To MAJOR GENERAL FRANK R. McCOY   August 16, 1936
                                                   In bivouac north of
                                                   Allegan [Michigan]

My dear General: As you alone are responsible for my present situation I want you to know that never have I had a more delightfully interesting bit of service in time of peace.

In the first place, the maneuvers are an outstanding, an impressive success. All observers, all officers concerned who knew anything about the Pine Camp and Knox affairs, are loud in their praise.[1] They say this is the first real, modern affair since 1918. It has gone off in splendid fashion, with a maximum of sustained interest and of, almost, wild excitement. The Mechanized Force has been great, and has learned a lot, operating for the first time on an extended front in strange terrain. Rail heads and generals have been captured, desperate situations created, and the National Guard given all of interest they are capable of absorbing.[2]

I started off with a command of my brigade, the 1st Bn. 14th Cav., 2d Bn. 3d F.A., all of the 106th Cavalry, and some loose companies. I also run a dump at the Allegan rail head, with a company as a Q.M. regiment.

We covered the first movement forward of the Corps, with the mechanized reconnaissance elements and the 106th Cavalry acting against my people. On a 17 mile front will [we] stopped all efforts at penetration and captured—without the aide of umpires—8 armored cars and a large bunch of motor cycles. That night my force jumped about [25?] miles, over to the Red side, and the following morning (less the 14th Cav.) attacked the front of the VI Corps moving across the Kalamazoo and into a defensive position. We drove in the heads of their flank columns—I left a 2 mile gap in my center—and prevented them from ever reaching their main line of resistance. Part of my infantry acted like horse cavalry. Palmer struck the flank and rear of the 33d, tore up their rail head and cut a swath through their rear.³ He almost—and should have captured the VI Corps C.P.

The following day was somewhat a repetition, Palmer striking the 32nd Div. with considerable success. I largely confined my attacks to the 33d, but had to be more careful about leaving gaps and deep open flanks—but had no difficulties. Tomorrow I defend a line of lakes and open country against the 32nd, while the 33d moves by truck to Custer. Palmer has promised me (on the QT) a platoon of armored cars and a platoon of tanks. If he delivers, I will strive for a genuine surprise, with a counter attack at the crucial moment—as I also have, for the first time, a decent reserve force, as well as the 14th Cav. with some scout cars. The 106th Cav. is enroute for Custer.

Really, the whole thing has been realistic to a remarkable degree. I am writing this in a granary of a little farm. Our message center is on the porch, the clerks in a wagon shed, and our office in the granary. Radio and cars are concealed under trees. We sleep in the open. Fleets of planes go overhead frequently, but so far no artillery fire has disturbed us. I move in the morning to a school house 2 miles from here.

Friday I tried to maintain our wide gap by personal reconnaissance and posting detachments, and just missed capture on three occasions. Today I learn that two regiments in the 33d had NCOs who know me with red hat bands from prisoners, in our lines trying to capture me—for a $25.⁰⁰ reward. If so, they don't place much of a price on my head.

I wish you could see this affair. It is great fun, and loaded with highly instructive situations. The men I have seen in the Guard are thrilled and morale never higher.

With affectionate regards   Faithfully,

G. C. Marshall

LC/F. R. McCoy Papers; H

1. The Fifth Corps Area maneuvers were held at Fort Knox, Kentucky, August 1-15.
2. The Sixth Corps Area maneuvers between Camp Custer and Allegan, Michigan, involved over twenty-six thousand officers and men divided into the Red Force (enemy) and Blue Force.

Marshall commanded the Twelfth Brigade (Reinforced). Most of his troops maneuvered with the Blue Force, Wednesday, August 12, and part of Thursday, until they joined the Red Force.

3. Colonel Bruce Palmer had been Marshall's friend since they were classmates at Fort Leavenworth's Infantry and Cavalry School and General Staff College (1906–8). During the 1936 maneuvers he commanded the Red Force's mechanized units.

REPORT TO THE COMMANDING GENERAL,   August 21, 1936
SECOND ARMY MANEUVERS   Camp Custer, Michigan

Report of operations, 2nd Army Maneuvers.

1. *a.* The 12th Brigade concentrated at Dunningville, northwest of Allegan, Michigan August 3 to 6, the headquarters on the 3d and the regiments arriving on the 6th. . . .

b. The brigade established a supply dump north of Allegan. . . .[1]

c. During the period August 8th to 12th the regular troops carried out a special training program. The National Guard regiment followed its own schedule.

2. *Maneuvers.*

a. Wednesday, August 12th, the 106th Cavalry left the brigade to join the Red force and the 3d Battalion, 2nd Infantry, reported to the Mechanized force for detached duty. During the afternoon of that day the brigade and attached troops took up the Blue covering position previously ordered. All were in place and communications established by 8:00 P.M., except the cavalry which was ordered to leave its bivouac at 1:00 A.M., August 13th, and move to its assigned position.

b. Thursday, August 13th,. from 6:00 A.M. to 3:00 P.M., the 12th Brigade and its attached troops covered the Corps front as directed, along a line 17 miles long, with advanced detachments from 1 to 5 miles to the front. The line was held secure, eight of the 18—1st Cavalry (Mechanized) armored cars were captured, along with several motorcycles. Communications were satisfactory except with the Cavalry.

The 2nd Infantry had in 28 miles of wire, the 6th Infantry 22 miles and the Brigade headquarters 15. One flight, 108th Observation Squadron furnished very effective cooperation from the air.

At 3:00 P.M. the 12th Brigade and attached troops stood relieved, under orders to proceed to region 10 or more miles to the east and join the Red side, ready to operate in the opposite direction at 3:00 A.M. Recovering the many miles of wire, and laying the wire for the Red deployment imposed a heavy burden on the communication crews. Few had any sleep between Wednesday morning and Friday afternoon.

c. Friday and Saturday, August 14th and 15th, the 12th Brigade (less 2 battalions and 2 companies) attacked the Blue Corps front, against both flanks on the 14th and against the Blue right wing on the 15th. The attached operation reports give an outline of the various events and movements. The zones of attack were selected because of the availability of leased ground. A gap of almost 2 miles between regiments in the attack on August 14th was left because of the barrier imposed by the unleased ground in that region. It was necessary for this brigade to move with celerity (without reserves, and with almost no supports, to meet the army commander's desire for activity along the front of both National Guard divisions) in order to prevent the enemy from forming a proper idea of our maneuver and of the deep vulnerable flanks, and the center, exposed to his counter attacks. Therefore, abnormal umpire controlled maneuvers in the zone covered with unleased property were not practicable. The gap was successfully covered with small detachments and active personal reconnaissance of enemy front lines by officers, including the brigade commander.

d. Monday, August 18th [*17th*], the brigade with 2nd Battalion, 3rd Field Artillery, and the 1st Squadron, 14th Cavalry attached, served by one army plane, defended its position along the front—ROUTE 434—SPECTACLE LAKE—DUMONT LAKE, against the attack of the 32nd Division. (See operation report attached.)

At 8:00 A.M. 2 platoons of Troop A, 1st (Mechanized) Cavalry, 8 armored cars, reported and were placed in a concealed position. The operations on this day were intensely interesting, since for the first time proper reserves could be held out—2½ battalions—and the terrain and lake formations afforded unusual facilities for launching sudden enveloping counter-attacks. Information from the air was so complete and so accurate that it was possible to conserve reserves to the last moment and to hold the cavalry almost intact until required for an offensive mission against a formation far to the flank of the Blues which had been under observation for several hours.

As the principal reserve was launched in a wide envelopment of the enemy's left, the armored cars were ordered to penetrate the hostile right, where the troops seemed to be in considerable confusion at the point selected.

The action terminated at noon.

3. The brigade and attached troops (less cavalry) now withdrew to widely separated bivouacs well to the east—except the 6th Infantry, which remained at Dumont Lake. The cavalry started immediately for Camp Custer, the artillery following on Sunday afternoon. The 12th Brigade proceeded by truck to Custer on Wednesday, moving its dump, or railhead, at the same time.

The date of first departure of the brigade is not known at this time.

4. *Comments.*

a. Morale: High throughout the maneuvers. The enlisted men were keenly interested, determined and, at times, considerably excited. They thoroughly enjoyed the operations. The excellent ration was an important morale factor.

b. Training: Regular troops lack opportunities for proper field training with other arms. They showed this in lack of experience with airplanes and artillery. The improvement was remarkable from day to day. On Saturday, August 15th, everything functioned from the headquarters staff, down through the regiments and attached units, in a splendid manner, without a hitch notwithstanding a widely dispersed assault against tremendously stronger forces. Air, ground, artillery, infantry, headquarters—all cooperated in a smooth satisfying manner. The same was true in the defensive action on Monday, August 17th.

Considering the fact that the brigade staff was largely composed of reserve officers, the air officer was a reserve officer and the executive and liaison officer of artillery was also from the reserve—all strangers to the brigade, as was its commander, executive, and headquarters captain—the smoothness with which operations were conducted was exceedingly gratifying.

c. Tactics and Technique:

(1) Trucks greatly increase the power of infantry to maintain distant reconnaissance and observation posts. They also permit rapid movement of reserves.

(2) Orders for a reenforced brigade in open warfare apparently should be largely oral, best indicated by the commander to his principal commanders graphically on their maps, so that they can proceed to develop the plan without delay. When reconnaissance or planning indicate desirable changes these can be incorporated orally. Finally, the order is issued, general in its nature—the details having been given direct by the commander to the regiments—more or less as a mere confirmation of what has already been arranged and partially carried out. If troops must await the receipt of a formal order they will have little time for the laborious business of their preparations.

It is evident that with voice radio service from a plane, or even the more limited message dropping service, changes of dispositions or deployments in daylight can usually be checked instantly, artillery concentrated on the vulnerable points, and troops prepared to take advantage of this knowledge.

All required a day or two to learn the important difference between the usual peace training command post procedure and technique, and that necessary to the successful conduct of actual operations. Orderly procedure in the almost constant use of staff officers to check movements and situations, the same service by the commander personally, freedom permitted regimental or separate organization commanders in developing their plans within general limits, etc., etc., familiarity with these and many more, similar matters could only be acquired with actual practice under the strain of uncertainties that exist in such maneuvers.

It seemed to be the opinion of officers generally that the regular components are in urgent need of such team training, and that it can only be obtained in maneuvers of this general character. All were enthusiastic over the opportunities afforded.

   d. Administration and Supply:

   The difficulties of the brigade lay almost entirely in the zone of administration. Charged with the supply and usually with the administration, of a number of units both regular and National Guard, and numerous small scattered army units of constantly changing strength, and lacking the trained clerical force, trucks, motor cars and motorcycle dispatch riders, necessary to a headquarters operating on such a basis, the problem became quite complicated and rather dwarfed tactical considerations.

   In this connection, it appeared to me that the most serious deficiency made evident by the maneuvers was the lack of organic or permanent groups as a basis of expansion for higher headquarters—such as a Corps or Army. Where all such organizations, as to most of their officer personnel and all of their enlisted personnel, are on an improvised basis, the difficulties of prompt and harmonious cooperation are vastly increased.

   Another point which requires attention was the matter of delaying until what seemed too late a date for establishing headquarters of higher units and all improvised headquarters of separate organizations. For example, it is believed that the 12th Brigade headquarters, considering its greatly enlarged obligations, should have been on the ground August 2nd and its Quartermaster personnel on August 1st.

   5. Recommendations—

   a. That such maneuvers be carried out at frequent intervals.

   b. That the infantry be given more modern signal equipment.

   c. That brigade and corps staffs in the regular service be put on a more stable basis.

   d. That the Army School staffs study the procedure actually followed in these maneuvers to determine the weak points of the present teachings in technique, and to reduce some matters to a more simple and workable basis.

   e. That artillery fire—direction and target—in maneuvers be graphically indicated by low flying planes—one to a regiment; and that no further attempt be made to handle this matter by ponderous umpire and signal communication set-ups.

   6. In conclusion I wish to report that in my opinion this was the most successful maneuver ever attempted in our Army. Its results should be far reaching.

NA/RG 407 (353, Bulky File)

   1. Several sentences of technical details have been omitted here.

To Major Matthew B. Ridgway   August 24, 1936
                                               [Chicago, Illinois]

My dear Ridgway: Sorry not to have seen you before you left Allegan for Washington.[1] I intended to write you a note from Custer but continuous series of callers prevented any attention to personal business. I wanted to thank you for the very vital services you rendered to me during the maneuvers in digging me out of a hole two or three times. It made things quite simple to know I, myself, could turn or send one of my staff to you if we got too hard pressed in some other direction. It is not particularly agreeable to have to make appeals and establish a reputation for not being able to "take it;" but in that affair up there I found "they" didn't have the least idea of the task they were imposing on us and the restrictions that were imposed on its execution. However, we got by, and other than that minor irritation the whole thing was a delightful enterprise. I have never enjoyed myself more in a training venture. As proof of that, even the umpires could not irritate me.

You personally are to be congratulated for the major success of all the tactical phases of the enterprise, and certainly Hayes has commendations coming for handling of a vast number of complications connected with setting up Supply and similar arrangements.[2] You two officers did such a perfect job that there should be some way of rewarding you other than saying it was well done.

I am concerned as to whether you have succeeded in relaxing. I know you have enough brains to perform your military duties in a superior fashion but I doubt very much whether you have enough sense to take care of the human machine— very few men have, and unfortunately when you burn out a fuse you cannot substitute another twenty minutes later. Seriously, you must cultivate the art of playing and loafing; there is no need for you to demonstrate any further you are an energetic, able workman. So I hope you will utilize the remaining days before the War College opens and the first week or two of the War College course to establish the reputation of being something of a dilettante.

With affectionate regards to Peggy, Virginia and yourself,   Faithfully yours,

GCMRL/G. C. Marshall Papers (Illinois National Guard)

1. Ridgway was stationed in Chicago as assistant chief of staff, G-3, of the Second Army and Sixth Corps Area until August 20, 1936. Following the Second Army maneuvers, he attended the Army War College and graduated in 1937.

2. Major George P. Hays was Sixth Corps Area assistant chief of staff, G-4.

From Captain Alfred R. W. DeJonge[1]   August 24, 1936
                                               Detroit, Michigan

My dear Colonel Marshall: Please accept my most sincere thanks for your kind letter of August 21.² I am certain that I am expressing the feelings of all the officers who had the honor of serving under you on the staff of the 12th Brigade when I say that the teamwork of which you speak so graciously was made possible solely by your inspiring leadership. I shall always treasure this tour of duty as the high point of my military career. If in the future I shall be enabled to serve my Country in a more efficient manner when the call does come, I shall never lose sight of the fact that such better performance of duty is due to your untiring efforts and your great patience in the face of the natural shortcomings of reserve officers.

I do hope that the War Department will see fit to continue the type of training which the Second Army maneuvers gave us, not only every four years for each of the four Armies, but every two years at least. I am convinced that this was training which one could not possibly get in ten years of other activities and I trust that the powers that be will see that the great benefits which were derived from it should be made available as frequently as possible to all members of the military service, especially as the very small extra expense is negligible in comparison with the outstanding results obtained.

It was a rare privilege to be allowed to serve under you and I hope that you will do me the honor to call upon me whenever your steps lead you to Detroit.   Very respectfully yours,

Alfred R.W. DeJonge

GCMRL/G. C. Marshall Papers (Illinois National Guard)

1. DeJonge, of *The Detroit Free Press* and a Michigan Reserve officer, was assistant chief of staff, G-2, of the Twelfth Brigade at the Allegan, Michigan, maneuvers.

2. No copy of Marshall's letter to DeJonge of August 21 has been found in the Marshall papers.

To Major General Frank R. McCoy   [August 28, 1936]
Chicago, Illinois

Dear General: Katherine and I got a great deal of satisfaction and a thrill out of your telephone call last evening. Your voices sounded so natural, so gracious and appealing, that it was almost as if you had been on the old divan in your oriental robes at 190 E. Chestnut. I deeply appreciated your congratulations,¹ especially since there has been no one who has gone so far out of their way to advance my interests as you did. Your concern over my promotion was not only flattering to me, but it was a source of profound satisfaction. For, your endorsement or good opinion is the last word with me on people, events or things.

I do wish Katherine and I could be with you and Francis again. Don't you need a brigadier at Governor's Island—sort of a Chief Dockmaster, or Gentleman Manager of the Grounds?

Katherine hardly returned from Canada late Wednesday evening to be greeted by the good news. K and I start east—by car—to Boston on the 6th or 7th, we will probably be at the Arts Club about the 12th; but I will send you word in advance of our arrival, as I want to be certain to see you.   Affectionately

G. C. Marshall

LC/F. R. McCoy Papers; H

1. Marshall was notified on August 26 of his promotion to brigadier general—effective on October 1, 1936—which he observed was "a very pleasant finale to the maneuvers to me." (Marshall to DeJonge, September 1, 1936, GCMRL/G. C. Marshall Papers [Illinois National Guard].)

To CAPTAIN CHARLES T. LANHAM   August 28, 1936
[Chicago, Illinois]

My dear Lanham: I am especially appreciative of your letter of warm congratulations which came this morning. The fact that men of your age in the army wish me so well is a great satisfaction to me. My only regret is I cannot do something to help unblock a system which leaves men like yourself to languish for years in spite of outstanding exhibitions of efficiency. However, we will have to wait and see.

With warm regards,   Faithfully yours,

GCMRL/G. C. Marshall Papers (Illinois National Guard)

To BRIGADIER GENERAL GEORGE V. H. MOSELEY   September 2, 1936
[Chicago, Illinois]

Dear General: I had planned to write to you to thank you for all you had done in my interest, without waiting for the congratulations I knew would be forth-coming. However, in the confusion of things here I did not get my note off before your nice letter of congratulations arrived.

I want you to know that I have a very sincere appreciation for all you personally did to promote my interests and I shall never forget your attitude and your willingness to advance my interests entirely on your own initiative. You have been a rare friend, and I deeply appreciate it.   Faithfully yours,

GCMRL/G. C. Marshall Papers (Illinois National Guard)

To General John J. Pershing   September 12, 1936
                                               New York, New York

Dear General: Your cable of congratulations was forwarded to Chicago by Adamson in time to reach me the night before I left on my present trip east.[1] Naturally I was very much gratified to have your message of good wishes at such long range, and I appreciate tremendously your cabling.

You had told me last May that I would be on the September list, but I had long ceased counting chickens before they were hatched; so I was delighted to have the matter settled.

Mrs. Marshall and I left Chicago by motor on the 4th enroute to Exeter to Emily Russell's wedding in Lewis Perry's house. We took the Buffalo boat at Detroit, paused at Saratoga Springs, made a house party in Vermont, and finally reached Exeter. Most of Milton was there, and Governor Forbes. Emily married a recent professor of law at the University of Penna, Renyolds Brown; a man of 68 years. Lewis Perry looked in fine shape and very happy in his marriage to Mrs. Adams—his first wife's sister.[2]

We reached New York late last night, and leave for Baltimore tomorrow— Washington Tuesday. Just returned from the McCoy's on Governor's Island and are headed for a dinner on 70th street and the theatre.

This goes to you on your birthday. I wrote my congratulations some weeks ago, but I supplement them today with my prayers for your health and continued happiness.

Thanks very deeply for your insistence on my promotion; I would still be waiting were it not for you.   Affectionately

                                               G. C. Marshall

LC/J. J. Pershing Papers (General Correspondence); H

1. Pershing to Marshall, August 27, 1936, LC/J. J. Pershing Papers (General Correspondence). There is no copy of this telegram in the Marshall papers.

2. Reynolds D. Brown (b. May 6, 1869), professor of law at the University of Pennsylvania from 1897 to 1936, and a resident of Milton, Massachusetts, married Emily Perry Russell on September 10, 1936. Lewis Perry, Sr., had married Juliette Hubbell Adams in June, 1935.

To Lieutenant Colonel George S. Patton, Jr.[1]   September 29, 1936
                                               [Chicago, Illinois]

Dear Patterson:[2]   I appreciated very much your fine note of congratulations, and I am particularly pleased to have expressions of approval on my promotion from a man with your standing in the Army. Should a situation develop where I could have your services, nothing would please me more, because you are very much the type who does things in spite of hell or high water.

With warm regards, and thanks,   Faithfully,

GCMRL/G. C. Marshall Papers (Illinois National Guard)

1. At this time Patton was assistant chief of staff, G-2, of the Hawaiian Department, at Fort Shafter, near Honolulu.

2. Marshall's secretary typed the name of another thank-you note recipient, Major General Robert U. Patterson, on this letter. Marshall may have changed it in his own handwriting, but the original was not found in LC/G. S. Patton, Jr., Papers.

To Major General Hugh A. Drum   October 1, 1936
                                                [Chicago, Illinois]

Dear Drum: I received your radio of congratulations and replied by the same means, but want you to know I deeply appreciate your congratulations and the promptness with which they were dispatched.

I have just been notified this morning that I go to Vancouver Barracks, Washington.[1] I welcome this in place of the desk, which I had feared; and I am very glad to have an opportunity to live in the beautiful Northwest.

With affectionate regards,   Faithfully,

GCMRL/G. C. Marshall Papers (Illinois National Guard)

1. Marshall was relieved from duty as senior instructor with the Illinois National Guard on October 5, 1936, and prepared to move to Vancouver Barracks, Washington, to assume command of the Fifth Brigade.

Vancouver Barracks

October 1936–June 1938

M ARSHALL arrived at Vancouver Barracks, Washington, on October 27, 1936, to assume command of the Third Division's Fifth Brigade and to supervise the district's Civilian Conservation Corps camps in Oregon and southern Washington. Having completed a leisurely three-week sightseeing drive west, accompanied by Mrs. Marshall and Molly, he was welcomed by Colonel Henry Hossfeld, commander of the Seventh Infantry and acting commander of the post prior to Marshall's arrival, and a formal ceremony (even though he had telegraphed that he wanted to enter the post quietly). Stationed at a historic post in beautiful country, Marshall was again back with troops. Mrs. Marshall later wrote: "Thus began two of the happiest years of our life." (K. T. Marshall, *Together*, pp. 22–24.)

Sixteen years later, Marshall pleasantly recalled his years at Vancouver Barracks. "Altogether, we experienced one of our most delightful periods of Army service and one that we look back on with additional warmth because there followed from the very month we left the Northwest long years of fearful strain and struggle with a world turmoil which has not yet subsided.

"Those days along the rivers of the Northwest, among its magnificent mountains, and by the picturesque seashore appealed to us as a pleasant dream in comparison with the troubled days that followed.

"The best that I can say today is that we would love to live those two years over again, each day as it was, each of our friends as they were." (Inclosure to Marshall to David W. Eyre, September 4, 1952, GCMRL/G. C. Marshall Papers [Retirement].) ★

TO GENERAL JOHN J. PERSHING   November 6, 1936
Vancouver Barracks, Washington

Dear General: I see by the papers that you are home again, and I suppose you are in Washington for a few weeks before going to the south west. I hope you returned in as fine health as you appeared to enjoy last May.

We took three weeks to a motor trip out here—used a Packard instead of a Ford—and had a gorgeous sight seeing time: Santa Fe, northern New Mexican Indian settlements, Petrified Forests, Painted Desert, Grand Canyon from both rims, Zion Park in Utah, Boulder Dam, Hollywood!, Yosemite, giant redwood groves along north coast road. At the Grand Canyon I tried to recall the details of your famous trip horseback so many years ago, but about all that I could remember was that you were in dire distress for water and uncertain of your course, and that you told the story at a campfire one evening on Lake Brandreth.

We found quarters, bordering on the palatial here as to size, convenience, gardens, views, etc. Arrived a week ago and were settled twenty four hours later.

Everything seems quite delightful, and we are charmed with our new surroundings.

My CCC inspections take me up the Columbia River gorge, out around Pendleton, and south to Eugene. I called on General Martin (Governor of Oregon) at Salem on my way here. He is an old and warm friend of mine. Looks well, and seems to be ace high as Chief Executive of the State.

With affectionate regards,   Faithfully yours,

G. C. Marshall

LC/J. J. Pershing Papers (General Correspondence); H

To Colonel Ralph D. Mershon   November 14, 1936 ⁄
Vancouver Barracks, Washington

My dear Colonel Mershon: Now that my military duties have carried me to the West Coast, I find that I can not serve on the Civilian-Military Education Fund to the extent desirable in a member of the committee. For me to attend meetings in the east would be prohibitively expensive and time consuming; therefore, with genuine reluctance, I tender my resignation.

I have been deeply interested in what has been accomplished during the past three years and the constantly increasing importance of the fund. Undoubtedly, without its influence and efforts, the cause of Civilian-Military education would have suffered some very serious blows. I feel that you have rendered a service of great value to the stability of our "institutions"—to employ a favorite political term for the purpose of expressing a sincere conviction. I wish I could have done more to help, but I am glad that I was given the opportunity to participate.

Incidentally, should you come out to the West Coast, I would be charmed to put you up and show you the military activities of the post, and the magnificence of this country—along the route of some thirty-five CCC camps for which I am responsible.

With assurance of my regard,   Faithfully yours,

GCMRL/G. C. Marshall Papers (Vancouver Barracks)

To Brigadier General Charles G. Dawes   November 21, 1936
Vancouver Barracks,
Washington

Dear General: This note is merely to report the arrival of the Marshalls in very delightful surroundings, and to express again my very real appreciation for your kindness to me, and bountiful hospitality, while I was in Chicago. It will be a long time before I forget those Saturday luncheons of yours, and the interesting conversation. Also, I think Mrs. Marshall feels as though she had known Mrs. Dawes for many years, and has in her a very dear friend.

We find our quarters here the most spacious and luxurious we have ever seen in the army. I believe the house was built for General Nelson Miles.[1] Then too, the trees and flowers, and the views are beautiful. Mt. Hood looms up with its snow crown in the vista from Mrs. Marshall's bedroom windows. My predecessor left a rose garden of sixty varieties, and a pretty good amateur dalhia show. The people are very cordial and hospitable.

General Martin immediately took me in hand and quickly established very valuable and agreeable relations for me with the Portland people. He is tremendously popular out here, with democrats and republicans alike. And he is great admirer of yours.

With affectionate regards to Mrs. Dawes and you,   Faithfully yours,

G. C. Marshall

NU/C. G. Dawes Papers; H

1. Brigadier General Nelson A. Miles—noted Indian fighter who engaged in campaigns against Sitting Bull, Crazy Horse, Chief Joseph, and Geronimo—commanded the Department of the Columbia, which had its headquarters at Vancouver Barracks, from 1881 to 1885. (Nelson A. Miles, *Serving the Republic: Memoirs of the Civil and Military Life of Nelson A. Miles* [New York: Harper and Brothers, 1911], pp. 210–15.)

TO GENERAL JOHN J. PERSHING   [November 26, 1936]
                                          Vancouver Barracks, Washington

My dear General: I have been waiting to see some notice of your annual trip to Tuscon. I wish we had a dryer climate here so that you might enjoy something of this lovely house we have and the gorgeous scenery of this region. They tell us that it rains all winter, but so far we have had perfect fall weather—the most unseasonable in the history of the northwest, according to the statistics.

I returned last night from a CCC inspection in the vicinity of Pendleton and Baker in eastern Oregon, very interesting country and quite new to me. Last week I battled fogs along the coast south of Astoria. I find the CCC intensely interesting and a welcome distraction from the routine of garrison administration.

We have an Irish Setter, raised from a pup in our Chicago apartment, that Mrs. Marshall and I take out in the woods on the reservation almost every afternoon and hunt pheasants—without any shooting. It makes a very pleasant arrangement for an afternoon walk.

Our house is the most attractive I have seen in the army, and we thoroughly enjoy it.

Gen. (Governor) Martin has made things very pleasant for me in Portland. He has a remarkable hold on these people, and is amusingly and daringly frank in his views on the present tendencies.

Please dictate a note and tell me how things go with you, and of your plans for the winter.

With affectionate regards,   Faithfully yours,

G. C. Marshall

LC/J. J. Pershing Papers (General Correspondence); H

FROM GENERAL MALIN CRAIG   December 1, 1936
Personal   Washington, D.C.

My dear George: I am delighted to have your cheerful note of November 26th.[1] I naturally have followed you from the time you left Chicago up to date, and I know you are getting along all right.

May I suggest that you take an early opportunity to drive over to Salem and call on General George White and General Tom Rilea, of the 41st Division.[2] White is one of the strongest backers we have and he has changed a good deal in his characteristics since shortly after the War, when he was a little hot headed. These men are both good soldiers and, as I say, will be worth a whole lot to you if you ever need any help. You will naturally find a great deal to interest you in Vancouver, and I personally believe that your contacts and experience will be worth far more to you eventually than had you gone back to take a brigade of the First Division, which might have seemed in order.

You are in a position, George, to keep me informed of your wishes, with the certain knowledge that I will accomplish them for you in so far as lies in my power. I think, between you and me and the fence, you will have to keep in touch with your Division Commander and put some thoughts into his head which will be calculated for him to consider as his own original ideas.[3]

Dave Stone is a classmate of mine and I love him dearly but he sometimes gives me a pain in the neck. Yesterday he wrote a long letter in here, some four pages, about the heart-breaking of an Aide of his who ought to go to Leavenworth; stated that the morale of these men was affected and that their careers were ruined if they could not go to these schools. I sent him word that he was peculiarly in a position to counteract this lowered morale by throwing out his chest and making the statement, which everybody knows is correct, that he himself managed to scrape through No. 59 in a class of 59 at West Point; that he had never been to any school in his life, and that he was, as everybody could see, a Major General in good standing.

As a matter of fact the school situation is a serious proposition and I am now working on a scheme to throw the onus from my own shoulders to the shoulders of the individuals who are so anxious to go to school. I believe we can figure it out so that each man who is eligible can be notified by the Adjutant General that he is eligible and that he is entitled to apply for an examination test if he desires to qualify, and then have his examination conducted in writing wherever the man is; the papers marked by the board at Leavenworth, and the winners, if their records are all right, given the call.

I can see that pretty house of yours and I believe that Mrs. Marshall will know how to keep the flowers growing and keep it more attractive. A large part of your time will be taken up with CCC inspections and activities. This may be an old story to you but the success of that movement depends upon constant inspections and holding up the standard. I seem to have drifted into a lecture, but I do not mean it that way.

Please remember me kindly to Mrs. Marshall and let me hear from you once in awhile. I always open my own mail and write my own letters, though naturally I am a little slow now and then, as my desk is pretty well crowded.

I saw General Pershing recently and the old gentleman looks quite as well as I have ever seen him look. He is, however, a little feeble, which is noticeable in his walk.

Again, with best wishes and good luck and thanks for your letter. Always sincerely,

Malin Craig

GCMRL/G. C. Marshall Papers (Vancouver Barracks)

1. This letter was not found in the Marshall papers.

2. Major General George A. White, the adjutant general of Oregon, commanded the National Guard's Forty-first Division. Brigadier General Thomas E. Rilea, commander of Oregon's Eighty-second Infantry Brigade, served as vice-president (1934–35) and president (1935–36) of the National Guard Association of the United States.

3. Major General David L. Stone (U.S.M.A., 1898) commanded the Third Division at Fort Lewis, Washington (September 22, 1936–March 30, 1937).

To Major General Frank R. McCoy   December 24, 1936
                                        Vancouver Barracks, Washington

My dear General: At letter writing I don't have much luck with you, but I cant allow Xmas to pass without wishing you all the good things of the season and for the New Year. And always I have a feeling of deep regret that we no longer can find you across the hall, with your warmth of hospitality and agreeable conversation.

Katherine has been extremely busy doing Xmas things, fixing up our tree, and contributing to the post effort. She has gone to bed, leaving me and Molly to go to the mid-night service. We had a dinner party of young people, who have gone on to some other place for variety and amusement.

We are charmed with our surroundings, especially with the people of Portland and with our house, which is the finest set of quarters I have seen in the army. Just now I am writing in library wing built, I understand, especially for General Miles. It is a huge place with six baths and a lavatory, and a gorgeous view of Mt. Hood.

I find Oregon fascinating, in inspecting the CCC. The coast is a succession of marvelous scenery, the gorge of the Columbia magnificient; and I find the semi-desert, mountainious country of eastern Oregon, a great and interesting contrast. I have 35 camps in all, which keeps me pleasantly occupied.

Give our love to Francis, and accept for the two of you our holiday greetings and every good wish for the New Year.   Affectionately,

G. C. Marshall

P.S. Ponty is splendid at pheasant hunting. We get up a half dozen almost every afternoon.

LC/F. R. McCoy Papers; H

TO THE PACKARD MOTOR COMPANY   December 26, 1936
                                               Vancouver Barracks, Washington

Gentlemen: In September I purchased a new Packard 120, touring sedan, from your Oak Park, Illinois agent. I was extremely careful to drive it at less than 25 miles per hour for the first 200 miles and at less than 35 for the first 1000. It was serviced by the selling agent at 500 miles, by your Springfield, Massachusetts agency at 1500; by the Oak Park agency at 2700 and by your Joplin, Missouri agency at 3700. As a matter of fact, I was on a brief tour in the East and then left Chicago for station at Vancouver Barracks. During this travel I several times went out of my way; altering my itinerary, in order to secure proper Packard service at the right time.

Notwithstanding these precautions, I found as I was approaching Amarillo, Texas that something was wrong in the differential. J. M. Wise, your agent at Amarillo, examined the car and found the differential almost completely lacking in grease and the gears injured. He, or rather, his mechanic and foreman, stated that evidently the differential had not been properly filled at the factory before delivery to your Oak Park agent. Also, quite evidently, the differential had not been properly checked at the successive servicing examinations. I asked Mr. Wise to put this in writing, but he told me that that was wholly unnecessary as there could be no possible question about the Packard service making good the damage. As he had no differential assembly he telegraphed ahead to your Albuquerque, New Mexico agency to secure the necessary parts and have them in readiness (see attached telegram). I then proceeded at less than 30 miles per hour to Albuquerque. There, Roland Sami and Company installed a new differential assembly. *But*, I was required to pay $9.40 (see attached bill and report indorsed on back).

I submit that no charge should have been made against me in this instance. Through the failure or oversight of the Packard Service, I had been delayed two days, with the expense involved for three people, and seriously inconvenienced.

Furthermore, at the time of purchase of the car I inquired particularly as to whether or not I would be charged for the routine 10,000 mile servicing at agencies en route—explaining where I was going. I was told that I would suffer no loss by dealing with the different agencies involved. Yet each agency imposed a charge, stating that I was only entitled to the free service in the local district in which I had purchased the car.

Furthermore, at the 500-mile servicing, after oiling and greasing, nothing was done to the car but stamping the plate under the hood. I, by accident, discovered this omission and only then secured, supposedly, the required service inspection.

I mention these details because they have pretty much destroyed my faith in the Packard service, which had been one of the determining reasons for my using a Packard since 1927.[1] The delay in reporting this affair was due to the papers being mislaid.   Very truly yours,

GCMRL/G. C. Marshall Papers (Vancouver Barracks)

1. Packard advertisements at the time said: "We sincerely believe that the Packard 120 is the most service-free car in America. Its finer materials, its better engineering, and the greater precision of its parts combine to reduce the need for service to an astonishingly low level." (*Saturday Evening Post* 209 [July 18, 1936]: 51.) The automobile cost between $950 and $1,150, depending upon optional accessories. No reply to this letter was found in the Marshall papers.

TO GENERAL JOHN J. PERSHING   January 27, 1937
                                         Vancouver Barracks, Washington

My dear General: I just happened on Westrate's book "Those Fatal Generals" and was delighted to see the write up he gave you.[1] To tell the truth, after I had read the dreadful panning he gave each man he touched I was fearful of what he might have to say about your work, knowing how these fellows strive to make their books newsy at whatever cost in accuracy or fairness. I have never heard of him until this book came along. Did you know him, or anything about him?

I am sending this to Tucson, though I am not at all certain that you are there. I sent you a note to that general address during the holidays, and I hope it reached you. General Dawes wrote that he had seen you on your way to Lincoln and the southwest.

Here we are clothed in a deep snow, thought it is not very cold. Every one is intent on skiing on Mt. Hood, which is only an hour and a half drive from the post.

I see by the papers that you are to go with Mr. Gerard to the coronation of King George in May.[2] I think you should have been named as the representative of the President. G. is nothing more that a rich man and a one time too talkative official in Berlin.

If you come out to the west coast in the Spring, please arrange to come up here and pay us a visit. You will find it delightful here at that season and the surroundings very beautiful. We would be so pleased and honore[d][3] to to have you, and I know we could make you very comfortable in this huge house.

Please bear with my typing. I have not done any for so long that I seldom seem to strike the right key. My clerk is too slow on dictation to be much of a comfort.

With affectionate regards,   Faithfully yours,

G. C. Marshall

LC/J. J. Pershing Papers (General Correspondence); T

1. Concerning his book on American generalship from 1776 to 1918, Edwin V. Westrate noted: "Its basic premise is that if there must be wars, they should be fought more efficiently. It has to do with the vicious toll which victory has not demanded but which we always have paid, the needless slaughter of those whose bitter sacrifice contributed nothing toward the victory but rather served only to prolong the desolating agony of the wars in which they were murdered." (*Those Fatal Generals* [New York: Knight Publications, 1936], p. 11.) In Westrate's opinion, America's outstanding generals had been George Washington, George H. Thomas, and John J. Pershing: "men who fought wisely, men who won brilliantly, men who never spent blood uselessly." (P. 288.)

2. President Roosevelt designated James W. Gerard—ambassador to Germany between 1913 and 1917—as "special ambassador" and General Pershing and Admiral Hugh Rodman (U.S.N.A., 1880) as the other United States representatives at the coronation of King George VI on May 12 at Westminster Abbey.

3. Marshall occasionally typed off of the right edge of the paper; the missing letters are supplied in brackets.

FROM GENERAL JOHN J. PERSHING   February 24, 1937
[Tucson, Arizona]

My dear George: I had quite a shock the other day when Mr. and Mrs. O'Laughlin reported to me that you were in Walter Reed Hospital.[1] I protested that it could not be, but he said that he had just come from Washington and that you were to be operated on for goiter. I told him that you could not possibly have a goiter, but he talked me down. I sent my best wishes and directed Adamson to go to the hospital and he reported back that you were not in the hospital with no further comment—so I am writing you today feeling that it was all a mistake.

General Dawes will be here sometime next week for a considerable stay but I am going to leave about the 8th of March for Hot Springs, Arkansas, to see if I can't get a lot of this rheumatism baked out.

I agree, this Coronation thing is difficult but it was hard to decline. However, I am quite content so long as we are going to have Jimmy Gerard at the head of the procession.

You were kind enough to say you were sending me Westrate's book "Those Fatal Generals". As I have not seen it I am sure it will give me pleasure if, and when, it arrives. Perhaps you haven't sent it yet.

Your typing is very good—keep it up.

Accept my affectionate regards for yourself and Mrs. Marshall.

Believe me, as always   Faithfully yours,

LC/J. J. Pershing Papers (General Correspondence)

1. John Callan O'Laughlin was a widely traveled author and publisher of the *Army and Navy Journal*.

To General John J. Pershing   March 4, 1937
                                                      San Francisco, [California]

My dear General: O'Laughlin was right about the goiter but wrong as to place.

I had had a slight swelling indicating goiter since about 1923, but tests—metabolism—always indicated it was quiescent. Last July my usual pulse of 72 grew irregular and rapidly worked up to from 90 to 105. Strange to say, I never felt better physically and gained, for the first time in my life, seventeen pounds between August and January. I took a thoro course of tests in Vancouver and Portland in December, had three wisdom teeth pulled, but still registered normal under a basal metabolism test. However, the leading specialist of the northwest believed that pressure of an enlarged thyroid was the trouble.

I came down here and they formed a similar conclusion. I was operated on three weeks ago, and a very much enlarged and partially diseased gland was removed.[1] The day following the operation my pulse fell into the eighties; the next day it struck the seventies and by the third morning it was registering about 68. For some days it continued to miss beats, but less frequently each day. I was up, dressed and around, but they put me to bed Sunday and started a quinidine treatment Monday, to give the heart a chance to fall into a regular rhythm.

However, the electro cardiogram of my heart, taken as they started the first dose Monday, but not available to examine until Monday night, showed my heart as normal, having fallen into time on its own recovery after the operative effects had subsided. The succeeding daily cardiograms show me as normal and they have cut the dosage one third and will probably stop it today and allow me to get up tomorrow.

Meanwhile, I feel fine and have regained five of the ten pounds I lost during the operation.

Usually patients for thyroid operations are much underweight, highly nervous, short of breath and generally unstrung. I was fortunate to be in fine shape, and was told that I was farther along the fifth day than most patients were after several months.

That's the state of affairs. I hope to return to Vancouver next week.

My fountain pen is out of commission, and I am writing in bed—hence this pencil.

I was to order you "Those Fatal Generals" in Portland, but left suddenly about that time. It will be along shortly.

I'm glad you are going to Hot Springs, but sorry you are not first heading in this direction. Hot Springs has a beautiful plant now and is rather a gentleman's club.

Give my best to General & Mrs. Dawes, and believe me, as always,   Affectionately,

G. C. Marshall

LC/J. J. Pershing Papers (General Correspondence); H

1. Marshall was writing from Letterman General Hospital. Lieutenant Colonel Norman T. Kirk told Marshall's Portland physician that he had performed a "subtotal thyroidectomy of both lobes" on Marshall on February 15, and that "his convalescence has been extremely mild." (Kirk to Dr. T. Homer Coffen, February 23, 1937, GCMRL/G. C. Marshall Papers [Vancouver Barracks].)

FROM MAJOR JOHN S. WINSLOW[1]   February 18, 1937
                                       Warsaw, [Poland]

My dear General Marshall: Remembering your attempt to give our army a modern drill regulation for close and open order work, I was much struck by the enclosed clipping from the Times which came out some days ago. Though the writer is Liddell Hart, in all probability, you may find some useful arguments to advance if you ever go after the War Department again.[2]

The Czechs use the modern column of threes whereas the Polish formation is similar to ours. The Poles have a regular force of about 260,000 men well disciplined, high morale, and in splendid physical condition but they have little modern equipment and no industrial system to produce it. Their political leaders, and I believe also the military, are tied to the past and their national vanity is so great that any idea from abroad meets intense opposition. They are highly secretive and suspicious and as I have not gained their confidence my supply of information from official channels is nil.

The Czechs on the other hand have a broad base of private industry which together with the Government arsenals provides a flow of first rate modern armament, but the appearance of their troops is much below that of the Poles.

A month ago I motored to Prague via Berlin and returned via Breslau. The German preparations are so great that any tourist must be impressed by them. The details of the military-political situation are very complex but the key to Europe's future is in Berlin and the problem which agitates every foreign office is simply when and where will Hitler embark on an inevitable military adventure. At the moment there is little expectation of war this spring or summer but though no one wants a war there is a general conviction that a German attack must be faced before many years.

To me it is apparent that every day the value of training mobility and skill becomes greater and the value of gross weight (numbers) becomes less. Our plans for great forces of militia and reserves are popular because they provide many jobs but confronted by a modern European army of even half their number they might stop bullets but nothing else. Training and physical condition were never at such a premium as now. . . .

Most sincerely,

John Winslow

GCMRL/G. C. Marshall Papers (Vancouver Barracks)

1. Winslow, a United States Naval Academy graduate (1914), served briefly with the New York National Guard (1916) before securing a commission in the United States Army Field Artillery. He knew Marshall from the time he served at Sixth Corps Area headquarters in Chicago, Illinois (mid-1934 until mid-1936). He was then detailed as military attache at the United States Embassy in Warsaw, Poland. Two paragraphs of personal greetings have been omitted from the letter printed here.

2. The unsigned column from the London *Times* by military correspondent Basil H. Liddell Hart is not in the Marshall papers.

To Major John S. Winslow   March 19, 1937
                                                 Vancouver Barracks, Washington

Dear Winslow: I have just received your interesting letter of February 18, and appreciate your giving me so many interesting details. The clipping from the "Times" was especially interesting to me.

In a letter the other day to General Craig, I made some comment on our effort to modernize our infantry drill, but I don't think he got the point I was trying to make.[1]

I was off in the hospital in San Francisco for 5 weeks, having an operation which had been due since July. I am back for duty now, feeling fine, and about 12 pounds heavier than when you last saw me.

I have just received a fine horse from Fort Riley which will add a great deal to our pleasure out here.

We are charmed out here and have the loveliest set of quarters I have seen in the Army, along with a rose garden of 65 varieties and about 200 plants.

My warmest regards to you both. Tell your wife that the spring flowers are in bloom here and skiing is active on Mt. Hood, an hour and 30 minutes drive distant from here.   Faithfully yours,

GCMRL/G. C. Marshall Papers (Vancouver Barracks)

1. No copy of this letter has been found in the Marshall papers.

To Major General Roy D. Keehn   March 19, 1937
                                                    Vancouver Barracks, Washington

My dear General: I appreciated very much your interesting and detailed letter
which I found on my return from San Francisco. I had had an operation due me
since last June or July, and should have had it in January, but the night before
they were to operate, the flu epidemic caused them to close down on all but
emergency cases, so I returned home for a month and went back to San Francisco in February. Came through in splendid shape, and already weigh about 10
pounds more than when you last saw me. Mine was a thyroid affair, which I had
been carrying about for some 15 years. Evidently pressure was getting in some
deadly work last summer. In any event, I am in splendid shape now, registering
normal in every respect—except probably, you would say, in some of my personal idiosyncrasies, which no operation could alter.

I note you desire to have me write you a lengthy letter suitable for publication
in a magazine. I will set about doing that right away, omitting medical details.
My duties here are in such marked contrast with those in Chicago, and the
country is so different, that possibly I can work up something of general interest.[1]

I am delighted that you are again feeling so vigorous, but I am sorry to learn
that you are having a bout with the flu. My family missed it out here, but
practically everybody else succumbed.

I am very glad to learn that you are so well satisfied with the progress Colonel
Ayer has been making.[2] Naturally, he was prepared to carry on in general the
ideas I had developed, or had, half baked in mind. Starting now, I think you
should be able to make an excellent selection, effective in September, after your
summer camp. Most of the turn-over in the Army of course is during the summer
months, and it is much easier to get a good man then than during the other
portions of the year. I suggest another try for September, for Colonel E. F.
Harding, Infantry, or Colonel William A. Ganoe, Infantry, or Colonel Oscar W.
Griswold, Infantry.[3] All of these men are of high efficiency, and Harding
particularly appealing and effective. I would suggest your writing a little personal
note to General Craig, giving him this list of names and asking him if it is possible
to get any one of these men for next September—but don't mention me.

I was much interested in what had happened to the 132nd Infantry. I had
known for a long time that this was an impossible situation, but you have gotten
rid of the two stumbling blocks who were located in the key positions.[4] Nothing,
absolutely nothing, but cold efficiency should ever be permitted to become involved in the selection of a colonel. We suffer from poor colonels in the Regular
Army, but the solidity, the disciplinary background and other special conditions,
serve to save us from the destructive effects that are completely demoralizing the
National Guard. Rewards for honest and faithful services, political obligations,
and other very human and common factors which are present in civil life, should
be paid or made in some other manner than designation to the leadership of a

regiment. A figurehead as lieutenant colonel can be carried, but never as colonel.

I find I am sermonizing at a great rate, but I have been very much impressed with their simple duty that would be the correctness and importance of my ideas on this subject.

With affectionate regards,   Faithfully yours,

GCMRL/G. C. Marshall Papers (Vancouver Barracks)

1. Marshall wrote Keehn a letter on March 25 (printed below) which was published in the April, 1937, *Illinois Guardsman*.

2. Lieutenant Colonel Wesley F. Ayer was acting senior instructor with the Illinois National Guard after Marshall left.

3. Lieutenant Colonel Edwin F. Harding was editor of the *Infantry Journal*. Colonel William A. Ganoe (U.S.M.A., 1907) had been commanding officer at Fort Screven, Georgia, since September 14, 1936. Lieutenant Colonel Oscar W. Griswold (U.S.M.A., 1911) had commanded a battalion of the Twenty-fourth Infantry at Fort Benning—October 10, 1931, to June 30, 1932—and at the time of Marshall's letter was detailed to the Office of the Chief of Infantry.

4. Two officers had resigned following an investigation of conditions in the 132nd Infantry ordered by General Keehn. (Keehn to Marshall, March 12, 1937, GCMRL/G. C. Marshall Papers [Vancouver Barracks].)

To Major General Roy D. Keehn   March 25, 1937
                                         Vancouver Barracks, Washington

My dear General Keehn: Since you have expressed curiosity regarding my new duties and surroundings I will endeavor to give you some idea of their contrast with those of a senior instructor for the 33d Division.

In the first place, I have three different jobs, the most immediate being the command of this post and the regiment and detachments stationed here. Vancouver Barracks is one of the old historic outposts of the army. Established in 1849 on the site of a Hudson Bay Company station, the traces of whose lookout station are still discernable in a tall fir tree, for more than fifty years it was the center for the development of the northwest. General Grant's log quarters are a part of the present post library building. Phil Sheridan left here a lieutenant to start his meteoric rise to fame. Pickett was a member of the garrison. My quarters were occupied by a succession of Civil War celebrities or Indian fighters. General Miles built the house, which was later occupied by Canby, Crook, Gibbon and Pope.[1]

During the past thirty years there has been little change in the outward appearance of the post, but the interior of barracks and quarters have been modernized to a degree and made reasonably attractive and comfortable. Giant fir trees ornament the parade; every yard has its holly trees and a profusion of shrubs. The original apple tree of the northwest, planted in the yard of the old trading post, still lives and is carefully fenced against possible harm. In my yard is a cherry tree of reported antiquity, with three grafted varieties of the fruit. All is in delightful contrast to the institution like appearance of many army posts.

The Columbia River, bordering our aviation field (we have four planes) in extension of the parade, emerges from its famous gorge a few miles above the post. In the distance the symmetrical cone of Mt. Hood stands covered with snow, summer or winter.

Another of my duties is the command of the 5th Brigade, one regiment of which occupies posts near Spokane, in Montana and in North Dakota. The local regiment has two companies at Chilkoot Barracks in Alaska. Except for inspections, training policies and periods of concentration, there is little for me to do with the troops of the brigade not stationed here.

My most pressing duty concerns the command of thirty-five CCC companies scattered through Oregon and southern Washington. These camps are beautifully organized, and the supply system and weekly motor transport convoys operate from here in a precise routine, under the capable direction of a staff of reserve officers.

The location of the camps contributes a great deal to the pleasure of my work, situated as they are along the coast, high in the mountains, on lakes, and at other points of scenic interest. Excellent fishing and hunting can usually be found in the vicinity of these camps—the steel head salmon are now running—but it is not necessary to go so far afield. A few evenings ago my orderly called my attention to four cock pheasants and six hens roosting in a tree in the yard.

To reach a large section of my district in Eastern Oregon I must traverse the Columbia River gorge, finally emerging from the dense green of the vegetation of the damp near-coastal region into the typical barrens of the dry western plains. In winter one passes, within a mile, from overcast skies, fogs or rain into the glare of cloudless skies. It is possible now, with the spring flowers blooming, to motor an hour and a half from here to the skiing slopes of Mt. Hood. Oregon is a region of contrasts.

The CCC companies are a source of keen interest. Near Pendleton, the scene of the famous annual "round up" or rodeo, is a company of Boston boys. Under Beacon Rock—except for Gibraltar, the largest monolith in the world, is a group of young fellows from the swamp regions of Arkansas. Providence, Rhode Island has a company near Tillamook on the shore of the Pacific. Their road sign reads, "Tillamook 18 miles. Providence, R. I., 3100." We have groups from New York, Connecticut, New Jersey, Ohio, Kentucky, Minnesota and the Dakotas.

The boys all seem to like this country, and I imagine that this peaceful invasion will have a marked effect on the future development of the region, as many of these young men remain out here to marry and settle down. As a whole they are a fine lot, hardworking, studious in following the educational courses we provide, and seeming to develop considerable ambition, along with the necessary energy and resolution.

I was very fortunate to find an old army friend in the Governor of Oregon, Major General Charles H. Martin, retired. He has done a great deal to help me in my contacts with the people of the State. I was also fortunate to find our old friend, General Rilea at Salem. The Adjutant General of Oregon and the Commanding General of the 41st Division, General George White, has been most cordial. We served together on an examining board last month. He and I will command the opposing forces in the army maneuvers next August, and I am trusting him not to put a price on my head as you did in the 2d Army Maneuvers in Michigan last summer.

The latter part of April we leave for a month of division maneuvers at Fort Lewis, some of the troops coming from as distant points as Salt Lake City and San Francisco. We will also have a brief joint maneuver with the Navy and Marine Corps, for which I am Chief Umpire.

June and July will be occupied with ROTC, CMTC, and Reserve regiment camps here and on our firing range fourteen miles away. And the last two weeks of August we return to the Fort Lewis reservation and vicinity for army maneuvers.

The town of Vancouver—some 15,000 people—adjoins the post. Portland is across the Columbia eight miles distant. The people are friendly and cordial. The country seems prosperous despite the recent prolonged marine strike which inflicted heavy losses on the lumber people, the apple growers and many other industries of this vicinity.

I have just read the descriptions in the last Guardsman of the work of the Illinois National Guard during the flood.[2] Colonel Davis and his command evidently did a magnificent job in a manner which should convince every citizen of the security guaranteed his home and his family by the maintenance of efficient state troops. The frequent employment of the National Guard in times of public disaster, to succor the distressed and to reestablish law and order, should have dispelled all feelings of hostility towards the military, and should win for it the determined support of citizens generally. It is the great non-political force in this country, state or federal, for the security of citizens.

I am deeply interested in the continued development of the 33d Division towards combat team efficiency. As commanders, and particularly staffs, acquire facility in the expeditious conduct of training and handling of troops, the efficiency of the division will reach a state not now considered possible of achievement. Without increase in working time and with less effort they will be able to accomplish twice as much. You have a splendid personnel, and the sky is the limit.   Faithfully yours,

Illinois Guardsman, April 1937

1. Marshall was referring to Ulysses S. Grant (U.S.M.A., 1843), Philip H. Sheridan (U.S.M.A., 1853), George E. Pickett (U.S.M.A., 1846), Edward R.S. Canby (U.S.M.A., 1839), George Crook (U.S.M.A., 1852), John Gibbon (U.S.M.A., 1847), and John Pope (U.S.M.A., 1842).

2. The Illinois National Guard went to the aid of victims of the flood of January-February, 1937, in the Ohio and Mississippi river valleys. Lieutenant Colonel Robert W. Davis commanded the Guardsmen at Cairo, Illinois, a critical flood area at the confluence of the Ohio and Mississippi rivers.

TO MAJOR GENERAL JOHN A. LEJEUNE   March 26, 1937
                                          Vancouver Barracks, Washington

Dear General: As you no doubt will understand, I have had numerous letters from would-be candidates for the position of superintendent at the Institute. To practically all of them I have had nothing to say, except in the case of Phil Peyton, who is a dear friend and was my roommate at the V.M.I., who I esteem highly and whose tact and brain rank far above the average.[1] Today, however, someone sent me a list of candidates, and, most confidentially, I have become so concerned over the possibility that one or two of these might receive serious consideration because of their Army positions, that I feel moved to tell you something of their disqualifications. I am referring to General Bolles and General McCloskey.[2] To appoint either of these men, in my opinion, would be a fatal error. In personality and in methods they are completely disqualified. There is not much else to say.

I dislike putting my oar into this matter, but my feelings for the Institute are too strong to permit me to sit quiet under these circumstances.

As I remarked above, please treat this as most confidential.   Faithfully yours,

GCMRL/G. C. Marshall Papers (Vancouver Barracks)

1. Colonel Philip B. Peyton commanded the Twenty-ninth Infantry at Fort Benning.
2. Marshall had received a list of ten possible candidates for the V.M.I. job from Peyton. Major General Frank C. Bolles (U.S.M.A., 1896) and Brigadier General Manus McCloskey (U.S.M.A., 1898), Peyton said, were actively campaigning for the post. (Peyton to Marshall, March 20, 1937, GCMRL/G. C. Marshall Papers [Vancouver Barracks].)

TO JOHN L. CABELL   March 29, 1937
                                          Vancouver Barracks, Washington

My dear John: Your letter of March 24th arrived too late for an answer to reach you in Lexington at Easter time—you gave no dates.[1]

General LeJeune informed me before the news of his retirement became public, that he had submitted my name to the Board of Visitors as one of the men recommended to succeed him. Beyond thanking him, I did not express any ideas on the subject. What you probably heard was the report of my declining to have my name considered when Cocke was urging me to retire and succeed him.[2]

At the present time I have had nothing to say since the Board of Visitors has had nothing to say to me. Confidentially, I would decline if offered the place, but I do not care to make any such announcement unless the Board tenders me the opportunity, or at least expresses some preliminary interest in the matter. I take this position as there may come a day a few years hence when I would be honored and happy to have such an opportunity. Were I a major general today I think I would accept such an appointment. But, I would not care to do it short of that commission.

I appreciate your interest very much, after all these years, and would prefer to thank you personally, and I congratulate you on being the proud father of a cadet captain. He certainly put it over on his Dad.

Buster Peyton is a candidate for the V.M.I. job and has asked me to help him. He is very able, and very tactful—to the highly necessary quality.   Faithfully yours,

GCMRL/G. C. Marshall Papers (Vancouver Barracks)

1. Cabell (V.M.I., 1901), an assistant professor at V.M.I., 1902–3, was a state and county tax collector in Savannah, Georgia. He was spending Easter in Lexington, Virginia, with his son, John B. Cabell, a first classman at V.M.I.

2. In February, Cabell had been in Lexington and had been told that Marshall would not consider accepting the superintendent's position to be vacated by Major General John A. Lejeune on October 1.

TO LEONARD K. NICHOLSON   March 30, 1937
                                              Vancouver Barracks, Washington

Dear Nick: While on the train for San Francisco several weeks ago I read a long and glowing account of you, and of your prominence in the newspaper publishing field, in one of the weeklies—"Today," I think.[1] Herewith I tender my congratulations. You lead our class in the distinction of your achievement. I intended to write you a note at the time, but became immersed in business and forgot. A letter from John Cabell this morning—not referring to you—reminded me of my omission.

I have lived in many parts of the country, including the west coast, but am now having my first experience in the Northwest. It is a fascinating country of gorgeous scenery and agreeable people.

Have you still all your hair; and is it grey; and how about the waist line? I have mine in much its original tint, but my belts are now 36 inches; weight, on the hoof, 185.

Let me hear from you.   Affectionately,

GCMRL/G. C. Marshall Papers (Vancouver Barracks)

1. Nicholson, one of Marshall's roommates at V.M.I., was president of the New Orleans Times-Picayune Publishing Company. An article on the centennial of the *Times–Picayune* was published in *Newsweek* 9(February 6, 1937): 33–35. *Today* was merged with *Newsweek* in early 1937.

To Major Paul E. Peabody[1]   April 6, 1937
                                                  Vancouver Barracks, Washington

Dear Peabody: I have been due to acknowledge your note of congratulations when this morning along came your letter inclosing the papers on the Command and General Staff School. Please tell General Embick that I will go over them immediately and give him my reaction.[2]

I appreciate your cordial expressions regarding my promotion, particularly as I have always appreciated your fine service since the early days in the 1st Division. I had rather lost track of you in the last two years and did not know you were in the War Department. As a matter of fact it has been so long since I have been in touch with the War Department that I know little about it. Posts, schools, and maneuvers are more down my alley. Incidentally, I commanded the Red forces, except the Mechanized troops, in the 2nd Army maneuvers last summer and I have never learned more in my life in a similar period of time. As a matter of fact, that is hardly a correct statement, because it was more a matter of having ideas confirmed than a question of learning. This may sound egotistical, but I think you know what I mean. There is no longer any doubt in my mind but that much, a tremendous amount, of the technical, formerly, and still to a certain extent, taught at Benning, will not hold water as a practical proposition in a warfare maneuver.

I attended the GHQ-CPX in New Jersey, and as I have just said, I attended the 2nd Army maneuvers—in a troop capacity and not as a staff officer or umpire or as a spectator. Among some of the little things exemplified, which we warred about at Benning, were these samples: two armies were involved in the GHQ-CPX and there was not a map co-ordinate and there were very few contours—certainly there was nothing resembling a Gettysburg map; in the 2nd Army maneuvers, proper, again there were no co-ordinates, only small-scale maps and usually no contours. Strange to say, the farmers' houses had no names on them, on the map. Orders, at least on my side, were almost entirely oral; staff officers were more actively engaged in checking troop executions and dispositions than in sitting at a table fooling with the usual CPX occupations.

All our school officers, certainly those who have not recently been on troop duty in Hawaii or Panama should be placed in a position, at least once in every two years, with troops in the field—off reservations—in a maneuver continuous over several days, and have some of the impractical technique and theories washed out.

Confidentially, and you must not betray my radical statement, it is a crime the way the higher staffs submerge the staffs and units below them with detailed instructions, endless paper reports, and other indications of unfamiliarities with troop doings. I have come almost to feel that my principal duty as a commander is to be out with the troops protecting them against my own staff, however good that staff, under the present state of mind.

I don't know how I got started on this declaration, except that I remember some of our discussions at Benning, but I have gotten to the point where the sight of paper inflames me. So many officers never seem happy unless they have two pages of highly paragraphed something or other. I find about four sentences will usually do the trick, expeditiously.

I was very fortunate in my hospital experience, though the flu epidemic caused me a delay of five weeks while I waited for them to resume operating. I went into the hospital with a pulse of a hundred, and a pretty rough hundred at that, and I came out registering the old 72 that had done business for me up till last June. Thyroid pressure seemed to have been the difficulty, and not the toxic poisoning that plays such hob with the nerves. My trouble seems to be a tendency to enjoy my food too much and to gain weight for the first time since college; however, a new horse which has just been sent me from Riley, already is beginning to solve my difficulty.

I leave on the 23rd for a month of division maneuvers at Fort Lewis, and am looking forward to this as an opportunity for enjoyable outdoor business. Faithfully yours,

GCMRL/G. C. Marshall Papers (Vancouver Barracks)

1. Peabody had been personnel officer and supply officer of the First Division during the World War. In 1927, he graduated from the Advanced Course at the Infantry School, and later he served there as an instructor (1928–31). At the time of this letter, he was a member of the General Staff Corps in the Office of the Deputy Chief of Staff.

2. Major General Stanley D. Embick (U.S.M.A., 1899) had been deputy chief of staff since May 29, 1936. He had sent Marshall a memorandum requesting his views on instruction at the Command and General Staff School. Marshall's reply of April 13 follows.

MEMORANDUM FOR THE DEPUTY CHIEF OF STAFF   April 13, 1937
Vancouver Barracks,
Washington

Command and General Staff School.

As a preliminary, I should explain that I have not been on duty at Leavenworth since relieved as an instructor there in 1910. In 1928, I visited Leavenworth and other schools to examine into the instructional systems. For five years at the Infantry School, where most of the seventy instructors were Leavenworth graduates, I was constantly engaged in efforts to modify or change the type of problems, the instructional methods, the marking system, and the method of securing accurate data for efficiency reports. I corresponded with General Brees (then Assistant Commandant at Leavenworth) over the type of problems, and had a lengthy correspondence on this subject with General Heintzelman. Since then I have observed the results of the school system in the work of Leavenworth graduates as instructors for the National Guard and Reserves, and at the GHQ-CPX and 2d Army Maneuvers.

1. *QUESTIONS.*
   a. Group instruction.
   b. Elimination of marked problems.
   c. Change of name of school.

To these three questions I find myself in general agreement with Colonel E. L. Gruber in his memorandum of March 30th, so there appears to be no need for detailed repetition by me of the various arguments.[1]

Colonel Gruber's comment regarding the method for effecting changes at Leavenworth is, in my opinion, of first importance in considering material or fundamental alterations. To issue an edict or regulation would probably do more harm than good. The job must be a personal one, to be effected slowly as faulty minds, physical means, and other tangible factors are gradually rounded into shape for each step. Sudden changes in an educational plant are bound to be destructive, and any material changes must be timed by the man on the ground.

As to marked problems: I am strongly opposed to the present type and system and, at the same time, I am strongly in favor of marked problems. (There may have been recent basic changes with which I am unfamiliar.)

2. *QUESTIONS.*
   a. Entrance Examinations.
   b. Substitution of extension courses for nongraduates.

a. Any system for the selection of officers for the Leavenworth detail will be opposed. This cannot be avoided. But, I think the introduction, as a two-year experiment, of some form of examination would be desirable. The efficiency report seems too valuable a criterion of an officer's character and ability to be ignored. Therefore I would propose a fifty-fifty combination between efficiency report rating and examination results.

b. I think *temporary* measures should be taken to meet the present abnormal situation regarding the large number of able men who have been passed over in the Leavenworth selection: by temporary I mean, a procedure to meet the present dilemma only, to be in force for a short period, about five years. A special extension course, developed with *some* consideration for the current work of officers, seems to be a desirable remedy for the present situation as to morale.

3. *GENERAL COMMENTS.*

Aside from the specific questions discussed, and without a basis of recent intimate contacts with the school, there seem to be certain fundamental practices or policies at Leavenworth which I believe seriously lessen the tremendous benefits which should accrue to the national defense through the graduates of that great institution, and which bear a direct relation to the type of problems employed and to the marking system.

In the first place, to base most of the instruction on well-trained units, of full strength and complete as to corps troops, materiel, etc., is to qualify officers for something they will never find during the first years of an American war. As a matter of fact, we must be experts in the technique—and the *special* tactics—of handling hastily raised, partially trained troops, seriously deficient in corps and army establishments and heavy materiel; we must be experts in the difficult technique suitable to small-scale maps lacking most of the convenient details common to the Gettysburg variety; we must be experts in meeting the confusion and chaotic conditions of the first methods of a war when discipline is poor, officers green and information of the enemy invariably lacking; we must be specially trained in *when* to make decisions rather than concentrating almost entirely on *what* decision to make. All these things are far more difficult to learn than the related ponderous technique and formal tactics of Leavenworth, and for which to an important extent, in my opinion, the marking system has been partially responsible. There may have been changes in recent years, but I am told that this is not the case.

GCMRL/G. C. Marshall Papers (Vancouver Barracks)

1. Colonel Edmund L. Gruber (U.S.M.A., 1904) was the chief of the Training Branch, G-3, at the War Department. He had been an instructor at Fort Leavenworth's Command and General Staff School (1927–32). His memorandum of March 30 is not in the Marshall papers.

To JOHN L. CABELL April 20, 1937
Vancouver Barracks, Washington

Dear John: I have given your letter of April 9 careful thought, and while I appreciate exceedingly the compliment implied, I find myself still of the same decision regarding the V.M.I. appointment.[1]

You missed my point of view a little on the reason I did not feel free to give favorable consideration to the possibility at this time. That was almost purely financial. In other words, after about 35 years service, I would be throwing away a matter of about $2,000 a year for the rest of my life, even should I become a centenarian. Having just viewed the hazards of a profound depression, I am loath to walk away from as sure a thing as the United States Government.

Of course, through all of this, there is the question of abandoning the possibilities of the next eight or nine years, so far as that pertains to a professional soldier. With the world in its present turmoil no one can prophesy what the outcome will be, and as I made my life occupation that of a soldier I hesitate to take any decision which might leave me eliminated at the critical moment.

Of course, all the foregoing is confidential; I am giving it to you because of your flattering interest in me.   Faithfully yours,

GCMRL/G. C. Marshall Papers (Vancouver Barracks)

1. Cabell wrote that Marshall was the best qualified of the candidates for superintendent and replied to Marshall's statement of not accepting the superintendency without first having a major general's commission. "It is only to be expected that a man, who, at your age, has made such an enviable record, must have mapped out a line of progress and, of course, towards a goal to be reached for the declining years. But, what if opportunity presents the final goal before it is to be expected in the regular order of things?

"Not being conversant with Army records, I do not know how many Major Generals there have been since 1839 but the number of Superintendents at V.M.I. can be counted on the fingers of one hand—an honor not often bestowed but very highly held—and one that should be appreciated more by a comparatively young man if it comes his way sooner than he might have expected it.

"At this time, the acceptance of the position might make it appear to you as a sacrifice. That may be, but in what better cause can the sacrifice be made than in the opportunity to serve in shaping the careers of thousands of young men! Where else can a man who is qualified for such a position really exert more beneficial influence than in this case?" (Cabell to Marshall, April 9, 1937, GCMRL/G. C. Marshall Papers [Vancouver Barracks].)

MEMORANDUM FOR THE ADJUTANT GENERAL   April 23, 1937
                                                      Vancouver Barracks,
                                                      Washington

Memoriam on Vancouver Barracks Reservation to Hudson Bay Post.

1. There has been some correspondence in the past over the desire of citizens of Vancouver to secure the agreement of the War Department for the erection on the reservation, through congressional appropriation, of a replica of the Old Hudson Bay Trading Post, at the site of an old (and now highly controversial) apple tree.[1] (See letter AGO—000.45, Vancouver Barracks, 3-25-35, Misc. D). Recently a committee of citizens of Vancouver called on me, in the hope of securing a reconsideration by the War Department.

2. I have examined the records on file, including General Parsons' statement in his indorsement of April 29, 1935,[2] and I have gone over the ground. Also I have had available a map of 1845 furnished from the records of the Hudson Bay Company in London, England (photostat enclosed).

The actual site of the trading post should not be made available for the erection of a replica, and it is not desired. The plot which the citizens desire to obtain is on the lane leading from the old landing to the trading post. It is very conveniently accessible from the town of Vancouver, at the eastern foot of 2nd street, and it is ground once intimately connected with the daily life and activities of the old trading post. That the much advertised apple tree happens to be on this piece of ground, is unimportant to the main issue. In my opinion the history and age of the tree is a matter of conjecture. It is very old and it is located on the edge of the trace of the lane which led (and still leads) up from the landing place on the Columbia to the site of the trading post. The blue print of the military reservation in 1859, made by Captain Geo Thom, topographical engineer, shows a tree or trees at the approximate site of the disputed tree.

3. The plot of ground desired for the replica of the post (blue print attached) is little used and until a few months ago was rather unsightly. It is a portion of the post—or reservation—rarely visited except by the working parties hauling coal or wood. The erection of a replica of the trading post—slightly reduced in size— would actually improve the appearance of the reservation and would introduce a very interesting feature, where now there is nothing to please the eye. I see no inconvenience to the post, provided the necessary stipulations were made to insure that no exits were permitted leading into the reservation from the stockade, and that its maintenance is properly guaranteed.

4. Since the War Department made formal statement in this matter on May 27, 1935, I am submitting this letter direct in rather a confidential manner, to ascertain if there is a possibility of favorable reconsideration before taking up the matter more formally.[3]

G. C. Marshall

NA/RG 407 (000.45, Vancouver Barracks[3-25-35])

1. In early 1935, a citizens group, led by Mrs. Fay G. Peabody, had asked the War Department to permit them to construct a half-sized replica on a portion of the Vancouver Barracks reservation near what was locally considered to be the oldest apple tree in the northwest. (Peabody to Dern, March 25, 1935, NA/RG 407 [000.45, Vancouver Barracks (3-25-35)].)

2. Responding to Mrs. Peabody's request, the Vancouver Barracks commander at that time, Brigadier General James K. Parsons, urged rejection of the petition on the grounds that the army would need the proposed site in the event of a mobilization and that there was no evidence that the apple tree in question had any historical significance. (Fourth Indorsement, Parsons to Commanding General, Ninth Corps Area, April 29, 1935, ibid.)

3. When the War Department turned down Mrs. Peabody's request, it was on the grounds that the actual site of the old fort was on that portion of the reservation "now used for a flying field and for other purposes." (Acting TAG to Peabody, May 27, 1935, ibid.) To Marshall's memoriam, Major General Edgar T. Conley (U.S.M.A., 1897), the army adjutant general, replied: "It appears that the new location now desired by the Vancouver citizens may meet the objections raised in the former refusal. While it is impossible to state now the final action upon a formal request, it appears worthwhile to have such a request resubmitted." (TAG to Marshall, May 22, 1937, ibid.)

To Major General Frank R. McCoy   May 16, 1937
                                                  Fort Lewis, Washington

Dear General: I forwarded your very welcome letter to Katherine while I
thought things over. This afternoon I received word from her that if I did not
accept your fine and complimentary offer I was something of a fool. Meanwhile
I had come to the same conclusion myself, not to mention considerations of
ingratitude and lack of appreciation.[1]

I will be delighted if you can arrange to have me designated to command the
First Division.

Frankly, I should think there would be difficulty in having this arranged, due
to my lack of rank. If there are three brigade commanders for the division, it
seems to me it will be difficult for you to find three available who are my juniors.
As a brigade proposition my present command is delightful—as to post, personnel, and especially as to the activities concerning the CCC which cover all of
Oregon and southern Washington.

Naturally the opportunity to command my old division appeals very strongly
to me; a special honor and a great satisfaction. Then also, there is nobody in the
army with whom I would prefer to serve so much as I would with you personally.
The mere prospect of a renewal of such association is delightful. I felt very sad
over your departure from Chicago as it appeared to be the end of our military
contacts. Your present proposal therefore is all the more appealing to me.

I have been here at Lewis since April 24th for 3d Division maneuvers. Sarted
out this morning—Sunday—at two o'clock on a maneuver which terminated at
noon. Hardly a restful Sunday. The past two weeks have been particularly
strenuous, and tomorrow the Corps Area inspection gets underway. We will be
out three nights this week, which means more here than in other regions with
which I am familiar, as the rains are almost daily affairs and it has been quite
cold at night with strong winds to cut the chill through your clothes.

I have enjoyed the maneuvers and the outdoor life tremendously. Brought my
new horse up here—one sent me from Riley—and have had fine rides, with
splendid views of Mt Ranier which towers over the reservation.

I came up here by way of the Columbia river gorge and Yakima, where I had a
dinner engagement. Katherine came along and spent one night here, returning to
Vancouver in care of my young CCC driver. She drove up again for a week end,
Molly coming up with some young people for a dance.

Physically I feel fine, except that I have gained too many pounds, which
Katherine thinks becoming, but which I deplore around the belt line. My
operation seems to have been a grand success. I suffered none of the usual
reactions and registered normal in heart action—which had been the only
symptom of any trouble—by the ninth day. Apparently pressure had caused the
trouble rather than toxic poisoning which shoots up the nervous system. Strange

to say I never felt better than when I went into the hospital, and I feel just as well now, and more impatient to get into everything with full energy. However, I am being very gradual about getting back to normal physical activities. They tell me not to work up to normal before the first of June. So long as I can ride horseback every day this precaution imposes no hardship.

Katherine has been a great success in Portland. Formerly the post had few contacts with the city, but already she seems to be the most sought after women about town. All the old conservatives are after here constantly, by telephone, motor and otherwise, to do this and that with them. I have been away so much that I am not very well known about town. I am merely Mrs. Marshall's husband—and much honored and pleased to be so considered. They have good taste.

Give my love to Francis, and believe me most appreciative and hopeful. Affectionately yours,

G. C. Marshall

LC/F. R. McCoy Papers; T

1. McCoy asked Marshall if he was interested in commanding the First Division after its commander, Brigadier General Perry L. Miles (U.S.M.A., 1895), retired in October. (McCoy to Marshall, May 6, 1937, LC/F. R. McCoy Papers.) Marshall did not receive the appointment. See Marshall to McCoy, July 4, 1937, below.

FROM LIEUTENANT COLONEL JOHN F. LANDIS[1]   May 18, 1937
Washington, D.C.

My dear General Marshall: I have just heard that you have been laid up recently although not seriously.

Colonel Spaulding in his recent book on the American Army in referring to General Morrison speaks of the early Leavenworth graduates who were proud to call themselves "Morrison men."[2] You may not know it but there are a number of your juniors who regard themselves as self-appointed "Marshall men." Speaking as one of these may I express the wish that you relax a bit and ease up for a while thus giving old dame nature a chance to get in a few good licks and set everything aright. I feel sure that that is everything that is necessary.

Trusting that by this time you are feeling much better, I am, Sincerely yours,

John Landis

GCMRL/G. C. Marshall Papers (Vancouver Barracks)

1. Landis was with the Historical Section at the Army War College. He had been an instructor at the Infantry School (1925–29).

2. Oliver L. Spaulding, *The United States Army in War and Peace* (New York: G. P. Putnam's Sons, 1937), pp. 397–98. See Marshall to Lentz, October 2, 1935, above, p. 45.

To Lieutenant Colonel John F. Landis   May 29, 1937
                                                        Vancouver Barracks,
                                                        Washington

Dear Landis: Thank you very much for your nice note of sympathetic inquiry.
I am quite all right, having just returned from a month of Division maneuvers at
Fort Lewis. They were pretty strenuous, but I took them in a philosophical
manner, leaving the younger men to do the wheel-horse work.

My trouble is, I feel so well that the desire to live actively is difficult to suppress; also, for the first time in my life I began to gain weight last July, and even
an operation does not set me back.

Thank you for your inquiry. I used to see Reed Landis quite frequently in
Chicago and of course we talked about you.[1] I have never forgotten our
mechanized warfare problem, for which you were largely responsible.

With warm regards to Mrs. Landis and yourself—tell her I have a new horse
from Fort Riley that is a dandy. I am going riding in a few minutes.   Faithfully
yours,

GCMRL/G. C. Marshall Papers (Vancouver Barracks)

1. Chicago business executive Reed G. Landis, John's cousin, had been a pilot during the
World War. He was the son of professional baseball commissioner Judge Kenesaw Mountain
Landis.

To Colonel Morrison C. Stayer[1]   May 30, 1937
                                                Vancouver Barracks, Washington

Dear Stayer: Your nice note has just come telling me of your conversation with
Kirk. He is a splendid surgeon and a dandy fellow. I felt very confident with
things in his hands, and he certainly seems to have done a marvelous job on me.

Last July my steady old seventy two pulse, winter or summer, walk or run,
suddenly developed an intermission—one beat in twelve. In a week or two it was
missing every fifth or sixth beat. Then, in a short time it went completely fluey, a
tumultuous 95 to 105. Strange to say, I never felt better in my life; gaining weight
steadily from June on, until I had run up from college poundage, and that of
practically all my service, to eighteen pounds additional. I had a terribly active
part in the 2d Army maneuvers, commanding the Red side, and attacking, with
from thre[e][2] to six thousand troops, a corps of eighteen thousand. Nearly got
captured three times, reconnoitering on foot. And gained three pounds during
the affair, whil[e] every one else lost from five to ten pounds!

As soon as I came out here I commenced a carefu[l] series of tests, finally
having the heart expert of the northwest—Homer Coffin,[3] go over me. Except

for pulse and cardiagram, all tests were normal, including BMR [Basal Metabolic Rate]. Coffin decided the trouble was undoubtedly thyroid, of which I had had a swelling for fifteen years. But he thought pressure was causing the functional disorder of the heart. They came to the same conclusion in San Francisco. Kirk has told you what they found.

He operated one Monday. On Tuesday my pulse was in the eighties; on Wednesday, in the seventies, and on Thursday, in the sixties! Ten days later the EKG [electrocardiogram] showed a normal heart beat, just as they were starting on a treatment with—, you know, a quinine derivative, I think. Apparently I missed all the nervous reaction which comes from toxic poison from the thyroid, as I fely fine, and not the least nervous, within four days of the operation.

I just returned three days ago from a month of 3d Division maneuvers at Fort Lewis. It was all very interesting. I commanded either a reenforced brigade or the division, but I allowed the boys to do all the running around, while I took things easily, except that I made the decisions and told the staff where to look next, and next, for trouble. The only strain was this business, in the field, of breakfast at two-thirty or thereabouts. Even so, I would curl up in my car, with the small seats covered with a blanket, and get in another snooze, early morning, mid-day or late afternoon. I had an EKG the morning after the last, and a three day, maneuver, and it showed a normal heart, with a pulse after a nights reast of 64.

I am telling you some details, so that you will realize that I am taking things slowly and carefully, though I feel like running all over the place. I have a horse, sent me from Riley in February, who furnishes me some fine rides in lovely country.

Katherine and I are doing frequent picnic lunches along with fishing ventures for steel head, bass, salmon and trout. We go out about three times a week; and I am taking her on my CCC inspections to the Snake River country, the Bend Valley, Crater Lake, and the region of Rouge River and the Uncompagr [*Umpqua*]. My work takes me into the most famous fishing country in the States, and where the scenery is magnificient. I park her at the little inn or hotel, and do the CCC in the vicinity. Then she and I fish and picnic. When Molly is not pressed with engagements here on the post, she goes along. It is a very delightful life.

Give my love to your wife and the Rogers,[4] and believe me, always,   Faithfully yours,

G. C. M.

Tell me how things line for you for Asst. Surgeon General and Surgeon General. It is time you were getting underway.

GCMRL/M. C. Stayer Papers; T

1. Stayer—who first met Marshall in Tientsin, China—was a 1930 graduate of the Advanced Course at the Infantry School. In 1931, Marshall appointed him head of the school's Third Section (weapons and physical training). While at Fort Benning, Stayer was Marshall's private physician and became acquainted with Marshall's fibrillation of the heart. (Major General

Morrison C. Stayer, interviewed by Forrest C. Pogue, January 20, 1960, GCMRL.) At the time of this letter, Stayer was stationed at Fort Riley, Kansas.

Because the state of his health, real or rumored, could influence his career, Marshall frequently typed or wrote by hand letters dealing with the subject. For example, see Marshall to Stayer, October 18, 1938, below.

2. Marshall occasionally typed off of the right edge of the paper; the missing letters are supplied in brackets.

3. Dr. T. Homer Coffen was a physician in Portland, Oregon.

4. Major and Mrs. Pleas B. Rogers were at Fort Riley, Kansas. He had been a student in the Infantry School's Advanced Course in 1929–30.

To Major Frank B. Hayne   June 3, 1937
                                    Vancouver Barracks, Washington

My dear Frank: Thanks for your note of May 27th, and my congratulations on your detail.[1] This should mean an intensely interesting period of your service. One suggestion, if I may make it, don't fall into the diplomatic state of mind as to the activities about you. Keep the American army in the forefront of your head all the time, and draw your deductions accordingly, from what you see. So frequently officers go off on such ventures and their view point becomes submerged in the strange and active social life, and their thoughts grow remote from the army at home they are supposed to serve with ideas and data.

General Pershing invited Mrs. Marshall and myself to go over in August and be present at the dedication of the Romagne cemetery—or rather, the Meuse-Argonne monuments. I have been delaying in answering in the hope that we could find it practicable to accept, but I fear now that we cannot make it, much as I should like to be there.

I have just returned from a month of division maneuvers at Fort Lewis, one hundred and fifty miles north of here. Had a very interesting time.

Commencing next Monday, Mrs. Marshall and I are off on a series of CCC inspections, which take me through the most famous fishing country of the northwest. And I plan to get in fishing every other day. We will gone a week this first trip, doing eastern Oregon as far out as the Snake River and down almost to Crater Lake. Two weeks later I do a series of camps along the sea shore south of Astoria, and have been loaned a summer cottage to utilize as headquarters, where I will park Mrs. Marshall and Molly. We will get in some ocean bathing and some steel head fishing. Then a week later, when it is warmer and the snows are largely melted, we go to Crater Lake.

We have made a habit lately, when ever we have no dinner date, to take a frying pan and some provender and go off fishing for the evening on some of the lakes or beautiful streams in this vicinity. We are going to a falls on the Lewis river this evening, for steel heads.

Write and tell me how things go in Russia. I will be much interested. If you see Truman Smith in Berlin, give him my regards. He knows his job.

You probably will not see Mrs. Dulany after you receive this, tho I am mailing it to Washington; but if you do, give them our love. I received a letter from her while I was on maneuvers.[2]

Good luck to you.   Faithfully yours,

G. C. M.

GCMRL/F. B. Hayne Papers; T

1. Hayne was to report in October as assistant military attache at the United States Embassy in Moscow.

2. Mrs. Dulany, who lived at "Oakley," near Upperville, Virginia, was Frank B. Hayne's mother-in-law.

To General John J. Pershing   June 5, 1937
                                          Vancouver Barracks, Washington

Dear General: I have delayed in answering your letter, written on the eve of sailing for England, while trying to figure out how Katherine and myself could accept your invitation to be present at the dedication of the Meuse-Argonne Memorials in August.[1] Naturally, I am terribly keen to go, and she is equally anxious; and for a time I thought we could work it out. But I now find it is not going to be practical for us to have this pleasure. I hate to think of this great work of yours coming to its final head, without my having seen anything of it on the ground. Also, it would give me a great thrill to stand on the Meuse-Argonne Field with you again.

We both have been scheming ever since April, to see our way clear to accept; but there are too many difficulties in the way at this particular time.

I am feeling fine, very fine; riding every day, fishing quite a few evenings each week, and gaining weight in spite of dieting. I had a month of quite strenuous maneuvers with the Third Division at Fort Lewis, and while I grew tired of having breakfast at 2:30 in the morning, nevertheless I enjoyed the affair tremendously.

Katherine and I are off tomorrow for a week of inspection of the CCC in eastern Oregon. I carry her along to fish with me between camps, leaving her at small hotels while I am actually inspecting. We will be trying for Rainbow Trout in the lake just north of Crater Lake, in a small crater lake in the mountains to the east, and in a famous lake near Snake River, east of Pendleton. A few days after we return here, we are off again to inspect camps on the coast south of Astoria. Someone has loaned me a beach cottage which Mrs. Marshall and Molly will enjoy and which I will use as a base for my inspections. It is, as you may see, a very healthy life, and a pleasant one. Do you remember Cameron Forbes jumping on me for my method of landing bass? I have a better technique now.

I have seen a number of photographs of you in England, and have heard over the radio several references to your impressive speech at Romagne on Decoration Day.[2] I hope that you have not been overdoing.

With affectionate regards,   Faithfully yours,

G. C. Marshall

McCoy has written, asking me if I care to have him apply for me to command the 1st Division—in October. I have replied that I would like such an arrangement, but I doubt whether it can be arranged, due to my lack of rank.[3]

LC/J. J. Pershing Papers (General Correspondence)

1. "It occurs to me that you and your attractive and charming better-half might well consider coming to France this summer for some of our dedications. The main one is to be held August 1st at Montfaucon, which has, as you know, already been classified as one of the fifteen decisive battles of the world by some writer of more or less importance, but whom we like to think of as being of considerable importance." (Pershing to Marshall, April 21, 1937, GCMRL/G. C. Marshall Papers [Vancouver Barracks].)

2. On May 30, General Pershing had dedicated the new chapel in the A.E.F. cemetery at Romagne-sous-Montfaucon.

3. This postscript was written in Marshall's hand.

COMMENTS FOR THE C.C.C. DISTRICT   [June, 1937]
REVIEW ON CAMP INSPECTIONS[1]   Vancouver Barracks,
Washington

I was much impressed by the uniform standard of excellence of the camps in eastern Oregon. Some camps, of course, were better than others; but as a general rule all came well up to the standard required for this particular district. The most important differences usually lay in the attitude of the boys towards self improvement. There were camps where practically every boy was definitely and determinedly trying to make up his deficiencies in education, or to fit himself practically for a position in civil life—and as rapidly as possible.

This matter of schooling, outside of the forestry, soil conservation, or other work of the companies, is in my opinion, the most important phase of the CCC program at the present time. The work in the woods, on the trails or otherwise, is the justification for the camps; but their primary purpose is to fit young men, now out of employment, to become more valuable and self supporting citizens. On every side it has become glaringly apparent during the past two years of business revival, that hereafter the unskilled man will have a desperately hard time succeeding, much harder than ever before. Today it is almost impossible in many regions for him to find any work that will be continuous or will pay enough to provide a decent living according to the much talked of American standard. At the same time, the skilled man can get work almost anywhere, and at a high wage. Labor saving devices and quantity production have combined to raise wages and eliminate unskilled labor. Fortunately, in America the opportunity is offered every boy in one way or another to fit himself for such work, if, and only if, he has the ambition and will power to drive him to the task of preparation. The CCC offers a rare opportunity; for here in the camps, bed, board and clothing are provided in a generous measure; healthy, outdoor work is the rule, the physical well being of the individual is taken care of to a degree not usually possible in the ordinary home; and an educational adviser, books and other facilities are made conveniently available. If a boy allows this opportunity to slip by, he will allow most of the remaining good things of life to slip past his door.

The weakest features of the camp system at present are involved in the "Spike" or "Trail" camps. Too frequently the leader or assistant leader in charge allows things to deteriorate—in morale, in personal and barracks cleanliness, and in the efficiency of the efforts of the kitchen force. These failures are usually due to one of two reasons: the company commander's lack of ability as a leader, his influence weakening with each mile of distance of the detachment from the main camp; or, his failure to select the right man as a leader, or to hold him to that duty. Corrective measures are going to be taken in this matter.

I found that the hard rains of last week had demonstrated that a portion of our tentage, in the temporary camps, had seriously deteriorated. This will be replaced. In the camp at Stanfield a severe wind storm had caused considerable damage.

What particularly impressed me was the ingenuity displayed in some of the temporary camps in arranging or fixing things in a convenient fashion. This was especially noticeable at Canyon City. The company near Ukiah has a difficult problem in transportation, which is being met in an efficient manner. The men at Odell Lake and at Enterprise have especially favorable sites, and are making the best use of them. Since my last inspection in Eastern Oregon, there have been marked improvements in several cases, notably at Zig Zag, at Hilgard and at Stanfield. Heppner continues to be a model camp, with Squaw Creek crowding it hard. Baker has been suffering from an epidemic of mumps and such a small enrollment that, with two Spike camps, the base camp has very few men for duty, which makes difficult the conduct of a bountiful mess. Unfortunately, thru lack of time, I was unable to inspect the camp at Moro. Incidentally, we have just received informal notice that there will be a new enrollment in July, and that the present restrictions are to be modified, permitting practically any boy over seventeen to enroll who needs a job. This should result in a material increase in numbers.

I have come in contact with young men here and there in the camps who display such outstanding efficiency, energy and determination, that I am making a special personal effort to locate for them good jobs in civil life. In doing this I have two things in mind—the boy deserves the break, and, what I believe is more important, he will be an excellent advertisement to convince employers that their

Cartoon published in the Vancouver Barracks C.C.C. District Review, June 1, 1938.

best labor or job market is in the CCC, if they want wholly dependable men who have demonstrated unmistakably that they have both the character and the ability. I am hopeful that good progress can be made in this matter, which will lead to a really effective system of placing men deserving of such consideration.[2]

Vancouver Barracks C.C.C. District *Review*, July 1, 1937

1. The week of June 7, Marshall traveled fourteen hundred miles inspecting the Civilian Conservation Corps camps of eastern Oregon.

2. The district C.C.C. newspaper later reported that Marshall had "urged sub-district commanders and staff members to be on the lookout for boys who are doing something well. Letters of commendation will be sent to boys achieving excellent records in camps. Last year General Marshall wrote to several hundred enrollees and in many cases such letters proved of value to those seeking employment at the expiration of their terms of service in the C.C.C." (C.C.C. District *Review*, March 1, 1938.)

To Brigadier General Thomas E. Rilea   June 16, 1937
                                                     Vancouver Barracks,
                                                           Washington

My dear General Rilea: I received your note this morning and am inclosing the necessary application blanks and instructions for your boy to enter the CMTC.[1]

I am delighted that he and you have seen fit to enter into this thing this summer. I am particularly pleased because I found it necessary to make a special canvas in order to obtain a higher grade of boys than had been secured in the past. I think we are going to have a fine camp; at any rate, I am sure I have arranged a more interesting program than has been the custom in the past. The boys will be taken away from the post for about ten days and will be more or less in the field at the target range and maneuver ground, about 14 miles from here, which has been greatly improved in the past year. I think they will find this much more interesting than the humdrum program on the post.

I am looking forward with a great deal of interest to seeing you and General White at Fort Lewis. Please give him my warm regards. Believe me,   Faithfully yours,

GCMRL/G. C. Marshall Papers (Vancouver Barracks)
    1. Rilea had requested an application for his son, Thomas, Jr., to attend the summer Citizens' Military Training Camp.

SHORTLY AFTER 5:00 P.M. (Pacific Standard Time) on June 17, 1937, three Russian fliers left Moscow to attempt the first non-stop flight to the United States by way of the North Pole. The single-engine monoplane headed for Oakland, California, carrying Pilot Valeri P. Chkalov, Co-pilot Georgi P. Baidukov, and Navigator Alexander V. Beliakov. Sixty-three hours later, the U.S. Army Signal Corps station at Seattle, Washington, received a message in international code that the craft had to make an emergency landing. Thus, on Sunday, June 20, at 8:22 A.M., under overcast skies, the plane set down on Pearson Field, Vancouver Barracks, having covered 5,288 miles. Inclement weather and poor visibility caused the premature stop, the pilot insisted, not a failing fuel pump. (Portland *Oregonian*, June 21, 1937; *New York Times*, June 21, 1937.)

The three weary fliers, unable to speak English, were met at the plane by a Russian-speaking Reserve officer and taken to Marshall's house for baths, breakfast, and sleep. Marshall ordered guards posted around the plane, the house, and in front of the fliers' bedroom doors. Meanwhile, reporters, photographers, news broadcasters, and various dignitaries were en route to the Marshall residence. Soviet Ambassador Alexander A. Troyanovsky arrived from Oakland, California, and that evening a radio broadcast was aired from Marshall's living room.

The ambassador compared the flight to Charles A. Lindbergh's, and the Soviet press asserted that the feat could have been accomplished only under a socialist regime. Telegrams and telephone calls from throughout the world poured into the Marshall residence. The local newspaper shouted in two-inch type: "Epochal Soviet Flight Ends." Complimentary references to Brigadier General and Mrs. Marshall were also printed. (Portland *Oregonian*, June 21, 1937.)

On Monday, the Vancouver Barracks garrison paid tribute to the airmen with a parade in their honor. In the afternoon Brigadier General Marshall, Ambassador Troyanovsky, and Governor Martin accompanied the Soviet heroes in a parade through Portland and to a Chamber of Commerce luncheon, prior to the fliers' departure for the east coast. (K. T. Marshall, *Together*, pp. 25–28; Portland *Oregonian*, June 22, 1937.) ★

TO ANNE LINDSEY[1]
June 27, 1937
Vancouver Barracks, Washington

My dear Nan: I found your nice note on my return from five days on the sea shore, where Mrs. Marshall had the loan of a cottage near Tillamook. Look that up on your map. It is famous for cheese, gorgeous scenery and the finest fishing in the northwest.

We were interested to know that you and May happened to hear the broad cast. I am sorry that you could not hear Katherine. The radio people were determined that she should say something, but she was adamant. The truth was, by that time of the evening she only wanted to sit and listen. The three fliers dropped in our lap at eight thirty of a Sunday morning; more than sixty press, radio and photographic peopl[e] had accumulated by ten or eleven; and the Ambassador, arriving at three thirty, only brought six in his party for lunch. Our house closely resembled a union station, except that all had but one object in view.

Entertaining the Russian air men would have been a ver[y] simple problem, except for getting them complete civilian outfits, altered and all, on a Sunday afternoon. It was the swarm of news people that we had to shelter—for it was raining hard all day and we could not leave them out in the weather. Three different broad cast setups were established in the house that evening. Fortunately we have an unusually large place—tremendous hall, one living room forty feet long and one about thirty feet square; also a detached library with phone, lavatory, etc., where we parked the press. In a large bed room at the back of the house we opened a complete clothing store, with outfits, in such quantites and sizes that any one could be satisfied. One item, there were fifteen pairs of shoes. Cheval glass, sewing machine, tailor to make alterations, three Russian interpreters to help the men in their choice and fitting. I think there were fourteen calls from Moscow in the first few hours. London had me on the phone within a half hour of the landing.

Enough of the Russians. Katherine and I have had a delightful time this late spring and early summer. Whenever we do not have a dinner date we take a frying pan, our fishing tackle, and drive off to some lovely lake or waterfall to fish and cook our supper. These places are so numerous and so close by that it is a delight to utilize them to the full; and the twilight lasts until almost nine o'clock. So we usually do not start out until after four.

Ten days ago we returned from a 1400 mile CCC inspection trip in Easter Oregon. I did the inspecting of camps, and she and I fished and did scenery in the intervals. We crossed mountain ranges seven times, cooked our lunch in mountain passes or by beautiful waters; spent one night in Canyon City, a famous tough, shooting gold mining town of the old days—one street wide, in a deep canyon—and only about two blocks long. The placer miners still line the stream, and a dredge is working the creek bottom. K. landed between four indians at the counter in the one little eat joint, and one of the braves was drunk. She got quite a thrill out of that. We rested up several days at a lodge on Wallola Lake, near the Idaho line, and fished for rainbows with a back ground of snow peaks and ridges. Next week we are off again toward central Oregon, and plan to fish the famous McKenzie River and spent several days at Crater Lake.

I was off at maneuvers for a month in April and May, near Tacoma, Washington; and I return for some largeer maneuvers the last two weeks in August. Katherine and Molly plan to meet me there at the close of the maneuvers, to motor up to Victoria and around Vancouver Island, British Columbia. Then the middle of August we are taking a party of young people to Wallola Lake for a week, to end up at the Pendleton Round Up for a day or two. I said August, but I meant September.

Katherine joins me in affectionate regards to you, May Catherine and the Armstrongs. We often talk of our delightful visit with you last September. K. objects strenuously to my draging her, impromptu fashion to see my friends; but you all made everything so charming for her that she has forgiven me my previous failures.

Incidentally, the lady whose wedding we were enroute through your place to attend at Exeter,[2] will be with us here in two weeks, enroute around the world.

With my love,   Faithfully yours,

G. C. M.

I fear poor Harry Cootes is in a sad way.[3]

GCMRL/C. L. Armstrong Papers; T

1. Anne (Nan) Lindsey and her sisters May and Catharine Lindsey (Mrs. Egbert) Armstrong were childhood friends of Marshall in Uniontown, Pennsylvania.
2. Mrs. Emily Russell Brown.
3. Colonel Harry N. Cootes retired at the end of June, 1937. He died on October 29, 1938.

FROM GENERAL MALIN CRAIG   June 28, 1937
                                                  Washington, D.C.

My dear George: I have your note of June 26th with the enclosed copies of letters from the Broadcasting people.[1]

I received a wild yell from the Columbia people in New York, who in effect gave me the idea that they were not allowed to use the broadcasting system to Russia and wished me to issue the order. I, of course, declined to do that and told them that all such matters were in the hands of the Corps Area Commander and that it would not be practicable for me to issue an order over his head,[2] especially when he has not been brought into the picture. I then called up Pratt and told him of the request and to handle it there on hearing from you.[3] From all I can hear, you did your part beautifully and I marvel at you and Mrs. Marshall being able to turn your house inside out even for an occasion of that sort. These same flyers are here in Washington now and are driving us crazy with receptions and visits and cocktail parties in their honor. I do not care when they go back to Russia.

I have no particular news for you, though it may interest you to know that our Appropriation Bill is being held up in conference by Ross Collins, who objects to the personnel increase on the ground that we are putting everything into pay envelopes and have nothing for materiel. Also Senator Copeland held up the bill until he could join it to the Rivers and Harbors Bill,[4] which latter bill was padded to the tune of $183,000,000 after it passed the House, and it makes our Army Appropriation bill look like a very war-like affair, when as a matter of fact it only carries $415,000,000, every cent of which can be defended for an army of 165,000 men. I do not believe the thing will be settled before the 1st of July, and we may be compelled to get along on a concurrent resolution continuing this year's appropriation until the matter is settled.

I hear only the finest things of you and Mrs. Marshall and your administration. While that was to be expected as far as I am concerned, it may please you to know that such is the fact. I hope that all goes well with you and that you are your usual active, cheerful and healthy self.

With every good wish for you and kind regards to Mrs. Marshall, believe me Sincerely,

Malin Craig

GCMRL/G. C. Marshall Papers (Vancouver Barracks)

1. Marshall's June 26 letter to Craig is not in the Marshall papers.
2. Major General George S. Simonds (U.S.M.A., 1899) was the Ninth Corps Area commander at the Presidio of San Francisco. He had been commandant at the Army War College (1932–35) and deputy chief of staff (February, 1935–June, 1936) before assuming command of the Ninth Corps Area.
3. Colonel Raymond S. Pratt (U.S.M.A., 1901) was chief of staff of the Fourth Army and Ninth Corps Area. Pratt wrote Marshall that he had received a call from General Craig and had replied "that there were no difficulties and that I had told the radio broadcasting company that I was sure you would do everything necessary on your own initiative but just to satisfy them I had called you up on the subject and found that you had done so. General Craig said he was sure that would be the case." (Pratt to Marshall, June 21, 1937, GCMRL/G. C. Marshall Papers [Vancouver Barracks].) In response, Marshall wrote: "Within two hours after the landing of the Russians I heard from NBC in New York, in San Francisco, and in Portland—as well as from the man on the ground. About the same procedure was followed by the Columbia people. They were all accorded permission immediately to run their wires into the house; my stipulation was that the manner of the broadcast would have to be determined by the ambassador." (Marshall to Pratt, June 26, 1937, ibid.)
4. Ross A. Collins, a Democrat representing Mississippi's Fifth District, was a member of the House Appropriations Committee. Senator Royal S. Copeland, a Democrat representing the state of New York, was a member of the Senate Appropriations Committee.

TO MAJOR GENERAL GEORGE S. SIMONDS

July 1, 1937
Vancouver Barracks,
Washington

Dear General: Thank you for your nice note of June 26. I appreciate very much your thanks, and am glad to know that the Russian affair seemed to go off satisfactory to your desires. As a matter of fact, the matter of entertaining the Russian fliers was no trouble at all. The trouble was the simultaneous looking after the Russian ambassador and his party of five, and none less than 60 members of the press and radio, who were under our roof until late Sunday night—and the Ambasssador of course was a house guest.

I found no difficulty in dealing with the radio people. They were most amenable. The reporters were as usual, but I long ago became familiar with them while traveling with General Pershing. The photographers were the ones that gave me gray hairs. In the interest of possible scoops, they of course tried to pull any stunt—trying to slip up stairs and photograph the fliers in bed etc., etc., and scrambling all over the plane the moment we relaxed. But however, we got through all right.

I am glad that you can find it possible to approve the Hudson Bay matter. I am in full agreement with the War Department in regard to chiseling in on Army posts, but this affair seemed to be justified.[1] The fact was, I contemplated it even before I heard of the movement, but I was going to do it with salvage lumber. Faithfully yours,

GCMRL/G. C. Marshall Papers (Vancouver Barracks)

1. Simonds had inclosed a copy of his indorsement approving Marshall's request for the construction of a replica of the Old Hudson Bay Trading Post. Simonds wrote: "I am not just sure how this will be received in the War Department. General Craig, as were his predecessors in office, is quite fed up with the continual chiseling in on Army reservations for all sorts of purposes throughout the Army of the United States. As a result of my tour of duty in the War Department, I cannot help but be quite in sympathy with their feeling. However, I think it is justified in this case and hope it goes through." (Simonds to Marshall, June 26, 1937, GCMRL/G. C. Marshall Papers [Vancouver Barracks].)

To Major General Frank R. McCoy   July 4, 1937
                                        Vancouver Barracks, Washington

My dear General: Your note has just come telling us that there is no hope of my being assigned to the 1st Division in October.[1] We are disappointed, primarily and most of all because we will not be with you and Francis this next year. Katherine, of course, is disappointed that she will not be closer to the family and her beloved Fire Island. However, she takes it like a veteran, and went down town immediatel[y] to buy some yard furniture and some other items she had let go by in the expectation that she would only be here a few months longer.

Fortunately the news came when the weather and the flowers, shrubs and trees were—and are—at their loveliest. Oregon is a beautiful state, and this time of the year the northwest is gorgeous. Each night we have free from a dinner engagement we go off about four thirty, with fishing tackle and a frying pan, seek some lovely lake or water fall, and fish and cook our supper; then drive home in the twilight, which carries us almost up to nine o'clock in this latitude. We enjoy these informal outings tremenduously, and some day Katherine will get a big steel head on her line.

A few days before the Russians descended on us K. and I returned from a 1400 mile CCC trip. We crossed mountain ranges seven times, cooked our lunches on mountain tops, stayed in delightful lodges, spent a night in famous old Canyon City—a one street mining town famous for its rough stuff, fished in lakes and rivers, made our way slo[w]ly through flocks of two and three thousand sheep a number of times; and had a delightful outing—all in eastern Oregon. As soon as the Russians left we lit out, with Molly for the sea shore south of Astoria, near Tillamook. A cottage had been loaned us and we stayed there for five days while I did some CCC inspections in that vicinity.

Next Thursday we start out on a weeks trip in southern Oregon. I am taking my executive and his wife, old friends of ours I brought out here, and my aide and Molly.[2] We men will do some camps and then all of us will fish the Mackenzie River, cross the mountain there and go on to Crater Lake. Then we plan to stop at East Lake—another, and smaller, crater affair famous for its rainbow trout fishing. We will stay there several days; then I will bring the women home while the other two men do some camps I saw on my last trip in that region.

I go up to maneuvers the middle of August and we plan to do Victoria and Vancouver Island as I go north to Tacoma. Molly and her mother will come back to Vancouver, and I will do two weeks at Lewis.

The Russian flyers were not much of a problem, except as to clothes on a Sunday; but the Ambassador with six in his. party and not less than sixty members of the press and radio in the house all of Sunday up to almost midnight! The Ambassador stayed with us, but I sent his attaches back to a hotel in Portland. Poor Katherine had to feed the news men coffee and sandwiches by the gallon and bale. All of this would not have been difficult with the resources of an army post, but when it develops in thirty minutes, and on a Sunday morning at breakfast time, there are some complications. London had me on the phone within twenty minutes—by name—and Moscow within the half hour! After that it was a constant phoning from all over the US and Europe.

Again, my thanks for your effort to get me the 1st Division. Maybe something yet will develop to bring our families together; but I had been planning on your assistance this fall in Katherine's birthday parade ceremony.[3]

With love to you both, from all of us,   Affectionately,

G. C. Marshall

LC/F. R. McCoy Papers; T

1. On June 28, McCoy wrote: "Since writing you I have had the chance to talk over things with the Chief of Staff, and am sorry to say that for the present there seems no probability of your being assigned to the 1st Division. However, he is as fully conscious as I of the appropriateness of it.

"I regret in a way that I brought up the subject, because it means not only a bitter disappointment to me, but I take it that it will mean so to you and especially to Katherine and Frances." (McCoy to Marshall, June 28, 1937, LC/F. R. McCoy Papers.)

2. Major Claude M. Adams assumed the position of executive officer on June 21, 1937. Marshall had requested Adams's transfer from the R.O.T.C. department at the University of Florida. Captain Edward C. Applegate, a 1932 graduate of the Infantry School's Company Officers' Course, had reported as Marshall's aide on June 24.

3. Mrs. Marshall's birthday was October 8. She noted that Marshall "loves to give surprises, but he does not like to receive surprises himself. Each birthday some unusual thing is sprung on me, I never know what, but something that has required thought and ingenuity to make the day wonderful." (K. T. Marshall, *Together*, p. 22.)

TO LIEUTENANT COLONEL ADOLF VON SCHELL   July 7, 1937
Vancouver Barracks,
Washington

My dear von Schell: I have just received your note from Fort Warren, and I can not tell you how sorry I am that you will not be able to visit me here.[1] In reply to my invitation through your military attache in Washington, I have already learned, before the receipt of your letter, that you would not be able to visit the Northwest.

I had several hopes in connection with your possible visit here. Mrs. Marshall and myself both looked forward to having you with us; I, of course, would have welcomed the opportunity to talk over the things in general, and military matters in particular; and, we had planned to take you on a trip through the gorgeous scenery of Washington and Oregon, ostensibly for me to inspect CCC installations, but actually to show you some of the magnificence of America, and give you some fine fishing. I am terribly disappointed that you can not come here.

I will always look back on our contacts at Fort Benning with a great deal of pleasure, and with realization that you brought me much that was highly important to my profession.

I have a letter this morning from General Pershing urging me to be present in France at the dedication in August of some of our war memorials. I am afraid I can not arrange to accept, but I particularly wish I could in order to run over to Germany to see you and Smith, and to pay my respects to your Minister of War.[2]

I think things must be in a very critical state abroad if they can not allow you an extra week in America.

Please present our compliments to Mrs. von Schell, and tell her that we will look forward to the pleasure of a possible meeting.   Faithfully yours,

GCMRL/G. C. Marshall Papers (Vancouver Barracks)

  1. Truman Smith wrote Marshall that von Schell, chief of staff of the German Army's Motor Corps, had left Germany on June 8 for a short tour of the United States and had specifically requested that his itinerary include Vancouver Barracks. (Smith to Marshall, June 9, 1937, GCMRL/G. C. Marshall Papers [Vancouver Barracks].)

  Writing from Fort Francis E. Warren near Cheyenne, Wyoming, von Schell expressed regrets for not being able to visit. "Having it thought over again and again I found out, that my time is too limited to go up so far to the North. I am somewhat in a hurry as I have to go from here to Salt Lake City, San Francisco, El Paso, San Antonio, New Orleans, Benning, being awaited back in Washington July 21st already. Mrs von Schell ordered me especially to remember her to Mrs Marshall and you." (Von Schell to Marshall, July 3, 1937, ibid.)

  2. Germany's minister of war was General Werner von Blomberg.

TO GENERAL JOHN J. PERSHING   July 16, 1937
Vancouver Barracks, Washington

Dear General: In my letter of last May, I explained that it would be impossible for me to be present at the dedication of the monument on Montfaucon. Since then I have received your very gracious letter of June 22 and your cable of June 29.[1]

I am at loss for words to express my regrets that I can not be near you on August 1st at Montfaucon. The expressions in your letter carried me back to those terrible days, now so happily of the past; and I feel that I am missing what would be a great moment in my life in not reporting again to you for duty on the Meuse-Argonne field.

Katherine is determined that I should go, but there really are too many complications to be circumvented. My heartfelt thanks for your invitation, and my deep regrets, go with this letter. May you be in the best of health during these ceremonies, so that you can enjoy to the full the immense satisfaction which should come to you on this final step in the completion of one of the greatest tasks ever carried from its first inception to completion by an American. Affectionately,

GCMRL/G. C. Marshall Papers (Vancouver Barracks)

1. On June 22 General Pershing again invited Marshall to attend the unveiling of the monument on Montfaucon if at all possible. "If you could realize the personal satisfaction it would give me to have you present with others who held important positions in the army during those grilling days of the Meuse-Argonne battle, I am sure your wish to be here would be all the greater. But whether you can come or not, you will know how sincerely I desire your presence." (Pershing to Marshall, June 22, 1937, GCMRL/G. C. Marshall Papers [Vancouver Barracks].)

To JOHN B. WILSON   July 27, 1937
                                                   Vancouver Barracks, Washington

Dear John: I appreciated your note of July 20th, and was very glad to hear from you direct.[1] I hope that we can get together, and that we will not have to wait a year.

My interest in Rose is very much from the heart, and I believe I am as well aware of her possibilities as her own family—possibly more so. She has the makings of a wonderful wife, and while this is no time for preaching, and that would hardly be tactful, I counsel you both to cultivate a wide degree of tolerance for this first year. Seemingly, in modern life, tolerance and loyalty play a small part in accepted requirements for the marital relation. As a matter of fact, they rank first.

I know you will be very happy, and I hope that prosperity for you two is just around the corner.

With my love to you both,   Faithfully yours,

GCMRL/G. C. Marshall Papers (Vancouver Barracks)

1. Marshall's goddaughter, Rose Page, had married Wilson in June, 1937. The July 20 letter is not in the Marshall papers.

REPORT TO MAJOR GENERAL GEORGE S. SIMONDS[1]   [August 28(?), 1937]
[Fort Lewis,
Washington]

Report of the Commanding General of the 5th Brigade.

1. The 5th Red Brigade, with the 1st Battalion, 10th Field Artillery and an additional battery, 1 platoon of engineers, the 116th Observation Squadron, and detachments of the ordnance, quartermaster and medical corps, had the problem of preventing a hostile Blue force from crossing to the north of the Nisqually River from 1:00 PM, August 23 until the arrival of Red re-enforcements at 7:00 AM on August 27.

2. In the initial field order the decision was announced "to take a position in readiness to defend the line of the river, with detachments, holding the bulk of the command, prepared to attack the enemy's columns as they emerged from the valley." The critical front was defined as from McKenna to Puget Sound. The two infantry regiments (each lacking a battalion) were placed abreast in columns of battalions, the 4th Infantry on the right. The artillery was directed to select positions from which fire could be delivered on the principal crossings of the Nisqually, and from which withdrawal to alternate positions could best be effected under cover. To all elements of the command it was announced that concealment of position and movement would be the factor of major importance.

With the command totaling 1900 men and an active front of 14 miles, not to mention possible surprise crossings to the east of McKenna, with an enemy almost three times as strong in infantry, more than eight times as strong in artillery and engineers, and with tanks, the problem for the Red commander was largely one of conservation of manpower, vigilance of reconnaissance, improvising means of communication, and concealment of artillery.

It was anticipated that the Blue artillery would seriously interfere with the Red artillery's program of fire. The artillery situation was further complicated by the necessity of detaching two guns for antitank use.

3. In the initial deployment, after moving forward to the river, the 4th Infantry held the Argonne Forest and the open valley to the east, including the 91st Division Prairie southwest of Nisqually Lake. The Marne Woods in the center of the front was left virtually undefended, except for a machine gun company of the 7th Infantry as Brigade Reserve, which was placed in the southern edge of the woods. A platoon of engineers to cover the guns was provided when the engineer tasks were completed Wednesday night. A battery of artillery was located in the same locality with its automatic rifles well advanced on the prairie. The 7th Infantry, based on Ficker Woods, covered the remainder of the front.

Very few machine guns were allowed as far forward as the edge of the river bluff, due to the small number available and the strong possibility of their being pinned to the ground by artillery fire or otherwise separated from the command as the enemy advanced. Such horses or mules as could be made available were used for messenger service for the advanced patrols. The latter could seldom be of greater strength than a cossack post.[2]

The artillery problem was largely one of locating concealed and unlikely positions from and to which rapid changes could be made under cover. It only proved practicable to provide fire for a limited period in the Northern Pacific Railroad area. The initial dispositions permitted two batteries to fire on possible bridging operations from Muck Creek to the vicinity of the Power House. It was not practicable to dispose the artillery in depth, until withdrawals from the most advanced infantry positions had been made.

4. The enemy's activities along the river bluffs and banks were observed in numerous localities from Tuesday until the actual crossings. On Wednesday afternoon bridging material, including pontoon boats, was brought to the river's edge in the open and work started. These activities were taken under observed artillery fire. No machine gun fire was permitted, as it would merely disclose positions which would be of much more importance later on. In an actual operation these guns would have been used, but under the necessary complications of umpiring and the fact that enemy casualties would be but a temporary embarrassment—if any, the possible price did not justify the disclosure of important positions under enemy observation, which were to be of great value later on.

Crossings were observed at dusk on Wednesday, and advanced Red detachments became engaged with Blue detachments along the western edge of the 91st Division Prairie. Liberal use of artillery was made at this time on the crossing sites in that vicinity.

The principal crossings were reported before dawn on Thursday morning. Numerous obstructions, mines, etc., had been prepared, theoretically, by the engineers, with the labor assistance of the Infantry. All possible artillery fire power was developed to hinder the actual crossing and the debouchment on to the plain. Not more than eight machine guns could be employed in this phase.

The functioning of both infantry and artillery observers was deserving of praise. Throughout Thursday morning practically every enemy movement, except for a time in the vicinity of the Northern Pacific Railroad bridge, was reported and kept under almost continuous observation.

The functioning of the 116th Observation Squadron, both as to ground administration and air activity, was splendidly carried out. Night missions thoroughly covered the Blue area, and during daylight hours provided such a constant stream of accurate information as to prove almost an embarrassment to the small intelligence personnel at Brigade headquarters. The work of observers showed a high degree of training and an extremely conscientious and enthusiastic performance of duty. The photographic missions were carried out with exactness and the results made available in a minimum of time. The work of this squadron in these maneuvers demonstrated the remarkable degree of efficiency possible of development in National Guard observation aviation during peacetime training.

With the information available the general development of the Blue action could be closely followed. However, contrary to expectations, the principal difficulties for the much dispersed Red force did not consist of artillery embarrassment, but rather of the rapidity of the Blue advance in the face of pre-arranged machine gun fires from intrenched positions, and the excellent maneuvering of the leading Blue elements, to outflank the small Red groups or to penetrate the many gaps in the line. The withdrawals required by the umpires quickly contracted the Blue front, especially as it became evident that there was no serious threat from the southwestern portion of the Argonne Forest or via the possible crossings in the vicinity of the Tighe Farm. Throughout the action the engineer platoon and reserve company of machine guns provided a liaison group between the two regiments, and guarded the Marne Forest Area.

At dusk and immediately thereafter on Thursday evening considerable activity developed all along the front and heavy night fighting soon created a confused situation. This finally reached so serious a condition, in my opinion, that I directed all Red troops to hold their positions, making no moves whatsoever.

5. *COMMENTS.*

Having commanded a Red force of from 3 to 5 thousand men in the 2nd Army Maneuvers in Michigan, and this year commanded a smaller but somewhat similar force in the 4th Army Maneuvers just completed, I am tremendously impressed with the instructional value of these exercises. The errors made evident, the forced reduction of theoretical technique to a more expeditious and practical basis, the experience in troop leading and troop reactions in confused situations, and the intimate association of various arms and services under approximate campaign conditions provided by such maneuvers as these, are inestimable value to all components of the army, and should be of similar value to the faculties of our service schools. I am strongly in favor of continued maneuvers of this nature.

I submit that the practice invariably followed in organizing these exercises, of absorbing, for outside use as it were, large numbers of men, vehicles, horses and materiel, is the one phase most urgently in need of a better solution than the present practice. It is not conceivable, under ordinary conditions, that American troops would have to operate in the field with the reduced number of motor vehicles that we are required to depend on in our maneuvers. The absence of horses and the lack of motorcycles and light cars renders normal reconnaissance, under modern conditions of fast-moving motor vehicles, the greatest embarrassment to a commander. The lack of even a dozen trucks in a force already short of sixty per cent of its field and combat motor transportation, is pitiful in its limitation on the power of a commander to move small bodies of his troops tactically. I am not referring to long motor convoys. I respectfully suggest the advisability of having a special study made as to how to stage such maneuvers without absorbing for other purposes such a large proportion of military facilities and personnel, of vital importance to field training.

There are attached hereto copies of field order and overlays of the successive positions occupied by the Red forces.[3]

G. C. Marshall

NA/RG 407 (353, Bulky File [12-13-35])

1. Regular, National Guard, and Reserve units participated in the Ninth Corps Area phase of the Fourth Army maneuvers held at Fort Lewis, Washington, August 17-27. Marshall commanded the Red Forces, the reinforced Fifth Brigade; and Major General George A. White commanded the Blue Forces, the reinforced Forty-first Division. During the river-crossing maneuver, following a command post exercise simulating the approach march, it was the Blue troops' goal to gain control of the river crossings along the Nisqually River defended by the outnumbered and outpowered Red troops. The high point in the maneuver came when the Blue army launched a surprise attack early Thursday, August 26, and by nightfall had most of its troops across the river. (Portland *Oregonian*, August 25-27, 1937.)

2. A "cossack post" was a four-man out-guard that posted a single sentinel.

3. The field order is not printed here, and the overlays were not in the file with the document.

To Leo A. Farrell[1]   September 2, 1937
                                               Vancouver Barracks, Washington

My dear Farrell: I found your letter on my return last evening from the 4th Army Maneuvers at Fort Lewis. You would know that I was greatly surprised to hear from you, but to find that your letter was inspired by a note of mine written fifteen years ago, was even more surprising.[2]

Your letter was a very moving document and touched me deeply. Few things that I have ever done have repaid me so fully as my brief action in your case, and never have I been so repaid in thanks and gratitude. As you probably have found out on many occasions, people have short memories, and those in deep trouble seem later to have the shortest memories of all. You, on the contrary, seem to magnify what little I did, with each year until now you almost have me thinking I am quite a fellow. General Mosely is the man; he did for you, as he generously met my request, without hesitation and in full measure.

Your remarks about your father and mother made the deepest impression for, strange to say, I had not thought of their connection with the brief tragedy of your army career. What you tell me of them makes me glad indeed that I had some part in straightening things out for you.

Your career seems fine, with still brighter prospects ahead. I knew Clark Howell and admired him.[3] He must have been an ideal boss in your particular field. Incidentally, my room mate for four years at school is the head of the Times Picayune in New Orleans, Leanord Nicholson.

Going back to your early difficulty, you will appreciate one I have just been trying to solve. My gardner here, a prisoner who had had his temporary blowup, was a young fellow about your age when I first saw you. Mrs. Marshall and I became interested in him and finally got his sentence of dishonorable discharge cancelled and had him restored to duty.[4] Then I had him as my orderly on the recent maneuvers, to take the place of another boy I sent down to the Presidio to prepare to take the examination for West Point. Which reminds me that I got an appointment for the orderly I had at Benning, and he is now a second lieutenant.[5] I'm afraid this last boy will not go that far, but I think he will make a useful citizen.

We are delighted with the northwest, and my duties with the CCC enable me to see every part of Oregon and southern Washington. The country is magnificient—and the fishing fine. I take my pole every where I go on inspection trips and have had some wonderful times. Horseback riding fills in the gaps, and altogether we find life out here a very pleasant business.

Please do not allow so much time to elapse before I next hear from you, for I am interested very sincerely in your circumstances and success.   Faithfully yours,

G. C. Marshall

GCMRL/L. A. Farrell Papers; T

1. Political editor for the *Atlanta Constitution*, Farrell had worked for the newspaper the past ten years.

2. In August, 1937, Major General George V.H. Moseley sent to Farrell a note he had received from Marshall written December 8, 1923. "I received a most grateful and appreciative letter regarding you from that boy, Leo Farrell," Marshall had written. "He told me that you had him tried by Summary Court, which certainly indicated a very generous attitude on your part. Who knows, you may have saved to the world a very celebrated journalist, even if erratic, though perhaps that is merely temperament." (Marshall to Moseley, December 8, 1923, GCMRL/L. A. Farrell Papers.) A summary court-martial is headed by a single officer, disposes of cases briefly and less formally, and imposes less severe penalties than special or general courts-martial. The incident involving Farrell (a charge of desertion was reduced to absent without leave) occurred in 1923 when Moseley commanded Fort Sheridan, Illinois.

3. Clark Howell had been president and publisher of the *Atlanta Constitution*. Farrell wrote, "I had long years of training under Clark Howell, who died last year, and I sure feel like he taught me the ropes." (Farrell to Marshall, August 23, 1937, GCMRL/G. C. Marshall Papers [Vancouver Barracks].)

4. "Private Jones," a pseudonym Mrs. Marshall used for the man in her memoirs, had been a school teacher prior to joining the army. He had been serving a sentence for desertion and was to receive a dishonorable discharge. (K. T. Marshall, *Together*, pp. 31–32.)

5. Second Lieutenant Clarence E. Gooding (U.S.M.A., 1936). See Marshall to Pershing, June 2, 1936, above.

TO GENERAL JOHN J. PERSHING   September 19, 1937
Vancouver Barracks, Washington

My dear General: Knowing the deluge of letters and cables you receive on each birthday I thought this time I would allow the flood to pass before tendering mine. Each year when I write my mind seems to go back to some particular occasion, different occasion of the years I was with you. This morning, out of a clear sky, their came the thought of another September morning in Ligny en Barrois when I met you in the street as I was enroute to my office. You held me up for a moment and asked me what I thought of the plans for the St Mihiel attack, if I thought it would be a go. I don't recall just what my reply was, but I do have in mind a perfect picture of you on that morning. It all seems so long ago, but what momentous days those were for the world and for you, in particular? I would like to have known your thoughts on the day of the dedication of the St Mihiel and Meuse-Argonne monuments. I studied your expression, in the movies, but they told little of what your real thoughts must have been.

I do hope that this birthday found you in fine shape and enjoying things. Your feeling of satisfaction and contentment should grow with the years, for each year adds increasingly to public appreciation of you and of what you did for America. Tho a great many years must pass before people generally will even in a small measure understand the gigantic nature of the task you undertook and the marvelously efficient manner in which you carried it through. In talking to writers I find that they will get a partially complete perspective of this or that phase, but none visualize the entire picture. I am afraid I have but a piecemeal idea of it myself.

I have been away from Vancouver most of the time this summer. I was off at maneuvers about five weeks in the late spring. Thereafter with long inspection trips, more maneuvers, and some purely pleasure trips, there has hardly been a week when I was here continuously.

Day before yesterday Katherine and I returned from the Pendleton Round-Up, where we had a great time watching an amazing spectacle. We revieed the great parade of some 2,000 Indians and all the spectacular phases of pioneers, trappers, a half dozen stage coaches, ancient vehicles of every character with occupants in appropriate dress, etc., we reviewed it with Governor Martin and the Episcopal Bishop of eastern Oregon. Then Governor Martin, Katherine and I had lunch with the young queen of the affair.

Enroute to Pendleton we had the good luck to find the Indians at the Dalles spearing and netting a run of huge salmon, and saw the fish leaping at the falls.

Tomorrow morning Katherine and I are off on another inspection, to cross the Cascades a couple of times, and I hope to pick up some fine fishing along the way. We will be gone until the end of the week. The President is due out here the 28th and I suppose I will have to be on hand for whatever is planned. He is to speak at Bonneville Dam, which is just now the political football of the northwest.[1]

Katherine had a letter from Mrs. Dawes a few days ago saying that she and the General and General Harbord were going over to see you some time in October. I am glad they are going for it should be a pleasant reunion for you. Dawes seems to pick up in energy of movement and of expression as things mend financially.

With my congratulations and my prayers for your continued well being, believe me always,   Affectionately,

G. C. Marshall

LC/J. J. Pershing Papers (General Correspondence); T

1. Political divisions regarding the Columbia River projects emerged as a result of philosophical differences over private versus public energy production and sale, over federally mandated regional versus state planning and control of resources, and over the wide distribution of and uniform charges for hydroelectric power versus preferential treatment for industries located near the dam sites. President Roosevelt touched upon each of these issues in his speech at the Bonneville Dam on September 28. (*Public Papers and Addresses of Franklin D. Roosevelt, 1937,* pp. 387–92.)

To Brigadier General Charles G. Dawes   October 8, 1937
Vancouver Barracks,
Washington

My dear General Dawes: This is an odd letter, but I became so irritated over an error of mine that I happened on this morning that I felt impelled to write to you forthwith and explain. A little over a year ago in Chicago I was in your office one morning and learnt that it was your birthday. Then and there I made a note of the date with the intention of remembering you with at least a message of congratulations on the following anniversaries. For some reason I got it into my head that it was in October, and when I went to look the matter up today I could not find my note, but I did find from Who's Who that August 27th was the great day, and I had completely missed out on my intentions.

Belated as this is I tender my congratulations, none the less sincere because of the faulty manner of their transmission. I only wish I could step in the elevator of 208 South LaSalle and drop off at the second floor to congratulate you in person. If your birthday fell like mine on New Years Eve, or on the 4th of July, I probably would not have so muddled things.

We are charmed with the northwest and have covered almost every part of Oregon and southern Washington on inspection-fishing trips. Now that the fall is here I can add shooting to the program. Mrs. Marshall and I are off Friday morning on an inspection trip of mine down the coast. Then we will loaf and fish on Saturday and Sunday near Gold Beach. On Monday morning at eleven I am to meet General, or rather, Governor Martin at Gold Beach and join him in a trip up the turbulent and famous Rogue River as the guests of a California oil millionaire, to spend three days at this fellow's lodge in the mountains, by the river. We will probably get some gorgeous steel head or jack salmon fishing. I have to leave Mrs. Marshall at Gold Beach, as this is a stag party; but she and I will do a couple of other ports after I come down the river.

General Martin is making a great name for himself out here for fearlessness, extreme frankness about the "crack pot ideas" of this day and age, etc. The radicals are trying to organize a heavy fight on him for the nomination next spring, and many republicans are changing their registration in order to vote for him. It is too early to predict the result.

I had to get out troops for Bonneville Dam and for Vancouver during the President's recent visit. I boarded his train at Bonneville and saw him off here in Vancouver after a very strenuous day. General and Mrs. Martin came here to the house with us after the train pulled out, for a drink, and finally for dinner. He lives at Salem sixty miles from here.[1]

I thought when I received my orders for this station that I was coming to a delightful but very quiet place, sort of a backwater. As a matter of fact about every one has appeared here, from the Russian fliers and the President, on down through a succession of important lesser notables. I have hardly had a moment to call my own. And now Jim Farley is scheduled for this vicinity. I do not suppose I will in any way become involved in his visit, but I am getting suspicious of any week that does not have some headliner due in this neighborhood. I would like a long rest, and more time for fishing and hunting.

With affectionate regards to Mrs. Dawes and you, and with my tardy congratulations, Faithfully yours,

G. C. Marshall

NU/C. G. Dawes Papers; T

1. Concerning the president's September 28 visit, Marshall told Pershing: "Had a few words with him [Roosevelt] and was much amused to watch the maneuvers of the various shades of New Dealers who were trying to appear before the public eye in his company. General Martin motored with him all of the day he was in this vicinity, and came here to the house for home dinner after seeing the President off for Seattle at the Vancouver station. It was interesting to see the impression made on General Martin by the tumultuous welcome accorded Mr. Roosevelt by the crowds in Portland and along other portions of his route. Quite apparently the Governor suffered a change of mind regarding the diminution of the President's hold on the people. He, Martin, has been pretty outspoken against what he calls 'crackpot schemes' and the something-for-nothing course of action." (Marshall to Pershing, November 17, 1937, LC/J. J. Pershing Papers [General Correspondence].)

COMMENTS ON VANCOUVER BARRACKS   [October, 1937]
DISTRICT C.C.C.[1]   [Vancouver Barracks, Washington]

The Vancouver District has been making preparations for the past few weeks to welcome the new arrivals from the southeastern portion of the United States. Heretofore we have had a great many men from New England, New York, New Jersey, and the middle west; but now half the district is to be composed of southerners.

It may interest the new men to know that the Ninth Corps Area, or the West

Coast, is the only sub-division of the Civilian Conservation Corps to receive companies from other portions of the United States. And the Vancouver District has the largest number of companies from other sections of the country.

This tremendous influx of strangers to this region presents many problems and some very interesting possibilities. Oregon and North Carolina, for example, are as dissimilar in climate and in the customs and attitude of their people as any two states in the Union. And we find in Oregon two totally different climates, with corresponding contrasts in vegetation and use of the soil. The farmer and orchard men of western Oregon compete with the cowboy rancher and sheep herder of the western [*eastern*] section of the state. Near the coast the winter is one of rains and fogs, with a deep green covering to the landscape. East of the Cascade Mountains the country is bare and open land typical of Wyoming and Colorado.

In the past it has been interesting to find boys from the same section of the east, some of them from the same city, located in the high mountains, some in the barren plains, and others along the sea coast. The first will be engaged in road construction and forestry work, those in the barren sections are usually employed in the construction of small dams and other checks to soil erosion. Along the Coast they are either engaged in forestry work or in attempting to pin down the great drifting sand dunes which have been engulfing fertile land. Each group seems to be happy in its peculiar surroundings, all of which form a striking contrast to the city life with which they have been familiar. The first month of rain usually lowers morale, but after that initiation all seem to accept this odd northwestern trick of the climate like the old timers.

This invasion of men from east of the Mississippi will probably have a marked effect on the future of this part of the country. Many of the newcomers grow to like it so well that they either remain here or return later to marry and settle down. In the 1840's the pioneers came into Oregon with horse and ox team, over the McKenzie Pass, across the Blue Mountains and down the Columbia. Today they come again, but this time by rail and under the auspices of the Civilian Conservation Corps. There is a great opportunity for the young men from the east in the CCC, to see a wonderful country, acquire healthful habits, and to prepare themselves for some specific work in civil life. I sincerely hope that each new member of the Vancouver District will make a definite plan for improving himself during his service in this region, so that he may graduate from the CCC into a position in civil life as a self-respecting, self-supporting citizen.

GCMRL/G. C. Marshall Papers (Pentagon Office, Speeches)

1. This article, with minor editorial changes, was published in the Vancouver Barracks C.C.C. District *Review*, October 15, 1937.

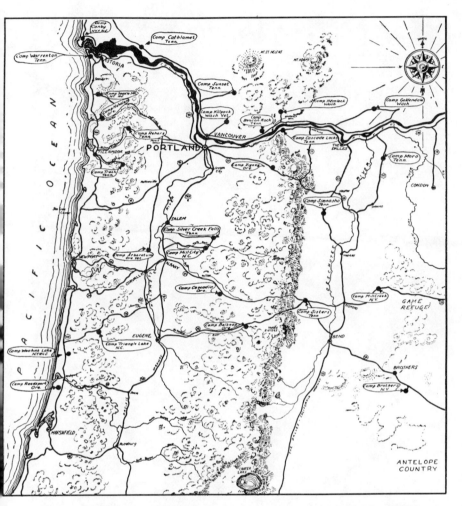

The Vancouver Barracks District Civilian Conservation Corps camps, October, 1937.

Brigadier General and Mrs. George C. Marshall during a fishing trip along the Metolius River, Oregon, 1938.

Mrs. Marshall, Major Claude M. ("Flap") Adams, Mrs. Adams, and Marshall relax at a fishing camp along the Metolius River, Oregon, 1938.

Brigadier General Charles H. Martin (c. 1923).

Brigadier General George C. Marshall, June, 1938.

Governor Charles H. Martin and Brigadier General George C. Marshall join the Russian fliers (with leis) in the Portland, Oregon, parade honoring the airmen, June, 1937.

George C. Marshall dining in his home with the three Russian airmen and the Soviet ambassador, June, 1937. Left to right: Alexander V. Beliakov, Soviet Ambassador Alexander A. Troyanovsky, George C. Marshall, Valeri P. Chkalov, and Georgi P. Baidukov.

The Marshalls' residence at Vancouver Barracks, Washington, 1936–38. (This photograph was taken in 1972.)

Brigadier General and Mrs. Marshall and Molly Brown pose with the Russian airmen and the Soviet ambassador, at Vancouver Barracks, Washington, June, 1937.

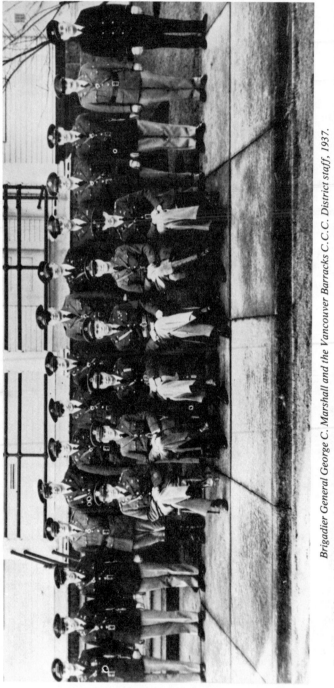

Brigadier General George C. Marshall and the Vancouver Barracks C.C.C. District staff, 1937.

Front row, left to right: Captain L. H. Hall, Lieutenant Colonel James A. Marmon, Captain J. D. Pomerene, Brigadier General G. C. Marshall, Lieutenant Colonel H. R. MacKellar, Captain W. E. Read.

Second row, left to right: Captain B. A. Johnson, Captain Jack W. Kittrell, Captain M. R. Simmonds, Captain A. H. Hopkins, Captain John E. Foley, Captain V. J. Gregory, Lieutenant Kenneth Horne, Captain F. F. Wolfer, Captain S. M. Kerron, Lieutenant M. E. Gilmore, Captain C. A. Hebert, Lieutenant W. F. Coughlin, Captain D. D. Todorovic, Captain B. O. Garrett, Mr. J. B. Kennedy (Coast Guard).

To Major General Frank R. McCoy   October 18, 1937
                                          Vancouver Barracks, Washington

My dear General: As a leading participant in the surprise birthday procession for Katherine two years ago I think that you and Francis will be interested in her most recent birthday celebration—October 8th last. She and I were due to leave that morning at nine on a week's trip down the coast, a departure which could not be postponed.

At seven in the morning I took her breakfast up stairs and gave her a present from Molly and me. This served to wipe out any suspicion she might have had about a possible surprise, as I have always tried to have one. Then Molly and I got busy down stairs.

Katherine came down at a quarter past eight, and as she reached the second landing on the steps the band on the lawn broke out with "Happy Birthday to You", and thirty breakfast guests joined in the chorus. It was not until she had shaken hands with every one that she saw the small breakfast tables and realized that the gathering was in the nature of a party. It went off with a great bang, and a complete surprise to her. Finally, they all gathered outside and gave us a send off as we left on our trip. It was rather like a wedding finish, lacking only the rice.

We have been going off from Monday to Friday about every other week. I inspect camps and she joins in the fishing and the enjoyment of the glorious scenery. This last trip was down to Gold Beach at the mouth of the famous Rogue River, near the California line. I did a few camps on the way down; then she and I trolled for chinook salmon at the river mouth, and finally I met Governor Martin and his fish and game commissions and we went up the Rouge to the lodge of a California oil millionaire to investigate the question of the pollution of the river by placer mining.

The trip up and down the river is a thriller, with wild rapids, rocks, etc. It is made in open boats with high powered motors. At the lodge in primitive surroundings, deer and wild turkey were wandering around in regular barnyard fashion.

Katherine waited two days for me at Gold Beach and then we went south to the California border and around to the Oregon Caverns, and on home. Had perfect weather and I never have seen more maginificient scenery. We are off again in about ten days to eastern Oregon, with pheasant and deer as a side line.

Katherine is deep in a Forty-Niner party the week end to raise funds for all our relief and Xmas purposes. Last year they got about $800 and this year she expects to clear between $1500 and $1800. The best part is, the soldiers have a great time and are anxious for the affair. We run the officers part separately, on another night. K. is having a lot of Portland high-lights in for the affair, for dinner at the house preliminary to the party. I find that most of these Portland people have either never been on the garrison or have had no social connection

571

with it for many years. And I find also that they get a great kick out of their army contacts when we renew them.

I wish you and Francis could join us for one of our trips. I know you would enjoy the country and the little inns or camps where we stay. Twelve of us are going up in the mountains on the McKenzie River to Belknap Springs for four days over Thanksgiving. The little hotel closes earlier in the season, but they have agreed to let us have it, we bringing our own cook and supplies. As they have a wonderful hot spring, there is no complication about heating the building or using the outdoor swimming pool along side of the river. We may get some good steel head fishing, and possibly some shooting; but I am certain we can have a lot of fun at a rediculously small expense.

Molly and I are riding before breakfast every morning. I got a fine horse from Riley last spring. Then Sweeney released the Riley thorobred mare he had at Douglas,[1] and I got that sent on. There was one three-quarter bred polo mount here in the headquarters stable and my aide, who is absent sick, has a fine thorobred. So Molly and I have a good stable to pick from. The North Woods above the post proper provide beautiful trails, and we usually scare up a few pheasants.

I hope that all goes well with you and Francis, and I am still regretful over the failure of the arrangement to get me to Fort Hamilton with the 1st Division.

My affectionate regards to you both.

G. C. Marshall

LC/F. R. McCoy Papers; T

1. Brigadier General Walter C. Sweeney was the commander at Fort Douglas, Utah.

To LIEUTENANT COLONEL WALTON H. WALKER[1]   December 21, 1937
                                                   Vancouver Barracks,
                                                   Washington

Dear Walker: I appreciated very much your letter inclosing the clipping.[2] What you have told me is all that I have heard aside from the newspaper reports.

Confidentially, there appears to be a little more to this than is evident on the surface. Fox Conner and myself were on the original organization board immediately after the passage of the National Defense Act in 1920. We stood out for a division of not to exceed 13,000 [men], but were finally forced to compromise with the proponents of a division of 27,000 on a limit of 18,000. For a time Conner contemplated submitting a minority report, but I persuaded him not to do this. In the end, we drafted a letter for General Pershing's signature which set forth our views, in which he concurred. As he was not Chief of Staff at the time, this was the only way we could legislate, and he was embarrassed in his action by reason of the fact that an AEF Board in 1919 recommended a large division.

Now, it would appear that this special board with only Conner and myself named, is sort of a "stacked deck" to secure the smaller division against the almost certain opposition of a large number of influential officers. Please treat this as for your eyes only, as it is only a mere conjecture and might seriously embarrass General Craig.[3] But it may serve to enable you to tip me off in advance of the course of events.

It is very good of you and Mrs. Walker to ask me to stay with you and I appreciate your hospitality. Moore told us that you had a beautiful and spacious apartment.[4]

I am giving Mrs. Marshall a surprise tomorrow by bringing on her elder boy from Chicago, for Christmas. He is driving out in order to sell his car out here; I have been much concerned about his crossing the continental divide in this season of the year, but he jumped from Cheyenne to Rupert, west of Pocatello in one hop yesterday. So I imagine he will spend tonight in Pendleton. He is picking up a friend in Boise, and no one in the house has any intimation of their approach.

With my Christmas greetings to you both and best wishes for the New Year, and a slap on the seat for Sam,[5] Faithfully yours,

GCMRL/G. C. Marshall Papers (Vancouver Barracks)

1. Walker (V.M.I., 1907–8; U.S.M.A., 1912) had been the Vancouver Barracks post executive (August, 1936–August, 1937) before being assigned to duty with the War Plans Division in Washington, D.C.

2. Neither the letter nor the clipping was found in the Marshall papers.

3. The *New York Times* had reported that General Craig was expected to set up a board composed of Marshall, Major General Fox Conner, and one other general officer to study the results of the reports of the "streamlined" division at Fort Sam Houston and to establish the organization for the new division. The new division was to be about half the size of the current twenty-two-thousand-man division, have increased mobility, and use modern equipment and arms. (*New York Times*, November 12 and December 13, 1937.)

4. Major William C. Moore was stationed at Vancouver Barracks with the Seventh Infantry.

5. Sam S. Walker, Lieutenant Colonel Walker's son.

To COLONEL RALPH D. MERSHON   December 22, 1937
                                      Vancouver Barracks, Washington

My dear Colonel Mershon: My Christmas greeting to you and my wish for your health and prosperity for the New Year.

Recently I had a letter from General Gignilliat, telling me of General Pershing's reception in Washington of the CMTC boys. Colonel Bishop is sending me some of the photographs. I am delighted to learn that the committee is making progress, and particularly that the office in Washington has been an increasingly helpful center, both for the War Department and for the interested civilian authorities. In all probability the fact that you have maintained that office has done more to protect and promote cause of civilian-military education than anything else could have done. Prior to that set-up there was no particular head to the business—none whatever on the outside and no chief of branch in the War Department. Since what is everybody's business tends to become nobody's business, the cause of civilian-military education always suffered accordingly. Now it is given what I believe is skillful and unobtrusive leadership, towards which all college authorities are steadily turning for both assistance and guidance.

The more I watched this work, the more I puzzled my brain to find a proper and enduring activity to promote this cause, the more I am impressed with the fact that leadership is the important thing. I believe that in due time it will be taken over in a large way by something like the Navy League; but at the present the time is not right and the business progresses very much better under your unselfish patronage.

I hope you are in good health, and that some day I may have the opportunity to talk things over with you. I was very sorry to leave the committee but it seemed that with my transfer to the Northwest affairs would go better, with a man in the East like Colonel Lowe to give active attention to the business, in frequent contact with other members of the committee.[1]

With regard and esteem, believe me, Faithfully yours,

GCMRL/G. C. Marshall Papers (Vancouver Barracks)

1. Lieutenant Colonel Frank E. Lowe succeeded Marshall as a member of the Civilian Military Education Fund Board.

To Major General Ewing E. Booth[1] December 23, 1937
Vancouver Barracks, Washington

Dear Booth: I have just come in from a before Breakfast ride to find your note of December 20th regarding my hospitalization. The facts are this: I went in the Letterman[2] last January feeling better than I ever had but due for a corrective operation for a minor goiter of about fifteen years standing. I made a very quick recovery and was back to normal in heart, blood pressure and BMR inside of ten days. As a matter of fact, all the preliminary tests would show me normal on the last two items, which made the diagnosis rather difficult for the doctors.

Since then I have done two big maneuvers, innumerable fishing and hunting trips, and am riding and playing golf daily. So, I am not the subject for much sympathy, but I do appreciate your interest.

I know how these rumors go. Recently I received a letter from a friend in Washington who said he understood I was crippled. I have often been crippled financially, but not yet physically. . . .   Faithfully yours,

October 1936–June 1938

GCMRL/G. C. Marshall Papers (Vancouver Barracks)

1. Booth, who had known Marshall since 1906, when Booth was an instructor at Fort Leavenworth, had written: "I had a rumor the other day that you had been in the hospital in Washington, D.C. I am sure that there was nothing serious but I would be delighted to hear from you regarding it any way. You know that as soon as we get along about 50 if we have a bad cold every one has us dying." (Booth to Marshall, December 20, 1937, GCMRL/G. C. Marshall Papers [Vancouver Barracks].) Rumors of ill health could, and a poor medical examination report would, significantly reduce if not eliminate a senior officer's chances of promotion. Marshall's care in this matter is evident in his letters to Morrison C. Stayer of October 18, 1938, January 15, and February 11, 1939, below. The omitted third of this letter was Christmas greetings to Major General and Mrs. Booth.

2. Letterman General Hospital, San Francisco, California.

To Colonel Horace F. Sykes[1]   December 27, 1937
                                        Vancouver Barracks, Washington

Dear Sykes: Major Klein gave me your nice message of greeting,[2] which I appreciated. However, I am writing this letter to you personally to seek your official influence in a case in which I am deeply interested.

There is going forward to your headquarters today the promotion board report on one 2nd Lieutenant Charles W.G. Rich, 7th Inf.[3] In it the doctors find him partially color blind. The facts are, he successfully entered West Point, successfully passed his physical examination there for his commission as a second lieutenant, failed to pass the air corps test, and has successfully reacted to thousands of red and green stop lights in the every-day business of driving a car.

More than this, he is an officer of unusual promise, who recently made a fine showing in the army maneuvers, commanding my only reserve in about ten engagements. He is far too good to lose and, in my military opinion, it would be a distinct loss to the government—while some slow witted fellow who knows "alice blue" is kept on.

The board, I understood, does not find his lack of color sense disabling. Please see if you can't maneuver this business so that we do not throw out a superior type over a technicality, and carry along the dead wood, as is usually the case.

I want to see you, one of these days, and talk things over. Motored through Fort Reno on my way west. Have not forgotten your fine note of congratulations.   Faithfully yours,

GCMRL/G. C. Marshall Papers (Vancouver Barracks)

1. Sykes was the Ninth Corps Area adjutant general.
2. Major John A. Klein was assistant adjutant general of the Ninth Corps Area.
3. Rich (U.S.M.A., 1935) was kept in the army, remaining at Vancouver Barracks until mid-1938, when he reported for student officer's duty at the Infantry School.

To Major General Fox Conner   January 7, 1938
                                      Vancouver Barracks, Washington

Dear Conner: I have just received your note and am very much interested to learn something at least semi-official regarding the Board which was referred to in the "New York Times." Up to the receipt of your note that was the only intimation of what was planned,[1] and a friend of mine in the War Department had written me that the G-3 Section thought there was nothing to it, as they had never heard anything regarding such a plan.

This business recalls vividly to my mind the struggle you and I made to get a small division in 1920. If poor old Tommy Heintzelman and Campbell King had not been quite such kindly characters we might have put over the smaller division at that time and avoided the prospect of a radical change eighteen years later.

I understand you saw the experimental division, and I read a newspaper statement quoting you on the subject. If you have any papers which you think it would be advisable for me to familiarize myself with in advance of arrival in Washington, or if there is any reading to which you could refer me to, I would appreciate your assistance.

With affectionate regards to Mrs. Conner and yourself, and continued pleasant memories of those October days at Brandreth Lake, Faithfully yours,

GCMRL/G. C. Marshall Papers (Vancouver Barracks)
  1. Conner had written: "I take it from the note on your Christmas card that you have heard rumors of the Board which Craig proposes to convene in Washington. According to what he told me when I was in Washington in December, you, Lesley McNair, and I are to meet as a Board to make recommendations on the final organization of the new division. Craig expects, I believe, to have the Board meet sometime in February." (Conner to Marshall, January 3, 1938, GCMRL/G. C. Marshall Papers [Vancouver Barracks].)

To Major General Roy D. Keehn   January 24, 1938
                                      Vancouver Barracks, Washington

Dear Keehn: I want you to know that I greatly appreciated your fine telegram. You were a very generous friend, and I derive a great deal of satisfaction from the warmth of your expressions.

We had a delightful Christmas, with a houseful, lovely weather, and a great deal to do. Immediately after New Years Mrs. Marshall and I went off on an inspection trip along the coast. All the Steelhead fishermen were in action for the winter run. We stopped for four days at a winter house party organized at a Seaside cottage by one of our Portland friends. We had a great time, and then I made some more inspections on my way back.

We are off this morning for Timberline Lodge—the WPA prodigal financial splash—8000 feet up on Mt. Hood. I am not going to try any skiing, merely going to enjoy the gorgeous winter scenery. The place is so convenient, that we can have lunch there and be back here before dinner.

I have been making entirely too many speeches lately, but there has been so little contact in the past between the Post and the people of Portland and other points in the State of Oregon, that I found it my duty to accept a great many invitations which involved talking for my supper. Eventually I will get my foot off the base, but I hope to cool down on this business before that occurs.

With warmest regards,   Faithfully yours,

GCMRL/G. C. Marshall Papers (Vancouver Barracks)

TO MAJOR LLOYD D. BROWN[1]   January 25, 1938
                                                  Vancouver Barracks, Washington

Dear Brown: I have just read your letter of January 20th and was delighted to hear from you and of you. I have noted your detail to the National Guard tour and intended to write you a line regarding it. You should be able to make a very valuable contribution from a desk in that office, but I imagine it will be six months or a year before most of them will understand what you are talking about.[2]

I am coming more and more to find, in the army, that if a thing has not been done it is tremendously hard to get anyone today in favor of doing it or opposed to stirring from the routine methods. Also, each thing they plan in the way of training is usually so damned elaborate in conception that if it is done at all, all is abandoned after one tremendous effort. They all preach about simplicity, and elasticity, but the burden of technique developed has submerged everybody, particularly as we apply training to the National Guard.

I know of your hopes and disappointments regarding the War College, and despite the fact that these things are settled seemingly on a cut and dried basis, I hope eventually to find the opportunity to help you to that detail.

With warm regards to Mrs. Brown and yourself,   Faithfully yours,

GCMRL/G. C. Marshall Papers (Vancouver Barracks)

1. Brown, a graduate of the 1927–28 Advanced Course at the Infantry School, had been an instructor with the Illinois National Guard's 131st Infantry in Chicago since 1934. Beginning on March 15, 1938, he was assigned to the Organization and Training Division of the National Guard Bureau in Washington, D.C.

2. In his letter to Marshall, Brown mentioned the planned division command post exercise. "This year they have a night withdrawal from action to a defensive position. The Division Staff made the decision and selected the position without being steered. The position is not so good, but I do not believe they will ever improve further if they are always to be led around." (Brown to Marshall, January 20, 1938, GCMRL/G. C. Marshall Papers [Vancouver Barracks].)

8

To Major General William D. Connor   January 28, 1938
Vancouver Barracks,
Washington

Dear Connor: When the notice in the service papers of the date of your relief from duty at West Point appeared,[1] I was absent on an inspection trip in the mountains of Oregon and did not learn of what was happening until too late to communicate with you at West Point. So now I am trying to reach you through the Adjutant General, on the general assumption that you are probably in Washington or in Memphis, prior to leaving for the coast.

I wanted particularly to send you some expression of my feelings on the day you hauled down your flag, and I am much distressed that I failed to do so. Your career has been so outstanding, such a fine model for the officers who follow you, and I have so valued your friendship, that it is difficult for me to put into words how much I deplore your departure from the active list and how splendid I think your army career has been. Also, there is the very personal side of the matter, and I think that you and your Elsa have given us a beautiful example of harmonious family life on the highest plane, both socially and in the way of culture.

You have much to be proud of and should enjoy a feeling of profound satisfaction with your course in the line of duty and of good citizenship.

I hope very much that we may have the opportunity of seeing you both out here. I want you to know Mrs. Marshall and I want you to honor our home with a visit.

With all good wishes for you in the coming years,   Affectionately yours,

GCMRL/G. C. Marshall Papers (Vancouver Barracks)

1. Connor had served as superintendent and commandant of the United States Military Academy (May 1, 1932–January 17, 1938), before retiring on February 28, 1938.

To Major General James K. Parsons[1]   January 31, 1938
Vancouver Barracks,
Washington

My dear General: I have had no occasion to write you for some time, but you may be interested in what has happened to the post, in the way of improvements, since your departure.

Last July we completed the new garages for the western half of the officers' quarters. All the old buildings to be demolished were gotten rid of by the end of May. The painting went ahead according to program and greatly improved the appearance of things, especially along the line of barracks. The heating plants and the electric wiring have been put in good shape. I got furnaces for those old buildings we were using for barracks, and their installation has just been completed.

Last September I shifted things in administrative set-up. The Regimental Commander is the Post Executive and is authorized to do practically all the various things that are covered for the Post Commander by regulations. He has his office where yours was, and his regimental staff includes the post administrative work along with the regimental.

I now have Hossfeld's old office as Brigade and CCC headquarters.[2] With the exception of Garrett and his immediate assistants,[3] all of the CCC people are in this building, and the space they formerly occupied has been turned over to the post and regiment.

I was cut from sixteen to five thousand in Barracks and Quarters money, but I got $37,000.00 WPA money from the State. Unfortunately the State held out practically all the money that might be spent for materials. However, I recently got $60,000.00 from the War Department allotment, which gives me a fair percentage for material. And I have just been notified that a further allotment of $61,000.00 is coming through, on the same basis.

The North Woods is being cleared and parked, and made much more available for training. The former radio station is now a double NCO set. We are about to level the floor in the Victory Theater, and insert two trusses, which will give us a fine basket-ball floor, with ample room for an audience, and a fine roller skating rink.

We succeeded in getting a Hammond electric organ for the Chapel, and this can be used in the Victory Theater for roller skating.

Our bowling crowd has so increased that we are putting in two new alleys, and the amateur boxing fills the theater.

Glass is a very good colonel, and Mrs. Glass is delightful.[4] We have an unusually fine crowd of officers here now, and the social life of the garrison is extremely active and very agreeable. The Club runs to capacity, and has something scheduled almost for every day. We are now enlarging and rearranging the kitchen and the bar to better accommodate people. We picked up two gas ranges for the Service Club so that we can serve dinner dance crowds there.

For the CCC end I am sending you a copy of our bi-weekly paper which will give you an idea of what has been going on.[5] The camps in eastern Oregon were transferred to the Boise district. I swapped Yakima for Canby and Cathlamet. The larger districts have been cut to provide sufficient camps for the smaller ones to enable them to maintain their overhead, under the present limiting budget.

I have thoroughly enjoyed my CCC inspections. Mrs. Marshall usually goes with me and I leave her in the towns while I inspect. We have covered practically every road and most of the trails in Oregon and southern Washington, fished most of the lakes and streams, and put up at most of the hotels, inns or motor camps. Belknap Springs hotel has become a favorite stopping place and several cottages have been placed at our disposal along the Coast where we rest up during our inspection trips. I spent four days two weeks ago in the Hamilton Corbett cottage next door to that nice little hotel in Gearhart.[6] Had a delightful house party.

With warm regards to you both,   Faithfully yours,

P.S.   You will be interested to know that we have made great strides at Camp Bonneville. Hogan has metamorphosed the reservation.[7] In early December the veteran camp at Arboretum was to be disbanded, but when they found they could not place the men elsewhere, they called on me to spend $2500 to rehabilitate an abandoned camp somewhere, for two month's occupation. I put over the proposition of giving me this company to house in the army cantonment at Bonneville, and I got $500 to put things in shape for winter occupation. Hogan managed the thing beautifully, and since then I have had about $700 more to spend. The buildings have been completely revamped and the camp put in splendid shape against the future.

GCMRL/G. C. Marshall Papers (Vancouver Barracks)

1. Parsons, whom Marshall succeeded as commander at Vancouver Barracks, was commanding the Second Division at Fort Sam Houston, Texas.

2. Colonel Henry Hossfeld had commanded the Seventh Infantry at Vancouver Barracks until Colonel Ralph R. Glass (U.S.M.A., 1904) assumed command in October, 1937.

3. Captain Byron O. Garrett, an Ordnance Corps Reserve officer, was the Vancouver Barracks C.C.C. District quartermaster.

4. Colonel Glass came to Vancouver Barracks from Atlanta, Georgia, where he had been G-3 at Fourth Corps Area headquarters. Shortly before Glass's arrival, Fourth Corps Area Commander Major General George V.H. Moseley wrote: "When Glass left I did not know I would be writing you so soon, so I sent messages by Glass, telling him that if I were elected President of the United States I would make you Chief of Staff on Inauguration Day—that is the best I can do." (Moseley to Marshall, September 9, 1937, GCMRL/G. C. Marshall Papers [Vancouver Barracks].)

5. With Marshall's vigorous encouragement, publication of the Vancouver Barracks C.C.C. District *Review* began on May 15, 1937.

6. Hamilton F. Corbett was president of the Portland Chamber of Commerce.

7. Reserve Infantry officer First Lieutenant Adellon H. Hogan.

To Captain Julius Klein[1]   February 3, 1938
                                Vancouver Barracks, Washington

My dear Julius: I would have replied to your Ms earlier, but I have been away on an inspection trip.

It is difficult for me to advise you about such matters, except to tell you where I think your fiction does not rhyme with fact. In chapter 13 you combine two things in the Intelligence or G-2, only one of which pertains to G-2 and was handled there. I refer to the map showing the locations of the German and the

Allied divisions. G-2 maintained the map showing the location of German divisions, and was responsible for obtaining the data on which it was based. The actual location determined for the German divisions was not a secret, and was furnished every division headquarters, and higher units, in the form of a lithographed copy which was issued at frequent intervals.

The map showing the Allied divisions was a responsibility of G-3, but even so, was not kept in the G-3 section, but at another point in the building and carefully guarded. The data for this map was not a matter of difficulty of determination, so long as the French and the British headquarters were willing to give us information as to the daily location of their divisions. Of course we knew where our own were. The information on this map was what the entire German Secret Service was striving to obtain, just as our G-2 section was striving to obtain the same data regarding the Germans.

The French and British at first hesitated to turn loose the data regarding their divisions, as we had no immediate use for such data, not having any field armies; and also, I suppose because it was such vital information that they did not wish to risk it in our headquarters until we had become pretty well established and GHQ affairs routinized.

This G-3 map, the replica of which is in the Smithsonian in Washington as it showed the divisions on November 11, was utilized by the Commander in Chief, the Chief of Staff and the G-3 for the determination of such plan of campaign as suited the directive of Marshal Foch.

Understand again, G-2 collects information about the enemy, and G-3 utilizes it. In one sense, G-2 was not at all concerned in what our own people were doing, except that it assisted them in obtaining information of the enemy.

I hope this rather involved information will clear things up, at least to the point where you can use such poetic license as necessary to your plot. Faithfully yours,

GCMRL/G. C. Marshall Papers (Vancouver Barracks)

1. Klein—a correspondent during the World War and editor for Hearst newspapers (1926–33)—joined the Illinois National Guard in 1933 and led an investigation of subversive activities in the middle west, 1933–34. On leave from the Illinois National Guard, he had been an executive for R.K.O. and Universal Pictures in Hollywood, California, since 1934. He was writing an American spy novel set during the World War and had sent Marshall parts of his draft for comment.

TO MAJOR GENERAL GEORGE S. SIMONDS   February 10, 1938
                                                 Vancouver Barracks,
                                                 Washington

My dear General: An item in the morning paper announces your retirement. Whether this merely means that the order has been issued for your retirement at some later date or that you actually are retiring ahead of time, I do not know.[1] But, I do want to comment on the fact before the day of your departure arrives.

I believe I remarked to you the other day that you and Heintzelman were the only two high-ranking officers I could recall, at the moment, whose advancement and whose entire careers had never been the subject of even envious criticism. I think I made an exception in the case of Heintzelman because I believe Bjornstad held some grudge regarding a Second Army matter. In your case, however, you have the unique and wonderful distinction of having run the race brilliantly, and with the unanimous good will and approval of every human being with whom you came in contact. That is a marvelous accomplishment, and I should think it would be a source of profound satisfaction to you, if your modesty permits you to admit the fact to yourself.

I am so glad I had this brief opportunity to serve under you, and am sorry that it could not have been in closer contact. In the War we were widely separated, and since then, except for this past year, I have never had the good fortune to be officially associated with you.

My admiration has been colored by the realization that you and I are such different types, and I heartily approve of yours. Frank McCoy and you are of the same stripe, and it is a very delightful thing to serve with you. Also, you add a great deal to the prestige of the army.

I hope that you find an interesting life beyond the active list; in fact, I know you will, because no one with your experience and qualifications will be allowed to effect a complete retirement. I want you to know that I sincerely appreciate the consideration with which you have treated me.[2]

Please give my warmest regards to Mrs. Simonds, and believe me always, Faithfully yours,

GCMRL/G. C. Marshall Papers (Vancouver Barracks)

1. Simonds, whose retirement became effective on March 31, was succeeded by Major General Albert J. Bowley (U.S.M.A., 1897). Bowley had commanded the Fifth Corps Area (May, 1934–October, 1935) and the Third Corps Area (October, 1935–February, 1938) before assuming command of the Ninth Corps Area in March, 1938.

2. On February 14, Simonds wrote: "You have a record and reputation which will insure that you are one of those who will be considered in the selection of the next Chief of Staff. You probably feel that you are too junior in rank for such consideration. Don't let that thought control you. If your selection for that office should not transpire you are certain to have assignments to high command and to positions carrying with them great responsibility. Of course I know that there is no need for me to give you that bit of advice for you have always been forward looking and keep yourself prepared for any duty that might come to you." (Simonds to Marshall, February 14, 1938, GCMRL/G. C. Marshall Papers [Vancouver Barracks].)

TO MAJOR GENERAL FRANK R. McCOY   [March 9, 1938]
Tucson, Arizona

Dear General: Katherine forwarded your recent letter—after reading it, apparently, and I was delighted to receive it here. I arrived Sunday after flying from Portland to Washington, and found General Pershing starting on the road to recovery—but pathetically weak. He has improved each day. At first I could see him only a few minutes at a time, but now I can visit with him for a half hour at a time. No one but Miss May Pershing, Warren and I have seen him—except the medical folk.[1]

Warren's fiancee is arriving by plane Friday morning. Adamson—his secretary—arrives tomorrow.

Katherine and I were due in Honolulu for February, but the N.Y. Times announcement of a board Fox Conner and I were to form a board for reorganization of the division in February [*sic*]. So we called off the trip. Then Conner went into the hospital and the board report from San Antonio was delayed, so Katherine and I arranged to leave for Del Monte and Carmel, Cal., a week ago last Monday. Molly had gone on to Honolulu. Instead, I left on an hours notice for Washington and Katherine is alone.

I plan to leave here Friday or Saturday.

I wish we could see you and Francis. We must get together. I fear I go to Washington this summer. If so Katherine will go to Fire Island until the fall, and then settle in Washington. I know she will insist on having you weekend with her down there, and I will get the chance to see you.

Craig talks of War Plans Division, but I am a country boy who rides every morning before breakfast, walks in the woods every evening, or runs about the mountains or down the sea coast inspecting and playing.

With affectionate regards to you both,   Faithfully,

G. C. Marshall

LC/F. R. McCoy Papers; H

1. Marshall was writing from the Desert Sanatorium, where General Pershing had been in critical condition. On February 26, Marshall had left Vancouver Barracks for Washington, D.C., soon after receiving an order from Chief of Staff Craig to report for special duty in connection with Pershing's affairs. Two days before, Captain George E. Adamson had written to Marshall: "Of course it is very difficult to think about the General being in a critical condition, but it is something to which we should now give some thought. He has always been so vital that it has never occurred to me that the time would come when his closest friends would be called upon to pay their last tribute of respect. Confidentially, I took up with General Craig's aide yesterday, Colonel Summers, who in turn talked it over with the Chief of Staff, the question of your being ordered to Tucson in case a critical situation arises. General Craig was rather of the opinion that this should be done at once, but in view of the more favorable reports I thought that it might be premature to take this action. The General has spoken to me about certain details, among which was that he desired you to take charge of arrangements in the event of his passing on." (Adamson to Marshall, February 24, 1938, LC/J. J. Pershing Papers [General Correspondence].)

To Lieutenant Colonel Guy W. Chipman[1]   March 16, 1938
[Vancouver Barracks,
Washington]

My dear Chipman: I have just returned from Tucson and will make a brief reply to your letter of February 16, because I find I will probably be away again and do not wish to postpone the matter indefinitely.

About the only advice I can give you is to keep very clearly in mind two or three factors, what I would call the dominant factors, in your work with the National Guard.

In the first place, whatever you do should be directed towards training them to do for themselves. For example, the Division staff was always glad to listen to a lecture. In fact, they preferred lectures. But I would very seldom if ever accommodate them because I found very little profit from such talking. I concentrated on training them to work as a team, expeditiously, smoothly and with a generous understanding of the human side of the troop situation. In other words, I found little opportunity to deal with the extension courses, because those were largely individual performances, and usually regarding purely tactical matters or momentary logistical incidents. What I wanted was a team that knew how to operate in the city, in the summer camp, in the field, or in a flood situation; and particularly, knew how to deal with troops without killing delays and unintentional impositions. In teaching the staff how to make inspections we finally developed one of the most efficient inspection routines I have ever seen, the principal point being that everything was done in an hour and 55 minutes, and that it was usefully done.

When it came to the infantry weapons, I found great inefficiency in their use. The larger responsibility for this lay with the War Department—or Benning—because the instructions are built for a permanent army with unlimited time available, and are an absurdity for those who only have an hour and a half a week. Our school of small arms reached that point of perfection where I had eliminated all regular instructors—and we started off with 38; and we not only eliminated the regulars from the setup, but at the same time improved the school, and vastly improved on Benning methods so far as expeditious work was concerned.

We developed the CPX procedure in camp far beyond what it had been, and managed it in a short half day instead of smearing it over 2½ days. Our winter CPX, I believe, was superior to anything attempted in the army.

Part of the foregoing discussion brings me to the second important consideration—the human interest factor. Nobody is interested in a mimeograph discussion, and only a military nut would be interested in these interminable complicated and stilted orders that are so common these days. Therefore we made brevity the soul of all our wit, and tried in every way to play up the interest factor. Hence the two-sided CPX with the enemy strength (reserves) unknown. In these matters I found that if I allowed preparations to take their normal course we were buried in papers and bored to death with formalities. Hence every effort was made by me to find simple expeditious ways for doing things.

The third factor concerns the time element and it should dominate everything you do with the National Guard. I had the best collection of regular instructors that I could imagine being gotten together with the National Guard, yet it was necessary for me to exert a constant and increasing pressure on them for doing things more expeditiously. I found that we often accomplished in 30 minutes what they at first thought would take a day, and did it much better. This may seem an exaggeration, but it is a fairly accurate statement, and today I am appalled at the waste of time involved in the training of regular troops. You can not secure more time for training in the armories, therefore it is vital that the training start on the dot and in a military manner throughout an armory, and that every by-product of this effort be realized. The ideal thing would be to have an armory transformed into a miniature West Point from the moment first call blew for drill until an hour and a half later. Now in this matter we were often at fault in imposing so much literature, or of such laborious requirements of the Leavenworth nature, that the troop commanders and staffs were largely concerned with purely administrative and tactical concerns.

I found it better to let the instructors act more as a faculty than officers isolated with the various regiments; and had them work in teams to demonstrate this or that. But avoid like you would the plague ponderous time-consuming didactic demonstrations.

Much of what I say you will find difficult to understand until you go over the past procedure after you reach Chicago. I offer this more or less confidential, and hope it will be of some benefit. Faithfully yours,

GCMRL/G. C. Marshall Papers (Vancouver Barracks)

1. Chipman (U.S.M.A., 1910), who had served with Marshall at Fort William McKinley in 1916, had received orders to report for duty in Chicago as senior instructor of the Illinois National Guard upon completion of his assignment as student officer, Special Advanced Course, at the Naval War College, in mid-May. He had written to Marshall: "Naturally, I am anxious to carry on this new work in the same efficient manner as you did. I would like very much to have suggestions from you about this particular detail, your method of putting the instruction across, the type and method of instruction, and anything else you believe would be of interest to me." (Chipman to Marshall, February 16, 1938, GCMRL/G. C. Marshall Papers [Vancouver Barracks].)

To Leo A. Farrell   March 26, 1938
                                        Vancouver Barracks, Washington

My dear Farrell: I found your letter on my return from an inspection trip down the coast, and as usual I was very much surprised—surprised to hear from you and more surprised by the subject of your note.[1] You and your expressions of good will, or evidences of your good deeds, always pop up in the most unexpected fashion after long silences. This last calm discussion of my being considered as a possible chief of staff, quite tops the lot. My worries have not been over that exalted office, but rather over the more prosaic problem of how-to-get-to-be a major general before I am too old or too junior in rank to amount to much of anything.

General Craig intimated to me while I was in Washington for two days recently, that I would be brought there to head the War Plans Division of the staff and I have been trying to compose myself to the loss of a dukedom out here in the magnificient northwest. I do wish you could come west before I am moved away. I would love to show you this CCC empire of mine and the magnificient scenery in which it is set. Not to mention the fascination of trying to do something constructive for these young boys. I have several thousand from the southeast—many from Georgia—and I am struggling to force their education, academic or vocational, to the point where they will be on the road to really useful citizenship by the time they return to their homes. I have done over my corps of civilian educators, and their methods, until I think we really have something supremely practical. To me it has been a fascinating side line, though it really takes the major portion of my time.

I spent a week with General Pershing at Tucson, lived in the Sanatorium cottage with him, and left only when his secretary arrived from Washington and Warren's fiance arrived from Palm Beach. The cottage was getting rather full, and it seemed to me that the possible excitement of some many different people looking in on the General might not be conducive to the complete rest and absence of emotional strain the doctors desired. So I came home. He was improving steadily and had reached the point of enjoying a good laugh. A remarkable recovery.

Thanks for your letter and kindly interest in my welfare. I will look forward to seeing you. Faithfully yours,

G. C. Marshall

GCMRL/L. A. Farrell Papers; T

1. Farrell's letter to Marshall was not found in the Marshall papers.

To Lieutenant Colonel Terry de la M. Allen[1]   March 26, 1938
[Vancouver Barracks,
Washington]

Dear Allen: I found your letter of March 1st on my return from Washington and Tucson—also the pamphlet of "Methods of Combat for Cavalry."[2]

I was much interested in glancing over what you had produced for the cavalry along this line. The procedure of the presentation impresses me very favorably, because I have come to believe that one of the most important considerations in all military training is brevity in the manuals, coupled with expeditious methods for accomplishing the training. My two years with the National Guard of Illinois was the final and convincing argument for me against our time consuming procedure and our wordy manuals. And when I finally rejoined the Regular Army I was even more impressed with the waste of time, in the midst of hard work, that is involved in the training of regular troops. So, from that viewpoint alone I was much interested in your manual.

As far as I can tell your text follows in general the teachings I was familiar with at the Infantry School. Your methods for combat correspond more or less to the "Offensive and Defensive Combat" of the Infantry School. In organization and equipment your horse cavalry squadron, with attached supporting weapons, in employment is much the same as our infantry battalion.

Off hand, I can think of no one better suited than you, temperamentally and by experience to be the guiding hand in preparing such a pamphlet, and I think you have done a fine job.

Reverting again to my earlier comments, I had an unusual group of instructors in Illinois—they would have made a splendid army corps staff, and more or less as a faculty they developed the most surprising technique for training that I have ever seen. The time element was the dominant factor, and next in importance was the interest factor. Hence, two-sided map problems, terrain exercises, command post exercises; maneuvers first handled as map problems, studied on the ground as terrain exercises and finally carried out as maneuvers—but always with a surprise factor, which usually upset the apple cart.

Utilizing available terrain and maps entered largely into our procedure. For example, within 45 minutes by motor car of the Loop district in Chicago we would carry out a terrain exercise—following an indoor winter CPX and picking it up at a certain hour in the CPX development—over a hundred square miles of country, with three or four hundred officers. They would deploy simultaneously at the point they had reached at a certain hour in the two-sided CPX, a month or two earlier, and go ahead over the actual ground. Organized Reserve units always provided the enemy. The right gun of every battery would be marked with a stake, the successive locations and movements of every special weapon would be traced, the OPs would be checked and the wire calculated, the command posts would be sketched in exact detail, the exact location of every kitchen, cart, dump and what not, would be actually determined. And all this between 10:00 a.m. and 1:30 p.m. of a Sunday, without the expenditure of a penny or leasing of an acre. I have seen the cavalry officers go over the ground involved in all the attacks and counter attacks of the CPX, with almost as much excitement as in a maneuver.

Now, given a regular command, and there was such a command within 15 minutes drive of this spot, and you would have had studies, estimates, funds to be secured, days to be allotted, and all the other time consuming training procedures of our laborious methods.

The School of Small Arms we developed, first for all the officers from brigadier generals down, including artillery and engineer officers, and division staff officers, lasted from 8:00 p.m. one Thursday until 6:00 p.m. on Sunday.

Some of my instructors had been Benning instructors and they told me that several of our courses, automatic rifle for example, proceeded more smoothly than at Benning. In one year we progressed from 38 regular instructors down to not a single regular acting as instructor at the second camp. The artillery and engineer field officers, the infantry plans and training and regimental staff officers, have all taken the machine gun course or the howitzer course or both. The division staff officers have also taken most of the courses. And when I say "taken" I mean turned out like West Point cadets at 5:45 for reveille and worked with absolute precision under careful direction, all day in blue denims, and fired a record course. And all of this in three days' time. Selected noncommissioned officers now go every year and all the newly commissioned officers.

The point I am trying to make is we found expeditious methods for doing what previously had been operations so time consuming that the National Guard simply would not attempt them or merely made a pretense.

I was very glad to hear from you, as I am always much interested in your military progress. Give my warmest regards to Mrs. Allen, in which Mrs. Marshall would join me if she were present at this dictation. Faithfully yours,

GCMRL/G. C. Marshall Papers (Vancouver Barracks)

1. A graduate of the Infantry School's Advanced Course in 1932, Allen had been stationed at the Cavalry School, Fort Riley, Kansas, since 1935, and had been chief of the Department of Weapons and Materiel since 1936.

2. Allen had sent Marshall a copy of the Cavalry School's text—*Methods of Combat for Cavalry* (Fort Riley, Kansas: Academic Division, The Cavalry School, 1938)—that included instructional matter on the execution of combat missions. "It has always seemed to me that service schools neglect instruction in methods of execution. It seems that instruction in methods of execution is equally as important as instruction in making tactical decisions. . . . By debunking the mystery connected with combat, by avoiding generalities and by stressing the needs of simplicity I believe we have evolved a text, the intelligent study of which will enable any smart corporal to lead a squadron in battle. As a matter of fact, this *same* text is now being used for N.C.O. Classes, Regular Classes, National Guard and Reserve Classes, Extension Courses and as a reference text by cavalry units. . . . I trust I may not seem troublesome in asking for your opinion on our innovation in school instruction. As a matter of fact I was actuated largely by what I learned at Benning in evolving the changes that we introduced here." (Allen to Marshall, March 1, 1938, GCMRL/G. C. Marshall Papers [Vancouver Barracks].)

To GENERAL JOHN J. PERSHING   April 6, 1938
                                    Vancouver Barracks, Washington

Dear General: I won't bother you with a long letter, merely a note to tell you how delighted we are to learn of the rapid progress of your recovery. It is a tribute to your constitution, the moderation of which you have controlled your diet, and your willpower.

I hear on all sides, and in so many of the letters I receive, of the deep interest of everybody in your welfare. It was one of the most amazing tributes of affectionate concern on the part of the people at large, that I know of; and it should be a great satisfaction to you, and help towards your recovery.

Warren writes me that the wedding will go off according to schedule. I had tried to promote a wedding at Tucson, but could not display much energy as his self-appointed manager, because I was injecting myself into a very personal affair. However, he and I got considerable amusement out of discussions.[1]

We are having Army Day here today,—a review of the troops for Governor Charles Martin, lunch for sixteen at our house, and 125 representatives of civic organizations in Portland and Vancouver have the noon-day meal with the men. Fortunately the sun is bright, the trees are leafing out or blooming and the post looks quite lovely.

With affectionate regards to you and Miss May,   Faithfully yours,

G. C. Marshall

LC/J. J. Pershing Papers (General Correspondence)

1. F. Warren Pershing and Muriel B. Richards were married in New York on April 22, 1938. Warren had written Marshall: "I have just returned yesterday from Tucson and hasten to get off this short note to tell you how much I appreciate your many kindnesses during the past few weeks. I can't tell you how much both Aunt May and I appreciated your stopping off and I am sure it did a great deal to hasten Father's recovery. I regret to tell you that your deep laid plot was not pulled off in Tucson, but that it is expected to go off on schedule on the 22nd of April and the Doctor announces that Father is entirely capable of attending the event." (Warren Pershing to Marshall, March 22, 1938, GCMRL/G. C. Marshall Papers [Vancouver Barracks].) Marshall replied, "I do think that as your manager I could have set you up to a wedding and a preliminary honeymoon that would put it all over anything those New York Socialites can do." (Marshall to Warren Pershing, March 29, 1938, ibid.)

To COLONEL CHARLES F. THOMPSON   April 28, 1938
[Vancouver Barracks, Washington]

Dear Charlie: Congratulations and many of them.[1] It is splendid to see men like you to be given appropriate rank in time to do something material for the Army. I will congratulate you even more heartily if I find that you are determined to throw away half the paper submitted by your staff, get rid of most of your mimeograph machines, and carry out training without months and miles of preparation and overpowering programs of procedure. I have gone through two army maneuvers, commanding the inferior "Reds" in each case, and am about fed up on fads and fancies.[2]

With my love to Laura and affectionate regards and congratulations to you both,   Faithfully yours,

GCMRL/G. C. Marshall Papers (Vancouver Barracks)

1. Assistant commandant at the Infantry School since February 1, 1937, Thompson was promoted to brigadier general effective September 1.

2. Thompson replied: "Your denunciation of our armament of mimeograph machines in our simulated warfare these days rings within me a sympathetic echo. I was on the Fourth Army Staff for the CPX in 1935 and I have thumbed the report on last year's maneuvers.

"The same bug is working in our schools. Here at Benning I flatter myself that we have made some progress in a campaign against elaborate written orders. You deserve some of the credit for what we may be accomplishing for I recall that you were sounding alarm on that subject when I had the good fortune to spend two weeks under your wing here in 1929." (Thompson to Marshall, May 4, 1938, GCMRL/G. C. Marshall Papers [Vancouver Barracks].)

To Major General James K. Parsons   May 6, 1938
[Vancouver Barracks,
Washington]

Dear Parsons: I am sending you under separate cover the answers and papers to your questions and requests of April 29th. I hope they prove to be what you want. Garrett has gone into considerable detail.[1]

There have been few changes made since your departure. Changing from our own convoys to commercial vans for deliveries beyond 100 miles has been the principal change. We started this experimentally in eastern Oregon, before we lost that part of the district, and found it more economical—though I had installed it in order to save our transportation and reduce the hazards involved in traversing the Columbia Gorge and the mountainous region of eastern Oregon during the winter months. It was so satisfactory there that we next moved into the Willamette Valley, and then included the coast camps, everything beyond 100 miles.

The other change of moment was the introduction of sub-district commanders. I have three sub-districts.[2] The officers are not allowed to have headquarters, and make no reports other than a rough diary once a week and a telephone message three times a week. They can go where they wish and when they wish. Their guiding mission is to raise the standard of poor camps to that of the best. They inspect the funds every other month. At first I did not have them do this, but found it advisable to inflict on them. We have found it more economical in the way of mileage than making all the inspections from here. They declare a great dividend when anything goes wrong, particularly a forest fire. Then I require them to be on the ground, to pick up several CCC boys and establish a command post for the coordination of effort and supply for all the detachments involved in the fire. It has removed the mixed up hurley-burley of this fire fighting business, and created order out of chaos in rear of the actual fire fighting activities. These sub-district fellows have informal schools for clerks, cooks, and for bakers; they take the best educational work in the sub-district and

590

make the other camps conscious of what is being done; they function very much as a battalion commander and I hold them accountable for the sub-districts. But, I have constantly to watch the staff here to see that they do not impose a lot of reports on the sub-district commanders. I find in the army every time I turn my back some staff officer calls on some poor devil for a report or an extra copy or some more damned papers—and I will not have it. I am off for maneuvers next week, and I am not going to allow a mimeograph machine in the war.

It would do your heart good to see what we have been able to do here for the post by the use of WPA money I got through Wilson in the War Department.[3] All of the married men's houses have been completely worked over inside and out, much needed additions made; the same thing has been done for all the junior officers' quarters, and in a general way for the barracks and for the senior officers. The North Woods has almost been grubbed out, the fence cutting it off from the post has been removed, and now troop training can be conveniently carried on from the vicinity of the officers' line to the north end of the woods. The post has been greatly beautified, a great deal of planting done—hedges, shrubs, etc.; all the old roads have been blotted out and resodding done; the Victory theater has about been converted into a splendid gymnasium, roller skating rink and basket-ball court. The road in rear of the officers' quarters has been made a very attractive street, widened and hedged, and the ball diamond and the vicinity of the CCC camp has been hand worked. The old radio house is now a double set of NCO quarters, and the former CMTC headquarters is about converted into a double set.

At Bonneville I picked up another veteran company—the one from Arboretum—for three months, pending its dissolution, and put it in the army cantonment. We transformed that place (This is strictly entre nous), making a splendid set of barracks, fine kitchens and mess halls, etc. out of the old setup. Drainage and wide streets were put in, an infirmary built, a first sergeant's office created, the front of the little club graded and planted, hedges distributed here and there, underpinning made permanent, reservoirs rebottomed, and the whole made a splendid installation.

The garden at my house is lovely now. They are spraying the roses this morning—for the third or fourth time this season.

Mrs. Marshall and myself leave for Fort George Wright Sunday morning thence to Missoula and thence to Fort Lewis, where she takes the train and I remain for maneuvers.[4]

With warm regards,   Faithfully yours,

GCMRL/G. C. Marshall Papers (Vancouver Barracks)

1. Parsons's April 29 letter to Marshall is not in the Marshall papers. According to Parsons's reply letter, Captain Garrett, the quartermaster, had sent him information concerning the Vancouver Barracks District C.C.C. Having recently assumed command of the Third Corps Area headquarters in Baltimore, Maryland, Parsons was striving to increase the authority of the district C.C.C. commanders and reduce interference from his Corps Area headquarters. "The other day I caught a letter calling for an explanation why a grease trap cover had been

changed without authority of Corps Headquarters. To prevent things of this kind I have directed that no one from Corps Headquarters will visit a CCC company without a specific order from me. I think I was a very good District Commander but I am sure I would have been a 'flop' if I had been in this Corps Area, since the District Commanders are not allowed any authority. This I am changing as fast as it is possible.'' (Parsons to Marshall, May 16, 1938, GCMRL/G. C. Marshall Papers [Vancouver Barracks].)

2. Infantry Reserve officers commanded the subdistricts: Captain Bernhard A. Johnson, Astoria; Captain James M. Carr, Hood River; and Captain Clarence A. Hebert, Eugene.

3. Major Arthur R. Wilson was on duty with the Office of the Chief of Staff.

4. Fort George Wright was located four miles west of Spokane, Washington. Marshall proceeded to Fort Missoula, Montana, for an inspection tour, May 11–13, and then came back to Fort Lewis, Washington, for the Fifth Brigade maneuvers that began on May 16.

TO BENJAMIN F. IRVINE[1] May 16, 1938
Fort Lewis, Washington

My dear Mr. Irvine: I am very sincere in the statement that the note from you and Mrs. Irvine made a deep impression on me and will be a source of gratification in my memories of Portland. I valued your good will, and your splendid efforts toward helping Vancouver Barracks, and now, since the receipt of your gracious note, I can enjoy the feeling of your friendly interest in me personally.[2]

Incidentally, I think we are actually on the way to the first favorable financial reaction from Washington for post construction. I have gotten $160,000 in WPA money out of the War Department in addition to $57,000 I secured through the State of Washington. With this money we are rehabilitating the post and grounds, and I think I am reasonably accurate in saying that Vancouver Barracks is the loveliest looking of the old posts in the entire army.

The bill for the construction of a replica of the old Hudson's Bay trading post has passed Congress and I have been meeting with the officials of Vancouver to arrange for the organization of a legal group to carry out the construction. I think this will be the most interesting historical monument in the Northwest, and both an asset to the region and a splendid thing to animate the pride and historical sense of the young people of Washington and Oregon.

I have been delayed in acknowledging your note due to my absence on an inspection trip in Montana.

With warm regards to Mrs. Irvine and you, and my appreciations and thanks, Faithfully yours,

GCMRL/G. C. Marshall Papers (Vancouver Barracks)

1. Until his retirement, Irvine had edited the Portland, Oregon, *Journal*, 1919–37.

2. On May 10 the War Department announced that Marshall was being detailed to the General Staff and would report for duty in the Office of the Chief of Staff in July. The same day, Irvine wrote Marshall and expressed regret at reading of his transfer to Washington, D.C.

To Colonel Ralph A. Fenton[1]   May 17, 1938
                                                         Fort Lewis, Washington

My dear Dr. Fenton: Your note has just reached me, in the field during maneuvers. I appreciate the nice things you say, and am very sad at the prospect of leaving the Northwest.

I do not look on the Washington detail with any favor. I am to be head of the War Plans Division of the General Staff, but that means purely a desk job, which is not to my taste.

You were very kind to write as you did and I appreciate it. I will see you before I leave, which will be about the middle of June. Faithfully yours,

GCMRL/G. C. Marshall Papers (Vancouver Barracks)

1. Fenton, a member of the American Medical Association's board of trustees, was an eye, ear, nose, and throat surgeon in Portland, Oregon. A colonel in the Medical Reserve, he had served in the United States Army Medical Corps, 1917–19. Fenton had written to Marshall: "Your administration has been most helpful to our community and many have voiced their regret that you must leave, even for a position of greater responsibility." (Fenton to Marshall, [May 13, 1938], GCMRL/G. C. Marshall Papers [Vancouver Barracks].)

To Reed G. Landis   May 17, 1938
                                                         Fort Lewis, Washington

Dear Landis: I found your letter of May 6th on my return from an inspection trip from Montana.

I see from the papers that the Reorganization Bill may come up again, and I was interested in your comments about joint purchasing, etc.[1]

In 1921 I represented the War Department and young Theodore Roosevelt (then Acting Secretary of the Navy) represented the Navy Department in the study of what might be done along the very line you refer to. The Brown Reorganization Project was then in view. We found then that many of the dissimilarities had been or were in process of being corrected, but there was much yet to be done. My principal proposal, which looks better to me today than it did then, got nowhere, because it did not have enough immediacy about it to provide potent political argument. However, I think it was and is the proper basis for relations between the army and navy, or any preliminaries to their consolidation.

I wanted to exchange officers from every section of the General Staff with equivalent officers of the Navy Department. Not as liaison officers, though they would have been this in effectiveness, but actually to exchange jobs. Only in this way, in my opinion, will the navy ever know intimately what, why and how the army does things—and vice versa. I would have carried a similar exchange between the supply departments, the medical departments, ordnance and communication services.

I found both army and navy officers—or officials, strongly opposed to such a measure, because they seemed to feel that the exchanged officer could never satisfactorily perform the job vacated by his opposite number. And, I do not think, they visualized the eventual good that I think would come of such procedure. As a matter of fact, I seem to be out of step with the rest of the world in this particular idea, but to me it is fundamental, and the only effective leadup to the proper coordination of the two services—don't quote me. Hastily yours,

GCMRL/G. C. Marshall Papers (Vancouver Barracks)

1. Landis had written of the need for standardization of supply items and the establishment of "some sort of a centralized joint purchasing office through which the requirements of both the Army and Navy could be coordinated. . . . There is little excuse for a Naval screw designed to do a certain job being required in a different material and thread than an Army screw which has to carry the same sort of loading." He also noted the possibility of the reorganization question resurfacing. "I believe it healthy for those of us who are intensely interested in a sound National Defense to spend a small part of our time in thinking about questions such as this, in the hopes that we can avoid being caught with our nether portions exposed in case of an emergency." (Landis to Marshall, May 6, 1938, GCMRL/G. C. Marshall Papers [Vancouver Barracks].)

To Brigadier General Charles G. Dawes   May 23, 1938
                                                 Fort Lewis, Washington

Dear General: I have learned nothing from the papers recently regarding the rate of your recovery. Will you please have Mr. Blyth send me a note, to Vancouver Barracks, telling me how you are progressing? I do not want to trouble Mrs. Dawes as I imagine she has been deluged with such inquiries.

I am hoping that this letter finds you in full force and vigor, and about ready for the same acute prediction regarding the trend of affairs, that you made so brilliantly in anticipation of the turning point in the first phase of the depression.

I have been ordered to Washington, to head the War Plans Division of the General Staff, sailing from San Francisco June 18th. I came here for Division maneuvers a week ago, direct from Missoula, Montana where I had been inspecting part of my Brigade. Mrs. Marshall was with me at Spokane and Missoula, and motored here with me via the Coulee Dam. Then she went on to Vancouver. We have our final maneuvers commencing tomorrow, and immediately thereafter—probably Thursday—I will return to Vancouver and get busy the final rites of breaking up a home.

We hate terribly to leave the Northwest, and I am particularly reluctant to go to a desk in Washington. I am a much more promising citizen, I think, in this sort of work than at a desk.[1]

I have marveled at General Pershing's remarkable recovery. I spent a week with him at Tucson, and it did not seem vaguely possible then, and in such a short time, that he would be on his feet en route to New York.

With deep interest in your welfare,   Affectionately yours,

G. C. Marshall

NU/C. G. Dawes Papers

1. Dawes, upon returning to Chicago following his recovery from an operation in New York City, wrote to Marshall: "I had heard at New York that you had been ordered to General Staff duty for which is particularly important at this time. The assignment in present world conditions is a distinctive honor." (Dawes to Marshall, June 25, 1938, NU/C. G. Dawes Papers.)

To Colonel James H. Van Horn[1]   May 23, 1938
                                                                Fort Lewis, Washington

Dear Van Horn: I was surprised and very much interested in your letter of May 16th, and appreciated greatly the extracts you had made for me from Liddell Hart's writing.[2] You know, if the General Staff in Washington could secure the services of Liddell Hart to convey their ideas and policies in his brand of English writing, they could get away with anything up to murder. He puts things beautifully, and so convincingly that so often he gets away with some things that are not justified by the cold, uninspiring facts. However, this present collection of extracts is most impressing.

Your suggestions were of great interest to me, and I should like very much to discuss them with you, particularly those regarding the National Guard and the Reserve Corps.[3] I don't quite agree with you as to the Reserve Corps. I think that half of its present weakness is due to our mishandling and our lack of vision in adapting the Reserve Corps to actual conditions. For example, I find I almost have to knock my officers down, particularly staff officers, to get them to use reserve officers in the actual job—and not half on-lookers. Personally I find that they can do it. I went into the 2nd Army maneuvers with a brigade staff of reserve officers, none of whom had seen each other, and none of whom I had seen. We handled up to 6000 troops on a more complicated basis than would have been the case on a Division staff. We lacked everything, and were given seemingly every possible administrative and supply responsibility, in addition to the tactical requirements. We covered 60 miles of country in a campaign against 20,000 troops. These reserve fellows did a beautiful job as 1, 2, 3 and 4 of my outfit. I have had other and similar experiences, and was entering the summer into a complete turnover, as it were, of all the leading jobs, line and staff, below the regiment, at Vancouver Barracks from the middle of June until the first of September. The only exceptions were in the matter of money and firing for record on the target range, and there all the subordinates are to be reserve officers. I want the regular officer to induct the reserve officer into his job in short order, as would be the case in war—I give the Post Adjutant two days, and permitting him only 30 minutes a day at his office thereafter. I have intended having most of the regular officers to seize this period for recreation, including leaves, instead of being confined to the post and camp more rigorously in the summer than at any other time. I am doing this last to make them like utilizing reserves.

I hope I get a chance to talk to you after I get to Washington. I have always been interested in your career and in your brain, which seems always on the make.   Faithfully yours,

GCMRL/G. C. Marshall Papers (Vancouver Barracks)

1. Van Horn was Signal Corps officer at First Corps Area headquarters in Boston, Massachusetts.

2. Extracts from Basil H. Liddell Hart, *Europe in Arms* (New York: Random House, 1937) had been inclosed.

3. Van Horn had written that he would like to see a new National Defense Act that would "1. Limit the composition of the Officers Reserve Corps (with few exceptions and during emergencies only), to Lieutenants; trained with Regular Army and National Guard Units; active for six or seven years only; paid a retaining fee instead of in prospects of, and encouragement for promotion. (The number of old timers should be confined to the Regular Service, where we have more than enough for the Army as a whole.) 2. Limit many of the key positions in National Guard Divisions to Regular officers." He also suggested reducing by fifty percent the number of Regular officers on duty with the R.O.T.C. and providing Regular officers with more service with troops. (Van Horn to Marshall, May 16, 1938, GCMRL/G. C. Marshall Papers [Vancouver Barracks].)

To Reed G. Landis
May 27, 1938
Vancouver Barracks, Washington

Dear Landis: I have just read your note of May 23rd, and while I am not going into further ramifications of my views on consolidation, I must comment on one item. Your reference to the difficulties in solution and interchange of Army and Navy officers, is an amusing confirmation of the attitude of most of the fellows in the War and Navy Departments. With this I disagree.[1]

I refer to the rank of the officers to be exchanged. We are so damned conservative in peace as to who can do what, that we seldom do any otherwise; and the hour war is declared we take a boy out of high school and give him a couple thousand of men. I am exaggerating somewhat, but merely to emphasize the point. In other words, we can exchange safely and efficiently officers of field rank, though I myself would prefer an outstanding captain of the army and commander of the navy. The new broom always sweeps clean, and usually sees things from a fresh and therefore from a more efficient point of view. He is not in a rut, and therefore is invaluable if he has good common sense and a sound military or naval basic education. A naval commander in the War Plans, G-3 or G-4 branches of the General Staff would quickly prove a very valuable General Staff officer of the army. But what is more to the point, he would bring across, by degrees, the best ideas of the navy, the best ideas of navy procedure point of view and vice versa, and would informally convey to the navy the better practices of the army that he observed and came to understand by his actual job of responsibilities. Hastily yours,

GCMRL/G. C. Marshall Papers (Vancouver Barracks)

1. Landis had written: "I presume that much of the routine action in both the Army and the Navy is based on the personal experience in the specific service enjoyed by the officers taking the action and that an Army officer suddenly dropped into a position of major responsibility in the Navy might have some difficulty in turning out the same amount of work that an experienced Naval file would turn out in a given period of time. This objection would, of course, completely disappear if the exchanged officers were started out in relatively low ranking jobs and worked their way up. The objection to this is that such officers would probably be young in service and not yet thoroughly experienced in their own branch. Because of this, it seems to me that it might possibly work out better and more quickly to set up joint offices where Army and Naval officers could handle the specific matters relating to their own services side by side and under coordinating influence experienced in both services. The result, I believe, would be eventually the same as you contemplate, without the initial difficulties." (Landis to Marshall, May 23, 1938, GCMRL/G. C. Marshall Papers [Vancouver Barracks].)

To Major General Charles H. Martin   May 27, 1938
[Vancouver Barracks,
Washington]

Dear General: The news of the election results reached me in the field at maneuvers at Fort Lewis, from where I just returned last night. I had a short time previously written a note of my feelings on the subject, and it really pains me to write to you now to express regrets.[1] Really what has happened is such a tragedy to the State of Oregon that I am without words on the subject. For you personally I feel a disappointment that I am sure is keener than yours, for I can not have your solace of feeling of work so well done and a vastly important service so well rendered.

I can not help but think that out of this black disappointment will come something much more important than we perceive at the present time. Meanwhile my deep regret that things have not gone entirely your way, and my deep regret that I am forced to leave the Northwest and the delightful intimacy I have had with you; in all of which Mrs. Marshall joins me. Faithfully yours,

GCMRL/G. C. Marshall Papers (Vancouver Barracks)

1. Governor Martin lost the Democratic gubernatorial primary in a close race against Henry L. Hess. Marshall had previously written to Martin: "I submit my prayers and hopes towards your success in the election on May 20th, and I wish that I could cast my first vote in your behalf. This note is merely to tell you that your success is dear to my heart and constantly in my mind." (Marshall to Martin, May 14, 1938, GCMRL/G. C. Marshall Papers [Vancouver Barracks].)

To General John J. Pershing   May 27, 1938
                                      Vancouver Barracks, Washington

Dear General: Your letter reached me in Montana where I was inspecting part of my Brigade.[1] From there I went to Fort Lewis for maneuvers of the 3rd Division, from which I just returned last night. There also reached me in Montana a radio ordering me to Washington on the General Staff.

I got a great thrill out of receiving a letter from you, the first since your illness. But I must admit that I got even a greater thrill out of seeing you at Warren's wedding, in Life.[2] The progress you made between my last visit at Tucson and the wedding is one of the most amazing recoveries, in point of speed, that I have ever heard of. I think the editorial in "The New York Times" on this subject was probably the finest tribute you received.

I had been very much in hopes that Muriel could be persuaded to move the wedding over to Tucson at the time of her visit there. I did not visualize the miraculously rapid recovery you would make. And I am now very glad that things turned out as they did, for your demonstration was the most effective that could have been conceived to bring the public to a realization of your true character and the degree of your backbone or courage.

As I have just gotten home, there has not been time to reach definite decisions as to plans. In all probability, we will sail from San Francisco June 18th, reaching Washington about July 6th. That is, I will reach Washington, Mrs. Marshall going directly from New York to Fire Island to spend the summer in her cottage there, or in the Adirondacks.

As far as I know, or as I was told by General Craig last February, I go to the War Plans Division.

One of the few redeeming features of this deal is the fact that I will be in close touch again with you. I am fond of Craig personally, but I loathe a desk. I would not mind much, except that I have so few years left for active service that I hate to lose them to desk instead of command work.

Please tell Adamson to send me a line with some frequency as to how you are getting along and of your plans and movements. Affectionately,

G. C. Marshall

LC/J. J. Pershing Papers (General Correspondence)

1. Pershing had written to Marshall on May 3: "I am just now getting around to writing briefly to a few of my friends to tell them how much their solicitude has meant to me in recent

weeks, and among the first is this note to you. You cannot know how much comfort and cheer your letters and telegrams, and above all your visit to Tucson, gave me.'' (Pershing to Marshall, May 3, 1938, GCMRL/G. C. Marshall Papers [Vancouver Barracks].)

2. The May 2, 1938, issue of *Life* featured photographs of General Pershing attending the wedding of his son and Muriel B. Richards on April 22 in New York City. (*Life* 4 [May 2, 1938]: 9–12.)

To Brigadier General John McA. Palmer   May 27, 1938
                                                    Vancouver Barracks,
                                                         Washington

Dear John: I have been absent for some weeks on an inspection trip to Spokane and Missoula, and at maneuvers at Fort Lewis. Just returned last night, and received your note this morning.

Thank you for your generous expressions regarding my movement east and a possible visit to New Hampshire. I certainly hope that the latter can be arranged.

I was interested in your letter to General Lynch, because I recall perfectly your explanation of the matter at the time you made the suggestions to the Senate Military Committee. And I remember your later comments, to the effect that the immediate result of the law had been a tremendous accelerant to the service schools, bringing the "old boys" into camp in short order.[1]

The years pass and conditions change. Leavenworth, its associations and what it gave me, remain a cherished memory, backed by a continued feeling of gratitude; but, strange to say, I am almost regarded today as an opponent to Leavenworth. I am so fed up on paper, impressive technique and the dangerous effect of masses of theory which have not been leavened by frequent troop experiences such as we had in the old days, and particularly in the summer maneuver camps. I have a feeling now that Leavenworth could be vastly improved, and the army saved the possibilities of bitter confusion and recriminations during the opening months of warfare of movement, if the instructors every other year could be poured into actual troop conditions for three weeks of maneuvers at Benning with that garrison of 7000, the cavalry from Oglethorpe, the 8th Brigade from the coast and McClellan, artillery from Bragg, and the mechanized forces from Knox. I believe this concentration could be made for $10,000, and I believe it would do, after several years, a hundred million dollars of good towards National Defense.

You'll be see'n me soon, I hope,   Affectionately,

                                                        G. C. Marshall

LC/J. McA. Palmer Papers

1. Palmer had inclosed a copy of his May 21, 1938, letter addressed to Major General George A. Lynch (U.S.M.A., 1903), the chief of Infantry. He wrote Lynch that he favored the proposal to amend the General Staff Eligibility List incorporated in the National Defense Act of 1920. It was needed in 1919 because a majority of the General Staff members had had no

special General Staff education. This was no longer the case in 1938. "But if a mandatory eligibility list is no longer necessary from the standpoint of general staff efficiency, there is a special reason for abolishing it. When the 'General Staff' school became a 'Command and Staff' school, I had serious misgivings. I feared that the same principle of academic eligibility would be applied to command and staffs assignments. Apparently this has taken place, and I assure you that this was never contemplated when the General Staff Eligibility list was written into the National Defense Act.

"A good General Staff officer is primarily a product of education, whether he gets his training in a staff school or by self-application. The gift of command is not. All history proves this. . . . Steuben's General Staff training made him Washington's indispensable assistant. But he lacked the rugged moral qualities that made Washington a great commander in spite of his limited military education. Steuben was largely the product of education, Washington was not." (Palmer to Lynch, May 21, 1938, inclosed in Palmer to Marshall, May 21, 1938, GCMRL/G. C. Marshall Papers [Vancouver Barracks].)

TO GENERAL MALIN CRAIG

May 27, 1938
Vancouver Barracks, Washington

Dear General: I returned to the post last night after an absence since May 8th, involving the tactical inspection at Wright and Missoula, and maneuvers with the Division at Lewis. My orders caught me at Missoula, and I have just returned now to start on the re-adjustment of my affairs toward pulling up stakes here and moving to Washington. I had been planning to sail from San Francisco on June 18th on the St. Mihiel as ordered, but a letter this morning indicates a possibility that on the small St. Mihiel I will not even rate a bathroom, as General Tracy and General Humphrey seem to be scheduled for that trip.[1] I have not talked to Mrs. Marshall yet, but I am loath to introduce her to her first transport trip on the basis of a little room in the tropics without a bath. Will you be very frank in telling me whether there will be any embarrassment in my applying for a month's leave, to carry me over to the sailing of the Republic?[2]

I do not even know that I want to do this, but before attempting to reach a decision, I would wish to know that any delay on my arrival in Washington would not be an embarrassment to you.

Mrs. Marshall will undoubtedly spend the summer at Fire Island, off Long Island, where she has a cottage, and I rather expect to locate myself on a temporary basis until the fall.

My recent trip was very interesting, and I learned a great deal of practical value to me in my inspection of the small units of the 4th Infantry, as well as in handling the pathetic little 15th Infantry during maneuvers. There is such a vast difference between our war contemplations and technique, and these dwindling infantry units, that it requires more brain and more cleverness—and above all, common sense, to handle these little fellows than to maneuver or train the large organizations contemplated.

I had a letter from Stone in Panama asking me to be prepared to talk over defense plans with him. He assumes that I am going to WPD. I have heard something from the people in San Francisco regarding Alaska and the Aleutians, again on the assumption that I am going to WPD. I am not making any assumptions, but if there is anything I should familiarize myself with en route, I would appreciate your having the appropriate party in the War Department advise me accordingly.[3]

Looking forward with a great deal of genuine pleasure to seeing you and Mrs. Craig in Washington,   Faithfully yours,

GCMRL/G. C. Marshall Papers (Vancouver Barracks)

1. Brigadier General Joseph P. Tracy (U.S.M.A., 1896) commanded the Ninth Coast Artillery District at the Presidio of San Francisco from January 1, 1937, to June 18, 1938. On leave beginning June 19 until his retirement on October 31, 1938, Tracy would be en route to his home in Washington, D.C. Brigadier General Evan H. Humphrey (U.S.M.A., 1899), having left his station in the Philippine Islands on April 30, was en route to Brooklyn, New York, to assume command of the New York Port of Embarkation on July 6.

2. "There is no objection in the world to your taking leave enough to keep you from sailing on the San Mihiel," Craig replied. "I would do the same thing if I were in your place." (Craig to Marshall, June 1, 1938, GCMRL/G. C. Marshall Papers [Vancouver Barracks].)

3. Major General David L. Stone had commanded the Panama Canal Department since April, 1937. Craig replied that he still planned on Marshall being assigned to War Plans, but that he should relax, sightsee, and not be concerned with any official business while en route to Washington, D.C. (Ibid.)

To General Malin Craig   June 7, 1938
                                   [Vancouver Barracks, Washington]

Dear General: I have just received a radio informing me that I will be ordered to proceed overland July first.

Your note of June second proposing this came by air mail ahead of your letter telling me that I could take my own time and pleasure in returning east. I could not tell from the note whether or not you wished me in Washington without undue delay, so I had to delay until the first letter arrived.

You have been very generous and understanding in this affair, and I really feel very embarrassed in having troubled the Chief of Staff of the Army about the minutiae of my change of station. The truth of the matter was I had traveled on the St. Mihiel, along with 105 children, as I recall. While I shared the best stateroom with a congressman, Lily and her mother had a red hot coop far removed from a bath. When I was told that the chances were that the only two desirable staterooms on the boat would be taken ahead of me, I dreaded Mrs. Marshall going to Panama on those metal decks at this time of year. She wanted to do it, though she had gone through there on a Dollar boat at one time, but knowing her susceptibility to extreme heat I was much concerned to avoid that possibility. Happily you have made everything quite delightful.

I am afraid that if these other general officers follow my example you would feel like shooting the lot of us. I hated to ask such favors, because I have tried to make it a practice to take on the nose whatever I was ordered to do. Therefore my apologies, and very sincere appreciations.

I propose leading a very idle life between now and July first, with most of my CCC inspections devoted to fishing streams. With affectionate regards, Faithfully,

GCMRL/G. C. Marshall Papers (Vancouver Barracks)

To Colonel Charles L. Sampson[1]   June 13, 1938
[Vancouver Barracks, Washington]

Dear Sampson: I am sending you direct, copies of my reports on tactical inspections of the troops of the 5th Brigade and the 15th Infantry. I am submitting the reports through 3rd Division, but I am attaching to these copies sent to you some additional papers which may be of interest, but did not seem necessary to the formal report.

There are two things that impressed me during these inspections, and I think we should do something about them:

The infantry combat firing is a little bit of a mess, and not in my opinion comparable to the artillery firing—which of course is much more easy to conduct. We go through so much of formality and time consuming preparation in our rifle and machine gun firing for the individual, that it is too bad that the ultimate test should be so unsatisfactory in the manner of its conduct. On most ranges it seems almost impossible to carry out ordinary tactical movements, leading up to combat firing, under the safety conditions imposed. Therefore I am of the opinion that we must frankly abandon our present method and find some new method of conduct which will not leave so many erroneous impressions and irritations. Also, much more time must be allowed for these affairs. Each of the observers should be involved in a solution. I did this, in a small measure, with all the observers at Fort Lewis. But it was only a makeshift.

Frankly and confidentially, I was shocked at Fort George Wright with the effect on young officers of trying to show intimate familiarity with Benning and Leavenworth technique which had little application to the minute affairs of the moment. If you check the orders of some of these young officers you would find that they were apparently in strict accord with the established technique of forms for orders. But, in dealing with such things as successive defensive lines, schemes of maneuver, and other matters of the same general nature, for the omission of which you get your heart cut out at the schools, they sometimes produced ridiculous solutions. The trouble invariably was that they had so few men to deal with. For example, in one outpost situation, after the advance detachments and the listening post had been provided for, there were about eleven men left. Now, when you involve yourself in formal expressions about a main line of resistance of about a half a mile and you only have eleven riflemen, it is very easy to produce an absurdity in orders. The trouble was, in their effort to show that they understood modern practice, they lost the fundamentals of tactics—which largely concerned direction, control, dispersion, and a few simple considerations of this sort. Their problem really was largely one of economy of force, which involved the careful selection of points which would serve to cover their mission, without undue dispersion or loss of control—which are much the same thing.

If these well educated regular officers have so much difficulty in applying fundamental tactical principles to driblets of troops, and largely because they have become involved in the elaborations of technique which are only easy of application to more or less normal units, what are temporary officers going to do?

Another thing, when we have problems for these anemic commands, I think we should either frankly skeletonize the command to represent larger units, or deal with it on a much simpler basis. The combination of embarrassingly limited terrain, little commands, absence of supporting weapons in fact, etc., etc., present too many confusions to the mind to permit of smooth running performance by the young officers concerned. I think we should try them out with a combination of Command Post–Terrain exercise, regarding the more elaborate combinations, which their actual command does not admit of.

I am discussing all this informally with you, because I do not want to involve my reports too much in the way of seeming criticism.   Faithfully yours,

GCMRL/G. C. Marshall Papers (Vancouver Barracks)

1. Sampson was assistant chief of staff for Operations and Training at Ninth Corps Area headquarters at the Presidio of San Francisco.

TO GENERAL MALIN CRAIG   June 16, 1938
                                        [Vancouver Barracks, Washington]

Dear General: Now that you have so graciously re-adjusted my affairs, I am leaving here July 2nd and will report to you on the morning of the 6th. Mrs. Marshall and Molly go on to Fire Island, New York.

With reference to your suggestion that I motor east: We motored west in coming out here and spent three weeks at it. Had a perfectly wonderful trip, and I notice the leading article in the "Saturday Evening Post" this week by Priestley, an English writer, is devoted to a description of that portion of our trip through the Painted Desert around to the north of the Grand Canyon.[1] That is the most wonderful drive I have seen in America, except for the Redwoods along the north coast of California, but even those lack the contrasts of northern Arizona.

I just got back an hour ago from four days leave down at Seaside, south of Astoria, and am off for the week end with Erskine Wood of Portland at his fishing camp east of McKenzie Pass. Incidentally, he is the brother of a Congresswoman Nan Honeyman and they are the children of a one time army officer. Wood was born on this post, and as a 14-year-old boy spent two summers in the tepee with Chief Joseph, who Wood's father assisted in securing permission to return to the Northwest, after his famous retreat.[2]

I am looking forward with keen pleasure to being with you in Washington. Faithfully yours,

P.S. I am so glad you sent Grunert here, for he will be able to do a great deal to improve conditions.[3] I think we are on the way to making Vancouver Barracks the most popular post, for both officers and men, in the West.

GCMRL/G. C. Marshall Papers (Vancouver Barracks)

1. J. B. Priestley, "Rainbow in the Desert," *Saturday Evening Post* 210 (June 18, 1938): 5–6.
2. Erskine Wood was a Portland lawyer. Nan Wood Honeyman, who had been a member of the Oregon House of Representatives (1934–36), represented the Third Oregon District in Congress. Their father was First Lieutenant Charles E. S. Wood, a graduate of the United States Military Academy in 1874.
3. Brigadier General George Grunert succeeded Marshall as commander at Vancouver Barracks in November, 1938.

To Brigadier General George P. Tyner[1]   June 21, 1938
[Vancouver Barracks,
Washington]

Dear Tyner: The Department of Labor is having a conference here at Vancouver Barracks of the selecting agents of the CCC for this Corps Area. The conference was moved from Portland to the Post because of the hotel strike. The purpose of this note is to pass on to you a suggestion made yesterday by the representative of the Grazing Service with regard to their camps in particular and the CCC in general.

In describing the work of the Grazing Service he commented on the fact that by its very nature the camps were invariably located in the most desolate country, far from streams and lakes, usually with a dearth or complete absence of trees, and almost always with a large population of snakes, desert insects and other unpleasant residents of such regions. Therefore, the problem of maintaining morale among the boys was a much more difficult one than in the other camps. I recalled, after he made this comment, that our particular grief and explosion out here was in a Grazing Service camp, and that a similar blow-up in California was also, I believe, in a Grazing Service camp.[2] Your statistics may show others of the same nature.

This being the case, it would seem that the general policy for camp construction and maintenance should ordinarily allow more money for installation of camp facilities and improvement of recreation rooms, and for recreational facilities. Also, since most of these camps are in such isolated localities the leave area situation should be treated as a special proposition. For my Grazing Service camp in the desert southeast of Bend I tried to locate an unoccupied store room in the town of Bend to set up temporary sleeping quarters and a cook stove, so that when the boys went to town in the winter—it goes to 40 below zero down there—we could send them in Friday evening and bring them back to camp Sunday night. While in town they would have a warm place to loaf, a place to sleep and very simple bulk meals, most of the food being prepared before they left camp. I had in mind little more than a stew and coffee, bread, apple sauce, or items of this general nature requiring almost no preparation.

I figured in this way the boys would get a reasonable break from the monotony of camp and would not be on the streets. I found that some of them had been making it a practice to get the police to allow them to sleep at the jail. This fact stirred me up to the necessity of some definite arrangement.

The other suggestion this man made was, that like the army, it would be better to allow a choice whenever possible, on the part of the enrollee as to the type of camp he wished to enter. Farm boys, for example would get much more benefit from a Grazing Service camp or a soil conservation project; whereas city boys have little aptitude for such work. I do not think they should be allowed a choice of camp, only a choice of type of work involved. And, of course, there would be no certainty that the choice could be met.

I pass these items along for such consideration as they are worth. By the time you receive this letter my CCC responsibilities will have terminated—but not my interest.   Faithfully yours,

GCMRL/G. C. Marshall Papers (Vancouver Barracks)
 1. Tyner was assistant chief of staff, G-4, in the War Department.
 2. In early February, 1938, thirty-seven C.C.C. enrollees had been discharged from Camp Frederick Butte, Brothers, Oregon, by the camp commander when they refused to work. A week following the incident, Captain Herman O. Lane filed an inspection report concluding that the discharge of the enrollees had been necessary to maintain discipline at the camp, but that the incident was the culmination of unfortunate circumstances. The recently organized camp consisted of enrollees from the metropolitan areas of New York and New Jersey, who had set up camp in inclement weather in a desolate area fifty-six miles from Bend, Oregon. A lack of properly prepared food in an atmosphere lacking leadership and efficiency on the part of the camp commander fueled the fires of discontent. Conditions had improved, however, by the time Captain Lane submitted his report: "The organization commander has been replaced

by a competent Ninth Corps Area Captain and experienced cooks have been transferred to the camp." Marshall, in his Second Indorsement, concurred with the findings of the report. (Lane's Memorandum to Commanding General, Headquarters Ninth Corps Area, NA/RG 407 [324.5, CCC (3–25–33)].)

To Major General James K. Parsons   June 23, 1938
                                                      [Vancouver Barracks,
                                                           Washington]

My dear Parsons: Before I leave here, July 2nd, I thought you would be interested in a summary of the present state of affairs on the post and at Camp Bonneville.

Through Major Wilson in the War Department I got a hold of almost $200,000 of WPA money, in addition to some $57,000 I had obtained from the State of Washington—though this last lacked any money for material. With these funds we have been able to bring practically everything on the post up to a fine standard of recondition.

Starting with the married soldiers' quarters we have fully repaired each set, replacing all defective lumber and underpinning, adding facilities and sometimes rooms, painting, etc., etc. We have had to tear down three or four sets, but have made the old radio station into two fine sets and have just completed transforming the former CMTC Headquarters into two splendid sets, beautifully finished inside. This repair work has been carried to practically every building on the post, and we have now just finished levelling up and the general rehabilitation of the library.

At the officers club we have added a store room, cut out partitions to provide an excellent pantry, enlarged the bar by removing the adjacent toilet and made an entrance from that side from a parking lot we have constructed behind the club. The removal of the partition between the dining room and the end or dancing room has transformed that portion of the club. Sidewalks have been laid outside, and a covered canvas way erected between the porch and the road on the parade ground side.

The Victory Theater has had the floor levelled and a fine maple flooring laid; with timbers and plans from Bonneville Dam we have widened the trusses so as to provide an excellent gymnasium, basket-ball, roller skating and dance floor. Bleacher seats have been erected along the sides, the windows cut down, the outside fire escape steps removed, a little sub-post exchange installed, and the building painted. It should be a tremendous morale booster for the winter season, particularly as we have a fine Hammond electric organ for the chapel, which can be used at the theater.

The road in rear of the officers' quarters has been widened, hedges planted, trees planted and the area generally beautified. The ball diamond has received the attention of a big league park.

The North Woods has been cleaned out, the trenches filled in, most of the stumps blown out—we used a ton and a half of dynamite on this—and the fence on the southern end was removed. The training area has thus been increased about 60%, troops can deploy near the main gate of the post and work clear through to the extreme northeastern corner of the woods. The old reservoir installations have been razed and the fences removed up there. That house has been put in excellent shape.

In the post proper all the roads have been trimmed up, gutters laid, shrubs planted—particularly in the vicinity of the post exchange and Quartermaster buildings. A new road has been laid down to the coal siding, the sewer lines completely reconditioned.

I have gotten the money and we have started on the erection of a CCC Headquarters adjacent to the Headquarters Company buildings—which incidentally, I have had siding put on and the buildings painted. This headquarters building will free the old band barracks for the use of the band. I have my office here now, but it is to be transferred to the library, and the library and a NCO Club established in the present District Quartermaster office building.

We have widened the main gate about ten feet, moved the flag pole down to the road between the band barracks and your aide's old house, improved the golf course, enlarged Pearson Field, and done so many things here and there that I can not recall them all. The trees have all been pruned, and the rotted places filled with cement. Someone said the other day the North Woods now looked like an English deer park.

Out at Bonneville we have metamorphosed the military cantonment area and buildings, installed a drainage system, widened the roads between the barracks, replaced the underpinning, braced the roofs, completely replaced all the old kitchen setup and mess tables with Hogan's best imitation of Camp Killpack. We have built a fine infirmary and first sergeant's office. 1500 acres have been completely cleared and parked, and the 1500 remaining acres has all the timber fallen and roads through it constructed. Unfortunately the company will be taken away from us on the 30th, leaving the final clearing of the remaining 1500 acres undone. The reservoir and the water system have been rebuilt to prevent leakage, and the roads oiled. You would not recognize the place. The area you planned for the Regimental Camp adjacent to Killpack has been completely cleared and levelled.

Knowing your interest in the place I thought this data would be of real interest to you. I will probably see you some time this summer.   Faithfully yours,

GCMRL/G. C. Marshall Papers (Vancouver Barracks)

War Department

July 1938–June 1939

MARSHALL reported for duty on July 6, 1938, as assistant chief of staff in charge of the War Plans Division of the War Department, a junior brigadier general in a protocol-conscious city where one-star generals were socially insignificant. (K. T. Marshall, *Together*, pp. 37–40.) In theory, each of the five divisions of the General Staff (G-1, G-2, G-3, G-4, and War Plans) was equal in stature; but in fact the War Plans Division was superior to the others. Army Regulation 10–15 (August 18, 1936), which defined the organization and general duties of the General Staff, designated the War Plans Division as the nucleus of the army's general headquarters in the event of mobilization. The brief period Marshall spent in that office (July 6–October 14, 1938) was essentially one of training for the post of deputy chief of staff.

On September 1, 1921, the post of deputy chief of staff was created, although prior to July, 1939, the office had no statutory basis. The deputy's jobs were to assist the chief of staff, to act for that officer in the War Department in his absence, and to report directly to the secretary of war in all matters not involving the establishment of important policies. His office was charged with "the preparation of plans and policies in connection with legislation and with military estimates for funds; with processing budgetary matters in the General Staff; with reports concerning legislation and requests for legislation that come within the purview of The General Council or that are referred to the General Staff; and with such other duties as the Chief of Staff may prescribe." The deputy also supervised and coordinated the activities of the five divisions of the General Staff. (War Department, *Army Regulations, No. 10–15* [Washington, D.C.: Government Printing Office, 1936], pp. 1–2.) The deputy's office was not an inevitable stepping stone to the chief's office. Since 1921, of the eleven men who had occupied the deputy's post before Marshall, only John L. Hines had become chief of staff.

Although it had increased in size by one-third since Marshall had left the Infantry School six years before, the army had made little progress toward rearmament or modernization. Marshall was anxious to proceed with those tasks and also to reconcile the divergent tactical and strategic views of the air and ground officers. When he became deputy chief of staff on October 15, 1938, he found that in addition he had to reconcile the divergent views of the various army branches with the realities of congressional budget appropriations. He told Major General Keehn of the Illinois National Guard: "I change jobs, on an order issued today making me Deputy Chief of Staff. I fear that this will carry with it a great deal of grief, because it will be my job to struggle with the budget, which is more or less the genesis of all ill feeling within the War Department and among the various components of the Army." (Marshall to Keehn, October 15, 1938, GCMRL/G. C. Marshall Papers [Pentagon Office, Selected].) A few weeks later, writing to invite some friends to visit him in Washington, D.C., he remarked: "All this, of course, if I am still here, because I am spending most of my time with my neck out, and there is a great deal of shooting going on." (Marshall to Mrs. William B. Tuttle, January 23, 1939, ibid.) ★

To Colonel Ralph R. Glass   July 7, 1938
                                                            [Washington, D.C.]

Dear Glass: I just arrived here yesterday and have been getting oriented this morning, but I want to tip you off immediately to the fact—at least I think it is a fact—that I have gotten you a double barrack (250 men) and a few sets of officers' quarters. I happened in on the fellow who was making adjustments for further expenditure of these funds and found that they were encountering considerable confusion in deciding from the present records here just what the conditions were at each post as to accommodations. I gave him immediately the facts on Vancouver Barracks, and took the liberty of telling him that the 15 sets of N.C.O. quarters would meet our present necessities and the remaining 15 should be put, I thought, at the bottom of the priority. I urged for two double sets of barracks, but found the War Department had only approved of one of these recommended by me. So I pressed for that as an immediate proposition, along with about $10,000 for a warehouse and as many of the sets of officers' quarters, up to the five approved, as he could manage. He thought all of this could be managed.

Please treat this as confidential, so far as Corps Area is concerned, as I am speaking out of turn, as it were.

We had a very pleasant and uneventful trip. It was 106 in Omaha, but the train was air-cooled. Washington is quite hot, but they tell me it's a cool day. Faithfully yours,

GCMRL/G. C. Marshall Papers (Pentagon Office, General)

To Major Claude M. Adams   [July (?), 1938]
                                                            [Washington, D.C.]

Dear Flap: I had a letter from Ruth the other day.[1] I really should answer it, but I will make this a joint affair.

My freight arrived yesterday and is being stored until I get located. I have my car, but have not yet used it, the license plates not being due until this afternoon. I am living temporarily with Colonel Walker, whose wife leaves tomorrow for Canada.

Washington is intensely hot and I have been equally busy, receiving official callers at the office, paying first office calls, and trying to find out about my business.

Mrs. Marshall finds Fire Island cool and delightful. Says she is feeling splendid. Her concern is over my house hunting.

Will you please tell the postmaster to ship magazines to me for the present at 2101 Connecticut Avenue, N.W., Washington, D.C. So far, none of my office papers have arrived, but I suppose Kendricks will start them shortly.

I have been drawn into a little CCC business, but nothing of importance, though I hear a good bit about what is going on from General Tyner, whose office is close by. If I learn anything of interest to the Staff I will let them know.

I will be interested to hear your reconnaissance report on the Uncle Sams. Ruth wrote that you had just left for a visit down there.

This is a hasty note. However, I did not want you two to think that I had forgotten you.

With my love,   Faithfully yours,

GCMRL/G. C. Marshall Papers (Pentagon Office, Selected)
1. This letter was not found in the Marshall papers.

To Major General Roy D. Keehn   July 13, 1938
                                                    [Washington, D.C.]

Dear Keehn: I got a great deal of satisfaction out of seeing you in Chicago the other day, and appreciated tremendously the fine reception you gave me. Increasingly I am looking back to my service with you and with the Illinois National Guard as one of the most instructive and valuable military experiences I have had, and one of the most agreeable in its human relations. I am quite serious about this, for I feel more and more, as I see what is going on, that, one way or another, we developed expeditious, economical, and effective methods of doing things that should in time have a far-reaching effect.

I was much concerned to hear what you had to tell me about your own affairs, and worried over your difficulties and prospects. I do hope that after all these knocks and bumps, you will straighten out into the stretch and have the breaks your way for the remaining innings.

I told Mrs. Marshall on the train of seeing you and she charged me to be sure and give you her affectionate regards. She is enjoying cool breezes up at Fire Island, while I am sweltering here in a climate of LaSalle Street.

With affectionate regards,   Faithfully yours,

GCMRL/G. C. Marshall Papers (Pentagon Office, Selected)

To General Adelbert de Chambrun   July 15, 1938
                                                   [Washington, D.C.]

Dear General: The Committee on Arrangements for the Annual Dinner of the Officers of the First Division are very anxious to have you as a guest of honor on that occasion, and they are in hopes that a note from me might help toward influencing you to a favorable decision. I don't know about that, but I do know that it would be a grand thing if your plans would permit you to accept.[1]

These fellows in the Division know that you were present at Headquarters during the Cantigny affair, but I doubt if practically any of them have any conception of the important part you played prior to Cantigny in bringing about a practical working solution of our scheme of communications, which remained virtually unchanged throughout the war and undoubtedly had a great deal to do with the successful performance of the Division on important battlefields. Also, I doubt if there are any who realize the calming and steadying influence of your presence during the affair at Cantigny, and the psychological benefits which resulted from your keen sense of humor. All that seems a long time ago—twenty years as a matter of fact—and it would be a delightful thing to listen to your comment on those days.

I was with General Pershing a week during his illness at Tucson, and saw him a few days ago at the Walter Reed Hospital. He is doing famously but moving carefully. He goes out for a short walk every day and for a ride. Will soon move into town. Fox Conner is across the hall from him—or was until day before yesterday when he went off on a final leave prior to retirement. He was operated on this spring for something in regard to his prostate gland, and while on sick leave recuperating from that developed coronary thrombosis. He seems very cheerful, but has a ticklish physical condition on his hands. He and I were to have been a special board this spring for final consideration of the reorganization—material reduction in strength—of the Infantry Division.[2] His illness blocked that, and I was not brought into Washington from the Northwest until a week ago.

With warm regards to Madame de Chambrun and yourself,   Faithfully yours,

GCMRL/G. C. Marshall Papers (Pentagon Office, General)

1. No reply to this letter has been found, but de Chambrun spoke at the dinner given on March 11, 1939, at New York City's Waldorf-Astoria Hotel. Marshall, master of ceremonies on that occasion, said of de Chambrun's contribution during the World War: "I doubt if any single individual, other than the highest commanders, played a more important part towards the general success of the Allies." (GCMRL/G. C. Marshall Papers [Pentagon Office, Speeches].)

2. See Marshall to Walker, December 21, 1937, and Marshall to Conner, January 7, 1938, above.

To Mrs. John B. Wilson[1] July 20, 1938
Washington, D.C.

Dear Rose: I have telephoned you no less than fifteen times and have never yet gotten an answer. This morning at 11:50 your line was busy, but when I got through at noon there was no answer. I have been trying to get you for luncheon with me so that we could talk things over. I have been out of town a little—down in the country for three days at Upperville—and the remainder of the time terribly busy here, house hunting in this heat, and with formal obligations at night. If you can't come for luncheon with me, invite me to dinner some night. I am on a diet, so you won't have to cook much.   Affectionately,

G. C. Marshall

P.S. My office is in the Winder Building at 17th and F Streets, Room 406; Telephone, National 2520—Branch 1304.

GCMRL/R. P. Wilson Papers
   1. Mrs. Wilson's account of the dinner that resulted from Marshall's letter is in *General Marshall Remembered*, pp. 204, 206.

To Major General Frank R. McCoy August 3, 1938
Washington, D.C.

My dear General: Your severance from the active list touches me more deeply than that of practically any other officer I have known in my Army career, and it makes me very, very sad to feel that I cannot serve under you and with you in the few years I have left. And I feel, too, a certain irritation with myself that I did not press my opportunities for association with you more determinedly while we were so close to each other in Chicago. That I did not do so was largely because of a fear of overdoing my opportunities.

   I believe I wrote Frances once that you were the model of how I felt command should be exercised in the Army, and that, of course, carries with it a large variety of implications concerning character, personality, consideration for others, mentality, and leadership. Since then I have become even more impressed with the correctness of my judgment, and I always felt a comfortable sense of gratification whenever you sought me out.

   Despite your desire to pursue coming years untrammeled by fixed obligations, I look forward to seeing you serve in highly important positions in public life.

   In all the above Katherine would join me, with many additions from a discerning heart, if she were here.

We hope and plan to see a great deal of the McCoys in the next few years. With my love and affectionate regards to you both, Faithfully yours,

G. C. Marshall

LC/F. R. McCoy Papers

To Rear Admiral Walter S. Anderson[1] August 8, 1938
[Washington, D.C.]

My dear Admiral: I was extremely pleased to have you remember me in your cordial note which came this morning. Both Mrs. Marshall and I have retained such pleasant recollections of our brief contact with you in Portland last summer that we commented on the fact that we would not have the opportunity of seeing you again this year. So I am much pleased to find that you still have me in mind, and I am very sorry that we did not have the pleasure of meeting and entertaining Mrs. Anderson.

I find Washington quite a contrast to the Northwest, and desk duty an even greater contrast to my duties out there. I am afraid I am a country boy when it comes to this city business.

I leave here early tomorrow morning by plane with General Andrews of the GHQ Air Force[2] and fly out to Spokane, Seattle, and Vancouver Barracks, then to Hamilton Field, near San Francisco, and March Field, near Los Angeles. From the last point we go up to Denver and then down to San Antonio and on by Louisiana to Washington. I expect to be gone until the 18th. I wish my stops on the West Coast, near Los Angeles, were not to be so brief, as I might have an opportunity to see you.

Mrs. Marshall did not stop in Washington, but continued on to her cottage on Fire Island, where she will be until the middle of September.

With warm regards, and trusting that I may have the pleasure of seeing you in Washington this winter, Faithfully yours,

GCMRL/G. C. Marshall Papers (Pentagon Office, General)

1. Anderson (U.S.N.A., 1903) commanded the Fourth Cruiser Division from the U.S.S. *Northampton* out of San Pedro, California.

2. One of the most significant changes in the War Department in the generation after the World War was the growth of a comparatively autonomous Army Air Force. In 1918 the Air Service became a branch of the army; in 1926 it received the name "Air Corps." General Headquarters Air Force was established in 1935 at Langley Field, Virginia, to coordinate and to command in combat the army's tactical air units. Colonel Frank M. Andrews (U.S.M.A., 1906) had been promoted to temporary major general on December 27, 1935, and given command of General Headquarters Air Force.

To General John J. Pershing   August 22, 1938
                                               Washington, D.C.

Dear General: I was extremely sorry to miss seeing you before your departure. Only by accident did I learn, the last hour before I left Washington, that you were leaving town, and when I called at your hotel I found that you were asleep. I sent you a bon voyage wire from Minneapolis, where I landed for the night on my air trip westward. Since my return Adamson tells me you had a very comfortable trip and arrived in fine shape.

I flew from here with General Andrews of the GHQ Air Force to Selfridge Field, Chanute Field, Minneapolis, then on to Billings, Montana, and across Yellowstone Park to Spokane, where part of the Air Force had concentrated. From there I flew over to Lewis, where another element of the First Wing was concentrated, did the Boeing Air Plant at Seattle, and stopped at Vancouver Barracks for the night, where another Wing of the First Group was concentrated. From the Northwest I flew to San Francisco, Sacramento, Los Angeles—the air plants there—Denver, San Antonio, Barksdale Field, Shreveport, and home. Altogether I had a very interesting trip professionally and a most magnificent one personally. We not only saw Yellowstone Park from the air, including Old Faithful, but saw Boulder Dam and flew up the Grand Canyon; saw Acoma Village and Meteor Crater from the air, also Santa Fe and Colorado Springs. I got back Thursday night and went to Baltimore for Saturday and Sunday with Parsons of the Third Corps Area. As he dragged me around to Fort Howard, Fort Meade, and Fort Hoyle, I did not find much relaxation there.

I have taken General Embick's house on Wyoming Avenue, just west of Connecticut Avenue, near old "2029".[1] We take over the house October first. I imagine Mrs. Marshall will come to town about the 15th of September.

I do hope you will find relaxation and renewed health in Sunny France. Adamson tells me you are going off to a spa.

With affectionate regards,   Faithfully yours,

G. C. Marshall

LC/J. J. Pershing Papers (General Correspondence)

1. Major General Stanley D. Embick was to become commander of the Fourth Corps Area and the Third Army, with headquarters in Atlanta, Georgia, on October 1. Senator and Mrs. Francis E. Warren formerly lived at 2029 Connecticut Avenue, N.W., Washington, D.C.

I HAD NOT known General Andrews at all well," Marshall recalled two decades after his Air Corps–inspired inspection trip. "While I was head of the War Plans Division, he called on me and said he was going around the country . . . , and invited me to go with him, and I accepted. As a matter of fact, there was some opposition to my going from the War Department. But I went ahead and took the trip, and I found it tremendously informing.

"I went to all the various plants and met the heads of the plants, particularly their chief engineers. I walked with one or the other through the plant while General Andrews was busy with the other fellow, and learned a great deal about construction and the difficulties and problems. I got an insight into what went on. I think we went to a [Boeing Airplane Company] plant in Seattle of which [Philip G.] Johnson was the head and where B-17s were being made. We also went to all the principal air stations, and at all of these I heard the comments of the officers. I heard their appeals to Andrews for better representation; I heard their appeals for things that they were being denied. I came to recognize a great many of the things as justified.

"When I got back to Washington, I looked into it, and I found out that they had almost no representation at all on the General Staff. I found the General Staff officers had little interest in the Air—mostly antipathy, and it was quite marked. . . . I found the young Air officers were dealing with Congress and stirring up everything, and there was a general muddle. They had something to complain about, because they were not getting recognition; the General Staff at that time had little understanding of the Air."

Few Air Corps officers wanted to attend the Army Service Schools at Fort Leavenworth. "In the first place it was hard work, but more particularly they were afraid of endangering their flight pay." But graduation from Fort Leavenworth was required in order to attend the Army War College, which itself was a prerequisite for a General Staff assignment.

On the other hand, ground staff officers did not like to fly. "They said it hurt their insurance. I believe it did. I think I had no insurance at all for some years there for Mrs. Marshall because of my flying."

In an effort to be of immediate assistance to the Air Corps, Marshall convinced Chief of Staff Malin Craig to approve the following proposition. But, he recalled, "when I became deputy chief of staff, I found this had never been put into effect." (Interview, January 22, 1957.) ★

MEMORANDUM FOR GENERAL EMBICK   August 22, 1938
[Washington, D.C.]

Retention of highly trained technical personnel.

A special policy or regulation is suggested to cover the matter of the present serious loss to the Air Corps, the Signal Corps, and possibly the Engineers and Ordnance Services, of enlisted men who have been provided, at material expense, with special training in various technical or mechanical pursuits. At the present time, the training of mechanics and similar specialists, weather men, etc., has been complicated by the fact that these men fail to reenlist, or that they purchase their discharges in order to accept more lucrative positions in civil life. To meet this considerable drain, classes have had to be larger and the Services have seldom been fully provided with the trained personnel required.

It would seem that men reporting for such training, which is usually sought by the individual, should be discharged and immediately reenlisted for three years, with the distinct understanding at the time that discharge by purchase would not be permitted. In this way, the Services concerned could be provided with trained men with something over two years to serve, and with the probability that many who would otherwise have purchased their discharges would continue on because of the increased ratings and rank that come with length of service. There is the possibility that the resulting economies would, in effect, provide an increase in available personnel for troops and depots.

The Congressional pressure for one-year enlistments which has been met by a generous policy in permitting discharge by purchase, could be satisfactorily met, I am sure, by the logic and resulting economy of the proposed exception.

GCMRL/G. C. Marshall Papers (Pentagon Office, Selected)

To Major General Ewing E. Booth   August 26, 1938
                                                                [Washington, D.C.]

Dear Booth: I was in Los Angeles the other day but so briefly that I did not even have a chance to telephone you. While on an 8,000 mile air tour with General Andrews, we came down to March Field late Sunday afternoon, August 14th, and on Monday morning flew directly to the Douglas plant, where I went over the plant with Douglas and his chief engineer. Then we flew to the Northrup plant and repeated the process; and continued on to the North American plant and walked miles through it. Then we took to the air, with some sandwiches in the plane for lunch, and flew directly to Denver. My entire period there was under such high pressure, and our schedule was so exacting, that I did not have a moment to myself and was not in a position to take exception to the arranged program. General Westover had sent out orders and requests covering my entire trip, and it was up to me to follow through.[1]

I am very sorry that when I was so close to you I did not have a chance to see you. Affectionately yours,

GCMRL/G. C. Marshall Papers (Pentagon Office, General)

1. Major General Oscar Westover, who had graduated immediately behind Frank M. Andrews at the United States Military Academy in 1906, had been chief of the Air Corps since December 24, 1935. On September 21, 1938, he was killed when the plane he was piloting crashed.

September 4, 1938
                                                            Clarksburg, West Virginia

It is always a pleasure to me to talk to men of the legion, particularly to a group in State Convention, because there is much that can be said to an audience of veterans which should not only be of interest but ought to be distinctly helpful to the cause of National Defense.

Today, with each issue of the press containing reports of battles here and there in the world and photographic records of the horrors resulting from the bombing of civil communities, practically every adult mind is directed toward the thought of what similar warfare might mean to us here in these United States.

You Legionnaires are probably more perturbed over this possibility than any other class of people, because most of you know from first-hand experience something of the meaning of war. You know that modern warfare has little of drama and romance, and is filled with hardships and horrors. Your views as to the method we should follow to render an attack against our nation both unlikely and unsuccessful, will have a determining effect on public opinion in this country. Therefore, it is of great importance that you know whereof you speak.

The problem of preparing the country to defend itself has reached the point in the matter of national effort, and especially in the matter of appropriations required, where it has become the business, I think, of every business man to inform himself as to our requirements for national safety. He should have a sufficient knowledge of the various factors involved in the problem to form a logical opinion as to how much money should be appropriated for the purpose of National Defense, and for what it should be spent. The subject is too complicated for the average citizen to become an expert of all phases of it, but he may so inform himself that he, and others similarly informed, can prevent public opinion from being led astray by the enthusiasms and theories of the moment. A complete understanding of essential mililtary requirements is complicated by the introduction of mechanical means to an extent never before realized in war, and by the effect of the reports of such activities on the public mind. A photograph of the bombing of women and children makes a profound impression on the public—attention is centered on aerial warfare, while the final results of more serious occurrences often go unnoticed. It is extremely difficult for the citizen to gain a perspective of the realities.

I think all of us are in agreement today that we must be prepared to defend ourselves; but we are not of one mind as to method and cost—the one is the corollary of the other. Such pointed references to money in connection with the National Defense may seem to accentuate unduly a sordid viewpoint, but the fact of the matter is that almost every War Department problem involves consideration of dollars and cents, just as the question of dollars and cents enters into the everyday problems of the average man.

We have today a very small Regular Army. The War Department does not regard a large standing Army as desirable. The first phase of any major military struggle in which we might unfortunately become involved will find the National Guard providing the bulk of the combat troops for immediate use, except in the air. There our splendid GHQ Air Force is rapidly being equipped and prepared to dominate. As the struggle develops, the ranks of the skeleton organizations of the Reserve Corps will be filled and trained, and a great National Army created.

So far as mere personnel is concerned, our plans and preparations have reached a fairly satisfactory degree of development; but it is in the field of materiel that the problem is productive of gray hairs, and the limitation is almost entirely a matter of money.

I am not advocating, by inference, vast appropriations for materiel, but I will try briefly to point out the necessity for adequate and modern materiel, and the necessity for the citizen and tax bearer thoroughly to understand what it is all about. Incidentally, I think it not inappropriate to dwell considerably on this particular phase of National Defense, because your former national commander, fellow townsman and West Virginian, the Honorable Louis Johnson, Assistant Secretary of War, is at the forefront of the drive to modernize the equipment of the Army and to prepare American industry for the rapid conversion of its production machinery from peace to war purposes.

The answer to the problem of materiel is comparatively simple from one point of view—we should have the most modern equipment for our Army and Navy; but when one delves into cost in relation to possible appropriations by Congress, and attempts to reach a decision as to what materiel is to be purchased, then a long look into the future, by a discerning mind, is necessary.

Allow me to give you a few examples of some of the factors involved. From the viewpoint of modern scientific and mechanical advances, combined with the powerful effect of public opinion on any action of Congress, we find a very special field concerned with the development of the Air Corps. We know pretty well, from examples that reach back into the earliest recorded history, what a man on foot can do. His effectiveness when mounted on a horse is well understood (though few nowadays understand the horse). The later phases of the World War gave us pointed evidence regarding the efficiency of tanks, or mechanized forces as we term them today; and we have witnessed quite a development since the War in the type and effectiveness of tanks. But great as this latter development has been, it is still within the grasp of the average military mind to forecast its practical effectiveness on the battlefield. However, when we come to aviation, the development has progressed with such leaps and bounds, such unbelievable advances in speed and distance, in altitude, and in size, that it staggers the imagination, and exercises a profound influence on public opinion as to the requirements for National Defense. The very nature of present air development and the uncertainty as to what this development will be in the future, makes it difficult to forecast the solution in military preparedness. New types of military planes cannot be designed and produced overnight. Development requires about five years, and later production at least a year, so that in some instances by the time we have gotten well into the production of a particular model its obsolescence is becoming apparent.

Now, as a business man, how would you meet that problem? We must have planes, and they cost millions. As I have said, they require about a year to produce after we have evolved and tested a model. We cannot wait until a year after the declaration of war to secure an adequate number of planes; and yet how heavily can we afford to plunge in building a certain type? Furthermore, and this is of high importance, against the pressure of public opinion in the solution of this problem, the War Department must consider the other equally vital, but less spectacular, less appealing, requirements of National Defense, which in their turn cost millions, but seldom make the pages of the newspaper or the pictorial magazines, but without which we would be militarily helpless.

Let us take another look at the example of an airplane. You gentlemen are undoubtedly interested in the number of planes we have, and vitally interested that they be of the most modern type. You would probably think of the funds involved in this problem arithmetically; that is, in terms of multiplying the number of planes that seem to be necessary by the cost of a plane. But the product of this computation covers only the first of many necessary expenditures. To this figure must be added the cost of elaborate and highly scientific equipment required by modern planes, the cost of replacement and maintenance equipment, and the cost of special operating and training facilities—all of which are very expensive.

But there is far more to it than that. A bomber needs bombs, is useless without them. Under present conditions, over a year is required for the manufacture of a bomb, which means that we should have sufficient bombs for each plane to provide for a year of active operations; otherwise, most of the money invested in the plane has been thrown away. Compare the far-reaching implications of the necessities of such a program with the present prospects for rapid changes in planes.

Recently, there has been a great deal said about anti-aircraft materiel, most of which requires nearly a year-and-a-half to produce, and is quite expensive. A tremendous public demand for this form of protection would develop the moment we became involved in a war. Those who recall or have read of the clamor of our coastal cities for heavy artillery at the time of the Spanish-American War can appreciate something of the furor that would be raised by practically all of our cities in the event of a future war. However, I hope with every fiber of my being that the horrible effect on civilian communities of recent air attacks will shock the civilized world into taking joint measures guaranteeing the immunity of such communities against bombing attacks in the future.

But, whatever the outcome, the necessity for anti-aircraft materiel makes a strong appeal today to the civilian mind. And here again, as in the case of aircraft, we must balance this appeal against other even more urgent requirements, which do not make the news pages and therefore are little considered outside of military circles.

While the need for adequate aircraft and anti-aircraft defense is appreciated, we must keep in mind that the defense of the nation depends on the adequacy and efficiency of all components of the mobile ground forces. These forces should be equipped with the most modern weapons, yet we find our National Guard, almost twenty years after the war, armed with rifles of the type produced thirty-five years ago and with machine guns of war vintage. Our light artillery is the famous old French soixante-quinze—the 75—though we have modernized its carriage and its field of fire.

The problem is not one of simply providing the most modern weapons for the National Guard and the Regular Army, but involves also the making of adequate provisions to equip promptly the reserve units that we would most assuredly need in a major emergency. Remember that the time element is a vital factor to American preparedness. Usually none of this materiel can be produced quickly, but the time lag in war can be reduced materially by peacetime planning and preparation. Tremendous progress has been made in the past year toward securing appropriations for the dies and jigs and other manufacturing devices essential to the quick conversion of industry to the production of war materiel. Again I would remind you of the fact that these phases of the general question, though vastly important, lack that dramatic appeal which secures the active backing of public opinion.

In brief, our major problem today is one of materiel—what types of equipment should we procure and in what quantities, considering the equipment on hand, the development of new types, and the need for a well-armed, balanced force, and how best to present to Congress the highly involved considerations which should govern the decision as to the money to be appropriated.

I should like to tell you something of the men who spend hours, days, months, and years studying the many factors that enter into the materiel problem, and working out ways and means to attain our objective—this symmetrical modernization and development of our military National Defense system.

First, we have the War Department General Staff, consisting of ninety-two officers (Regular, National Guard and Reserve), working under the direct supervision of the Chief of Staff, General Craig. This group constitutes our military faculty. Among its many other duties, the War Department General Staff is responsible for preparing and submitting to the Secretary of War, Mr. Woodring, our military requirements in both materiel and personnel. The solution of this problem, as well as the solution of many other allied problems, involves the General Staff not only in most difficult decisions, but in numerous decisions which disappoint or irritate those who have decided views regarding our military set-up, and, being Americans, we all have a plenitude of individual views and opinions. Scarcely a question comes to the General Staff that does not involve money—money to be obtained from Congress or the spending of money that has already been appropriated. We never have, nor can we get, money enough to buy everything the various activities of the War Department desire, hence, of necessity, decisions are made that cause countless disappointments and irritations, if not actual hostilities. It is the unfortunate duty of the General Staff to ride these dilemmas and stoically to accept the hard feelings unavoidably engendered.

The General Staff must adjust the demands of many different agencies to the means available. We deal in time of peace with forty-eight Governors of States, forty-eight Adjutants General, and a number of Division Commanders of the National Guard, to none of whom the War Department can issue an order in a strict military sense. Our national policy demands a citizen army, and this is exactly as it should be, but such an organization does not provide a bed of roses for the coordinating General Staff, particularly when money is involved.

Within the Regular establishment itself there is just as much grief for the General Staff, because if in the interest of a better balanced Army, you take a million or so dollars from one Chief of Branch and give it to another Chief of Branch, you immediately create resentment. The more intensely a man has concentrated on the development of his particular arm or branch, the greater is his disappointment when funds for that arm or branch are reduced. So the General Staff can hardly be classed as a popular body in our military system, yet I personally believe it to be one of the most, if not the most, highly educated and technically prepared group of individuals serving the Government today. I do not think this opinion is prejudiced by my service on the General Staff, since I only reported for duty a few weeks ago and had not been on duty with the War Department for fourteen years.

As you will hear references to the War Department General Staff in the future, it might be interesting to outline the preparation an officer of the Regular Army must go through in order to receive such an assignment. Several years after being commissioned in the Army he is sent to a special school for his arm of the service where he passes through an intensive course of ten months of instruction. If he has stood unusually well and makes an outstanding reputation for himself during the following five or ten years, he is selected for a strenuous course of instruction at our Command and General Staff School at Fort Leavenworth, Kansas, which also lasts about ten months. There he enters into a competition which, from the standpoint of severity, is unique among American educational institutions. Later on, if his records warrant, he may be one of the eighty-eight officers selected each year to attend the Army War College in Washington. Heretofore, under the law no officer could be assigned to the War Department General Staff who was not a graduate of the Army War College. This past year Congress removed that legal restriction, but the majority of the members of the War Department General Staff will usually be selected from graduates of the Army War College.

So the Regular Army officer on the War Department General Staff, unlike the business or professional man, except possibly the doctor, goes to school or college on a competitive basis until he is fifty years old, and he works as hard and seriously through these courses of instruction as any business man does to survive in the business world. This is little understood among civilians, who do not realize that the officers who are carefully selected for General Staff duty are the product of the most extensive educational system in America.

There is a second group of officers who play the leading part in our materiel problem. After the military requirements are approved, the materiel must be procured as rapidly and as economically as possible. Here we enter the field of business. Any purchasing agent who spends approximately $250,000,000 a year and does it well has no simple task. This phase of War Department activity is carried out by officers working under the Assistant Secretary of War, Colonel Johnson. Many of these officers have been through the same course of schooling as the personnel of the War Department General Staff and most of them are graduates of the Army Industrial College which·operates under the Assistant Secretary of War.

In addition to current procurement activities, the Assistant Secretary of War is charged with assuring adequate provision for the mobilization of materiel and industrial organizations essential to increased wartime needs. This responsibility requires on the part of his organization a tremendous amount of long-range planning, covering all industrial problems from the procurement of raw materials to the delivery of finished products. This planning, in coordination with business, is essential if we are to avoid a complete upset of our industrial and commercial life when war comes.

It is hardly necessary for me to tell you that the two groups of officers I have just discussed do not work in separate water-tight compartments, but by daily collaboration endeavor to adjust the military demands to the capabilities of industry.

I have gone somewhat into particulars with you gentlemen, possibly uninteresting particulars, regarding the War Department's problem of National Defense, in the hope that I might be able to give you a purely practical slant on the general question, because it is a very practical proposition, if we can only succeed in having it treated as such. You have had enough of war. All of us wish to avoid war. If adequate National Defense is our best insurance against war, then let us have it established on the most sensible basis consistent with economy and the character of our people and institutions.

GCMRL/G. C. Marshall Papers (Pentagon Office, Speeches)

1. Marshall was asked to deliver this address to the West Virginia State American Legion Convention by Assistant Secretary of War Louis A. Johnson, who was a Clarksburg lawyer and a former national commander of the American Legion (1932–33).

To Major General George V. H. Moseley   September 9, 1938
[Washington, D.C.]

Dear Moseley: I read with pointed regret the order announcing your retirement. A long time ago, thirty-three years to be exact, I reported to you on my
way to see General Jesse M. Lee. When I came into your office, a young
lieutenant who had been mapping on the Pecos, feeling that I had had a pretty
hard time, not only as a result of the climate and a harsh terrain, but largely
because of the dyed-in-the-wool spirit of the commissary staff—we darn near
starved—I have never forgotten your kindly greeting at that time. Three years
later you reported for duty as a student at Leavenworth and I recall that when
you found I was being ranked out of quarters you offered me a share of yours. I
have never forgotten that. And of course I have many recollections of the war
period and since.

You have the satisfaction of leaving the active list of the Army after a most
unusual and splendid career. I know you will leave behind you a host of younger
men who have a loyal devotion to you for what you have stood for. I am one of
that company, and it makes me very sad to think that I cannot serve with you
and under you again.   Affectionately yours,

GCMRL/G. C. Marshall Papers (Pentagon Office, Selected)

To Major General Fox Conner   September 9, 1938
[Washington, D.C.]

Dear Conner: When I read the order announcing your retirement memories of
those earliest days in the A.E.F. and our later delightful relationship were
aroused. I am deeply sorry, both personally and officially, to see you leave the
active list, because you have a great deal yet to give the Army out of that wise
head of yours. General Pershing was talking about you a few days before he
sailed for France, and as always in the most complimentary terms possible
regarding your wisdom and judgment.

I was very sorry that we could not have had more of a talk out at the Walter
Reed, but I felt hesitant about talking shop to you at that time. I do hope that
you are feeling very much better, and that you are enjoying the beautiful fall
weather on Brandreth Lake as I did in 1919.

With affectionate regards to Mrs. Conner and yourself, and to Paulina if she is
there, believe me always   Faithfully yours,

GCMRL/G. C. Marshall Papers (Pentagon Office, General)

To Miss May Pershing   September 15, 1938
                                                  [Washington, D.C.]

My dear Miss May: I wrote the General a note of congratulations on his birth-day, but I thought that you were possibly more entitled to congratulations than anybody else, for I think your devoted care and ministrations are largely ac-countable for the opportunity of congratulating him on his 78th birthday.

I was very sorry to miss seeing you before you left town. As a matter of fact I also missed seeing the General. I did not know he was leaving, and called to see him twice without success and accidentally found out from Adamson that he was leaving in three days. Unfortunately, I was leaving within the hour to be gone a week, and when I stopped at the hotel he was taking a nap, so I missed him for the third time.

I wish you would be good enough to write me a note and tell me how you are getting along at Lincoln. Also if there is any chance of your coming to Washington for the winter.

The next time I am in New York, I will try to look up Warren and his bride. Evidently, they had a marvelous trip and I would like to hear something of it at first hand.

I have been away pretty constantly and hope to get really settled down shortly. I managed to have a week with Mrs. Marshall on Fire Island—she does not come to town until October 1st; then I had to run off to West Virginia to make a talk; I was about to leave for Leavenworth when that trip was postponed until October 1st or thereabouts; and now I am off Saturday to make a talk before the Air Corps Tactical School at Montgomery, Alabama. I think I made my long 8000 mile trip around the United States while you were here. It was very busy on the ground, but delightful in the air—I saw Yellowstone Park, Boulder Dam, Grand Canyon and a number of other interesting geological and historical points.

We have taken a house at 2118 Wyoming Avenue, N.W., that was General Embick's (he is now Deputy Chief of Staff) and will settle there on October 1. I hope very much to have the great pleasure of entertaining you before very long.

With affectionate regards,   Faithfully yours,

GCMRL/G. C. Marshall Papers (Pentagon Office, Selected)

To Brigadier General Charles H. Cole[1]   September 17, 1938
                                                       [Washington, D.C.]

Dear Cole: Replying to your telephone message of yesterday requesting data as to our necessities in corps and army troops as a basis for a resolution to be in-troduced at the coming National Guard convention towards securing additional personnel for the Guard: the factors involved are so numerous, basically involve continuing increases in appropriations, that it is not possible for me to give you an immediate answer, and it must be immediate, if at all, as I leave today for the Air Corps Tactical School at Montgomery, Alabama and you leave Wednesday for the convention.

I will summarize some of the involvements—

It would not be permissible for me, off hand as it were, to initiate action towards increasing appropriations. That, of necessity, is taboo. Only after careful study, General Staff concurrence and formal approval by the Chief of Staff and Secretary, would I be free to act towards that particular end.

But there are other important factors involved. In the first place, the War Department is committed—and the Congressional Committees partly so—to a National Guard increase of 5000 men in April, for which funds have been appropriated, and for another 5000 a year later, for which funds must be secured in the next Army appropriation bill. Our pressure, and yours too I should think, must be concentrated on securing the 5000 men allotted for 1940. That will not be so easy as there is an increasing demand in Congress to expend more money for materiel and less for personnel. I quote from a portion of the last hearing before the Sub-Committee on Military Appropriations of the House:

"AMOUNT REQUIRED FOR AN ADDITIONAL 5,000 MEN

"Mr. Snyder.[2]   General, this budget provides for doing in the next fiscal year what the Congress had intended would be done during the present fiscal year; that is, it looks to giving you a 5,000 increase just 1 year later; is that right?

"General Blanding.[3]   That is correct.

"Mr. Snyder.   General, you have a number of important and really urgent materiel matters for which this budget makes no provision, and which were stressed very forcibly by the representatives of the National Guard Association at their recent hearing. What would be the additional expense in the fiscal year 1940 to take care of the 5,000 increase in personnel effective from April 1, 1939?

"General Blanding.   Roughly, about a million dollars.

"Mr. Snyder.   Now, without going beyond 1940, that would mean an additional expense of $500,000 for 1939 plus $1,000,000, or a total of $1,500,000. Would you advise that expenditure in the face of your deficiencies in antiaircraft equipment, animals, motors, clothing, and so forth?

"General Blanding.   Yes, sir; I would.

"Mr. Snyder.   Why would you?

"General Blanding.   Because I think we should complete our program of 210,000 men, completing the organization of the 18 infantry divisions and the 10 antiaircraft regiments, and certain other forces, and have the set-up and the complete organization.

"Mr. Collins.[4]   And have our Army more like the Chinese than it has ever been?

"General Blanding.   No, sir.

"Mr. Collins.   You would just have men and no implements? You would have them fight with their fists?

"General Blanding.   We are providing the implements.

"Mr. Collins.   You do not have a decent rifle in the National Guard, and now you want more men.

"General Blanding.   Well, if there was any way that I knew of to get the new automatic rifle—

"Mr. Collins.   You are never going to do that as long as you spend all your money in paying your men."

Similar reactions have occurred in other portions of the hearings.

Further, as to personnel, the existing Regular establishment is approaching a distressing situation in this regard, especially in the infantry, artillery and Air Corps, and for which there apparently is to be no legislative remedy. To go before Congress for still additional National Guard personnel, in view of the foregoing, would not be consistent with the urgent requirements, so long as the approaching authorized and anticipated National Guard increases are not devoted to what appears very plainly to be the logical necessities of the situation, rather than to large organizations for which there is no urgent need. This is a frank, but confidential statement for you personally, though I said as much to your Committee the other afternoon.

I recognize, I think as fully as any member of the National Guard, the necessity of many compromises in this matter, but there are limits beyond which we should not go, and especially at this time with vital needs which could be met next April and a year later; and in the light of a possible reorganization based on a reduction in the size of divisions.

I am enclosing a copy of the letter of February 10, 1938, to the Chief of the National Guard Bureau listing the first priority of corps troops whose activation the War Department urgently desires to secure.[5] This last is the definite answer to your request, to the extent it is possible for me to go in this hurried note.

I am intensely interested in this problem and I am much relieved to sense your deep personal interest in its solution. Please send me a note with your reactions to my comments.[6]   Hastily yours,

GCMRL/G. C. Marshall Papers (Pentagon Office, Selected)

1. When Marshall was inspector-instructor with the Massachusetts Volunteer Militia (1911–12), he had met Cole, who was an officer with the First Corps of Cadets. During the World War, Cole commanded the Fifty-second Brigade, Twenty-sixth Division (1917–19). In 1928 he was the Democratic party candidate for governor. When Cole failed to secure the nomination again in 1934, Marshall wrote: "I was terribly disappointed over the recent nomination campaign in Massachusetts. I had hoped to see you Governor, and for that matter I still feel certain you will end up in that chair. Certainly you deserve it, and more certainly, the Commonwealth needs it." (Marshall to Cole, October 31, 1934, GCMRL/G. C. Marshall Papers [Illinois National Guard].)

Cole had been appointed adjutant general of Massachusetts on January 7, 1937. He was the chairman of the Committee on Cavalry Organization of the Adjutants General Association. Marshall had met with Cole and his committee in Washington on September 15, 1938.

2. Representative J. Buell Snyder was a Democrat from the Twenty-fourth District of Pennsylvania.

3. Major General Albert H. Blanding had been chief of the War Department's National Guard Bureau since January 31, 1936.

4. Representative Ross A. Collins was a Democrat from the Fifth District of Mississippi.

5. The letter stated that while revision was needed in the War Department's 1923 program on the strength and organization of the National Guard, it should be postponed until the new division and corps organization tables became available. Moreover, any increases in National Guard strength should come primarily in the Field Artillery and the Engineer, Signal, and Medical Corps. (Captain Frank M. Smith to the Chief of the National Guard Bureau, February 10, 1938, GCMRL/G. C. Marshall Papers [Pentagon Office, Selected].) Cole had hoped for an increase in the size of the Cavalry.

6. Cole replied that Marshall had convinced him that "we should go very slowly before asking for more personnel at this time; therefore, I shall not present any resolution [at the National Guard Convention] because it might endanger the fourth 5,000 increment. . . . I believe it is possible to get an increase of personnel both for the regular service and the National Guard in *addition* to the materiel requirements if both the Army and National Guard really got to work on the subject." (Cole to Marshall, September 20, 1938, ibid.)

T HE AUTHORITATIVE formulation of United States Army combat doctrine in the 1920s and 1930s was the field service manual issued in 1924. That document stated that the destruction in battle of the enemy's armed forces by the combined offensive employment of the army's six combat arms—Infantry, Artillery, Cavalry, Signal Corps, Engineer Corps, and Air Service—was the prerequisite to victory in war. But while teamwork was essential, the Infantry was the key to success. "The special missions of other arms are derived from their powers to contribute to the execution of the infantry mission." (War Department, *Field Service Regulations, United States Army, 1923* [Washington, D.C.: Government Printing Office, 1924], pp. 11, 77.) The role of the Air Service— called the Air Corps beginning in 1926—was to control the sky over the battlefield, to attack the enemy on the battlefield and beyond the range of the Field Artillery, and to gather information about the enemy. (Ibid., p. 21.)

In the two decades following the World War, air-minded people around the world began to believe that the primacy of the infantry on the ground and of the battleship at sea had passed; the airplane was the new queen of battles. The United States Army Air Corps was strongly influenced by the ideas enunciated by Brigadier General William Mitchell. Victory in war, Mitchell asserted, was achieved by destroying the enemy's homefront resources for making war and his civilian population's morale. This would be accomplished by the destruction rained by fleets of bombers. "Aircraft operating in the heart of an enemy's country will accomplish this object in an incredibly short space of time, once control of the air has been obtained and the months and even years of contest of ground armies with a loss of millions of lives will be eliminated in the future." (William Mitchell, *Winged Defense: The Development and Possibilities of*

Modern Air Power—Economic and Military [New York and London: G. P. Putnam's Sons, 1925], pp. 126–27.)

Air Corps leaders chafed increasingly at the restraints imposed upon them by the War Department General Staff. The rapid growth and increasing sophistication of air forces in Europe—particularly in Germany—after the mid-1930s contrasted unfavorably with the slow progress in the United States. Assistant Secretary of War Louis A. Johnson observed in the War Department's 1938 annual report that "our former technical superiority in aeronautical development is no longer clearly apparent. Recent advances in other countries have equaled if not exceeded our efforts. We have known for some time that foreign nations far surpassed us in the number of military aircraft at their disposal but we also knew that we led the field technically. It now appears that our research and development programs must be accelerated if we are to regain our position of technical leadership." (*Annual Report of the Secretary of War, 1938* [Washington, D.C.: Government Printing Office, 1938], p. 26.)

The fountainhead of American military air power doctrine was the Air Corps Tactical School at Maxwell Field, Alabama. The ideas taught there are summarized in Wesley Frank Craven and James Lea Cate, editors, *The Army Air Forces in World War II,* volume one, *Plans and Early Operations* (Chicago: University of Chicago, 1948), pp. 51–52. After he arrived at the school to present his speech, Marshall found it advisable to make certain changes in the text he had brought with him. No copy of the original draft has been found. Upon returning to Washington, he rewrote the speech as printed below. ★

SPEECH

September 19, 1938
Maxwell Field, Alabama

My first duty is to express General Craig's keen regret that he could not fill his engagement to be here this morning. He really wanted to have the opportunity to talk to you and had completed his preparations for that purpose. However, duties in Washington made it impossible for him to come and he sends you his very genuine regrets by me.

Though but a poor substitute for the Chief of Staff, I am glad to be here for several reasons. In the first place, I was in immediate charge of the school at Fort Benning for five years but unfortunately had to leave there just as the Air Corps Tactical School was transferred to Maxwell Field.[1] I had visited the school at Langley Field and had gone over the course taught at that time. Also later we had received at Fort Benning a visit from the faculty and students of the school, which proved highly informative for us at Benning and, I believe, for the Air Corps personnel as well. What I wished for was the opportunity to go along for a year or two at Benning in close contact with the school here at Maxwell Field, because I believe that the proximity of the two schools presented a grand opportunity for the development of an understanding of our air requirements in relation to the ground forces. In other words, to reach, through the close contact possible here, a genuine appreciation of the Army problem—a problem which includes all the arms and services.

Then there is another, rather non-professional, reason for my keen interest in the Air establishment in general, and this school in particular. Years ago I was present at a lecture delivered by the Head of the Signal School at Fort Leavenworth. During his talk he made the startling statement, that two brothers, named Wright, were actually reaching the solution of flight by heavier-than-air machines. I knew nothing of this at the time, having seen no reference to it in the press, and I have never forgotten the profound impression it made on my mind.

Only a little later, I happened to be staying for the night in Washington with a young lieutenant who had made, that very afternoon at Fort Myer, the historic test flight of the Wright plane for its acceptance by the Government. Members of the cabinet, ambassadors and diplomats were present to see the miracle—an effort to fly twenty miles, with two passengers, at a speed of at least forty miles per hour, with a bonus for each additional mile per hour. At the apartment that evening a group of reporters appeared to secure some newsworthy comments. The lieutenant was your recent chief, General Foulois.[2]

And then a little later, during the first concentration of our troops on the Mexican Border in 1911, I was detailed as Assistant to the Chief Signal Officer of the field division. Under that officer were the activities of the two Army planes which then composed our air force, the historic Wright machine and a highly modernized Curtiss production. I turned out every morning at 5:30 in the cold of a Texas winter to avoid a possible calamity, as the planes in taking off barely cleared my tent. I saw the Curtiss crash, and I saw the Wright run through a horse and buggy, or rather I saw the horse run over the machine.

In 1918, while G-3 of the First Army in the Meuse-Argonne operations, two squadrons of planes were placed at my disposal for emergency missions. Then shortly before the Armistice, I watched a group of 164 American planes pass over the German lines. On the morning following the Armistice, I looked over the ground in No-Man's-Land to see the effect of the bombing by that great air armada.

So, by the mere accident of position, I attended the birth and was present during much of the childhood of your Air Corps. More recently, in a flight around the United States with General Andrews, I inspected most of the air installations in this country, and the splendid GHQ Air Force. Professionally, as head of the War Plans Division, I am intimately concerned with the development of the Air Corps, and personally I am deeply interested in everything pertaining to it. Therefore it is a special pleasure to have this opportunity to visit the Air Corps Tactical School and to meet the faculty and the students.

Yesterday afternoon the senior members of your faculty gave me an outline of your course. I was much impressed by what they are doing to carry out the principal purpose of the school—the education of Air officers in a knowledge of the combined arms.

Young Air officers probably consider their future as irrevocably tied to air activities, and do not visualize service not intimately connected with the Air Corps. These are quite logical reasons why their approach to the national military problem may sometimes lack consideration of the multitude of other factors involved. Military victories are not gained by a single arm—though the failures of an arm or service might well be disastrous—but are achieved through the efforts of all arms and services welded into an Army team.

There is still another point of view for the younger officers. Many will be called upon to fill positions as principal staff officers or as high commanders with mixed forces; positions which require an intimate knowledge of the combined arms, and a breadth of vision impossible to the man who devotes his entire interest to a single arm. General Pratt, the former Commandant of the Air Corps Tactical School, is an example of an officer trained and experienced in the Air Corps who is on his way to high command. Now en route to the Philippine Islands, he will serve with the ground forces of that command.[3]

The most difficult problem for the War Department is the determination of the best organization for the Army, within the limits of the funds available. Fortunately, in some respects, we are not like European nations who clearly recognize potential enemies and therefore can plan for national defense along definite lines. The size and character of the military organizations that will best meet their special situations can be accurately determined.

With us, geographical location and the international situation make it literally impossible to find definite answers for such questions as: who will be our enemy in the next war; in what theatre of operations will that war be fought; and, what will be our national objective at the time? These uncertainties lead inevitably to the conclusion that the only sensible policy for us to follow is to maintain a conservatively balanced force for the protection of our territory against any probable threat during the period the vast but latent resources of the United States, in men and materiel, are being mobilized.

To illustrate the complete uncertainty as to future wars, take, for example, the situation at Fort Leavenworth thirty years ago. Our principal, in fact our only, text on Applied Tactics was a German production by Colonel Griepenkerl, who presented his tactical problems on a map of the terrain in the vicinity of Metz.[4] There was much derision in the Army, along with active hostility towards Leavenworth, at the idea of teaching of American officers in Kansas the tactics outlined by a German officer on a map of terrain 5000 miles away. Yet, but a few years later, the principal operations of our Army in the World War were located on that very terrain, and the names of the villages, the hills, the streams, and even the larger woods were familiar to our staff officers.

Now, it is a very simple matter to say that we need a balanced force, but the headache develops when we work out the detailed composition of such a force, that is within the financial means available. There are no series of facts that will lead to the one perfect solution, and short of war, there is no method for testing a solution. The decision must be based largely on opinions, and opinions will necessarily vary.

It is no exaggeration to state that the War Department is devoting more study to the size and composition of the Air Corps component of the Army team than to any other single subject, because aviation is a new arm and there is only a meagre background of major war experience to guide us in its use. Also, in its rapid development, the theories of today are often in the discard tomorrow, and the question of dollars and cents absolutely dominates the field. That there is no neglect of aviation is evidenced by the fact that almost one-third of the total funds appropriated for the Army are expended on the Air Corps.

Sit down sometime and try to balance all the factors concerned with the national defense—including limited appropriations—and then attempt to outline the organization for a balanced Army. Divorce yourself for the moment from the Air Corps and assume that the responsibility for the decisions regarding national defense rests solely on your shoulders. Conscientiously consider the limitations imposed by annual appropriations—and weigh carefully the necessity and requirements for each arm, including the present problem of archaic equipment for which there are no replacement funds. Having reached a general conclusion, which checks with probable appropriations and the basic law, then set up, within those limits, the air force that you feel will best meet our requirements. Be conservative as to the powers of aviation and honest as to its limitations.

Your first decision will probably be to equip your air organizations with modern materiel. That is a sound decision, but how are you going to carry it out? Aviation materiel is extremely costly; it takes a long time to produce; and, remember this, is rapidly outmoded. Can you afford to discard the expensive materiel you have on hand for yet more modern types? Another consideration: the more costly the plane, the fewer of them you can have, and for each plane, guns, instruments, bombs, ammunition, and maintenance must be provided. Study the emergency situations you think we may be required to meet, and then decide on the proportion of plane types to meet those situations. Is it more desirable to have a large number of small planes or a small number of large planes? Consider the major emergency problem of training of pilots rapidly; that you will have to use rapidly trained pilots; and that your air force may be required to operate in theatres where airdromes are limited in number and size. In view of these factors, are combat planes—simple to operate and rugged in construction—indicated? Is it wise to sacrifice desirable technical features in order to obtain planes with special characteristics? There are almost unlimited permutations and combinations to resolve into a solution.

You must set aside funds for research and development, and for the maintenance and training of personnel, year in and year out. We have a very fine commercial aviation system and splendid Naval aviation. What effect will these have on the solution of your problem? The questions I have outlined are not academic—far from it, they are before the War Department for consideration every day.

Saturday morning, before leaving for Maxwell Field, it was necessary for me to pass on the proposition of a further allocation of funds for bombs. A great bombing plane without bombs—and it requires a year to make a bomb—would be a most expensive futility in the scheme of national defense. The project before me was to increase the number of missions of bombs to be procured. It was favorably acted upon. But—and this is the point I wish to make—at the same time that I was considering the dollars and cents involved in aviation munitions, I had in mind the fact that the rifle for the troops of our first war Army is of a type thirty-four years old, yet we have developed a semi-automatic shoulder rifle which is at least the equal of any similar weapon in the world. You gentlemen in the Air Corps would have no hesitation about the matter of bombs. But what about the thirty-four-year-old type rifle?

I leave this problem with you. Please give it serious thought and contribute towards its solution, for it is my firm conviction that aerial supremacy in the next war will not be merely a matter of technical excellence and tactical skill, but will depend fundamentally on the soundness of our peacetime planning and preparations.

We have the finest pilots in the world and planes that are at least equal in efficiency to those of any other nation. You can be justly proud of your contribution to these achievements. But you are now about to enter into a broader field of study where consideration is given to the role the Air Corps plays as a component part of the Army. Seek to obtain a clear picture of every aspect of national defense, so that you may think straight and advise wisely. The more outstanding you become as an officer of the Air Corps, the more important it is that you thoroughly understand the requirements and operation of the combined arms. The War Department needs Air experts who understand the Army, for we must have a team.

GCMRL/G. C. Marshall Papers (Pentagon Office, Speeches)

1. In 1931, the school moved from Langley Field, near Hampton, Virginia, to Maxwell Field, near Montgomery, Alabama.

2. Major General Benjamin D. Foulois was chief of the Air Corps from December 22, 1931, until December 21, 1935, when he retired.

3. Brigadier General Henry C. Pratt (U.S.M.A., 1904) was commandant from March 15, 1937, to August 6, 1938. After leaving the Tactical School, he commanded the Twenty-third Brigade at Fort William McKinley, Philippine Islands.

4. In 1906, the Fort Leavenworth schools adopted as a textbook, Otto F.W.T. Griepenkerl, *Letters on Applied Tactics*, sixth edition (Kansas City, Missouri: Franklin Hudson, 1906).

To General John J. Pershing   September 26, 1938
                                               Washington, D.C.

Dear General: . . . I have had a rather busy time since my last letter to you. I managed to get a week with Mrs. Marshall on Fire Island and then had to make a talk at Clarksburg, W. Va., for The Assistant Secretary of War. Shortly after that I went down to Maxwell Field to address the new class of the Air Corps Tactical School at the opening of the session. From there I flew over to Benning and spent a day and a half there seeing what a magnificent place it has been made since my departure in 1932. I returned to Washington Wednesday afternoon, and Thursday morning learnt of the terrific hurricane in the Northeast. The Western Union people told me I could not hope to communicate with Bay Shore, L.I., the point from which one takes a boat for Fire Island, where Mrs. Marshall has her cottage, for at least 24 hours; and as nothing was known of what had occurred on Fire Island, I took a plane and flew up to see what had occurred. From the air, I saw the cottage had not been destroyed, though most of the houses in the vicinity had collapsed or been demolished. Many on the bay side of the island—which is about 600 yards wide—had floated out in the water. On the ocean side, the dunes had been broken through by heavy seas and most of the cottages in that vicinity were destroyed. I flew over to Mitchel Field and procured a small training plane, and succeeded in landing on the beach. I found Mrs. Marshall and Molly all right, but they had had a terrific night and escaped from the cottage in water up to their waists, and in a 50–90 mile an hour gale. My orderly was with them and he did his part nobly. The next morning they took stock and found that the cottage had not been harmed, though destruction elsewhere had been terrific, and quite a few lives were lost. The adjacent community of Saltaire was completely destroyed, except for 6 cottages. I remained on the island and got Mrs. Marshall over to the Long Island side. On Friday evening I took her and Molly in to New York, where they now are, apparently none the worse for their experience.

I get my house, 2118 Wyoming Ave., on October 1st, and they arrive that day.

The weather is lovely now. I spent the week-end down near Upperville with Mrs. Rozier Delany, and had a delightful rest and a little fishing on Sunday morning. I drove through Bluemont, and got the gorgeous view looking over the Shenandoah.

I had a nice letter from Miss May a few days ago. She seems to be getting along famously. However, she is uncertain as to her winter plans.

Please be careful of yourself and do not overdo, and do not allow people to impose upon you.

With affectionate regards,   Faithfully yours,

                                               G. C. Marshall

I know nothing about the major general business. Rumor is destroying me, I fear. I am announced by Tom, Dick and Harry as Deputy Chief of Staff and

Chief of Staff to be, the Asst. Secretary makes similar announcements. Probably antagonizing Woodring & Craig.[1]

LC/J. J. Pershing Papers (General Correspondence)

1. Marshall added this handwritten postscript in response to a comment General Pershing had made: "Incidentally, please let me know confidentially just when you expect to be promoted to the grade of Major General. It might, though not necessarily will, have some effect upon your future. So far as I can make out it will be at least a year, although I have not gone into the details." (Pershing to Marshall, September 1, 1938, GCMRL/G. C. Marshall Papers [Pentagon Office, Selected].)

To Brigadier General John W. Gulick
September 28, 1938
[Washington, D.C.]

Dear Gulick: Just read the announcement of the orders for your approaching retirement.

I am very sorry to see you leave the active list. Personally sorry that this should occur without further promotion for you; and officially regretful because I have always felt that you had one of the wisest military heads in the Army. I have heard many fine things regarding you since the time when you were a captain, and especially covering the very difficult period when you were Executive Officer of the Bureau of the National Guard. This last, I regarded as something of a triumph, because there is no more difficult spot in the Army.[1]

I hope very much that you will have a pleasant course outlined for the future, and I will always look back on my brief contacts with you with a great deal of pleasure.   Faithfully yours,

GCMRL/G. C. Marshall Papers (Pentagon Office, General)

1. Gulick served in the Militia Bureau from February 27, 1926, to March 1, 1930, when he became the chief of Coast Artillery. He retired as a major general on November 30, 1938.

To Major General Stanley D. Embick
October 17, 1938
[Washington, D.C.]

Dear Embick: I appreciated your radio very much, though I knew I had your good will long before.[1]

Was just talking to Dunlap in the Club and he spoke of your going up to the recent air-ground maneuvers.[2] I suppose you had to do this, but aren't you making a very rapid start in the opposite direction to that restful period I counseled? I do hope you spread out and enjoy yourself in that gorgeous fall weather, which is particularly impressive around Asheville. Remember that is in the center of your command, just as Key West will be in the winter, and Biloxi.

Mrs. Marshall is charmed with the house, and I find it much more attractive than I had anticipated. The upstairs sitting room has made the greatest hit and evidently we are going to spend nine-tenths of our time there while we are in Washington, and I am not at the War Department.

We kept Henry until Saturday night and he left then at his own election, to accept a job at sixty dollars a month at the Soldiers' Club or mess. We found him most satisfactory, a splendid cook, and very agreeable to have around. Molly was very much opposed to his leaving, and I think Henry would have stayed with the least encouragement. But Mrs. Marshall thought that he ought to take the higher wages offered. He may be back before many months go by—at least, he gave us that impression—and as he engaged and located in position our cook, I suppose he retains the right to dislocate the lady if necessary.

With warm regards to you both,   Faithfully yours,

GCMRL/G. C. Marshall Papers (Pentagon Office, Selected)

1. Embick's radiogram said: "Delighted by the news of your designation as Deputy." (Embick to Marshall, October 15, 1938, GCMRL/G. C. Marshall Papers [Pentagon Office, Selected].)

2. The conversation that Marshall mentions presumably occurred in the Army and Navy Club in Washington, D.C., with Lieutenant Colonel Robert H. Dunlop (U.S.M.A., 1910), assistant chief of staff, G-1, Fourth Corps Area. The maneuvers took place at Fort Bragg, North Carolina.

To Colonel Morrison C. Stayer   October 18, 1938
Personal   Washington, D.C.

Dear Stayer: I have just read your note of October fifteenth, and want to thank you for your kindly congratulations. I knew that I had them without any letter to tell me so.

As to our scheme, just now I am not doing anything about it—in fact, I dropped the matter about ten days ago. A mild attack of summer "flu" upset me a little but, while I am a little choked up now and somewhat sniffly, I seem to be quite normal again. However, my departure from normal was not extreme. I plan to get busy again as soon as this "flu" has passed on.

Mrs. Marshall and Mollie had a wild experience in the hurricane. They were on Fire Island and escaped from their cottage in water up to their waists, with the wind blowing between fifty and ninety miles an hour. After a wretched night, huddled up with all the dogs, children, and men and women in the village, they got back to their cottage at noon the next day and found it entirely intact, * practically no damage at all, while everything in the neighborhood was pretty generally destroyed.

They came to town October first, I having opened the house September thirtieth, and we are now pretty well settled and have already reached one hundred callers. It is even worse than Benning, though I had forty there my first night.

With affectionate regards to Mrs. Stayer and yourself, Faithfully yours,

See attached sheet.[1]

*I flew up the next morning and managed to land on the beach.

P.S. I stopped my medecin ten days ago, to let 2 weeks elapse before resuming. Meanwhile I developed mild flu. I think this last was responsible for an irregular pulse, rather than sessation of medecine. I found that when I walked to the office my pulse would skip a beat every fifth to tenth beat. Sometimes it did this in the morning when I had ridden to the office. But usually in the afternoon in settled down to a steady pulse of 68 to 78, depending on how much I moved about.

This all took place after the first two days of the flu—a light summer type—from which I am still suffering in chest congestion, which is developing to the sneezing phase today. But my pulse now is much more regular, usually without intermissions, and I have had to be unusually busy, getting orie[nted] in the most pressing job in the W.D. I thought it best to wait until my flu effects had passed before starting up on the medecine again, as I wanted to see if my pulse would be regular.

I have seen the doctors twice, and my pulse and temperature were normal—my blood pressure 122. The last is usually 132 or thereabouts. My pulse was not intermitting when the doctors saw me.

GCMRL/M. C. Stayer Papers

1. This note, the asterisk in the margin above, and the postscript were all added in Marshall's hand and do not appear on the carbon copy in the Marshall papers. Stayer's letter of October 17, 1938, said in part: "Have not heard from you relative to our scheme. Would be glad to hear from you in this matter. Perhaps, if necessary, we can change the scheme a little." (GCMRL/G. C. Marshall Papers [Pentagon Office, General].) Stayer began visiting Washington periodically in late 1938 and early 1939 to see Marshall in regard to his heart condition. (Major General Morrison C. Stayer, interviewed by Forrest C. Pogue, January 20, 1960, GCMRL.)

To Mrs. John C. Newton
October 21, 1938
[Washington, D.C.]

Dear Ada: I have just finished reading your letter of October sixteenth, and I was greatly interested in all the news you had to give me, and very glad to learn that you are so comfortably and agreeably settled.

Now as to John's detail to Leavenworth, as you know, the policy was announced the day before he arrived in Washington, and the chances for its modification this year are, I would say, exceedingly remote. I will keep close check on what is going on and see if there is any device by which he could be worked in.

But I would say this, back in 1921, I think, I personally got them to put an age limit on the War College. It then was a collection of old men of about my age, the majority over fifty. The policy announced was on the basis of none over forty-eight the first year, none over forty-seven the next year, and so on down for six years until forty-two was the limiting figure—or thereabouts. Now the point is, this has been changed any number of times, and they have gone up and down the scale, older and then younger; half and half, and then sixty of one and forty of the other. So do not be disheartened, and do not allow him to be depressed, because there is considerable water yet to go over the dam.[1]

I am writing this hastily. With warm regards to you both, and to those lovely daughters of yours, Faithfully,

GCMRL/G. C. Marshall Papers (Pentagon Office, General)

1. Major Newton had been a student at the Infantry School's Company Officers' Course, 1928–29. At this time he was forty-four years old and an instructor with the Ohio National Guard in Toledo.

To DOUGLAS C. ARNOLD[1]   October 28, 1938
                                                            [Washington, D.C.]

My dear Mr. Arnold: I received a letter dated October twenty-sixth from Mr. Elmo Roper, regarding my attendance at a meeting of the Pelham Men's Club on November fifteenth.[2] In his letter he asked me to communicate directly with you regarding several questions he raised.

As to whether or not I prefer my talk to be "just a personal address", or "would it serve better any purposes you had in mind if we arranged for the presence of newspaper reporters?", I very much prefer that no reporters be involved. With them present I would have to be exceedingly conservative, so much so that there would be little interest, probably, in what I had to say.

Mr. Roper states that you will meet me at any train; therefore, I would appreciate your giving me the convenient hour for my arrival, and the train time departure from New York.

Also, I would appreciate your telling me whether I should appear in ordinary business clothes, or a dinner coat.

Thanking you for your consideration, Faithfully yours,

GCMRL/G. C. Marshall Papers (Pentagon Office, General)

1. Arnold was the president of the Keystone Varnish Company and a resident of Pelham, in Westchester County, New York.
2. Elmo B. Roper, Jr., was a marketing consultant and the research director of the *Fortune*

Survey of Public Opinion. He wrote, "Your talk will be billed as 'America and the Need for Armament' and we shall leave the treatment of this subject to your own good judgment. Our talks usually last from forty-five minutes to an hour. There will probably be about two hundred in attendance and the membership is composed largely of men who are managing New York businesses. From this you may safely assume it is a somewhat conservative group." (Roper to Marshall, October 26, 1938, GCMRL/G. C. Marshall Papers [Pentagon Office, General].) No copy of a prepared address has been found in the Marshall papers.

To COLONEL ROY A. HILL[1]   October 28, 1938
                                                              [Washington, D.C.]

Dear Hill: I appreciated very much your fine letter of congratulations, and the interesting comments regarding your present duties. I would like very much to talk things over with you, following your experience there, preceded by your particular duties here in Washington.

   Confidentially, I have this in mind: The possible accumulation under the present representative of the Reserve Corps in Washington, General Thompson, matters of the ROTC and the CMTC. My purpose would be to give more dignity and prestige to ROTC affairs. I would appreciate very much your letting me know, confidentially, what your reaction to this would be; particularly as you are intimately familiar with the way things are managed at the present time. I do not have in mind any administrative set-up under General Thompson, and I do not think he has any such set-up for the Reserve Corps.[2]

   Let me hear from you on this.

   With warm regards to you and Mrs. Hill, and my best to that sweet daughter of yours,   Faithfully,

GCMRL/G. C. Marshall Papers (Pentagon Office, General)

   1. Hill (U.S.M.A., 1908) had been P.M.S.&T. at Louisiana State University since August, 1936. Prior to that assignment, he served four years in the War Department's G-3 section.

   2. Brigadier General Charles F. Thompson had become the War Department's executive for Reserve Affairs on September 16, 1938.

To LEO A. FARRELL   October 31, 1938
                                                            Washington, D.C.

Dear Farrell: Thanks for your fine letter of October 28th, and your items of news and opinion.[1] I am doing my reply in long hand for evident reasons.

   Reference any publicity regarding me, or "build up" as it is called; I am now, in my particular position with low rank, on the spot in army circles. The fact of my appointment as Deputy while a brigadier general, junior to other generals of the general staff, makes me conspicuous in the army. Too conspicuous, as a matter of fact.

My strength with the army has rested on the well known fact that I attended strictly to business and enlisted no influence of any sort at anytime. That, in army circles, has been my greatest strength in this matter of future appointment, especially as it is in strong contrast with other most energetic activities in organizing a campaign and in securing voluminous publicity. Therefore, it seems to me that at this time the complete absence of any publicity about me would be my greatest asset, particularly with the President. And the army would resent it, even some of those now ardently for me. In other words, it would tar me with the same brush to which they now object.

The National Guard knows me now. The Reserve Corps know me well. The ROTC people, including many college presidents, know me. And the Regular Army know me. It is not time for the public to be brought to a view of my picture.

How does the logic of this strike you? But in any event, be assured that I greatly appreciate your desire to do me a service.

However, we can talk this all over when you come to town.

Meanwhile, and hurriedly, my thanks and warm regards, Faithfully yours,

G. C. Marshall

GCMRL/L. A. Farrell Papers; H

1. Farrell's letter was not found in the Marshall papers.

To Brigadier General Leigh R. Gignilliat   November 4, 1938
[Washington, D.C.]

Dear Gignilliat: I have delayed answering your letter of October twenty-fifth until I had something specific I could tell you.[1] At the moment I have no prepared speech that might be furnished for your purpose, but as the date is rapidly approaching for your talk at Muncie, I have to tell you something immediately.

In brief, here is the basis on which we operate in all our planning at the present time:

"Our defense policy is to maintain an immediately available force, adequate to defend the continental United States, Panama, and Hawaii (in conjunction with the Navy), during the period our vast resources in personnel, materiel, and industry are mobilized for war. This calls for a *balanced Army*, equipped with modern planes, weapons, and munitions suitable to our particular problem."

In solving our defense problems, we have our greatest advantage in the vast difference between our geographical location and that of European countries, the more impressive since the appearance of the long range bombing plane. Modern developments do not modify the fact that to attack the United States an enemy must cross an ocean.

Our great necessity at the present time is in materiel. Of course, we are in sore need of personnel for manning additional planes to be delivered, and particularly for creating some anti-aircraft units. But, far outweighing these necessities is the matter of materiel, almost every item of which cannot be produced under a year, and many of them—such as directors for anti-aircraft firing—require almost a year and a half.

At the present time most of the Infantry of the Regular Army, and all of the Infantry of the National Guard have a rifle thirty-four years old, at the same time that we have in models for production the most effective semi-automatic shoulder rifle in the world.

Our Regular Infantry and National Guard Infantry are without anti-tank guns, 37s, and more than a year will be required to manufacture these. The Artillery of the small Regular Army is just being modernized in 75s and 155s. In the National Guard it has not been touched, except to permit towing. And of course, in the above items of materiel and in the modernization of artillery to suit perspective battle conditions, we must have enough on M-day for the full expansion of the Regular Army and the National Guard, or for seven hundred thousand odd men, plus several hundred thousand replacements.

Our initial Protective Mobilization Plan contemplates the smallest force to be mobilized that we think could safeguard the continental United States until the full Protective Mobilization Plan gets under way. We deal with the smallest force in order to obviate every possible burden and complication of initial effort.

Another item which we need to lay in heavy stocks is powder. This is pretty confidential and should not be touched upon except by implication. But the point is, the powder we need is practically all non-commercial.

Now, all the above items, once on hand, are good for about twenty-five years at a minimum of maintenance charge—a most important consideration with us, particularly when we view the approaching years of drastic economy. The ordinary Ordnance materiel only involves about one percent, the powder three percent, for maintenance.

When we come to aircraft, we are of course involved in heavy maintenance charges and the factor of obsolescence. Our problem is to have enough planes on hand on M-day to maintain us through the first losses until heavy production can get under way.

I am not asking you to treat the foregoing as confidential, but it is not to be quoted as coming from here except that I do not mind your using the one quoted paragraph on our defense policy in its exact wording.

This is a very hasty business, but I hope it will be of help. Faithfully yours,

GCMRL/G. C. Marshall Papers (Pentagon Office, Selected)

1. Gignilliat had written that he had to speak to the Rotary Club of Muncie, Indiana, on November 8, on the status of national defense measures. He asked Marshall for "a pointer so that I may drive it home and that might prove helpful to the cause." (Gignilliat to Marshall, October 25, 1938, GCMRL/G. C. Marshall Papers [Pentagon Office, Selected].)

SPEECH[1]

November 6, 1938
Brunswick, Maryland

As I understand it, this gathering today is to celebrate the Armistice of twenty years ago, which brought to a close the active fighting of the World War. The anniversary of so momentous an occasion should be observed, not to celebrate a victory, but in consecration of the sacrifice of the young Americans in France, and to bring to mind the conditions of that frightful conflict, in an effort to provide for the avoidance of such a catastrophe in the future.

Unfortunately these present days, particularly these past few months, have involved a series of events frightening to every citizen, in their threats or implications.

No one of us wants war. I believe that is axiomatic in this country—certainly on the part of any veteran of the World War. There is nothing romantic, dramatic, or satisfying in modern conflict. It is all horrible, profoundly depressing; and now it carries with it a dreadful threat to civil populations. I think we are in general agreement regarding the statements I have just made, but the trouble, the difficulty of the problem, is what is to be done about it.

We honor our dead of past wars; we encourage the ideal of patriotic self-sacrifice of the individual; but, we must be far-sighted and sound in our attitude as to just what is the proper thing for this Government to do in the way of national defense.

You know, a photograph in a weekly magazine depicting some horror—like the bombing of a city in China or in Spain—not only creates a profound impression upon every civilian who examines it, but it more or less fixes in his mind a specific remedy—practical or impractical. But there is far more to this business than the bombing of cities—far, far more—and my desire today is to find the words to make clear the real issue, from a Governmental point of view, of a matter of vast importance to every citizen. Possibly by utilizing some homely examples, I might better be able to make clear the complications of the problem and the difficulties which are inherent in its solution.

In the first place, national defense under modern conditions has become a tremendously expensive business, so much so that I think it is the business of every mature citizen to acquaint himself with the principal facts, and form a general idea as to what he or she thinks is the wise course for this country to follow.

I am not discussing the evil of war, or what brings about war, or whether or not I think there is any possibility of our being involved in a war in the near future. I want merely to present the problems involved from the viewpoint of the professional soldier on duty in the War Department.

Allow me to give you a few examples of this so-called unpreparedness:

All of our military strength developed during the Revolutionary War had been disbanded at the time of the outbreak of the War of 1812. I think we had then some eighty-nine soldiers, and it therefore became necessary to create an army out of whole cloth. Public opinion, and mark that well—public opinion forced us immediately to an invasion of Canada, and we enjoyed a series of the most humiliating military episodes on record. Fortunately, or maybe unfortunately, our school boys have had their attention diverted from these tragedies by the splendid but local victories of American privateers on the high seas in conflict with isolated English naval vessels, and by the magnificent performance of General Jackson at New Orleans.

The Mexican War had a slow approach, giving us time for preparation of an army in the field in Texas. We were dealing with a weak country and had every advantage in means and men. But even here we find some remarkable examples of American military policy. For instance, we find General Scott's army hurrying up from the coast at Vera Cruz to cross the fever district of the plains before the hot season developed, forcing its way into the mountains at Cerro Gordo in order to secure the passage of this high mountain range before the time of service of a large portion of his men expired, to leave him in Mexico, in the enemy's country, with the mere remnant of an army. He had to wait there until the new men arrived. Fortunately, the enemy was not capable of taking advantage of what might well have been a fatal dilemma.

The Civil War was so full of illustrations of our lack of preparation that it is useless to recite them.

However, when we come to the Spanish American War, which is within the day of many of us here, we find most surprising situations. Out in San Francisco an expedition was embarking to sail to the Philippines, to back up Admiral Dewey. They lacked all knowledge of the country, of the people, of the general necessities; they lacked training and organization; and yet they sailed off across the broad Pacific to fight, seven thousand miles from their base, with only one hundred and fifty rounds of ammunition available per man, just about one day of rifle fire on a battlefield. What was to happen the morning following the first encounter had to be completely ignored.

In those days we had nothing, literally, but small garrisons at old frontier posts, and little units along the coast to man ancient guns. There were no reserves of war supplies, and practically no modern equipment. Our losses, due to ignorance of leadership on the part of troop commanders, and poor sanitation on the part of an untrained medical personnel, were greater in the camp and hospital than they were on the battlefield.

Following this disgraceful display, in which the questions of personal courage and patriotic energy were never questioned, a deliberate effort was made for the first time to remedy conditions. Mr. Elihu Root stepped into the picture as Secretary of War, and out of his great mind came a revolutionary step in the modernization of the American Army—the introduction of the military school system which culminates in the War College at Washington, the creation of a General staff which consists of a group of highly trained officers to coordinate all military effort towards the best preparation of the army for its ultimate purpose. These growing pains brought about many difficulties, as was natural, and we reached the World War in the midst of the transition of the National Guard— our principal immediate available forces—and before we had had time to develop organizational methods for handling large bodies of troops. Our part in the World War is well known to all of you, but many of our blundering steps are unknown to the general public.

Allow me to give you a few examples within my own experience. I sailed from New York on the first ship of the first convoy, in June, 1917. This was the First Division, a unit which eventually had 27,000 men in its ranks and suffered 25,000 casualties in France. It went over with the first convoy and it returned with the last in September, 1919. We embarked hurriedly in Hoboken, put out from the dock in the several boats, and anchored awaiting the completion of the installation of naval guns, and the preparation of convoy arrangements for crossing the Atlantic. The Staff of that Division, of which I was a member, immediately got together—having assembled for the first time on the boat—to study our situation. We found, while anchored in the Hudson River, that the organization of the troops was entirely new to us, that there were four regiments of infantry in the division instead of the nine of our previous experience; that there were units of which we had never before heard, armed with weapons of which we knew nothing. And like that expedition from San Francisco to the Philippines in 1898, with only 150 rounds per man, we were sailing 3,000 miles from home to fight on foreign soil, and not until we arrived in France did the Division Commander and the members of the Division Staff learn that these new weapons were non-existent, and that the troops which on paper were charged with operating those weapons had never seen even a model of one. We found that eighty percent of the men in ranks were recruits, to many of whom rifles had been issued on the trains between the Mexican Border and Hoboken. They were all good men, they were all splendid Americans—but they were not soldiers.

The day we landed in France I saw the French General in command of that region, in his full dress uniform, with his medals on his chest, arrive at our headquarters, which had been hastily established in a stubble field. He was calling on our Commanding General to extend the welcome of France to the first unit of American soldiers to arrive on the soil of France, to repay our debt to Lafayette. He was calling on an organization of the Regular Army, as he thought. The sentinel at the gate was a tall, rangy, Tennessee mountain type. As the General approached, the Tennessean did his best with a salute—and I was concerned to see that not only was his blouse partly unbuttoned, but he had a watch chain stretched from one pocket to the other. The French General made an evident comment regarding the rifle, and our sentry handed his gun over to the Frenchman and seated himself on a nearby post to roll a cigarette.

I am not depreciating the quality of those men. I saw them on a series of terrible battlefields where they established an outstanding reputation in the AEF, and a world-wide reputation in Europe. Finer soldiers you could not have found, but the point is, at this moment, they were not soldiers; but our peculiar fortune in that war was, that our Allies protected us on the field of battle for a long year while we slowly got ready—for we landed in France on June 26, 1917, and it was not until September 12, 1918, that an American Army deployed in a battle. Prior to that time there were engagements in which smaller detachments of American troops were engaged. The First Division made the first American attack at Cantigny on May 28, 1918, and participated in the famous counterattack at Soissons, the turning point of the war, on July 18, 1918. Other divisions operated in the Marne Salient that summer. But, more than a year elapsed after our declaration of war before our first divisional unit engaged in battle, and seventeen months before an American Army appeared on the field.

I emphasize these time elements because the implications of the past few weeks have indicated that war is a sudden and terrible business, with the accent on the sudden.[2] Nothing that has recently been said or printed seemed to indicate that we would have a year in which to get ready. Now, what we are interested in, as our simple duty in the War Department, is the development of logical plans suitable to our national characteristics and adequate for our protection.

There are a few thoughts I would ask you to keep in mind. Remember that almost every weapon of war, certainly every gun—big or little—and every device for aiming and firing that gun, like the elaborate instruments necessary for anti-aircraft artillery, require a year to a year-and-a-half to manufacture. So, no matter how many billions of dollars Congress places at our disposal on the day war is declared, they will not buy ten cents worth of war materiel for delivery under twelve months, and a great deal of it will require a year-and-a-half to manufacture. In other words, whatever your son and my son is to use to defend himself and to defend us and the Country, has to be manufactured in time of peace.

We have models of the best weapons and mechanical devices, we think, in the world, and we have the finest aircraft in design and performance; but what we must have is the accumulation of an adequate reserve of this materiel, not just some popular item, but a balanced program suitable for the instant arming of our first modest war army, in the event of trouble.

Our primary need is materiel, everything else is of secondary importance.

Our policy is, I think, thoroughly in keeping with American thought and characteristics—only the means necessary to defend ourselves until the vast resources of this country, in men and industry, can be mobilized. We want nothing today for armed invasion, we want no huge forces on foot or wing; but we do want the materiel and the nucleus for the rapid equipping and expansion of the Regular Army and the National Guard to a strength adequate to protect us; that is, the United States, Panama, and Hawaii, while our great industrial plants are set going towards the production of war materiel, and our vast resources in men can be organized and trained.

GCMRL/G. C. Marshall Papers (Pentagon Office, Speeches)
1. Marshall spoke to the American Legion at Brunswick, Maryland.
2. The Germany-Czechoslovakia crisis of September, 1938, appeared to be drifting rapidly toward war until Great Britain, France, Germany, and Italy signed an agreement at Munich, Germany, on September 30.

To COLONEL ROY A. HILL   November 10, 1938
Confidential   Washington, D.C.

Dear Hill: I have just read your letter of November eighth and I am still in some doubt as to your reactions. As you filled the job in G-3 of looking after ROTC affairs, and you now are on such duty—and in a most important post—I am particularly interested in just what you think of the idea I suggested.

I am aware of the objections you mentioned, and very much aware of the latent power of the combined Reserve Corps, ROTC and CMTC.[1] What I want to know is your precise view as to how best to handle the matter. Do you think it could best be done as it was done for the ROTC through you in a subordinate position, in the G-3 Section; and, by the same token, do you think the Reserve affairs should be handled in that fashion, rather than having the prestige of a General with the ear of the Chief at his disposal? If you do think these matters should be handled after that fashion, have you any fear that sooner or later in their urgings for consideration, these various groups, through Congress, might obtain a powerful office in the War Department, of the type of the present National Guard Bureau, which would be a powerful agency for interference with the ordinary routine of the General Staff?

I was impressed during your tenure of office and my connection with the Mershon Committee, that your voice and influence in ROTC matters was very weak because of the fact that you were submerged in a large section with its multiplicity of interests. When a college president came to town, he could not find the Chief of Staff intimately familiar with the ROTC problems, and his problem in particular, and he would find almost the same situation with the General officer at the head of G-3. Unless he burrowed down to a comparatively low ranking subordinate at a desk well in the background, he never could have the feeling of having reached headquarters regarding the solution of his difficulties. Apparently, you and such important men found little difficulty in reaching an amicable solution or agreement, but you yourself had difficulties in making the problem understood by your immediate chief, by the Executive of the Section, and finally the Assistant Chief of Staff, G-3. Is this correct, or have I been laboring under a misapprehension?

I was much impressed in my few months' work in the General Staff to find, comparatively speaking (and this is most confidential), the small importance, or rather the little thought given to such tremendous agencies as the National Guard of two hundred thousand men, the ROTC of one hundred sixty-five thousand men, and the Reserve of one hundred thousand men. The larger interests seemed to be centered in construction problems, installations of foreign garrisons, promotion questions, decentralized training problems—mostly of Regular Army concern—and routine business of the day, while the affairs of what concerned 80% of the first war army appeared to be secondary thoughts, though every one, theoretically at least, would immediately admit the importance of the activity.

Now I am writing most confidentially, for your eye alone. But because of your particular experience here, and where you are, I want your frankest reaction. You are a most important witness by reason of your particular experience.

Let me hear from you further. Faithfully yours,

GCMRL/G. C. Marshall Papers (Pentagon Office, General)

1. Regarding the proposal to place R.O.T.C. and C.M.T.C. affairs under the War Department's executive for Reserve Affairs, (see Marshall to Hill, October 28, 1938, above) Hill commented: "It is not necessary for me to tell you that such an organization violates the principles of General Staff organization. This in itself is not an objection which should prevent establishing such an organization if the ends to be accomplished justify it. However, the objection which does occur to me and which you have undoubtedly considered is the question as to where such an organization may lead. It is possible in time the tail may wag the dog. You will recall the difficulties encountered by former Chiefs of Staff in attempting to set up an organization which would run the Army for the best interests of the National Defense rather than for those of a particular branch or bureau of the Army. You are more familiar than I am with the functioning of the present National Guard Bureau and with the methods employed by it in securing special consideration at the expense of the National Defense as a whole." (Hill to Marshall, November 8, 1938, GCMRL/G. C. Marshall Papers [Pentagon Office, General].)

TO MAJOR MARK W. CLARK

November 16, 1938
[Washington, D.C.]

Dear Clark: I have just read your letter of November twelfth and am much interested in what you had to say about your prospective maneuvers. I hope you get the money for rentals; but, had you considered the possibility of maneuvering entirely off the reservation in one of the National Forest Ranges—in other words, out of sight of the Post water tower?[1] Motorized as most of your Lewis crowd is, is there not some Government land convenient for such a concentration.

Please treat this suggestion as entirely confidential, because it is far from my business to be sending hints to General Sweeney about the training of his division. It is for your eye only. I am merely interested in the possibilities of getting off the home grounds and doing things on a more warlike basis. Hastily yours,

GCMRL/G. C. Marshall Papers (Pentagon Office, Selected)

1. At this time, Clark (U.S.M.A., April 1917) was assigned to Third Division headquarters at Fort Lewis, Washington. He commented in his letter on the need for money to rent land for the division's spring maneuver at Fort Lewis. (Clark to Marshall, November 12, 1938, GCMRL/G. C. Marshall Papers [Pentagon Office, Selected].)

T HE SEPTEMBER war scare in Europe forced Britain, France, and the United States to reevaluate their military positions with regard to Germany. The latter's air superiority emerged as the most threatening aspect of the imbalance of power. United States Ambassador William C. Bullitt was told by French Intelligence that Germany had sixty-five hundred modern planes, two-thirds of them bombers. France was unprepared to meet such a massive assault.

For a time, to help redress the balance of power in Europe while avoiding the prohibitions of the United States Neutrality Act of 1935, Bullitt sought President Roosevelt's support for a scheme to build factories in Canada to produce planes for sale to France and Britain using United States tools, machines, and designs. Bullitt unsuccessfully sought to convince Charles A. Lindbergh to return from England to the United States to assist in the enterprise. (Bullitt to Roosevelt, September 28, 1938, in Orville H. Bullitt, editor, *For the President, Personal and Secret: Correspondence Between Franklin D. Roosevelt and William C. Bullitt* [Boston: Houghton Mifflin, 1972], pp. 297–99; Charles A. Lindbergh, *The Wartime Journals of Charles A. Lindbergh* [New York: Harcourt Brace Jovanovich, 1970], pp. 80–81, 83, 87.)

Evidence of White House concern over the growing power of the German-Italian alliance surfaced immediately after Ambassador Bullitt returned to Washington, D.C., on October 13. Bullitt helped to convince Roosevelt that United States aircraft production had to be stimulated at once. The president's private remarks led to conjectures in the press that he would soon ask Congress to appropriate money for ten thousand aircraft plus increased production facilities. (Mark S. Watson, *Chief of Staff: Prewar Plans and Preparations*, a volume in the *United States Army in World War II* [Washington, D.C.: Historical Division, Department of the Army, 1950], pp. 131–32.)

One of the most important of the meetings on military policy Marshall attended as deputy chief of staff occurred in the White House on the afternoon of November 14, one month after he took over the post. The Western Hemisphere was vulnerable to attack, President Roosevelt asserted, and this situation demanded the immediate creation of a huge air force so that the United States would not need to have a huge army. It was politically impossible to send a large army abroad. A powerful air force was essential to back up the administration's foreign policy. The United States needed ten thousand airplanes and the capacity to produce twenty thousand more per year. (See Herman Oliphant's account of the meeting in the Henry Morgenthau, Jr., Diary, 150: 337–42, FDRL/H. Morgenthau, Jr., Papers. See also Memorandum for the Chief of Staff by Henry H. Arnold, November 15, 1938, NA/RG 165 [OCS, Conferences].)

Marshall believed that the president's new program was unbalanced and underfunded. Not only did it favor the Air Corps over the army as a whole, it concentrated too much on machinery at the expense of other Air Corps needs. The White House meeting, he recalled, was "quite an assembly of men and a great many of the New Deal protagonists; it had to do with these appropriations we were trying to get of a military way. There was a great difference of opinion as to what it should be. The president, of course, was all for the increase in the air, but he wasn't much for getting the men to man the airships nor for the munitions and things that they required. He was principally thinking at that time of getting airships for England and France." (Interview, March 6, 1957.)

Marshall remembered sitting "on a lounge way off to the side" in the White House meeting room. Roosevelt finished his presentation and began asking the other participants' opinions. "Most of them agreed with him entirely, had very little to say, and were very soothing in their comments. He, of course, did the major portion of the talking. He finally came around to me, . . . and I remember he called me 'George.' I don't think he ever did it again. That rather irritated me, because I didn't know him on that basis. Of course, the president can call you pretty much what he wants to, but nevertheless I wasn't very enthusiastic over such a misrepresentation of our intimacy. So he turned to me at the end of this general outlining . . . and said, 'Don't you think so, George?' And I replied, 'Mr. President, I am sorry, but I don't agree with that at all.' I know that ended the conference, and the president gave me a very startled look.

"When I went out, they all bade me goodbye and said my tour in Washington was over. But I want to say in compliment to the president that that didn't antagonize him at all. Maybe he thought I would tell him the truth so far as I personally was concerned—which I certainly tried to do in all of our later conversations. He thought I was too intent on things, of course, and he was having a very hard time raising the public backing for the money, and there was a debt limitation during these early periods. But my job was to see that the country was armed, if it was possible to do so, which meant large appropriations." (Ibid.)

The day following the meeting, Assistant Secretary of War Johnson sent Army Chief of Staff Craig a memorandum instructing him to prepare budget estimates for a rearmament program which went significantly beyond the president's airplanes-only approach. On November 17, Marshall wrote to Major General Embick: "As you can tell from the papers, things are very, very busy here.

Occasionally I have time to turn around, but not often." (GCMRL/G. C. Marshall Papers [Pentagon Office, Selected].) Marshall, who was in charge of the army's appropriations requests, called in his assistants and apportioned the work. ★

STATEMENT TO THE ASSISTANT CHIEFS OF STAFF   November 17, 1938
Secret   [Washington, D.C.]

Supplementary Estimates, Fiscal Year 1940.

1. Each of you has been furnished a copy of a memorandum from the Acting Secretary of War to the Chief of Staff directing that estimates of costs be prepared for the objectives prescribed therein. This memorandum, so far as practicable, will be regarded as SECRET.

2. You will notice that the costs for the several programs are to be calculated on a two-year basis. The Chief of the Air Corps has already done a great deal of work on the objectives set forth in sub-paragraphs 1, *a, b, c,* and *d.*[1] It is desired that the General Staff Divisions should now participate in this study in accordance with their functional responsibilities and also in order to assist General Arnold in the burden of work that has been placed upon him. There is no time for normal General Staff procedure. Speed is essential and your efforts should be informal. Papers will not be entrusted to messengers.

3. I will discuss each of the objectives in turn and indicate the action which each of the General Staff Divisions should take:—

a. Subparagraph a.—It is desired that the War Plans Division, in conjunction with the Chief of the Air Corps and G-3, determine and recommend what the Army airplane strength of 10,000 planes by balanced types shall be.

b. Subparagraph b.—The War Plans Division, in conjunction with the Chief of the Air Corps and G-3, will determine and recommend what 50% of airplane strength on an operating basis shall be. A memorandum on these two paragraphs should be submitted to the Chief of Staff at the earliest practicable moment. Upon the approval of these recommendations the necessary data will be furnished G-4 and G-1. G-4 in conjunction with the Air Corps will determine the rate of procurement of each type and the costs. G-1 will then, in conjunction with the Chief of the Air Corps, determine the required strength of the Air Corps to operate 50% of the airplane strength and the necessary rate of procurement of trained personnel to meet the procurement in planes. G-1 will then in conjunction with the Chief of Finance determine the cost of the increased personnel.

c. Subparagraph b (latter part) and subparagraph c.—G-4, in conjunction with the Chief of the Air Corps, will determine the additional cost for the maintenance and operation of 5000 active airplanes and of 5000 in storage, and, in conjunction with The Quartermaster General, the cost of all additional construction required therefor.

d. Subparagraph d.—The Assistant Secretary of War will be requested to furnish this office with estimates of costs for these objectives.

e. Subparagraph e.—G-4 will coordinate the estimates of all services concerned and determine the additional costs in accordance with the enlarged program.

f. Paragraph 2.—The total of the estimates heretofore prepared to meet the deficiencies in the Protective Mobilization Plan was $579,500,000. We can now deduct $110,000,000 from this total for the procurement of airplanes and $42,000,000 for aids to manufacture for which provision has been made elsewhere. This leaves a total of $427,500,000. It is desired that G-4 prepare and submit a statement, similar to the one previously presented to the President which shall provide for this amount.

g. Paragraph 3.—The Assistant Secretary of War will be requested to prepare a statement of costs under this paragraph.[2]

4. All estimates of costs will provide for the complete two-year program. They will show the cash appropriation required (based upon the estimated amount which will be withdrawn from the Treasury in the Fiscal Year 1940), the remainder to be covered by contract authorizations.

5. All estimates will be submitted by appropriation title to the Budget Officer for the War Department and will be separated into three categories:—

a. The airplane program.

b. Requirements for the Protective Mobilization Plan.

c. Industrial Preparedness.

6. All estimates will be submitted at the earliest practicable date. It is understood that these estimates of cost will be submitted to the President for approval before formal estimates will be submitted to the Bureau of the Budget.

7. It is to be understood that the functions of the General Staff should be restricted to supervision and coordination, and that the actual estimates of cost should be prepared by the respective operating services. Time does not permit the preparation of a formal directive, and the purpose of this conference is to insure that these operating services have information as precise as practicable as a basis for their respective estimates.

NA/RG 407 (580, Increase of the Air Corps [10-19-38])

1. The subparagraphs of Johnson's memorandum were: "*a.* An Army airplane strength of 10,000 planes properly balanced as to types. *b.* 50% of airplane strength to be on an operating basis including operating personnel, installations, materials, etc. *c.* Remainder of planes to be provided with satisfactory storage conditions and care. *d.* Provision for 7 Government aircraft factories with an average production capacity of 1200 planes per year each, on assumptions that land will be obtained from that at present available or from funds other than those contained in Army Appropriations Acts, that buildings will be constructed from relief funds, but that machinery, upkeep, operation, etc., must be provided from Army

funds.   *e.* Provision for necessary supporting materials and services such as Ordnance, Signal Corps, Quartermaster, Pay, etc." (Johnson Memorandum for General Craig, November 15, 1938, NA/RG 407 [580, Increase of the Air Corps (10–19–38)].)

2. In paragraph 3, Johnson requested budget estimates to provide "for assistance to Governmental Production and Industrial Preparedness as follows: *a.* Completion of Educational Order Program. *b.* Rounding out present Government Arsenals and Plants with up-to-date machinery. *c.* Completion of the making of factory plans for critical items of supplies. *d.* Acceleration of Procurement Planning by completing industrial surveys, drawings, specifications, etc. *e.* Special machinery as reserve for manufacture of essential munitions. *f.* Stock piles of strategic materials." (Ibid.)

To General John J. Pershing   November 23, 1938
                                                        [Washington, D.C.]

Dear General: Enclosed is a draft of a letter which we would like you to consider sending to The President. I think it reflects your views, and I know that it would have a powerful effect. There is no one else in the country who can speak as you do. Mr. Harry Hopkins the other day expressed to me his regret that you were not here to discuss some of the aspects of the present situation with The President.[1] Possibly you will consider doing it in the manner here suggested.

I realize that this is taking a great liberty, but the importance of the issue outweighs the other factors to be considered, it seems to me.

I talked this over with Adamson, testing it against his ultra-conservative mental process, and found him acquiescent. So I place the suggestion in your hands.

There are enclosed some clippings which came to me this morning from Governor Martin's office, requesting that if convenient I show them to you.[2]

Adamson tells me that you are in fine shape, and Katherine received a letter from Miss May yesterday, written in Atlanta, to the effect that the trip so far had been most enjoyable and you had been standing it beautifully. Please move on the careful side, and don't fall for invitations to tiresome affairs.   Affectionately yours,

[Inclosure]

The President,   November ____, 1938.

My dear Mr. President: In thinking over our Armistice Day conversation regarding military necessities in the light of the present European situation, I fear that my views may not have been clearly expressed. With your permission, I would like to summarize what appear to me to be the most important considerations.

As to large additions to our present air force, there can be no question but that it is highly advisable to have more planes available, and especially to bring about the coordination of our aeronautical industries so that they can quickly respond to tremendous increases in the production of what the Government requires. I will not discuss this phase as you are fully informed.

My concern at the moment is directed towards those requirements, or I should say essentials, in which the General Staffs of the world know that we are pathetically deficient, and particularly to those features of the defense mechanism that are vital necessities to air operations, though not organically of the air service. Ground forces will bear exactly the same relation to large air fleets of bombers that they do to the Navy for the protection of its bases. If we are to be prepared to extend a long and powerful air arm to the southward, we must have instantly available the means to maintain that air activity by establishing the necessary advance bases.

I am not intimately familiar with the present situation of our ground forces, but I do know that our deficiencies for their current equipment and for their first war expansion are so serious that whatever is done in the near future to strengthen your hand, these deficiencies should be made good, and at the earliest possible moment. I am referring specifically to modern materiel which requires a year or more to produce, especially artillery, which, I believe, is in a lamentable state. What our situation is with regard to ammunition I do not know, but it is highly important that there be no shortages.

The requirements I have mentioned have always been overlooked, and have never been available at the outbreak of war. My embarrassment in France regarding these matters was continuous from the date of my arrival until the Armistice. We were literally beggars as to every important weapon, except the rifle.

I hope you will pardon the liberty I am taking in writing you thus informally. I not only have a natural patriotic interest, but I have had the problem of meeting the dreadful deficiencies of military armament on the outbreak of war.

Believe me, Mr. President,   Most respectfully,

GCMRL/G. C. Marshall Papers (Pentagon Office, Selected)

1. About this time, Secretary of the Interior Harold L. Ickes, whose rivalry with Hopkins was of long standing, noted in his diary that "Harry Hopkins is described as the person who is closest to the President and there is no doubt that this is the fact. He is extraordinarily close. He all but lives at the White House and he seems to be in the complete confidence of the President." (Harold L. Ickes, *The Secret Diary of Harold L. Ickes*, 3 vols. [New York: Simon and Schuster, 1953–54], 2: 508.) Hopkins had recently returned from an inspection of West Coast aircraft factories. Concerning his activities and his emerging relationship with Marshall, see Robert E. Sherwood, *Roosevelt and Hopkins, An Intimate History* [New York: Harper and Brothers, 1948], pp. 100–101.

2. The editorials from two Oregon newspapers (the *Medford Mail Tribune* of November 9 and the *Corvallis Gazette-Times* of November 10) praised Governor Martin as one who had sacrificed his own political fortunes for the good of the state.

To Colonel Roy A. Hill   November 30, 1938
Confidential   [Washington, D.C.]

Dear Hill: With further reference to the ROTC, I wish you would read the article in the November-December number of the Infantry Journal,[1] and let me have your reactions. I am not referring to his final recommendation as to the War Department set-up, as we have already discussed that.

However, in regard to my last comment and with reference to your last letter, you have never expressed yourself as to what is liable to happen here in case we leave the organization in its present set-up. My view had a double purpose—a stronger voice in ROTC affairs here and, at the same time, the avoidance of an unfortunate office being created seriously to interfere with the proceedings of the General Staff.   Faithfully yours,

GCMRL/G. C. Marshall Papers (Pentagon Office, General)

1. Captain Edward Y. Blewett, "Behind the ROTC Scene," *Infantry Journal* 45 (November-December 1938): 543–48. Blewett's thesis was that the value, role, and future of college R.O.T.C. programs were being questioned by students, faculty, and administrators because of insufficient support by the War Department. R.O.T.C. programs were not getting a sufficient number of instructors of suitable quality and disposition; the R.O.T.C. curriculum was being criticized on campus as of dubious quality; the corps area R.O.T.C. heads were failing to impress university leaders with the program's seriousness of purpose; and the quality of equipment available to the R.O.T.C. was low. The author suggested that the War Department create a board of three Reserve officers—somewhat like the military academies' boards of visitors—to direct the program.

To Colonel Henry R. Richmond[1]   December 3, 1938
                                                      [Washington, D.C.]

Dear Richmond: I am writing you informally and direct to get the benefit of your opinion regarding ROTC affairs. I wish you would glance through an article in the last issue, the November-December number, of the Infantry Journal, written apparently by a member of the College Faculty who is also a Captain in the Reserve Corps.

I had in mind writing you some time back, but I now add this reference because the author of the article has quite a bit to say on the subject. I am intensely interested in the sound development of the ROTC and the practical improvement of the Reserve Corps. We have lots of studies available here, but frankly I am interested in the informal opinion of men on the ground like yourself. So I would appreciate the frankness of your reply and I will treat all of it as confidential, just as I will ask you to treat this direct approach to you as confidential.[2]

It is a long time since I have seen you, and therefore a long time since I have heard one of your gorgeous stories. I wish we could get together again, and if you ever come near Washington please let me know in advance.   Faithfully yours,

GCMRL/G. C. Marshall Papers (Pentagon Office, General)

1. Richmond was the Civilian Components Affairs officer at Fourth Corps Area headquarters in Atlanta, Georgia.

2. Marshall sent similar letters to Colonel Hill (printed above), to the officer in charge of R.O.T.C. in the Ninth Corps Area, and to the professor of military science and tactics at Georgetown University in Washington, D.C. The four officers responded quickly and at considerable length. Richmond, the respondent most critical of the essay, thought Blewett was overly critical and impatient. In general, all four men agreed that the War Department was neglecting the R.O.T.C. program, that the corps area Civilian Components Affairs officers were frequently not interested in it, and that something had to be done soon to improve it. None wanted anything resembling the proposed overseeing of R.O.T.C. affairs by a board of Reserve officers in the War Department. Marshall marked these responses "confidential" and sent them to the executive for Reserve Affairs.

MEMORANDUM FOR GENERAL GRUNERT[1]   December 5, 1938
                                                     [Washington, D.C.]

CCC DISTRICT STAFF

I inherited this Staff, except the Educational Advisor, Donald Mace, from General Parsons. All in all, it was the best Staff with which I have ever worked, because it was a homogeneous group gathered together by the stern process of selection and elimination, and naturally aware of the fact that only high efficiency would permit continuance in office.

If you have not worked with the CCC before, and particularly in recent years, your difficulty will be to realize the vast number of considerations which do not appear on paper or in regulations. Here is where the efficiency of the Staff is most evident. The contacts they must have with officials in other government services, with business men, contractors and so forth, are extremely numerous and highly important. A new Staff officer is lost for about six months, as to this phase of the business, to the great disadvantage of the District.

Like all Staffs, they wish to centralize business and to reduce everything to routine. A good bit of this was anathema to me, and I had to find a compromise. This is particularly apparent when it comes to the judicious expenditure of money. Higher government agencies—the Quartermasters and the Finance people—seldom admit consideration of losses in morale due to delays in approving expenditures, or adopting the recommendations of the man on the ground, the Camp Commander. Of course, a more uniform, and possibly economical, result will come from a strictly supervised procedure. But along with such strict supervision goes serious losses in morale, which are not measured in money, except that it frequently required a tremendous expenditure to recover the situation.

I have this suggestion to make: I found the Post officers so completely ignorant of what was going on in the CCC District, so unaware of the tremendous Staff problems handled with high efficiency, that I had the Staff of the CCC prepare a little lecture-demonstration which involved two meetings of an hour and a half each. Though this came towards the end of my tour I learned a good bit from it. So I would suggest that you have Pomerene or Hall arrange to do this for you personally,[2] because it will give you more data and information in two short sessions than you would normally pick up in a year or more.

EDUCATIONAL SERVICE

Mr. Mace is probably about the best District Educational Advisor in the CCC. He is also a splendid Staff officer, though he doesn't wear uniform. He is an excellent publicity man. He has the courage of his convictions, and is loyal when you have made the decision.

We have found the District with a lot of lame ducks as Educational Advisors —sort of "bread ticket" fellows. We raised the standard by eliminating poor men and built up the morale until I think we had a splendid Educational Service. Measured by the number of boys who secured certificates for higher grades, particularly those from the Southeast, and measured by the number of men who worked up to real efficiency in vocational jobs, I think a splendid thing was done for these boys. However, it will not run by mere regulation, because it is all voluntary and comes at the end of a hard day's work. Unless the Staff, and particularly the Camp Commanders, feel that there is no eye-wash about this business, and nothing less than a high standard of performance will be accepted by you, the procedure is rather futile. I regard the educational part of the program as the most important, because the other matters are pretty well routinized, you have no control over the project work, and the educational part does prepare a boy for a job in civil life, which is the real purpose of the CCC. The common tendency is to call for reports, but they don't amount to much and merely divert attention from the real issue, which is performance and results.

SUB-DISTRICT COMMANDERS

I instituted the business of Sub-District Commanders more or less over the protest of the entire Staff and with the reluctant approval of Corps Area Headquarters. To me, the thing was fundamental, the very bedrock of any military organization. Centralized control over a large number of camps, scattered over a wide area, is all right on a fair day, but all wrong in a storm. The Staff would like to saddle various reports on the Sub-District Commanders. I opposed this in every way, though I finally permitted an inspection of funds and books every other month. The diaries of the Sub-District Commanders were helpful, but were growing into lengthy reports which I think the Sub-District Commanders felt they must submit to keep on the good side of the Staff. In all this business the Staff wanted everything done the same way, while I wanted—with the necessary limitations as to ordinary matters of administration—the Sub-Districts and the camps to somewhat express the leadership and personality of their respective commanders.

INSPECTIONS

I have found in the CCC that it is very important in all inspections to have the camp officers feel that your main purpose is to help them. While I was pretty ruthless about getting rid of the poor fish, I felt, on the other hand, that it was highly important to build up confidence and trust on the part of the others whose commissions—or livelihood—are at your mercy. Camp officers live a very isolated life and have an amazing complicaton of difficulties to meet. The boys as groups differ widely. They require totally different methods of handling. I have found that all respond in remarkably fine fashion to almost any desire, once they have confidence that you are trying to help them and not being merely hard-boiled.

GENERAL POLICIES

As the CCC has grown older, of course, the regulations and policies have increased in number. Where I found it difficult was in planning matters so as to produce a uniform standard of service. For example, as simple a matter as the use of white paint would be objected to as unnecessary. Yet it is very necessary in the long dull rainy season for boys unaccustomed to that climate. It is not necessary out in the plains east of the Cascades. So it is difficult to meet the demands of a policy which admits only of uniformity in conditions.

Then too, conditions in one camp are very much more difficult than in another. Therefore, I always struggled to give the poor camp the advantage in money and other services, which were not so necessary to other camps. For example, a camp of local boys who practically all week-end at home does not require nearly the recreational facilities as the isolated camps—like that southeast of Bend—where the boys are from distant parts of the country and wholly unaccustomed to the locality.

I found the CCC the most instructive service I have ever had, and the most interesting. The results one could obtain were amazing and highly satisfying—and they have it all over the results one endeavors to obtain here at a desk.

POST MATTERS

So far as the regiment is concerned, I tried to treat it like I was in another county—just as far from it as I was from the Fourth Infantry. If anything, the troops are usually over-trained so far as routine matters go. My concern would have been to give the lieutenants more of a show. We have too much rank. I found I could have little effect on the troops at Wright and Missoula. The last mentioned certainly need your sympathetic interest. Whitley has made a tremendous improvement out there in living conditions and morale,[3] and he needs your hearty support towards getting WPA and other money, which none of the higher Army Staffs are enthusiastic about because they all are thinking only of the abandonment of the Post. Politically it can't be abandoned, though we tried to trade it off the other day—this is confidential.

Sweeney was telling me yesterday that he wanted to fly in bombers the Missoula garrison over to Lewis. I think that would be a fine thing to do and it would give those isolated boys a great kick.

As to Post installations and problems, we had things pretty well fixed up when I left, but I believe you can get much more WPA money if you go after it strong with the State people. Wilson, here in the Budget Section, suggests that we try to put up small buildings, like tool houses and things of that nature, out of WPA funds. Larger buildings, of course, cannot be built as there is not enough money for material. If you can open up a stone quarry out there, then it is possible to do a lot of building. It took me almost a year to get any WPA funds, and then we ran it up to something over $300,000. I thought here I had you a new double barrack, a warehouse, and a couple of quarters, but it got chiseled out before it reached there. However, I have my eye on it.

I was particularly interested in getting the Liberty Theatre organized so that the men had some place to go for amusement in the evenings during the long rainy winter, and I hope that goes forward on that basis and is not entirely committed to basketball. I also hope that they do not try to make it a money-making enterprise but then spend all the profits for lighting up and brightening up the building. You will find this the best recruiting agency that you have.

I had an excellent Chaplain who did tremendously fine work among the married personnel and generally among the soldiers. He worked fourteen hours a day at it, and completely relieved me of those considerations. The maintaining of a room at the hospital where women and children could be treated, I regarded of great importance—because otherwise the people were being overwhelmed with debt for medical services, to the great loss of morale.

From Camp Bonneville and in the North Woods we got a great deal of fire wood for the married soldiers. Whether you can do this again this year I don't know but, with the slow promotion, you have splendid men as sergeants who have had many years of service and who are without the right to allowances for quarters. I used to find them all Saturday afternoon and most of Sunday during the winter, week in and week out, sawing and chopping wood in the North Woods. Old sergeants with eighteen to twenty years' service, fine men. Fortunately, with the WPA and the CCC company at Camp Bonneville, I was able to get wood for them. Whether you can manage it or not I don't know, but out in the Northwest it is pretty important.

CIVILIAN CONTACTS

Flap Adams has a list, I think, of practically every body with whom I was in contact. I had to build up almost all my contacts in Portland, as there were practically none when I went there.

First, I would suggest that you call on Governor Martin, with your Aide, and have your wife drive down with you and call at the same time on Mrs. Marshall [*Martin*]. Then I would suggest that you call on Major General George White, at the Adjutant General's office in Salem. You can waive formalities and call on him first.

Then call on Joe Carson, Mayor of Portland. Joe is a fine fellow and he can be of great help.

Over in Vancouver the Mayor undoubtedly will call on you, and Adams can give you the other names. They are nice plain people in Vancouver who are very responsive, and the contact furnishes a good base of departure for influencing the Washington senators who are only interested in the military activities of the northern part of the State.

In Portland there are about three groups of people to consider: The official ones, the head of the Military Order of the World War, the head of the Reserve Regiments, Judge (Flap will give you his name) who is a retired Reserve officer, and other similar people. Then, the middle-aged group, who are gay and interesting and very pleasant—the Hamilton Corbetts, the Smiths, and about a dozen other couples whose names I can't remember but who are very agreeable.

Then, there is an older group which I think it is important for you to know—Doctor and Mrs. Fenton, the Peter Kerrs, Mrs. Tom Kerr, Miss Failing (about 75 and will talk your ear off), the Ainsworths, president of the big bank, and others whose names I cannot recall.

I think it highly desirable that Mrs. Grunert accept membership in the Town Club. It is a delightful women's club which she can use to advantage, and the contacts are valuable.

In this connection, I think it is important to have one of your Post Staff represented in the Chamber of Commerce and another in the Junior Chamber of Commerce in Vancouver. Baumeister and Nave used to be these two representatives.[4]

This is a very hurried memorandum, but it may be of some help. However, I must ask you not to quote me, even to your wife.

GCMRL/G. C. Marshall Papers (Pentagon Office, Selected)

1. George Grunert had risen from the rank of private in 1898, to lieutenant colonel in the General Staff Corps (1921–24), to brigadier general in 1936. He had recently been relieved of duty in the Philippines to take Marshall's former command at Vancouver Barracks, Washington. He wrote to Marshall to ask his advice regarding C.C.C. matters and for "a memorandum touching on important matters that need most attention, and projects which you had in mind for the future, and those which were prominent when you left and had not time to finish. Also, advise me as to the people I should contact in the best interests of the [C.C.C.] District and the Post." (Grunert to Marshall, November 29, 1938, GCMRL/G. C. Marshall Papers [Pentagon Office, Selected].) This memorandum was inclosed in a brief letter (not printed) from Marshall to Grunert of the same date.

2. Captain Joel D. Pomerene, Seventh Infantry, was the adjutant and public relations officer for the C.C.C. District. Captain Lester H. Hall, Infantry Reserve, was personnel adjutant and welfare officer.

3. Colonel F. Langley Whitley (U.S.M.A., 1908) had been an officer of the Twenty-fourth

Infantry at Fort Benning from August, 1932, until May, 1933. He then served as a military attache in Yugoslavia, Greece, and Rumania until May, 1937. Since that time, he had been commanding officer at Fort Missoula, Montana.

4. Captain Theodore A. Baumeister, of the Quartermaster Corps, had attended the 1927–28 Company Officers' Course at the Infantry School. First Lieutenant William L. Nave (U.S.M.A., 1929) was assigned to the Seventh Infantry.

NOTES FOR THE CHIEF OF STAFF   December 7, 1938
                                                                [Washington, D.C.]

Meeting with Major Generals at 10:00 A.M. Thursday, December 8, 1938.

Reserve Corps Affairs

Reserve Corps affairs are handled somewhat differently in each Corps Area, though in keeping with general War Department policy. However, the efficiency of the results apparently finally depends very largely on the intimate scheme for promoting this activity. General Thompson, Executive for Reserve Affairs, was much impressed by the arrangements in the Fifth Corps Area, so I am asking Van Voorhis here to give us a brief statement of just how he goes about this particular phase of the business.[1]

Married Enlisted Men

We have had up for final consideration the last few days recommendations as to a new War Department regulation regarding the handling of the married question among the enlisted men. Of course, like everything else of this kind, the proposed result is considerable of a compromise—you know what I think of a compromise, though it is unavoidable in this instance.

The most important stipulations in the proposed revision are:

1. No man with dependents will be accepted for original enlistment.

2. Marriage will not affect re-enlistment of those in the first three grades.

3. Corps Area Commanders may authorize, in worthy cases, the marriage of 4th grade men with eight years' service, and air mechanics. This takes the decision from local commanders. Incidentally, there is a saving clause to protect the rights now possessed by married men in the service, provided the enlisted man can maintain his dependents on his pay.

4. The enlistment contract will contain an agreement by the individual that he will not marry except under the conditions of the new regulations. No man will be accepted for enlistment or re-enlistment conditional upon any implied promise to allot part of his pay to any person.

5. Finally, in the future, soldiers who marry without authority will be immediately discharged.

General Sweeney has some very definite views with regard to this matter, particularly as relates to classifying a certain group of soldiers as "professional", who would thereby be entitled to be married regardless of rank.

Including the 4th grade with eight years' service has been our effort to meet this view.

New Legislation

The papers have much to say about an enlarged program for National Defense. Unfortunately, I cannot talk this over with you at this time. I merely mention this to explain why I can't answer any questions.

New Construction

It is desired that as much necessary construction be secured through WPA and PWA funds as it is possible to arrange for. Here, again, we are impressed in the War Department by the difference in results obtained in various Corps Areas, both as to the amount of funds secured for construction or similar purposes, and especially as to the efficiency with which the various projects are organized and carried through. The difficulties seem to reflect two opposite points of view. In some Posts or Corps Areas there has been, undoubtedly, the reaction that the War Department has delayed approval of projects to such an extent as to jeopardize the particular enterprise. On the other hand,—and this is the item I would like particularly to call your attention to—it is evident in the War Department that instructions regarding the methods to be followed in submitting projects of this nature have been very carelessly observed, with the result that so much essential data is omitted that approval has to be delayed until we can secure the complete statement of the essential facts regarding the project.

I would like to see as much advantage taken of these funds for the benefit of the Army as possible, so I wish you would make certain that your Staff and various commanders understand the requirements in order that there may be no more of the delays to which I have referred.

ROTC

I am told that in some quarters there is a feeling developing among college authorities that the War Department is not sufficiently interested in the further development of the ROTC; that our support of this activity is not strong enough; and that its future is somewhat imperiled. Now, there is no question about the tremendous value of the ROTC. We do lack officers in sufficient numbers for this activity; we lack funds for the creation of new units; and we have little in assistance that we can give existing units. We have increased the number of men permitted to take the Advanced Courses, but we have no available funds for further additions.

The War Department regards the ROTC as one of the most valuable adjuncts to our personnel problem for National Defense. Everything possible should be done to give it encouragement. I merely mention this matter in view of the critical attitude to which I refer.

Training

I think the training of the Army, particularly as to field work, has developed steadily during the past few years, and this preceding season was no exception.

However, I think it is of great importance that we find more economical methods for much more extensive training activities. The Navy has a great advantage in not having to hire an ocean, or to assemble the fleet from forty-nine different States. But we must constantly work on the problem of how to assemble and train large bodies of troops without prohibitive expense, and over varied terrain permitting of wide turning movements or the rapidity of motorized movements that we now contemplate.

I am wondering if a region dotted with governmental tracts, like the National Forests such as we find up and down the West Coast, would not lend itself to inexpensive maneuvers off the reservations. Benning offers a very fine concentration point in the Southeast, where large bodies of troops can be brought together with a minimum of expense.

I think we must progress more rapidly along this particular line, and I am hoping that some of our younger officers may come forward with an acceptable economical solution. I think the main trouble is, we feel that we cannot do anything out of sight of the Post water tower.

GCMRL/G. C. Marshall Papers (Pentagon Office, Selected)
1. Major General Daniel Van Voorhis commanded the Fifth Corps Area.

To Lieutenant Colonel Frederick Palmer[1]   December 8, 1938
Confidential   [Washington, D.C.]

Dear Palmer: I received your note of November twenty-third, with the proposal of Hawthorne Daniel regarding the development of the ROTC idea to produce trained Reserve officers.[2] The matter was carefully gone over in the related Section of the General Staff, and General Craig replied yesterday, either to you or to Mr. Daniel, I have forgotten which, as to the difficulties in the plot. What he said I concur in, so there is no point to repetition here.

I might add this—the ROTC at present is, I think, the most valuable personnel asset in our National Defense scheme. Also, at present it suffers from lack of funds to a serious extent, which is producing unfavorable comments from college authorities. Here are the facts: We are so short of officers that we cannot give nearly enough to the existing ROTC units, which means that the course of instruction is seriously hampered by the tremendous numbers of boys or men that a single officer has to handle each day.

I will give you some concrete examples. Following the Communistic—anti-ROTC demonstrations at the University of Chicago several years ago, the University of Illinois ROTC swelled the following term from twenty-five hundred to thirty-five hundred boys. Now this was a splendid answer to the University of Chicago demonstration, but we could not give them an additional officer to help instruct this tremendous increase in numbers. As a matter of fact, we have had to cut down the number of officers at the ROTC plants in schools below the college grade. Culver, for instance, has only one Regular officer where it used to have a number; yet it has a large group of splendid young fellows taking intensive military instruction.

Then, there is the limitation of funds which restricts us as to the number of boys we can carry in the Advanced Course. The first year in some colleges is compulsory, in others voluntary, but in all a large group of men. Following that, a drastic selection has to be made, due to lack of funds to carry a larger number through the remaining two years' schedule of instruction, including the six months' intensive training camp. A number of costs are involved in this,—the daily ration allowance, the clothing allowance, equipment, more precise instruction which means more instructors, ammunition for target practice—which is a considerable item in Field Artillery units—etc., etc.

Our situation at the present time compels us to refuse to accept any new units, though a large number of schools and colleges wish to create an ROTC department. We simply have not the money.

My particular job includes all budget questions and it is a continuous matter of robbing Peter to pay Paul. In one sense, the Army runs on a shoe-string.

General Craig, in his letter, referred to the possible attitude towards a strongly militarized unit such as that suggested by Mr. Daniel. I think this is a serious objection because we are in a continual battle with the people who resent any form of military instruction. In the CCC we are barred from every form of military instruction and have to maintain discipline by what you might call remote control. Until a few months ago the boys in the CCC did not even have to get up, and few of them did get up, when you would come into their barrack or other room to inspect. Now, when an eighteen year old, undeveloped lunk can sit on the small of his back, with his feet on the table, during the inspection of that particular room by a General commanding that district, you can see how far we have to go to avoid antagonizing a large number of people. I might say, very privately, that they didn't sit on the small of their back around me—but the regulations were quite another affair.

I must ask you not to quote me, but you and Mr. Daniel are interested in a very important matter and I want you to know that your interest is deeply appreciated and will be given every consideration. Faithfully yours,

GCMRL/G. C. Marshall Papers (Pentagon Office, General)

1. Palmer was a well-known writer and military correspondent. During the World War he had had staff assignments with the A.E.F. For General Pershing's opinion of Palmer's book *Newton D. Baker: America at War,* see above, pp. 375–76.

2. Daniel, managing editor of *The Commentator* (New York City), a monthly journal of essays on political and social issues, proposed that the War Department erect military dormitories at selected colleges to accommodate a special corps of scholastically and physically qualified college-age men who would enlist in the Regular Army, receive military and scholastic training for four years at army expense, receive Reserve officer's commissions upon graduation, and be required to maintain that status for ten years. This, he supposed, would in time create a large body of well-trained officers while avoiding the deficiencies of the World War training camp system.

Left to right: Colonel John B. Brooks, Brigadier General Barton K. Yount (assistant to the chief of the Air Corps), Marshall, and Major General Frank M. Andrews, at Randolph Field, Texas, August 17, 1938.

Deputy Chief of Staff Marshall testifies before the House Committee on Military Affairs in support of the Roosevelt Administration's proposed defense budget, January 19, 1939.

The army chief of staff and his assistants. Seated left to right: Major General Stanley D. Embick, deputy chief of staff; General Malin Craig, chief of staff; Brigadier General Lorenzo D. Gasser, G-1. Standing left to right: Brigadier General George P. Tyner, G-4; Brigadier General Robert McC. Beck, Jr., G-3; Brigadier General George C. Marshall, WPD; Colonel E. R. Warner McCabe, G-2. Washington, D.C., September 28, 1938.

Marshall's reception in a Brazilian city; early June, 1939. (Marshall is the saluting figure on the right near the front of the black automobile in the center.)

Marshall and General Monteiro at a Brazilian Embassy reception in Washington, D.C., June 21, 1939. Standing is Brazilian military attache Major Jose Biana Machado. Seated are General Pedro Aurelio de Goes Monteiro, Brazil's army chief of staff, and Marshall.

Retiring Chief of Staff Malin Craig congratulates Marshall, who is to become acting chief of staff on July 1, 1939.

669

To Lieutenant Colonel Truman Smith   December 8, 1938
                                                                [Washington, D.C.]

Dear Smith: I was very glad to receive your letter of November twentieth, and tremendously impressed by the news regarding von Schell, to whom I have just written a note as suggested by you. His selection is another indication of the current advantages of that particular form of Government, and it is conspicuous evidence of the wisdom with which they choose their leaders. I am delighted that von Schell has risen to such important posts, and I agree with you that his future may reach the highest military altitude.[1]

I have noted your desires regarding assignment and I will do what I can to bring about an acceptable job and station.[2] While I have not looked into the matter yet, I know that other Lieutenant Colonels here in the War Department— Gerow, for instance, have been denied troop assignments because they have had three years in the past twelve, or something of that sort. Gerow is being sent to Benning on the Infantry Board, because he could not get another station.[3]

Incidentally, I am told that if one picks out a very unpopular Post he usually can get it. If this is the case, feel towards Fort Francis E. Warren at Cheyenne? The Artillery people tell me they can always get troops if they will choose that Post. I admit it would be a tremendous contrast to Berlin, and I must comment on the despair of the wife of the present Commanding Officer at Fort Missoula,[4] who proceeded there direct from Budapest, I believe. I am talking about Mrs. Whitley, a lovely Greek, who sees no charm in the mountain scenery, the high winds, and the local populace. She told me her dinner partner the other day was the undertaker. Whitley, however, is doing great things there and is making quite a reputation for himself.

Fort Lincoln, North Dakota, is another spot that usually goes begging. I looked at it from the air the other day but only know the ground conditions from gossip and rumor. They say it is a sad spot, and I have found it rather interesting to make over such blemishes.

Would you be interested in Leavenworth, or a staff position with troops—the Third Division or the Second Division? Let me hear from you very frankly. I will regard what you say as confidential.

With warm regards to Mrs. Smith and yourself, and thanks for your letter, Faithfully yours,

P.S.   The data regarding German air personnel was very interesting. I had G-2 ask the questions for me while I was head of War Plans Division.

GCMRL/G. C. Marshall Papers (Pentagon Office, General)

1. Smith had written that a few lines of congratulations from Marshall would please von Schell greatly and "help my position immensely." Von Schell had just been promoted to colonel, appointed head of the German automobile industry, inspector of Tank Corps, and inspector of Army Mobilization. His rise "has been so meteoric in the last two years that it almost staggers one." (Smith to Marshall, November 20, 1938, GCMRL/G. C. Marshall Papers [Pentagon Office, General].)

2. He would be coming back to the United States in August, 1939, Smith wrote. "I have grown very tired mentally this year and shall need a very regular and active physical life for about a year after I get home. . . . You may believe me when I say that the Military Attache job in Germany in the last two or three years has been no lead pipe cinch. We have lived more or less on a volcano here and the strain on one's nerves has been tremendous." (Ibid.)

3. Lieutenant Colonel Leonard T. Gerow (V.M.I., 1911) had served in the Office of the Chief of Infantry from February, 1921, until July, 1923. Between May, 1936, and March, 1939, he served as executive officer of the War Plans Division.

4. Colonel F. Langley Whitley.

MEMORANDUM FOR THE CHIEF OF STAFF   December 9, 1938
Washington, D.C.

Field Training.

You commented the other morning to the General Officers of the Eligible List Board on the necessity for larger and more economical maneuvers. A satisfactory solution to the problem involves many ramifications, which I would like to discuss in writing and then orally, with a view, at some later and less crowded date, of having a study made on the subject.

PRESENT SITUATION:

In the first place, practically no military reservation today is sufficiently large to permit of the type of maneuvers which I believe are essential to the development of tactics, technique, and leadership. Motorization, mechanization, and planes have spread military problems all over the map, as it were.

———

Next in order, the law and regulations governing the leasing of ground have been drawn up, I believe,—though I have not investigated this in the War Department—from the viewpoint of the convenience and certainty of administrative procedure at Corps Area and War Department headquarters, rather than with the primary object of facilitating field maneuvers. If I am correct, this would mean that we are limiting the development of training and tactics, for the convenience of distant staffs and for the too secure protection of higher officials from possible reclamas.

The complications involved in this are numerous. I can elaborate on them orally.

———

Next, there is the cost of concentrations, and the time consumed. I do not know what can be done about this, but it should be studied. Offhand, I am inclined to the idea that for short hauls box cars are sufficient for the purpose of moving troops. What the legal involvements are I do not know, but I do not imagine they are beyond cure. Anyway, too much money is tied up in this phase of the business.

671

Along with this goes the cost of assembling officers for a variety of special jobs, the creation of temporary staffs, etc. I think we must turn to the air for economies in this direction. The flying is done as a matter of practice, so in one sense the passenger costs nothing.

FUTURE DEVELOPMENT:

The necessary terrain should be acquired on some form of lease permitting the right to trespass, including a simple method for determining damages and making immediate settlement on the ground for those under certain amounts, and not involving disputes. Leases in quintuplicate and other time-consuming and irritating procedures should be studied with a view to their simplification. The law, I think, should be changed to accomplish some of these purposes, certainly to give an Army Commander more authority than he now possesses, and to remove from the War Department the restriction on the settlement of damages, except in extraordinary cases. In other words, everything should be done to make it a simple matter to acquire the right of trespass from the property owners. I have done this personally on a large scale, and therefore I know it can be done satisfactorily.

The timing of large maneuvers should be made to fit in with other activities, which should be included. For example, the ROTC would receive tremendous impetus if the Advanced Students in the region where Army maneuvers are being conducted, serve their last two weeks of field training attached to various Headquarters units as orderlies, couriers, and scouts, and to combat organizations with the Headquarters group.

Large maneuvers should be so arranged that the strategical and tactical approaches can be considered in the winter instruction of the National Guard and the Reserve. Temporary commands and staffs should be completed in skeleton form months before the maneuvers in order that a team will take the field, rather than a disturbing group of hastily assembled officers. The more brilliant the officer the more dangerous he becomes in an improvised headquarters.

Again, this subject has too many involvements to burden you on paper. I can cover it orally.

The business of umpiring needs re-doing to put it on a more practical basis. It is entirely too ponderous, requires too many people, is therefore too expensive, and ignores too largely the importance of flash decisions. The procedure has been reduced to a mathematical formula. That may be all right for calculating ship gun firing, but it completely ignores the surprise element, the uncertainty factors of military contacts in open warfare. This has particular application to mechanized forces, bombing, artillery and machine gun concentrations in rear areas. It is important that we develop a device for conveying information of distant machine gun fire, and for portraying artillery fire in the rear areas other than by impractical telephonic or radio procedure. The life in the rear of the front line is going to be a devastating business, as to nerves and judgment. We cannot afford to have our training regulations ignore this factor.

———

To sum up, I think we are too ponderous and too infrequent in our maneuver efforts; that we are too limited as to terrain and play too much on the home grounds; that we do not obtain sufficient appropriations for this vitally important business; that a determined effort must be made to amend laws, change regulations, and evolve systems which will enable us to offset the present theoretical training (due to too many desks and details, mostly unavoidable) in order that the Army may properly train for its real purpose, as a matter of annual routine.[1]

G. C. Marshall

NA/RG 407 (353 [12-9-38])

1. Marshall's idea was "100% sound and a change is vitally needed," Malin Craig wrote on a note attached to the original document. "Let's go to it."

To Brigadier General Leigh R. Gignilliat   December 10, 1938
[Washington, D.C.]

Dear Gignilliat: Lieutenant Colonel Harold R. Bull, Infantry, now Secretary of the General Staff,—to be relieved next summer—told me yesterday that Paul had been talking to him about possible detail to Culver.[1] Bull wants to go to troops, though doubts whether he can obtain the assignment. I think the Chief of Infantry wants to send him as Instructor at the Infantry School, and Bull would not be very keen about this.

I am telling you that if you can get Bull you will have about the best man in the Army, even better than Paul. He is a small, trim, red-headed fellow, of charming personality; business all over, yet attractive about it; about the most popular instructor I had at Benning, certainly among the most able; understands boys thoroughly, and practically had charge of a boys' camp in Vermont for three or four seasons, utilizing his academic leave from Benning. I would pick him as Chief of Staff of an Army, so certainly he ought to be good enough for Culver.

I have been talking to Bull about the business, and I think he is trying to find out definitely from the Office of the Chief of Infantry whether or not they will give him a troop assignment.

I am passing this on to you for your information.   Faithfully yours,

GCMRL/G. C. Marshall Papers (Pentagon Office, Selected)

1. Bull (U.S.M.A., 1914) had been an instructor at the Infantry School between August, 1928, and July, 1932. When Marshall arrived at the War Department in mid-1938, Bull was in

the Statistics Branch of the Office of the Chief of Staff. From November 10, 1938, to July 2, 1939, he was secretary of the General Staff. The "Paul" mentioned is Major Willard S. Paul—in 1929–30 a student in the Infantry School's Advanced Course—who was in the Adjutant General's Department.

To Brigadier General Philip B. Peyton   December 12, 1938
                                                         [Washington, D.C.]

Dear Buster: I was about to write you a Christmas note when your gracious letter of November twenty-second arrived this morning. You always do the delightful thing in the delightful manner, and I welcome such communications because they promote morale and smooth over the rough edges. You need have no fear that I am going to run myself ragged. I ceased doing real onerous work a long time ago and, as I read pretty rapidly and make up my mind even more so, I think I can economize considerably on the time requirements of the job.[1]

At a dinner at the Army Navy Country Club the other night R. C. Marshall was present.[2] The host was his nephew, Geoffrey Marshall, so there was plenty of VMI spirit. I hear a great deal of that Institute these days. I am sorry I could not go up there for the last game of the season. "Stow" Stuart wanted us to drive up with himself and his wife, but I could not get away. They struck miserable weather, and Mrs. Stuart was stormbound there with the car, while he returned to New York by rail. He is quite successful and, confidentially, is in the market now for the Ambassadorship to Russia. I wouldn't be surprised to see him get it. McIntyre, the President's Secretary, is a close friend, and he has a great many prominent backers—and unlimited nerve. I admire him very much, and he certainly is generously disposed towards me.[3]

I envy you your delightful climate and peaceful surroundings, and daily duties. You are very fortunate. We live at 2118 Wyoming Avenue, in the Embick's house. It is just two doors off Connecticut and very convenient to the office.

With my most affectionate regards to you both,   Faithfully yours,

GCMRL/G. C. Marshall Papers (Pentagon Office, Selected)

1. Peyton, at this time commanding the Hawaiian Separate Coast Artillery Brigade at Fort DeRussy, Hawaii, wrote: "If you are going to stay behind that desk and attempt to handle every detail yourself, you have undertaken an extremely hard task. I should regret extremely to hear that you had become a slave to a job that might possibly prove to be extremely detrimental to your health. I certainly hope that you will have ample time for exercise and recreation because when the time comes I want to see you go straight to the top where I have many times predicted you would finally land." (Peyton to Marshall, November 22, 1938, GCMRL/G. C. Marshall Papers [Pentagon Office, Selected].)

2. Richard C. Marshall had been a Regular Army officer from 1902 to 1920, reaching the rank of brigadier general during the World War. He was a construction engineer and lived in Chicago, Illinois.

3. Charles E. Stuart (V.M.I., 1901) was a construction engineer. He had been a consultant to the government of the U.S.S.R. (1926–32), a director of the American-Russian Chamber of Commerce, executive vice-president of the Export-Import Bank of Washington, D.C., (1934–36), and had numerous other duties pertaining to foreign trade.

MEMORANDUM[1]   December 14, 1938
                                                       [Washington, D.C.]

Every discussion of the new defense program seems to involve this question, "Why did not the War Department long ago make known these tremendous deficiencies in Ordnance weapons, ammunition, and similar items?" It did, and here is the explanation of the present misunderstandings:

First, the present world situation and the recent restatement of the Monroe Doctrine introduced new factors into our military problem, which everyone admits demand increased means of defense.

However, the reasons why we find ourselves at the present time so seriously lacking in materiel, and in personnel, are these:

The Chiefs of Staff, year in and year out, have stated our necessities in general terms, and have testified to them before Committees of Congress. In loyal deference to the current administrative policy, they have tempered their language, and held their requests for funds within the limits of the total sum allotted to the War Department.

The War Department devotes about ten months to the preparation of the estimates for the annual Army appropriations. An increase over the preceding year's appropriation is usually found inadvisable, and requests for similar amounts are frequently pared down by the Bureau of the Budget in the Treasury Department to meet the requirements of the general directive regarding the grand total of annual appropriations. National and international considerations govern in this matter, the Executive making the initial decision, and Congress taking final action.

Reductions in the War Department estimates are often made by the Bureau of the Budget, and here we find the most important reason why we are short of vital munitions. The War Department administers the Army on a parsimonious basis. Unlike the Navy Department, it has many, varied and powerful interests outside of the small regular army: A National Guard of 210,000, a Reserve Corps of 120,000, an ROTC of 165,000, and an annual month of CMTC for about 40,000 young men. In addition, are the requirements of industrial mobilization, which cost money. Therefore the Department must trim its sails with meticulous attention to matters of economy wherever possible. So, when the Bureau of the Budget is required to trim the Army estimates, there is literally no fat meat available. You cannot well cut rations and you cannot easily cut pay; it is difficult to deny adequate housing to people living in tents, as some Army units did for more than ten years after the war; and the pressure, political and otherwise, from the various States, numerous Associations, and the heads of the colleges and universities with ROTC units, all combine to make an extremely difficult matter of the allocation of funds. The Bureau of the Budget, therefore, finds itself reduced to the necessity of eliminating items involving materiel. So, year after year, we receive but a small percentage of our necessities for munitions, until today we find ourselves in the present predicament.

For example, in the current budget of the War Department, the preparation of which started almost a year ago, less than 9% of the requirements in munitions for our mobilization necessities, are included, but even so, there have been cuts.

In times like these, the habit of the press is to point to this person or to that person on which to pin the fault. The fact of the matter is, the fault lies with the general public. They are not interested until a crisis arises, and even then the particular matter must have some dramatic appeal, such as the photograph of a line of battleships, or of a squadron of huge bombing planes, or of the tragedy of women and children being bombed in Spain or China. The public reacts to these with a specific demand for planes and for anti-aircraft artillery, but they are not interested in Army Ordnance—field artillery, anti-tank guns, automatic rifles, powder, etc.—which are the vital necessities at the present date if there is to be modern equipment available for our peace time army and its first war increment.

GCMRL/G. C. Marshall Papers (Pentagon Office, Selected)

1. There is no addressee on this memorandum, and it may not have been sent to anyone. It was probably precipitated by Assistant Secretary of War Johnson's letter of December 10 to Chief of Staff Craig. Johnson observed that during the next several months the army would have to spend considerable time defending and supporting the new preparedness program. "The study recently submitted to the President gave cost data on a four-point, two-year program consisting of (1) augmentation of air force to 10,000 airplanes of which 50% would be on an operating status; (2) procurement of the equipment, munitions, and supplies essential to the support of the Protective Mobilization Plan Army; (3) aids to industrial mobilization; (4) increases of ground forces to the extent of some 58,000 men for the Regular Army and 35,000 men for the National Guard." Johnson asked Craig to "have prepared for me a justification of the four-point program as submitted to the President." (Copies of Johnson's letter and the reply are in NA/RG 165 [War Plans Division, File 3674].)

MEMORANDUM FOR THE CHIEF OF THE AIR CORPS   December 16, 1938
Secret   Washington, D.C.

Dear Arnold:[1]   In addition to the routine justifications that the Chief of Staff must present at any budget hearings, it will be necessary, in connection with this Two-year Program, to provide him with data to meet the numerous questions which are probably going to be asked. I am listing below requests for some of the data that it seems to me he should have available. And I am addressing you informally, because I would like to have a trial effort made as to the style in which the data might be presented for his use. Then, if that is acceptable, we will go about the business of exact calculations.

So, will you please have some one make a hurried stab at this, using rough estimates only, flash figures as we recently have become fond of saying, and send up the result for General Craig and myself to look over prior to any serious calculations.

I would first like answers to the following questions along with a terse explanation in each pertinent case, as a background for his oral explanations or answers during the hearings.

Here is the list:

1. What is the proper proportion of types of combat aircraft of say, in a block of 1,000? What is this proportion based upon? What tactical and strategical considerations are involved?

2. If we include combat, training and miscellaneous types in a block of 1,000 airplanes, what is the proportion of each? Discuss the proportion of training and miscellaneous types required to combat types.

3. Should the percentages of airplanes in reserve be the same for all types? Discuss the relative needs for reserve of combat types vis-a-vis the need for a reserve of training types.

4. In a block of 1,000 combat airplanes properly balanced as to types, what should be considered a proper rate of obsolescence to maintain this force a modern and effective combat factor? Consider varying rates for the types involved.

5. Based upon the above rate of obsolescence, what replacement in each type which would be required to maintain the Air Corps under the 10,000 airplane program in a state of modern combat efficiency?

6. What do you consider the minimum number of replacements annually required under the 10,000 plane program from the aircraft industry to maintain that industry on a sound basis, both from the standpoint of development and production, which would permit rapid and healthy expansion in a war emergency?

7. To what extent do the two above requirements coincide: Would the satisfaction of these requirements result in a surplus of obsolescent aircraft? If so, how much annually over a period say of five years?

8. Will it be practicable to dispose of these surplus without injury to our aircraft industry? Please give your opinion of the problem with which Germany will be faced in this regard if she does not become involved in war before her present air force begins to become obsolescent. How would this situation affect sales of our obsolescent military aircraft?

9. The cost data on 1,000 planes (50% in reserve), in proper proportion of types in accordance with the general proposal for the 10,000; everything to be

677

included (and items indicated), such as plane crew, ground crew, proportionate number of mechanics in the depots, proportionate number of men in training elsewhere; bombs, if a bombing plane; fuel, hangar space where required, etc. etc. I think the general overhead could be ignored.

10. The same data as above for different types of planes. For example, take a B-17, give its original cost, the cost of the spare parts, the annual maintenance charge, the plane crew, ground crew, the proportionate number of mechanics in the depots, fuel operating cost in training, etc., etc. Also, the same data for that plane if kept in reserve.

11. What is involved in the cost of a military airplane (the B-17 for example)?

    a. The bare airplane.

    b. Airplane spares.

    c. Engines.

    d. Engine spares.

    e. Government furnished equipment—What does it consist of—and where, if any, are the choke points?

    f. Armament (including war reserve of ammunition).

    g. Radio.

12. What do you estimate the annual replacement cost of aircraft to be provided for under the requirement for a modern air force of 10,000 planes and a healthy industry for the 10,000 airplane program.

13. Cost of training a pilot under our present system and under the proposed system—

    a. For pursuit or attack plane purposes.

    b. For the heavy bomber purpose, if different.

You probably have these figures to a certain extent but I want all the factors included so as to get a clean-cut unit cost. I think the wear and tear on pilots should be considered, that is, the percentage of loss to the Service; and of course the original cost for examinations, washouts, etc. etc.

14. In addition to the above, I would like some information on the following points; in connection with the 10,000 airplane program:

    a. To what extent do the personnel provided in the program meet the war requirements of the tactical operating units? Would it be necessary in an emergency to augment this personnel materially? If so, to what extent, and why?

    b. Do you visualize the necessity for dual crews in an emergency?

15. What are our immediate resources in critical personnel, i.e., pilots and mechanics. What is proposed to meet deficiencies in this regard? Will the Air Corps have to train more mechanics and pilots than are necessary for replacements in peace in order that we may have an adequate reserve for war?

16. To what extent can the use of civilian mechanics and pilot schools for preliminary training be utilized for continued peacetime training of Air Corps personnel, and to what extent do you estimate the load on Air Corps facilities could be reduced thereby?

17. What scheme would you propose for the operation of seven government factories during the program? Upon the completion of the program? Where do you believe they should be located, and why?

18. What do you visualize as the future for the labor which will be built up to meet the requirements for accelerated aircraft production in the period of the program?

Could these factories, if they are provided in accordance with the program, be economically and practically utilized after the program is completed, to produce articles which now represent choke points in the production of military aircraft, with a viewpoint of increasing our ability to produce airplanes rapidly in a war emergency?

19. What do you estimate the labor surplus in the industry will be as a result of accelerated production to meet the program and how are these personnel to be utilized when the program is completed and the production drops off?

20. What is the average cost of concrete runways on a modern field?

G. C. Marshall

NA/RG 18 (Office of the Chief of the Air Corps, Library Document File D 00.17)

1. Major General Henry H. Arnold (U.S.M.A., 1907) had been chief of the Air Corps since September, 1938.

To Major General Charles E. Kilbourne[1]   December 19, 1938
[Washington, D.C.]

Dear Kilbourne: I have just read your letter of December seventeenth, and I am disturbed by the fact that you were disturbed over my suggesting the possibility that a temporary shift from a VMI graduate to a West Pointer might be a good thing. Please forget it. Bull knew nothing of my writing you and had no thought whatever regarding VMI; I merely thought that he was so far above almost anyone I know that, when I was reminded of the coming vacancy by the appearance of Burress, my mind immediately turned to Bull.[2]

I might say that it has been in my mind for some time that it would be a good thing at West Point to have a VMI superintendent. However, they never offered it to me, and I imagine it would be "rather disturbing", as you wrote, for them to consider such a possibility. But aside from the personal angle, I think it would be a damn good thing. Somewhat the same line of reasoning prompted my suggestion regarding Bull and you.   Faithfully yours,

GCMRL/G. C. Marshall Papers (Pentagon Office, Selected)

1. General Kilbourne had been superintendent of the Virginia Military Institute since October 1, 1937.

2. Major Withers A. Burress (V.M.I., 1914), the commandant of cadets at V.M.I. since 1935, visited Marshall on December 14, and said that he would probably be relieved soon. Marshall wrote to Kilbourne to recommend Colonel Harold R. Bull as a possible replacement

for Burress: "I picked him out at Benning years ago . . . as one of the two men I would reach for to be my Chief of Staff in case I landed with the high command. . . . I realize he is a West Pointer and not a VMI graduate, but I think an occasional change would be a good thing, and he would be perfect for such purpose." (Marshall to Kilbourne, December 15, 1938, GCMRL/ G. C. Marshall Papers [Pentagon Office, Selected].) Kilbourne responded: "My own feeling is that it is far better to have a V.M.I. graduate if one of the proper characteristics is available. . . . Your feeling that a shift from a V.M.I. graduate to a West Pointer occasionally would be a good thing is rather disturbing because I have such confidence in your judgment." (Kilbourne to Marshall, December 17, 1938, ibid.)

To General John J. Pershing   December 20, 1938
                                                Washington, D.C.

Dear General: I appreciated your letter, and was gratified to learn that my proposal for a note from you to The President had been acceptable. I do not believe you appreciate just how important the results from that may be.[1]

We are hoping that you reached Tucson in fine shape and that you are comfortably settled there. While not exactly Christmasy in appearance, yet I envy you your surroundings for the Christmas season.

I saw in the morning paper the other day that Warren had been in town the night before for the Gridiron Dinner, but I did not get to see him personally. I hope the next time he comes down, or that I go to New York, I can have a talk with him. He is a fine boy.

With my affectionate regards to you and Miss May, and holiday greetings from the Marshall family,   Faithfully yours,

G. C. Marshall

LC/J. J. Pershing Papers (General Correspondence)

1. General Pershing had written: "I signed and sent forward, within a day or two after its receipt, the letter that you had prepared for my signature, but I doubt sincerely whether it will have much effect." (Pershing to Marshall, December 9, 1938, LC/J. J. Pershing Papers [General Correspondence].) The letter Marshall had prepared for Pershing is printed on pp. 654–55.

To General Malin Craig   December 30, 1938
Secret   [Washington, D.C.]

Dear General: Welcome home, I trust in fine spirits and all well with the world.[1]

Lest you be bored over the week-end until the War Department re-opens Tuesday morning, I am sending you some light reading matter in four volumes:

First,—A confidential journal of important conferences I had with the Secretaries.

Second,—Questions and answers in connection with the 10,000 airplane program.

Third,—Questions about special matters concerned with the increased defense program.

Fourth,—Statement of the Chief of Staff and the Secretary of War to Military Sub-committee reference regular military estimates, FY 1940.[2]

I think these will occupy your full time until Tuesday morning. Other papers are being prepared, and these I am giving you are being more carefully worked up against the necessity for their formal employment in the near future.

Everybody in the office is well and all will be delighted to welcome you back. Lee and Parks have been most helpful.[3]   Faithfully yours,

G. C. M.

GCMRL/G. C. Marshall Papers (Pentagon Office, Selected)

1. Craig had been vacationing in Fort Myers, Florida.
2. The following was written on both the original and the carbon copy: "The above papers were destroyed by Col. W. T. Sexton at C/S direction 1/4/44."
3. Major Carnes Lee and Captain Floyd L. Parks.

MEMORANDUM FOR THE CHIEF OF THE AIR CORPS[1]   January 14, 1939
[Washington, D.C.]

Attached is a rough outline of the War Department's plans to carry out the terms of the Presidential message on National Defense of January 12, as a guide for the Chief of Staff in an informal hearing before the House and Senate Military Committees on Tuesday, January 17.[2]

Please rework those portions pertaining to aviation.

As the Military Committee of the House is primarily interested in legislation, rather than appropriation, an additional paragraph should be added outlining— very briefly—the legislative requirements necessary to carry out our plans for aviation.

Also, please attach such lists of special data as you may deem advisable, such as, character and number of permanent structures to be erected at bases, along with a list of temporary buildings also involved.

All must be completed by 11:30 AM, Monday [January 16].

NA/RG 165 (War Plans Division, File 4132)

1. This version of the document was attached to a similar memorandum of the same date addressed to Brigadier General George V. Strong (U.S.M.A., 1904) of the War Plans Division.
2. The president's message is printed in *The Public Papers and Addresses of Franklin D. Roosevelt, 1939,* pp. 70-74. The president asked Congress to appropriate approximately $525,000,000 for the next two years, $450,000,000 of which was for the army. Two-thirds of the army appropriation was for airplane purchases.

To Colonel Morrison C. Stayer   [January 15, 1939]
                                                 Washington, D.C.

Dear Stayer: I have waited until Sunday morning to answer your last letter, and also the question in your preceding letter.[1]

In the first place, I took my physical last Tuesday, unexpectedly and on but a half hours notice.

We have been terribly busy, and I more than most, and involved in difficult conferences with many of importance. Things got so hectic that while we were having a sandwich luncheon in General Craig's office on Tuesday and the conversation got around to the start of the physicals the following afternoon, he remarked that I would never find time then or for some days to come; that he had had his going over the previous day out at Ft. Myer; and that he thought it would be best, and more private for me to do the same thing. Picking up the phone he made the appointment with his friend at Myer—a 1st Division, DSC, lieut. colonel, and a very fine fellow.

This threw out my schedule, as I had just resumed the regular dosage the day before, and planned to go up for my physical a week later, as you all instructed. Also, I intended arranging to take things very quietly the morning of that day. As it was I had had a tumultuous morning, whith much emphatic arguement.

I do not know yet just how I got by. It was the most thoro exam I have had—very well done. He even went up and down my back bone, investigated my prostate gland, and similar unusual details. He found a slight irregularity in my pulse before exercise, and none after exercise. Regular pulse 68; after exercise 88; and a minute or two later 66. Blood pressure 78—132. He remarked that if I wrote my own ticket I could not beat that. Said all organs sound, heart in no way enlarged, arteries in good shape, prostate normal. The only comment was on the irregularity of pulse which he thought was probably due to smoking, until I told him that I no longer smoked. He agreed with me that it was due to too much desk and two little exercise of the type to which I had been accustomed. Said I would have to fight a "desk belly", tho I was pretty well off at the time, being six pounds lighter than when you first saw me, and in better shape, both as to hardness and figure. He told me to try and sit as erect as possible at the desk, something I never do. I rather imagine that he gave me a pretty good report. I will let you know as soon as I hear. I could easily check up on it thru the AGO, but I am not drawing any attention to my thoughts on the subject.[2]

I think that any pulse remark would be credited by Craig as a more or less natural reaction to the really terrific strain of the past three weeks, during which I have had to work like lightening, compromise endless disagreements, sit in on most difficult scenes, etc. The chief burden of the War Department plot has been mine, so I approached my physical under unusually heavy pressure. As a matter of fact, I feel fine and in high spirits—in contrast to most of the others.

I have taken no treatment since the exam and at present, this morning, my pulse is about 70, with slight wavers every twenty or thirty beats, but no intermissions.

Now as to your affairs. I hardly know what to advise as to bringing in outside pressure. In all the cases I hear of here it has merely been an irritant. Unless it is from a very powerful source and to a powerful source, on a most intimate basis, it gets you know where and only seems to do harm. Letters to the President are just sent over for the WD to prepare answers.

I have absolutely nothing to go on, but I am beginning to suspect that Ireland and his associates will exert the greatest influence, and possibly thru the Medical assn. Now it just happens that I think that Assn is not popular at the moment, because of the struggle to set up other medical arrangements which the Administration favors.

Why not try this method or approach: Write frankly to Bob Patterson, refering to the difficult position he put you in at Carlisle, and part of its consequences, and request him to indorse you to the American Medical Assn. Also, if he can find a normal reason for writing to General Craig, to include in it a strong and complimentary reference to you. I fear that a letter for that purpose alone would merely irritate—tho maybe not. In any event, make the strong selling points your outstanding ability as an administrator, as a leader and influencer of morale—your demonstrated ability to handle hospitals and to handle men. Also emphasize your loyalty, to offset in no uncertain terms any implications Dulaney may have spread around.[3]

If there is any one of great influence who stands in with the Administration, that would be willing, on a very personal basis to put in a strong indorsement for you, you might try that.

Another consideration is the timing. I think now it is a little too early, that anything now would give too much the impression of a campaign. You must avoid that; tho what I am advising is a campaign, but one of only two, or at most three blows, and those hard and determined ones. Routine indorsements are to be avoided like the plague.

I fear that I have not been able to be very helpful. Also, there is this possibility, that later on I might be consulted, and if so my lips are sealed from then on. My best advise is to consider the points I suggest to be made in any recommendation of you, and that only powerful sources should be brought into this.

I sent you a photograph the other day, which I hope reached you all right. It is very handsome, if you view it as a mother.

Give my best regards to Mrs. Stayer, and believe me, Faithfully,

G. C. M.

GCMRL/M. C. Stayer Papers; T

1. Neither of these letters is in the Marshall papers.

2. Marshall was examined by Lieutenant Colonel Albert W. Kenner. Marshall was five feet, eleven and three-quarters inches tall (without shoes) and weighed 175 pounds.

3. Stayer was seeking a new station. The nature of the problem in which he became embroiled while stationed at Carlisle Barracks, Pennsylvania, in the early 1930s is not known, but it involved the current (1931–35) army surgeon general, Major General Robert U. Patterson, and the former (1918–31) surgeon general, Major General Merritte W. Ireland.

To General John J. Pershing

January 16, 1939
Washington, D.C.

Dear General: I feel sure when you read The President's message that you must have appreciated the importance of your contribution in this matter. Some time I want to go over all the details with you, but for the moment you can judge from the message what has happened. Let us hope that out of this will come genuine and lasting advantage to the National Defense. Speaking for those who know nothing of what you did, and would be eternally grateful if they did understand what had happened, I want to thank you rather formally for going out of your way and troubling yourself to assist us.

I learned from Adamson that things are going well with you. He turned over the other day some tickets to the National Geographic Society, which I understand you had told him to make available for Mrs. Marshall and myself. We went to the lecture and greatly enjoyed it, and she has asked me to thank you particularly for your thoughtfulness—in which I join.

I have just completed a statement for the Secretary of War to make before the Military Committee of the House tomorrow morning, the first War Department hearing regarding the new National Defense program. He and General Craig and myself go up there at ten-thirty, and at three in the afternoon appear before the Senate Military Committee. Of course, this is only a preliminary hearing, for the general orientation of the Committee members before they go to work on the details. I will be interested in their reactions. Judging from the press there will be not nearly so much opposition as was anticipated, but undoubtedly there will be decided opposition.

I was very sorry to see the New York papers starting discussions as to the next Chief of Staff, in which my name was mentioned. I suppose this is inevitable but it certainly is distasteful to me—and I think not at all helpful.

We received your Christmas telegram, and New Year's and, I believe birthday greetings from Miss May. Mrs. Marshall gave me a surprise party on New Year's Eve—my birthday—which did not break up until three in the morning. We had six members of the family with us during the holidays, quite a houseful.

I wrote Warren that his office announcement card was very striking in the name, number, street, and city—Pershing, No. 1 Wall Street, New York City. I want to try to see Warren in New York when I go up for the First Division Dinner, for which I am Toastmaster. Incidentally, if you have any little personal message I could give the officers of that Division, it would give me great satisfaction to present it in my opening remarks.

With affectionate regards to you both,   Faithfully yours,

G. C. Marshall

LC/J. J. Pershing Papers (General Correspondence)

TO RUFUS C. HOLMAN   January 18, 1939
                                                     [Washington, D.C.]

My dear Senator Holman: I have just received your note of January sixteenth, with the copies of letters from Judge Kanzler and Muthersbaugh of the Portland Chamber of Commerce regarding Vancouver Barracks.[1] I will probably see you this afternoon when I accompany General Craig to a hearing of the Military Committee of the Senate, but in any event I will get in touch with you regarding the details of this matter as soon as they come up.

I might say now, without having seen their proposed plans, that it all is a matter of priorities—that is, which post needs the buildings most; and in view of the present defense program of the President, I fear that all the money for shelter will go for new Air Corps installations and those required for anti-aircraft and seacoast defenses in Panama. Certainly the War Department will, under the terms of the President's program, have to give first priority to those matters. However, I can talk this over with you when I see you and when I know more of the details of the plot.

I might say that I have the deepest interest in the development of Vancouver Barracks. When I went there, I found a garrison which had not had a new building provided by the Government for thirty-three years, and before I left we had gotten an appropriation for sixteen non-commissioned officers' quarters, and about three hundred thousand dollars in WPA money. With the latter fund I reconditioned the post and got it in excellent shape, with many improvements to boost morale. The completion of these non-commissioned officers' quarters will, of course be important assistance to that effect.[2]   Faithfully yours,

GCMRL/G. C. Marshall Papers (Pentagon Office, Selected)

1. A native of Portland, Holman was the newly elected Republican senator from Oregon and a member of the Senate Military Affairs Committee. Holman's letter to Marshall of January 16 inclosed copies of letters from Phil H. Muthersbaugh, secretary of the Portland Chamber of Commerce's Council of National Defense, and Judge Jacob Kanzler of the Circuit Court of Oregon.

2. On January 24, Marshall sent a confidential letter by special messenger to Senator Holman inclosing "drafts of letters or statements regarding various matters we talked about the other day: A letter to the Secretary of War urging further construction at Vancouver Barracks. A letter to General George White [printed below]. . . . A statement regarding the military advantages of the development of the new municipal airport on the Columbia [River]

near Portland. . . . An outline of the existing defenses at the mouth of the Columbia, together with a statement of the provisions, under the 'Five-year Project', for the further development of these defenses." (Marshall to Holman, January 24, 1939, GCMRL/G. C. Marshall Papers [Pentagon Office, Selected].)

TO BRIGADIER GENERAL PHILIP B. PEYTON   January 23, 1939
                                                          [Washington, D.C.]

Dear Buster: I am enclosing a letter from Nick, along with some enclosures he sent me.[1] I thought they would interest you.

I intended this letter to go by air mail as a birthday greeting, but became so involved with three different committees of Congress in this hectic National Defense business, and the re-orienting of numerous officers in the War Department after each change of front, that I have lost all track of my own personal affairs. So I merely send you the report from the third of the old room-mates, which rather shows that he tops the list in the importance of position and achievement. However, I think as a rule we hit a high average—being not at all modest.

Wouldn't it be a grand thing if we could get together and celebrate a sort of joint birthday party, or anniversary of some kind or another?

Nick seems to have been "nicked" in the gall bladder, so each of us have had a turn on the operating table. But at the moment at least we are all here and steaming ahead.

I am going before a string of Committees of Congress today and tomorrow, with reporters thicker than flies.

With my affectionate regards,   Faithfully yours,

GCMRL/G. C. Marshall Papers (Pentagon Office, Selected)

1. Leonard K. Nicholson, a member of the Board of Directors of the Associated Press, had written to Marshall on January 18.

TO MAJOR GENERAL GEORGE A. WHITE [s. Holman][1]   January 24, 1939
                                                     [Washington, D.C.]

My dear General White: While I have had but a brief opportunity to familiarize myself with matters here in Washington, yet so much has been happening in the way of proposals for the national defense that I have progressed rather rapidly along that line.

A great deal has been said to me about the defenses of the Columbia, in respect to a submarine station, and regarding the further development of the coast defenses. I am soliciting detailed information from the Navy Department regarding their phase of the matter, and am asking the Chief of Coast Artillery for information regarding the coast defensive measures necessary. However, I find that the recent War Department proposal, in consequence of the President's message, provides $110,000,000 for the purchase of modern equipment for the ground forces. I am told that this means not only tremendous improvement in our materiel situation for anti-aircraft defense but that it will permit the placing in the hands of your Division, for example, the new rifles, anti-tank and anti-aircraft guns; that it will permit the modernization of all of your artillery, and will provide a proper reserve of ammunition. It seems to me that this particular phase of the proposed measure will have a more important effect on the national defense than anything else that is being attempted, not even excepting an increase in the Air Corps; because, as I understand it, the ground forces are the very foundation of our defense, Navy, Air or Coast.

I would like to have your advice and suggestions in this matter.   Very sincerely,

GCMRL/G. C. Marshall Papers (Pentagon Office, Selected)

1. Marshall inclosed this draft in a letter to Senator Rufus C. Holman dated January 24, 1939. (GCMRL/G. C. Marshall Papers [Pentagon Office, Selected].)

TO MAJOR GENERAL CHARLES H. MARTIN   January 30, 1939
[Washington, D.C.]

Dear General: I have just read your note of January twenty-third, and hasten to inform you that I have already met Senator Holman, have had several long conversations with him—and *most confidentially*, have prepared letters for his signature and arguments for his tongue. We are getting along famously, and I hope nothing occurs to upset the present agreeable relations.[1]

I have been spending a good bit of my time now before Committees of Congress, mostly in Executive Session; and it is a difficult business in this present controversial situation—which has always behind it motives towards future elections, and things of that sort.

With most affectionate regards to Mrs. Martin and yourself, whom we miss seeing more each month that goes by,   Faithfully yours,

GCMRL/G. C. Marshall Papers (Pentagon Office, Selected)

1. Martin had written: "My buddy on the State Board of Control for the past four years, Rufus Holman, is the new Senator from Oregon, and he has written me that he wants me to advise him on his activity as a member of the Senate committee on military affairs. Now Rufus is a sound, courageous, honest and capable business man and will want to do what is right regardless of politics. He is a man of intense friendships and what goes with it, intense hatreds. If you people in Washington can get him enlisted in your cause, and you can if you handle him right, you will have a strong champion for your cause." (Martin to Marshall, January 23, 1939, GCMRL/G. C. Marshall Papers [Pentagon Office, Selected].)

To Major General William N. Haskell[1]   January 30, 1939
[Washington, D.C.]

Dear Haskell: I am very appreciative of the invitation in your letter of January 26th, from the New York Society of Military and Naval Officers of the World War, to be the guest and principal speaker at the annual dinner on April 18th.

Due to the pressure of business here at this particular period, I have been declining all such invitations, and for that reason I feel that it would be best for me to express my regrets for the annual dinner of your Society.

To be perfectly frank, and most confidentially, I am principally influenced by the desire to avoid publicity, in the light of all this talk about the next Chief of Staff—which is very distasteful to me, and I think equally harmful. And for that reason alone, I hesitate to mix up with this talking business, though under ordinary conditions I would really enjoy the opportunity you extend.

Please treat my rather personal comments as confidential. I am writing frankly because I did not want you to think me unappreciative.[2]

With warm regards,   Faithfully yours,

GCMRL/G. C. Marshall Papers (Pentagon Office, Selected)

1. Haskell (U.S.M.A., 1901) had resigned from the Regular Army in January, 1926, and had been appointed a major general and the commanding general of the New York National Guard.

2. Malin Craig may have encouraged Marshall's negative reply. At the top of Haskell's January 26 letter, Marshall wrote: "Gen Craig—What do you think about my doing this— aside from the question of the time consumed? GCM"

Memorandum for the Chief of Infantry[1]   February 2, 1939
Confidential   [Washington, D.C.]

The preparation and presentation of the special defense program, along with certain related studies which have to be quickly prepared, has overburdened the General Staff. The services of additional qualified officers are necessary immediately to meet the demands of the next month. This has particular application to the War Plans Division.

The Chief of Staff desires to draw temporarily on less heavily pressed sections of the War Department for the necessary assistance, as additional officers are not to be ordered for duty in Washington. He recognizes that such action may delay the completion of certain of your projects.

Below are listed the names of two officers on duty in your office. It is desired that you furnish this office the name of one of the officers listed, who can best be spared for temporary duty at this time:

Lieut. Colonel L. C. Allen

Major R. G. Tindall

Similar request has been made of other Chiefs of Arms.

NA/RG 165 (War Plans Division, File 3354)

1. Similar memorandums requesting one officer from a list given went to the chiefs of Coast Artillery, Engineers, Cavalry, and Field Artillery. This was probably precipitated by General Strong's memorandum of January 27: "The situation in regard to commissioned personnel in the War Plans Division is critical. The present personnel is inadequate properly to carry out the duties assigned with a reasonable degree of promptness and efficiency." (Strong to Chief of Staff, January 27, 1939, NA/RG 165 [War Plans Division, File 3354].)

SPEECH[1]   February 3, 1939
                                                          [Washington, D.C.]

General Reckord has asked me to talk to you on any subject that I might select, but he mentioned his interest, and the purpose of this organization, in keeping alive a realization of the importance of the rifleman in the settlement of any war—especially in these days of myriads of planes, of mechanized cavalry, and of submarines and mysterious gases.

And I am glad to take that as the text for some informal remarks this evening, though I admit to embarrassment in holding forth on any military subject in the presence of the Assistant Secretary of War and the Chief of Staff of the Army. When my invitation for this evening was delivered, no mention was made of the fact that I would be called upon to talk under these circumstances, so, while complimented and honored by the invitation, it seems inappropriate, as it certainly is embarrassing, for me to be advising on military matters in the presence of these two high officials of the Army.

The world is air-minded today, all thoughts turn to attack from the air. A glance through military history shows a monotonous repetition of such special interests. Chariots were once heralded as the dominators of the battlefield, then elephants; the mechanized force of the Macedonian Phalanx played a brief determining part, but the short-sword of the Roman infantryman brought back to the battlefield its basic factor. Hordes of horsemen, comparable to the threatened hordes of airplanes, carried Genghis Khan across Asia to the gates of Vienna; and through a series of changes we reach the period of the armored knight. Then came the crossbowman to dominate the field; and artillery appeared, to reach a peak in employment under Napoleon. This special arm again reached dominating importance in the World War, when the infantry casualties became prohibitive in prolonged attacks. For the same reason the tank put in an appearance and played a leading part in the last phase of the World War. But meanwhile, the airplane, starting with shotgun and revolver armament, rapidly developed into a carrier of synchronized machine guns and a dropper of bombs, though remaining of value largely as a reconnaissance weapon. The air fights in France were almost entirely concerned with the gathering of information.

But in all these struggles, as the smoke cleared away, it was the man with the sword, or the crossbow, or the rifle, who settled the final issue on the field. Probably the most impressive exception could be made to this statement in connection with the completely horsed armies of Genghis Khan,—this was one of those exceptions that prove the rule.

To return to the airplane. Since the World War its development has gone ahead by leaps and bounds, due to its suitability for commercial usage, and its adaptability to offset sea power, on a quick production basis. Anti-aircraft measures have lagged for the opposite reason, being entirely of a non-commercial character and dependent upon military appropriations.

We now come to a most unusual development in world armaments. A nation which had been disarmed, and deprived of practically all of its military materiel, a nation which had been barred from the development of aviation and of tanks, suddenly throws off the yoke and launches a huge program of military preparation.

People generally do not comprehend the far-reaching effect of this unusual base of departure for the rearmament of Germany. Had that country possessed an accumulation of World War weapons, it would probably have suffered the necessity of compromising the desire to procure more modern equipment, with the more economical possibility of modernizing some of the existing materiel, and of utilizing the remainder unaltered—a procedure in which the other nations of the world were and are engaged, and which never produces even an approximation of a complete modernization of munitions.

But Germany had nothing with which to start, except the little force of 100,000 men permitted to her by treaty; her cannon decorate the public parks of the Allies, her wartime machine guns had largely been destroyed, she was prohibited planes and tanks. But, she was spared the expensive procedure of the development and outmoding of airplanes or tanks or mechanized cavalry. When the yoke of the Versailles Treaty was discarded, Germany started from scratch, as it were, without necessity for compromise, and initiated the development of a complete armament program, closely integrated with civil industry. She had the full benefit of the experimentation of the world in planes and tanks; in artillery, mechanized vehicles, and in the production of ammunition. Evidently, during her period of restricted military activities following the World War, she had concentrated on experimental research along military lines. Her sudden departure on a program of rearmament was not so revolutionary as might appear, because it is apparent that she had carefully laid a sound basis for the initiation of the program. It was no hastily improvised affair.

Had the great nations grown old together, in the gradual elimination of outmoded weapons, planes and equipment, no single country could have gained such a long lead in the matter as attained by Germany. Contradictory as it may seem, she actually profited by the forcible wiping out of her World War armament. She also profited by the forced reduction of her army, because in the rapid swelling of numbers to her present standing army, she was free of the normal resistance to changes in organization, and has therefore approached her ideal of military power.

There are a world of controversial phases of this matter that might be discussed, but which time and restraint cause me to avoid, but I will say that it is most important in judging these matters to gain a proper perspective, and not permit the trees to obscure the woods.

For example, there is nothing dramatic about industrial preparedness, except in its appeal to the manufacturer; but it is evident that unless we set up a practical program in this respect we will be impotent, even if we have a collection of Galahads in the ranks. The same thought applies to the equally undramatic business of reserve stocks of critical materials.

In all this present welter of conflicting information as to what is happening in Europe, the dramatic features have been widely publicized while other equally important measures have been ignored. I might illustrate this phase of the matter by a single example. We have all heard how many planes Germany has and what vast numbers she can produce, but I doubt if very many have learned that for more than two years she has turned out a million rounds of artillery ammunition a week! Now you, of the National Rifle Association, would be primarily interested in what she has done in terms of the rifle and the man. Whatever that is, will be of no public interest, lacking all dramatic quality, until we find an Horatius at the bridge.

Those of you who fought in France will remember that the daily communiques of all the Allies—and of the Central Powers—usually cited by name some gallant knight of the air who had driven down an opponent in flames or to a crash. Practically never did you read a similar public reference to the poor devil with the infantry platoon, who labored in the cold and mud, under shell and machine gun fire, was bombed and gassed, and who carried the battle to the enemy, and actually conquered the disputed ground. Yet it was this soldier who forced the issue to the Armistice. I only recall one exception to these comments, and that was in the case of an infantry lieutenant of the German Army who was cited by name in the radio communique in April, 1918, for having forced a river crossing ahead of schedule and permitted the German advance down the Valley of the Lys to proceed so rapidly that it resulted in a near catastrophe for a portion of the British Army.

I have at last arrived in this talk at the point of discussing the activities of the National Rifle Association in the promotion of National Defense.

Without giving much thought to the matter, we all know that the old days of the squirrel hunter and the pioneer have departed, and with their departure has been lost that intimate knowledge of the rifle common to early American history. Your association undertakes to keep alive this knowledge, and to develop better technique, better weapons, and better powders for the rifle.

Almost thirty years ago I got myself ordered to Camp Perry for duty as an official of the National Rifle Matches, in order that I might see for myself just what was accomplished there. At the time I was an instructor at Leavenworth, and so supercharged with theoretical conceptions of making war that I thought it would be an excellent thing to get a more practical slant on certain aspects of the battlefield. I was much impressed by that experience. While not a high-powered rifleman, I had on at least one occasion been high gun of the Post, but my duties had carried me away from the target range, and I never found opportunity to develop myself into anything of a rifle shot; that is, according to the standards necessary for an Army officer who enters the lists at Camp Perry. Before I found the time and opportunity, my eyes had settled the question with finality.

Every hour of my experience in France impressed me more and more with the importance and potential power of the infantryman on the battlefield, *if* and *provided* the man was hardened and disciplined, and *if* he was trained to use his weapon with efficiency under the conditions of combat. It was clear to all present in France that the burden of the war fell on the shoulders of the members of the infantry platoon. No other group competed with them in hardships and casualties. But they received little public recognition for their work and sacrifices.

There is another aspect to this matter which, I think, is not fully understood, and possibly I can illustrate my particular view of this phase by a comparison with the present development of the National Guard. I must ask you to treat the following statement as somewhat confidential, because it is purely my personal opinion, gained from intimate contact with those troops.

Under the conditions controlling the development of the National Guard as to limited time, restricted training facilities, etc., it has seemed to me that the units most readily developed to a high point of efficiency have been, strange to say, the observation squadrons of the Guard air force; next, the Engineer regiments; and then the Field Artillery. I won't go further down the list, but will merely mention my opinion that the most difficult unit to develop satisfactorily in the National Guard is the infantry regiment. And there is a very simple reason for this situation.

The infantryman on the battlefield is distinctly on his own, without a horse or a motor to turn to, and lacking the anchor of a field gun or tank, or other heavy equipment. Once the field of action has been reached and the deployment completed, the infantry soldier becomes an isolated individualist, with all the frailties of the individual magnified a thousandfold. Only a corporal remains nearby to back him up, upon whom he can depend for reassurance. He lacks a physical rallying point—no ship, no heavy gun, no fortification, nothing but a few scattered buddies. He is a young fellow, depressed by a heavy physical burden on his back, exhausted by long marches of concentration and deployment, and lack of food, and he is virtually alone under the terrific pounding of hostile fires of every character. Of himself, by himself, he can apparently do very little, though collectively he can win the war.

He must be supported by artillery, which means in turn that his platoon commander must have a skilled knowledge of topography and able to report exactly where his line is established—on ground never seen before and of which he probably has no map. This information, coupled with accurate observations of the enemy's opposing installations—which usually are at a distance and on a decided angle from the front of the platoon—must be communicated through an elaborate but hastily established communications system, by runner, telephone, radio, through company, battalion, and regimental headquarters, to some distant battery of artillery, probably a mile to the rear, and which the platoon commander has never seen and possibly never will see. It may be necessary to coordinate his isolated activities with an infantry cannon or Stokes mortar, and certainly with distant machine guns. He may even have to initiate procedure to secure the support of tanks still miles to the rear. All of this he does, lying on his stomach, under a hostile fusillade—with a diet of gas thrown in for good measure. And what he proposes must be coordinated with the scattered units along a regimental, a brigade, a divisional front, and through its depth of supports and reserves. Altogether, it is *the* most complicated problem of troop leadership, and requires a higher degree of training and discipline, I believe, than for any other military preparation—except for the actual flying of the airplane. There are no convenient electrical buttons as on a battleship to launch a broadside; no hot meals, no rest, seemingly no end to a long drawn out battle of endurance.

Yet with all this, we seldom hear this phase of the matter referred to. As a matter of fact, I think the common belief is that the most quickly created instrument of war is the infantry regiment. Yet, I would say that we have lost more lives and been delayed more in battle by the acceptance of this doctrine than for any other purely military reason.

There is another aspect of this same matter. In ordinary training little that the infantryman does closely simulates what actually happens on the battlefield and, what is most important, the most serious errors or lacks of the peace-time training can seldom be made apparent in that training, or even in maneuvers; because until the leader or individual has once been submerged with hostile fire— bullet, shell, and bomb—and left apparently unsupported in an exposed position, and has found himself utterly unable to secure any artillery fire or machine gun fire, or other supporting action, he will never appreciate the special importance to infantry—above all other arms or services—of discipline and leadership, and of communications; and their absolute determining effect on the battlefield.

Today, when people think of bombs dropping like hail, certainly not like the gentle dew from heaven, they probably dispose of the infantryman's problem with the thought that, "Certainly he has no defense against such war-making methods." Well, one wounded infantry sergeant in the old 69th Regiment in New York, infuriated by the return a second time of a German low-flying strafing plane which had disabled him on its first passage—that man, lying on his back, fired at the plane, killed the pilot and crashed the ship, which fell on another German plane flying under it, a single rifle shot bringing down two planes. He was not mentioned, like the successful aviator, in the day's communique, but he did receive the Distinguished Service Cross.

I am not implying that we expect to shoot down many planes with rifle bullets. But recently the infantry has forced the rather low-flying tactics of the air people into higher altitudes because of the recorded effectiveness of fire from trained infantry riflemen.

I do mean, by implication, that the foundation on which a successful war is carried to conclusion, aside from the character and resolution of the people, eventually rests with the infantry soldier, no matter what the scientific developments and clever gadgets developed for making war. Of course, without air support he is doomed, just as he cannot live on the battlefield without the fire of his own artillery; and frequently could never advance without the support of tanks; and usually would be completely in the dark without the reconnaissance of plane or car, or cavalry, or humble foot patrollers. He will never be the subject of wide acclaim, but he will continue to be the solid rock on which wars are finally settled; and everything we can do to give him prestige, to develop his weapons, to afford a general knowledge of the use of those weapons, are just so many steps exactly in the right direction. Therefore, the justification for the National Rifle Association.

GCMRL/G. C. Marshall Papers (Pentagon Office, Speeches)

1. This speech was delivered to the convention of the National Rifle Association in Washington, D.C., at the request of Major General Milton A. Reckord, commanding general of the Maryland National Guard and president of the National Rifle Association.

To Major General John L. De Witt[1]   February 6, 1939
Confidential   [Washington, D.C.]

Dear DeWitt: I am enclosing herewith a draft of a directive for a study on Brazil, as prepared by the War Plans Division.[2] They are in urgent need of two such studies, one on Brazil and one of a similar nature on Venezuela. If you can handle one after February 15th under the terms we discussed, it will be very much appreciated. If you can handle two, all the better.

I have instructed General Strong to treat this as confidential, so that no one in the General Staff generally will be aware of the fact that we have broken your precedent at the War College;[3] I have told him that Major Bonham's relations with him will be on a confidential basis, and that the work was to be promulgated from your desk.

Under these conditions, it is quite possible that this study may be undertaken without any particular knowledge of the fact that the War Plans Division has been responsible for it, except, of course, that Bonham would have to know.[4]

I trust this will not embarrass you, and I will greatly appreciate your assistance. Faithfully yours,

NA/RG 165 (War Plans Division, File 4115)

1. De Witt had been commandant of the Army War College since July, 1937.
2. The secret, undated, unsigned directive read: "Prepare a complete strategic survey of Brazil to include a detailed consideration of the most effective military operations that the United States could undertake should it become necessary to assist that country in the maintenance of its independence and integrity in the face of internal or external operations, undertaken, fostered or assisted by non-American countries. This survey will include a thorough analysis of those political, geographical, economic and military and naval factors that have pertinent bearing upon the operations in question, and an indexed assembly of factual data in support of the conclusions drawn in this survey." (NA/RG 165 [War Plans Division, File 4115].)
3. Since Major General James W. McAndrew's reorganization of the Army War College in the early 1920s, college policy had been to pursue its academic mission and to avoid becoming a study and planning adjunct for the War Department's General Staff.
4. Major Francis G. Bonham (U.S.M.A., April 1917) was an instructor at the Army War College. He had graduated from the Infantry School's Advanced Course in 1929; between 1931 and 1934, he was a tactics instructor at the Infantry School. Bonham was head of the special committee of War College students who prepared the "Special Study—Brazil" between February 17 and March 29, 1939. (Ibid.)

MEMORANDUM FOR GENERAL BECK[1]　　　　　　　　　February 7, 1939
[Washington, D.C.]

Dear Beck:　I think it is time we got started on a possible reorganization of the mobile ground forces of the Army in the event that a new organization for the Infantry Division proves acceptable.[2] I have in mind the necessity for a preliminary outline only of the redistribution of troops both in the regular service and the National Guard, particularly as concerns the development of an increase in corps and army units.

Should a new Division be authorized for the National Guard, I realize that it will be necessary to have the new allocations reported on by a special committee representing the National Guard but, in the meantime,—and confidentially—I would like you to have your people work out a rough outline of the possible new set-up—as to number and location of divisions, the same regarding corps and army troops, and other general details which would be involved.

I think it is very important to have this preliminary study available, in order that we may answer the inevitable pressure that will soon develop for the creation of new anti-aircraft units in the National Guard, or corps and army troops as referred to by the Secretary of War in his statement before the Military Committees of Congress.

Don't have your people go into exhaustive details in this. All I want at the present time is a rough outline which will permit us to form some conclusion as to probable necessity for creating entirely new units for which additional personnel would have to be provided by Congress. I rather think that the authorization of the new Infantry Division should afford us most of the personnel required for other purposes.

GCMRL/G. C. Marshall Papers (Pentagon Office, Selected)

1. Major General Robert McC. Beck, Jr., (U.S.M.A., 1901) had been assistant chief of staff for Operations and Training (G-3) since March 7, 1938.

2. The army had been testing various aspects of a new, smaller, three-regiment ("triangular") infantry division which, being about half the size of the A.E.F. four-regiment ("square") division, would be easier to maneuver and administer. The actual creation of new-type divisions did not begin until after war broke out in Europe in September, 1939.

To Colonel Morrison C. Stayer   February 11, [1939]
                                               Washington, D.C.

Dear Stayer: Your long hand note came this morning and I will make immediate reply.

In the first place, I seem to be improving despite a violation of the doctors orders. I seemed to be feeling so much brisker and energetic for several weeks that I decided to drop the medecine and watch the effect for a short time. I had been having occasional skip beats, usually about one in thirty, or rather fumbled beats; sometimes as often as once in fifteen. But since I have gotten well started on walking rapidly both ways, down to the office and home at night, rain or shine, my pulse seems to have largely straightened out. I have noticed for some days that it goes steadily and strongly. Tonight it is a steady 69 while I am lazing around.

I had been walking home at night, but intentionally at a rather slow rate, but once I got started on walking down also, and feeling so sprightly, I began to hustle along as was my custom, with the apparent result that my pulse has steadied down. Maybe it comes about through loss of more weight. I am now down to 172 from that 182 of last September when you first examined me.

The work has been strenuous, with frequent hearings on the Hill, but it comes easy and the rush and pressure does not disturb me. As a matter of fact, the time I get restless, or nervuous, is when the desk is clear.

As to your affairs: Guy V. Henry was talking about you at lunch out at Myer yesterday, and praising you very highly; also little Patty, who voiced her praise rater accurately in her description of the Riley hospital. I dropped a discrete hint that some of these medical fellows here I thought were jealous of your success in administration and in handling people. I would have coached him direct in what he might say to General Craig had I been certain that he does not air such matters to Mrs. Henry.[1]

Then this morning Barney Legge came in for a moment and spoke of seeing you recently, and stating his hope that you would be surgeon general.[2] I am afraid that what you need is a management of line officers rather than of medical fellows. The more I see of what is going on the more it become apparent to me that the deliberate recommendation or urging is destructive. The informal praise, by chance as it were, is what seems to do the trick, at least to the extent of giving one man the edge on others of approximately identical records. All straight pressure seems merely to irritate and stiffen resistance. . . .[3]

With warm regards,   Faithfully yours,

G. C. M.

GCMRL/M. C. Stayer Papers; T

1. Major General Guy V. Henry (U.S.M.A., 1898) had commanded Fort Riley, Kansas, between July, 1934, and his retirement in January, 1939. Patricia V. Henry was his younger daughter.

2. Lieutenant Colonel Barnwell R. Legge (The Citadel, 1911) was an instructor at Fort Leavenworth's Command and General Staff School at this time. He had been an officer in the First Division's Twenty-sixth Infantry during the World War. During the 1929-30 and 1930-31 school years, he had been a member of the Infantry Board at Fort Benning.

3. One paragraph regarding some of the activities of various members of Marshall's family has been omitted.

To COLONEL JOHN N. GREELY[1]   February 13, 1939
Confidential   [Washington, D.C.]

Dear John: I have just this moment opened your letter of February 10th, and will answer immediately.[2]

In the first place, I should tell you that I know little or nothing about these makes, except information picked up from time to time, which would indicate that the matter is handled on a very exact basis as to age, position on the Eligible

List, probable period of availability for the grade of major general, and allotments to arms. As you have not been passed by anybody in the Field Artillery, my advice would be, by all means, to continue business as at present. I must make it perfectly clear to you that I have no information of any kind on the subject. But I should add one more item to the foregoing—from what I have been able to learn influence has been completely negligible and only an irritation. General Craig tells me that every make is his, in other words, that he is completely responsible for each one.

I want to ask you to treat the foregoing as highly confidential, and I question whether I should have commented this freely. He has had to take a terrible beating in the feeling aroused by the procedure followed in going down the list for brigadiers, and this feeling grows more, I imagine, with each successive announcement.

I wish that I had had an opportunity to see you when I was flying through San Antonio last August, but you were on maneuvers. Maybe I will get down there by air again before the year is out, but certainly not this winter as things are terrific here in the way of business.

With affectionate regards to both of you,   Faithfully yours,

GCMRL/G. C. Marshall Papers (Pentagon Office, Selected)

1. Greely, at this time commander of the Fifteenth Field Artillery at Fort Sam Houston, Texas, was the son of noted Arctic explorer Major General Adolphus W. Greely. During the World War he served with the First Division's Seventh Field Artillery in 1917, before moving to the division's Operations Section to work for Marshall. Subsequently, he served as head of the Operations Section, then division chief of staff, and as a member of the Operations Section at A.E.F. General Headquarters. Between 1921 and 1924 he was detailed to the Operations and Training Division of the War Department General Staff.

2. Greely wrote that he was worried that the promotion to brigadier general of an officer in another branch who was junior to him meant that he was being passed over for promotion. If so, he thought he might "turn to writing with a view to retiring as soon as I can afford it, to give my whole time to this. I believe that I would be financially and mentally better off than hanging on in a futile hope that lightning would some day strike. I had a lot of big jobs in my time, and I should hate to see them get less and less important. Please let me know your advice if you feel free to do so. Say either—hang on—or—you better prepare to get out." (Greely to Marshall, February 10, 1939, GCMRL/G. C. Marshall Papers [Pentagon Office, Selected].)

MEMORANDUM FOR GENERAL BECK   February 15, 1939
                                               [Washington, D.C.]

With reference to the consideration you are now giving to the matter of command and supply for the GHQ Air Force, I am sending you informally—and confidentially—a memorandum on the subject, prepared by Colonel Maxwell, now in the Office of the Assistant Secretary of War.[1]

General Craig has not seen this memorandum, and I have avoided showing it to him for fear that he might feel that Maxwell was putting his foot into something that was none of his business; and I wish to avoid inadvertently harming Maxwell in that manner.

What brought about the memorandum was this: Maxwell was Ordnance officer for the Cavalry Division during the period of its principal development as to munitions. He has been Ordnance officer of the GHQ Air Force during its great development. Therefore his personal experience has been rather unique, and he was talking to me about his estimate of the present situation without any knowledge of the fact that a new decision might be made.

To me, an interesting aspect of his experience was this: In the Cavalry Division the horse—as compared with the plane in the GHQ Air Force—was not a debatable question. There was no question of supercharging his engine and refiguring his aerodynamics. Also there was not much question about matters of Cavalry tactics, or of weapon technique and practices. The main thing that had to be accomplished was the proper equipment of the Cavalry as to weapons, reserves, and things of that sort; and I understand from Maxwell that the Cavalry Division exercised the determining influence in this matter, rather than the Office of the Chief of Cavalry.

Now in the GHQ Air Force, the situation has been almost entirely reversed. The Office of the Chief of Air Corps has been directly involved in the development of planes, constantly of a more modern type; but in questions of tactics, of bombing, of technique of weapons—and the consequent training of personnel in those matters, and the development of discipline towards those ends, and policies of leadership—almost everything had to be done. Therefore it was most fortunate that the command relationship was not set up under the Chief of the Air Corps.

Now Maxwell fears that we may step back to a situation where materiel and mere assignment of personnel become the dominant factors, rather than the ultimate purpose of the GHQ Air Force, which is its war efficiency—leadership, tactics, bombing, and the use of other weapons. Incidentally, he tells me that when it comes to the technique of weapons, other than bombing, the Air Corps has everything to learn and little standardization, and a different opinion from almost every individual as to how the weapons should be handled.

I talked to Arnold about this and he accepted most of the statements, but thought in view of the tremendous program now about to be realized, that it would be impossible to carry it out without a more intimate and direct relationship and well-ordered arrangement of authority between the Office of the Chief of the Air Corps and the GHQ Air Force.[2]

In view of Maxwell's unusual service, and the clarity with which he expresses his ideas, I told him to reduce it to paper, and I pass it along to you. But I would prefer that you keep his name out of it.

GCMRL/G. C. Marshall Papers (Pentagon Office, Selected)

1. Since 1935, the Army Air Corps command had been divided between the G.H.Q. Air Force, which exercised combat responsibility, and the Office of the Chief of the Air Corps,

which had charge of training and indoctrination of crews and of the development and procurement of equipment. The two agencies were on the same command echelon and reported separately to the army chief of staff. After considerable debate within the Air Corps, consolidation of the two was effected on March 1, 1939, and the G.H.Q. Air Force was made subordinate to the chief of the Air Corps. (Craven and Cate, *The Army Air Forces in World War II*, 1: 31–32, 114–15.)

The subject of Lieutenant Colonel Russell L. Maxwell's memorandum to Marshall was "Chain of Command, GHQ Air Force." Maxwell argued that the divided responsibility should continue, because the conflict was "a symptom of a healthy growing condition," and because the current chain of command was reasonable and proper. "The Chief of Staff has agencies available for the performance of referee duty, and if he should abdicate in favor of the Chief of the Air Corps, it will only be a matter of time until the now dormant clamor for a separation of the Air Arm from the Army, would again be heard, and the Army as a whole would be less well prepared to meet the issue than it is today."

Maxwell urged increased contact between the airmen and the rest of the army, particularly with the General Staff. "There is only one way to know the Air Force, and gain a sympathetic understanding of its needs, powers, limitations, aims, hopes and ambitions, and that is to live with it and *fly* with it. I cannot overemphasize *flying* as the fundamental requirement for anyone who seeks to gain the confidence of an Air Corps officer, whose main interest in life is flying." (Maxwell Memorandum for Marshall, February 13, 1939, GCMRL/G. C. Marshall Papers [Pentagon Office, Selected].)

2. The chief of the Air Corps since General Westover's death in September, 1938, had been Major General Henry H. Arnold. He had first met Marshall during the January, 1914, maneuvers in the Philippine Islands. "When I returned from the maneuvers," Arnold recalled, "I told my wife I had met a man who was going to be Chief of Staff of the Army some day. . . . The young lieutenant was George Catlett Marshall." (Henry H. Arnold, *Global Mission* [New York: Harper and Brothers, 1949], p. 44.)

To MAJOR GENERAL DAVID L. STONE[1]   February 18, 1939
Confidential   [Washington, D.C.]

My dear Stone: . . . Walker has come back tremendously enthusiastic over Panama,[2] and especially over the manner in which you made it possible for him to get a fine picture of the situation. I might tell you—and this is most confidential—that the increases for Panama in the way of quarters, personnel, and for the antiaircraft coast defense, were not in the picture at all, and had to be handled with considerable finesse. Actually, the President's message did not include the appropriation requirements involved there, in the total he proposed in his bill. He merely referred to the importance of rectifying the situation, and the amount of money involved. We succeeded in having the matter handled in this manner, trusting that once it reached Congress from such an authoritative source, there might not be any quibble over increasing the totals involved. And this seems to be the case, so there should be no trouble about getting what is required. Of course, in this connection, there was never any question whatsoever in regard to the air increments, except as to the funds for the fields, the quarters, and the personnel. However, these are now on the program, and I hope will stay there.

In considering this whole matter, our great trouble is to maintain interest in the materiel items, because they lack all dramatic appeal; and therefore the money involved is always subject to the risk of being cut. However, we are making quite a struggle in regard to this phase of the affair, in the hope that for at least once in our history, in time of peace we can have modern equipment for the ground forces—though only for those now in the ranks in the Regular Army and the National Guard.[2]

The maneuvers I have described above, please treat as most confidential—that is, for your eye only. Possibly I should not have included them in such a letter, but I knew you would be much interested. Faithfully yours,

GCMRL/G. C. Marshall Papers (Pentagon Office, Selected)

1. Stone had commanded the Panama Canal Department since April, 1937. In the omitted thirty percent of this letter, Marshall requested Stone to extend certain small courtesies to two friends who would be passing through the Canal Zone.
2. Lieutenant Colonel Walton H. Walker was on duty in the War Plans Division.

To COLONEL JOHN N. GREELY   February 20, 1939
                                             [Washington, D.C.]

Dear John: Replying to your discussion of the relative merits of tabular charts and T of O's, I don't think my point of view has been made clear to you.[1]

In brief, it is this: The War Department never seems to have caught up with its T of O's to the existing situation or proposed organization. This has been a continuing embarrassment at Leavenworth and at the Service Schools, and was so embarrassing to the War Plans Division here recently that something had to be done immediately to remedy the situation.[2]

Offhand, and without stating the various qualifications pertinent to the matter, I would say that the T of O's represent an ideal proposition and therefore an impractical one for our Army.

My thought was to find some way that the G-3 Section could keep abreast of conditions in its published organizational prescriptions, and not be eternally laboring over long and involved columns of this and that, and footnote "h", to show that he carries a revolver, or a pickaxe, or some other damn thing.

I wanted an outline chart of the organization with only enough of detail on the outline to show the type organization approved. Then, to include the briefest possible list of war strength personnel, armament, equipment, and transportation. Attached to this chart would be the yearly layout, which varies with every appropriation bill and has to be published yearly, in any event.

In the main, my method would leave to the colonel of the regiment the decision as to whether this particular sergeant will be here or there, and not have the War Department indulging in minutiae of this character when organizations differ so materially here and there about the country.[3]

For example, in the Infantry branch, about which I know the most, we have a war strength regiment less a battalion at Benning; three battalion regiments at a service strength in Hawaii; regiments at another strength in Panama; three battalion regiments at still another strength in the United States; two battalion regiments here and there in the United States; and finally, the 15th Infantry of less than two battalions, and each battalion of a different organization from all other battalions.

Now, the point I would like to make is, this is not abnormal in the sense that it seldom happens with us. It always happens, and our system should be adapted to the facts rather than to the theories. Above all, it should be a simple proposition—and even above that, it should permit the local commander to use his brains a little bit and not have everything dictated from a desk in Washington.

As I am airing myself quite freely from the desk of the Deputy Chief of Staff, I will have to ask you to treat this as confidential, because I cannot afford to advertise my views in this manner. Hastily yours,

GCMRL/G. C. Marshall Papers (Pentagon Office, Selected)

1. Greely had written: "I understand that you favor tabular charts showing strength in place of formal T. of O.s [Tables of Organization]. Either will work practically, but to secure some uniformity the T. of O.s seem more valuable." (Greely to Marshall, February 16, 1939, GCMRL/G. C. Marshall Papers [Pentagon Office, Selected].)

2. In his June 30, 1939, annual report, Chief of Staff Craig stated: "Since my last report a restudy has been made of our Tables of Organization and 249 of these tables have been revised, bringing them up to date and in accord with modern equipment and modern means of transportation." ("Annual Report of the Chief of Staff," in *Report of the Secretary of War to the President, 1939* [Washington, D.C.: Government Printing Office, 1939], p. 28.)

3. Marshall's influence on the complexity of the army's tables of organization was slight. In 1941, the "Headquarters, Field Army" (T/O 200-1) had a twenty-three-column, seventy-eight-row table with seventeen lettered footnotes for slightly less than seven hundred men. The table for "Infantry Regiment, Rifle (Motorized)," contained thirteen columns and forty-eight rows (T/O 7-61), and the table for "Infantry Company, Prisoner of War Escort," (ninety-six men) had seven columns and twenty-eight rows. (*Tables of Organization of Infantry Units*, [Washington, D.C.: Infantry Journal, 1941], pp. 68–69, 105, 118–19.)

To Brigadier General Lesley J. McNair   February 23, 1939
[Washington, D.C.]

Dear McNair: You have probably already learned that the Chief of Staff has decided to detail you as Commandant of the Command and General Staff School, to succeed Bundel, who goes on leave March 23d.[1]

I am now telling you, and most confidentially, that considerable feeling has developed regarding the courses at Leavenworth and that the Secretary of War is determined that something should be done immediately to modernize the school methods of instruction. He has heard a great many comparisons unfavorable to

Leavenworth with regard to the Air Corps Tactical School especially and to Fort Benning and other Special Service Schools. The Chief of Staff feels that Leavenworth is frozen, as it were, in its routine procedure, and he has noticed that most officers selected for detail as instructors there are opposed to such service; and that this reaction is not true of the other Army schools.

As I said above, it is desired that you treat this as confidential, for your sole information, as General Craig is very desirous that no gossip or publicity be stirred up regarding rumored drastic changes, etc. The Secretary of War wished to have a board appointed to go over the whole situation but we have successfully resisted this idea in order to avoid the disadvantages of the discussion which will be bound to follow.

General Craig has therefore directed me to send you herewith some comments regarding the school which General Embick collected so that you may read these over immediately. If you are agreeable to flying, he would like to send his plane down to fly you to Barksdale Field, Langley Field and Maxwell Field, en route to Washington, where you could have all or a portion of the day at each place to familiarize yourself somewhat with present air developments, particularly at the GHQ Air Force at Langley Field, as to the principles and theories being taught at the Air Corps Tactical School. After some conferences here in the War Department with the Chief of Staff, General Beck and myself, and with the Secretary of War, you could fly on out to Leavenworth for a brief preliminary survey and then proceed to San Antonio preparatory to final departure for Leavenworth.

The Chief of Staff wishes me to tell you that he desires that your arrival at Leavenworth be several days in advance of General Bundel's departure. It may be, after a preliminary stop there, if you make the flight I am suggesting, that this early arrival will be unnecessary. You could report for duty there on General Bundel's departure.

Please do not hesitate to send me any inquiries that suggest themselves to you and I will answer by Air Mail. Also, please let me know as early as possible, whether you wish to undertake the plane trip.   Faithfully yours,

GCMRL/G. C. Marshall Papers (Pentagon Office, Selected)

1. At this time, McNair was commanding the Second Field Artillery Brigade at Fort Sam Houston, Texas. Brigadier General Charles M. Bundel (U.S.M.A., 1899) was preparing to go on leave prior to his retirement at the end of June. Bundel had been commandant at Fort Leavenworth's Command and General Staff School since June, 1936.

To Colonel Edwin T. Cole   February 24, 1939
                                                                 [Washington, D.C.]

My dear Colonel Cole: I really have been deeply affected by your letter of February 20th.[1] It recalled the days of Salt Creek Valley and Sentinel Hill—my first real beginning towards a career in this Army, because it opened my eyes to the broader viewpoint of Military development and education which was to be necessary for any officer who hoped to achieve position in later years.

Also, I was touched by your comments about me personally. I have always been grateful for the distinction of your selecting me, an inconspicuous and overslaughed second lieutenant, to be an instructor at Leavenworth in those days when everyone was my senior. It was the first step, and therefore the most important step to me personally.

Then, another thing, I have always felt personally grateful to you for my topographic education. It was of such tremendous value in the War that there can be no offhand rating of its importance. On one occasion, the intimate knowledge you ground into me of the ground forms and critical points and limits, saved me from walking into German lines during a reconnaissance in the dark preliminary to the fight at Cantigny. There was no wire to restrict one and I had never seen the ground in the day time and incidentally never have seen it by daylight. Booth had a similar experience in an automobile drive south down the Meuse River towards St. Mihiel before we took the salient.

However, I never fully realized the advantage we had in our ground knowledge as a result of your course at Leavenworth, until I came into intimate contact with junior officers of the Army after the War; especially during the period I was running the Infantry School at Benning the principal difficulty was to secure instructors who understood the thing as we of the pre-war Leavenworth crowd had been trained to do. It was an odd situation, where almost every general officer was an expert topographer and the young men had merely a theoretical knowledge of map reading.

Most of the trouble today has been due to the fact that there are so many specialties which must be learned and highly technical subjects to be mastered, such as modern communications and innumerable infantry weapons—cannons, mortars, machine guns, automatic rifles; firing at high speed targets, etc., that there is little time to give to the laborious business of making maps. And that is the only way I know how to teach one to read a map.

I have been busier the last three months than at any time since the World War and with just about as many conflicting interests and problems to deal with.

Yesterday was Washington's birthday and I spent practically all day at the Capitol in connection with the final vote by the Senate committee on the Army Bill. Today I am at it again, but at this end of the line. Everything has grown so complicated and one must have so much detailed knowledge of many side lines, scientific, mechanical, technical, political etc.—that I look back with envy on the peaceful days of the old Army when we debated the relative merits of a chuck wagon attachment for the escort wagon, and carefully considered its advantages for hunting trips. You can't even march on the road today without being sideswiped by an automobile. All the glamour, if there ever was any, has gone out of the business of war, and it becomes more and more a proposition of horrible possibilities, with an extremely complicated approach in each instance.

I appreciate all the kind things you had to say about me personally, more than I can express in such a letter, but I appreciate more than anything else the fact that you wrote as you did.

One reference I would like to make regarding an interesting comment you made about General Pershing—I had a letter from him two days ago. You wrote that you had heard "Some claim that he was inclined to wear a very high hat", and was difficult of approach. Exactly the opposite is the case. I have always found him as informal and as unpretentious almost as a boy and as youthful in his reactions. He could listen to more opposition to his apparent view than any man I have ever known, and show less personal feeling than anyone I have ever seen. He was the most outstanding example of a man with complete tolerance towards all discussions regarding the matters in which he was considering, regardless of what his own personal opinions seemed to be. In that quality lay a great part of his strength. Of course, hard common sense and backbone were his cardinal attributes.

As to General Sumner—I knew him and Mrs. Sumner well, and called on them with General Pershing.[2] Her favorite story was how, when General Sumner refused to get a trunk out of a warehouse for her to wear to a reception at Oklahoma City because she had made up her mind so late in the day, Captain Pershing broke into the warehouse and got the trunk. She said General Sumner did not think this so funny at the time, but it was Mrs. Sumner's greatest compliment.

With most affectionate regards,   Faithfully yours,

GCMRL/G. C. Marshall Papers (Pentagon Office, General)

1. Cole, formerly Marshall's superior in the Engineering Department at Fort Leavenworth (1908-10), had written a long letter which had been stimulated by Marshall's February 16 address on National Defense Week on the NBC radio network. Concerning his former pupil, Cole observed: "I have for years predicted that if we again went to war when you were not too young or too old to be considered that you would undoubtedly be the Commander in Chief." (Cole to Marshall, February 20, 1939, GCMRL/G. C. Marshall Papers [Pentagon Office, General].)

2. Major General Samuel S. Sumner, who served in the army from 1861 until 1906, had once been Cole's as well as Pershing's commanding officer. Sumner died on July 26, 1937.

To Brigadier General Asa L. Singleton[1]   February 27, 1939
[Washington, D.C.]

Dear Singleton: General McNair is to be the next Commandant at Fort Leavenworth. To prepare him, the Chief of Staff is sending him by air to

Barksdale Field, the Air Corps Tactical School, Langley Field, on route to the War Department and to Leavenworth for a preliminary survey.

I doubt if he has more than one day at Benning, but I hope that in that brief time, you can give him a good idea of the practical tactics and technique taught there. I think it very important to have brought to his attention any apparent differences between Benning tactical technique and that at Leavenworth.

For example, during my period, a Leavenworth Infantry battalion order would be two or three pages long, where a similar order at Benning would be less than a page in length. The same applied to G-2 summaries, supply details and so forth. The one was ponderous and cumbersome, while the other at least showed struggle towards simplicity. Benning used geological survey maps and Leavenworth was more inclined to the Gettysburg variety. Bennings procedure suggested more of contact with soldiers and the soil, than did the Leavenworth production. I am writing you most informally to give you some idea as to why McNair is being sent to Benning.

Times have changed and maybe there is not the difference today that there was in my day.

Please treat all that I have said here as confidential.   Faithfully yours,

GCMRL/G. C. Marshall Papers (Pentagon Office, Selected)
   1. Singleton had been commandant of the Infantry School at Fort Benning since July, 1936.

MEMORANDUM FOR GENERAL WESSON[1]   March 3, 1939
[Washington, D.C.]

With reference to your telephone conversation of the other day regarding a release on plans for certain Ordnance materiel, for Holland I believe, and with regard to the recent developments in this matter: What do you think of the proposition of reconsidering all items of Ordnance—and other munitions—on the basis of the relative advantages of secrecy versus the opportunities for civil industry to become familiar with the manufacture of the items concerned?

We had a discussion the other day over the French query as to 3-inch anti-aircraft guns, whether or not it was best to release the plans for the private manufacture in this country of the present 3-inch piece, or the plans for the new lighter weight 3-inch piece. In this connection, it seems to me that it would be distinctly to our advantage to have the more modern, that is, the light weight piece, in manufacture in civil industry, particularly if it can be done without expense to us.

I want to get your general idea, on a purely informal basis, before taking the matter up with the Chief of Staff towards having a definite study made of all material on that particular basis.

It may be that you have already had such a study prepared, but I am not clear on the subject.

GCMRL/G. C. Marshall Papers (Pentagon Office, Selected)

1. Major General Charles M. Wesson (U.S.M.A., 1900) had been army chief of Ordnance since June, 1938.

To Brigadier General Lesley J. McNair   March 4, 1939
                                                                                        [Washington, D.C.]

Dear McNair: A radio has come in from Gruber stating your desire to stop and see the Mechanized Force at Knox. This will be arranged.

He also inquired, I think, as to how long you are to be here. I should imagine three days would suffice in Washington, but we can determine that once you have arrived. I am assuming that many factors concerned with schedules at Leavenworth, lack of provision in the course for instruction relative to the GHQ Air Force, etc., would have been discussed in considerable detail by you and Gruber before you reach Washington, and so should require very little time here towards reaching a solution.[1]

In this whole business, I think the main thing is to give you great freedom of action, after you have learned what the consensus of opinion seems to be as to the state of affairs at Leavenworth—and I do not mean the consensus of opinion in the faculty at Leavenworth—they are too close to the trees to see the woods, and too many of them are only theoretically familiar with the air component and the National Guard.

With relation to the last named force, I think our instruction is the most defective, and for these reasons: We must be prepared the next time we are involved in war, to fight immediately, that is within a few weeks, somewhere and somehow. Now that means we will have to employ the National Guard for that purpose, because it will constitute the large majority of the war army of the first six months.

This being so, it seems fundamental to me that the training of our officers, our staff procedure, and our manuals, should primarily be based for use in connection with such force. Regular officers should be experts regarding every consideration involved in the training and the leadership of partially trained troops; they should be intimately familiar with the employment of organizations below war strength and lacking in artillery and similar components, as well as supply echelons. They should be most familiar with the technique involved in working on poor maps of the Geological small scale variety—rather than the Leavenworth fourth-year-of-a-war type.

Our text should present in the simplest possible manner the absolute essentials necessary to the National Guard on M[obilization]-day, along with the most expeditious methods for giving that instruction or training. We can never take more time from the business men and the workers in the National Guard for military training, therefore we must develop more expeditious methods of giving the training we think necessary, and we should eliminate everything that is not absolutely essential. What we do today at Leavenworth, as I understand it, is to consider complete organizations of trained troops, and usually on special maps, when none of these conditions exist during the first six months or even the first year of war.

The tactics appropriate in open warfare to a highly trained experienced unit, are not usually at all appropriate in open warfare to a partially trained inexperienced unit, and the latter form of tactics for leadership should be the first consideration of every Regular officer on the outbreak of war.

After an intimate experience with the National Guard in large numbers during three years, and participation in two Army Maneuvers, in which I commanded the smaller Red side, and a look as observer at the procedure in the GHQ Command Post Exercise in New Jersey some years back—I have been horrified by the methods taken by Regular officers in handling these partially trained troops, and also I have been depressed by the laborious stabilizing command post technique and procedure displayed. In frequency and length of orders, and in the detail of orders, in the continuous and voluminous reports required, and the absurd amount of G-2 information supplied, one could not help but be impressed with the idea that stabilized or semi-siege warfare conditions were influencing everything that was done.

Now, we know what kind of an army we are going to have on M-day, and we must presume that open warfare will be the rule rather than the exception; therefore, it seems to me that should govern the basic policy for the training of our people, because if we can successfully survive the first three or four months, we will have plenty of time to absorb the technique of leadership adapted to full war strength organizations, with completely equipped ranks of seasoned, disciplined men.

I did not intend when I started this letter to elaborate on this Leavenworth question, but having started I thought it best to go ahead and get this off my chest. However, please treat these frank statements as confidential, between the two of us.

I hope you are having a fine trip.   Faithfully yours,

GCMRL/G. C. Marshall Papers (Pentagon Office, Selected)

1. In a letter to McNair on February 27 (not printed), Marshall sent copies of Colonel Edmund L. Gruber's views to General Embick on the Fort Leavenworth situation and on how best to correct it, as well as his own response to Gruber's memorandum. (See above Memorandum for the Deputy Chief of Staff [Embick], April 13, 1937.) Marshall arranged to have Gruber meet McNair in San Antonio, Texas, and to accompany him back to Washington. "This will give us some one in the G-3 Section who will have had ample opportunity to talk to you, and who will have seen the new air installations and equipment." (Marshall to McNair, February 27, 1939, GCMRL/G. C. Marshall Papers [Pentagon Office, Selected].)

To MAJOR GENERAL STANLEY D. EMBICK   March 10, 1939
                                                      [Washington, D.C.]

Dear Embick: You came to my mind a few minutes ago when the old custodian of the records concerning Joint Army and Navy action, came in here with an amendment to go in the binder under that title. He said it was a confidential document that was probably in the safe, but we found it on the table with the Congressional Directory and the Army Register. I accepted his reprimand, but privately pass it on to you because I have never seen the darn thing before, so you must have left it there. So, deal lightly with any of your people who throw secret volumes around!

The down spouts on the side of the house next to the alley fell down, and I notice two places where the guttering has broken loose, so I will get the Barrett Roofing Company to make an estimate and repair this. Also, the two outside lights, one near the kitchen and one outside the dining room door, are both loose from the wall, and I fear are a fire hazard, with the exposed wires getting wet. I will have these fixed.

We are in the midst of a hectic legislative situation, and the pressure seems to continue without interruption. The conference committees are now at work on the Army authorization bill for the special program. We are also having hearings on the appropriation items of the special program, though the calculations on the airplane have not yet been made.

Everyone here continues to miss you, and speak of you frequently. I do hope you have taken recreation in the lovely country included in your domain. Faithfully yours,

GCMRL/G. C. Marshall Papers (Pentagon Office, Selected)

MEMORANDUM[1]   March 22, 1939
                                                      Washington, D.C.

Mr. Green, Division of Controls, State Department, is preparing a recommendation to the Secretary of State for a law to facilitate the restriction of the exportation of scrap iron. I sent a memorandum to the Secretary of War today, via General Craig, to that effect, and said that I would give the Secretary a copy of Mr. Green's proposal, which is to be ready tomorrow.[2]

(This paper should be gotten from the State Department, given to Colonel Bull for the Chief of Staff and the Secretary of War).

Colonel Rose, G-4 Division, is the proper officer to be consulted about it.[3]

The Secretary of State, Secretary of War, and Attorney General were to draw up the law.

This was a kind of emotional proposition brought up in Cabinet meeting, when, as a matter of fact, it had been incited, I think, by the iron and steel men, who want the price of scrap kept low for their use during the filling of big contracts at this time.[4]

GCMRL/G. C. Marshall Papers (Pentagon Office, Selected)

1. This memorandum was not specifically addressed to any person or office. On the bottom of the page someone wrote: "This memo by Gen. Marshall prior to departure on air trip."
2. Joseph C. Green was chief of the Division of Controls and executive secretary of the National Munitions Control Board.
3. Colonel John B. Rose (U.S.M.A., 1907), of the Ordnance Corps, had been in the Logistics Division (G-4) since July, 1935.
4. On this subject, Secretary of the Interior Ickes commented: "The subject of selling scrap iron to foreign nations was raised at Cabinet meeting last Friday [March 17] by the Secretary of War. He thought that we ought not to sell this abroad and the President thought well of the suggestion. He asked the Vice President what he thought of it, and his reply was that sales should have been prohibited long ago." (Ickes, *Secret Diary*, 2: 599.)

TO BRIGADIER GENERAL LESLEY J. MCNAIR   March 28, 1939
[Washington, D.C.]

Dear McNair: I have already thanked you for your nice note regarding the air reconnaissance. Personally, I was gratified to learn from you that the affair worked out so well. I think that very important results, for the general good of the Army, will flow from that beginning. At the moment I am concerned over the preliminary estimates being made for maneuvers and demonstrations to be financed out of fiscal year 1941 funds, and I thought it might be just as well to discuss one of the phases with you direct, at this particular time.

Each year, faculty and students at Leavenworth are taken up to Fort Riley for a demonstration of artillery fire and air bombing. The proposals for 1941 have expanded the affair to six days, at a cost of about $57,000.

The same paper discussed the movement of the mechanized force to Fort Riley for a demonstration before the Cavalry School. The cost of this would be about $168,000. G-3 decided that it would be better to move the faculty and students to Fort Knox and hold the demonstration there, as this would cost only, all told, $15,000.

I find in the estimates such pathetically small amounts as $4,000 for the maneuvers in the First Corps Area and a similar amount for maneuvers in the Third Corps Area, and only $16,000 for the Corps Area concentration at Benning, which is a very large affair; etc., etc. Considering that the ultimate training of the Army is supposed to be taken care of in the maneuvers, these minute appropriations indicate a rather futile basis for the development of genuine field efficiency and leadership.

Now the thought occurred to me—and this is the reason for my letter to you—

that to spend $57,000 for a demonstration to the students at Leavenworth dignifies that affair out of all proportion to its importance, when we consider the matter of field training and leadership, as indicated by the small appropriations I have just referred to. And then there is another consideration—the fact that most of the officers at Leavenworth have witnessed similar demonstrations, certainly at Benning, and, I imagine, also at Sill and possibly at Riley.

We discussed with G-3 the advisability of sending the Leavenworth crew complete to the demonstration at Fort Knox, previously referred to as being set up for the Cavalry School people. Firing conditions, on account of trees, are not so satisfactory at Knox, but in view of the fact that most of these people have already seen such firing, it would appear that great economy could be effected, and at the same time very satisfactory results obtained. I believe movement from Leavenworth to Knox and return could be managed for a comparatively small sum of money, which would release important amounts to give the Corps Areas reasonable allocations of funds to carry out their most important work.

I am not asking you for a reply to this letter, and I should prefer that you do not discuss with others the views I am expressing, that is, as my conclusions or those of the War Department, but I want you to have this in mind when you go to Leavenworth so that I may obtain your opinion later as to what you think about things.   Faithfully yours,

GCMRL/G. C. Marshall Papers (Pentagon Office, Selected)

TO FRANK MURPHY[1]   April 7, 1939
                                                     [Washington, D.C.]

My dear Mr. Attorney General: There was mailed to me from your office a copy of your radio broadcast of March 27th on Civil Liberties.[2] The logic of the discussion is impressive. To me, however, the manner of your presentation is the more important contribution to the subject, considering the exceeding difficulty of making a definite or lasting impression on the public mind regarding either the meaning or the importance of Civil Liberties. For that reason, it seems to me, the simplicity of your argument together with the interest of your illustrations, should really have an important effect on the public mind. The trouble, of course, generally lies in the very human trait of complete indifference to a problem until ones particular ox is being gored.

If I am indebted to you for the copy of the broadcast, please accept my thanks. Faithfully yours,

GCMRL/G. C. Marshall Papers (Pentagon Office, Selected)

1. President Roosevelt had appointed Murphy, a former governor of Michigan, as attorney general of the United States in January, 1939.

2. No copy of Murphy's speech was found in the Marshall papers, and it was not reported in the *New York Times*. On May 15, Murphy gave a speech to the United States mayors' conference; having described civil liberties, he said: "These are ordinary things to a people that has done them pretty much without interruption for a century and a half. They seem elementary and commonplace—so simple that it seems unnecessary to speak of them. But actually they are not ordinary things. They are the hallmarks of civilization." (*New York Times*, May 16, 1939.)

TO BRIGADIER GENERAL LESLEY J. MCNAIR   April 19, 1939
                                                    [Washington, D.C.]

Dear McNair: I have been considering the invitation in your letter of April 15th since its receipt day before yesterday.[1] It would give me a great deal of pleasure to go out to Fort Leavenworth on June 20th for the purpose of talking things over with you, and if the price of admission is a talk to the Class, then I am very glad to accept. But I must state that the uncertainty of developments in the War Department at the present time makes me afraid to give any promises about movements of mine more than six hours in advance of the time set. I hope no complication will arise in June. Whether I will fly out or go out by rail will have to be decided later on.

I would like you to treat what follows as *most confidential*.

If possible, I wish that the fact of my acceptance might be kept confidential for the present; for, if the President should announce the new Chief of Staff in the meantime, then undoubtedly you should invite that officer to make the graduation talk, and there should not be the embarrassment of having had my name previously involved.

Despite these various exceptions, thank you very much for the compliment of the invitation.   Faithfully yours,

GCMRL/G. C. Marshall Papers (Pentagon Office, Selected)
    1. McNair had written to ask Marshall to speak at the graduation of the current class of the Command and General Staff School on June 20.

PRESIDENT ROOSEVELT was expected to announce the name of the next army chief of staff before the summer of 1939. At the end of June, General Malin Craig, who had held that post since October 2, 1935, would take his final leave prior to retiring on August 31. Tradition demanded that the man named to be chief of staff or to be the chief of any branch have at least four years to serve before his retirement. There were sixty-seven general officers on active duty, according to the April 20, 1939, edition of the semiannual *Army List and Directory*. Of this group, twenty major generals (excluding Malin Craig) and eleven brigadier generals ranked ahead of Marshall. But when the four-years-to-serve rule was applied, Marshall was fifth, behind Major Generals Hugh A. Drum, John L. De Witt, Frank W. Rowell, and Walter Krueger.

Hugh Drum was widely considered to be the leading candidate for the chief's job, and he actively campaigned for the position. De Witt, Rowell, and Krueger had neither mounted active campaigns, nor had powerful supporters who lobbied in their behalf. There was no assurance, however, that the president would not reach below Marshall on the eligiblity list for a younger man.

The strength of Drum's own campaign may have worked against him. In May, Boake Carter, a syndicated newspaper columnist who favored Drum and was critical of the Roosevelt Administration, wrote: "Tremendous pressure was exerted upon Mr. Roosevelt to appoint General Drum. But perhaps Hugh Drum's friends should have read the history of the last seven years and known better. The greater the pressure exerted on Mr. Roosevelt for an appointment to an office, the greater the determination of the President not to yield, regardless of the merits of the candidate involved." ("FDR Wanted a 'Yes-Man'," New York *Daily Mirror*, May 5, 1939.)

Marshall was instructed to meet President Roosevelt in the White House on Sunday, April 23. He arrived at approximately 3:35 P.M. and stayed forty minutes. (FDRL/White House Usher's Diary.) He was to be the new chief of staff, the president said; even Secretary of War Woodring had as yet not been informed. As soon as Malin Craig took his leave of absence prior to retirement— at the end of June—Marshall would become acting chief of staff. He would be sworn-in officially on September 1, 1939. Although General Pershing was in France at this time, his influence over the years had undoubtedly been to Marshall's benefit. A more recent acquaintance, Harry L. Hopkins, also admired him and had strongly recommended him to the president. (Robert E. Sherwood, *Roosevelt and Hopkins: An Intimate History,* [New York: Harper and Brothers, 1948], p. 11.)

Seeking to avoid the interviews with the press and the congratulatory publicity that would inevitably follow the announcement of his promotion, Marshall asked the president to postpone the release of the news until April 27. By that time he expected to be gone on a week-long inspection trip of West Coast installations. (K. T. Marshall, *Together*, pp. 42–43.) ★

To Leo A. Farrell

[April 27, 1939]
Denver [Colorado]

Dear Farrell: Now that my selection has been announced I want you to know that your much more than friendly interest has been deeply appreciated. For a good many years you have generously blown my horn, in season and out, and I am happy that your partiality to me finds some justification today.

I landed here an hour ago from Dayton, Ohio, and am off again early tomorrow for Ogden and San Francisco.

I will need your prayers for the next few years. Hastily and faithfully,

G. C. Marshall

GCMRL/L. A. Farrell Papers; H

To Brigadier General Lesley J. McNair   May 3, 1939
[Washington, D.C.]

Dear McNair: I have just gotten back from the West Coast and am off Tuesday to sail for South America. As I will not be back before the end of June, it will not be possible for me to accept your invitation to the graduation exercises at Leavenworth.

I am very sincere in telling you that this is a real disappointment, because as the next Chief of Staff I would have liked the opportunity to be at Leavenworth before the breakup of the present term.

Please accept my apologies and regrets.

They tell me there is a fine letter of congratulations from you, which I have not yet seen, so I will not delay in expressing my appreciation.

You at the head of Leavenworth are one of the great satisfactions I have at the moment in visualizing the responsibilities of the next couple of years. And, as I told you here, speaking merely as Deputy Chief of Staff, I now tell you as a prospective Chief of Staff that your judgment in what is to be done quietly at Leavenworth is to govern.   Faithfully yours,

GCMRL/G. C. Marshall Papers (Pentagon Office, Selected)

To Franklin D. Roosevelt   May 10 [1939]
From Katherine T. Marshall   [Washington, D.C.]

My Dear Mr. President,   Ever since your appointment of my husband—as your next Chief-of-Staff—I have wanted to write to you. It is difficult for me to put into words what I really feel. For years I have feared that his brilliant mind, and unusual opinion, were hopelessly caught in more or less of a tread-mill. That you should recognize his ability and place in him your confidence gives me all I have dreamed of and hoped for. I realize the great responsibility that is his. I know that his loyalty to you and to this trust will be unfailing. It is with the deepest feeling of gratitude and happiness that I send you this note of thanks.   Very Sincerely Yours,

Katherine Marshall

FDRL/F. D. Roosevelt Papers (OF 25-T); H

714

T HE THREAT of German and Italian commercial, political, and military penetration of Latin America "was no mere conjuring by an excited fancy," Secretary of State Cordell Hull asserted several years later; "our diplomatic representatives in Latin America had given us literally hundreds of concrete instances." (*The Memoirs of Cordell Hull*, 2 vols. [New York: Macmillan, 1948], 1: 601.) Brazil—with its large, well-organized German and Italian communities (variously estimated at between three and four million persons), its history of revolts and coups, and its twenty-five hundred miles of largely undefended coastline containing several excellent harbors—particularly worried United States military planners. There were no doubts in Washington regarding Brazil's traditional friendship and trade with the United States or its support of the principles of hemispheric independence. The chief problem, from the point of view of the United States, was how to counter German-Italian propaganda and influence, particularly in the strategic southern states and in the field of aviation. (Colonel E. R. W. McCabe, G-2, Memorandum for the Assistant Chief of Staff, WPD, January 25, 1939, NA/RG 165 [War Plans Division, File 4115].)

Internal dissent involving pro-Fascist and pro-Nazi groups might lead to an attempt to overthrow the government—as had happened in May, 1938. One possibility was the establishment of a pro-Fascist regime in part of Brazil which would be gradually reinforced by Germany and Italy, as had been the case in Spain since 1936. "If successful in establishing a Fascist regime in Brazil, our vital interests would immediately be affected and the Panama Canal menaced. The movement would also tend to spread to neighboring countries. It is this trend of events which is believed to create the real danger to stability in South American countries and security in the Western Hemisphere." (Ibid. See also the unsigned, undated attachment "Attitude of Brazil toward the United States and Intrusion of the Axis States in Brazil.")

Shortly before Marshall arrived in Washington in mid-1938, the State, War, and Navy Departments had begun sending representatives to meetings of the Standing Liaison Committee. The committee, which was strongly influenced by Under Secretary of State Sumner Welles, was chiefly concerned with Latin American military problems, particularly with the defense of Brazil. Marshall became involved in the committee's work when he became deputy chief of staff. In February, 1939, Brazil's Foreign Minister Oswaldo Aranha visited the United States, where he had been ambassador from 1934 to 1938. In Washington, he talked with Chief of Staff Craig and other military leaders. A few weeks after Aranha returned home, Chief of Staff-designate Marshall was invited to Brazil. (Stetson Conn and Byron Fairchild, *The Framework of Hemisphere Defense*, a volume in the *United States Army in World War II* [Washington, D.C.: Office of the Chief of Military History, Department of the Army, 1960], pp. 174, 266–67.)

While on his western trip, Marshall learned that he was to leave on May 10 aboard a cruiser for Rio de Janeiro, Brazil, with stops on the way at Puerto Rico and Trinidad. "I received very brief instructions for the trip," Marshall recalled later. General Pedro Aurelio de Goes Monteiro, Brazil's army chief of staff, had praised the German Army and had been invited to visit Germany. "In order to suppress these intimacies, I was sent to Brazil on a goodwill tour." (Interview, December 7, 1956.) ★

To General Malin Craig   May 26, 1939
                                                                       Rio de Janeiro, Brazil

Dear Chief: As this airmail costs 25¢ a sheet I will crowd my report into a few pages.

We landed, or docked, at 9-30 yesterday morning alongside a park like enclosure at the foot of the principal avenue—with a club building at the foot of the gangway, for reception purposes. A band of 100 pieces was alongside and gathered in the reception club were about 25 generals—all of this vicinity, the Ambassador,[1] the Mayor, representatives of the President and minister of foreign affairs, the head of the Navy, etc, etc.

In the Presidents open car I was taken up the avenue, which was lined with troops—and several bands, for about ten blocks—maybe [less?]. The people thronged in rear of the troops and applauded rather generously. The Ambassador said this was most unusual, as they were generally silent. I am being impersonal as I personally was unknown.

At the hotel they put us up luxuriously—I have 2 sitting rooms and a balcony overlooking the beach. The calls—President, Mayor, minister of Foreign Affairs, Ministers of War and Navy, and General Monteiro were as usual, but pretentiously arranged. All the officers of the War Dept received me at Gen. Monteiro's office—and he served champagne. Each of us has a car and a Brazilian aide—I have 2, a colonel of aviation and a major. All the aides are put up at the hotel. All our hotel and travel expenses are covered by the Government. They are doing this in great style.

Aranya is the guiding hand, and is both charming and utterly frank. He states his desires, solicits my assistance in influencing Brazilian Generals, advises me, explains the things he would like Monteiro to see in U.S., etc. etc. He is crazy about Col. Smith and hopes Monteiro will see him in U.S.

The present mission seems to be working out *OK*, from all I hear— Ambassador, Aranya, Monteiro.

I find Gen. Monteiro appears at all luncheons, receptions, dinners; but delegates other Generals to accompany me. That being so, I could start out with him and then return to Washington if you care to get away.

I had a long strenuous day today—walked miles. At 7 P.M. go to Palace to reception for Countess Ciano—Mussolinis daughter.[2] At 8 P.M. I go on to a military reception for me. Tomorrow noon I leave—by plane—for Sao Paulo and Southern Brazil.

The Pan-American is offering free transport north, so I am sending Col. Chaney and Ridgeway ahead of time to mouth of Amazon and intermediate ports.[3] They return to Pernambuco and the Nashville (and I) pick them up there. The ambassador insisted on the importance of Gen. Monteiro and I sailing from here on the Nashville, with the maximum of ceremony. Under this arrangement we should reach Annapolis June 20th—noon. I will radio tomorrow the definite decision.

I suggest the Langley Field and Mitchell Field air forces meet the Nashville about 9 A.M. and escort the boat a half hour or so.

Aranya wants to have a larger mission and more senior officers, the extra ones to go by commercial boat. He wants them, the seniors, to see our methods, people, etc.

This will be hard reading. It has been hard writing on this paper.

You certainly have been good and kind about Katherine, and I deeply appreciate and will never forget.[4] I have had 4 letters from her here.

Affectionately,

G. C. M.

NA/RG 407 (210.482, Brazil [4-29-39]); H

1. The United States ambassador to Brazil since August, 1937, had been Jefferson Caffery.

2. Countess Edda Ciano, daughter of Italian leader Benito Mussolini and wife of Italy's foreign minister, arrived in Brazil at nearly the same time as Marshall. One United States magazine cited Brazilian sources as saying that her visit was directly connected with the German-American competition for trade supremacy in Brazil. (*Time* 33 [May 22, 1939]: 29.)

3. Major Matthew B. Ridgway, a General Staff officer attached to the Fourth Army Staff in San Francisco, had been personally selected by Marshall for the trip. General Arnold had proposed Colonel James E. Chaney (U.S.M.A., 1908), former assistant chief of the Air Corps (1934–38).

4. Marshall's wife had contracted an acute case of poison-ivy rash and was in Walter Reed Hospital. (K. T. Marshall, *Together,* p. 43.)

To General Malin Craig

June 1, 1939
Bello Horizonte, Brazil

Dear Chief: Your radio of May 29th reached me here in the mountains last night.[1] Thanks for the news and especially for the greeting.

I have been traveling since last Wednesday, six days ago—all by air, with a very strenuous program everywhere and a devilish number of speeches a day—and under any and every condition. The reception given us has been remarkable, with a steadily increasing enthusiasm. It worries me because these people are very sensitive and comparisons are odious, and what they have done personally we cannot duplicate. Therefore I fear the result of comparisons which might well defeat the purpose of the exchange of visits. To illustrate my meaning, let me give you an outline of my last two cities—Porto Allegro in southern Brazil—and here at Bello Horizonte, north of Rio some 200 miles.

Arrived in Porto Allegro—Governor of State, Military Commanders, Arch Bishop, Cabinet civil officials, etc. at field. Guard of Honor, Cavalry escort surrounding my car, motorcycle police. Main street bordered by thousands of school children in uniform, 50 or 75,000 people crowded in rear of children, confetti and paper, like Broadway, for a half mile of blocks, four or five bands.

Another guard of honor at palace of governor, all civil officials present, champagne, etc. The same at headquarters of General. Tour of city with Mayor and general. Dinner by Governor—100 guests, usual variety of wines, elaborately printed menus in form of memento. Then a ball or dance. Civil guards in plume, jackboots, etc at entrance, all guests grouped to receive me, Governor as escort, national anthems, a dais at which to sit. It sounds like a joke or a bit of stage business, but it was all in deadly earnest in their desire to do the gracious thing.

Inspection of a frontier regiment at its barracks. Regiment paraded along road in advance of barracks, wide road leading 400 yards to barracks carpeted with flowers, sign across archway in letters two feet high "Welcome General Marshall", complete inspection, including layout of all programs and schedules of instruction, welcome by officers in their club, formal speech—written—by Colonel, champagne; another inspection of an airfield, same arrangements, another formal speech, more champagne; return to city, luncheon by General for 60 guests—as formal in arrangements, menu, speeches, music, as dinner night before; visit to femal academy (this, I think was probably arranged for you), indoor amphitheatre filled with girls, front row ones with flowers—they sing a welcome in English, do their flag stunt, sing some Brazilian chants and present me with 50 bunches of flowers—all sent later to my hotel. The whole thing was beautifully arranged and executed. Then a parade of 6000 school children, in school uniforms, 2 army bands, followed by 2000 men of various sport clubs. All this last was a hurried arrangement due to publicity regarding my contact with school children at Curitiba where I sent candy for 200 boys of agricultural orphanage who had paraded.[2] The sport clubs insisted on being let in, which involved all the German rowing clubs—to the intensive satisfaction and amusement of Brazilians.

Then a reception and lastly the ball referred to. The next morning all the officials were at the airport. I arrived in Rio to change planes, at 2:30 PM—not to leave the airport. The minister of airways, roads and railroads received me and was host at a stand up buffet lunch—champagne. The Chief of Staff, the minister of War, a representative of the Minister of Foreign Affairs, the General ADC to the President (Pa Watson)[3] and others welcomed me. I left in 30 minutes for Bell Horizonte, arriving there at dusk. The same reception at the airport, a

718

troop of cavalry surrounded my car as escort. When I reached the principal street or avenue I found the school children bordering my route, so over protest of Brazilian staff, I got out of car and walked 1½ miles thru the streets. About 12,000 children, with all the city packed in behind—really a very inspiring sight. The applauded at first by clapping their hands but I soon got them going, as it were, and the thing developed into an uproar of cheering. The Ambassador tells me they receive people always in respectful silence, so the compliment or expression of friendly feeling was be measured accordingly. Call on Governor with another guard of honor. He returns call and takes me to see some of his special interests prior to banquet. Moving pictures of industries during banquet—100 guests. Box at prize fight later. Ovation there repeated for 3 or 4 minutes. The a formal ball of the "high society". Another speech affair at midnight supper. The following morning the usual program of military inspections. A luncheon and then to plane. Governor hands me a small package which I did not open until the plane was "taking off". I found a case containing 3 aquamarines and one quite sizeable gold nugget. They tell me the stones are worth about $300 to $400. I should say the gold nugget was worth $75 or $100. I went through a gold mine yesterday. Please don't advertise this gift business; I am merely trying to give you an idea of how much is being done. The Governor was a business type, deeply concerned in the direction and development of industries. No funny business about him—a very able, direct, to the point sort of person.

Friday noon Rio

Since 8-30 a.m. I have been inspecting ordnance plants, a guard regiment of infantry and a guard regiment of cavalry. Tell Wesson that they serve champagne and cakes in the middle of a shell manufacturing shop. They are making rapid strides in manufacturing processes and their workmen quickly develop technical skill. Unfortunately, all schooling has been in Germany or France—therefore machinery from those countries.

I do not think it at all necessary for me to travel with Gen. Monteiro. He does not make a pretense of traveling with me. I might start him off by going to Langley Field, and meet him later at West Point, or some such arrangement. He sends Generals with me who are concerned with the region or the installations I am looking over. We might well do it that way: For example, Emmons from Langley to Barksdale and Randolph Field; Brees from Sam Houston to Fort Bliss; Bowley to meet him in Los Angeles and to San Francisco; Chaffee at Knox and me at West Point; Drum in New York. He sends aides with me, 2 for me and 1 for each member of mission. I would not do this: Let Col. Miller and Captain North manage affairs,[4] assisted by 2 good orderlies to look after baggage, and do clerical. Have aides report at each place for the day.

I have written this at odd hours and hurriedly, so it is for you, and *not* for general circulation—too hastily and frankly written for the latter. I must leave now for luncheon by Minister of F.A—Arayana. Four speeches so far today, and 3 more yet to do.   Hastily,

G. C. M.

NA/RG 407 (210.482, Brazil [4-29-39]); H

1. This message was not found in the Marshall papers.
2. For an account of Marshall's diplomatic coup at Curitiba, see K. T. Marshall, *Together*, pp. 48–49.
3. Edwin M. ("Pa") Watson (U.S.M.A., 1908) had been President Roosevelt's military aide since 1933. On April 1, 1939, he was promoted to brigadier general and given the additional title and duties of secretary to the president.
4. Lieutenant Colonel Lehman W. Miller (U.S.M.A., 1915) had been a member of the United States military mission to Brazil between 1934 and 1938 and was able to act as an interpreter. Marshall chose Captain Thomas North for the mission because he was a "geographic expert and good linguist." (Marshall to the Chief of Staff, May 1, 1939, NA/RG 407 [210.482, Brazil (4-29-39)].)

To the Secretary of War   June 21, 1939
Washington, D.C.

Dear Mr. Secretary: In compliance with your instructions, my staff and I boarded the U.S.S. "Nashville," Captain W. W. Wilson commanding, in the Hudson River at New York City on May 10th last, and sailed that day for Brazil. Leaving Rio de Janeiro on June 7th, and Recife, the last Brazilian port of call, on June 10th, my staff and I returned on the "Nashville," disembarking at Annapolis on June 20th. General Goes Monteiro, Chief of Staff of the Brazilian Army, and a staff of five accompanied me on the return journey from Rio de Janeiro.

Throughout the period spent on the "Nashville" Captain Wilson surrounded my officers and me with every possible courtesy and consideration, placing at our disposal every administrative and recreational facility available in his ship, and contributing through informal lectures by himself and his officers to a better understanding of the problems of the two services.

The fine impression created by the officers and the conduct of the men ashore in Rio de Janeiro reflected the greatest credit on both the ship and the Naval Service, and were borne out by the high morale exhibited by every individual in the execution of his daily duties at sea.

I would appreciate having the Secretary of the Navy advised of our appreciation of the unfailing courtesy and consideration shown by the Commanding officer of the "Nashville," and by his officers and men, which reflected their high morale and fine appearance.   Respectfully,

G. C. Marshall

NA/RG 407 (210.482, Brazil [6-21-39])

FROM GENERAL MALIN CRAIG
June 30, 1939
Washington, D.C.

My dear George: When I tell you goodbye I shall not be able to say the many things in my heart that should be said. It isn't my nature, but the feelings are there, and I hope you realize it. I have always admired you a great deal, but the close association with you the past year has given me a far greater insight into your splendid character and able mind. Your work as Deputy has been outstanding. I have leaned heavily upon you, and you have always responded with strength and wisdom.

In addition to a feeling of gratitude for the splendid official support you have given me, I have derived great pleasure and mental stimulus from our informal conversations and discussions, and I shall miss these daily contacts more than I can tell you. They have meant much to me.

In departing I leave with you my hearty thanks for loyal services well done and warm good wishes for a future career even more brilliant than the past.
Sincerely,

Craig

NA/201 File

WAR DEPARTMENT, SPECIAL ORDERS, NO. 149
June 27, 1939
Washington, D.C.

. . . 2. Brigadier General *George C. Marshall,* General Staff Corps, is detailed as Acting Chief of Staff, effective 1 July, 1939, and will report for duty accordingly. (A.G. 210.61, Gen. Staff.) . . .

NA/201 File

Index